AF324266

# ECONOMIC GROWTH
## OF SINGAPORE IN
## THE TWENTIETH CENTURY

Historical GDP Estimates and Empirical Investigations

# Economic Growth Centre Research Monograph Series
(ISSN: 2010-0760)

**Editor-in-Chief:** Euston Quah, *Nanyang Technological University, Singapore*
**Editor:** Rosalind Chew, *Nanyang Technological University, Singapore*
**Associate Editor:** Ho Kong Weng, *Nanyang Technological University, Singapore*

---

Vol. 1   Economic Growth and Transition:
Econometric Analysis of Lim's S-Curve Hypothesis
*by Hui Ying Sng (Nanyang Technological University, Singapore)*

Vol. 2   Economic Growth of Singapore in the Twentieth Century:
Historical GDP Estimates and Empirical Investigations
*by Ichiro Sugimoto (Soka University, Japan)*

Economic Growth Centre Research Monograph Series – Vol. 2

# Economic Growth of Singapore in the Twentieth Century

## Historical GDP Estimates and Empirical Investigations

### Ichiro Sugimoto

Soka University, Japan

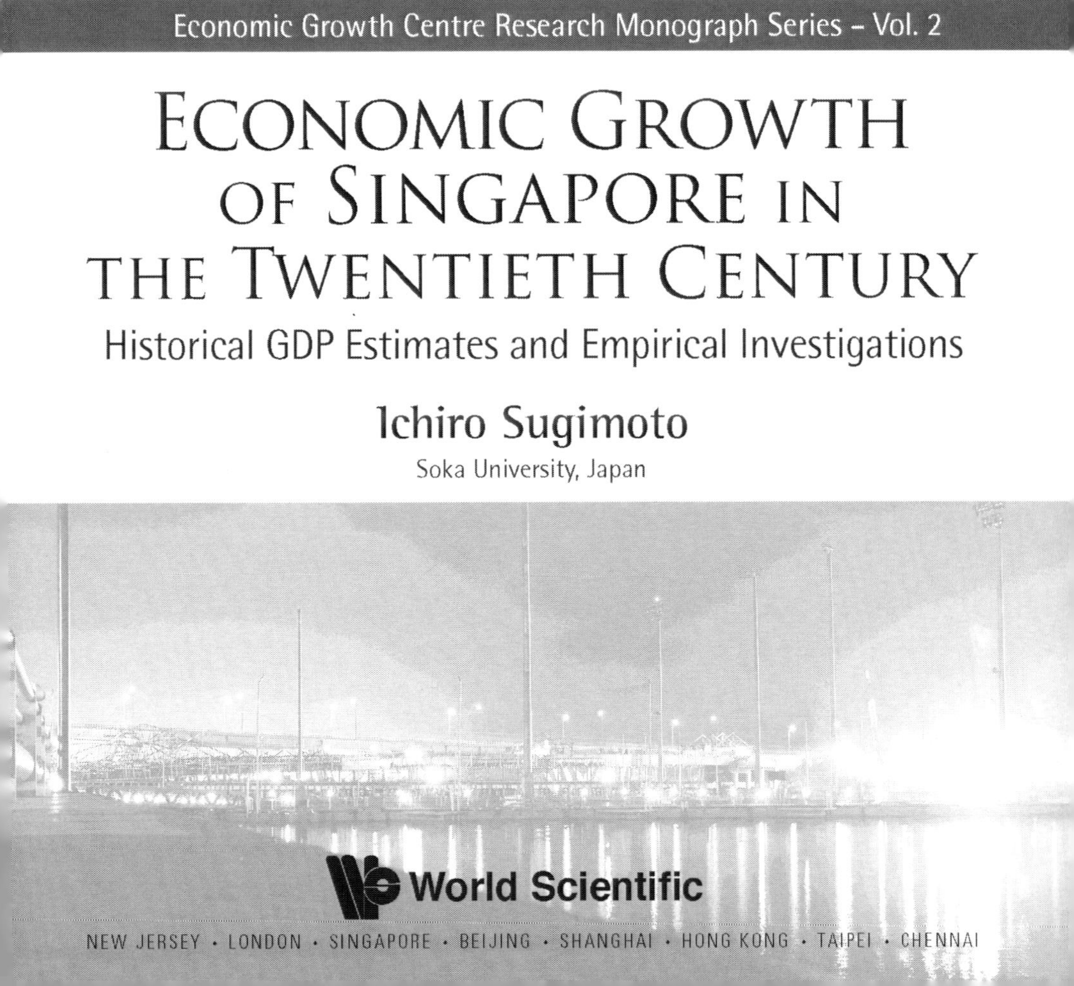

**World Scientific**

NEW JERSEY · LONDON · SINGAPORE · BEIJING · SHANGHAI · HONG KONG · TAIPEI · CHENNAI

*Published by*

World Scientific Publishing Co. Pte. Ltd.

5 Toh Tuck Link, Singapore 596224

*USA office:* 27 Warren Street, Suite 401-402, Hackensack, NJ 07601

*UK office:* 57 Shelton Street, Covent Garden, London WC2H 9HE

**British Library Cataloguing-in-Publication Data**
A catalogue record for this book is available from the British Library.

**Economic Growth Centre Research Monograph Series — Vol. 2**
**ECONOMIC GROWTH OF SINGAPORE IN THE TWENTIETH CENTURY**
**Historical GDP Estimates and Empirical Investigations**



ISBN-13 978-981-4317-91-7
ISBN-10 981-4317-91-8

Typeset by Stallion Press
Email: enquiries@stallionpress.com

Printed in Singapore.

This Book is dedicated to

*Dr. Daisaku Ikeda, Founder of
Soka University*

# Preface

Research on the long-term economic growth of Singapore has been hampered until now largely because of the virtual absence of economics-related statistics prior to 1956, which conformed to the definitions as outlined in the System of National Accounts. Keeping in view this limitation, the first part of this study is devoted to providing the methodologies employed for the construction of Singapore's historical GDP estimates for the periods 1900–39 and 1950–60. The "expenditure approach" was applied to derive GDP data series in current and constant prices for these periods. Subsequently, these time-series data were extended to cover the entire twentieth century using a single base year (1990 prices).

Using this historical GDP series, two types of empirical investigations were attempted to examine the economic growth experiences of Singapore. The first type deals with the relationship between economic instability and economic growth. Three related issues, namely, extent, sources, and consequences of economic instability during the twentieth century were examined. It was observed that the extent of output volatility in the pre–World War II period was greater than that of the post–World War II period. In relation to sources of output volatilities, explanatory variables such as the share of government deficit/surplus to GDP, changes in trade as a share of GDP, and changes in terms of trade were found to be statistically insignificant for both the pre-WWII and post-WWII periods. With regard to the effect of economic instability on economic growth, export instability has negatively affected the real per-capita GDP growth for the entire twentieth century, but the coefficient has fallen over time as the structure of the economy became more diversified.

The second type deals with government fiscal behavior toward economic growth. It focuses on notable differences or similarities in fiscal behavior between the British colonial period and the period of self-government that ensued. This study primarily identifies the nature of colonial government finance behavior and then goes on to trace the changes in revenue raising, expenditure allocation, and budget balance management patterns in the twentieth century. A major structural change was observed after WWII due to the shift of the source of revenue from the sales of opium to revenue obtained from income tax. This transition affected the revenue-raising capacity and subsequently the size of government expenditure. Nevertheless, the share of government expenditure to GDP during the British colonial period and the period of self-government remained small, whereas that of other developed countries increased during same period. In fact, both the British colonial government and the self-government attempted to establish balanced or a surplus budget structure. For analytical purposes, the validity of Wagner's law was empirically tested. The result of the Granger causality test found that economic growth nurtured the expansion of government expenditure in the pre-WWII period, whereas economic expansion during the post-WWII period could mainly be attributed to astute macroeconomic management.

# Acknowledgments

This work (Sugimoto, 2009) was originally submitted for a Ph.D degree at the University of Malaya, Kuala Lumbur and the research was carried out during my Ph.D candidature at the University of Malaya.

I am greatly indebted to Prof. Tan Eu Chye, who was my supervisor. I thank him for his intellectual support, patience, encouragement, advice, and guidance. With his support and encouragement, I presented part of this book at some of the notable conferences, namely, "The Economic History Society Annual Conference 2005" (Leicester, UK), "The Socio-Economic History Society Annual Conference 2007" (Tokyo, Japan), and "The Singapore Economic Review Conference 2007" (Singapore).

I would also like to express my deep appreciation to His Royal Highness Raja, Dr. Nazrin Shah, Crown Prince of Perak and Pro-Chancellor, University of Malaya, for providing me great encouragement and opportunity to be a part of his research project entitled "Historical National Accounts of Pre-Independence Malaya Since 1998." The experience gained from this project as well as the accessibility accorded me to his personal collections of colonial documents was of immense help in completing studies presented in this book.

I would like to thank Prof. Lim Cheng Yah and Prof. Rosalind Cheng who encouraged me to get this book published.

I would like to thank Dato' Dr. Shaharil Talib, former executive director, Asia–Europe Institute, for his encouragement and for sharing his knowledge on colonial history of Singapore.

Mr. Gnaseagarah, C. Kandaiya, and Mr. Harbans Singh, with their profound experience, have guided me in studies related to the construction of historical statistics. I also received valuable comments at various stages from Prof. Riitta Hjerppee, Dr. Reino Hjerppee, Dr. Pierre van der Eng, Prof. Jan Luiten van Zanden, Dr. Thomas Linblad, Prof. Om Prakash, Prof. Anne Booth, Prof. Yoshihiro Tsubouchi, Prof. Konosuke Odaka and Prof. Osamu Saito, and Dr. Choy Keen Meng.

The Asia–Europe Institute, University of Malaya, headed by Prof. Datuk Dr. Roziah Omar, provided the best facility and resources to complete my studies. I am grateful to my former research colleagues Ruhana, Nazli, Anita, Tuah, Tin, Laili, Zul, Suhaimi, and Quang. They been a great source of motivation.

My most heartfelt gratitude to Dr. Daisaku Ikeda, founder of the Soka University for his encouragement and support. He supported me wholeheartedly when I decided to pursue further studies in Malaysia.

I am grateful to Prof. Masami Kita, Prof. Yoshihisa Baba, Prof. Hirotomo Teranishi, Prof. Tsuyoshi Kato, Prof. Yosuke Nihei, Dr. Motoko Kawano, Mr. Choo Kong Fei, Mrs. Choo Aiko, Prof. Christopher Boey, Mrs. Chang Lee Leng, Mrs. Lim Suat San, Mr. Haji Ibrahim, Mr. Fumio Nakano, Mr. Hiroyuki Azuma, Mr. Mitsuharu Mori, Mr. Futoshi Ozaki, Mr. Tomohito Gyota, and Mr. Kazunori Wakayama for their continued moral support.

Finally, I am forever indebted to my wife, Mieko, and my son, Yoichi, for their understanding, endless patience, and encouragement when it was most required. I am also grateful to my late father, Yoshio Sugimoto, my mother, Kazuko Sugimoto, my parents-in-law, Fumio Murayama and Tokiko Murayama, for their unflagging support.

# Contents

| | | |
|---|---|---|
| **Chapter Three** | **The Result of GDP Estimates in Singapore and Overall Patterns of Growth for the Twentieth Century** | **139** |

# List of Tables

# List of Figures

# List of Maps

# List of Abbreviations

| | |
|---|---|
| ADB | Asian Development Bank |
| ADF | Augmented Dickey-Fuller |
| ARTSS | Appendix to the Report on the Trade, Straits Settlements |
| ASHSTAT | Asian Historical Statistics Project |
| BM | Returns of Foreign Imports and Exports, British Malaya |
| BOP | Balance of Payments |
| CO | Colonial Office |
| CPI | Consumer Price Indices |
| DF | Dickey-Fuller |
| FMS | Federated Malay States |
| FTM | Foreign Trade of Malaya |
| GCF | Gross Capital Formation |
| GDP | Gross Domestic Products |
| GNP | Gross National Products |
| GFCE | Government Final Consumption Expenditure |
| GFCF | Gross Fixed Capital Formation |
| GFS | Government Financial Statistics |
| HP | Hodrick Prescott Method |
| NBER | National Bureau of Economic Research |
| NETEX | Net Exports of Goods and Services |
| PFCE | Private Final Consumption Expenditure |
| PP | Phillips-Perron |
| PPP | Power Purchasing Parity |

| | |
|---|---|
| SNA | System of National Accounts |
| SS | Straits Settlements |
| SSBB | Blue Book, Straits Settlements |
| STBCPP | Statistical Tables Relating to British Colonies, Possessions and Protectorates |
| STCOPUK | Statistical Tables Relating to the Colonial and Other Possessions of the United Kingdom |
| STCPP | Statistical Tables Relating to the Colonial and Other Possessions and Protectorates |
| TGE | Total Government Expenditure |
| UMS | Unfederated Malay States |
| UN | United Nations |
| WWII | World War II |

# Chapter One

# Introduction

## 1.1 Objective of Study

The objective of this study is to examine the long-term economic growth of Singapore during the twentieth century. According to official statistics released since 1960, the economic indicators of Singapore show a sustained and relatively rapid economic growth over this period. For the period 1960–2000, real GDP (1990 prices) rose at an average annual rate of 7.7 percent. With population growth at 2.2 percent, real per capita GDP increased by 5.5 percent on average each year. In fact, real per capita GDP has increased 9.7 times within 40 years. Out of 107 countries, Singapore registered the highest growth performance[1] during 1960–2000 (Ghesquiere, 2007, p. 14). This phenomenon was frequently cited as an "economic miracle". On the other hand, economic performance of Singapore prior to 1960 was not the same due to non-availability of comparable economic statistical indicators such as GDP and other relevant statistical time-series. Given these serious constraints of data availability for the earlier period, the existing literature on the pre-1960 economic development of Singapore has been confined merely to studies on specific sectors. Admittedly, though these specific studies help to shed some light on certain aspects of the economic activities in Singapore during this period they certainly are not enough to give any detailed insight into the long-term economic growth of Singapore during the last 100 years.

---

[1] National Income expressed in PPP dollars.

The first part of this book focuses on the construction of historical GDP estimates of Singapore in both current and constant prices for the time periods 1900–39 and 1950–60. It should be noted here that the World War II period (1941–45) and the years immediately after WWII are not covered in this book because of the difficulties in estimating historical GDP time-series due to non-availability of data for some of the components of GDP. The construction of historical GDP of Singapore involved three major steps. First, it required identification and collection of existing statistical records published by the British colonial authority. Second, the data required evaluation and subsequently estimates were made by employing several methodologies, while at the same time ensuring that the concepts and definitions, conformed to those outlined in *A System of National Accounts (SNA) 1968*[2] for each component of GDP. Third, the reliability and validity of the estimated statistical series had to be checked by tracing supportive information which could possibly explain the upturns and downturns of each component of GDP in both current and real terms.

Based on this newly derived historical GDP and official time-series database for the post-1960 period, the second part of this book focuses on the empirical investigation with regards to Singapore's long-term economic growth during the entire twentieth century by applying modern econometric techniques. It first discusses the economic instability and economic growth and related issues, namely, (i) extent of real GDP volatility (ii) source of the real GDP volatility and (iii) the effects of economic instability on economic growth.

It then discusses government fiscal behavior towards economic growth. This study firstly identifies the ramifications of colonial

---

[2] Three different versions of SNA were released by United Nations for the years 1953, 1968 and 1993 respectively. In this study, the SNA 68 was utilized for the estimation of each component of historical GDP. This is mainly because all official GDP estimates of Singapore for the period 1960–2000 were constructed based on the SNA 68.

government finance and subsequently observes the transition of government fiscal behavior from the British colonial rule to the period of self-government. Based on the observations, this chapter focuses on whether there existed any notable differences or similarities between various types of government expenditure and economic growth. For analytical purposes two econometric techniques of cointegration and Granger causality tests are applied.

The structure of the remaining part of this chapter is organized as follows: Section 1.2 provides a literature review on the economic history of Singapore, construction of historical statistics and lastly the concept of GDP and the three different approaches that can be used in its estimation. Section 1.3 explains the data required for the construction of historical GDP estimates. Finally, the layout of the book is briefly presented in Section 1.4.

## 1.2 Literature Review

This section briefly conducts a literature review relevant to this study. Three areas of literature review are identified, namely, [1] economic history of Singapore prior to Independence, [2] the construction of historical GDP estimates and [3] concept of GDP.

### 1.2.1 *Literature Review on Economic History of Singapore Prior to Independence*

Wong Lin Ken (1979) provided a literature review on the economic history of Malaya (inclusive of Singapore) in his article *Twentieth-Century Malayan Economic History: A Select Bibliographic Survey*. He stated that "research in this region is still on the frontier area of the social sciences. Analytical methodology grounded in economic theory was lacking". Two decades later, Drabble, John H (2000), in his book *Economic History of Malaysia*, which covered the period 1800–1990, elaborated the progress of economic history of Malaysia by stating that "from the standpoint of the economic historian the situation is still to a large extent as Wong described". Loh Wei Leng (2005) also stated that "(quantitative) data found in official documents are seldom questioned and are yet to be closely scrutinized as to their likely use in support of specific policies. There is an obvious need to be more sensitive to these implications in future work". These statements make it clear that research in this field of economic history saw little progress.

Table 1.1 provides a slew of previous studies on Singapore in the field of socio-economics during the British colonial period. Studies on economic history of Singapore ranged from trade, commercial activity, money, government finance and financial development to economic conditions during the Depression in early 1920's and 1930's. Apart from this, studies on demographic changes, labour conditions, infrastructure development in terms of construction of water supply and port facilities as well as opium revenue collection by the British administration were also conducted. In these studies, the economic importance of Singapore as an entrepôt and a regional trading centre was often highlighted. For example, Kaoru Sugihara studied the statistics of intra-Asian trade during the nineteenth and early half of 20th century and clarified the nature of the western impact and the role of regional trade in Asia's economic development (Sugihara, 1980, 1996, 1998). In a related study, Lindblad, J. Thomas (1997, 1998) examines the role of foreign direct investment (FDI) in Southeast Asia from the late nineteenth century. He contrasts the statistical evidence pertaining to the late 1930s and the late 1980s and identifies features of change and continuity between these two periods.

Nevertheless, very few researchers have attempted to investigate the overall economic activities of Singapore. The following three studies, however, provided various statistical databases and interpreted Singapore's economy during the British colonial period.

First, a study by Emerson, Rupert (1964) entitled *Malaysia: A study in direct and indirect rule* examines the similarities and

**Table 1.1:**  List of Previous Studies on Singapore Relating to Socio-Economic Issues Prior to Independence

| Field of Research | Author/Year | Period |
| --- | --- | --- |
| Trade | Chiang, Hai Ding (1963 and 1965) | 1870–1915 |
| | Sharom Ahmat (1965) | 1819–1865 |
| | Blake, DJ (1968) | 1961–1966 |
| | Choo, Eng Kang (1976) | 1920–1922 |
| | Wong Lin Ken (1978) | 1819–1941 |
| | Wong Lin Ken (1991) | Pre-WWII period |
| | Huff, WG (1993) | Pre-WWII period |
| | Huff, WG (1994) | Pre-WWII period |
| Economic Conditions | Hernaikh Singh Dhaliwal (1989) | 1920–30s |
| | Huff, WG (2001) | Early 1930's |
| | Kratoska, Paul H (1990) | 1917–1921 |
| Population | Saw, Swee Hock (1999) | 1871–1940 |
| Infrastructure | Teo, Mary Celine Kiew Ting (1962) | 1819–1959 |
| (Water Supply | Hanizah Idris (1995) | 1819–1941 |
| and Port Facilities) | Huff, WG (1994) | Pre-WWII period |
| | Ruhana Padzil (1999) | 1819–1941 |
| Municipality | Khoo, Kay Kim (1960) | 1887–1940 |
| | Yeoh, Brenda SA (1993 and 1996) | Early 20th Century |
| Government Finance | Lee Soo Ann (1974) | 1948–60 |
| | Edward, CT (1970) | 1948–60 |
| Money and Banking | Lee, Sheng Yi (1990) | Early 20th Century |
| | Hicks, George H (eds.) (1993) | 1910–1940 |
| | Huff, WG (2003a) | Pre-WWII period |
| | Huff, WG (2003b) | Pre-WWII period |
| Labour | Warren, James Francis (1986) | 1900–1940 |
| | Huff, WG (2007) | Pre-WWII period |
| Commercial Activities | Shimizu, Hiroshi and Hirakawa, Hitorchi (1999) | 1870–1965 |
| | Brown, Ian (1994) | 1930's |
| Opium | Trocki, Carl, A (1990) | 1800–1910 |
| | Cheng, U Wen (1961) | 1867–1910 |

differences in economic activities between the colonial administered territories of British Malaya (See Map 1.1)[3] and Netherland
Indies. Subsequently, Lim Chong Yah's book (1967) entitled
*Economic Development of Modern Malaya* examined the socio-
economic development of Malay states from various aspects such
as the role of major export commodities (e.g., rubber and tin),
trade as well as government revenue and expenditure allocation.

These two studies by Emerson, R (1964) and Lim Chong Yah
(1967) provided well documented statistical databases and identified Singapore as a major regional entrepôt. These studies also
described the economic structure of Singapore as entirely different from that of the other states of Malaya which concentrated
on the production of primary export commodities. The island of
Singapore formed a part of the Straits Settlements during the
period of the British colonial administration.[4]

---

[3] Prior to World War II, the territory of British Malaya was administrated as
three different entities, namely the Straits Settlements, Federated Malay States
and Unfederated Malay States. Frequently, the term "British Malaya" was
considered as the summation of these three administrative units.

[4] The establishment of the Straits Settlements followed the Anglo-Dutch Treaty
of 1824 between the United Kingdom and the Netherlands, by which the Malay
archipelago was divided into a British zone in the north and a Dutch zone in the
south. This resulted the exchange of the British settlement of Bencoolen (on
Sumatra) for the Dutch colony of Malacca and undisputed control of Singapore.
Its capital was moved from Penang to Singapore in 1832. In 1867, the
Settlements became a British Crown Colony, making the Settlements answer-
able directly to the Colonial Office in London instead of the Calcutta government based in India on April 1. Earlier on February 4, a "Letters Patent"
granted the Settlements a colonial constitution. This allocated much power to
the Settlements' Governor, who administered the Colony of the Straits
Settlements with the aid of an Executive Council, composed wholly of official
(i.e., *ex-officio*) members, and a Legislative Council, composed partly of official
and partly of nominated members, of which the former had a narrow permanent majority. The work of administration, both in the Colony and in the
Federated Malay States, was done through civil service in which members were
recruited by competitive examination held annually in London. Penang and
Malacca were administered, directly under the Governor, by resident
councilors.

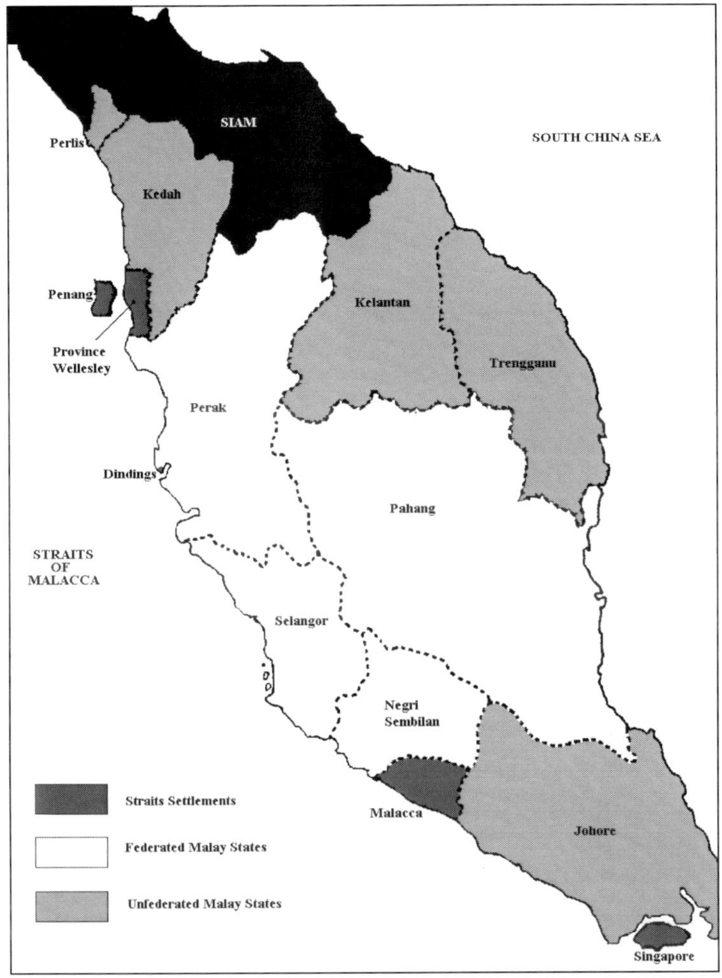


**Map 1.1:**   The Malay Peninsula, c. 1925

The third study was conducted by WG Huff (1994) and documented in his book *The Economic Growth of Singapore, Trade and Development in the Twentieth Century*. This is the first major research work which traces the long-term economic development of Singapore as an economic entity during the twentieth century. "The history of Singapore is written mainly in statistics" is the opening sentence in Huff's book. Huff gathered significant statistical material through several primary, secondary and even obscure data sources. The result is a systematic attempt at tracing economic link between the metropolis and its hinterland and connections between agriculture, trade, banking and industry. He argues that Singapore was essentially a port dealing with staple commodities. It built its original development on tin exports from Malaya and the Netherland East Indies. However, frequent fluctuations in the international demand of rubber had a serious impact on the economy of Singapore.

Apart from tin and rubber, the other major export commodity of Singapore in the 1930's was petroleum, which was imported from the Dutch East Indies. But this did not have much impact effect on the Singapore economy as it created little employment and its installations were confined to offshore islands. It did, however, create employment opportunities in the extensive shipyard facilities which the British had established. In this study, Huff highlights the fact that Singapore achieved economic development without having the manufacturing industry as a driving force.

These three studies mentioned above have, in fact, immensely contributed to a better understanding of the economic history of Singapore. However, their scope of research was basically determined by the availability of relevant statistical information compiled by the British colonial authority. At this juncture, it would be important to take note of Wong Lin Ken's comment on analytical methodology grounded in economic theory which was described as being still on the frontier area. This existing fundamental research gap was purely due to the lack of analytical work grounded on macroeconomic data. The field of economic history of Singapore was treated as such and no compatible analysis was conducted to identify the long-term economic growth of Singapore. The twentieth century witnessed the "rubber boom", which was driven by the requirements of the automobiles industry.

This phenomenon is not restricted to Singapore. In fact, most of the former colonies faced a similar predicament. Michael Havinden and David Meredith's work (1996) entitled *Colonialism and Development: Britain and Its Tropical Colonies, 1850–1960* considers policy decisions of Great Britain with regard to the economic development of its tropical possessions from 1860 through to 1960. This study, however, used "size of foreign trade" as a proxy to measure the economic development of the respective colonies with the author acknowledging with a caveat that foreign trade was not a reliable proxy to indicate economic growth. This implies that deficiencies in relevant economic indicators did not permit a modern quantitative economic analysis. Thus, the collection and construction of macroeconomic time-series data of Singapore such as GDP, which is an integral part of this study represents a fundamental yet crucial step towards filling this void, notwithstanding the painstaking and tedious task of compiling the required raw data from various official publications and records.

### 1.2.2 *Literature Review on the Construction of Historical Statistics*

Unlike developing countries, the construction of historical national accounting has been regarded as one of the most dynamic branches of economic history (Heikkienen, Sakari and Luiten Van Zanden, 2004) in western countries. This was closely associated with the creation of the System of National Accounts (SNA). The first major research in the field of historical national accounts was conducted by Clark (1937) and Kuznets (1934). Subsequently, the first standardized SNA was designed and formulated largely by Maede and Stone (1941). They made the first official estimates of national income for the United Kingdom in 1941. Subsequently, the United Nations, in 1953, released its first recommendations on a standardized SNA. This has been widely applied in most countries. Following this, the

United Nations published two revised versions of SNA in 1968 and 1993.

In line with this development of SNA in the 1950's, the methodology employed in the construction of historical GDP and formulation of economic theory has made incremental improvements. Most of the empirical research since then has focused on expanding and deepening the database on which the comparative and summarizing studies of Kuznets were based, while much of the theory-oriented research has concentrated on refining the growth accounting framework. This quantification of past economic activities using the SNA approach was crucial in seeking general characteristics related to structural transformation, technological change, income distribution and population growth.

The empirical research has expanded to other countries, by updating the previous work in order to comply with the procedures as set out in the SNA. Among these prominent research studies are those initiated by Craft (1984, 1987, 1988, 1995, 1999), Broadberry, (1986, 1988, 1997a, 1997b), Craft, and Broadberry (1990a, 1990b).

While both "old" and "new" economic historians emphasized the importance of empirical investigation for economics, *cliometricians*[5] equated 'fact' with measurable phenomena. Empirical facts meant quantitative facts (Rouvray, 2004, 157).

Reconstruction of historical national accounts was made available for almost all OECD countries by the 1970s. This reconstruction exercise has been carried out in several countries by teams of researchers and in other countries by individual scholars.

Angus Maddison, whose work on historical national accounts is frequently referred, collected a voluminous vast data, interpreted them in a consistent way, and made them internationally comparable to a siginificant extent. Expansion of the database

---

[5] Historical researchers using economic models and advanced mathematical methods of data processing and analysis.

has been one of the major achievements of the worldwide network of historical national accountants. Refinements in methodology, in particular concerning the measurement and analysis of productivity growth, has been another major field of research. The Purchasing Power Parity (PPP) method was aimed at resolving the problem caused by exchange rates, which are not good indicators of the relative values of currencies of different countries. Kravis *et al.* (1975) initiated a system for international comparisons of GDP and this made it possible to integrate the long-term growth of GDP into one global database.[6]

Unlike these OECD countries, the relative unavailability of database on historical national accounts and related empirical growth studies in developing countries represented a severe handicap. From Angus Maddison's efforts in compiling data on real GDP time-series (Maddison, 2001, 2003) it was obvious that there was gap in availability of historical GDP estimates in Asian countries was found wanting (See Table 1.2).

In Asian countries, historical GDP estimates pertaining to the period prior to World War II was initiated by two major research teams. The first major collaborative research project was *The Long-term Economic Statistics of Japan 1867–1965*,[7] led by the Institute of Economic Research, Hitotsubashi University and was carried out over the period 1957–88. This project also covered former Japanese colonies such as Korea and Taiwan. The second research group undertook a study of the Netherland Indies, and was led by Creutzberg and Boomgaard (1975–96)

---

[6] It must be noted here that historical GDP estimates of Singapore conducted in this study cannot be converted into international comparative prices such as PPP or Geary-Khamis Prices due to lack of data to initiate this study.

[7] In 1957, professors Ohkawa, Shinohara, Umemura and others of the Institute of Economic Research at the Hitotsubashi University launched a monumental project to estimate GDP series of Japan since the Meiji period. The project was completed in 1988, when the last volume in the series *Long-term Economic Statistics of Japan*, 1867–1965 was published. This project was mainly financed by the Rockefeller Foundation.

**Table 1.2:** Historical GDP Estimates Available in Asian Countries prior to World War II.

| Region | Country | 1870 | 1880 | 1890 | 1900 | 1910 | 1920 | 1930 | 1940 |
|---|---|---|---|---|---|---|---|---|---|
| East Asia | Japan | 1870– | | | | | | | |
| | China | | | | | | | 1929-38 | |
| | Korea | | | | | 1911– | | | |
| | Taiwan | | | | | 1912– | | | |
| | Hong Kong | | | | | | | | |
| Southeast Asia | Indonesia (Java) | 1870-1941 | | | | | | | |
| | Philippines | | | | 1902-40 | | | | |
| | Peninsular Malaysia | | | | 1900-39 | | | | |
| | Singapore | | | | 1900-39 | | | | |
| | Thailand | | | | | | | | |
| | Burma | | | | | | | | |
| | Vietnam | | | | | | | | |
| | Laos | | | | | | | | |
| | Cambodia | | | | | | | | |
| South Asia | India | | 1884– | | | | | | |
| | Sri Lanka | 1870– | | | | | | | |
| | Bangladesh | | | | | | | | |
| | Nepal | | | | | | | | |
| | Pakistan | | | | | | | | |

*Sources*:

| | |
|---|---|
| Japan | Ohkawa, Shinohara and Umemura (eds.) (1974) |
| China | Maddison, Angus (1998) |
| Korea | Mizoguchi and Umemura (eds.) (1988) |
| Taiwan | Mizoguchi and Umemura (eds.) (1988) |
| Indonesia (Java) | Eng, P Van Der (2002) |
| Philippines | Hooley, Richard (2005) |
| Peninsular Malaysia | Nazrin, Raja (2000, 2002 and 2006) |
| India | Sivasubramonian, S (2000) |
| Sri Lanka | Snodgrass, D R (1966) |

from the Royal Tropical Institute. They compiled 16 volumes of historical statistics on the Netherland Indies entitled *The Changing Economy of Indonesia*.

These two research efforts were regarded as one of the first long-term projects in the Asian region. Other than these two collaborative research projects, other studies were made by individual scholars. The commencement of all these research work started in the 1960's. Unfortunately, other countries did not initiate similar research. In the 1960's, in fact, Simon Kuznets visited some Asian countries and investigated the possibility of starting a project on the construction of historical GDP estimates in Asian countries but proceeded no further as it was ascertained that the project would require skilled statistical specialists who were in short supply in these countries.[8] In fact, reliability of GDP estimates in the early 1950's in selected countries were highly questionable (Oshima, 1956). Attention was focused on the creation of reliable modern GDP estimates rather than historical GDP estimates (Goh, 1956).

Since then, no collaborative large-scale research on the construction of historical GDP in Asian countries was attempted for many decades. The rapid and sustained economic growth witnessed in East Asian countries since the 1970's further encouraged research in the area. In 1995, the Economic Research Institute, Hitotsubashi University, organized the *Asian Historical Statistics Project* for the period 1995–2000 with Konosuke Odaka as its project director.[9] In 1998, HRH Raja Dr Nazrin Shah embarked on a study to compute GDP estimates of Peninsular Malaysia for the period 1900–39.[10] In fact, this study on the GDP estimates of Singapore relies heavily on the research project initiated by HRH Raja Dr Nazrin Shah.

As is shown in Table 1.3, data on national income was only available for the entity of British Malaya (incorporating the territories of the Federation of Malaya and Singapore) for the period 1947–55. Subsequently, the official estimates of the

---

[8] According to Oshima (1997), upon the request of the Ford Foundation, Kuznets embarked on a trip to explore the possibilities of studying pre-war Asian economic conditions soon after World War II. However, his conclusion was that with the exception of Japan, this would not be a feasible project. He suggested to the Ford Foundation that before undertaking any economic analysis, it would be necessary to start with training statistical survey specialists in the various Asian countries.

[9] The interim Report on the Asian Historical Statistics Database project was released (Odaka, Konosuke, 2007). The listed countries are Taiwan, Vietnam, Mainland China, Korea, Thailand, India/Pakistan, Indonesia, Russia, Egypt and Turkey, Philippines, Central Asia and Russia and Japan. Malaya and Singapore are not included in this project.

[10] Nazrin (2000, 2002, 2006).

**Table 1.3:** Malaya and Singapore: Gross National Product and Gross Domestic Product, 1947–60 (At Market Prices $ Million)

| | GDP at Current Market Prices | | | | | | | GNP at Current Market Prices | | |
| --- | --- | --- | --- | --- | --- | --- | --- | --- | --- | --- |
| | British Malaya (Federation of Malaya and Singapore) | | Federation of Malaya | | | | Singapore | Singapore | | |
| 1947 | 3,531 | [1] | | | 2,601 | | | | | 1947 |
| 1948 | 3,619 | | | | 2,612 | | | | | 1948 |
| 1949 | 3,550 | | | | 2,635 | | | | | 1949 |
| 1950 | 5,345 | | | | 4,075 | | | | | 1950 |
| 1951 | 7,520 | [2] | | | 5,686 | | | | | 1951 |
| 1952 | 6,350 | | | | 4,670 | | | | | 1952 |
| 1953 | 5,780 | | | | 4,137 | [4] | | | | 1953 |
| 1954 | | | | | 4,273 | | | | | 1954 |
| 1955 | | | 4,992 | | 4,880 | | | | | 1955 |
| 1956 | | | 5,060 | | 4,933 | | | 1,685 | [7] | 1956 |
| 1957 | | | 5,126 | [3] | 4,985 | | | 1,797 | | 1957 |
| 1958 | | | 4,896 | | 4,764 | | | 1,967 | [8] | 1958 |
| 1959 | | | 5,527 | | 5,393 | | 1,968 [5] | 1,886 | | 1959 |
| 1960 | | | 5,866 | | 5,876 | | 2,150 [6] | 2,001 | | 1960 |

*Sources*: [ ] implies published sources.

[1] Benham, Frederick (1951).    [5] Goh Keng Swee (1995).

[2] IBRD (1955).    [6] Department of Statistics (1996).

[3] Department of Statistics, Malaysia (1999).    [7] Benham, Frederick (1959).

[4] Rao, B (1976).    [8] Lee Soo Ann (1981).

Federation of Malaya for the period 1956–60 were computed by the Department of Statistics, Federation of Malaya. Additionally, Rao (1976) provided another set of GDP estimates for the Federation of Malaya for the period 1947–55. In the case of Singapore, the first estimate of the national income of Singapore was prepared by Benham (1959) for the year 1956. Subsequently, the unofficial GNP figure was constructed by the Department of Statistics, Singapore, for the years 1957–60. For the same period, no GDP figures were available for Singapore.[11] Official GDP figures were computed by the Department of Statistics from 1960 onwards.

---

[11] Maddison (2001, pp. 293, 299 and 305) provided figures on GDP, GDP percapita and population since 1950. The figures, however, provided in the International Geary Khamis dollars and the methodology used in the computation was not explained in detail.

### 1.2.3 *Literature Review on GDP Concepts and Approaches*

In SNA, there are four accounts of the nation, namely Gross Domestic Product Account, Income and Outlay Account, Capital Transactions Account and Balance of Payments Account. The basic measure of the output arising from economic activity is known as the Gross Domestic Product (GDP). It is important to determine what constitutes an economic activity, as this determines the scope of the national accounting system. There is no difficulty in defining activities that result in the production of goods and services for sale on the market as economic activities. There is also a general agreement that government activities in the areas of public administration, law and order, health, education, and social services (and activities in similar areas carried out by private non-profit organizations) should be counted as economic activities, even though their output is not sold. However, the SNA does not include unpaid services rendered by housewives and other household members. Once the boundary of economic activity has been established, as illustrated in Table 1.4, the GDP can be derived by using three approaches.

The first approach measures the contribution of the output made by each producer by deducting from the total value of its output the value of the goods and services it purchases from other producers and uses these in producing its own output. The remainder is the value added by the producer in question; what is used in production is intermediate consumption. With some minor adjustments (less imputed bank services plus import duties), the total value added by all producers equals GDP at market prices. This method of GDP compilation is commonly known as the production approach to GDP.

The second approach, also known as the income approach, considers the costs incurred by the producer within his own operation: compensation to employees, net indirect taxes less subsidies, consumption of fixed capital, and the operating surplus. The third approach, known as the expenditure

**Table 1.4:** The Components of GDP from Production, Income and Expenditure Approach

| A | B | C |
|---|---|---|
| Gross domestic product by type of economic activity | Cost components of gross domestic product | Expenditures on gross domestic product |
| 1. Agriculture, hunting, forestry and fishing | 1. Indirect taxes, net<br>Indirect taxes paid<br><br>Less: subsidies received | 1. Private final consumption expenditure, Resident households, Private non-profit institutions serving households |
| 2. Mining and quarrying | | |
| 3. Manufacturing | | |
| 4. Electricity, gas and water | | |
| 5. Construction | | |
| 6. Wholesale and retail trade, and restaurants and hotels | 2. Consumption of fixed capital<br>Compensation of employees | 2. Government final consumption expenditure |
| 7. Transport, storage and communication | | |
| 8. Financing, insurance, real estate and business services | 3. Operating surplus | 3. Gross capital formation<br>Increase in stocks<br>Gross fixed capital Formation |
| 9. Owner-occupied dwellings | | |
| 10. Community, social and personal services | **Gross domestic product in purchaser's value** | 4. Net exports of goods and services |
| Less: imputed bank service charges | | |
| Sub-total: Domestic product of industries | | **Gross domestic product in purchaser's value** |
| 11. Producers of Government Services | | |
| 12. Producers of private non-profit services to households | | |
| 13. Domestic services of households | | |
| Adjustments:<br>Plus: import duties | | |
| **Gross domestic product in purchaser's value** | | |

approach, considers a country's output for private final consumption expenditure, government final consumption expenditure, gross capital formation and net export of goods and services. In other words, it shows what becomes of the output once it has been produced.[12] Conceptually, the results derived from each of these three approaches should be identical. However, different methods of estimating GDP will not yield similar statistical results due to leakages.

Table 1.5, which is a simplified version of what in national accounting is known as an input-output table, shows production and cost inter-relationships. It also shows how the various types of input into economic activity (listed in the rows of the chart) flow through the economy and are purchased by various users (listed in the columns). The chart is divided into three quadrants. Quadrant I shows intermediate consumption of producers. Across the top, producers are grouped by the kind of activity in which they engage. The right side of the table shows goods and services which they purchase for use in production are listed by type. Although the labels on the columns and rows of this quadrant are the same, their content is not. For example, non-agricultural goods, for example, may be produced by establishments classified under agriculture and, conversely, establishments classified under agriculture may produce some goods and services classified elsewhere. The column heading refer to whole establishments, classified by their principal activity. The rows, on the other hand, refer to goods and services, classified as per their own nature. The subtotal row at the bottom of this quadrant shows total intermediate consumption of producers engaged in each kind of activity. The sub-total column on the right side of this quadrant shows same total intermediate consumption by the types of goods and services of which it is composed. Quadrant III (the lower left-hand corner) shows the rest of production costs of producers (that is, costs that do not arise

---

[12] Department of International Economic and Social Affairs, United Nations (1986: 1).

**Table 1.5:** Integrated Framework for Measurement of GDP

| Types of Goods and Services | | | Intermediate consumption by kind of activity — Industry | | | | | | | | | | Producers of government services | Producers of private non-profit services to households | Domestic services of households | Total All Activities (Column 1–13) | Final demand — Government Final Consumption Expenditure | Private Final Consumption Expenditure | Gross Capital Formation | Exports of Goods and Services | Less: Imports of Goods and Services | Total Final Expenditure (Column 11–15) | Gross Output (Column 14+20) |
|---|---|---|---|---|---|---|---|---|---|---|---|---|---|---|---|---|---|---|---|---|---|---|---|---|
| | | | Agriculture, hunting, forestry and fishery | Mining and quarrying | Manufacturing | Electricity, gas and water | Construction | Wholesale and retail trade and restaurants and hotels | Transport, storage and communication | Financing, insurance, real estate and business services | Owner-occupied dwellings | Community, social and personal services | | | | | | | | | | | |
| | | | 1 | 2 | 3 | 4 | 5 | 6 | 7 | 8 | 9 | 10 | 11 | 12 | 13 | 14 | 15 | 16 | 17 | 18 | 19 | 20 | 21 |
| Industry | Agriculture, hunting, forestry and fishery | 1 | | | | | | | | | | | | | | | | | | | | | |
| | Mining and quarrying | 2 | | | | | | | | | | | | | | | | | | | | | |
| | Manufacturing | 3 | | | | | | Quadrant I (Intermediate Consumption) | | | | | | | | | Quadrant II (Final Expenditure) | | | | | | |
| | Electricity, gas and water | 4 | | | | | | | | | | | | | | | | | | | | | |
| | Construction | 5 | | | | | | | | | | | | | | | | | | | | | |
| | Wholesale and retail trade and restaurants and hotels | 6 | | | | | | | | | | | | | | | | | | | | | |
| | Transport, storage and communication | 7 | | | | | | | | | | | | | | | | | | | | | |
| | Financing, insurance, real estate and business services | 8 | | | | | | | | | | | | | | | | | | | | | |
| | Owner-occupied dwellings | 9 | | | | | | | | | | | | | | | | | | | | | |
| | Community, social and personal services | 10 | | | | | | | | | | | | | | | | | | | | | |
| Producers' of government services | | 11 | | | | | | | | | | | | | | | | | | | | | |
| Producers of private non-profit services to households | | 12 | | | | | | | | | | | | | | | | | | | | | |
| Domestic services of households | | 13 | | | | | | | | | | | | | | | | | | | | | |
| Total (goods and services) (Column 1–13) | | 14 | | | | | | | | | | | | | | | C | | | | | GDP | |
| Costs | Indirect taxes, minus subsidies | 15 | | | | | | | | | | | | | | | | | | | | | |
| | Consumption of fixed capital | 16 | | | | | | Quadrant III (Value Added) | | | | | | | | B | | | | | | | |
| | Compensation of employees | 17 | | | | | | | | | | | | | | | | | | | | | |
| | Operating surplus | 18 | | | | | | | | | | | | | | | | | | | | | |
| Total Value Added (Column 15–18) | | 19 | | | | | | A | | | | | | | | GDP | | | | | | | |
| Gross Input (Column 14+19) | | 20 | | | | | | | | | | | | | | | | | | | | | |

*Source:* Department of International Economic and Social Affairs, United Nations (1986: 6).

from purchases from other producers). These remaining costs are the components of value added as listed in (B) of Table 1.4 and comprise of indirect taxes (net), consumption of fixed capital, compensation for employees, and operating surplus.

Adding the contents of rows of this quadrant yields the column at the right — the entries in Table 1.5. Adding down the columns yields, in the total row at the bottom of Quadrant III, the entries in (A) of Table 1.4. The grand total row, Gross Input, at the bottom of the chart, is the sum of all production costs and profits of the producers classified under each kind of activity. This is equal to the sum of intermediate consumption and value added. Thus, another way of deriving (A) of Table 1.4 is by subtracting the total row of Quadrant I (intermediate consumption), from the grand total row representing Gross Input. Quadrant II (the upper right-hand corner) shows the final uses of GDP. Across the top, the column headings are the categories of final expenditure that appear in Table 1.5. The column at the right side of this quadrant shows entries of (C) of Table 1.4.

The grand total column (Gross Output), at the extreme right of the chart is the sum of intermediate purchases by producers (shown in Quadrant I) and final purchases by others (shown in Quadrant II), classified according to the type of goods and services. Total gross output is, by definition, equal to total gross input. In rare occasions the national accountant will be able to use all three approaches for making complete and independent estimates of GDP, particularly in developing countries where there is a dearth of data. However, it is advisable to use more than one approach because of the analytic usefulness of the figures and as a check on the reasonableness of the estimates.

## 1.3 Statistical Sources and Possible Approach for the Construction of GDP of Singapore

Compared to modern estimates of GDP, the construction of historical GDP estimates suffers from serious constraints because the estimating procedure depends on the availability of statistical information. The gathering and preparation of statistical material and compiling a time-series database represents a basic yet an important step in constructing GDP estimates. Ideally, deriving estimates using the three different approaches would be advisable since the credibility of the results of these estimates can be evaluated one against the other. However, this is constrained by the availability of data.

Prior to World War II, the British colonial authority compiled statistical information on British Malaya based on constituent administrative units, namely the Straits Settlements, Federated Malay States and the five individual Unfederated Malay States. Among these, the Straits Settlements had the most complete and comprehensive time-series statistical information for the period 1900–39. The statistics for Singapore was recorded as a part of the Straits Settlements.

The British authorities published four kinds of reports containing socio-economic data on Singapore prior to World War II, namely, the *Blue Book, Straits Settlements, 1899–1938, Statistical Tables Relating to the Colonial and Other Possessions of The United Kingdom,* 1900–01, *Statistical Tables Relating to the Colonial and Other Possessions and Protectorates,* 1902–07 and *Statistical Tables Relating to British Self-Governing Dominions, Crown Colonies, Possessions and Protectorates,* 1908–1912. These reports provided detailed statistical figures on trade, market prices, agricultural planting, demography and government finance (revenue, expenditure, assets and liabilities).

*Annual Report, Straits Settlements,* 1899–1938 summarized economic data pertaining to the Straits Settlements and provided descriptive explanations on various socio-economic events. Finally, the *Straits Settlements, Departmental Reports,* (namely on *Education, Electrical, Post and Telegraph, Trade, Financial Statement, Land Office, Chinese Protectorate, Labour and Indian Immigration, Public Works, Medical, Forest and Government Monopoly) 1888–1938* provided descriptive explanations and statistical data with regards to education, health care, public works, and post and telecommunications. Apart from these reports, the British colonial administration also released other specific data on Singapore. For matters pertaining to economic indices, the *Average Prices, Declared Trade Values, Exchange, Currency and Cost of Living, Malaya, 1929–38 and 1948–51* provided average market prices on major consumer items and cost of living indices as reflected by consumption standards which were based on ethnicity and occupation. In the case of trade, *the Appendix to the Report on Trade, Straits Settlements, 1896–1906, 1908–17, 1921–28; British Malaya, Return of Foreign Imports and Exports, 1921–39 and Foreign Trade of Malaya, 1929–30, 1932, 1934, 1936–39* provided information on Singapore's trade by (i) class of goods and (ii) country of origin and destination. Private investment in perennial crops was compiled and published in the *Malayan Agricultural Statistics, 1931–39, 1947–49. The Reports on Population Censuses (Straits Settlements, 1871, 1881, 1891, 1901 and 1911)* and *British Malaya, (1921, 1931, 1947 and 1957)* provided detailed information on the characteristics of the population and its geographical distribution. During the inter-censal years, the yearly reports entitled *Registration of Births and Deaths, Straits Settlements, 1899–1939* and the *Administration Report on the Singapore Municipality, 1899–1939* gave annual population estimates by ethnicity and gender.

The end of World War II and the Japanese occupation of British Malaya in 1945 marked the end of the Straits Settlements as an administrative unit. Singapore was reconstituted as a British Crown Colony and continued to be so up to 1955. This administrative transition ushered in an era whereby Singapore began collecting, compiling and publishing its own statistical data. *Annual Report, the Colony of Singapore* provided a wide range of statistical figures and descriptive information while the *Financial Statement of Singapore* and *Singapore's External Trade* contained detailed data on government finance and trade respectively. The British colonial authority had in place devices to collect and compile a wide range of statistical information which improved over time.

Table 1.6 illustrates the availability of relevant statistical information for the computation of each component of GDP (expenditure approach). As is described above, statistical information on government expenditure and merchandize trade was relatively well documented. This information helped in estimating the final consumption expenditure and net of exports of goods (merchandize). Other than these two components, unfortunately, no direct statistical information was available to comply with the definitions of *SNA 68*. Therefore, alternative methods were adopted depending on the availability of the relevant statistical data.

Keeping in view the nature of data that was available, the expenditure approach was selected. The other two approaches, namely the production approach and the income approach, were found to be not feasible since the data required as inputs for these two approaches were generally not available or incomplete.

## 1.4 Layout of the Book

This book is organized as follows. Chapter 1 provides an introduction to the issue at hand. Chapter 2 shows the methodology employed for the construction of each component of GDP, namely Private Final Consumption Expenditure by Resident Households (PFCE), Government Final Consumption Expenditure (GFCE), Gross Capital Formation (GCF) and Net Exports of Goods and Services in both current and constant (1914) prices. Chapter 3 examines the result of GDP estimates by conducting consistency checks between estimated figures and official figures and also by comparing with available historical GDP estimates of other countries. Subsequently, possible reasons of upturns and downturns of each component of GDP are provided. The overall pattern of Singapore's GDP growth for the entire twentieth century is commented upon. Based on this, two types of empirical investigations were conducted to examine the economic growth of Singapore in the twentieth century.

**Table 1.6:** Singapore: List of Source Materials Utilized for the Computation of Each Component of GDP, (Expenditure Approach), 1900–39 and 1950–60

| | Private Final Consumption Expenditure by Resident Househoulds | Government Final Consumption Expenditure | Gross Fixed Capital Formation | | | Net Exports of Goods and Services | |
|---|---|---|---|---|---|---|---|
| | | | Investment on Construction | Investment on Machinery and Equipments | Investment on Cultivated Assets | Net Exports of Goods (Merchandize) | Net Exports of Services |
| 1900–39 | AP<br>ARCPSS<br>AREDSS<br>ARGMSS<br>ARIISS<br>ARMDSS<br>ARRBDSS<br>ARSM<br>ARSS<br>CSS<br>CBM<br>SSBB | ARSM<br>FSSS<br>SSBB | ARTCFMS<br>ARTSS<br>BM<br>FTM<br>STCOPUK<br>STCPP<br>STBCPP | ARTSS<br>FTM<br>STCOPUK<br>STCPP<br>STBCPP | MAS<br>SSBB | ARTSS<br>BM<br>FTM<br>SSBB<br>STCOPUK<br>STCPP<br>STBCPP | ARSHB<br>ARSM<br>FTM<br>SSBB |
| 1950–60 | AP<br>AREDS<br>ARLDS<br>ARMDS<br>ARRBDMS<br>CMU<br>CS<br>MSBFM | ARCCS<br>ARCS<br>ARS<br>FSCS | ARS<br>SET | MSBFM<br>SET | | SET | ARCCS<br>ARSHB |

*Abbreviations*:

| | |
|---|---|
| AP | Average Prices, Declared Trade Values, Exchange, Currency and Cost of Living, Malaya. |
| ARCCS | Administration Reports on City Council, Singapore. |
| ARCPSS | Annual Report, Chinese Protectorate, Straits Settlements. |
| ARCS | Annual Report, Colony of Singapore. |
| AREDS | Annual Report, Education Department, Colony of Singapore/State of Singapore. |
| AREDSS | Annual Report, Education Department, Straits Settlements. |
| ARGMSS | Annual Report, Government Monopoly Department, Straits Settlements. |
| ARIISS | Annual Report, Indian Immigrations, Straits Settlements. |
| ARLDS | Annual Report, Labour Department, Colony of Singapore. |
| ARMDS | Annual Report, Medical Department, the Colony of Singapore/State of Singapore. |
| ARMDSS | Annual Report, Medical Department, Straits Settlements. |
| ARRBDMS | Annual Report, Registration of Births and Deaths Marriages and Persons, Singapore. |
| ARRBDSS | Annual Report, Registration of Birth and Death, Straits Settlements. |

(*Continued*)

**Table 1.6:** *(Continued)*

| | |
|---|---|
| ARSHB | Annual Report, Singapore Harbour Board. |
| ARSM | Administration Report on the Singapore Municipality. |
| ARS | Annual Report, the Colony of Singapore/State of Singapore. |
| ARSS | Annual Report, Straits Settlements. |
| ARTCFMS | Annual Report, Trade and Custom, Federated Malay States. |
| ARTSS | Appendix to the Report on Trade, Straits Settlements. |
| BM | British Malaya, Return of Foreign Imports and Exports. |
| CSS | Population Census, Straits Settlements. |
| CBM | Population Census of British Malaya. |
| CMU | Population Census of Malayan Union. |
| CS | Population Census of Colony of Singapore. |
| FSCS | Financial Statements, the Colony of Singapore. |
| FSSS | Financial Statements, Straits Settlements. |
| FTM | Foreign Trade of Malaya. |
| MAS | Malayan Agricultural Statistics. |
| MSBFM | Monthly Statistical Bulletins, Federation of Malaya. |
| SET | Singapore External Trade. |
| SSBB | Straits Settlements, Blue Book. |
| STCOPUK | Statistical Tables Relating to the Colonial and Other Possessions of the United Kingdom. |
| STCPP | Statistical Tables Relating to the Colonial and Other Possessions and Protectorates. |
| STBCPP | Statistical Tables Relating to British Colonies, Possessions and Protectorates. |

Chapter Four examines economic instability and economic growth. It deals with four related issues: (i) whether the degree of output volatility has dampened over time (ii) the explanatory variables for the decline in output volatility (iii) the means by which economic instability has impacted on economic growth and (iv) a comparison of Singapore's situation vis-à-vis other countries.

Chapter Five examines the long-term transition of government finance structure and empirically investigates the relationship between government fiscal behavior and economic growth. It primarily identifies the features of the fiscal policy during the British colonial period and describes the transition of government fiscal behavior in terms of budgetary process, revenue raising, government expenditure and budget management (surplus/deficit management). It then proceeds to explain the empirical analysis where in the validity of Wagner's Law is tested. For analytical purposes, two econometric techniques, namely, cointegration test and Granger causality test, are employed.

As a conclusion, Chapter 6 encapsulates the major findings and limitations of the study as well as suggestions for future research in this field.

# Chapter Two

# The Construction of Historical Gross Domestic Product Estimates of Singapore, 1900–39 and 1950–60 at Current and Constant Prices

## 2.1 Introduction

This chapter discusses estimating procedures for each component of GDP, namely Private Final Consumption Expenditure by resident households (PFCE), Government Final Consumption Expenditure (GFCE), Gross Capital Formation (GCF) and Net Exports of Goods and Services. Each component is discussed as follows: First, the definition of each component is explained. Subsequently, we identify the data availability for the period being studied. Third, the methodologies employed for the construction of the respective components of GDP in current prices is explained. Finally, we discuss about a suitable deflator that can obtain constant prices for each component. We note that for the periods 1900–39 and 1950–60, 1914 was selected as the base year. This is because the cost of living index, which was used for the construction of Consumer Price Indices, set 1914 as a base year. The year 1914 was deemed to be a relatively stable year for the period under study.

### 2.1.1 *Overview on the Methodology Employed for Estimation of Each Component of GDP*

Before explaining the methodology employed for the estimation of each component of GDP, it is necessary to understand the background. As discussed in Chapter One, the concept and definition of each component of GDP were clearly described in SNA. Nevertheless, published statistical data series in the British colonial documents are not fully available to construct each component of GDP. Thus, various creative methodologies were applied. These conformed, as closely as was possible, to the definitions outlined in *The System of National Accounts (SNA) 1968*.

Currently, household budget surveys and commodity flow tables are widely utilized for the computation of PFCE. However, these approaches could not be employed due to the dearth of such data. As such, alternative techniques had to be utilized in arriving at these estimates. As shown in Table 2.1, two distinctive approaches were employed via the direct and indirect approach. In the direct approach, data on consumption expenditure pertaining to opium, education, medical fees and utilities (gas, water supply and electricity) were gathered independently from various official sources. The indirect approach involved the estimate of PFCE on food, beverages and tobacco, clothing, rent, domestic servants and transport. By adding the expenditures derived from these two approaches we arrive at the PFCE in current and constant prices.

The estimation for indirect approach involved a number of steps. First, six consumption standards were classified based on the fact that there are significant differences in consumption levels and expenditure patterns which exist among different ethnic groups. Subsequently, the current per capita consumption expenditure of each major object of consumption was identified for each standard. These figures were then deflated by the consumer price indices of each major object of consumption to obtain the expenditure in constant prices. Real per capita consumption expenditure of each major object of consumption for each standard was then adjusted based on the changes in real

**Table 2.1:** Steps of Estimating Private Final Consumption Expenditure, 1900–39 and 1950–60

| Direct Component | Indirect Component | | | |
|---|---|---|---|---|
| | Food | Beverage & Tobacco | Clothing | Rent |
| Opium | Transport | Servants | Clubbing | Miscellaneous |

| | |
|---|---|
| **Step 1** | Estimation of mid-year population by consumption standards |
| **Step 2** | Estimation of per capita consumption expenditure of major objects of consumption and standards in current prices for selected years |
| **Step 3** | Estimation of Price Indices for Major Objects of Consumption and Consumption Standards, Malaya |
| **Step 4** | Estimating the per capita final consumption expenditure of major objects of consumption and standards in 1914 prices for selected years |
| **Step 5** | Estimations of real wage index, 1900–39, 1947–60 |
| **Step 6** | Deriving Total Private Final Consumption Expenditure in Constant and Current Prices, 1900–39 |

(Direct Component column also lists: Education, Medical, Utilities)

| | |
|---|---|
| **Step 7** | Aggregation of Direct and Indirect Component to obtain the PFCE in the Domestic Market |
| **Step 8** | Deriving PFCE by resident household by deducing non-resident consumption made in the domestic market |

income over time, taking into account the income elasticities of demand by each major object of consumption. For example, annual figures on PFCE were computed for food as per the European standard in both constant and current prices as follows:

If in the base year ($t$), the real per capita expenditure on food for European standard is $RPCF_t$ and if the real wage indices[13]

---

[13] Data on household income was not available. The movements of the nominal weighted wage indices of the agriculture and non-agriculture sectors were then used as surrogates for household income changes. The real wage index for the period 1900–39 was then computed by dividing the linked series from 1900–39 by the overall Consumer Price Indices with base year 1914 = 100.

increase from 1 in year $t$ to 1.2 in year $t + 1$, real per capita expenditure on food in year $t + 1$ ($RPCF_{t+1}$) is calculated as follows:

$$RPCF_{t+1} = RPCF_t + ((RPCF_t \times 1.2/1.0) \times 0.7).$$

If the real earnings index increases to 1.5 in year $t + 2$, per capita food expenditure in year $t + 2$ is calculated as follows:

$$RPCF_{t+2} = RPCF_{t+1} + ((RPCF_{t+1} \times (1.5 - 1.2)/1.2)) \times 0.7)).$$

Real per capita expenditure of the European standard on food for the period 1900–39 is then multiplied by the population of each year under the European Standard to obtain the real PFCE of the European Standard on food for each reference year. The derived figures are then inflated by the food indices to arrive at the PFCE in current prices. Similar procedures are applied for each major object of consumption for the six consumption standards. PFCE in the domestic market is then derived by aggregating the figures of the direct components and indirect components. In order to obtain PFCE by resident households, adjustment are made.

Government final consumption expenditure (GFCE) is derived by deducting from the government output (goods and services), the sales of other goods and services produced by the producers of government services (See Table 2.2). Output of producers of government services is computed by summing up the compensation for employees (personal emoluments), intermediate consumption of goods and services and depreciation

**Table 2.2:** Steps involved for the Estimation of GFCE, 1900–39 and 1950–60

| | |
|---|---|
| *Step 1* | Estimation of output of producers' government services at current prices |
| *Step 2* | Estimation of government sales (Education and Medical) at current prices |
| *Step 3* | Deriving estimated government final consumption expenditure (Government Output of Producer's Government Services-Government Sales) at Current Prices |

allowances of all producers of government services. These estimates include the expenditure incurred by Colony of Singapore, Municipality/City Council of Singapore and Rural Boards.[14] In the case of government sales of goods and services, school fees and hospital fees are identified and deducted from government output to arrive at the GFCE.

The estimates of Gross Capital Formation (GCF) include investments made in construction, machinery and equipment and cultivated assets. Inventories include stocks of goods held by producers to meet temporary or unexpected fluctuations in production or sales, and work in progress other than construction.

In the case of construction output capitalized, as presented in Table 2.3, total construction output is first derived by using input-output coefficients of cement to total construction output based on the first construction survey in 1972. Total construction expenditure that was incurred in fixed capital formation is then derived by deducting from total output of construction, the expenditure incurred on repairs and maintenance.

In the case of investment on machinery and equipment (M&E), it is assumed that the M&E produced locally during the period was negligible for the period under study. This means that the total net imports valued at market prices is equivalent to total investments in M&E. Net imports of M&E at c.i.f.

**Table 2.3:** Steps involved for the Estimation of Construction Output Capitalized, 1900–39 and 1950–60

| *Step 1* | Estimation of net imports of cement retained in Singapore |
|---|---|
| *Step 2* | Identification of input-output coefficient of cement to total output |
| *Step 3* | Estimation of total output for Construction |
| *Step 4* | Identification of weights on repairs and maintenance against total output |
| *Step 5* | Deriving estimated Construction Output Capitalized |

---

[14] Military expenditure on capital formation items have been treated as intermediate consumption of goods and services and form part and parcel of output.

**Table 2.4:** Steps involved for the Estimation of Machinery and Equipment Capitalized, 1900–39 and 1950–60

| | |
|---|---|
| *Step 1* | Estimation of net imports of machinery and equipment retained in Singapore |
| *Step 2* | Identification of market margin and transport margin |
| *Step 3* | Estimation of total output of Machinery and Equipment |
| *Step 4* | Identify the weight of output capitalized for investment on Machinery and Equipment |

values are obtained from official trade statistics. No commodity taxes were levied against M&E which meant that the c.i.f. (basic) and producers' values were identical. As shown in Table 2.4, trade and transport margins are added to producers' value to arrive at market prices. The final step is to determine the proportion of net imports to be capitalized. Some of these imports would have been used as inputs into construction activity and some as part of private final consumption expenditure.

In preparing estimates on investments cultivated assets, only rubber and coconut were selected since other perennial crops were found to be negligible. All expenses sunk into perennial crops prior to their reaching the bearing age were treated as part and parcel of capital expenditure. As shown in Table 2.5, three types of information were utilized for the above computation. They are newly planted acreage for each year, number of years it takes for the crop to reach bearing age and annual cost per acre of getting the crop ready for production. The yearly estimates of expenditure on cultivated assets at different years of maturity are derived by multiplying the total immature acreage with the corresponding base year estimates of cost of investment per acre at different stages of maturity. These yearly estimates were then aggregated to arrive at yearly estimates of real capital expenditure. Total real investment in cultivated assets is then inflated by the nominal rubber tapper's earnings indices. For rubber and coconut, distinction made between smallholding and estate cultivation.

**Table 2.5:** Steps involved for the Estimation of Investment for Cultivated Assets, 1900–39 and 1950–60\

| *Step 1* | Estimation of newly planted acreage for smallholding and estimate |
|---|---|
| *Step 2* | Estimation of cost of production up to maturity for various period (Smallholding and Estate) |
| *Step 3* | Computation of Cultivated Assets for various period with different base year |
| *Step 4* | Estimation of Nominal Agricultural wage Index as deflator |
| *Step 5* | Adjustment for deriving Cultivated Assets in Current Prices |

Inventory, as defined in SNA 68, consists largely of raw materials and supplies, finished or partly finished products awaiting sale and unpaid work in progress on assets which takes a long time to produce. The colonial government records, however, do not provide sufficient information on how to construct reliable estimates. Keeping in view the limitations of data availability, the official figures available after 1960 are utilized. It is observed that there is a positive correlation between GDP growth and value of changes in stock (See Table 2.6). Taking into account prevailing economic conditions, as reflected in the level of GDP growth rate, the percentage contribution of changes in stock to GDP are assigned values ranging from –3.0 percent to 3.0 percent.

Export and import statistics cover transactions of goods and services between the residents of one country and non-residents of another. Data on merchandize imports and exports of Singapore are available for the period 1900–27. For the period 1928–39, 50–60, WG Huff's (1994) estimates were applied. Exports and imports of services are captured in this estimate by using port and other related statistics (See Table 2.7).

Real GDP figures are derived by deflating each component of aggregate demand in current prices by various deflators into constant 1914 prices for the period 1900–39 and 1950–60. Table 2.8 shows various deflators used in the deflation process. For example, CPI and Import and Export Unit Value Indices are

**Table 2.6:** Steps involved for the Estimation of Changes in Stock, 1900–39 and 1950–60

| | |
|---|---|
| *Step 1* | Observe relationship between GDP growth and level of change in stock for post-war Singapore |
| *Step 2* | Apply appropriate weights on change in stocks to GDP |

**Table 2.7:** Steps involved for the Estimation of Imports and Exports of Goods and Services, 1900–39 and 1950–60

| | |
|---|---|
| *Step 1* | Deriving Merchandize Imports and Exports from official record |
| *Step 2* | Estimating trade in services on port services and non-resident consumption expenditure made in domestic market. |

computed using the Laspeyres Price Indices.[15] Unit values of commodities are derived from the quotients of values and quantities. As it is not feasible to derive an outright continuous unit value indices series due to changing composition of exports, the sample period is broken down into several but overlapping intervals with different base years. The criteria for the selection of intervals and their base years include relative stability of the shares of commodities and a relatively tranquil year. In this exercise, the base year of each interval is identified based on the proximity of the price of the commodity that commands

---

[15] Laspeyres Price Indices is computed using the following formula;

$$\frac{\sum PnQo}{\sum PoQo} = \frac{\sum \frac{Pn}{Po} * PoQo}{\sum PoQo}$$

where $Pn$ = Price in current period

$Qo$ = Quantity in base period.

Currently, Department of Statistics, Singapore uses the Laspeyres method in computing Consumer Price Indices as well as Import and Export Unit Value Indices.

**Table 2.8:** Summary of Deflator Employed by Each Component of GDP

| GDP Components | Method Applied / Deflators |
|---|---|
| Private Final Consumption Expenditure | |
| Indirect Approach | Consumer Price Indices for each major object of consumption |
| Direct Approach | Consumer Price Indices |
| Government Final Consumption Expenditure | |
|   Government Output | |
|     Compensation of Employees | Consumer Price Indices |
|     Intermediate Consumption | Consumer Price Indices |
|   Sales of Government Services | Consumer Price Indices |
| Gross Capital Formation | |
|   Cultivated Assets | Indian Rubber Tapper's Wage Indices |
|   Construction | Import Unit Value Indices of Cement |
|   Machinery and Equipment | UK Indices of Machinery and Plant |
|   Changes in Stock | Import Unit Value Indices |
| Exports of Goods and Services | |
|   Merchandize | Export Unit Value Indices |
|   Port (goods and services) | UK Weighted Indices for Fuel and Light, Transport, Communication and Other Services |
|   Non-residents consumption in domestic market | Consumer Price Indices |
| Imports of Goods and Services | |
|   Merchandize | Import Unit Value Indices |

the largest weight to its average price level during the corresponding interval.

## 2.2 Private Final Consumption Expenditure by Resident Households, 1900–39 and 1950–60

### 2.2.1 *Definition*

Private final consumption expenditure (PFCE) by resident households as defined in the SNA68 is the actual total consumption of private households and non-profit making institutions[16] on current goods and services less sales of similar goods and services. PFCE by resident households include purchases of goods and

---

[16] Private non-profit institutions are private organizations such as clubs, clan associations, religious organizations and trade unions. This series, however, does not take into account the PFCE of private non-profit making institutions because the magnitude of their final consumption expenditure is rather small or negligible.

services made abroad by resident households[17] which excludes purchases by non-resident households (e.g., by foreign tourists) made in the domestic market. Normally, PFCE made in the domestic market would be constructed first, before adjustments are subsequently made to derive PFCE by resident households.

### 2.2.2 *Sources and Methods of Estimation at Current Prices*

PFCE in the domestic market is generally constructed using a number of approaches, namely (i) household budget survey method,[18] (ii) commodity flow approach,[19] (iii) retail valuation method[20] and

---

[17] In addition, net value of gifts sent abroad is taken into account.

[18] Household budget survey method is the summation of household consumption expenditure to cover all households by inflating the data collected in a sample household survey. However, the use of data from the household expenditure survey are subject to three major constraints. First, the household survey is based on a small sample of households and/or may refer to particular groups of the population only. Second, respondents are reluctant to the provide actual expenditure pattern. Third, the household survey does not cover the rent of owner-occupied dwellings.

[19] The commodity flow approach can only be adopted if we have fairly good statistics on production, imports, exports, capital formation, intermediate consumption, stocks and other related statistics. The commodity flow table traces the use of a particular commodity by various end-users, e.g., household consumers, intermediate consumption by industries, producers of government services or other final demand. Based on the commodity flow table, it is relatively easy to construct an input/output table which can then be used to determine the PFCE based on the movements of production of commodities, imports, etc. However, the coefficients of the input/output tables should be revised from time to time but the construction of a commodity flow table itself is admittedly time consuming.

[20] Retail value method is used when primary information on household consumption is available in terms of quantities. The household expenditure is then computed by multiplying the quantity consumed by the households by the retail prices paid by the consumers. However, the compilation of appropriate average retail prices to value the quantities of commodities that households consume or acquire may be difficult to obtain. Correct weights for geographical price differences, adjustments for variations in quality, etc., are not available.

(iv) retail sales method.[21] However, in this exercise, none of the methodologies described above could be used for the estimation of the PFCE for the years 1900–39 and 1950–60 due to the dearth of data. No household budget surveys or wholesale, retail and catering trades censuses were conducted during the period 1900–39 in Singapore. In fact, the first household budget survey in Singapore was only conducted in 1947/48. This survey, however, was not comprehensive since it only covered the expenditure pattern of Europeans and the higher income Asiatic group. Consumption by institutional population was also not included.

In Singapore, the first attempt at estimating PFCE in the domestic market was made by Benham (1959) in the year 1956. He took into account net imports (quantity) of non durable, semi-durable and durable goods which were consumed by households and multiplied them by the respective retail prices. In addition, locally produced goods (quantity) consumed by households were multiplied by their respective retail prices. The own-account consumption of produce by fishermen and farmers was obtained by multiplying the quantity consumed by producer's price (See Table 2.9).

Unfortunately, this methodology could not be employed for the period under study since the required data was not available for this period. Hence, we had to adopt an alternative method of constructing the PFCE in the domestic market.

The remainder of this section attempts to describe the data and methods used to put together the PFCE series according to constant and current prices. Basically, two approaches were combined to estimate the PFCE. PFCE on opium, education, medical

---

[21] Retail sales method takes into account data on sales gathered from retailers and other outlets selling goods and services direct to household consumers. Issues of apportioning items of expenditure between final consumption expenditure of households and the intermediate consumption or gross capital formation of industries arises in instances of goods utilized by professional practitioners and other individual proprietors both in production and in household consumption.

**Table 2.9:** Singapore: Summary of Expenditure by Private Households at Market Prices, 1956

| Item | Straits $ (millions) | Percentage |
|---|---|---|
| Food | 641 | 40.2 |
| Alcoholic Drink | 59 | 3.7 |
| Tobacco | 76 | 4.8 |
| Clothing | 163 | 10.2 |
| Durable Consumer Goods | 78 | 4.9 |
| Other Manufactured Goods | 167 | 10.5 |
| Passenger Transport | 124 | 7.7 |
| Entertainment | 20 | 1.3 |
| Other Services | 98 | 6.1 |
| Housing (including rates) | 170 | 10.6 |
| Total | 1,596 | 100.0 |

*Source:* Benham (1959:1).

services, utilities and passenger rail transport were compiled for each year using current prices, via the direct approach. Expenditure on food and groceries, beverages and tobacco, clothing, rent, domestic services, clubs, passenger transport (other than rail and ferry) and other miscellaneous household expenditures were compiled using an indirect approach. Adding the expenditures from these two approaches in current and constant prices gives us the PFCE in the domestic market according to both current and constant prices. Further adjustments were made by taking into account consumption made by residents outside Singapore and deducting consumption of non-residents (e.g., foreign tourists) made in the domestic market.

### 2.2.2.1 *Direct Components*

Under the category of direct components, data on consumption expenditure on opium, education, medical fees, utilities (gas, water supply and electricity) was gathered independently. Information related to this relatively well documented in official British colonial government reports. For the years which data was not available, the methodology was then applied in the ensuing paragraphs.

### 2.2.2.1.1 Opium Consumption

Opium consumption in Singapore prior to World War II was not unlawful and data pertaining to household consumption of opium could be obtained from various official sources. Therefore, for the purpose of this study, estimates of PFCE incorporating household opium consumption were made for Singapore for the period prior to World War II. However, after World War II with household opium consumption not being sanctioned by the government, there was no data available whatsoever on the household consumption of opium. The paucity of this data meant that this component of PFCE was not taken into account for the post-war period.

The distribution and sale of opium in Singapore prior to World War II underwent many stages of transitions. As shown in Table 2.10, purchases and sales of opium were entirely operated by Chinese revenue farms since the early nineteenth century. It was not until 1910 that the British colonial authority took over the right for purchasing and selling opium from Chinese revenue farms. Nevertheless, a majority of retail shops that sold opium to consumers were operated by licensed private (Chinese) retailers. At the same time, Singapore gradually increased its government-owned retail shops.

Between 1910 and 1926, the proportion of government retail shops increased significantly. Eventually, licensed private retail shops were abolished by 1926 and fully monopolized by the government.

For the computation of the PFCE on opium in Singapore, three different procedures were applied based on the availability of data on opium consumption (See Figure 2.1(b)). For the period 1899–1922, statistical information on the quantity of opium sold to consumers and its retail price was utilized from the two reports by the Opium Committee for the years 1908 and 1924. Subsequently, due to the lack of information on quantity sold and retail prices, government revenue figures on the sales of opium provided in the *Annual Report, Government Monopoly*

**Table 2.10:**

(a) Singapore: Transformation of Revenue Collection from Final Consumption the Sales of Opium, 1899–1939

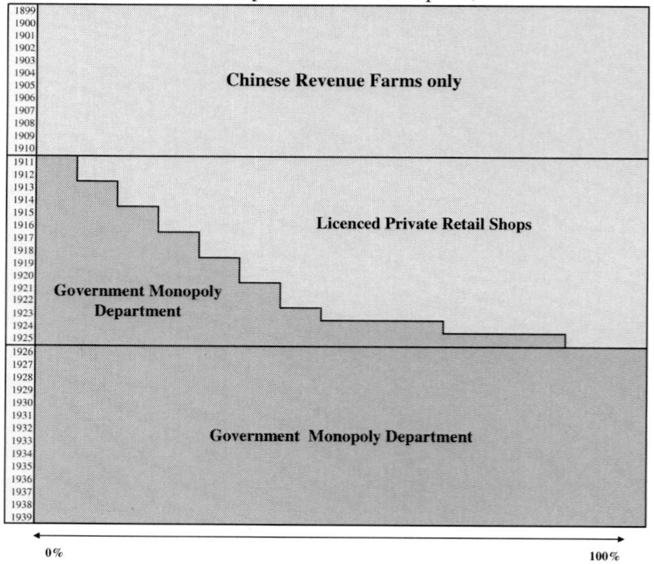

(b) Singapore: Methods Adopted to Estimate The Private Expenditure of Opium / Chandu, 1899–1939

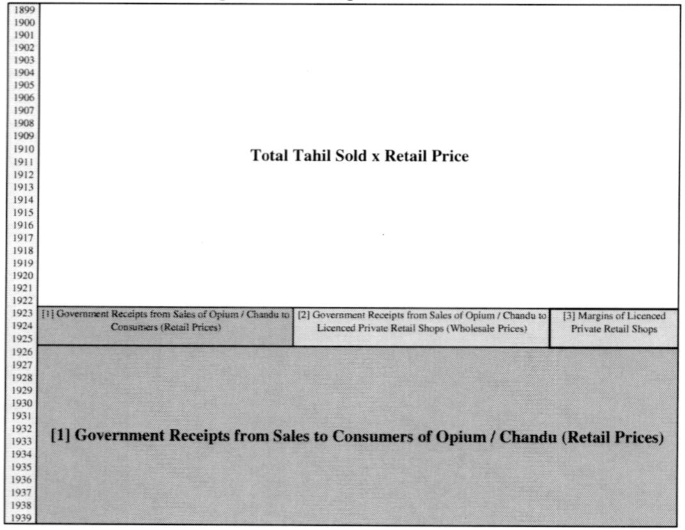

*Sources*: Based on the *Straits Settlements and Federated Malay States Opium Commission*, (1908) *Commission Appointed to Inquire into Matters Relating to the Use of Opium in the Straits Settlements and the Federated Malay States* and *British Malaya Opium Committee* (1924), *Proceedings of the British Malaya Opium Committee.*

**Table 2.11:** Singapore: Methodology Adopted to Estimate PFCE on Opium for the period 1923–25

| | Gross Government Revenue Receipts from the Sales of Opium / Chandu ($) | Gross Government Revenue Receipts from the Sales of Opium / Chandu to Consumers (Retail Prices) ($) | | Gross Government Receipts from the Sales of Opium / Chandu to Retail Shops (Wholesale Prices) ) ($) | | Trade and Transport Margins (%) | Dealers Receipts from Consumers (Retail Prices) ($) | Total Private Final Consumption of Opium / Chandu ($) |
|---|---|---|---|---|---|---|---|---|
| | [1] | [2] | [3]= [1]x[2] | [4] | [5]=[1]x[4] | [6] | [7]=[5]x(1+[6]) | [8]=[3]+[7] |
| 1923 | 10,137,264 | 60% | 6,082,358 | 40% | 4,054,906 | 4.2% | 4,225,212 | 10,307,570 |
| 1924 | 9,033,157 | 70% | 6,323,210 | 30% | 2,709,947 | 4.2% | 2,823,765 | 9,146,975 |
| 1925 | 9,306,725 | 90% | 8,376,052 | 10% | 930,672 | 4.2% | 969,761 | 9,345,813 |

*Department, Straits Settlements* and the *Blue Book, Straits Settlements* were used to estimate the PFCE on opium for the period 1923–25, details of which are given in Table 2.11. It should be noted that government revenue figures on the sale of opium as contained in these two reports for the period 1923–25 did not fully represent the actual consumption figures. The revenue figures for this period were estimated using a combination of (i) government receipts from sales of opium to consumers in retail prices and (ii) government receipts from sales of opium to licenced private retail shops at wholesale prices. The wholesale price was adjusted to obtain the retail price by making use of the 1922 trade and transport margin which was estimated to be approximately 4.2 percent. For the remaining period between 1926–39, the figures pertaining to government revenue from the sale of opium to household consumers were directly obtained from the *Annual Report, Government Monopoly Department, Straits Settlements*.

### 2.2.2.1.2  Education and Medical Fees

Total school fees collected by the Department of Education and Education Board were used as expenditure on education. The figures for the period 1900–39 were extracted from the *Blue Book, Straits Settlements* and *Annual Report, Education Department, Straits Settlements*. Subsequently, the *Annual Report, Education Department, Colony of Singapore* and *Annual Report, Education Department, States of Singapore* were utilized to obtain the information for the period 1948–56 and 1957–60 respectively.[22]

For medical expenditure, revenue collected in the form of hospital fees by the Medical Department was defined as consumption expenditure. Figures were compiled from the *Blue Book, Straits Settlements, Annual Report, Medical Department, Straits Settlements, Annual Administration Report, Malacca* and *Annual Administration Report, Penang*. For some years, the relative information was not available. Estimates were derived by employing the average ratio of Singapore's revenue collected from hospital fees relative to that of Penang. For the period 1947–60, figures on hospital fees were compiled from *Annual Report, Medical Department, Colony of Singapore*, 1947–56 and *State of Singapore*, 1957–60.


### 2.2.2.1.3 Utility (Gas, Water Supply and Electricity)

In the case of Singapore, revenue collection for utilities was undertaken by the Singapore Municipality. Revenue collection from households on electricity, gas and water was considered as final expenditure on utilities. Expenditure by businesses and public authorities was excluded, as far as possible. However, it must be noted that in some instances, the government publications did not clearly distinguish the revenue obtained from private as against public users. In such instances, the average ratio of private usage against total usage was used to interpolate and derive the estimated figures. For the period between 1900–39, figures were compiled from the *Annual Administration Report on Singapore Municipality*. As for the years 1947–60, the *Annual Administration Report on Singapore City Council* was used to obtain these figures.

---

[22] For the period of 1953–58, unfortunately, no figures were presented in *The Colony of Singapore, Report of the Educational Department*. Considering these contraints, a compound growth rate (11.6 percent) was derived from given figures for 1952 and 1959 respectively. The figures for the years 1953–58 were then computed based on this compound growth rate.

### 2.2.2.2 *Indirect Components*

In this category, major components of PFCE such as food, beverages, tobacco, clothing, rent, servant, transport and miscellaneous expenditure were computed by an entirely different method. The remainder of this section will explain the process of computation (See Table 2.12).

#### 2.2.2.2.1 Estimate of Population and Consumption Standards (STEP 1)

(I) Estimation of Mid-year Population of Singapore for 1900–39 and 1947–60

In most countries, population censuses are normally carried out on a decennial basis. Due to prohibitive high costs associated with it, this has deterred countries from conducting it on a more frequent basis. In modern times, a Post-enumeration Survey (PES) is often carried out as soon as a population census enumeration is completed. It is to evaluate the completeness and accuracy of the data on population characteristics in terms of the coverage and content collected in the census (Muhsam, 1960). The results of the PES often serve as a basis for adjusting the population census count for under-enumeration. This count is then adjusted to mid-year. In principle, there are two approaches to conducting a population census, namely the *de facto* and *de jure* methods. Whereas the *de facto* method enumerates persons in terms of the place where they were physically present on Census Night, the *de jure* method involves enumerating persons according to their usual place of residence at the time of the census irrespective of their physical presence.[23] The Censuses of British Malaya, of which Singapore was a constituent entity, were all conducted on *de facto* basis.

---

[23] Department of Economic and Social Affairs Statistics Division, United Nations (1997, 63).

**Table 2.12:** Flow Chart for Computation of PFCE in Domestic Market at Current Prices, 1900–39

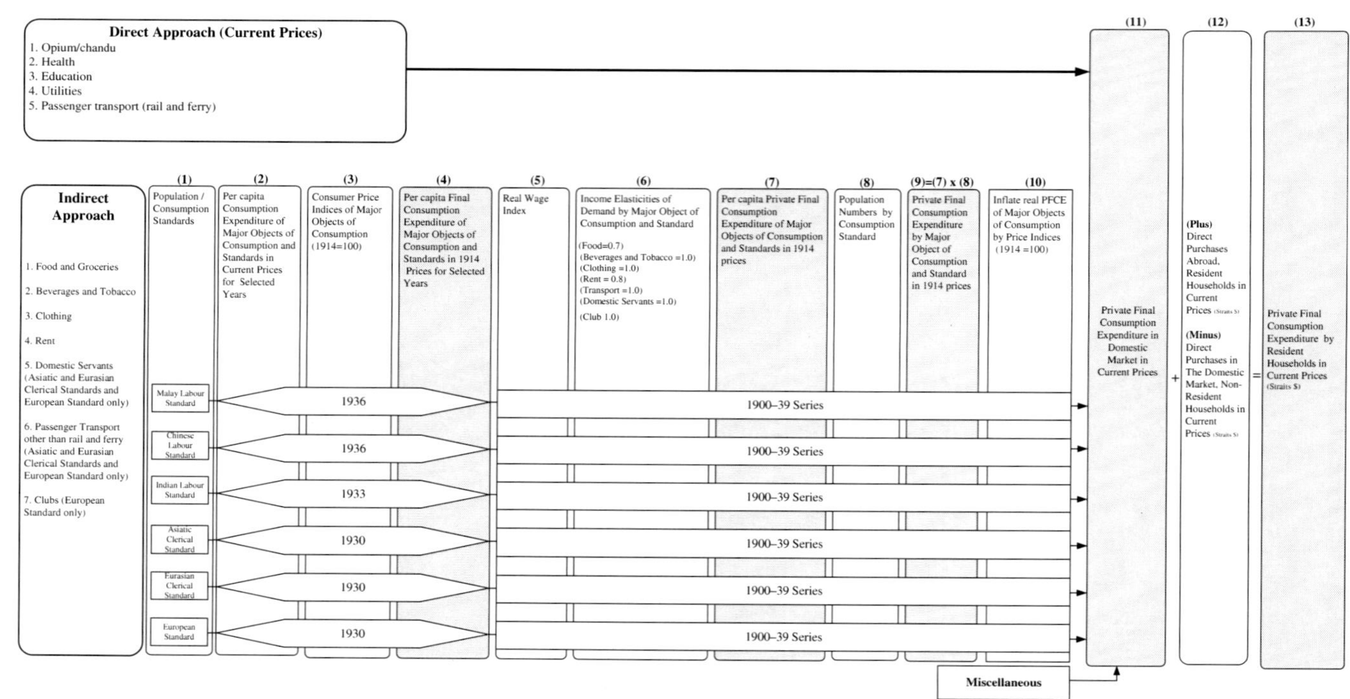

This population figure derived from the population census was then used as a base to derive post-censual annual population estimates by adding to it natural increase (i.e., excess of births over deaths) and net immigration (i.e., excess of immigration/ arrivals over emigration/departures) that had occurred over the one-year period. This method of estimating annual population continues until the next population census is held, whereby figures from the latest census are used as a new base to make post-censual annual population estimates.

It should be noted here that although the population censuses were generally conducted in March or April, for the purpose of this exercise, the population census count has been taken to represent the population as at 1st January in the year in which the census was conducted. It was felt that, to a certain extent, this would neutralize the phenomenon of undercounting that is generally prevalent in a population census.

For the period 1900–30, the total estimated population of the Colony of Singapore was available in the *Annual Report, Registration of Birth and Death, Straits Settlements*. This report provided the total estimated end-year population as well as the number of births and deaths. The figure presented in this report yielded relatively steady rates of population growth for the period 1901–10 (2.3–2.4 percent) and 1911–20 (2.8 percent). However, kinks in population growth rates were observed between the Census year and the year preceding it, much of it being attributed to the rather inaccurate data pertaining to net immigration. Information related to the issue of net immigration was documented in the *Annual Report, Chinese Protectorate, Straits Settlements*. This report provided the number of Chinese arrivals into Singapore.[24] These figures, however, did not reflect the actual number of immigrants to Singapore. *Annual Report, Indian Immigrations, Straits Settlements* provided figures on

---

[24] Chinese immigrants who were examined on board in Singapore mainly proceeded to FMS, Penang and Malacca in the territory of British Malaya and Bangkok and Rangoon (outside of British Malaya).

Indian arrivals at and departures. The coverage of this report, however, was limited only to immigrants arriving at and departing from Penang. Moreover, the number of Indians who proceeded to Singapore was not available from this report.

Given the above data constraints, the following estimation procedure was applied: First, the population numbers recorded in The *Report of the Population Census of 1947* for the years 1901, 1911, 1921, and 1931 was set as the anchor figure.[25] Second, the inter-censual annual population estimates were obtained by adding to the census base population the natural increase and net migration that occurred over each year. While the figures on births and deaths were deemed to be reasonable, the same could not be said of net migration obtained by deducting departures from arrivals.[26] As a result, there was a big difference between the inter-censual population estimate and the census figure for the same year. Since it was strongly believed that the figures obtained from the censuses must be given more credence than the constructed inter-censual figures, the inter-censual figures were adjusted to bring them in line with the census figures. To clarify this estimation procedure, we shall use Table 2.13 as an example, to illustrate the adjustments applied for the period 1921–31. To begin with, the 1921 census population count was used as the base figure representing the population as at 1st January 1921. Subsequently, the annual natural increase and net immigration figures were added year by

---

[25] The census data ordinarily pertained to the months of March and April. This is, however, assumed to pertain to 1st January of the relevant years. It is hoped that this procedure would largely neutralize the phenomenon of undercounting of the population in the census years.

[26] *Annual Report, Chinese Protectorate Department, Straits Settlements* provided the number of Chinese arrivals and departures during the year. This number of net immigrants is, however, far different from the figures in *Annual Report, Registration of Birth and Death, Straits Settlements*. This is because *Annual Report, Chinese Protectorate Departments, Straits Settlements* regards Singapore as the entry and exit point of Chinese migration to British Malaya.

**Table 2.13:**  Singapore: Methodology to Derive Adjusted Total Population

| | | | |
|---|---|---|---|
| Estimated Net Immigration (1st Jan.1921–31st Dec.1930) | Adjusted Net Immigration (1st Jan.1921–31st Dec.1930) | | |
| Esimated Natural Increase (1st Jan.1921–31st Dec.1930) | Esimated Natural Increase (1st Jan.1921–31st Dec.1930) | Total Census Population 1931 (1st January 1931) |
| Total Census Population 1921 (1st January 1921) | Total Census Population 1921 (1st January 1921) | Total Census Population 1921 (1st January 1921) | |

year from 1st January 1921 to 1st January 1931. Logically, intercensual–derived figure on 31st December 1930 (or 1st January 1931) should be identical to that of the 1931 Census figure, but the derived inter-censual figure was found to be much higher than the 1931 Census figure. Thus, an exercise had to be undertaken to reconcile these figures. Meanwhile, the birth and death figures were left unchanged, while net migration bore the full brunt of the adjustments.

The adjustment was made in the following manner: First, the net immigration for the period 1st January 1921–1st January 1931 was obtained as a residual by taking the population growth (obtained by taking the 1931 census population minus the 1921 census population) less the natural increase during the period 1st January 1921–1st January 1931. The ratio of this residual net migration figure in relation to the sum of yearly net immigration for the period 1921–31 (1st January) was then used as an adjustment factor and applied to the latter. The resulting adjusted net immigration figures when added to the figures of natural increase for each year (of the 10-year period, respectively), using 1921 census population as the base, would yield inter-censual population estimates in line with the 1931 Census figure.

For the period 1931–60, *Report on the Registration of Birth and Deaths, Malayan Union, 1940–1946* and *Annual Report, Registration of Births and Deaths Marriages and Persons for the year 1965*, Singapore, provided figures on mid-year population. These figures, particularly those pertaining to net immigration, which hitherto had been deemed to be grossly inaccurate, were then accepted as reliable figures on the basis of the statements made in the Population Census Report of 1947.[27] The estimated mid-year population for Singapore for individual years as well as annual population growth rates for the period 1900–39 and 1947–60 are given in Table 2.14.

### (II)  Consumption Standards

It is generally accepted that there were significant differences in consumption levels and expenditure patterns between ethnic groups, between rural and urban areas and between households in different income/occupational brackets. In constructing our expenditure series, an attempt was made to take into account these differences in population characteristics. To derive this, expenditure patterns were classified into six consumption standards for the periods 1900–39 and 1950–60. In this exercise, occupations were first classified into professional/managerial, clerical and manual, and this classification scheme was then used alongside the information on ethnicity to establish the total number of employed for the various consumption standards mentioned above. For example, it was assumed that Eurasian

---

[27] It is only fair to point out that the pre-1930 figures for China did not even purport to be migration statistics. They were merely departmental records kept by the Chinese Protectorate in Singapore of arrivals there of deck passengers from China, including passengers in transit to other Malaysian ports or other countries and of departures to China alone. Naturally, the use of these figures on the assumption that they were genuine migration statistics provided absurdly high estimates. There was gross undercounting of departures (Census Report 1947, 28). However, the whole system of collecting migration statistics had been completely overhauled in 1930, and subsequently, the figures were as complete as could reasonably be expected though, doubtless, small movements by junk or boat to and from China and Indonesia and over the Siamese border went unrecorded (Census Report, 1947, 28).

**Table 2.14:**   Singapore: Mid-year Population, 1900–39 and 1947–60

| | Mid-year Population | Growth Rate (%) | | Mid-year Population | Growth Rate (%) | | Mid-year Population | Growth Rate (%) |
|---|---|---|---|---|---|---|---|---|
| 1900 | 226,100 | | 1920 | 411,849 | | 1947 | 938,144 | |
| 1901 | 231,845 | 2.5 | 1921 | 427,026 | 3.6 | 1948 | 960,800 | 2.4 |
| 1902 | 238,508 | 2.8 | 1922 | 446,426 | 4.4 | 1949 | 978,700 | 1.8 |
| 1903 | 245,328 | 2.8 | 1923 | 462,792 | 3.6 | 1950 | 1,022,100 | 4.3 |
| 1904 | 252,345 | 2.8 | 1924 | 479,462 | 3.5 | 1951 | 1,068,100 | 4.4 |
| 1905 | 259,591 | 2.8 | 1925 | 500,229 | 4.2 | 1952 | 1,127,000 | 5.4 |
| 1906 | 267,042 | 2.8 | 1926 | 520,163 | 3.9 | 1953 | 1,191,800 | 5.6 |
| 1907 | 274,717 | 2.8 | 1927 | 540,660 | 3.9 | 1954 | 1,248,200 | 4.6 |
| 1908 | 282,626 | 2.8 | 1928 | 561,434 | 3.8 | 1955 | 1,305,500 | 4.5 |
| 1909 | 290,754 | 2.8 | 1929 | 582,519 | 3.7 | 1956 | 1,371,600 | 4.9 |
| 1910 | 299,096 | 2.8 | 1930 | 575,435 | −1.2 | 1957 | 1,445,929 | 5.3 |
| 1911 | 308,378 | 3.1 | 1931 | 562,866 | −2.2 | 1958 | 1,514,000 | 4.6 |
| 1912 | 318,630 | 3.3 | 1932 | 545,988 | −3.0 | 1959 | 1,579,600 | 4.2 |
| 1913 | 329,169 | 3.3 | 1933 | 514,500 | −5.9 | 1960 | 1,634,100 | 3.4 |
| 1914 | 340,005 | 3.2 | 1934 | 525,228 | 2.1 | | | |
| 1915 | 351,144 | 3.2 | 1935 | 572,310 | 8.6 | | | |
| 1916 | 362,602 | 3.2 | 1936 | 603,163 | 5.3 | | | |
| 1917 | 374,393 | 3.2 | 1937 | 651,486 | 7.7 | | | |
| 1918 | 386,530 | 3.2 | 1938 | 710,037 | 8.6 | | | |
| 1919 | 399,013 | 3.2 | 1939 | 727,564 | 2.4 | | | |

manual workers shared the same lifestyle as their Indian counterparts and were subsequently placed in the Indian labor standard. Non-Europeans holding professional/management positions were classified under the European standard. Altogether, six benchmark years are involved and it generally corresponds with the availability of data on the total number of employed by occupation and by ethnic group in Singapore. Those years include 1901, 1911, 1921, 1931, 1947 and 1957. Figures for inter-censual years were estimated on the basis of approximations from benchmark years as no breakdown on the figures of employment is available for those years. Hence, 1901 has been used as the reference year for the period 1900–10, 1911 for 1911–20, 1921 for 1921–30, 1931 for 1931–39, 1947 for 1947–56 and 1957 for 1957–60. However, census data of 1901 and 1911 do not provide information on population by occupation. Therefore, the population by occupational categories for the years 1900–20 was estimated using the assumption that its distribution would be very much akin to that observed in the 1921 Population Census.[28]

Table 2.15 lists out the six consumption standards on the basis of the above-mentioned ethnicity–employment (occupational) data. Adjustments were made on numerous occasions to the data obtained from source documents when it was felt that the number of persons of a specific ethnic group reported, for a particular occupational category, was incredibly large. For instance, of the total Malays employed as accountants and book-keepers, it would be deemed that not all of them were actually in the professional/managerial category and thus were adopting the European lifestyle. Instead, it would be assumed, based on local knowledge, that only a certain percentage of them actually fell in the professional/managerial category (European standard), while the rest were in the clerical category (Asiatic clerical standard). This table also a lists out the six consumption standards based on the above-mentioned ethnicity–employment (occupational) data.

### 2.2.2.2.2 Per-capita Consumption Expenditure by Standard for Base Year (STEP 2)

The second step involved the determination of the annual consumption expenditure of a "representative" individual of each of

---

[28] For the years 1900–10 and 1911–20, the distribution of six consumption standards was based on the 1921 Census with slight adjustments being made for 1901 and 1911 (See Table below). It was assumed that the composition of European Standard, Asiatic clerical, Chinese labor standard and Indian labor standard was slightly smaller prior to 1921. On the other hand, the composition of Malay labor standard was assumed to be higher on the basis that substantial immigration of this group occurred in the early 20th century.

| Census Year | European Standard (%) | Asiatic Clerical Standard (%) | Eurasian Clerical Standard (%) | Chinese Labor Standard (%) | Indian Labor Standard (%) | Malay Labor Standard (%) | Total (%) |
|---|---|---|---|---|---|---|---|
| 1901 | 6.0 | 8.5 | 1.0 | 59.5 | 7.0 | 18.0 | 100.0 |
| 1911 | 6.0 | 8.8 | 1.0 | 60.2 | 7.0 | 17.0 | 100.0 |
| 1921 | 6.5 | 11.0 | 1.0 | 60.5 | 8.0 | 13.0 | 100.0 |

**Table 2.15:** Singapore: Population by Consumption Standard, 1899–1939 and 1947–60

|  | European Standard | Asiatic Clerical Standard | Eurasian Clerical Standard | Chinese Labor Standard | Indian Labor Standard | Malay Labor Standard | Total |  |
|---|---|---|---|---|---|---|---|---|
| 1899 | 13,667 | 19,362 | 2,278 | 135,535 | 15,945 | 41,002 | 227,790 | 1899 |
| 1900 | 13,566 | 19,219 | 2,261 | 134,530 | 15,827 | 40,698 | 226,100 | 1900 |
| 1901 | 13,911 | 19,707 | 2,318 | 137,948 | 16,229 | 41,732 | 231,845 | 1901 |
| 1902 | 14,310 | 20,273 | 2,385 | 141,912 | 16,696 | 42,931 | 238,508 | 1902 |
| 1903 | 14,720 | 20,853 | 2,453 | 145,970 | 17,173 | 44,159 | 245,328 | 1903 |
| 1904 | 15,141 | 21,449 | 2,523 | 150,145 | 17,664 | 45,422 | 252,345 | 1904 |
| 1905 | 15,575 | 22,065 | 2,596 | 154,457 | 18,171 | 46,726 | 259,591 | 1905 |
| 1906 | 16,023 | 22,699 | 2,670 | 158,890 | 18,693 | 48,068 | 267,042 | 1906 |
| 1907 | 16,483 | 23,351 | 2,747 | 163,456 | 19,230 | 49,449 | 274,717 | 1907 |
| 1908 | 16,958 | 24,023 | 2,826 | 168,162 | 19,784 | 50,873 | 282,626 | 1908 |
| 1909 | 17,445 | 24,714 | 2,908 | 172,999 | 20,353 | 52,336 | 290,754 | 1909 |
| 1910 | 17,946 | 25,423 | 2,991 | 177,962 | 20,937 | 53,837 | 299,096 | 1910 |
| 1911 | 18,503 | 27,137 | 3,084 | 185,643 | 21,586 | 52,424 | 308,378 | 1911 |
| 1912 | 19,118 | 28,039 | 3,186 | 191,815 | 22,304 | 54,167 | 318,630 | 1912 |
| 1913 | 19,750 | 28,967 | 3,292 | 198,160 | 23,042 | 55,959 | 329,169 | 1913 |
| 1914 | 20,400 | 29,920 | 3,400 | 204,683 | 23,800 | 57,801 | 340,005 | 1914 |
| 1915 | 21,069 | 30,901 | 3,511 | 211,389 | 24,580 | 59,695 | 351,144 | 1915 |
| 1916 | 21,756 | 31,909 | 3,626 | 218,286 | 25,382 | 61,642 | 362,602 | 1916 |
| 1917 | 22,464 | 32,947 | 3,744 | 225,385 | 26,208 | 63,647 | 374,393 | 1917 |
| 1918 | 23,192 | 34,015 | 3,865 | 232,691 | 27,057 | 65,710 | 386,530 | 1918 |
| 1919 | 23,941 | 35,113 | 3,990 | 240,206 | 27,931 | 67,832 | 399,013 | 1919 |
| 1920 | 24,711 | 36,243 | 4,118 | 247,933 | 28,829 | 70,014 | 411,849 | 1920 |
| 1921 | 27,757 | 46,973 | 4,270 | 258,351 | 34,162 | 55,513 | 427,026 | 1921 |
| 1922 | 29,018 | 49,107 | 4,464 | 270,088 | 35,714 | 58,035 | 446,426 | 1922 |
| 1923 | 30,082 | 50,907 | 4,628 | 279,989 | 37,023 | 60,163 | 462,792 | 1923 |
| 1924 | 31,165 | 52,741 | 4,795 | 290,074 | 38,357 | 62,330 | 479,462 | 1924 |
| 1925 | 32,515 | 55,025 | 5,002 | 302,638 | 40,018 | 65,030 | 500,229 | 1925 |
| 1926 | 33,811 | 57,218 | 5,202 | 314,698 | 41,613 | 67,621 | 520,163 | 1926 |
| 1927 | 35,143 | 59,473 | 5,407 | 327,100 | 43,253 | 70,286 | 540,660 | 1927 |
| 1928 | 36,493 | 61,758 | 5,614 | 339,668 | 44,915 | 72,986 | 561,434 | 1928 |
| 1929 | 37,864 | 64,077 | 5,825 | 352,424 | 46,602 | 75,727 | 582,519 | 1929 |
| 1930 | 37,403 | 63,298 | 5,754 | 348,138 | 46,035 | 74,807 | 575,435 | 1930 |
| 1931 | 36,586 | 61,915 | 2,814 | 354,606 | 50,658 | 56,287 | 562,866 | 1931 |
| 1932 | 35,489 | 60,059 | 2,730 | 343,972 | 49,139 | 54,599 | 545,988 | 1932 |
| 1933 | 33,443 | 56,595 | 2,573 | 324,135 | 46,305 | 51,450 | 514,500 | 1933 |
| 1934 | 34,140 | 57,775 | 2,626 | 330,894 | 47,271 | 52,523 | 525,228 | 1934 |
| 1935 | 37,200 | 62,954 | 2,862 | 360,555 | 51,508 | 57,231 | 572,310 | 1935 |
| 1936 | 39,206 | 66,348 | 3,016 | 379,993 | 54,285 | 60,316 | 603,163 | 1936 |
| 1937 | 42,347 | 71,663 | 3,257 | 410,436 | 58,634 | 65,149 | 651,486 | 1937 |
| 1938 | 46,152 | 78,104 | 3,550 | 447,323 | 63,903 | 71,004 | 710,037 | 1938 |
| 1939 | 47,292 | 80,032 | 3,638 | 458,365 | 65,481 | 72,756 | 727,564 | 1939 |

|  | European Standard | Malay Clerical Standard | Chinese, Indian, Eurasian Clerical Standards | Chinese Labor Standard | Indian Labor Standard | Malay Labor Standard | Total |  |
|---|---|---|---|---|---|---|---|---|
| 1947 | 56,289 | 14,072 | 126,649 | 562,886 | 93,814 | 84,433 | 938,144 | 1947 |
| 1948 | 57,648 | 14,412 | 129,708 | 576,480 | 96,080 | 86,472 | 960,800 | 1948 |
| 1949 | 58,722 | 14,681 | 132,125 | 587,220 | 97,870 | 88,083 | 978,700 | 1949 |
| 1950 | 61,326 | 15,332 | 137,984 | 613,260 | 102,210 | 91,989 | 1,022,100 | 1950 |
| 1951 | 64,086 | 16,022 | 144,194 | 640,860 | 106,810 | 96,129 | 1,068,100 | 1951 |
| 1952 | 67,620 | 16,905 | 152,145 | 676,200 | 112,700 | 101,430 | 1,127,000 | 1952 |
| 1953 | 71,508 | 17,877 | 160,893 | 715,080 | 119,180 | 107,262 | 1,191,800 | 1953 |
| 1954 | 74,892 | 18,723 | 168,507 | 748,920 | 124,820 | 112,338 | 1,248,200 | 1954 |
| 1955 | 78,330 | 19,583 | 176,243 | 783,300 | 130,550 | 117,495 | 1,305,500 | 1955 |
| 1956 | 82,296 | 20,574 | 185,166 | 822,960 | 137,160 | 123,444 | 1,371,600 | 1956 |
| 1957 | 86,756 | 14,459 | 267,497 | 788,031 | 144,593 | 144,593 | 1,445,929 | 1957 |
| 1958 | 90,840 | 15,140 | 280,090 | 825,130 | 151,400 | 151,400 | 1,514,000 | 1958 |
| 1959 | 94,776 | 15,796 | 292,226 | 860,882 | 157,960 | 157,960 | 1,579,600 | 1959 |
| 1960 | 98,046 | 16,341 | 302,309 | 890,585 | 163,410 | 163,410 | 1,634,100 | 1960 |

the six standards by each major object of consumption. The methodology involved for estimating the per-capita consumption expenditure for major objects of consumption of the various consumption standards can be described as follows.

## (I) Pre–World War II Period
### (a) The European Standard (1930)

From the *1930 Family Budget Survey* of Singapore, it was established that a typical European standard household of three persons would incur a monthly expense of $649.10, as given in Table 2.16.

This figure ($649.10) excludes expenditure on certain consumption items (e.g., health, education, and utilities) that has already been estimated via the direct approach. This European budget also excludes consumption of a non-resident family member. At the same time, the miscellaneous expenditure would only be taken into account in the final stages in the computation of PFCE of all standards. The monthly and yearly per-capita consumption of this household was also subsequently derived.

### (b) The Eurasian/Asiatic Clerical Standards (1930)

It should be noted here that for the Eurasian and Asiatic clerical standards in Singapore, the procedure of deriving monthly and yearly per-capita consumption expenditures was similar to that adopted for the European standard as described above. The source data were again obtained from the Family Budget Survey of 1930 for Singapore, taking into account the variations in household size.

### (c) The Indian Labour Standard (1933)

The consumption of an adult of this standard was obtained from the Indian Labourer's Specimen Monthly Budget (1933) as contained in the Annual Report, Johore (1933), which amounted to $4.525 per month as shown in Table 2.17.

This figure does not include miscellaneous expenses incurred on items such as soap, kerosene, pots and pans, mats, pillows, etc. The monthly and yearly weighted per-capita consumption

**Table 2.16:** Singapore: European Family Budget, 1930

| Major Objects of Consumption | Straits $ |
|---|---|
| **Food** | **157.00** |
| Market and cold storage | 120.00 |
| Groceries | 30.00 |
| Bakery | 7.00 |
| **Beverages and Tobacco** | **47.63** |
| Whisky, gin, vermouths, port, sherry, liquers, bitters and wine | 36.03 |
| Aerated waters | 4.40 |
| Tobacco | 7.20 |
| **Servant** | **170.00** |
| Boy, cook, tukang ayer, gardener, amah and syce | 170.00 |
| **Transport** | **53.47** |
| Petrol, tyres, insurance covering car, lubricating oil and repairs | 53.47 |
| **Clothing** | **80.00** |
| Man | 25.00 |
| Wife | 40.00 |
| Child in Malaya | 15.00 |
| **Club** | **61.00** |
| Entrance fees, subscriptions and expenses (caddies, etc) | 61.00 |
| **Rent** | **80.00** |
| Rent | 80.00 |
| **Total** | **649.10** |

*Source:* Milles (1930, 14–16 and 20–23).

expenditure was then derived on the basis of the assumption that an adult female would consume the same amount of food and clothing as the adult male. Meanwhile, a child's consumption of these items would be two-thirds of that of an adult.[29] It should be noted that the figure for food was revised upwards to account for own-account consumption.[30] The per-capita consumption of

---

[29] This information was derived from the Health and Nutrition Information Infrastructure Database System (1995) developed by the National Institute of Health and Nutrition (NIHN) in collaboration with the Japan Science and Technology Agency (JST). Annual mean of the total amount of food, both animal food and vegetable food, for an adult (30–39 years old) and child (1–6 years old) were 1,479.8 grams and 983.4 grams, respectively. Using this available information, it was decided that consumption of food by a child was almost two-third of an adult.

[30] For example, this includes consumption of home-grown poultry and livestock products, vegetables, etc.

**Table 2.17:** A Labourer's Specimen Monthly Budget (1933)

| Items | Amount | Unit of Quantity | Price in Cents per Gantang, Chupak or Kati | Cost (Straits $) |
|---|---|---|---|---|
| **Food** | | | | **3.855** |
| Rice | 6 | Gantang | 20 | 1.200 |
| Salt | 1.5 | Chupak | 3 | 0.045 |
| Chillies | 0.5 | Kati | 17 | 0.085 |
| Coriander | 0.75 | Chupak | 6 | 0.045 |
| Tamarind | 1.5 | Kati | 7 | 0.105 |
| Dhal | 1.5 | Chupak | 12 | 0.180 |
| Green peas | 1 | Chupak | 8 | 0.080 |
| White beans | 0.5 | Chupak | 10 | 0.050 |
| Onions | 1 | Kati | 6 | 0.060 |
| Garlic | 0.5 | Kati | 8 | 0.040 |
| Thalippu | 0.5 | Chupak | 24 | 0.120 |
| Pepper | 1.25 | Chupak | 5 | 0.060 |
| Turmeric | 1.25 | Chupak | 16 | 0.040 |
| Curry masala | | | | 0.040 |
| Coconut oil | 1 | Bottle | 10 | 0.100 |
| Salted fish | 1 | Bottle | 19 | 0.190 |
| Mutton | 1 | Kati | 48 | 0.480 |
| Vegetables | | | | 0.400 |
| Potatoes | 1 | Kati | 5 | 0.050 |
| Coffee | 1 | Tin | 12 | 0.120 |
| Sugar | 1 | Kati | 4.5 | 0.045 |
| Tin milk | 1 | Tin | 18 | 0.180 |
| Gingelly oil | 0.5 | Bottle | 28 | 0.140 |
| **Tobacco** | | | | **0.420** |
| Betel nut and tobacco | | | | 0.420 |
| **Clothing** | | | | **0.250** |
| Clothing | | | | 0.250 |
| **Per-capita Adult Consumption** | | | | **4.525** |

*Source:* Annual Report, Johore (1933), Labourer's Specimen Monthly Budget (1933), p. 27.

tobacco was based solely on the consumption made by an adult male. Data on rent for the Indian standard were not available for any of the years during this period. Expenditure on rent was, therefore, estimated using surrogate data. The cost-of-living index of the Eurasian Clerical standard (1914–39) hold a weightage of 8 percent for rentals for the base year, in relation to all goods and services consumed. This was taken into account and an assumption was made that the rental expenditure for the

Indian standard would account for about 5 percent of all goods and services consumed. The treatment of miscellaneous items was similar to that of the Eurasian and Asiatic clerical standards mentioned earlier.

## (d) The Malay and Chinese Labour Standards (1936)
## (i) Food (1936)

The food consumption pattern of a full-meat diet of a Malay and a Chinese adult was based on the 1936 diet scale of government hospitals. Since food provisions in government hospitals were deemed to be the minimum dietary requirements, the food consumption data were adjusted upwards to reflect the normal intake of an adult. Subsequently, the monthly and yearly weighted per-capita consumption for the Malay and Chinese standards were derived with a procedure similar to that as described for the Indian labour standard.

## (ii) Tobacco, Clothing and Rent (1936)

No data were available for 1936 on the per-capita consumption of tobacco, clothing and rent. Given this predicament, estimates for the various major objects of consumption in 1936 were made on the basis of per-capita consumption of such objects (except rent) in the year 1949, for which only then the data were available. It was assumed that the proportion of expenditure, in nominal terms, on these major objects of consumption in relation to food as observed in 1949 would remain unchanged in 1939. Using this assumption, the consumption of food in 1939 was computed. However, the changes in real consumption due to changes in real income were not taken into account. Having determined the per-capita consumption of food in 1939, the per-capita consumption of tobacco and clothing for 1939 was computed using the relationship of these major objects of consumption to food in 1949. The data for 1936 were then obtained by deflating each major object of consumption by the relevant price index to reflect price changes for the two years (1936 and 1939) using 1914 as the base year.

Data on rent were not available for the year 1949. It was noted that rent constituted 8 percent of the per-capita expenditure of the Eurasian clerical standard in 1914. It was then posited that the percentage of expenditure on rent for the Malay and Chinese labor standards would certainly be less than the Eurasian clerical standard. An assumption was therefore made that the percentage would only be about 5 percent for the Malay labor standard and about 6 percent for the Chinese labor standard. As for the miscellaneous items of consumption, its treatment is similar to that of the European/Eurasian clerical/Asiatic clerical standards as described earlier. By now, I have so far described the manner in which annual per-capita consumption expenditure of a "representative" individual in each of the six consumption standards has been constructed, for each major object of consumption in current prices for the selected years. The results of the above exercise are summarized in Table 2.18 (A).

## (II) Post–World War II Period
### (a) The European, Malay Clerical and Chinese, Indian, Eurasian Clerical Standards

The publication entitled *Average Prices, Declared Trade Values, Exchange, Currency and Cost of Living, Department of Statistics, Straits Settlements and Federated Malay States, 1948, Malaya* provided a detailed structure of household consumption expenditure by major object of consumption for the European, Malay Clerical and Chinese, Indian, Eurasian Clerical standards, respectively. The original data provided quantity consumed on food, tobacco and transport and also the total value of consumption for beverages, clothing, clubs and rents at 1948 prices. To derive the value in 1948 for food items, tobacco and transport, available market prices of that particular year were derived from the *Monthly Statistical Bulletin, Federation of Malaya* and *Malayan Statistics Monthly Digest of Economic and Social Statistics Relating to the Colony of Singapore and the Federation of Malaya.*

**Table 2.18A:** Singapore: Annual Per-capita Private Consumption Expenditure by Standard, Selected Years

(A) 1900–39 Series

| Consumption Standard / Major Objects of Consumption | European Standard (1930) | Eurasian Standard (1930) | Asiatic Clerical Standard (1930) | Malay Labour Standard (1936) | Chinese Labour Standard (1936) | Indian Labour Standard (1933) |
|---|---|---|---|---|---|---|
| Food and Groceries | $601.20[1] | $195.48[1] | $184.56[1] | $84.54[2] | $88.01[2] | $79.79[6] |
| Bevarages and Tobacco | $171.48[1] | $8.64[1] | $8.64[1] | $10.19[3] | $8.14[3] | $16.36[6] |
| Clothing | $288.00[1] | $31.20[1] | $31.20[1] | $11.58[4] | $11.42[4] | $10.18[6] |
| Rent | $288.00[1] | $72.00[1] | $72.00[1] | $5.57[5] | $7.03[5] | $9.49[7] |
| Domestic Servants | $655.20[1] | $24.00[1] | $24.00[1] | Not applicable | Not applicable | Not applicable |
| Transport (Other than Railway) | $192.48[1] | $26.50[1] | $26.50[1] | Not applicable | Not applicable | Not applicable |
| Clubs | $219.60[1] | Not applicable | Not applicable | Not applicable | Not applicable | Not applicable |

*Notes*:

1. Per-capita consumption was derived on the basis of household size of each standard household.
2. Per-capita consumption is assumed to be 25 percent more than the full-meat diet scale of adults in government hospitals. Male and female adults consume the same amount whereas children consume two-third of adult amount.
3. Applied the ratio of beverages and tobacco to food in 1949 to 1939 and deflated to 1936.
4. Applied the ratio of clothing to food in 1949 to 1939 and deflated to 1936.
5. Applied the ratio of rent to food in 1949 to 1939 and deflated to 1936.
6. Per-capita consumption is assumed to be 20 percent more than that of Labourer's Specimen, Johore, 1933. Male and female adults consume the same amount whereas children consume two-third of adult amount.
7. Computed as a 5 percent of total expenditure on food, clothing, beverages and tobacco.

*Sources*:

[1] Milles (1931, 14–16 and 20–23).

[2] *Annual Report, Johore 1933, Laborer's Specimen Monthly Budget*, p. 27.

[3] *Allen, A (1938, 1705)*.

[4] *Annual Report Labor Department, Colony of Singapore* (1949, 74–76).

## (b) Chinese, Malay and Indian Labor Standards for the Year 1949

*Annual Report, Labour Department, the Colony of Singapore, 1949* provided information on quantity consumed by an adult male for each item, namely food, tobacco, and clothing. The monthly and yearly weighted per-capita consumption expenditure was then derived on the assumption that an adult female would consume the same amount of food and clothing as the adult male. Meanwhile, a child's consumption of these items would be two-thirds of that of an adult. As for the estimation of consumption expenditure on rent, an assumption was therefore made that the percentage would only be about 5 percent for the Malay and Indian labour standards and around 6 percent for these Chinese labour standard. The results of these estimates are presented in Table 2.18 (B).

### 2.2.2.2.3 Construction of Consumer Price Indices 1900–39 and 1950–60 (1914 = 100) (STEP 3)

Consumer price indices (CPI) form a basis for measuring the rate of inflation and are a useful tool for deflating PFCE, wage

**Table 2.18B:** Singapore: Annual Per-capita Private Consumption Expenditure by Standard, Selected Years

(B) 1947–60 Series

| Major Objects of Consumption | European Standard (1948) | Malay Clerical Standard (1948) | Chinese, Indian and Eurasian Clerical Standard (1948) | Malay Labour Standard (1949) | Chinese Labour Standard (1949) | Indian Labour Standard (1949) |
|---|---|---|---|---|---|---|
| Food and Groceries | $1,245.82[1] | $451.33[1] | $419.13[1] | $300.42[2] | $356.03[2] | $407.74[2] |
| Beverages and Tobacco | $708.90[1] | $20.70[1] | $20.70[1] | $39.94[2] | $36.33[2] | $38.80[2] |
| Clothing | $951.82[1] | $57.74[1] | $54.46[1] | $48.22[2] | $54.14[2] | $31.43[2] |
| Rent | $672.65[1] | $60.50[1] | $60.50[1] | $22.95[3] | $32.97[3] | $28.94[3] |
| Domestic Servants | $1,357.69[1] | $108.08[1] | $108.08[1] | Not applicable | Not applicable | Not applicable |
| Transport (Other than Railway) | $470.32[1] | $81.09[1] | $72.09[1] | Not applicable | Not applicable | Not applicable |
| Clubs | $456.00[1] | Not applicable | Not applicable | Not applicable | Not applicable | Not applicable |

*Notes*:

1. Per-capita consumption was derived on the basis of household size of each standard household.
2. Male and female adults consume the same amount whereas children consume two-thirds of adult amount.

Computed as a percentage of expenditure on food, clothing, beverages and tobacco: Malay and Indian Labor 5 percent, Chinese Labor 6 percent.

*Sources:*

[1] Department of Statistics, Federation of Malaya (1949, 74–77).

[2] *Annual Report, Labor Department, the Colony of Singapore, (*1949, 74–76).

rates, etc. They provide a measure of the average rate of change in prices of a fixed basket of consumer goods and services which represent the household expenditure pattern.[31] For this purpose, CPI by major object of consumption were required to obtain the respective real per-capita consumption expenditure. Additionally, the overall CPI were utilized to compute real wage indices. The following actions were taken to compute the CPI.

First, estimate the private final consumption expenditure of each major object of consumption for each consumption standard using (1914 = 100) as the base year. Second, compute the base weights of private final consumption using the total private final consumption expenditure of each major object of consumption by each consumption standard. The weights of private final consumption of each consumption standard within a particular major object of consumption should add up to unity. Subsequently, multiply the base weights of private final consumption of each consumption standard within a particular major object of consumption by the relevant price indices of each year. Using the above procedures, derive the overall price index of each major object of consumption by adding up the weighted index of each standard.

This will give you the overall price index for each major object of consumption for each year. The details on how the price indices for each major object of consumption were estimated and the results of such an exercise are presented in Appendices 1–3. It will be apparent from these appendices that there are essentially two series of price indices. The first series covering the period 1900–39 had 1914 as its base year (1914 = 100), while the second series encompassing the period 1939, 1947–60 had 1949 as the

---

[31] A base weighted price index, i.e., a Laspeyres Price Index, was used in the computation. It can be computed using the following formula:

$$\text{Laspeyre's Index} = \frac{\sum P_n Q_o}{\sum P_o Q_o} = \frac{\sum \frac{P_n}{P_o} * P_o Q_o}{\sum P_o Q_o}$$

where $P_n$ = Price in current period and $Q_o$ = Quantity in base period.

base year. With 1939 being common to both the series of price indices, it was then possible to reconstruct one continuous series for the period 1900–39 and 1950–60 with 1914 as the base year (1914 = 100) by using the overlapping 1939 price indices expressed as a conversion factor and applying it to the period 1950–60.

The weights of private final consumption expenditure in the base year of each major object of consumption (irrespective of standard) were computed by using the total private final consumption expenditure. These weights should add up to unity. Subsequently, multiply the base weights so derived by the price indices of each major object of consumption for each year. Finally, calculate the overall price index by adding up the base weighted index for each major object of consumption for each year. The estimated CPI derived for the year 1900–39 and 1950–60 are presented in Table 2.19. The computation of procedures of CPI for the various periods, namely 1899–1914, 1914–39 and 1939, 1947–60 are presented in Appendix Table 3–5.

### 2.2.2.2.4 Estimating the Per-capita Final Consumption Expenditure of Major Objects of Consumption and Standards in 1914 Prices for Selected Years (STEP 4)

By utilizing the consumer price indices constructed in Step 3, figures on real per-capita consumption expenditure by each major object of consumption and each standard, using 1914 as the base year, were derived and the results are presented in Table 2.20.

### 2.2.2.2.5 The Real Wage Indices (STEP 5)

Ideally, a real wage index should be constructed using the weighted average of wages in all sectors of the economy. Unfortunately, no such detailed time series data were available. As an alternative approach, the following estimation procedure

**Table 2.19:** Singapore: Price Indices by Major Object of Consumption and Consumer Price Index, 1899–1939 and 1947–60 (1914 = 100)

| | Price Indices by Major Object of Consumption | | | | | | | Overall CPI |
|---|---|---|---|---|---|---|---|---|
| | Food & Groceries | Tobacco | Clothing | Rent | Servants | Transport | Club | |
| 1899 | 81.12 | 81.32 | 76.31 | 75.02 | 69.64 | 109.66 | 88.18 | 81.23 |
| 1900 | 81.97 | 83.55 | 78.94 | 76.46 | 75.00 | 107.87 | 88.88 | 82.73 |
| 1901 | 82.91 | 81.61 | 84.45 | 77.93 | 73.21 | 107.44 | 89.10 | 83.57 |
| 1902 | 85.51 | 86.19 | 86.79 | 79.43 | 82.14 | 107.23 | 90.99 | 86.73 |
| 1903 | 85.51 | 91.42 | 92.79 | 80.96 | 82.14 | 107.34 | 91.66 | 87.79 |
| 1904 | 87.28 | 86.94 | 90.19 | 82.53 | 78.57 | 107.23 | 91.97 | 87.89 |
| 1905 | 90.18 | 89.41 | 87.98 | 84.12 | 78.57 | 107.12 | 93.74 | 89.51 |
| 1906 | 87.80 | 86.21 | 84.42 | 85.74 | 82.14 | 107.23 | 92.14 | 88.13 |
| 1907 | 85.69 | 89.90 | 82.99 | 87.40 | 91.07 | 105.07 | 91.55 | 88.04 |
| 1908 | 87.02 | 90.40 | 86.31 | 89.09 | 91.07 | 104.64 | 92.28 | 89.25 |
| 1909 | 85.83 | 87.90 | 76.42 | 86.37 | 91.07 | 103.67 | 91.37 | 87.13 |
| 1910 | 87.09 | 90.09 | 84.38 | 86.05 | 91.07 | 103.24 | 92.28 | 88.78 |
| 1911 | 102.81 | 88.10 | 84.03 | 84.75 | 91.07 | 102.91 | 99.88 | 97.35 |
| 1912 | 105.84 | 88.64 | 83.07 | 85.45 | 91.07 | 103.02 | 101.47 | 99.03 |
| 1913 | 105.09 | 99.12 | 99.53 | 90.86 | 91.07 | 99.46 | 102.43 | 101.09 |
| 1914 | 100.00 | 100.00 | 100.00 | 100.00 | 100.00 | 100.00 | 100.00 | 100.00 |
| 1915 | 104.73 | 91.83 | 138.32 | 100.28 | 103.82 | 101.83 | 91.31 | 106.54 |
| 1916 | 106.47 | 135.91 | 161.28 | 102.44 | 103.82 | 103.13 | 103.77 | 113.14 |
| 1917 | 115.77 | 127.84 | 144.02 | 102.29 | 113.09 | 108.64 | 113.88 | 117.78 |
| 1918 | 139.48 | 174.54 | 189.80 | 114.34 | 116.80 | 112.50 | 134.00 | 140.43 |
| 1919 | 183.87 | 201.99 | 229.60 | 124.90 | 116.80 | 122.90 | 147.40 | 172.28 |
| 1920 | 243.98 | 236.50 | 291.60 | 160.76 | 155.50 | 126.80 | 163.50 | 221.30 |
| 1921 | 167.96 | 237.22 | 237.20 | 168.16 | 155.50 | 122.80 | 176.70 | 174.82 |
| 1922 | 144.20 | 233.57 | 182.80 | 186.66 | 155.50 | 112.00 | 177.40 | 156.16 |
| 1923 | 144.28 | 201.55 | 163.60 | 209.64 | 155.50 | 94.80 | 169.20 | 152.11 |
| 1924 | 144.61 | 188.81 | 157.10 | 217.54 | 155.50 | 99.40 | 164.10 | 151.49 |
| 1925 | 149.58 | 186.19 | 158.10 | 225.57 | 155.50 | 105.30 | 164.20 | 155.07 |
| 1926 | 158.49 | 187.93 | 157.50 | 236.04 | 155.50 | 103.50 | 161.70 | 160.33 |
| 1927 | 154.85 | 180.99 | 155.40 | 253.41 | 155.50 | 94.20 | 159.50 | 158.00 |
| 1928 | 150.77 | 181.13 | 151.90 | 275.75 | 155.50 | 93.10 | 159.50 | 156.66 |
| 1929 | 147.73 | 176.61 | 141.00 | 277.40 | 155.50 | 89.70 | 155.30 | 153.27 |
| 1930 | 138.26 | 170.09 | 139.80 | 255.60 | 152.90 | 85.50 | 156.10 | 145.73 |
| 1931 | 104.59 | 174.80 | 136.57 | 221.46 | 138.00 | 96.20 | 160.50 | 124.49 |
| 1932 | 89.18 | 168.76 | 121.38 | 181.20 | 124.70 | 89.00 | 160.10 | 109.58 |
| 1933 | 82.36 | 155.09 | 115.68 | 159.06 | 115.80 | 85.40 | 158.40 | 101.76 |
| 1934 | 86.41 | 156.31 | 110.78 | 159.06 | 123.70 | 84.50 | 159.50 | 104.44 |
| 1935 | 94.68 | 147.01 | 109.81 | 159.06 | 127.40 | 82.40 | 157.70 | 108.53 |
| 1936 | 92.21 | 146.72 | 109.12 | 159.06 | 125.70 | 80.00 | 157.40 | 106.70 |
| 1937 | 101.76 | 146.72 | 112.79 | 161.78 | 130.00 | 81.40 | 157.70 | 113.08 |
| 1938 | 94.29 | 145.90 | 113.92 | 169.58 | 128.20 | 81.50 | 159.40 | 109.42 |
| 1939 | 91.81 | 154.10 | 123.83 | 182.26 | 128.20 | 82.18 | 152.87 | 110.16 |
| 1947 | 394.16 | 493.82 | 628.50 | 549.01 | 366.43 | 181.50 | 423.73 | 409.33 |
| 1948 | 361.21 | 404.61 | 385.91 | 460.76 | 306.70 | 151.91 | 444.09 | 344.50 |
| 1949 | 336.79 | 417.66 | 389.07 | 510.58 | 322.29 | 150.46 | 437.21 | 338.58 |
| 1950 | 360.41 | 444.64 | 415.49 | 527.05 | 334.74 | 155.63 | 469.31 | 359.02 |
| 1951 | 480.24 | 506.62 | 525.93 | 642.35 | 380.93 | 173.46 | 546.51 | 451.51 |
| 1952 | 502.13 | 514.31 | 514.47 | 680.78 | 423.69 | 171.95 | 564.09 | 469.80 |
| 1953 | 477.30 | 521.93 | 472.64 | 719.21 | 448.21 | 166.69 | 556.45 | 458.41 |
| 1954 | 433.27 | 542.23 | 448.54 | 735.68 | 454.64 | 164.20 | 546.51 | 436.94 |
| 1955 | 415.99 | 540.39 | 439.15 | 724.70 | 457.59 | 165.87 | 544.22 | 427.08 |
| 1956 | 418.47 | 542.24 | 438.15 | 768.62 | 459.05 | 168.29 | 549.57 | 431.66 |
| 1957 | 436.83 | 549.94 | 444.86 | 790.58 | 459.05 | 174.01 | 558.74 | 444.20 |
| 1958 | 430.04 | 550.13 | 443.56 | 807.05 | 459.05 | 174.83 | 561.80 | 441.93 |
| 1959 | 419.57 | 547.50 | 436.17 | 818.03 | 459.05 | 177.47 | 567.15 | 436.87 |
| 1960 | 418.89 | 547.21 | 438.13 | 818.03 | 459.05 | 179.24 | 572.82 | 437.05 |

**Table 2.20:**  Singapore: Real Per-capita Private Consumption Expenditure by Standard, Selected Years

**(A) 1899–1939 (1914 Prices)**

| Major Object of Consumption \ Consumption Standard | European Standard (1930) $ | Eurasian Standard (1930) $ | Asiatic Clerical Standard (1930) $ | Malay Labour Standard (1936) $ | Chinese Labour Standard (1936) $ | Indian Labour Standard (1933) $ |
|---|---|---|---|---|---|---|
| Food and Groceries | 434.85 | 141.39 | 133.49 | 91.68 | 95.45 | 96.88 |
| Beverages and Tobacco | 100.82 | 5.08 | 5.08 | 6.95 | 5.55 | 10.55 |
| Clothing | 206.01 | 22.32 | 22.32 | 10.61 | 10.47 | 8.80 |
| Rent | 112.68 | 28.17 | 28.17 | 3.50 | 4.42 | 5.97 |
| Domestic Servants | 428.52 | 15.70 | 15.70 | Not applicable | Not applicable | Not applicable |
| Transport (Other than Railway) | 225.12 | 30.99 | 30.99 | Not applicable | Not applicable | Not applicable |
| Clubs | 140.68 | Not applicable | Not applicable | Not applicable | Not applicable | Not applicable |

**(B) 1947–60 (1914 Prices)**

| Major Object of Consumption \ Consumption Standard | European Standard (1948) $ | Malay Clerical Standard (1948) $ | Chinese, Indian and Eurasian Clerical Standard (1948) $ | Malay Labour Standard (1949) $ | Chinese Labour Standard (1949) $ | Indian Labour Standard (1949) $ |
|---|---|---|---|---|---|---|
| Food and Groceries | 344.90 | 124.95 | 116.12 | 89.20 | 105.71 | 121.07 |
| Beverages and Tobacco | 175.21 | 5.12 | 5.12 | 9.56 | 8.70 | 9.29 |
| Clothing | 246.65 | 14.96 | 14.11 | 12.39 | 13.92 | 8.08 |
| Rent | 145.99 | 13.13 | 13.13 | 4.49 | 6.46 | 5.67 |
| Domestic Servants | 442.68 | 35.24 | 35.24 | Not applicable | Not applicable | Not applicable |
| Transport (Other than Railway) | 309.60 | 53.38 | 47.46 | Not applicable | Not applicable | Not applicable |
| Clubs | 102.68 | Not applicable | Not applicable | Not applicable | Not applicable | Not applicable |

was applied to compute the real wage indices. For the period 1899–1939, the wage index was constructed using the daily wage rates of carpenters, joiners, blacksmiths, bricklayers in Singapore and the Indian factory workers in Singapore to capture wage movements in the non-agriculture sectors.[32]

---

[32] Wage data of carpenters, joiners, blacksmiths and bricklayers was only available from 1899–1923, while that of Indian factory workers only from 1925–39. To link the two wage series, it was necessary for us to make an educated guess

Meanwhile, the Indian rubber estate tappers' wage rate was used to reflect wage movements in the agriculture sector.

A weighted wage index was constructed on the basis of the employment data of the agriculture and non-agriculture sectors in accordance with the 1921 Population Census.[33] Real earnings index was then derived by deflating the earnings index with the overall CPI.

For the period 1947–57, the information on number of laborers by industry for the years 1947 and 1957 was provided in the *Population Census 1957, the Colony of Singapore.* According to this census report, more than half of the working population was employed in the manufacturing and services sectors for both 1947 and 1957. With this observation, minimum daily wage information was extracted from the *Annual Report, Labour Department, the Colony of Singapore.* The data presentation, however, has changed over time. Therefore, synchronizations needed to be made. These selected representative wage rates for each industry were then converted to a wage index using 1957 as

---

on the level of wages of Indian factory workers relative to that of carpenters, joiners, blacksmiths and bricklayers. It was assumed that the wage rates of carpenters, joiners, blacksmiths and bricklayers was about 2.27 times that of the Indian factory workers.

[33] The weighting of the nominal wage indices for agriculture and non-agriculture sectors for both periods (1900–14 and 1914–39) was based solely on the 1921 Population Census data on employment across sectors given the absence of such data for the base year, 1914. As shown in the table below, weights on agriculture and non-agriculture sectors for 1921 and 1931 were relatively stable. Therefore, the weights from the 1921 Census were used to represent base year (1914) weights.

|      | Agriculture<br>Sector (%) | Non-agriculture<br>Sector (%) |
| --- | --- | --- |
| 1921 | 13.8 | 86.2 |
| 1931 | 12.9 | 87.1 |
| 1947 | 8.1 | 91.9 |
| 1957 | 6.9 | 93.1 |

**Table 2.21:** Singapore: Weighted Real Wage Indices, 1899–1939 and 1947–60 (1914 = 100)

| 1899–1939, 1947–1960 (1914=100) | | | | | |
|---|---|---|---|---|---|
| 1899 | 116.03 | 1920 | 89.13 | 1947 | 164.71 |
| 1900 | 113.92 | 1921 | 112.82 | 1948 | 179.65 |
| 1901 | 112.77 | 1922 | 123.66 | 1949 | 220.02 |
| 1902 | 108.67 | 1923 | 126.94 | 1950 | 203.15 |
| 1903 | 107.35 | 1924 | 127.47 | 1951 | 181.26 |
| 1904 | 107.24 | 1925 | 124.53 | 1952 | 176.19 |
| 1905 | 105.29 | 1926 | 120.44 | 1953 | 206.53 |
| 1906 | 106.94 | 1927 | 127.57 | 1954 | 208.97 |
| 1907 | 107.05 | 1928 | 131.90 | 1955 | 204.74 |
| 1908 | 107.87 | 1929 | 131.51 | 1956 | 230.57 |
| 1909 | 110.50 | 1930 | 129.23 | 1957 | 215.81 |
| 1910 | 108.44 | 1931 | 115.38 | 1958 | 215.37 |
| 1911 | 98.90 | 1932 | 122.09 | 1959 | 194.19 |
| 1912 | 97.22 | 1933 | 136.87 | 1960 | 230.48 |
| 1913 | 95.24 | 1934 | 130.38 | | |
| 1914 | 100.00 | 1935 | 137.02 | | |
| 1915 | 93.86 | 1936 | 148.89 | | |
| 1916 | 88.38 | 1937 | 150.08 | | |
| 1917 | 100.72 | 1938 | 155.10 | | |
| 1918 | 104.36 | 1939 | 154.06 | | |
| 1919 | 92.87 | | | | |

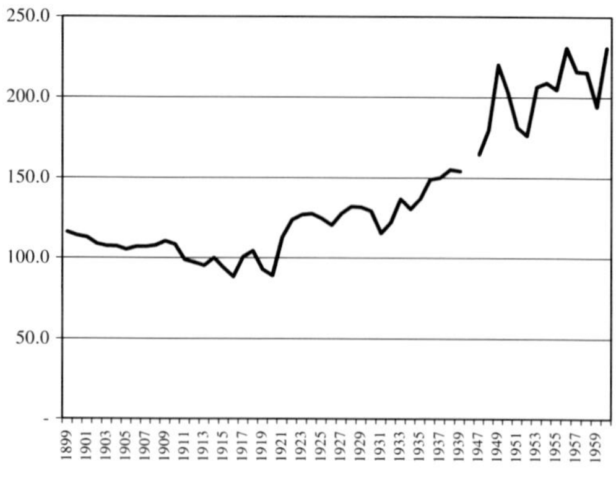

the base year. Subsequently, the weighted wage index was computed based on the 1957 Census. The derived nominal weighted wage index was then deflated by the overall CPI. The real wage indices for the period 1899–1939 and 1947–60 were thus obtained and are presented in Table 2.21.

### 2.2.2.2.6 Deriving Private Final Consumption Expenditure in Constant and Current Prices, 1900–39 and 1948–60 (STEPS 6–11)

In steps 1–5, the necessary statistical information was prepared, namely population by consumption standard, per-capita consumption expenditure by major object of consumption and standard in current prices, consumer price indices by major object of consumption (1914 = 100), per-capita consumption expenditure by major object of consumption and standard in 1914 prices and real wage indices. In deriving yearly private consumption expenditure in both 1914 and current prices (Steps 6–11), the element of changes in real income levels, which have an impact on the consumption patterns, needs to be factored in. As a result, certain assumptions were made with regard to income elasticities of demand to adjust the expenditure series for changes in real income over time: the assumed income elasticities of demand being 0.7 for food,[34] 1.0 each for beverages, tobacco, clothing, domestic servants, and transport (other than railway), and 0.8 for rent. To give an example, if in the base year ($t$) real per-capita expenditure on food for the European standard is $RPCF_t$ and if the real wage indices increases from 1 in year $t$ to 1.3 in year $t + 1$, then the real per-capita expenditure on food in year $t + 1$ ($RPCF_{t+1}$) is calculated as follows:

$$RPCF_{t+1} = RPCF_t + ((RPCF_t \times (1.3 - 1.0)/1.0) \times 0.7).$$

If the real earnings index increases to 1.5 in year $t + 2$, real per-capita expenditure in year $t + 2$ is calculated as:

$$RPCF_{t+1} = RPCF_{t+1} + ((RPCF_{t+1} \times (1.5 - 1.3)/1.3)) \times 0.7)).$$

This computation is illustrated in more detail in Table 2.22, (Columns (1) to (5)) taking the consumption expenditure on food for the European Standard, as an example. The real per-capita expenditure of the European standard on food for the period 1899–1939 (Column 5) was then multiplied by the population of the European standard (Column 6) to obtain the real private consumption expenditure on food for the Europeans standard in 1914 prices (Column 7). This was finally inflated by food indices (Column 8) to obtain private final consumption expenditure on food for the European standard in current prices (Column 9).

---

[34] The basis for using an income elasticity of demand of 0.7 for food was very much guided by other related studies. In this regard, Derkson, JBD and Tinbergen, J (1945) established that the income elasticity of demand on food was 0.7 for the Netherlands. In the case of pre-war Malaya, a study by Nazrin (2006) set 0.8 as elasticity of demand on food. In the light of this, it was assumed that elasticity of demand on food for Singapore ought to be lower than pre-war Malaya and not too dissimilar to that of the Netherlands.

**Table 2.22:** Singapore: Computation of PFCE in the Domestic Market, 1900–39 and 1948–60, European Standard — Food in Current and 1914 Prices

(Straits $)

| Year | Annual Per Capita Private Final Consumption Expenditure in Real Terms (1914 Prices) (Straits $) | Weighted Real Wage Indices of Agriculture and Non-agriculture Sectors (1914=100) | Changes in Real Wages (%) | Changes in Real Consumption (%) | Real Per Capita Private Final Consumption Expenditure based on Real Wages and Income Elasticities of Demand (1914 Prices) (Straits $) | European Population Standard (Numbers) | Total Real Private Final Consumption Expenditure on Food in the Domestic Market (1914 Prices) (Straits $) | Food Price Indices (1914=100) | Total Private Final Consumption Expenditure on Food in the Domestic Market (Current Prices) (Straits $) |
|---|---|---|---|---|---|---|---|---|---|
| | STEP 4 | STEP 5 | STEP 6 | STEP 7 | | STEP 8 | STEP 9 | STEP 10 | STEP 11 |
| | [1] | [2] | [3] | [4] | [5] | [6] | [7]=[5]x[6] | [8] | [9]=[7]x[8]/100 |
| 1899 | | 116.03 | | | 397.96 | 13,667 | 5,439,107 | 81.12 | 4,412,406 |
| 1900 | | 113.92 | −1.81% | −1.27% | 392.91 | 13,566 | 5,330,194 | 81.97 | 4,369,042 |
| 1901 | | 112.77 | −1.01% | −0.71% | 390.14 | 13,911 | 5,427,068 | 82.91 | 4,499,325 |
| 1902 | | 108.67 | −3.64% | −2.55% | 380.20 | 14,310 | 5,440,909 | 85.51 | 4,652,316 |
| 1903 | | 107.35 | −1.21% | −0.85% | 376.97 | 14,720 | 5,548,916 | 85.51 | 4,744,669 |
| 1904 | | 107.24 | −0.11% | −0.07% | 376.69 | 15,141 | 5,703,397 | 87.28 | 4,977,968 |
| 1905 | | 105.29 | −1.82% | −1.27% | 371.91 | 15,575 | 5,792,605 | 90.18 | 5,223,634 |
| 1906 | | 106.94 | 1.56% | 1.09% | 375.97 | 16,023 | 6,024,044 | 87.80 | 5,289,017 |
| 1907 | | 107.05 | 0.10% | 0.07% | 376.24 | 16,483 | 6,201,579 | 85.69 | 5,313,974 |
| 1908 | | 107.87 | 0.77% | 0.54% | 378.27 | 16,958 | 6,414,603 | 87.02 | 5,582,067 |
| 1909 | | 110.50 | 2.44% | 1.71% | 384.73 | 17,445 | 6,711,682 | 85.83 | 5,760,682 |
| 1910 | | 108.44 | −1.86% | −1.30% | 379.72 | 17,946 | 6,814,297 | 87.09 | 5,934,800 |
| 1911 | | 98.90 | −8.80% | −6.16% | 356.32 | 18,503 | 6,592,851 | 102.81 | 6,778,183 |
| 1912 | | 97.22 | −1.70% | −1.19% | 352.09 | 19,118 | 6,731,180 | 105.84 | 7,124,071 |
| 1913 | | 95.24 | −2.04% | −1.43% | 347.07 | 19,750 | 6,854,720 | 105.09 | 7,203,681 |
| 1914 | | 100.00 | 5.00% | 3.50% | 359.21 | 20,400 | 7,327,950 | 100.00 | 7,327,950 |
| 1915 | | 93.86 | −6.14% | −4.30% | 343.76 | 21,069 | 7,242,660 | 104.73 | 7,585,155 |
| 1916 | | 88.38 | −5.83% | −4.08% | 329.73 | 21,756 | 7,173,622 | 106.47 | 7,638,020 |
| 1917 | | 100.72 | 13.95% | 9.77% | 361.94 | 22,464 | 8,130,391 | 115.77 | 9,412,300 |
| 1918 | | 104.36 | 3.61% | 2.53% | 371.09 | 23,192 | 8,606,305 | 139.48 | 12,003,667 |
| 1919 | | 92.87 | −11.01% | −7.70% | 342.50 | 23,941 | 8,199,725 | 183.87 | 15,077,106 |
| 1920 | | 89.13 | −4.03% | −2.82% | 332.84 | 24,711 | 8,224,894 | 243.98 | 20,066,803 |
| 1921 | | 112.82 | 26.58% | 18.61% | 394.78 | 27,757 | 10,957,825 | 167.96 | 18,404,853 |
| 1922 | | 123.66 | 9.60% | 6.72% | 421.32 | 29,018 | 12,225,691 | 144.20 | 17,628,945 |
| 1923 | | 126.94 | 2.66% | 1.86% | 429.16 | 30,082 | 12,909,727 | 144.28 | 18,626,209 |
| 1924 | | 127.47 | 0.41% | 0.29% | 430.40 | 31,165 | 13,413,301 | 144.61 | 19,396,465 |
| 1925 | | 124.53 | −2.31% | −1.62% | 423.44 | 32,515 | 13,768,225 | 149.58 | 20,594,430 |
| 1926 | | 120.44 | −3.28% | −2.30% | 413.71 | 33,811 | 13,987,688 | 158.49 | 22,169,479 |
| 1927 | | 127.57 | 5.93% | 4.15% | 430.87 | 35,143 | 15,141,927 | 154.85 | 23,446,884 |
| 1928 | | 131.90 | 3.39% | 2.38% | 441.10 | 36,493 | 16,097,336 | 150.77 | 24,270,469 |
| 1929 | | 131.51 | −0.30% | −0.21% | 440.19 | 37,864 | 16,667,209 | 147.73 | 24,622,799 |
| 1930 | 434.85 | 129.23 | −1.73% | −1.21% | 434.85 | 37,403 | 16,264,686 | 138.26 | 22,486,856 |
| 1931 | | 115.38 | −10.72% | −7.50% | 402.22 | 36,586 | 14,715,907 | 104.59 | 15,391,167 |
| 1932 | | 122.09 | 5.82% | 4.07% | 418.60 | 35,489 | 14,855,891 | 89.18 | 13,248,386 |
| 1933 | | 136.87 | 12.10% | 8.47% | 454.06 | 33,443 | 15,185,011 | 82.36 | 12,505,866 |
| 1934 | | 130.38 | −4.74% | −3.32% | 439.00 | 34,140 | 14,987,527 | 86.41 | 12,950,916 |
| 1935 | | 137.02 | 5.09% | 3.56% | 454.65 | 37,200 | 16,913,087 | 94.68 | 16,013,727 |
| 1936 | | 148.89 | 8.66% | 6.06% | 482.21 | 39,206 | 18,905,496 | 92.21 | 17,432,618 |
| 1937 | | 150.08 | 0.80% | 0.56% | 484.91 | 42,347 | 20,534,128 | 101.76 | 20,895,697 |
| 1938 | | 155.10 | 3.35% | 2.34% | 496.27 | 46,152 | 22,904,054 | 94.29 | 21,596,868 |
| 1939 | | 154.06 | −0.67% | −0.47% | 493.94 | 47,292 | 23,359,018 | 91.81 | 21,445,527 |
| 1947 | | 164.71 | | | 324.32 | 56,289 | 18,255,364 | 394.16 | 71,954,987 |
| 1948 | 344.90 | 179.65 | 9.067% | 6.347% | 344.90 | 57,648 | 19,882,898 | 361.21 | 71,818,963 |
| 1949 | | 220.02 | 22.473% | 15.731% | 399.16 | 58,722 | 23,439,406 | 336.79 | 78,941,707 |
| 1950 | | 203.15 | −7.666% | −5.366% | 377.74 | 61,326 | 23,165,302 | 360.41 | 83,489,050 |
| 1951 | | 181.26 | −10.776% | −7.543% | 349.25 | 64,086 | 22,381,866 | 480.24 | 107,486,516 |
| 1952 | | 176.19 | −2.797% | −1.958% | 342.41 | 67,620 | 23,153,681 | 502.13 | 116,261,314 |
| 1953 | | 206.53 | 17.217% | 12.052% | 383.68 | 71,508 | 27,435,948 | 477.30 | 130,950,539 |
| 1954 | | 208.97 | 1.183% | 0.828% | 386.85 | 74,892 | 28,972,205 | 433.27 | 125,527,001 |
| 1955 | | 204.74 | −2.023% | −1.416% | 381.38 | 78,330 | 29,873,146 | 415.99 | 124,269,457 |
| 1956 | | 230.57 | 12.617% | 8.832% | 415.06 | 82,296 | 34,157,654 | 418.47 | 142,939,681 |
| 1957 | | 215.81 | −6.401% | −4.481% | 396.46 | 86,756 | 34,395,185 | 436.83 | 150,249,636 |
| 1958 | | 215.37 | −0.205% | −0.144% | 395.89 | 90,840 | 35,962,661 | 430.04 | 154,652,705 |
| 1959 | | 194.19 | −9.837% | −6.886% | 368.63 | 94,776 | 34,937,265 | 419.57 | 146,586,615 |
| 1960 | | 230.48 | 18.691% | 13.084% | 416.86 | 98,046 | 40,871,439 | 418.89 | 171,204,779 |

| | |
|---|---|
| Percentage Change in Real Wage Indices, 1906–1905 | 1.56% |
| Percentage Change in Real Consumption, 1906–1905 | 1.09% |

$$\frac{C_{1906}}{C_{1905}} - 1 = 1.09\%$$

$$\frac{C_{1906}}{C_{1905}} = 1.09\% + 1$$

$$\frac{375.97}{C_{1905}} = 1.0109$$

$$C_{1905} = \frac{375.97}{1.0109}$$

$$C_{1905} = 371.91$$

Similar procedures were applied to compute PFCE on food, tobacco, clothing, rent, domestic servants, and clubs, wherever applicable, for each standard in both current and constant prices using their respective income elasticities of demand (See Appendix Table 6). The summation of each of the major objects of consumption for each standard in constant and current prices gave us the total PFCE of those items in both constant and current prices, respectively (See Appendix Table 7).

The miscellaneous items expenditure was then computed for each year using the indirect approach of computing the total PFCE in current prices. The miscellaneous items included, among others, furniture and furnishings, household equipment and operations such as furniture, curtains, cooking appliances, glassware, tableware, household utensils and other non-durable goods, e.g., matches, soap, candles and shoe polish. It also included cultural services and other goods and services, including personal care, e.g., barbers, laundry, etc., using the indirect approach. On the basis of statistical evidence, the miscellaneous expenditure was taken to be 10.0 percent of the total private final consumption expenditure in current prices using PFCE derived from the indirect approach.[35] The estimates are, therefore, subject to errors. The miscellaneous expenditure in constant terms for each year was determined by dividing the miscellaneous expenditure in current terms by the overall CPI. The overall PFCE in the domestic market for each year was then

---

[35] Department of Statistics, Singapore (1983), provides the figures on private final consumption expenditure in the domestic market by major objects of consumption for the period 1960–82 at current prices. According to this time series data, a weight on the other goods and services (expenditure on personal care, restaurants, cafes and hotels) for the period 1960–65 was in the range of 15–16 percent. However, this category includes the consumption expenditure on clubs. The weight on this specific consumption was approximately 3–5 percent. Using this, 10 percent was assigned for deriving miscellaneous expenditure. It will be noted in Nazrin's (2006) estimates of private consumption expenditure for pre-war Malaya that a figure of 7 percent was applied for miscellaneous expenditure.

derived by summing up the major objects of consumption in both current and constant prices via direct and indirect approaches (including the miscellaneous expenditure based on the indirect approach, See Table 2.23).

### 2.2.2.3 *Private Consumption Expenditure by Resident Households*

As discussed above, PFCE in the domestic market was computed on the basis of the procedures as outlined in steps 1–10. This derived estimate, however, required further adjustment to derive PFCE by resident households. Ideally, direct purchases abroad by resident households and direct purchases of non-resident households in the domestic market should be calculated independently but it was difficult to construct such data. As an alternative option, the available official figures for the period 1960–70 were used as a guide. As is presented in Table 2.24, 10–15 percent of total PFCE in the domestic market was non-resident consumption made in the domestic market. On the other hand, direct purchases abroad by residents were around 1 percent. Using this observation, it was decided that 20 and 15 percent of the PFCE[36] in the domestic market was taken to represent purchases in the domestic market by non-resident households for the period 1900–32 and 1933–60, respectively. The results are presented in Table 2.25. It should be noted here

------

[36] It was assumed that the weights on the non-resident consumption made in the domestic market were higher in the period after the formation of self-government due to the relatively free flows of migration. Since the early 1930s, the Colonial government of Straits Settlements had imposed restrictions on Chinese immigration from China (*Annual Report, Chinese Protectorate, Straits Settlements*). Using this observation, weights on resident household consumption in the domestic market have been taken to increase from 80 to 85 percent. These figures must be treated with great reserve. However, it is important to note here that non-resident consumption made in the domestic market was regarded as exports of services. Therefore, the total GDP figure remained unchanged.

**Table 2.23:** Singapore: Private Final Consumption Expenditure in the Domestic Market, 1900–39 and 1950–60 at Current and Constant Prices

| | Private Final Consumption Expenditure in the Domestic Market by Resident and Non-resident Households | | | | Per-capita Private Final Consumption Expenditure in the Domestic Market by Resident and Non-resident Households | | | |
|---|---|---|---|---|---|---|---|---|
| | Current Prices (Straits $) | Growth Rate (%) | 1914 Prices (Straits $) | Growth Rate (%) | Current Prices (Straits $) | Growth Rate (%) | 1914 Prices (Straits $) | Growth Rate (%) |
| 1900 | 42,103,116 | | 50,867,089 | | 186.21 | | 224.98 | |
| 1901 | 43,224,674 | 2.6 | 51,708,242 | 1.6 | 186.44 | 0.1 | 223.03 | –0.9 |
| 1902 | 45,130,696 | 4.3 | 52,021,265 | 0.6 | 189.22 | 1.5 | 218.11 | –2.2 |
| 1903 | 46,597,537 | 3.2 | 53,072,229 | 2.0 | 189.94 | 0.4 | 216.33 | –0.8 |
| 1904 | 47,674,674 | 2.3 | 54,244,611 | 2.2 | 188.93 | –0.5 | 214.96 | –0.6 |
| 1905 | 49,407,615 | 3.6 | 55,200,986 | 1.7 | 190.33 | 0.7 | 212.65 | –1.1 |
| 1906 | 50,344,313 | 1.9 | 57,105,288 | 3.4 | 188.53 | –1.0 | 213.84 | 0.6 |
| 1907 | 51,953,202 | 3.1 | 58,969,568 | 3.2 | 189.12 | 0.3 | 214.66 | 0.4 |
| 1908 | 54,441,481 | 4.7 | 60,963,806 | 3.3 | 192.63 | 1.8 | 215.71 | 0.5 |
| 1909 | 55,398,248 | 1.7 | 63,525,899 | 4.1 | 190.53 | –1.1 | 218.49 | 1.3 |
| 1910 | 58,374,612 | 5.2 | 65,715,977 | 3.4 | 195.17 | 2.4 | 219.72 | 0.6 |
| 1911 | 61,657,716 | 5.5 | 63,318,932 | –3.7 | 199.94 | 2.4 | 205.33 | –6.8 |
| 1912 | 64,088,347 | 3.9 | 64,692,236 | 2.1 | 201.14 | 0.6 | 203.03 | –1.1 |
| 1913 | 66,565,286 | 3.8 | 65,855,277 | 1.8 | 202.22 | 0.5 | 200.07 | –1.5 |
| 1914 | 70,238,013 | 5.4 | 70,238,013 | 6.4 | 206.58 | 2.1 | 206.58 | 3.2 |
| 1915 | 73,289,375 | 4.3 | 68,826,758 | –2.0 | 208.72 | 1.0 | 196.01 | –5.3 |
| 1916 | 77,541,495 | 5.6 | 68,664,206 | –0.2 | 213.85 | 2.4 | 189.37 | –3.4 |
| 1917 | 92,493,914 | 17.6 | 78,609,260 | 13.5 | 247.05 | 14.4 | 209.96 | 10.3 |
| 1918 | 116,860,527 | 23.4 | 83,392,017 | 5.9 | 302.33 | 20.2 | 215.75 | 2.7 |
| 1919 | 134,334,722 | 13.9 | 78,080,370 | –6.6 | 336.67 | 10.8 | 195.68 | –9.8 |
| 1920 | 172,156,775 | 24.8 | 77,821,030 | –0.3 | 418.01 | 21.6 | 188.96 | –3.5 |
| 1921 | 177,206,263 | 2.9 | 101,716,229 | 26.8 | 414.98 | –0.7 | 238.20 | 23.2 |
| 1922 | 177,376,184 | 0.1 | 113,684,635 | 11.1 | 397.32 | –4.3 | 254.65 | 6.7 |
| 1923 | 181,144,588 | 2.1 | 119,178,513 | 4.7 | 391.42 | –1.5 | 257.52 | 1.1 |
| 1924 | 185,897,887 | 2.6 | 122,754,643 | 3.0 | 387.72 | –0.9 | 256.03 | –0.6 |
| 1925 | 194,814,805 | 4.7 | 125,693,013 | 2.4 | 389.45 | 0.4 | 251.27 | –1.9 |
| 1926 | 203,283,357 | 4.3 | 126,960,364 | 1.0 | 390.81 | 0.3 | 244.08 | –2.9 |
| 1927 | 217,979,220 | 7.0 | 138,128,353 | 8.4 | 403.17 | 3.1 | 255.48 | 4.6 |
| 1928 | 230,014,025 | 5.4 | 146,879,422 | 6.1 | 409.69 | 1.6 | 261.61 | 2.4 |
| 1929 | 229,670,817 | –0.1 | 149,860,839 | 2.0 | 394.27 | –3.8 | 257.26 | –1.7 |
| 1930 | 214,289,817 | –6.9 | 146,942,993 | –2.0 | 372.40 | –5.7 | 255.36 | –0.7 |
| 1931 | 163,923,019 | –26.8 | 131,160,777 | –11.4 | 291.23 | –24.6 | 233.02 | –9.2 |
| 1932 | 148,784,340 | –9.7 | 135,065,402 | 2.9 | 272.50 | –6.6 | 247.38 | 6.0 |
| 1933 | 143,273,992 | –3.8 | 139,775,888 | 3.4 | 278.47 | 2.2 | 271.67 | 9.4 |
| 1934 | 145,253,521 | 1.4 | 138,216,342 | –1.1 | 276.55 | –0.7 | 263.15 | –3.2 |
| 1935 | 170,007,793 | 15.7 | 155,815,301 | 12.0 | 297.06 | 7.2 | 272.26 | 3.4 |
| 1936 | 188,072,989 | 10.1 | 175,116,863 | 11.7 | 311.81 | 4.8 | 290.33 | 6.4 |
| 1937 | 214,810,368 | 13.3 | 189,079,124 | 7.7 | 329.72 | 5.6 | 290.23 | –0.0 |
| 1938 | 230,461,017 | 7.0 | 209,108,433 | 10.1 | 324.58 | –1.6 | 294.50 | 1.5 |
| 1939 | 236,976,709 | 2.8 | 213,456,021 | 2.1 | 325.71 | 0.3 | 293.38 | –0.4 |
| 1948 | 870,785,958 | | 252,774,860 | | 906.31 | | 263.09 | |
| 1949 | 1,030,867,837 | 16.9 | 304,461,754 | 18.6 | 1,053.30 | 15.0 | 311.09 | 16.8 |
| 1950 | 1,073,862,182 | 4.1 | 299,061,922 | –1.8 | 1,050.64 | –0.3 | 292.60 | –6.1 |
| 1951 | 1,272,003,340 | 16.9 | 281,946,415 | –5.9 | 1,190.90 | 12.5 | 263.97 | –10.3 |
| 1952 | 1,366,152,822 | 7.1 | 290,898,659 | 3.1 | 1,212.20 | 1.8 | 258.12 | –2.2 |
| 1953 | 1,609,481,462 | 16.4 | 351,634,837 | 19.0 | 1,350.46 | 10.8 | 295.05 | 13.4 |
| 1954 | 1,626,152,653 | 1.0 | 372,052,806 | 5.6 | 1,302.80 | –3.6 | 298.07 | 1.0 |
| 1955 | 1,639,802,301 | 0.8 | 383,467,220 | 3.0 | 1,256.07 | –3.7 | 293.73 | –1.5 |
| 1956 | 1,921,470,437 | 15.9 | 444,809,033 | 14.8 | 1,400.90 | 10.9 | 324.30 | 9.9 |
| 1957 | 2,014,487,496 | 4.7 | 455,456,344 | 2.4 | 1,393.21 | –0.6 | 314.99 | –2.9 |
| 1958 | 2,093,107,385 | 3.8 | 475,456,393 | 4.3 | 1,382.50 | –0.8 | 314.04 | –0.3 |
| 1959 | 1,988,598,796 | –5.1 | 456,342,816 | –4.1 | 1,258.93 | –9.4 | 288.90 | –8.3 |
| 1960 | 2,371,715,294 | 17.6 | 544,423,403 | 17.6 | 1,440.55 | 13.5 | 330.68 | 13.5 |

**Table 2.24:** Singapore: Direct Purchases Made Abroad by Resident Households and Direct Purchases in the Domestic Market Made by Non-resident Households as a percentage of Total PFCE in the Domestic Market, 1960–70

| | | 1960 | 1961 | 1962 | 1963 | 1964 | 1965 | 1966 | 1967 | 1968 | 1969 | 1970 |
|---|---|---|---|---|---|---|---|---|---|---|---|---|
| [1] | PFCE in the Domestic Market | 2,111.5 | 2,305.7 | 2,419.2 | 2,593.8 | 2,565.3 | 2,733.2 | 2,991.0 | 3,288.2 | 3,618.0 | 3,922.3 | 4,474.4 |
| [2] | Direct Purchases Made Abroad by Resident Households | 32.3 | 33.3 | 34.4 | 30.6 | 30.9 | 32.3 | 33.6 | 37.6 | 40.8 | 50.5 | 54.7 |
| [3] | Direct Purchases in the Domestic Market Made by Non-resident Households | 222.3 | 230.2 | 258.5 | 297.8 | 358.0 | 424.9 | 468.4 | 473.2 | 479.1 | 533.1 | 609.5 |
| [4] = [1] + [2] + [3] | Total Private Consumption Expenditure | 1,921.5 | 2,108.8 | 2,195.1 | 2,326.6 | 2,238.2 | 2,340.6 | 2,556.2 | 2,852.6 | 3,179.7 | 3,439.7 | 3,919.6 |
| [2] / [1] | Percentage Contribution of [2] against [1] | 1.5% | 1.4% | 1.4% | 1.2% | 1.2% | 1.2% | 1.1% | 1.1% | 1.1% | 1.3% | 1.2% |
| [3] / [1] | Percentage Contribution of [3] against [1] | 10.5% | 10.0% | 10.7% | 11.5% | 14.0% | 15.5% | 15.7% | 14.4% | 13.2% | 13.6% | 13.6% |

*Source*: Department of Statistics, Singapore (1996, 77).

that resident household expenditure incurred overseas was assumed to be negligible. To derive the PFCE in the domestic market by resident households in 1914 prices, current price data were then deflated by overall CPI.

## 2.3 Government Final Consumption Expenditure

### 2.3.1 *Definition*

Government final consumption expenditure is defined in the SNA68 as the value of the gross output of general department (producers of government services),[37] less the value of

---

[37] The producers of government services (General Department) include all bodies, departments and establishments of government-central, state or provincial, district or country, municipal, town or village, which engage in a wide range of activities, e.g., administration, defense and regulation of the public order, health, educational, cultural, recreational and other social service. The legislative executive, departments, establishments and other bodies of government are also included. However, government expenditure incurred by industries (trading departments), e.g., post and telegraph, electricity, public works, printing, drainage and irrigation and the like was not included on the ground that the nature of activities of these departments deals purchases and sales.

**Table 2.25:** Singapore: PFCE in the Domestic Market, PFCE by Resident Households and Non-resident Household Consumption Expenditure made in the Domestic Market, 1900–39 and 1950–60 at Current Prices

| | Current Prices | | | | 1914 Prices | | | | |
|---|---|---|---|---|---|---|---|---|---|
| | PFCE in the Domestic Market by Resident and Non-resident Households | (*) | PFCE in the Domestic Market by Resident Households | PFCE in the Domestic Market by Non-resident Households | PFCE in the Domestic Market by Resident and Non-resident Households | CPI | PFCE in the Domestic Market by Resident Households | PFCE in the Domestic Market by Non-resident Households | |
| | [1] | [2] | [3] = [1] * [2] | [4] = [1] − [3] | [5] | [6] | [7] = [4] / [6]*100 | [8] = [5] − [7] | |
| 1900 | 42,103,116 | 80% | 33,682,493 | 8,420,623 | 50,867,089 | 82.73 | 40,713,842 | 10,153,247 | 1900 |
| 1901 | 43,224,674 | 80% | 34,579,739 | 8,644,935 | 51,708,242 | 83.57 | 41,377,221 | 10,331,021 | 1901 |
| 1902 | 45,130,696 | 80% | 36,104,557 | 9,026,139 | 52,021,265 | 86.73 | 41,630,535 | 10,390,730 | 1902 |
| 1903 | 46,597,537 | 80% | 37,278,029 | 9,319,507 | 53,072,229 | 87.79 | 42,461,783 | 10,610,447 | 1903 |
| 1904 | 47,674,674 | 80% | 38,139,740 | 9,534,935 | 54,244,611 | 87.89 | 43,397,230 | 10,847,381 | 1904 |
| 1905 | 49,407,615 | 80% | 39,526,092 | 9,881,523 | 55,200,986 | 89.51 | 44,158,159 | 11,042,827 | 1905 |
| 1906 | 50,344,313 | 80% | 40,275,451 | 10,068,863 | 57,105,288 | 88.13 | 45,698,299 | 11,406,988 | 1906 |
| 1907 | 51,953,202 | 80% | 41,562,561 | 10,390,640 | 58,969,568 | 88.04 | 47,206,706 | 11,762,862 | 1907 |
| 1908 | 54,441,481 | 80% | 43,553,185 | 10,888,296 | 60,963,806 | 89.25 | 48,798,861 | 12,164,945 | 1908 |
| 1909 | 55,398,248 | 80% | 44,318,599 | 11,079,650 | 63,525,899 | 87.13 | 50,866,768 | 12,659,131 | 1909 |
| 1910 | 58,374,612 | 80% | 46,699,690 | 11,674,922 | 65,715,977 | 88.78 | 52,602,070 | 13,113,906 | 1910 |
| 1911 | 61,657,716 | 80% | 49,326,173 | 12,331,543 | 63,318,932 | 97.35 | 50,669,872 | 12,649,060 | 1911 |
| 1912 | 64,088,347 | 80% | 51,270,678 | 12,817,669 | 64,692,236 | 99.03 | 51,774,227 | 12,918,009 | 1912 |
| 1913 | 66,565,286 | 80% | 53,252,229 | 13,313,057 | 65,855,277 | 101.09 | 52,680,481 | 13,174,796 | 1913 |
| 1914 | 70,238,013 | 80% | 56,190,410 | 14,047,603 | 70,238,013 | 100.00 | 56,190,410 | 14,047,603 | 1914 |
| 1915 | 73,289,375 | 80% | 58,631,500 | 14,657,875 | 68,826,758 | 106.54 | 55,030,406 | 13,796,352 | 1915 |
| 1916 | 77,541,495 | 80% | 62,033,196 | 15,508,299 | 68,664,206 | 113.14 | 54,827,165 | 13,837,042 | 1916 |
| 1917 | 92,493,914 | 80% | 73,995,131 | 18,498,783 | 78,609,260 | 117.78 | 62,827,025 | 15,782,235 | 1917 |
| 1918 | 116,860,527 | 80% | 93,488,421 | 23,372,105 | 83,392,017 | 140.43 | 66,572,058 | 16,819,959 | 1918 |
| 1919 | 134,334,722 | 80% | 107,467,778 | 26,866,944 | 78,080,370 | 172.28 | 62,378,416 | 15,701,954 | 1919 |
| 1920 | 172,156,775 | 80% | 137,725,420 | 34,431,355 | 77,821,030 | 221.30 | 62,236,003 | 15,585,027 | 1920 |
| 1921 | 177,206,263 | 80% | 141,765,011 | 35,441,253 | 101,716,229 | 174.82 | 81,091,031 | 20,625,198 | 1921 |
| 1922 | 177,376,184 | 80% | 141,900,947 | 35,475,237 | 113,684,635 | 156.16 | 90,870,685 | 22,813,950 | 1922 |
| 1923 | 181,144,588 | 80% | 144,915,671 | 36,228,918 | 119,178,513 | 152.11 | 95,268,174 | 23,910,339 | 1923 |
| 1924 | 185,897,887 | 80% | 148,718,310 | 37,179,577 | 122,754,643 | 151.49 | 98,170,886 | 24,583,757 | 1924 |
| 1925 | 194,814,805 | 80% | 155,851,844 | 38,962,961 | 125,693,013 | 155.07 | 100,505,831 | 25,187,183 | 1925 |
| 1926 | 203,283,357 | 80% | 162,626,685 | 40,656,671 | 126,960,364 | 160.33 | 101,429,843 | 25,530,520 | 1926 |
| 1927 | 217,979,220 | 80% | 174,383,376 | 43,595,844 | 138,128,353 | 158.00 | 110,369,534 | 27,758,820 | 1927 |
| 1928 | 230,014,025 | 80% | 184,011,220 | 46,002,805 | 146,879,422 | 156.66 | 117,457,064 | 29,422,358 | 1928 |
| 1929 | 229,670,817 | 80% | 183,736,654 | 45,934,163 | 149,860,839 | 153.27 | 119,880,132 | 29,980,707 | 1929 |
| 1930 | 214,289,817 | 80% | 171,431,854 | 42,857,963 | 146,942,993 | 145.73 | 117,632,905 | 29,310,088 | 1930 |
| 1931 | 163,923,019 | 80% | 131,138,415 | 32,784,604 | 131,160,777 | 124.49 | 105,343,984 | 25,816,793 | 1931 |
| 1932 | 148,784,340 | 80% | 119,027,472 | 29,756,868 | 135,065,402 | 109.58 | 108,621,325 | 26,444,077 | 1932 |
| 1933 | 143,273,992 | 85% | 121,782,894 | 21,491,099 | 139,775,888 | 101.76 | 119,672,423 | 20,103,465 | 1933 |
| 1934 | 145,253,521 | 85% | 123,465,493 | 21,788,028 | 138,216,342 | 104.44 | 118,216,791 | 19,999,552 | 1934 |
| 1935 | 170,007,793 | 85% | 144,506,624 | 25,501,169 | 155,815,301 | 108.53 | 133,147,850 | 22,667,450 | 1935 |
| 1936 | 188,072,989 | 85% | 159,862,041 | 28,210,948 | 175,116,863 | 106.70 | 149,821,047 | 25,295,816 | 1936 |
| 1937 | 214,810,368 | 85% | 182,588,812 | 32,221,555 | 189,079,124 | 113.08 | 161,461,646 | 27,617,477 | 1937 |
| 1938 | 230,461,017 | 85% | 195,891,864 | 34,569,153 | 209,108,433 | 109.42 | 179,024,728 | 30,083,705 | 1938 |
| 1939 | 236,976,709 | 85% | 201,430,203 | 35,546,506 | 213,456,021 | 110.16 | 182,848,975 | 30,607,046 | 1939 |
| 1948 | 870,785,958 | 85% | 740,168,064 | 130,617,894 | 252,774,860 | 344.50 | 214,850,296 | 37,924,564 | 1948 |
| 1949 | 1,030,867,837 | 85% | 876,237,662 | 154,630,176 | 304,461,754 | 338.58 | 258,796,929 | 45,664,825 | 1949 |
| 1950 | 1,073,862,182 | 85% | 912,782,854 | 161,079,327 | 299,061,922 | 359.02 | 254,244,530 | 44,817,393 | 1950 |
| 1951 | 1,272,003,340 | 85% | 1,081,202,839 | 190,800,501 | 281,946,415 | 451.51 | 239,464,811 | 42,481,604 | 1951 |
| 1952 | 1,366,152,822 | 85% | 1,161,229,899 | 204,922,923 | 290,898,659 | 469.80 | 247,177,082 | 43,721,577 | 1952 |
| 1953 | 1,609,481,462 | 85% | 1,368,059,242 | 241,422,219 | 351,634,837 | 458.41 | 298,436,369 | 53,198,467 | 1953 |
| 1954 | 1,626,152,653 | 85% | 1,382,229,755 | 243,922,898 | 372,052,806 | 436.94 | 316,341,017 | 55,711,790 | 1954 |
| 1955 | 1,639,802,301 | 85% | 1,393,831,956 | 245,970,345 | 383,467,220 | 427.08 | 326,361,963 | 57,105,257 | 1955 |
| 1956 | 1,921,470,437 | 85% | 1,633,249,872 | 288,220,566 | 444,809,033 | 431.66 | 378,360,750 | 66,448,283 | 1956 |
| 1957 | 2,014,487,496 | 85% | 1,712,314,371 | 302,173,124 | 455,456,344 | 444.20 | 385,479,118 | 69,977,226 | 1957 |
| 1958 | 2,093,107,385 | 85% | 1,779,141,277 | 313,966,108 | 475,456,393 | 441.93 | 402,588,812 | 72,867,580 | 1958 |
| 1959 | 1,988,598,796 | 85% | 1,690,308,977 | 298,289,819 | 456,342,816 | 436.87 | 386,911,225 | 69,431,592 | 1959 |
| 1960 | 2,371,715,294 | 85% | 2,015,958,000 | 355,757,294 | 544,423,403 | 437.05 | 461,262,368 | 83,161,035 | 1960 |

*Note:*

(*) = Represents the total private final consumption expenditure by resident households only in the domestic market.

government sales[38] and less the value of any own-account capital formation that is included in gross output. Government final consumption expenditure is thus equal to the value of goods and services produced by the government for its own current use. Since government output is mainly not sold, SNA68 measures its value by the cost of producing it, namely the sum of four component items, i.e., (i) compensation of employees (personal emoluments),[39] (ii) intermediate consumption of goods and services by producers of government services and estimates of fixed capital,[40] (iii) consumption of fixed capital,[41] (iv) net indirect taxes paid and own-account construction, if any.[42] In most cases, units classified as governmental do not pay indirect taxes nor do they receive subsidies. As such, only the first three components need to be considered in the Singapore context.

### 2.3.2 *Source Materials and Methodology for Estimates*

Prior to World War II, British colonial authority formed *six* separate general governmental administrative bodies at different points of time in line with the development of public administration in Singapore, namely the Colony of Straits

---

[38] Government sales include receipts from reproduction of museums, publications sold by statistical office, fees for medical and hospital treatment, sales of maps and charts, etc. Fees that are levied for regulating purposes are excluded such as passport and driving licenses.

[39] Compensation of employees consists of personal emoluments (wages and salaries in cash), payment in kind and contributions to social security.

[40] Intermediate consumption is defined as the non-durable goods and services that are purchased by producers and used up in the process of production. Fixed capital formation on defense (exclusive of private dwelling) was treated as intermediate consumption.

[41] Consumption of fixed capital is a cost of production. It may be defined as the decline in the current value of the stock of fixed assets owned and used by a producer as a result of physical deterioration, normal obsolescence or normal accidental damage.

[42] Department of International Economic and Social Affairs, United Nations (1986, 118).

Settlements (1868), Municipality (1886), Rural Board (1908), Education Board (1909) and Hospital Board (1910). In the case of Municipality and Rural Board, individual government expenditure accounts were available for Singapore alone. On the other hand, in the case of government expenditure account pertaining to the Colony of Straits Settlements, Education Board and Hospital Board, government expenditure account figures were consolidated and presented for the Straits Settlements as a whole.

After World War II, due to the dissolution of Straits Settlements, Singapore was reconstituted as an independent Crown Colony. The Municipality of Singapore was renamed as the City Council. Due to the increasing urbanization of Singapore, the trading activities of City Council, namely electricity, gas and water, were subsequently separated from that of the City Council and were reconstituted as part of the newly created Utility Board. The Rural Board was continuously in existence under the Municipal Ordinance. With elected self-government under the 1959 Constitution, the PAP Government abolished these two levels of local government and these functions were integrated as part of the Central Government on the ground that Singapore was too small to afford such differentiation in roles.

Detail expenditures recorded in conventional government accounts varied among administrative bodies and also within each administrative body over time. However, there were no systematic presentations of the expenditure incurred. In view of this, it was necessary to set up a coding system that would identify for estimating compensation of employees, intermediate consumption, capital formation, transfers and others.[43] For

---

[43] Government Finance Statistics Manual (GFS Manual) defines the coding system for all headings of government expenditure incurred by all government bodies. For the construction of GFCE, GFS transaction category on (1) compensation of employees [Code 21], (2) use of goods and services (intermediate consumption) [Code 22], (3) consumption of fixed capital [Code 23] and (4) Sales of government services [Code 142] could be utilized. (Department of Statistics, IMF, 2001, Appendix 3–4). In this exercise, however, the coding system is not followed exactly due to the fact the available information during the research period were rather limited. (Department of Statistics, IMF, 2001, Appendix 3–4).

**Table 2.26:** Singapore: Coding System for Identifying the Different Classes of Government Expenditures

| | Major Code | Sub Code |
|---|---|---|
| **Compensation of employees** | 1 | |
| Emoluments (proper) | 1 | 1 |
| Annual recurrent expenditure | 1 | 2 |
| Special expenditure | 1 | 3 |
| Special services | 1 | 4 |
| Other charges | 1 | 5 |
| Blank | 1 | 6 |
| Others | 1 | 9 |
| **Intermediate consumption** | 2 | |
| **Fixed Capital Formation** | 3+4 | |
| Construction | 3 | |
| Residential building | 3 | 1 |
| Non-residential building | 3 | 2 |
| Other construction | 3 | 3 |
| Residential and non-residential building | 3 | 4 |
| Residential and other construction | 3 | 5 |
| Non-residential and other construction | 3 | 6 |
| Residential, non-residential and other construction | 3 | 7 |
| Others | 3 | 9 |
| Machinery and Equipment | 4 | |
| Transport | 4 | 1 |
| Others | 4 | 9 |
| **Transfer Payments and Others** | 5 | |

convenience, major codes of 1–5 were assigned for personal emoluments, intermediate consumption expenditure, government fixed capital formation, transfer payments and others respectively as presented in Table 2.26. In addition to expenditure incurred under the major code, further detailed breakdown were made based on the availability of data.

To meet the definitions of SNA68, the following steps were taken to identify the government final consumption expenditure. In general, the government expenditure accounts presented expenditure incurred by each department. Within the department, two major classifications were made, viz. personal emoluments (compensation of employees) and other charges (annual recurrent and special expenditure). Under this broad classification, details were provided. Unfortunately, no systematic presentation of the expenditure incurred was available. In view of this, it was necessary to set up a coding system that would identify for our purpose, compensation of employees, intermediate consumption, capital formation, transfers and others.

First, information on revenue received by class of account was utilized to identify the sales of other goods and services by producers of government services. For the compilation of the government final consumption expenditure, the expenditure incurred by the following departments were excluded:

  (i)  Drainage and Irrigation Department
  (ii)  Electric Supply Department
 (iii)  Gas Supply Department
 (iv)  Government Monopolies Department
  (v)  Post and Telegraph Department
 (vi)  Printing Department
 (vii)  Public Works Department
(viii)  Railway Department
 (ix)  Water Supply Department

Second, from the producers' of government services, independent transfer items recorded under the head of department such as pensions, purchase of land, payment of loans are also excluded. Having done these deductions, the output of producers of government services which constitute compensation of employees and intermediate consumption expenditure were identified (See Table 2.27).

Consumption of fixed capital, however, is very difficult to trace due to the dearth of data. Therefore, based on the available post independent information, it was assumed that 1 percent of gross output of producers of government services would be classified as depreciation allowance.[44]

---

[44] Information on this which was available for the 1960s was used as an indicative guide. The data on consumption of fixed capital and its percentage share of government output for Singapore for the years 1960–170, was in the range of 1 percent to 2 percent. Based on this statistical evidence it was assumed that the percentage share of consumption of fixed capital to total government output for Singapore during the study period 1900–39, 1950–60 would have been in the region of 1 percent.

**Table 2.27:** Singapore: Classification for Total Output of Producers of Government Services

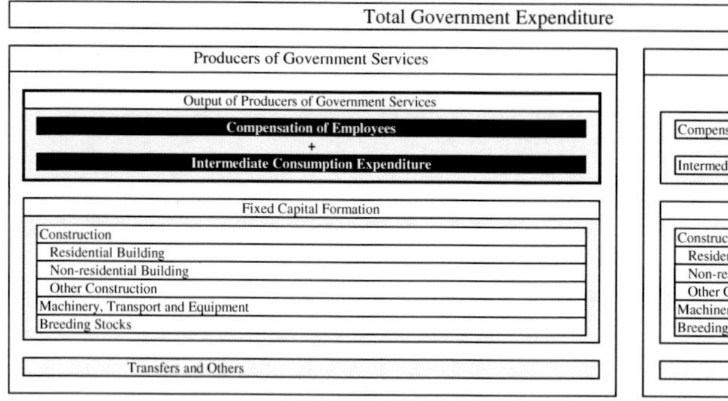



**LIST OF MAIN DEPARTMENTS**

| | |
|---|---|
| Administration of Justice | Labor Department |
| Agricultural | Land and District Office |
| Analyst | Legal |
| Appeal Court | Light Houses |
| Assistant Adviser | Liquors |
| Audit | Malayan Civil Service |
| Bands | Malayan Establishment Office |
| Bankruptcy | Marine |
| Botanical Gardens and Museum | Marine Survey |
| British Adviser | Markets |
| Chandu Monopoly | Medical and Health |
| Charitable Allowances | Military Expenditure |
| Chinese and Indian Immigrants Protection | Mines |
| Chinese Protectorate | Miscellaneous Services |
| Chinese Secretariat | Monopolies and Customs |
| Civil Service | Mosques |
| Clerical Services | Mosquito Destruction Boards |
| Collector of Land Revenue | Municipal |
| Colonial Secretary | Museum and Library |
| Commissioner of Lands and Mines | Native States |
| Conservancy | Office of Registrar of Titles |
| Contribution to Imperial War Funds | Official Assignee |
| Co-operative Societies | Penghulus |
| Courts, Civil and Criminal | Pensions and Retired Allowances |
| Customs and Excise | Police |
| Demarcation | Political Intelligence Bureau |
| Religious Affairs | Post Office |
| District and Land office | Printing Office |
| Ecclesiastical | Prisons |
| Education | Public Trustee |
| Estate Duty Office | Rent |
| Exchange | Revenue Services |
| Excise | Sanitary Board |
| Fire Brigade | Secretary to High Commisioner |
| Fisheries | State Council |
| Food Control | State Secretary |
| Forest | Statistics |
| Game Warden | Stores and Workshops |
| Gaols | Subventions |
| Geological Survey | Supreme Court |
| Government Gardens | Survey Department |
| Government Monopolies | The Federal Secretary |
| Government Printing Office | The Governor |
| Government Town Planner | The High Commissioner |
| Government Vessels, | The Residents |
| H.H.The Sultan's Office | The Rulers and Chiefs |
| Hackney Carriage, Jinrikisha and etc. | Town Hall and Municipal Offices |
| Hackney Carriages and Jinrikisha Dept | Town Lighting and Street Watering |
| Harbour Department | Town Planning |
| Health Branch, Singapore | Transport |
| Hospitals and Dispensaries | Transport Licensing Board |
| Immigration Department | Treasury |
| Imports, Exports and Statistics | Valuer General |
| Income Tax | Veterinary Department |
| Indian Immigration | Volunteer Force |
| Judicial | War Expenditure |
| | Widows and Orphans's |

**LIST OF MAIN DEPARTMENTS**

| |
|---|
| Drainage and Irrigation Department |
| Electric Supply Department |
| Gas Supply Department |
| Government Monopolies |
| Post and Telegraph Department |
| Printing Department |
| Public Works Department |
| Railway |
| Water Supply Department |

Third, government sales were deducted from gross output of producers of government services. Sales of other goods and services produced by the producers of government services were refered to as school fees, hospital fees, etc.

These standard procedures, however, were not fully applicable for all government accounts due to the deficiencies of data. Therefore, the following approach was applied on the basis of the availability of data.

### 2.3.2.1 *Colony of Singapore, 1900–39 and 1950–60*

The government expenditures for the Colony of Singapore are published in the yearly *Blue Book, Straits Settlements* for the period 1900–38. For the year 1939, the data are available in the *Financial Statements of the Colony of the Straits Settlements*, while for the years 1950–56, the data are available from the *Financial Statements of the Colony of Singapore* and for the years 1957–60 in the *Financial Statements of the State of Singapore*. Availability of expenditure details varied over time. For the period 1900–09, the expenditures incurred were presented in a manner that was quite different from that of 1910–39. For the period 1900–09, detailed expenditure by heads of departments was available for each of the settlements with regard to personal emoluments, annual recurrent and special expenditures. From the detailed expenditures incurred, we were able to identify emoluments, intermediate consumption, capital formation and "transfers and others". In the case of "Crown Agents", we were also able to assign, in most cases, the expenditure incurred in each of the settlements wrong the information provided in the source documents. Only in some cases were we not able to assign with precision the expenditure incurred by the "Crown Agents". The magnitude of these expenditures was relatively negligible. Overall, it could be said that the estimated expenditures incurred by the "Crown Agents" in the respective settlements were fairly reliable. The detailed transactions made by producers' of government services and other trading departments (industries) were available on a departmental basis. The output of producers of government services was computed by summing up the emoluments and intermediate consumption of goods and services of the producers of government services (major code of 1 and 2 in Table 2.6), although initially it did not take into the consumption of fixed capital formation (depreciation).

For the period 1910–39, data on personal emoluments and input were available by heads of departments on a consolidated basis for the Colony of the Straits Settlements. In addition, detailed transactions of "recurring" and "special" expenditure, in some instances, were available only on a consolidated basis. This being the case, the consolidated personal emoluments of each department from 1909 to 39 were apportioned on a simple average basis to each of the Settlements in the colony on the basis of the structure of each department for the period 1900–09 (See Appendix Table 8). In cases where a particular department that existed in 1910–39 but not in the period 1900–09, we had to find an alternative approach to identify the proportion of emoluments that ought to be allocated to each entity of the settlements in the colony. The apportioning of the emoluments in this instance was based on the input structure (intermediate consumption of goods and services) of each department for which data were available. This methodology was adopted as it was felt that there was a stable relationship within each department between compensation of employees and intermediate consumption (See Appendix Table 9). Relevant information was also available to distinguish the producers of government services from that of industries.

In cases where sufficient data on inputs were not available, estimates of emoluments were made for each of the regions on the basis of local knowledge of the department (See Appendix Table 10). It should be noted that in the accounts of the Straits Settlements proper, government contributions to Hospital Board, Education Board and Rural Boards were excluded in the computation of government final consumption expenditure. However, they were incorporated in government final consumption expenditure of Municipalities and local bodies.

After World War II, the island of Singapore was treated as a separate entity (British Crown Colony of Singapore) due to the dissolution of the Straits Settlements. *Financial Statements of Colony of Singapore*, 1950–56, and *Financial Statement of the State of Singapore*, 1957–60, were used to obtain the government final consumption expenditure.

### 2.3.2.2 *The Municipality of Singapore, 1900–39, and the City Council of Singapore, 1950–60*

For the computation of government final consumption expenditure at the local government level, the yearly *Annual Administration Report on Singapore Municipality* 1900–02, 1904–09 and 1911–39 was used to obtain government accounts. In the pre–World War II period, the local government of Singapore was known as the Singapore Municipality and subsequently was renamed as the Singapore City Council. For the pre-war period, two different formats of accounts were provided. For the period 1900–16, the *Annual Administration Report of Singapore Municipality* provided total expenditure by department and crude classification of departmental expenditure was presented under the heading of [1] personal emoluments, [2] other charges and [3] special services. No further detailed expenditure breakdown was available. Personal emoluments can in its entirety be classified as compensation of employees. On the other hand, other charges and special services generally contain a whole host of expenditures. However, most of the expenditure appearing under the heading of other charges was intermediate consumption expenditure. At the same time, the expenditure on special services was not classified as compensation of employees or intermediate consumption expenditure.

For the period 1917–39, the figures for the Colony of Singapore were relatively well documented. Detailed expenditure of each department was available and personal emoluments and intermediate consumption expenditure were then summed up to obtain government output of goods and services of Singapore Municipality. For the post-war period, the *Annual Administration Report on City Council of Singapore* provided government accounts by department. The accounts of each department, however, were provided in different formats and the classifications used were rather crude. As an alternative option, *Singapore's City Council Estimate for the year 1954* was used. This report provided very detailed expenditure accounts for the year 1952 for each department. The percentage distribution of each expenditure item for each department by object was identified. These distribution patterns were then applied to the other years. The derived figures are, therefore, inevitably crude estimates considering that a fixed (1952) percentage distribution pattern was applied for the period 1950–60. In contrast to the Colony of Singapore, the City Council of Singapore did not have any kind of government sales of goods and services such as education and hospital fees. Therefore, the government final consumption expenditure was treated as equal to the expenditure on government output.

### 2.3.2.3 *Rural Boards*

The Rural Boards existed only in the settlements of Singapore, Penang and Malacca, having their origin in the Municipal Ordinance of the former Straits Settlements. Actual operation of Rural Boards started since 1908.[45] In effect, they cover the whole

---

[45] [1] In December 1907, the Secretary of State signified his approval of the institution of Rural Boards in the Country Districts outside Municipal limits (Source: Straits Settlements (1909) Proceeding's of the Legislative Council of the Straits Settlements for the year 1908, p.C149). [2] The institution of Rural Boards outside Municipal limits I (Secretary of State) mentioned last year (1908), and I am glad to be able to say that hitherto they have worked well. (Source: Straits Settlements (1910) Proceeding's of the Legislative Council of the Straits Settlements, for the year 1909, p.C.97).

area of Singapore with the exception of the municipal areas.[46] Unfortunately, only total expenditure figures were available in *Blue Books, Straits Settlements* for the period 1911–38. For the post–World War II period, the *Annual Report of Singapore* provided the account of expenditure with breakdowns by major classification of accounts for the years 1950–57. As detailed information on expenditure was not available for the years 1911–39, there was no other option but to apply the percentage distribution of expenditure by class of accounts (emoluments, intermediate consumption, capital formation and "transfers and others") as observed for Rural Boards in the early 1980s. For the years 1908–10, the average ratio between rural boards and municipality for compensation of employees and intermediate consumption was applied to obtain the estimated figures.

For the period 1950–60, the *Annual Report of Singapore* provided the breakdown of expenditure by its various departments. These figures on expenditure were then reclassified by objects and total expenditure on personal emolument and intermediate consumption expenditure were then summed up to derive the government output of goods and services.

### 2.3.2.4 *Education Board*

The Education Board of Straits Settlements was formed for the following reasons: First, to determine the amount of fees to be charged in government schools and to receive all such fees. Second, to submit to the government the annual estimates for educational purposes and to make recommendation thereon. Third, to advise the government as to the purposes for education should be expended upon any matters connected with education which may, from time to time, be referred to it by the Governor.

The percentage distribution by class of account was known in respect of the Education Department in Singapore. The

---

[46] Taylor, WC (1949, 61).

expenditure pattern of the Education Department and Education Board by class of account for Singapore was then estimated for the period 1910–39 on the basis of average share of the expenditure by class of account of Singapore in relation to the Straits Settlements expenditure for the period 1900–09. Having determined the expenditure by class of account for the Education Department and Education Board on a consolidated basis for Singapore, we were able to determine the expenditure by class of account for the Education Board proper for Singapore. We can further deduct from the consolidated account of the Education Department and Education Board of Singapore the expenditure pattern by class of account of the Education Department. In the case of the Education Board proper, the data available were only in respect to total expenditure on a consolidated basis for the period 1900–39 without breakdown by class of account. Estimation by class of account for each of the entity within the Straits Settlements was estimated as follows.

For the period 1900–09, the total expenditure on education was the sole responsibility of the Education Department (SS). With the setting up of the Education Board in 1909, the expenditure on education became the joint responsibility of the Education Department and the Education Board (SS). For the period 1911–39, the expenditure by class of account of the Education Department (SS) was available. However, no such data were available in the case of Education Board (SS) whereby only the total expenditure was known. The percentage distribution from 1900 to 09 of the Education Department (SS) was then used to determine the pattern of expenditure of the Education Board (SS) and the Education Department (SS) on a consolidated basis for the period 1910–39. Having identified the total expenditure pattern by class of account on a consolidated basis, the expenditure pattern of the Education Board proper (SS) was derived by isolating from the expenditure pattern of the Education Department (SS) and the Education Board (SS) on a consolidated basis. In the post-war period, unfortunately, expenditure on Education Boards was no longer available in the *Annual Report, Financial Statement of Singapore* and *Annual Report, Education Department, Singapore.* Therefore, there was no other option but to estimate the figures by extrapolation.

### 2.3.2.5 *Hospital Board*

The Hospital Board was formed for a number of reasons, namely (a) to determine the amount of fees to be charged in all hospitals and asylums, (b) to disburse all sums voted by Governor in Council for the purposes of hospitals and asylums and (c) to advise the Government on any matters in connection with hospitals and asylums. In the case of Hospital Board, separate data on total expenditure incurred were available for Singapore. The assignment of expenditure incurred by the Medical Department of Singapore and the Hospital Board of Singapore by class of account for the period 1910–39 was derived using the expenditure pattern by class of account from 1900 to 09 of the expenditure incurred by Medical Department of Singapore. Having identified the total expenditure pattern of the Medical Department and the Hospital Board on a consolidated basis, the expenditure pattern by class of account of the Hospital Board was derived by isolating the consolidated expenditure pattern of the Medical Department and the Hospital Board, the expenditure of the Medical Department for the period 1910–39. In the post-war period, expenditure on Hospital Boards was not available in the relevant reports — a situation similar to that of the Education Board as has been mentioned earlier. Therefore, the extrapolation method was applied under these circumstances to obtain the estimates.

### 2.3.2.6 *Total Government Output of Producers' of Government Services, 1900–39 and 1950–60*

Table 2.28 presents the total expenditure incurred for (1) compensation of employees and (2) intermediate consumption by

**Table 2.28:** Singapore: Gross Output of Producers of Government Services, 1900–39 and 1950–60

(Straits Millions $)

| Year | A: Colony | | | | | B: Municipality | | | | | C: Rural Board | | | | | D: Education Board | | | | | E: Hospital Board | | | | | Total | | | | | Percentage Share:- | | | | | Year |
|---|---|---|---|---|---|---|---|---|---|---|---|---|---|---|---|---|---|---|---|---|---|---|---|---|---|---|---|---|---|---|---|---|---|---|---|---|
| | [1] | [1]/[3] | [2] | [2]/[3] | [3]=[1]+[2] | [1] | [1]/[3] | [2] | [2]/[3] | [3]=[1]+[2] | [1] | [1]/[3] | [2] | [2]/[3] | [3]=[1]+[2] | [1] | [1]/[3] | [2] | [2]/[3] | [3]=[1]+[2] | [1] | [1]/[3] | [2] | [2]/[3] | [3]=[1]+[2] | [1] | [1]/[3] | [2] | [2]/[3] | [3]=[1]+[2] | A | B | C | D | E | |
| 1900 | 0.88 | 69 | 0.40 | 31 | 1.28 | 0.20 | 20 | 0.77 | 80 | 0.96 | | | | | | | | | | | | | | | | 1.08 | 48 | 1.17 | 52 | 2.25 | 57 | 43 | | | | 1900 |
| 1901 | 0.99 | 67 | 0.48 | 33 | 1.47 | 0.23 | 19 | 0.99 | 81 | 1.23 | | | | | | | | | | | | | | | | 1.22 | 45 | 1.48 | 55 | 2.70 | 55 | 45 | | | | 1901 |
| 1902 | 1.11 | 67 | 0.54 | 33 | 1.66 | 0.26 | 28 | 0.67 | 72 | 0.93 | | | | | | | | | | | | | | | | 1.37 | 53 | 1.21 | 47 | 2.58 | 64 | 36 | | | | 1902 |
| 1903 | 1.25 | 61 | 0.82 | 39 | 2.07 | 0.27 | 22 | 0.94 | 78 | 1.21 | | | | | | | | | | | | | | | | 1.52 | 46 | 1.76 | 54 | 3.28 | 63 | 37 | | | | 1903 |
| 1904 | 1.27 | 57 | 0.96 | 43 | 2.24 | 0.28 | 19 | 1.18 | 81 | 1.46 | | | | | | | | | | | | | | | | 1.56 | 42 | 2.15 | 58 | 3.70 | 60 | 40 | | | | 1904 |
| 1905 | 1.32 | 68 | 0.61 | 32 | 1.93 | 0.31 | 22 | 1.12 | 78 | 1.43 | | | | | | | | | | | | | | | | 1.63 | 49 | 1.73 | 51 | 3.36 | 57 | 43 | | | | 1905 |
| 1906 | 1.24 | 67 | 0.62 | 33 | 1.86 | 0.33 | 25 | 1.00 | 75 | 1.32 | | | | | | | | | | | | | | | | 1.57 | 49 | 1.62 | 51 | 3.19 | 58 | 42 | | | | 1906 |
| 1907 | 1.26 | 67 | 0.62 | 33 | 1.88 | 0.35 | 27 | 0.93 | 73 | 1.28 | | | | | | | | | | | | | | | | 1.61 | 51 | 1.55 | 49 | 3.16 | 60 | 40 | | | | 1907 |
| 1908 | 1.41 | 70 | 0.59 | 30 | 2.00 | 0.37 | 28 | 0.94 | 72 | 1.31 | 0.03 | 44 | 0.04 | 56 | 0.06 | | | | | | | | | | | 1.81 | 54 | 1.57 | 46 | 3.38 | 59 | 39 | 2 | | | 1908 |
| 1909 | 1.53 | 74 | 0.54 | 26 | 2.07 | 0.38 | 32 | 0.82 | 68 | 1.20 | 0.03 | 48 | 0.03 | 52 | 0.06 | | | | | | | | | | | 1.94 | 58 | 1.39 | 42 | 3.33 | 62 | 36 | 2 | | | 1909 |
| 1910 | 1.61 | 77 | 0.49 | 23 | 2.11 | 0.41 | 26 | 1.14 | 74 | 1.55 | 0.03 | 42 | 0.04 | 58 | 0.07 | 0.02 | 41 | 0.03 | 59 | 0.05 | 0.04 | 26 | 0.12 | 74 | 0.17 | 2.12 | 54 | 1.83 | 46 | 3.95 | 53 | 39 | 2 | 1 | 4 | 1910 |
| 1911 | 1.55 | 81 | 0.36 | 19 | 1.91 | 0.43 | 23 | 1.46 | 77 | 1.89 | 0.03 | 38 | 0.04 | 62 | 0.07 | 0.05 | 56 | 0.04 | 44 | 0.09 | 0.03 | 20 | 0.12 | 80 | 0.15 | 2.09 | 51 | 2.02 | 49 | 4.11 | 47 | 46 | 2 | 2 | 4 | 1911 |
| 1912 | 1.67 | 83 | 0.35 | 17 | 2.01 | 0.43 | 25 | 1.29 | 75 | 1.72 | 0.04 | 38 | 0.07 | 62 | 0.11 | 0.05 | 54 | 0.04 | 46 | 0.09 | 0.01 | 10 | 0.12 | 90 | 0.14 | 2.20 | 54 | 1.86 | 46 | 4.07 | 49 | 42 | 3 | 2 | 3 | 1912 |
| 1913 | 1.76 | 84 | 0.35 | 16 | 2.10 | 0.56 | 22 | 1.98 | 78 | 2.54 | 0.04 | 38 | 0.07 | 62 | 0.11 | 0.07 | 59 | 0.05 | 41 | 0.12 | 0.01 | 9 | 0.14 | 91 | 0.16 | 2.45 | 49 | 2.59 | 51 | 5.03 | 42 | 51 | 2 | 2 | 3 | 1913 |
| 1914 | 1.82 | 82 | 0.41 | 18 | 2.23 | 0.66 | 28 | 1.71 | 72 | 2.37 | 0.08 | 38 | 0.12 | 62 | 0.20 | 0.05 | 53 | 0.05 | 47 | 0.10 | 0.03 | 17 | 0.16 | 83 | 0.19 | 2.64 | 52 | 2.45 | 48 | 5.09 | 44 | 47 | 4 | 2 | 4 | 1914 |
| 1915 | 1.76 | 83 | 0.37 | 17 | 2.13 | 0.50 | 24 | 1.58 | 76 | 2.08 | 0.06 | 38 | 0.10 | 62 | 0.16 | 0.06 | 54 | 0.05 | 46 | 0.11 | 0.03 | 15 | 0.15 | 85 | 0.17 | 2.40 | 52 | 2.25 | 48 | 4.65 | 46 | 45 | 4 | 2 | 4 | 1915 |
| 1916 | 1.71 | 63 | 1.00 | 37 | 2.72 | 0.43 | 27 | 1.16 | 73 | 1.59 | 0.05 | 38 | 0.09 | 62 | 0.14 | 0.12 | 65 | 0.06 | 35 | 0.18 | 0.03 | 18 | 0.15 | 82 | 0.19 | 2.35 | 49 | 2.47 | 51 | 4.82 | 56 | 33 | 3 | 4 | 4 | 1916 |
| 1917 | 1.78 | 84 | 0.35 | 16 | 2.13 | 0.61 | 29 | 1.52 | 71 | 2.13 | 0.06 | 38 | 0.10 | 62 | 0.16 | 0.06 | 53 | 0.05 | 47 | 0.11 | 0.04 | 20 | 0.17 | 80 | 0.21 | 2.55 | 54 | 2.18 | 46 | 4.73 | 45 | 45 | 3 | 2 | 4 | 1917 |
| 1918 | 2.20 | 58 | 1.56 | 42 | 3.76 | 0.59 | 26 | 1.69 | 74 | 2.28 | 0.07 | 38 | 0.12 | 62 | 0.20 | 0.07 | 55 | 0.06 | 45 | 0.13 | 0.06 | 25 | 0.19 | 75 | 0.25 | 3.00 | 45 | 3.61 | 55 | 6.61 | 57 | 35 | 3 | 2 | 4 | 1918 |
| 1919 | 2.98 | 72 | 1.15 | 28 | 4.13 | 0.77 | 36 | 1.40 | 64 | 2.17 | 0.09 | 38 | 0.14 | 62 | 0.22 | 0.09 | 58 | 0.07 | 42 | 0.16 | 0.13 | 33 | 0.27 | 67 | 0.39 | 4.06 | 57 | 3.01 | 43 | 7.07 | 58 | 31 | 3 | 2 | 6 | 1919 |
| 1920 | 5.55 | 82 | 1.25 | 18 | 6.80 | 1.15 | 34 | 2.25 | 66 | 3.40 | 0.09 | 38 | 0.14 | 62 | 0.23 | 0.44 | 72 | 0.17 | 28 | 0.61 | 0.11 | 24 | 0.33 | 76 | 0.44 | 7.34 | 64 | 4.14 | 36 | 11.49 | 59 | 30 | 2 | 5 | 4 | 1920 |
| 1921 | 6.11 | 81 | 1.40 | 19 | 7.51 | 1.69 | 36 | 3.06 | 64 | 4.75 | 0.09 | 38 | 0.15 | 62 | 0.24 | 0.22 | 61 | 0.14 | 39 | 0.37 | 0.19 | 30 | 0.46 | 70 | 0.66 | 8.31 | 61 | 5.21 | 39 | 13.53 | 56 | 35 | 2 | 3 | 5 | 1921 |
| 1922 | 5.48 | 80 | 1.35 | 20 | 6.84 | 1.29 | 27 | 3.46 | 73 | 4.75 | 0.08 | 38 | 0.12 | 62 | 0.20 | 0.17 | 55 | 0.14 | 45 | 0.31 | 0.10 | 22 | 0.36 | 78 | 0.46 | 7.12 | 57 | 5.43 | 43 | 12.56 | 54 | 38 | 2 | 2 | 4 | 1922 |
| 1923 | 5.05 | 80 | 1.29 | 20 | 6.34 | 1.34 | 26 | 3.74 | 74 | 5.08 | 0.09 | 38 | 0.15 | 62 | 0.24 | 0.19 | 56 | 0.14 | 44 | 0.33 | 0.11 | 23 | 0.37 | 77 | 0.48 | 6.78 | 54 | 5.69 | 46 | 12.47 | 51 | 41 | 2 | 3 | 4 | 1923 |
| 1924 | 5.43 | 78 | 1.49 | 22 | 6.93 | 1.41 | 27 | 3.88 | 73 | 5.29 | 0.11 | 38 | 0.17 | 62 | 0.28 | 0.21 | 56 | 0.16 | 44 | 0.37 | 0.15 | 30 | 0.36 | 70 | 0.51 | 7.31 | 55 | 6.07 | 45 | 13.38 | 52 | 40 | 2 | 3 | 4 | 1924 |
| 1925 | 5.63 | 83 | 1.12 | 17 | 6.75 | 1.49 | 33 | 2.98 | 67 | 4.48 | 0.13 | 38 | 0.21 | 62 | 0.34 | 0.23 | 56 | 0.18 | 44 | 0.41 | 0.04 | 6 | 0.53 | 94 | 0.57 | 7.53 | 60 | 5.02 | 40 | 12.55 | 54 | 36 | 3 | 3 | 5 | 1925 |
| 1926 | 5.84 | 83 | 1.21 | 17 | 7.06 | 1.53 | 29 | 3.70 | 71 | 5.23 | 0.11 | 38 | 0.18 | 62 | 0.29 | 0.32 | 61 | 0.21 | 39 | 0.52 | 0.02 | 3 | 0.54 | 97 | 0.56 | 7.82 | 57 | 5.84 | 43 | 13.66 | 52 | 38 | 2 | 4 | 4 | 1926 |
| 1927 | 5.79 | 83 | 1.21 | 17 | 7.00 | 1.61 | 27 | 4.26 | 73 | 5.87 | 0.18 | 38 | 0.29 | 62 | 0.47 | 0.36 | 61 | 0.23 | 39 | 0.58 | 0.15 | 17 | 0.76 | 83 | 0.91 | 8.08 | 55 | 6.74 | 45 | 14.83 | 47 | 40 | 3 | 4 | 6 | 1927 |
| 1928 | 6.14 | 82 | 1.35 | 18 | 7.50 | 1.74 | 31 | 3.93 | 69 | 5.67 | 0.15 | 38 | 0.24 | 62 | 0.39 | 0.37 | 61 | 0.24 | 39 | 0.61 | 0.08 | 9 | 0.79 | 91 | 0.87 | 8.49 | 56 | 6.56 | 44 | 15.05 | 50 | 38 | 3 | 4 | 5 | 1928 |
| 1929 | 6.76 | 80 | 1.67 | 20 | 8.43 | 1.85 | 32 | 4.00 | 68 | 5.86 | 0.24 | 38 | 0.39 | 62 | 0.64 | 0.39 | 60 | 0.26 | 40 | 0.64 | 0.03 | 4 | 0.73 | 96 | 0.76 | 9.28 | 57 | 7.05 | 43 | 16.33 | 52 | 36 | 4 | 4 | 5 | 1929 |
| 1930 | 6.96 | 79 | 1.86 | 21 | 8.82 | 1.82 | 30 | 4.28 | 70 | 6.10 | 0.24 | 38 | 0.39 | 62 | 0.64 | 0.41 | 60 | 0.28 | 40 | 0.69 | 0.03 | 4 | 0.75 | 96 | 0.78 | 9.47 | 56 | 7.56 | 44 | 17.03 | 52 | 36 | 4 | 4 | 5 | 1930 |
| 1931 | 7.14 | 78 | 1.97 | 22 | 9.10 | 2.03 | 34 | 3.89 | 66 | 5.92 | 0.24 | 38 | 0.39 | 62 | 0.64 | 0.41 | 58 | 0.30 | 42 | 0.71 | 0.03 | 4 | 0.75 | 96 | 0.78 | 9.85 | 57 | 7.30 | 43 | 17.15 | 53 | 35 | 4 | 4 | 5 | 1931 |
| 1932 | 6.51 | 80 | 1.60 | 20 | 8.11 | 2.07 | 38 | 3.40 | 62 | 5.46 | 0.14 | 38 | 0.22 | 62 | 0.36 | 0.35 | 55 | 0.29 | 45 | 0.64 | 0.04 | 5 | 0.67 | 95 | 0.71 | 9.10 | 60 | 6.18 | 40 | 15.28 | 53 | 36 | 2 | 4 | 5 | 1932 |
| 1933 | 6.26 | 83 | 1.26 | 17 | 7.52 | 1.73 | 37 | 3.00 | 63 | 4.73 | 0.14 | 38 | 0.22 | 62 | 0.36 | 0.32 | 54 | 0.27 | 46 | 0.59 | 0.04 | 7 | 0.56 | 93 | 0.59 | 8.48 | 61 | 5.32 | 39 | 13.80 | 55 | 34 | 3 | 4 | 4 | 1933 |
| 1934 | 6.10 | 87 | 0.92 | 13 | 7.02 | 1.60 | 38 | 2.58 | 62 | 4.18 | 0.11 | 38 | 0.18 | 62 | 0.30 | 0.27 | 51 | 0.26 | 49 | 0.53 | 0.04 | 6 | 0.56 | 94 | 0.60 | 8.13 | 64 | 4.51 | 36 | 12.64 | 56 | 33 | 2 | 4 | 5 | 1934 |
| 1935 | 6.58 | 87 | 0.97 | 13 | 7.55 | 1.70 | 39 | 2.66 | 61 | 4.36 | 0.14 | 38 | 0.22 | 62 | 0.36 | 0.28 | 51 | 0.27 | 49 | 0.54 | 0.05 | 7 | 0.67 | 93 | 0.72 | 8.75 | 65 | 4.79 | 35 | 13.54 | 56 | 32 | 3 | 4 | 5 | 1935 |
| 1936 | 6.54 | 82 | 1.42 | 18 | 7.97 | 1.80 | 44 | 2.26 | 56 | 4.06 | 0.16 | 38 | 0.26 | 62 | 0.41 | 0.32 | 53 | 0.28 | 47 | 0.60 | 0.04 | 6 | 0.69 | 94 | 0.73 | 8.86 | 64 | 4.92 | 36 | 13.77 | 58 | 29 | 3 | 4 | 5 | 1936 |
| 1937 | 7.35 | 82 | 1.62 | 18 | 8.97 | 1.82 | 46 | 2.12 | 54 | 3.94 | 0.17 | 38 | 0.27 | 62 | 0.43 | 0.34 | 53 | 0.30 | 47 | 0.64 | 0.03 | 4 | 0.69 | 96 | 0.72 | 9.71 | 66 | 5.00 | 34 | 14.71 | 61 | 27 | 3 | 4 | 5 | 1937 |
| 1938 | 7.29 | 80 | 1.84 | 20 | 9.13 | 1.86 | 41 | 2.73 | 59 | 4.59 | 0.21 | 38 | 0.35 | 62 | 0.56 | 0.38 | 55 | 0.32 | 45 | 0.70 | 0.06 | 6 | 0.82 | 94 | 0.87 | 9.81 | 62 | 6.05 | 38 | 15.85 | 58 | 29 | 4 | 4 | 6 | 1938 |
| 1939 | 7.01 | 75 | 2.32 | 25 | 9.32 | 1.90 | 40 | 2.84 | 60 | 4.73 | 0.25 | 38 | 0.40 | 62 | 0.65 | 0.43 | 56 | 0.34 | 44 | 0.76 | 0.02 | 2 | 0.93 | 98 | 0.95 | 9.60 | 58 | 6.82 | 42 | 16.43 | 57 | 29 | 4 | 5 | 6 | 1939 |
| | | 76 | | 24 | | | 30 | | 70 | | | 39 | | 61 | | | 56 | | 44 | | | 14 | | 86 | | | 55 | | 45 | | 54 | 38 | 3 | 3 | 4 | |
| 1950 | 41.31 | 73 | 14.92 | 27 | 56.23 | 5.04 | 38 | 8.21 | 62 | 13.25 | 0.29 | 20 | 1.16 | 80 | 1.45 | 0.96 | 56 | 0.74 | 44 | 1.70 | 0.29 | 14 | 1.83 | 86 | 2.12 | 47.89 | 64 | 26.86 | 36 | 74.76 | 75 | 18 | 2 | 2 | 3 | 1950 |
| 1951 | 50.21 | 72 | 19.30 | 28 | 69.51 | 6.30 | 38 | 10.28 | 62 | 16.59 | 0.30 | 17 | 1.43 | 83 | 1.73 | 1.15 | 56 | 0.89 | 44 | 2.04 | 0.35 | 14 | 2.19 | 86 | 2.54 | 58.32 | 63 | 34.09 | 37 | 92.41 | 75 | 18 | 2 | 2 | 3 | 1951 |
| 1952 | 58.37 | 73 | 21.85 | 27 | 80.22 | 7.26 | 38 | 12.09 | 62 | 19.35 | 0.39 | 20 | 1.56 | 80 | 1.95 | 1.29 | 56 | 1.00 | 44 | 2.29 | 0.39 | 14 | 2.46 | 86 | 2.85 | 67.70 | 63 | 38.96 | 37 | 106.66 | 75 | 18 | 2 | 2 | 3 | 1952 |
| 1953 | 68.55 | 72 | 26.33 | 28 | 94.88 | 7.80 | 38 | 12.49 | 62 | 20.28 | 0.55 | 22 | 1.94 | 78 | 2.49 | 1.65 | 56 | 1.27 | 44 | 2.93 | 0.50 | 14 | 3.15 | 86 | 3.65 | 79.06 | 64 | 45.17 | 36 | 124.23 | 76 | 16 | 2 | 2 | 3 | 1953 |
| 1954 | 73.34 | 66 | 37.07 | 34 | 110.41 | 8.66 | 38 | 14.18 | 62 | 22.84 | 0.51 | 17 | 2.43 | 83 | 2.93 | 1.95 | 56 | 1.50 | 44 | 3.44 | 0.59 | 14 | 3.71 | 86 | 4.30 | 85.04 | 59 | 58.89 | 41 | 143.93 | 77 | 16 | 2 | 2 | 3 | 1954 |
| 1955 | 84.63 | 73 | 31.58 | 27 | 116.21 | 10.35 | 38 | 16.74 | 62 | 27.08 | 0.58 | 19 | 2.56 | 81 | 3.14 | 2.08 | 56 | 1.60 | 44 | 3.69 | 0.63 | 14 | 3.97 | 86 | 4.60 | 98.28 | 64 | 56.44 | 36 | 154.72 | 75 | 18 | 2 | 2 | 3 | 1955 |
| 1956 | 93.84 | 79 | 25.04 | 21 | 118.88 | 12.05 | 37 | 20.79 | 63 | 32.83 | 0.57 | 16 | 3.10 | 84 | 3.67 | 2.43 | 56 | 1.87 | 44 | 4.31 | 0.74 | 14 | 4.63 | 86 | 5.37 | 109.63 | 66 | 55.43 | 34 | 165.06 | 72 | 20 | 2 | 3 | 3 | 1956 |
| 1957 | 98.98 | 79 | 25.65 | 21 | 124.63 | 12.08 | 46 | 14.12 | 54 | 26.20 | 1.02 | 22 | 3.53 | 78 | 4.55 | 3.02 | 56 | 2.32 | 44 | 5.34 | 0.92 | 14 | 5.75 | 86 | 6.66 | 116.02 | 69 | 51.36 | 31 | 167.38 | 74 | 16 | 3 | 3 | 4 | 1957 |
| 1958 | 106.55 | 79 | 27.66 | 21 | 134.21 | 13.01 | 46 | 15.23 | 54 | 28.23 | 1.11 | 23 | 3.75 | 77 | 4.86 | 3.22 | 56 | 2.48 | 44 | 5.71 | 0.98 | 14 | 6.14 | 86 | 7.12 | 124.87 | 69 | 55.27 | 31 | 180.14 | 75 | 16 | 3 | 3 | 4 | 1958 |
| 1959 | 106.54 | 75 | 34.61 | 25 | 141.14 | 13.00 | 41 | 19.05 | 59 | 32.05 | 0.96 | 25 | 2.85 | 75 | 3.82 | 2.53 | 56 | 1.95 | 44 | 4.48 | 0.77 | 14 | 4.82 | 86 | 5.59 | 123.81 | 66 | 63.28 | 34 | 187.09 | 75 | 17 | 2 | 2 | 3 | 1959 |
| 1960 | 105.16 | 75 | 35.05 | 25 | 140.21 | | | | | | | | | | | | | | | | | | | | | 105.16 | 75 | 35.05 | 25 | 140.21 | 100 | | | | | 1960 |
| | | 74 | | 26 | | | 40 | | 60 | | | 20 | | 80 | | | 56 | | 44 | | | 14 | | 86 | | | 66 | | 34 | | 75 | 17 | 2 | 3 | 3 | |

*Notes:* [1] Compensation of Employees, [2] Intermediate Consumption Expenditure and [3] Output of Producers of Government Services.

*Source:*

each government body. Two features can be highlighted here. First, the share of personal emoluments for the Colony was very high (in the region of over 70 percent) during the period under review, while the share of total personal emoluments for all government bodies averaged about 55 and 66 percent for the period 1900–39 and 1950–60, respectively. Second, the share of that of the local bodies, particularly the Municipality, was relatively high, particularly during the period 1900–39 (46 percent), compared to the 1950s (25 percent).

### 2.3.3 *Government Final Consumption Expenditure in Current Prices*

Gross output of producers of government services was then derived by summing up the output from all government bodies. As is presented in Table 2.29, each government administration showed different weights on the compensation of employees and intermediate consumption expenditure, but its aggregated weight provides relatively similar weights with the official figure. As stated earlier, a depreciation rate of 1 percent was applied against gross output of producers of government services. Finally, to obtain the estimate of government final consumption expenditure (GFCE), from the estimate of gross output were all of the elements entering into it that were not final consumption; that is, amount received for any part of government gross output that in fact is sold on the market. In these estimates, only school fees and hospital fees which appeared in the *Blue Books, Straits Settlements* and *Annual Report, Financial Statement* were used as government sales.

### 2.3.4 *Government Final Consumption Expenditure in 1914 Prices*

As has been mentioned above, output of producers of government services was derived by summing up the compensation of employees (personal emoluments), intermediate consumption of goods

**Table 2.29:** Singapore: Government Final Consumption Expenditure, 1900–39 and 1950–60, at Current and 1914 Prices

(Straits Millions $)

| | Current Prices | | | | | | | | 1914 Prices | | | |
| | Government Output | | | | Sales of Government Services | | | | | | | |
| Year | Compensation of Employees | Intermediate Consumption | Depreciation | Total | School Fees | Hospital Fees | Total | Govt. Final Consumption Expenditure | Government Output | Sales of Govt. Services | Govt. Final Consumption Expenditure | Year |
| | [1] | [2] | [3]= [4]-[1]-[2] | [4]= ([1]+[2]) / 0.99 | [5] | [6] | [7] = [5] + [6] | [8]=[3]-[4]-[7] | A | B | C = A- B | |
|---|---|---|---|---|---|---|---|---|---|---|---|---|
| 1900 | 1.08 | 1.17 | 0.02 | 2.27 | 0.01 | 0.03 | 0.04 | 2.23 | 2.74 | 0.05 | 2.70 | 1900 |
| 1901 | 1.22 | 1.48 | 0.03 | 2.72 | 0.01 | 0.03 | 0.04 | 2.69 | 3.26 | 0.04 | 3.21 | 1901 |
| 1902 | 1.37 | 1.21 | 0.03 | 2.61 | 0.01 | 0.04 | 0.05 | 2.56 | 3.01 | 0.06 | 2.95 | 1902 |
| 1903 | 1.52 | 1.76 | 0.03 | 3.32 | 0.03 | 0.04 | 0.07 | 3.25 | 3.78 | 0.08 | 3.70 | 1903 |
| 1904 | 1.56 | 2.15 | 0.04 | 3.74 | 0.03 | 0.04 | 0.07 | 3.67 | 4.25 | 0.08 | 4.18 | 1904 |
| 1905 | 1.63 | 1.73 | 0.03 | 3.39 | 0.08 | 0.04 | 0.12 | 3.27 | 3.79 | 0.13 | 3.66 | 1905 |
| 1906 | 1.57 | 1.62 | 0.03 | 3.22 | 0.03 | 0.05 | 0.08 | 3.14 | 3.65 | 0.09 | 3.56 | 1906 |
| 1907 | 1.61 | 1.55 | 0.03 | 3.20 | 0.04 | 0.04 | 0.08 | 3.12 | 3.63 | 0.09 | 3.54 | 1907 |
| 1908 | 1.81 | 1.57 | 0.03 | 3.41 | 0.04 | 0.05 | 0.09 | 3.32 | 3.82 | 0.11 | 3.72 | 1908 |
| 1909 | 1.94 | 1.39 | 0.03 | 3.37 | 0.18 | 0.05 | 0.23 | 3.14 | 3.86 | 0.26 | 3.60 | 1909 |
| 1910 | 2.12 | 1.83 | 0.04 | 3.99 | 0.12 | 0.06 | 0.18 | 3.81 | 4.49 | 0.20 | 4.29 | 1910 |
| 1911 | 2.09 | 2.02 | 0.04 | 4.15 | 0.13 | 0.07 | 0.20 | 3.95 | 4.26 | 0.20 | 4.06 | 1911 |
| 1912 | 2.20 | 1.86 | 0.04 | 4.11 | 0.14 | 0.06 | 0.20 | 3.91 | 4.15 | 0.20 | 3.95 | 1912 |
| 1913 | 2.45 | 2.59 | 0.05 | 5.08 | 0.16 | 0.06 | 0.22 | 4.86 | 5.03 | 0.22 | 4.81 | 1913 |
| 1914 | 2.64 | 2.45 | 0.05 | 5.14 | 0.16 | 0.06 | 0.22 | 4.92 | 5.14 | 0.22 | 4.92 | 1914 |
| 1915 | 2.40 | 2.25 | 0.05 | 4.69 | 0.17 | 0.08 | 0.25 | 4.44 | 4.41 | 0.24 | 4.17 | 1915 |
| 1916 | 2.35 | 2.47 | 0.05 | 4.87 | 0.05 | 0.10 | 0.15 | 4.72 | 4.30 | 0.13 | 4.17 | 1916 |
| 1917 | 2.55 | 2.18 | 0.05 | 4.78 | 0.05 | 0.13 | 0.18 | 4.60 | 4.06 | 0.15 | 3.91 | 1917 |
| 1918 | 3.00 | 3.61 | 0.07 | 6.68 | 0.05 | 0.16 | 0.21 | 6.46 | 4.75 | 0.15 | 4.60 | 1918 |
| 1919 | 4.06 | 3.01 | 0.07 | 7.14 | 0.06 | 0.20 | 0.26 | 6.88 | 4.15 | 0.15 | 3.99 | 1919 |
| 1920 | 7.34 | 4.14 | 0.12 | 11.60 | 0.07 | 0.25 | 0.32 | 11.28 | 5.24 | 0.14 | 5.10 | 1920 |
| 1921 | 8.31 | 5.21 | 0.14 | 13.66 | 0.08 | 0.32 | 0.39 | 13.27 | 7.82 | 0.22 | 7.59 | 1921 |
| 1922 | 7.12 | 5.43 | 0.13 | 12.68 | 0.08 | 0.40 | 0.48 | 12.21 | 8.12 | 0.31 | 7.82 | 1922 |
| 1923 | 6.78 | 5.69 | 0.13 | 12.60 | 0.09 | 0.50 | 0.59 | 12.00 | 8.28 | 0.39 | 7.89 | 1923 |
| 1924 | 7.31 | 6.07 | 0.14 | 13.52 | 0.10 | 0.26 | 0.36 | 13.16 | 8.92 | 0.24 | 8.68 | 1924 |
| 1925 | 7.53 | 5.02 | 0.13 | 12.68 | 0.12 | 0.34 | 0.47 | 12.21 | 8.18 | 0.30 | 7.88 | 1925 |
| 1926 | 7.82 | 5.84 | 0.14 | 13.80 | 0.12 | 0.38 | 0.50 | 13.30 | 8.61 | 0.31 | 8.29 | 1926 |
| 1927 | 8.08 | 6.74 | 0.15 | 14.98 | 0.12 | 0.37 | 0.50 | 14.48 | 9.48 | 0.31 | 9.16 | 1927 |
| 1928 | 8.49 | 6.56 | 0.15 | 15.20 | 0.14 | 0.39 | 0.53 | 14.68 | 9.70 | 0.34 | 9.37 | 1928 |
| 1929 | 9.28 | 7.05 | 0.16 | 16.49 | 0.15 | 0.46 | 0.61 | 15.88 | 10.76 | 0.40 | 10.36 | 1929 |
| 1930 | 9.47 | 7.56 | 0.17 | 17.20 | 0.16 | 0.55 | 0.72 | 16.48 | 11.80 | 0.49 | 11.31 | 1930 |
| 1931 | 9.85 | 7.30 | 0.17 | 17.32 | 0.18 | 0.66 | 0.83 | 16.49 | 13.91 | 0.67 | 13.24 | 1931 |
| 1932 | 9.10 | 6.18 | 0.15 | 15.43 | 0.19 | 0.78 | 0.97 | 14.46 | 14.08 | 0.88 | 13.20 | 1932 |
| 1933 | 8.48 | 5.32 | 0.14 | 13.94 | 0.18 | 0.79 | 0.97 | 12.97 | 13.70 | 0.95 | 12.75 | 1933 |
| 1934 | 8.13 | 4.51 | 0.13 | 12.77 | 0.19 | 0.91 | 1.10 | 11.67 | 12.23 | 1.05 | 11.17 | 1934 |
| 1935 | 8.75 | 4.79 | 0.14 | 13.67 | 0.20 | 0.81 | 1.01 | 12.66 | 12.60 | 0.93 | 11.67 | 1935 |
| 1936 | 8.86 | 4.92 | 0.14 | 13.91 | 0.21 | 0.86 | 1.07 | 12.84 | 13.04 | 1.00 | 12.04 | 1936 |
| 1937 | 9.71 | 5.00 | 0.15 | 14.86 | 0.23 | 0.81 | 1.04 | 13.82 | 13.14 | 0.92 | 12.22 | 1937 |
| 1938 | 9.81 | 6.05 | 0.16 | 16.01 | 0.22 | 0.86 | 1.08 | 14.93 | 14.64 | 0.99 | 13.65 | 1938 |
| 1939 | 9.60 | 6.82 | 0.17 | 16.59 | 0.21 | 0.91 | 1.13 | 15.47 | 15.06 | 1.02 | 14.04 | 1939 |
| 1950 | 47.89 | 26.86 | 0.76 | 75.51 | 0.33 | 0.73 | 1.06 | 74.45 | 21.03 | 0.30 | 20.74 | 1950 |
| 1951 | 58.32 | 34.09 | 0.93 | 93.34 | 0.50 | 0.92 | 1.42 | 91.92 | 20.67 | 0.31 | 20.36 | 1951 |
| 1952 | 67.70 | 38.96 | 1.08 | 107.74 | 0.54 | 0.99 | 1.53 | 106.21 | 22.93 | 0.33 | 22.61 | 1952 |
| 1953 | 79.06 | 45.17 | 1.25 | 125.48 | 0.56 | 1.15 | 1.71 | 123.77 | 27.37 | 0.37 | 27.00 | 1953 |
| 1954 | 85.04 | 58.89 | 1.45 | 145.38 | 0.56 | 1.18 | 1.74 | 143.64 | 33.27 | 0.40 | 32.87 | 1954 |
| 1955 | 98.28 | 56.44 | 1.56 | 156.28 | 0.63 | 1.19 | 1.82 | 154.47 | 36.59 | 0.43 | 36.17 | 1955 |
| 1956 | 109.63 | 55.43 | 1.67 | 166.73 | 0.70 | 1.20 | 1.90 | 164.83 | 38.63 | 0.44 | 38.19 | 1956 |
| 1957 | 116.02 | 51.36 | 1.69 | 169.07 | 0.78 | 1.46 | 2.24 | 166.83 | 38.06 | 0.51 | 37.56 | 1957 |
| 1958 | 124.87 | 55.27 | 1.82 | 181.95 | 0.87 | 1.52 | 2.39 | 179.56 | 41.17 | 0.54 | 40.63 | 1958 |
| 1959 | 123.81 | 63.28 | 1.89 | 188.98 | 0.98 | 1.35 | 2.32 | 186.65 | 43.26 | 0.53 | 42.73 | 1959 |
| 1960 | 105.16 | 35.05 | 1.42 | 141.63 | 1.23 | 1.31 | 2.54 | 139.09 | 32.41 | 0.58 | 31.82 | 1960 |

and services (inputs) and depreciation allowances. Unfortunately, an appropriate wage index of government employees for deflating personal emoluments was not available. As an alternative option, CPI were applied as an alternative deflator for both output of producers of government services and government sales. Government final consumption expenditures in constant prices are presented in Table 2.29.

## 2.4 Gross Capital Formation

### 2.4.1 *Definition*

Gross capital formation contains two major components, namely gross fixed capital formation and increase in stocks during a period which do not enter into the intermediate consumption during the period. The fundamental distinction between intermediate consumption and gross capital formation is whether commodities are considered to be used up during the account period or to yield benefits in the future.[47] The 1968 SNA provides for the classification of gross fixed capital formation according to the kind of economic activity of the owner and the type of fixed assets. The classification according to the type of fixed assets is given in Table 2.30.[48]

Currently, data on fixed capital formation may be obtained from specialized surveys or general production surveys. But in the case of government and public corporations, it is obtained directly from the accounts. Changes in inventories, however, are more difficult to estimate, especially because of the related

---

[47] Department of Economic and Social Affairs, Statistical Office of the United Nations (1968, 110).

[48] The coverage of gross fixed capital formation has changed from SNA68 to SNA93. For example, SNA93 has recommended that computer software which are used in the production of goods and services for more than one year are to be treated as investment instead of intermediate consumption.

**Table 2.30:** The Components of Gross Capital Formation (SNA68)

**By Type of Capital Goods**

1. Residential building
2. Non-residential building
3. Other Construction except land improvement
4. Land improvement and plantation and orchard development
5. Transport equipment
6. Machinery and equipment

**Gross fixed Capital Formation**

1. Goods producing industries
2. Wholesale and retail trade
3. Other industries
4. Government services

**Gross Capital Formation**

*Source*: Department of Economic and Social Affairs, Statistical Office of the United Nations (1968, 173).

problems of stock valuation.[49] Nevertheless, in most cases, the indirect approach is used by employing the commodity flow table. Estimates of gross capital formation by the commodity flow method, however, do not lend themselves to classification according to the kinds of economic activity of the purchasers. Generally, in practice, in most cases, the indirect approach is the only way of estimating gross fixed capital formation simply because data on gross fixed capital formation occurring in all sectors of the economy are generally not available. In the case of Singapore, the first estimates were provided by Benham (1959). As is presented in Table 2.31, the figures on capital formation were constructed based on the aggregations of retained imports, domestic production, new building and public works and animal

---

[49] Department for Economic and Social Affairs, Statistics Division, United Nations (1999: 9–10).

**Table 2.31:** Singapore: Estimates of Capital Formation for the Year 1956

|  | Straits $ (millions) | % |
|---|---|---|
| **I. Retained Imports** | **91** | 46.9 |
| 1. Machinery, excluding parts | 44 | 22.7 |
| 2. Implements and tools | 7 | 3.6 |
| 3. Industrial electrical equipment | 19 | 9.8 |
| 4. Telegraph and telephone equipment and transmitting | 8 | 4.1 |
| 5. Commercial vehicles | 13 | 6.7 |
| **II. Domestic Production** | **8** | 4.1 |
| 1. Machinery and equipment | 6 | 3.1 |
| 2. Ships and sailing vessels | 2 | 1.0 |
| **III. New Building and Public Works** | **94** | 48.5 |
| 1. Public authorities | 63 | 32.5 |
| 2. Private | 31 | 16.0 |
| **IV. Animal Husbandry** | **1** | 0.5 |
| 1. Animal husbandry | 1 | 0.5 |
| **Total** | **194** | 100.0 |

*Source*: Benham (1959, 23–24).

husbandry.[50] It is important to note that weights on domestic production were small as Singapore heavily relied on imports from overseas due to the lack of domestic production.

Investments in cultivated assets were omitted since they were deemed to be negligible in 1956. In the pre-war period,

---

[50] In these estimates, other capital formation (roads, etc.) was included in the current expenditure of the city council and Rural Board. Part of the plant and machinery, etc., included in this estimate was used for renewals and replacements. On the other hand, the estimates for local output of machinery and for increase in local livestock are on the low side, and attap houses are excluded. Hence the figure of $194 million may be taken as about equal to net capital formation. The above value for machinery, etc., includes the costs and profits of distribution. Domestic production of machinery and equipment for export (mainly to the Federation) is excluded. Domestic production of implements and tools was less than $1 million. Animal husbandry represents mainly the increase in the number of pigs. Poultry are excluded. Other agricultural investment (apart from roads, etc., included in Public Works) was relatively small. Durable consumer goods such as private motor cars, furniture and refrigerators have been shown under a separate heading. Owing to the lack of information, changes in stock were omitted.

cultivated assets were regarded as a component of Gross Capital Formation (GCF) despite the small weight attached to it. In this estimate, GCF was classified into (1) construction, (2) machinery and equipment, (3) cultivated assets and (4) changes in inventories.

### 2.4.2 *Investment in Construction*

#### 2.4.2.1 *Definition*

By definition, construction output that is to be capitalized is computed by taking into account the output of the characteristic products of the construction industry at purchaser's values, less the sum of construction for military uses except family buildings (dwellings), plus construction on own account and for sale by other kinds of activities less the characteristic output of construction activity that is for maintenance and current repairs. According to UN recommendations, gross fixed capital formation on buildings and other construction is often estimated as the sum of the estimated value of the building and construction materials used, overhead costs and value added, based on information from a number of contractors. Alternatively, the data are estimated by inflating the value of a few basic materials used, such as cement, sawn timber, plywood, mild steel bars and rods, floor tiles (terrazzo, mosaic, etc.), bricks, roofing tiles, etc., by coefficients from input–output studies.[51] The gross output of the construction industry is also frequently taken as a measure of gross fixed capital formation in construction. It should be noted, however, that gross output of the construction industry and gross fixed capital formation in construction are not equal; some of the output of the construction industry consists of maintenance and current repairs. As such, it should not be capitalized.

---

[51] Department of International Economic and Social Affairs, Statistical Office, United Nations (1986, 141).

## 2.4.2.2 *Investment in Construction in Current Prices*

For the period 1900–39 and 1948–60, it is not possible to compute the value of construction output that goes into capital formation due to the paucity of data. No survey on construction output was carried out during this period. The first survey of construction in respect of Singapore was only carried out in 1972. Thereafter, surveys were carried out on an annual or biennial basis. The only information on construction for the period 1900–39 and 1948–60 that could be used to estimate part of the construction output was the information that was incorporated in the financial statements of government accounts in relation to the general government departments and the government trading departments. One other option to estimate the total construction output was to inflate the value of a few basic materials used in construction, such as cement, sawn timber, plywood, mild steel bars and rods, floor tiles, bricks, etc., by coefficients from the input–output studies. Unfortunately, again we noted that information on the inputs mentioned above for the period was scarce and no continuous series of data was available except for cement. Even in this case, net imports of cement retained in the territory of Singapore were available only for the period 1900–12 and 1933–39. They were provided for in the *Statistical Tables Relating to the Colonial and Other Possessions of The United Kingdom* for the period 1900–01, *Statistical Tables Relating to the Colonial and Other Possessions and Protectorates* for the period 1902–07 and *Statistical Tables Relating to British Self-Governing Dominions, Crown Colonies, Possessions and Protectorates* for the period 1908–12. For the period 1933–39, the *Annual Report, Returns of Imports and Exports, British Malaya* and *Malayan Statistics* provided figures on imports, exports and net imports retained in Singapore. Unfortunately, figures for the years 1913–27 and 1928–32 were not available. As illustrated in Table 2.32, figures on net imports of Singapore for the period 1913–27 were calculated using two steps: First, the figures of net imports of cement for Singapore for the period 1913–27 were treated as 80 percent

**Table 2.32:** Net Imports Value of Cement Retained in Singapore, 1900–39

(Straits $)

| | Straits Settlements [a] | [b] /[a] | Singapore [b] | [c]/[b] | British Malaya [c] |
|---|---|---|---|---|---|
| 1900 | | | 137,601 | | |
| 1901 | | | 174,859 | | |
| 1902 | | | 231,109 | | |
| 1903 | | | 266,285 | | |
| 1904 | | | 456,583 | | |
| 1905 | | | 341,007 | | |
| 1906 | | | 243,722 | | |
| 1907 | | | 361,569 | | |
| 1908 | 731,979 | 0.8 | 588,755 | | |
| 1909 | 1,012,271 | 0.9 | 935,311 | | |
| 1910 | 1,021,781 | 0.9 | 884,914 | | |
| 1911 | 1,033,553 | 0.7 | 729,444 | | |
| 1912 | 1,311,534 | 0.8 | 1,011,788 | | |
| 1913 | 1,437,048 | 0.8 | 1,170,209 | | |
| 1914 | 1,127,613 | 0.8 | 918,232 | | |
| 1915 | 1,025,719 | 0.8 | 835,258 | | |
| 1916 | 1,263,359 | 0.8 | 1,028,772 | | |
| 1917 | 1,314,887 | 0.8 | 1,070,732 | | |
| 1918 | 2,062,321 | 0.8 | 1,679,379 | | |
| 1919 | 1,918,128 | 0.8 | 1,561,960 | | |
| 1920 | 3,764,525 | 0.8 | 3,065,508 | | |
| 1921 | 3,391,003 | 0.8 | 2,761,344 | | |
| 1922 | 1,571,905 | 0.8 | 1,280,026 | | |
| 1923 | 1,567,542 | 0.8 | 1,276,473 | | |
| 1924 | 1,380,399 | 0.8 | 1,124,079 | | |
| 1925 | 1,899,811 | 0.8 | 1,547,044 | | |
| 1926 | 2,076,033 | 0.8 | 1,690,544 | | |
| 1927 | 3,193,865 | 0.8 | 2,600,812 | | |
| 1928 | | | 4,214,191 | 0.5 | 8,428,382 |
| 1929 | | | 3,788,160 | 0.5 | 7,576,319 |
| 1930 | | | 2,583,546 | 0.5 | 5,167,092 |
| 1931 | | | 2,411,288 | 0.6 | 4,018,813 |
| 1932 | | | 1,641,887 | 0.6 | 2,736,479 |
| 1933 | | | 1,223,569 | 0.7 | 1,849,716 |
| 1934 | | | 885,452 | 0.6 | 1,516,025 |
| 1935 | | | 1,568,647 | 0.7 | 2,396,194 |
| 1936 | | | 1,814,001 | 0.6 | 2,795,513 |
| 1937 | | | 2,486,377 | 0.6 | 4,003,490 |
| 1938 | | | 2,449,133 | 0.6 | 4,289,340 |
| 1939 | | | 3,534,574 | 0.6 | 5,480,500 |

*(Continued)*

of Straits Settlement's total figure based on experiences of 1908–12. For the period 1928–32, similar procedures were applied on the basis of the relationship between net value of imports of cement into Singapore and total net cement imports into British Malaya as a whole for the period 1933–39. It was decided that 50 and 60 percent of the total value of net imports of cement of British Malaya be allocated to Singapore for the period 1928–30 and 1931–32, respectively.

Subsequently, the net import value of cement in Singapore for the period 1950–60 was computed by employing a different methodology due to the paucity of information. The *Report on the Colony of Singapore* and *Singapore's External Trade* provides the quantity of cement exports and imports for the period 1953–58, but the value data were not available. As an alternative option, weights of cement import and export values to that of total merchandize imports and exports were applied to estimate data for missing years. In the case of imports, 0.5 percent of total merchandize imports was treated as cement for the period 1950–56 based on the 1957 figure.

---

**Table 2.32:** *(Continued)*

*Sources*: (Singapore)
1900–01: Statistical Tables Relating to the Colonial and Other Possessions of the United Kingdom.
1902–07: Statistical Tables Relating to the Colonial and Other Possessions and Protectorates.
1933–37: Returns of Imports and Exports, British Malaya.
1938–39: Foreign Trade of Malaya.
(Singapore and Straits Settlements).
1908–12: Statistical Tables Relating to British Self-Governing Dominions, Crown Colonies, Possessions and Protectorates.
1913–15: Appendix to the Report on the Trade, Straits Settlements.
1916–27: Blue Book, Straits Settlements.
(British Malaya).
1928–37: Returns of Imports and Exports, British Malaya.
1938–39: Foreign Trade of Malaya.

**Table 2.33:** Singapore: Estimating Net Imports of Cement, 1950–60

(Straits $)

| | Imports of Cement (Singapore) | [a]/[b] | Total Merchandize Imports (Singapore) | Exports of Cement (Singapore) | [c]/[d] | Total Merchandize Exports (Singapore) | Net Imports of Cement (Singapore) |
|---|---|---|---|---|---|---|---|
| | [a] | | [b] | [c] | | [d] | [a]-[c] |
| 1950 | 16,176,492 | 0.5% | 3,273,497,000 | 6,090,184 | 0.2% | 3,025,750,000 | 10,086,308 |
| 1951 | 17,353,987 | 0.5% | 5,027,204,000 | 6,265,155 | 0.2% | 4,745,242,000 | 11,088,832 |
| 1952 | 18,531,482 | 0.5% | 3,750,056,000 | 6,440,127 | 0.2% | 3,199,610,000 | 12,091,356 |
| 1953 | 14,927,286 | 0.5% | 3,020,706,000 | 5,342,160 | 0.2% | 2,654,114,000 | 9,585,126 |
| 1954 | 14,947,779 | 0.5% | 3,024,853,000 | 5,405,370 | 0.2% | 2,685,518,000 | 9,542,409 |
| 1955 | 19,088,308 | 0.5% | 3,862,736,000 | 6,780,466 | 0.2% | 3,368,699,000 | 12,307,842 |
| 1956 | 19,417,486 | 0.5% | 3,929,349,000 | 6,901,789 | 0.2% | 3,428,975,000 | 12,515,697 |
| 1957 | 20,220,446 | 0.5% | 4,091,837,000 | 7,519,418 | 0.2% | 3,478,133,000 | 12,701,028 |
| 1958 | 18,700,325 | 0.5% | 3,740,065,000 | 5,852,524 | 0.2% | 3,140,343,000 | 12,847,801 |
| 1959 | 19,538,350 | 0.5% | 3,907,670,000 | 3,134,997 | 0.1% | 3,440,263,000 | 16,403,353 |
| 1960 | 20,388,430 | 0.5% | 4,077,686,000 | 1,967,923 | 0.1% | 3,477,053,000 | 18,420,507 |

*Sources*: 1950–56: Annual Report, Colony of Singapore.
1957–60: Singapore's External Trade.

Subsequently, 0.4 percent and 0.3 percent were applied for the years 1958 and 1959, respectively on the basis that weight on cement imports against total merchandize imports was 0.2 percent for the year 1960. Similar procedures were employed to estimate cement exports for the periods 1950–56 and 1958–59 (See Table 2.33).

Estimated figures on the value of net imports of cement for the territory of Singapore for the periods 1900–39 and 1950–60 were then used to compute the investment figure. According to the production accounts of the construction sector in Singapore for the year 1972, the input value of cement and concrete products to total output value was 9.1 percent, as given in Table 2.34.

In these estimates, it was assumed that the input value of cement to total output value was 6 percent, 8 percent, and 9 percent for the periods 1900–07, 1907–27, and 1928–60, respectively. These coefficients were assigned on the basis of the conventional premise that input value of cement was lesser in the earlier period. The total construction that would go into fixed capital formation was derived by deducting from total output of construction, the repairs and maintenance and those used by the

**Table 2.34:** Singapore: Production Account — Construction, 1972

| | | |
|---|---:|---:|
| **Purchase of Materials and Services** | 644 | 48.8% |
| | | |
| Wood and wood products | 76 | 5.8% |
| Granite, bricks, and tiles | 69 | 5.2% |
| *Cements and concrete products* | *120* | *9.1%* |
| Metal and metal products | 210 | 15.9% |
| Machinery and equipment | 87 | 6.6% |
| Other materials and services | 82 | 6.2% |
| | | |
| **Indirect Taxes** | 17 | 1.3% |
| **Value Added** | 660 | 50.0% |
| | | |
| **Total Cost** | 1,321 | 100.0% |

*Source*: Department of Statistics, Singapore (1975, 17).

military (except family dwellings). These percentages were used to estimate total investments in construction, the results of which are presented in Table 2.35.

### 2.4.2.3 *Investment in Construction in 1914 Prices*

The output of construction in real terms is arrived at by deflating the current output by using the movements of price increase or decrease in cement imports with 1914 as the base year (See Table 2.36). Undoubtedly, the deflator used is rather weak. A more appropriate deflator should be used that takes into account price movements, salaries and wages paid, and inputs used to generate the construction output.

Investment of construction in constant prices for the periods 1900–39 and 1950–60 is presented in Table 2.37.

### 2.4.3 *Investment in Transport, Machinery, and Equipment*

#### 2.4.3.1 *Definition*

Fixed capital formation in machinery and equipment (M&E) by producers consists of the value of their acquisitions of new

**Table 2.35:** Singapore: Total Investment in Construction (Construction Output Capitalized) in Current Prices, 1900–39

(Straits $)

| | Net Imports of Cement in Singapore | Total Output by Different Input–Output Ratios | | Repairs and Maintenance | | Investment in Construction (Construction Output Capitalised) |
|---|---|---|---|---|---|---|
| | [A] | [B] | [C] = [A]/[B] | [D] | [E] = [C] × [D] | [F] = [C] − [E] |
| 1900 | 137,601 | 6.0% | 2,293,350 | 2.0% | 45,867 | 2,247,483 |
| 1901 | 174,859 | 6.0% | 2,914,317 | 2.0% | 58,286 | 2,856,030 |
| 1902 | 231,109 | 6.0% | 3,851,817 | 2.0% | 77,036 | 3,774,780 |
| 1903 | 266,285 | 6.0% | 4,438,083 | 2.0% | 88,762 | 4,349,322 |
| 1904 | 456,583 | 6.0% | 7,609,717 | 2.0% | 152,194 | 7,457,522 |
| 1905 | 341,007 | 6.0% | 5,683,450 | 2.0% | 113,669 | 5,569,781 |
| 1906 | 243,722 | 6.0% | 4,062,033 | 2.0% | 81,241 | 3,980,793 |
| 1907 | 361,569 | 6.0% | 6,026,150 | 2.0% | 120,523 | 5,905,627 |
| 1908 | 588,755 | 8.0% | 7,359,438 | 3.0% | 220,783 | 7,138,654 |
| 1909 | 632,344 | 8.0% | 7,904,306 | 3.0% | 237,129 | 7,667,177 |
| 1910 | 679,161 | 8.0% | 8,489,514 | 3.0% | 254,685 | 8,234,829 |
| 1911 | 729,444 | 8.0% | 9,118,050 | 3.0% | 273,542 | 8,844,509 |
| 1912 | 1,011,788 | 8.0% | 12,647,350 | 3.0% | 379,421 | 12,267,930 |
| 1913 | 1,170,209 | 8.0% | 14,627,615 | 3.0% | 438,828 | 14,188,786 |
| 1914 | 918,232 | 8.0% | 11,477,898 | 3.0% | 344,337 | 11,133,561 |
| 1915 | 835,258 | 8.0% | 10,440,728 | 3.0% | 313,222 | 10,127,506 |
| 1916 | 1,028,772 | 8.0% | 12,859,649 | 3.0% | 385,789 | 12,473,860 |
| 1917 | 1,070,732 | 8.0% | 13,384,150 | 3.0% | 401,524 | 12,982,625 |
| 1918 | 1,679,379 | 8.0% | 20,992,232 | 3.0% | 629,767 | 20,362,465 |
| 1919 | 1,561,960 | 8.0% | 19,524,501 | 3.0% | 585,735 | 18,938,766 |
| 1920 | 3,065,508 | 8.0% | 38,318,856 | 3.0% | 1,149,566 | 37,169,290 |
| 1921 | 2,761,344 | 8.0% | 34,516,800 | 3.0% | 1,035,504 | 33,481,296 |
| 1922 | 1,280,026 | 8.0% | 16,000,319 | 3.0% | 480,010 | 15,520,310 |
| 1923 | 1,276,473 | 8.0% | 15,955,908 | 3.0% | 478,677 | 15,477,231 |
| 1924 | 1,124,079 | 8.0% | 14,050,992 | 3.0% | 421,530 | 13,629,462 |
| 1925 | 1,547,044 | 8.0% | 19,338,053 | 3.0% | 580,142 | 18,757,911 |
| 1926 | 1,690,544 | 8.0% | 21,131,805 | 3.0% | 633,954 | 20,497,851 |
| 1927 | 2,600,812 | 8.0% | 32,510,145 | 3.0% | 975,304 | 31,534,840 |
| 1928 | 4,214,191 | 9.0% | 46,824,344 | 3.0% | 1,404,730 | 45,419,614 |
| 1929 | 3,788,160 | 9.0% | 42,090,661 | 3.0% | 1,262,720 | 40,827,941 |
| 1930 | 2,583,546 | 9.0% | 28,706,067 | 3.0% | 861,182 | 27,844,885 |
| 1931 | 2,411,288 | 9.0% | 26,792,087 | 3.0% | 803,763 | 25,988,324 |
| 1932 | 1,641,887 | 9.0% | 18,243,193 | 3.0% | 547,296 | 17,695,898 |
| 1933 | 1,223,569 | 9.0% | 13,595,211 | 3.0% | 407,856 | 13,187,355 |
| 1934 | 885,452 | 9.0% | 9,838,356 | 3.0% | 295,151 | 9,543,205 |
| 1935 | 1,568,647 | 9.0% | 17,429,411 | 3.0% | 522,882 | 16,906,529 |
| 1936 | 1,814,001 | 9.0% | 20,155,567 | 3.0% | 604,667 | 19,550,900 |
| 1937 | 2,486,377 | 9.0% | 27,626,411 | 3.0% | 828,792 | 26,797,619 |
| 1938 | 2,449,133 | 9.0% | 27,212,589 | 3.0% | 816,378 | 26,396,211 |
| 1939 | 3,534,574 | 9.0% | 39,273,044 | 3.0% | 1,178,191 | 38,094,853 |
| 1950 | 10,086,308 | 9.0% | 112,070,093 | 3.0% | 3,362,103 | 108,707,991 |
| 1951 | 11,088,832 | 9.0% | 123,209,245 | 3.0% | 3,696,277 | 119,512,968 |
| 1952 | 12,091,356 | 9.0% | 134,348,397 | 3.0% | 4,030,452 | 130,317,945 |
| 1953 | 9,585,126 | 9.0% | 106,501,398 | 3.0% | 3,195,042 | 103,306,357 |
| 1954 | 9,542,409 | 9.0% | 106,026,771 | 3.0% | 3,180,803 | 102,845,968 |
| 1955 | 12,307,842 | 9.0% | 136,753,795 | 3.0% | 4,102,614 | 132,651,182 |
| 1956 | 12,515,697 | 9.0% | 139,063,305 | 3.0% | 4,171,899 | 134,891,406 |
| 1957 | 12,701,028 | 9.0% | 141,122,533 | 3.0% | 4,233,676 | 136,888,857 |
| 1958 | 12,847,801 | 9.0% | 142,753,344 | 3.0% | 4,282,600 | 138,470,744 |
| 1959 | 16,403,353 | 9.0% | 182,259,478 | 3.0% | 5,467,784 | 176,791,693 |
| 1960 | 18,420,507 | 9.0% | 204,672,300 | 3.0% | 6,140,169 | 198,532,131 |

**Table 2.36:** Singapore: Import Unit Value Indices of Cement, 1900–39 and 1950–60 (1914 = 100)

| 1900–39 and 1947–60 (1914 = 100) | | | | | | | | | |
|---|---|---|---|---|---|---|---|---|---|
| 1900 | 134.40 | 1910 | 100.15 | 1920 | 300.09 | 1930 | 102.64 | 1950 | 262.29 |
| 1901 | 132.96 | 1911 | 94.64 | 1921 | 279.44 | 1931 | 84.89 | 1951 | 330.69 |
| 1902 | 125.01 | 1912 | 100.39 | 1922 | 176.26 | 1932 | 81.46 | 1952 | 377.29 |
| 1903 | 131.06 | 1913 | 112.24 | 1923 | 132.11 | 1933 | 72.49 | 1953 | 351.30 |
| 1904 | 123.58 | 1914 | 100.00 | 1924 | 128.77 | 1934 | 58.51 | 1954 | 325.31 |
| 1905 | 115.78 | 1915 | 111.67 | 1925 | 121.10 | 1935 | 57.42 | 1955 | 331.00 |
| 1906 | 90.63 | 1916 | 131.44 | 1926 | 122.59 | 1936 | 56.53 | 1956 | 320.32 |
| 1907 | 104.27 | 1917 | 176.55 | 1927 | 122.99 | 1937 | 58.12 | 1957 | 314.21 |
| 1908 | 105.29 | 1918 | 242.95 | 1928 | 121.89 | 1938 | 68.55 | 1958 | 269.95 |
| 1909 | 102.16 | 1919 | 248.81 | 1929 | 118.52 | 1939 | 76.28 | 1959 | 271.47 |
| | | | | | | | | 1960 | 241.55 |

*Sources*:

(FMS)

1903–32: Annual Report, Trade and Custom, Federated Malay States.

(Singapore)

1900–01: Statistical Tables Relating to the Colonial and Other Possessions of the United Kingdom.

1902–07: Statistical Tables Relating to the Colonial and Other Possessions and Protectorates.

1908–12: Statistical Tables Relating to British Self-Governing Dominions, Crown Colonies, Possessions, and Protectorates, Straits Settlements.

1916–27: Appendix to the Report on Trade, Straits Settlements.

(British Malaya)

1921–27: Returns of Foreign Imports and Exports, British Malaya.

1928–39: Foreign Trade of Malaya.

existing transport, machinery, and equipment less the value of disposals of existing ones. It covers transport equipment and other machinery and equipment, including office equipment, furniture, etc. New M&E that have not yet been sold form part of additions to inventories of finished goods held by the producers of the assets. Similarly, imported M&E are not recorded as gross fixed capital formation until they are acquired by the unit that intends to use it. M&E such as vehicles, furniture, kitchen equipment, computers, and communications equipment that are acquired by households for the purpose of private final consumption are not fixed assets. Not only so, their acquisition is not

**Table 2.37:**   Singapore: Construction Investment, 1900–39 and 1950–60 in 1914 Prices

(Straits $)

| 1900–39 and 1950–60 (1914 = 100) | | | | | | | | | |
|---|---|---|---|---|---|---|---|---|---|
| 1900 | 1,672,225 | 1910 | 8,222,647 | 1920 | 12,385,907 | 1930 | 27,128,671 | 1950 | 41,445,484 |
| 1901 | 2,148,013 | 1911 | 9,345,441 | 1921 | 11,981,683 | 1931 | 30,615,392 | 1951 | 36,140,083 |
| 1902 | 3,019,550 | 1912 | 12,219,773 | 1922 | 8,805,342 | 1932 | 21,723,699 | 1952 | 34,540,107 |
| 1903 | 3,318,515 | 1913 | 12,641,360 | 1923 | 11,715,038 | 1933 | 18,192,688 | 1953 | 29,406,546 |
| 1904 | 6,034,725 | 1914 | 11,133,561 | 1924 | 10,584,176 | 1934 | 16,310,505 | 1954 | 31,614,434 |
| 1905 | 4,810,708 | 1915 | 9,069,382 | 1925 | 15,490,189 | 1935 | 29,441,597 | 1955 | 40,075,494 |
| 1906 | 4,392,325 | 1916 | 9,490,320 | 1926 | 16,721,087 | 1936 | 34,585,492 | 1956 | 42,111,745 |
| 1907 | 5,663,897 | 1917 | 7,353,695 | 1927 | 25,639,347 | 1937 | 46,103,537 | 1957 | 43,566,392 |
| 1908 | 6,779,901 | 1918 | 8,381,259 | 1928 | 37,262,057 | 1938 | 38,507,737 | 1958 | 51,295,409 |
| 1909 | 7,505,372 | 1919 | 7,611,772 | 1929 | 34,447,940 | 1939 | 49,943,553 | 1959 | 65,124,024 |
| | | | | | | | | 1960 | 82,190,271 |

treated as gross fixed capital formation. Proceeds of sales by resident producers of their used and scrapped fixed assets of the same type and the cost net of dealers' margins and other transfer charges of purchases of these secondhand items by resident producers for uses are classified as fixed assets (Department of Economic and Social Affairs, Statistical Office of the United Nations, 1968, 115).

### 2.4.3.2 *Investment in M&E in Current Prices*

Commodity flow analysis is often used in estimating gross fixed capital formation in transport, machinery, and equipment on the basis of statistics on foreign trade and domestic production.[52] In this estimate, it was assumed that there were no M&E produced locally during the periods 1900–39 and 1950–60 and all M&E supplies came as imports from abroad. This means that total expenditure on M&E equals to net imports valued at market prices. This assumption is deemed to be not unrealistic. Official published figures on the net import value of M&E for Singapore were available for the periods 1900–12, 1924–27, 1933–39, and

---

[52] Department of International Economic and Social Affairs, Statistical Office, United Nations (1986, 142).

1956–60 using seven different sources. These sources include the *Statistical Tables Relating to the Colonial and Other Possessions of the United Kingdom* for the period 1900–1901, *Statistical Tables Relating to the Colonial and Other Possessions and Protectorates* for the period 1902–1907, *Statistical Tables Relating to British Self-Governing Dominions, Crown Colonies, Possessions and Protectorates* for the period 1908–12, *Appendix to the Report on Trade, Straits Settlements* for the period 1924–27, the *Annual Report, Returns of Import and Exports, British Malaya and Malayan Statistics* for the period 1933–39, and the *Annual Report, Singapore's External Trade* for the period 1956–60. Unfortunately, a complete set of data on net imports of M&E for Singapore was not available for many years. This being the case, it was necessary to make estimates of M&E for the missing years. In the case of pre–World War II period, a two-step estimation procedure was used. First, Singapore's import value of M&E for the periods 1913–23, 1928 and 1932 was estimated using the average ratio against the total import value of M&E for Straits Settlements as provided in Table 2.38. However, in 1920, 90 percent of total imports on M&E for the Straits Settlements were distributed to Singapore on the grounds that large amounts of M&E were purchased for Singapore for infrastructure building, such as the Singapore harbour dock.[53]

Second, total export values on M&E for the periods 1913–23 and 1928–32 were estimated using the average percentage between import and export values on M&E for the years 1910–12 and 1924 (See details in Table 2.39). Finally, net imports were derived by subtracting the value of exports from imports for the period 1900–39.

In the postwar period, the presentation of trade data changed significantly. *The Report on External Trade of Singapore* treated Singapore as an entity and provided figures on net imports of machinery for the period 1956–60. However, prior to

---

[53] Annual Report, Straits Settlements (1920, 51).

**Table 2.38:** Estimating Singapore's Imports of Transport, Machinery, and Equipment for the Periods 1913–23 and 1928–32

(Straits $)

| | Singapore | [1]/[2] | Straits Settlements |
|---|---|---|---|
| | [1] | | [2] |
| 1900 | 2,789,534 | 100% | 2,789,534 |
| 1901 | 2,844,144 | 95% | 2,989,628 |
| 1902 | 1,996,283 | 85% | 2,348,134 |
| 1903 | 3,107,048 | 92% | 3,364,716 |
| 1904 | 1,762,233 | 85% | 2,065,266 |
| 1905 | 1,902,332 | 77% | 2,456,378 |
| 1906 | 2,493,448 | 84% | 2,985,329 |
| 1907 | 2,967,486 | 80% | 3,690,461 |
| 1908 | 3,368,956 | 80% | 4,199,327 |
| 1909 | 3,087,451 | 78% | 3,973,806 |
| 1910 | 3,875,828 | 71% | 5,466,342 |
| 1911 | 3,644,147 | 73% | 4,993,771 |
| 1912 | 4,294,793 | 63% | 6,771,441 |
| 1913 | *4,707,839* | *69%* | 6,813,000 |
| 1914 | *3,169,654* | *69%* | 4,587,000 |
| 1915 | *2,017,744* | *69%* | 2,920,000 |
| 1916 | *4,683,653* | *69%* | 6,778,000 |
| 1917 | *5,395,392* | *69%* | 7,808,000 |
| 1918 | *3,953,949* | *69%* | 5,722,000 |
| 1919 | *9,075,010* | ▼ *69%* | 13,133,000 |
| 1920 | *29,519,100* | **90%** | 32,799,000 |
| 1921 | *12,013,056* | ▲ *73%* | 16,435,000 |
| 1922 | *5,227,854* | *73%* | 7,152,200 |
| 1923 | *8,735,505* | *73%* | 11,951,000 |
| 1924 | 12,566,154 | 73% | 17,191,691 |
| 1925 | 22,650,025 | 72% | 31,669,998 |
| 1926 | 28,861,834 | 73% | 39,338,957 |
| 1927 | 23,421,318 | 68% | 34,607,035 |
| 1928 | *22,647,239* | *60%* | 37,630,239 |
| 1929 | *23,832,851* | *60%* | 39,600,229 |
| 1930 | *14,731,930* | ▼ *60%* | 24,478,305 |
| 1931 | *7,618,502* | ▲ *53%* | 14,459,288 |
| 1932 | *5,530,315* | *53%* | 10,496,082 |
| 1933 | 5,815,076 | 53% | 11,036,535 |
| 1934 | 12,031,077 | 94% | 12,765,495 |
| 1935 | 13,787,495 | 55% | 24,908,410 |
| 1936 | 13,597,542 | 51% | 26,688,037 |
| 1937 | 19,222,710 | 48% | 40,424,359 |
| 1938 | 17,317,989 | 53% | 32,486,643 |
| 1939 | 15,459,511 | 51% | 30,544,750 |

☐ Estimated Figure

(*Continued*)

**Table 2.38:**  *(Continued)*

*Sources*:

(Singapore)

1900–12: Statistical Tables Relating to the Colonial and Other Possessions of the United Kingdom.

1902–07: Statistical Tables Relating to the Colonial and Other Possessions and Protectorates.

1908–12: Statistical Tables Relating to British Self-Governing Dominions, Crown Colonies, Possessions, and Protectorates.

1924–27: Appendix to the Report on the Trade, Straits Settlements.

1933–37: Report on Foreign Imports and Exports, British Malaya.

1938–39: Foreign Trade of Malaya.

(Straits Settlements)

1900–27: Appendix to the Report on the Trade, Straits Settlements.

1928–39: Foreign Trade of Malaya.

1956, no statistical data on net imports of M&E into Singapore were available. Alternatively, two different methods were employed for the periods 1953–55 and 1950–52, respectively. For the period 1953–55, the ratio of total imports to exports on M&E in Singapore against the Federation of Malaya's imports to exports recorded in 1956 was applied. Subsequently, the percentage contribution of imports and exports of M&E against Singapore's total merchandize imports and exports for the year 1953 was applied for the period 1950–52 (See Table 2.40).

No commodity taxes were levied on imports on M&E during this period so that cost, insurance, and freight (c.i.f) and producers' values were identical. Estimated trade and transport margins of 16 percent and 2 percent,[54] respectively, were added to the producers' values to arrive at market prices. The final step was to determine what proportion of net imports to capitalize. Some of these imports would have been used as inputs in construction

---

[54] Due to the complete absence of information, this study used similar margins introduced by Nazrin (2002, 26).

**Table 2.39:** Estimating Singapore's Net Imports of Transport, Machinery, and Equipment for the Periods 1913–23 and 1928–32

(Straits $)

|  | Imports [1] | [1]/[3] | Exports [2] | [2] / [3] | Total Trade [3] | Net Imports [1] – [2] |
|---|---|---|---|---|---|---|
| 1900 | 2,789,534 | 77% | 828,767 | 23% | 3,618,301 | 1,960,767 |
| 1901 | 2,844,144 | 77% | 867,112 | 23% | 3,711,256 | 1,977,032 |
| 1902 | 1,996,283 | 73% | 750,491 | 27% | 2,746,774 | 1,245,792 |
| 1903 | 3,107,048 | 79% | 841,909 | 21% | 3,948,957 | 2,265,139 |
| 1904 | 1,762,233 | 71% | 710,643 | 29% | 2,472,876 | 1,051,590 |
| 1905 | 1,902,332 | 69% | 853,504 | 31% | 2,755,836 | 1,048,828 |
| 1906 | 2,493,448 | 75% | 843,608 | 25% | 3,337,056 | 1,649,840 |
| 1907 | 2,967,486 | 70% | 1,282,859 | 30% | 4,250,345 | 1,684,627 |
| 1908 | 3,368,956 | 81% | 801,176 | 19% | 4,170,132 | 2,567,780 |
| 1909 | 3,087,451 | 77% | 917,596 | 23% | 4,005,047 | 2,169,855 |
| 1910 | 3,875,828 | 72% | 1,515,728 | 28% | 5,391,556 | 2,360,100 |
| 1911 | 3,644,147 | 68% | 1,740,194 | 32% | 5,384,341 | 1,903,953 |
| 1912 | 4,294,793 | 67% | 2,123,872 | 33% | 6,418,665 | 2,314,790 |
| 1913 | 4,707,839 | 69% | 2,132,350 | 31% | 6,840,188 | 2,575,489 |
| 1914 | 3,169,654 | 69% | 1,435,651 | 31% | 4,605,305 | 1,734,004 |
| 1915 | 2,017,744 | 69% | 913,909 | 31% | 2,931,653 | 1,103,835 |
| 1916 | 4,683,653 | 69% | 2,121,395 | 31% | 6,805,049 | 2,562,258 |
| 1917 | 5,395,392 | 69% | 2,443,767 | 31% | 7,839,159 | 2,951,625 |
| 1918 | 3,953,949 | 60% | 2,635,966 | 40% | 6,589,915 | 1,317,983 |
| 1919 | 9,075,010 | 60% | 6,050,007 | 40% | 15,125,017 | 3,025,003 |
| 1920 | 29,519,100 | 60% | 19,679,400 | 40% | 49,198,500 | 9,839,700 |
| 1921 | 12,013,056 | 60% | 8,008,704 | 40% | 20,021,759 | 4,004,352 |
| 1922 | 5,227,854 | 60% | 3,485,236 | 40% | 8,713,090 | 1,742,618 |
| 1923 | 8,735,505 | 60% | 5,823,670 | 40% | 14,559,175 | 2,911,835 |
| 1924 | 12,566,154 | 60% | 8,288,299 | 40% | 20,854,453 | 5,253,258 |
| 1925 | 22,650,025 | 61% | 14,577,710 | 39% | 37,227,735 | 10,535,117 |
| 1926 | 28,861,834 | 73% | 10,739,152 | 27% | 39,600,986 | 15,789,544 |
| 1927 | 23,421,318 | 63% | 13,924,529 | 37% | 37,345,847 | 11,553,270 |
| 1928 | 22,647,239 | 68% | 2,812,682 | 32% | 25,459,921 | 19,834,558 |
| 1929 | 23,832,851 | 68% | 1,970,445 | 32% | 25,803,295 | 21,862,406 |
| 1930 | 14,731,930 | 68% | 1,541,426 | 32% | 16,273,355 | 13,190,504 |
| 1931 | 7,618,502 | 71% | 1,294,530 | 29% | 8,913,032 | 6,323,971 |
| 1932 | 5,530,315 | 71% | 1,036,928 | 29% | 6,567,243 | 4,493,387 |
| 1933 | 5,815,076 | 71% | 2,387,656 | 29% | 8,202,732 | 3,427,420 |
| 1934 | 12,031,077 | 82% | 2,668,216 | 18% | 14,699,293 | 9,362,861 |
| 1935 | 13,787,495 | 81% | 3,196,168 | 19% | 16,983,663 | 10,591,327 |
| 1936 | 13,597,542 | 80% | 3,355,608 | 20% | 16,953,150 | 10,241,934 |
| 1937 | 19,222,710 | 80% | 4,737,509 | 20% | 23,960,219 | 14,485,201 |
| 1938 | 17,317,989 | 78% | 4,812,617 | 22% | 22,130,606 | 12,505,372 |
| 1939 | 15,459,511 | 77% | 4,591,334 | 23% | 20,050,845 | 10,868,177 |

☐ Estimated Figure

*(Continued)*

**Table 2.39:**   (*Continued*)

*Sources*:

1900–01: Statistical Tables Relating to the Colonial and Other Possessions of the United Kingdom.

1902–07: Statistical Tables Relating to the Colonial and Other Possessions and Protectorates.

1908–12: Statistical Tables Relating to British Self-Governing Dominions, Crown Colonies, Possessions, and Protectorates.

1924–27: Appendix to the Report on the Trade, Straits Settlements.

1933–37: Returns of Foreign Imports and Exports, British Malaya.

1938–39: Foreign Trade of Malaya.

**Table 2.40:**   Estimating Singapore's Net Imports of Transport, Machinery, and Equipment, 1948–60

(Straits $)

| | Imports of Transport, Machinery, and Equipment | | | | Total |
| | Federation of Malaya | [a]/[b] | Singapore | [b]/[c] | Merchandize Imports |
| | [a] | | [b] | | [c] |
|---|---|---|---|---|---|
| 1950 | | | 199,738,539 | 6.1% | 3,273,497,000 |
| 1951 | | | 306,744,250 | 6.1% | 5,027,204,000 |
| 1952 | | | 228,816,678 | 6.1% | 3,750,056,000 |
| 1953 | 172,800,000 | 94% | 184,314,024 | 6.1% | 3,020,706,000 |
| 1954 | 148,700,000 | 94% | 158,608,191 | | 3,024,853,000 |
| 1955 | 174,300,000 | 94% | 185,913,972 | | 3,862,736,000 |
| 1956 | 231,500,000 | 94% | 246,925,327 | | 3,929,349,000 |
| 1957 | 244,900,000 | | 281,354,832 | | 4,091,837,000 |
| 1958 | 222,700,000 | | 254,978,710 | | 3,740,065,000 |
| 1959 | 242,500,000 | | 225,009,047 | | 3,907,670,000 |
| 1960 | 330,300,000 | | 287,421,374 | | 4,077,686,000 |

| | Exports of Transport, Machinery, and Equipment | | | | Total |
| | Federation of Malaya | [a]/[b] | Singapore | [b]/[c] | Merchandize Exports |
| | [a] | | [b] | | [c] |
|---|---|---|---|---|---|
| 1950 | | | 143,266,747 | 4.7% | 3,025,750,000 |
| 1951 | | | 224,683,264 | 4.7% | 4,745,242,000 |
| 1952 | | | 151,498,874 | 4.7% | 3,199,610,000 |
| 1953 | 14,100,000 | 11% | 125,670,091 | 4.7% | 2,654,114,000 |
| 1954 | 9,600,000 | 11% | 85,562,615 | | 2,685,518,000 |
| 1955 | 13,700,000 | 11% | 122,104,982 | | 3,368,699,000 |
| 1956 | 17,600,000 | 11% | 156,864,795 | | 3,428,975,000 |
| 1957 | 25,500,000 | | 172,293,132 | | 3,478,133,000 |
| 1958 | 19,100,000 | | 166,727,342 | | 3,140,343,000 |
| 1959 | 18,100,000 | | 181,928,013 | | 3,440,263,000 |
| 1960 | 30,800,000 | | 232,912,385 | | 3,477,053,000 |

| | Imports | Exports | Net Imports |
|---|---|---|---|
| 1950 | 199,738,539 | 143,266,747 | 56,471,792 |
| 1951 | 306,744,250 | 224,683,264 | 82,060,987 |
| 1952 | 228,816,678 | 151,498,874 | 77,317,804 |
| 1953 | 184,314,024 | 125,670,091 | 58,643,932 |
| 1954 | 158,608,191 | 85,562,615 | 73,045,575 |
| 1955 | 185,913,972 | 122,104,982 | 63,808,989 |
| 1956 | 246,925,327 | 156,864,795 | 90,060,532 |
| 1957 | 281,354,832 | 172,293,132 | 109,061,700 |
| 1958 | 254,978,710 | 166,727,342 | 88,251,368 |
| 1959 | 225,009,047 | 181,928,013 | 43,081,034 |
| 1960 | 287,421,374 | 232,912,385 | 54,508,989 |

*Sources*:

(Federation of Malaya)

1953–60: Monthly Statistical Bulletin, Federation of Malaya.

(Singapore)

1956–60: Singapore's External Trade.

activity, some as part of final consumption expenditure, some as intermediate consumption (repairs and maintenance), and some as current consumption in the case of military expenditure. It was not possible to determine these values from historical records. Consequently, 10 percent of net import was assigned for the above and the remaining 90 percent capitalized.[55] The results are presented in Table 2.41.

### 2.4.3.3 *Investment in M&E in 1914 Prices*

No proper price indices were available for Singapore during the British colonial period. As an alternative option, UK price indices for capital goods on plant and machinery provided by Feinstein (1972) were used on the grounds that Singapore had imported M&E to a large extent from UK (See Table 2.42). These deflators were then applied to obtain investment in M&E in constant prices; the data are presented in Table 2.43.

### 2.4.4 *Cultivated Assets*

### 2.4.4.1 *Definition*

Expenditure on cultivated assets of estates/smallholdings, orchards, and vineyards consists of trees (including shrubs) which will be cultivated and take more than a year to become productive for the products which they yield yearly. Cultivated assets produced on own account are valued by the value of cost incurred in their production during the period. For example, the calculation takes into account the cost of preparing the ground (including felling, clearing, stumping and burning, soil conservation, draining, and chankolling), lining, holing and planting (including seedlings and plants), staking, protection from weather or disease (including insecticides, pesticides, and fertilizers applied), pruning, weeding, upkeep, and draining until the trees reach maturity and start to yield a product.

### 2.4.4.2 *Investment in Cultivated Assets in Current Prices*

The perennial crops investment in Singapore examined are rubber and coconut. No estimates were made for other perennial

---

[55] Because of the complete absence of information, this study used similar margins introduced by Nazrin (2002, 26).

**Table 2.41:** Singapore: Transport, Machinery, and Equipment Investment, 1900–39 and 1950–60 in Current Prices (Straits $)

| | Singapore: Net Imports of M&E (CIF) | Plus 18% [Trade Margin (16%) and Transport (2%)] | Investment in Machinery, Transport, and Equipment |
|---|---|---|---|
| | [1] | [2] = [1] × 1.18 | [3] = [2] × 90% |
| 1900 | 1,960,767 | 2,313,705 | 2,082,335 |
| 1901 | 1,977,032 | 2,332,898 | 2,099,608 |
| 1902 | 1,245,792 | 1,470,035 | 1,323,031 |
| 1903 | 2,265,139 | 2,672,864 | 2,405,578 |
| 1904 | 1,051,590 | 1,240,876 | 1,116,789 |
| 1905 | 1,048,828 | 1,237,617 | 1,113,855 |
| 1906 | 1,649,840 | 1,946,811 | 1,752,130 |
| 1907 | 1,684,627 | 1,987,860 | 1,789,074 |
| 1908 | 2,567,780 | 3,029,980 | 2,726,982 |
| 1909 | 2,169,855 | 2,560,429 | 2,304,386 |
| 1910 | 2,360,100 | 2,784,918 | 2,506,426 |
| 1911 | 1,903,953 | 2,246,665 | 2,021,998 |
| 1912 | 2,314,790 | 2,731,452 | 2,458,307 |
| 1913 | 2,575,489 | 3,039,077 | 2,735,169 |
| 1914 | 1,734,004 | 2,046,125 | 1,841,512 |
| 1915 | 1,103,835 | 1,302,525 | 1,172,273 |
| 1916 | 2,562,258 | 3,023,465 | 2,721,118 |
| 1917 | 2,951,625 | 3,482,917 | 3,134,625 |
| 1918 | 1,317,983 | 1,555,220 | 1,399,698 |
| 1919 | 3,025,003 | 3,569,504 | 3,212,554 |
| 1920 | 9,839,700 | 11,610,846 | 10,449,761 |
| 1921 | 4,004,352 | 4,725,135 | 4,252,622 |
| 1922 | 1,742,618 | 2,056,289 | 1,850,660 |
| 1923 | 2,911,835 | 3,435,965 | 3,092,369 |
| 1924 | 5,253,258 | 6,198,844 | 5,578,960 |
| 1925 | 10,535,117 | 12,431,438 | 11,188,294 |
| 1926 | 15,789,544 | 18,631,662 | 16,768,496 |
| 1927 | 11,553,270 | 13,632,859 | 12,269,573 |
| 1928 | 19,834,558 | 23,404,778 | 21,064,301 |
| 1929 | 21,862,406 | 25,797,639 | 23,217,875 |
| 1930 | 13,190,504 | 15,564,795 | 14,008,315 |
| 1931 | 6,323,971 | 7,462,286 | 6,716,057 |
| 1932 | 4,493,387 | 5,302,197 | 4,771,977 |
| 1933 | 3,427,420 | 4,044,356 | 3,639,920 |
| 1934 | 9,362,861 | 11,048,176 | 9,943,358 |
| 1935 | 10,591,327 | 12,497,766 | 11,247,989 |
| 1936 | 10,241,934 | 12,085,482 | 10,876,934 |
| 1937 | 14,485,201 | 17,092,537 | 15,383,283 |
| 1938 | 12,505,372 | 14,756,339 | 13,280,705 |
| 1939 | 10,868,177 | 12,824,449 | 11,542,004 |
| 1950 | 56,471,792 | 66,636,715 | 59,973,043 |
| 1951 | 82,060,987 | 96,831,964 | 87,148,768 |
| 1952 | 77,317,804 | 91,235,009 | 82,111,508 |
| 1953 | 58,643,932 | 69,199,840 | 62,279,856 |
| 1954 | 73,045,575 | 86,193,779 | 77,574,401 |
| 1955 | 63,808,989 | 75,294,608 | 67,765,147 |
| 1956 | 90,060,532 | 106,271,428 | 95,644,285 |
| 1957 | 109,061,700 | 128,692,806 | 115,823,525 |
| 1958 | 88,251,368 | 104,136,614 | 93,722,953 |
| 1959 | 43,081,034 | 50,835,620 | 45,752,058 |
| 1960 | 54,508,989 | 64,320,607 | 57,888,546 |

**Table 2.42:** Singapore: Deflators for Investment for Machinery, Equipment, and Transport (1914 = 100)

| 1900–39 and 1947–60 (1914 = 100) | | | | | | | | | | | |
|---|---|---|---|---|---|---|---|---|---|---|---|
| 1900 | 101.96 | 1910 | 93.77 | 1920 | 253.37 | 1930 | 123.48 | 1947 | 295.68 | 1957 | 489.30 |
| 1901 | 96.81 | 1911 | 96.81 | 1921 | 178.82 | 1931 | 115.40 | 1948 | 328.55 | 1958 | 502.32 |
| 1902 | 92.72 | 1912 | 100.91 | 1922 | 135.31 | 1932 | 115.08 | 1949 | 334.11 | 1959 | 503.90 |
| 1903 | 90.72 | 1913 | 105.00 | 1923 | 128.42 | 1933 | 110.57 | 1950 | 343.14 | 1960 | 509.88 |
| 1904 | 90.72 | 1914 | 100.00 | 1924 | 130.83 | 1934 | 117.39 | 1951 | 368.24 | | |
| 1905 | 90.72 | 1915 | 127.47 | 1925 | 130.41 | 1935 | 120.23 | 1952 | 409.40 | | |
| 1906 | 90.72 | 1916 | 151.94 | 1926 | 127.79 | 1936 | 128.21 | 1953 | 423.99 | | |
| 1907 | 93.77 | 1917 | 195.72 | 1927 | 130.10 | 1937 | 147.00 | 1954 | 425.04 | | |
| 1908 | 96.81 | 1918 | 215.15 | 1928 | 131.88 | 1938 | 147.84 | 1955 | 445.62 | | |
| 1909 | 93.77 | 1919 | 251.79 | 1929 | 135.45 | 1939 | 154.46 | 1956 | 471.77 | | |

*Source*: Based on Feinstein (1972, T136).

**Table 2.43:** Singapore: Transport, Machinery, and Equipment Investment, 1900–39 and 1950–60 in 1914 Prices

(Straits $)

| 1900–39 and 1950–60 (1914 = 100) | | | | | | | | | |
|---|---|---|---|---|---|---|---|---|---|
| 1900 | 2,042,406 | 1910 | 2,673,094 | 1920 | 4,124,390 | 1930 | 11,344,603 | 1950 | 17,477,718 |
| 1901 | 2,168,792 | 1911 | 2,088,625 | 1921 | 2,378,224 | 1931 | 5,820,059 | 1951 | 23,666,617 |
| 1902 | 1,426,987 | 1912 | 2,436,259 | 1922 | 1,367,683 | 1932 | 4,146,661 | 1952 | 20,056,793 |
| 1903 | 2,651,651 | 1913 | 2,604,923 | 1923 | 2,408,106 | 1933 | 3,292,109 | 1953 | 14,688,992 |
| 1904 | 1,231,028 | 1914 | 1,841,512 | 1924 | 4,264,282 | 1934 | 8,470,362 | 1954 | 18,251,082 |
| 1905 | 1,227,795 | 1915 | 919,646 | 1925 | 8,579,322 | 1935 | 9,355,782 | 1955 | 15,206,936 |
| 1906 | 1,931,360 | 1916 | 1,790,975 | 1926 | 13,122,429 | 1936 | 8,484,017 | 1956 | 20,273,714 |
| 1907 | 1,908,040 | 1917 | 1,601,587 | 1927 | 9,431,241 | 1937 | 10,464,819 | 1957 | 23,671,270 |
| 1908 | 2,816,840 | 1918 | 650,583 | 1928 | 15,972,324 | 1938 | 8,983,161 | 1958 | 18,658,017 |
| 1909 | 2,457,619 | 1919 | 1,275,886 | 1929 | 17,141,288 | 1939 | 7,472,729 | 1959 | 9,079,681 |
| | | | | | | | | 1960 | 11,353,367 |

crops since the investments were negligible.[56] Additionally, fruit-bearing trees such as durians, rambutans, chikus, langsat, mangosteens and mangoes were not estimated because of data unavailability. In preparing the estimates, all expenses sunk into

---

[56] For the period 1900–39, total newly planted acreage of perennial crops was almost negligible except rubber and coconut as it is illustrated. Total planted acreage of perennial crops became negligible after the World War II. On the basis of this recognition, estimates of investment on perennial crops were confined only to rubber and coconut in this exercise for the period 1900–39. It is necessary to note that investments on cultivated assets were omitted from official accounts after 1960. This is because planting of perennial crops was negligible in Singapore.

perennial crops prior to their reaching the fruit-bearing age were treated as an investment expense. Once the trees began to yield an income, expenditures on fertilizers and other maintenance were treated as production expense. The following information was compiled for rubber and coconuts:

(1)  Newly planted acreage each year from 1900 to 1939
(2)  Number of years it takes for the crop to reach bearing age
(3)  Cost per acre of bringing the crop into production

The yearly estimates of real investment in cultivated assets at different years of maturity are derived by multiplying the total acreage (newly planted) with the corresponding base-year estimates of cost of development per acre at different stages of maturity. These yearly estimates are then aggregated to arrive at the yearly estimates of real investments. Subsequently, these estimates of total real investment in cultivated assets are transformed into nominal investment figures using the nominal earnings index of rubber tappers (See Table 2.44). This procedure was resorted to in the absence of price indices of other components of investment in cultivated assets. Nevertheless, this

**Table 2.44:** Singapore: Format for Calculating Investment on Coconut Planting at Current Prices, 1910–16

| | | 1910 | 1911 | 1912 | 1913 | 1914 | 1915 | 1916 |
|---|---|---|---|---|---|---|---|---|
| Newly Planted Acreage for 1910 | [1] | 10 | 10 | 10 | 10 | 10 | 10 | |
| Cost per Acre (1911 Prices) | [2] | 50 | 20 | 20 | 20 | 20 | 20 | |
| Value | [A] = [1] × [2] | 500 | 200 | 200 | 200 | 200 | 200 | |
| | | 1910 | 1911 | 1912 | 1913 | 1914 | 1915 | 1916 |
| Newly Planted Acreage for 1911 | [3] | | 30 | 30 | 30 | 30 | 30 | 30 |
| Cost per Acre (1911 Prices) | [4] | | 50 | 20 | 20 | 20 | 20 | 20 |
| Value | [B] = [3] × [4] | | 1500 | 600 | 600 | 600 | 600 | 600 |
| | | 1910 | 1911 | 1912 | 1913 | 1914 | 1915 | 1916 |
| Investment (1911 Prices) | [C] = [A] + [B] | 500 | 1700 | 800 | 800 | 800 | 800 | 600 |
| Rubber Tappers Indices (1911 Prices) | [D] | 90 | 100 | 110 | 120 | 130 | 140 | 150 |
| Investment (Current Prices) | [E] = [C] × [D]/100 | 450 | 1,700 | 880 | 960 | 1,040 | 1,120 | 900 |
| Rubber Tappers Indices (1914 Prices) | [F] | 69 | 77 | 85 | 92 | 100 | 108 | 115 |
| Investment (1914 Prices) | [G] = [E]/[F]*100 | 652 | 2,208 | 1,035 | 1,043 | 1,040 | 1,037 | 783 |

was not a major drawback, since wages of rubber tappers were the single largest component of total investments in cultivated assets. Data series on newly planted acreage for rubber and coconut were obtained by taking the year-to-year changes in total planted acreage. This method should give a fairly accurate picture of new plantings as long as there was not much replanting activity being undertaken. Consider the following example: If old coconut trees were completely removed and the land replanted with coconut seedlings, the records will show no change in total planted acreage of coconuts and our estimates will understate the actual investment in coconut planting.

Instead, if the land was converted to rubber, the records will show an increase in total rubber acreage and this new investment in rubber will be included in our estimates. The historical records indicate that there was no significant replanting undertaken for the crops considered here, except in the case of rubber.

There were some years in which data on planted acreage were not available and it was necessary to make some broad assumptions. The method of estimation employed was to assume constant annual increases in newly planted acreage for the missing years. If the records show a reduction in total acreage planted between any two years, these estimates show no new plantings and hence no investment in those years. For both rubber and coconut, a distinction was made between smallholding and estate cultivation. This is because the cost structure of the estate was considerably higher than that of the smallholding, necessitating the use of different cost-per-acre estimates when calculating investments. In some years in particular, the breakdown of total acreage into smallholding and estate cultivation could be obtained directly from source materials. In other years, this information was not directly available and the breakdown was derived in two stages.

First, estate acreage was established on the assumption that its share of total acreage was the same as that of the nearest year for which data on both total acreage and estate acreage were available. Second, smallholding acreage was obtained by taking the difference between total and estate acreage. The cost-per-acre estimates used were governed by data availability. The calculations took into account the cost of land preparation (including felling, clearing, stumping and burning, soil conservation, and draining), lining, holing and planting, protection from weather and disease (including use of insecticides, pesticides, and fertilizer), pruning, weeding, and upkeep until the trees reached maturity. Contemporary estimates were used wherever possible. Since our study period spans 40 years (1900–39), an attempt was made to use varying cost estimates for different subperiods in order to more accurately take into account changes in costs over time. For the rubber estate, three sets of cost estimates were used, respectively, for the entire period. In the case of rubber smallholdings, however, only one period was selected because of the general unavailability of data. The estimates for estates rubber tabulated in Tables 2.45, 2.46, and 2.47 were used in the calculations covering the periods 1900–20, 1921–30, and 1931–39, respectively. Table 2.48 shows the estimates for rubber smallholdings for the period 1900–39.

In the case of coconuts, different cost production estimates were used for estates and smallholdings. In the case of the former, two sets of estimates were used: one for the period 1900–27 (Table 2.49) and the other for the period 1928–39 (Table 2.50).

**Table 2.45:** Rubber: Cost-per-Acre Estimates, Estate, 1900–20 in 1911 Prices

| Item | Year | | | | | | Total |
|---|---|---|---|---|---|---|---|
| | 1 | 2 | 3 | 4 | 5 | 6 | |
| Survey | 1.00 | | | | | | 1.00 |
| Felling, clearing, and burning | 15.00 | | | | | | 15.00 |
| Cleaning up after burning | 7.50 | | | | | | 7.50 |
| Weeding | 18.00 | 12.00 | 9.00 | 5.00 | 5.00 | 5.00 | 54.00 |
| Draining | 5.00 | | | | | | 5.00 |
| Holing, lining, and filling | 4.00 | | | | | | 4.00 |
| Planting and supplying | 2.00 | | | | | | 2.00 |
| Two-year-old plants | 4.00 | | | | | | 4.00 |
| Tools | 10.00 | | | | | | 10.00 |
| Management | 12.50 | 12.50 | 12.50 | 12.50 | 12.50 | 12.50 | 75.00 |
| Hospital, medical attendance | 3.75 | 3.75 | 3.75 | 3.75 | 3.75 | 3.75 | 22.50 |
| Contingencies | 2.00 | 2.00 | 2.00 | 2.00 | 2.00 | 2.00 | 12.00 |
| Cultivated Assets | 84.75 | 30.25 | 27.25 | 23.25 | 23.25 | 23.25 | 212.00 |

*Source*: Figart (1925, 90).

**Table 2.46:**  Rubber: Cost-per-Acre Estimate, Estate, 1921–30 in 1924 Prices

| Item | Year | | | | | | Total |
|---|---|---|---|---|---|---|---|
| | 1 | 2 | 3 | 4 | 5 | 6 | |
| Preliminary expenses | 3.00 | | | | | | 3.00 |
| Felling | 12.00 | | | | | | 12.00 |
| Clearing and burning | 40.00 | | | | | | 40.00 |
| Stumping and burning | 80.00 | | | | | | 80.00 |
| Sundry expenses in connection with clearing | 4.00 | | | | | | 4.00 |
| Soil conservation, draining, and chankolling | 30.00 | | | | | | 30.00 |
| Lining, holing, and planting including nurseries | 17.00 | | | | | | 17.00 |
| Upkeep | 12.00 | 20.00 | 20.00 | 15.00 | 15.00 | 15.00 | 97.00 |
| Miscellaneous purchases, etc. | 7.00 | | | | | | 7.00 |
| General charges: Superintendence, $130, labor charges (recruiting, medical expenses, etc.) $60, other $25 | 35.00 | 37.00 | 35.00 | 36.00 | 36.00 | 36.00 | 215.00 |
| Cultivated Assets | 240.00 | 57.00 | 55.00 | 51.00 | 51.00 | 51.00 | 505.00 |

*Source*: Figart (1925, 52).

**Table 2.47:**  Rubber: Cost-per-Acre Estimate, Estate, 1931–39 in 1934 Prices

| Item | Year | | | | | | Total |
|---|---|---|---|---|---|---|---|
| | 1 | 2 | 3 | 4 | 5 | 6 | |
| Survey | 1.00 | | | | | | 1.00 |
| Felling, clearing, and burning | 10.50 | | | | | | 10.50 |
| Cleaning up after burning | 5.25 | | | | | | 5.25 |
| Weeding | 12.60 | 8.40 | 6.30 | 3.50 | | | 30.80 |
| Draining | 3.50 | | | | | | 3.50 |
| Holing, lining, and filling | 4.00 | | | | | | 4.00 |
| Planting and supplying | 2.00 | | | | | | 2.00 |
| Two-year-old plants | 4.00 | | | | | | 4.00 |
| Tools | 8.00 | | | | | | 8.00 |
| Management | 6.66 | 6.66 | 6.66 | 6.66 | 6.66 | 6.66 | 40.00 |
| Hospital, medical attendance | 2.00 | 2.00 | 2.00 | 2.00 | 2.00 | 2.00 | 12.00 |
| Contingencies | 1.08 | 1.08 | 1.08 | 1.08 | 1.08 | 1.08 | 6.48 |
| Cultivated Assets | 60.59 | 18.14 | 16.04 | 13.24 | 9.74 | 9.74 | 127.53 |

*Source:* Bauer, PT (1948, 129–130).

**Table 2.48:**  Rubber: Cost-per-Acre Estimate, Smallholdings, 1900–39 in 1924 Prices

| Item | Year | | | | | | Total |
|---|---|---|---|---|---|---|---|
| | 1 | 2 | 3 | 4 | 5 | 6 | |
| Clearing and burning | 50.00 | | | | | | 50.00 |
| Soil conservation, draining, and chankolling | 5.00 | | | | | | 5.00 |
| Lining, holing, and planting including nurseries | 5.00 | | | | | | 5.00 |
| Upkeep | 10.00 | 8.00 | 8.00 | 8.00 | 8.00 | 8.00 | 50.00 |
| Cultivated Assets | 70.00 | 8.00 | 8.00 | 8.00 | 8.00 | 8.00 | 110.00 |

*Source*: Figart (1925, 90).

The estimates for smallholdings are provided in Table 2.51. The period to maturity was 6 years for estates and 8 years for smallholdings. These tables present the estimates on private investment in coconut planting in each year from 1900 to 1939.

**Table 2.49:** Coconuts: Cost-per-Acre Estimate, Estate, 1900–27 in 1908 Prices

| Item | Year | | | | | | Total |
|---|---|---|---|---|---|---|---|
| | 1 | 2 | 3 | 4 | 5 | 6 | |
| Felling and clearing | 10.00 | | | | | | 10.00 |
| Draining | 12.00 | | | | | | 12.00 |
| Cost of seed | 6.40 | | | | | | 6.40 |
| Fencing | 2.00 | | | | | | 2.00 |
| Lining and planting | 2.00 | | | | | | 2.00 |
| Tools | 2.00 | | | | | | 2.00 |
| Stationery and postage | 0.10 | | | | | | 0.10 |
| Medical | 0.10 | | | | | | 0.10 |
| Weeding | 6.00 | 12.00 | 8.40 | 7.00 | 7.00 | 7.00 | 47.40 |
| Contingencies | 1.00 | | | | | | 1.00 |
| Superintendence | 6.00 | 6.00 | 6.00 | 6.00 | 6.00 | 6.00 | 36.00 |
| Supplying | | | 0.60 | | | | 0.60 |
| Cultivated Assets | 47.60 | 18.00 | 15.00 | 13.00 | 13.00 | 13.00 | 119.60 |

*Source*: Straits Settlements and Federated Malay States (1909). *Agricultural Bulletin*, 8(5), Appendix. B, 237–238.

**Table 2.50:** Coconut: Cost-per-Acre Estimate, Estate, 1928–39 in 1928 Prices

| Items | Year | | | | | Total |
|---|---|---|---|---|---|---|
| | 1 | 2 | 3 | 4 | 5 | |
| Tools | 0.40 | 0.40 | 0.40 | 0.40 | 0.40 | 2.00 |
| Felling, burning, and clearing | 27.00 | | | | | 27.00 |
| Seeds | 2.00 | | | | | 2.00 |
| Lining, holing, and planting | 3.00 | | | | | 3.00 |
| Supplying | 0.60 | 0.60 | 0.60 | 0.60 | 0.60 | 3.00 |
| Circle cultivation of seedlings | 3.00 | | | | | 3.00 |
| Weeding | 4.20 | 4.20 | 4.20 | 4.20 | 4.20 | 21.00 |
| Cover crops | 0.80 | 0.80 | 0.80 | 0.80 | 0.80 | 4.00 |
| Pests and diseases | 2.00 | 2.00 | 2.00 | 2.00 | 2.00 | 10.00 |
| Survey fees, suprintendence, medical and contingencies, and quit-rent* | 7.52 | 7.52 | 7.52 | 7.52 | 7.52 | 37.60 |
| Total | 50.52 | 15.52 | 15.52 | 15.52 | 15.52 | 112.60 |

*Note*:
The above estimate does not take into account cost of premium on land, survey fees, permanent buildings, renticing and bunding (at present 20 cents per foot) and other overhead charges.
* Item 1–9 excludes (i) survey fees, (ii) suprintendence, (iii) medical and contingencies, and (iv) quit-rent. Item 10 [(i) survey fees, (ii) suprintendence, (iii) medical and contingencies, and (iv) quit-rent] — estimates based on coconut estates cost structure, 1908.
*Source*: Grist, DH (1950, 113).

Even for the same crop at the same point in time which employed the same type of cultivation, the costs of opening up an acre of land could vary considerably depending on location, type of land, and other local circumstances. It is, of course, not

**Table 2.51:** Coconuts: Cost-per-Acre Estimate, Smallholdings, 1900–39 in 1934 Prices

| Item | Year | | | | | | | | Total |
|---|---|---|---|---|---|---|---|---|---|
| | 1 | 2 | 3 | 4 | 5 | 6 | 7 | 8 | |
| Seeding | 7.00 | | | | | | | | 7.00 |
| Copra sun-dried nuts | 2.00 | | | | | | | | 2.00 |
| Tools and stores | 5.00 | | | | | | | | 5.00 |
| Cover crop | 1.00 | | | | | | | | 1.00 |
| Pest and disease | 0.62 | 0.62 | 0.62 | 0.62 | 0.62 | 0.62 | 0.62 | 0.62 | 4.96 |
| Contingencies | 0.75 | 0.75 | 0.75 | 0.75 | 0.75 | 0.75 | 0.75 | 0.75 | 6.00 |
| **Cultivated Assets** | 16.37 | 1.37 | 1.37 | 1.37 | 1.37 | 1.37 | 1.37 | 1.37 | 25.96 |

*Source*: Federated Malay States (1932) *Third Inter-Departmental Agricultural Conference*, Kuala Lumpur: Government Printing Office, Appendix p. 5.

possible to cover all cases. Instead, it was necessary to resort to some generalizations. Subsequently, these estimates of total real investment in cultivated assets were transformed into nominal investment figures on the basis of the nominal rubber tappers' wage indices.[57] The nominal figures of investments for rubber and coconut planting with breakdown on estates and smallholdings are presented in Tables 2.52 and 2.53.

### 2.4.4.3 *Investment in Cultivated Assets in 1914 Prices*

The aggregated nominal investments of cultivated assets were then deflated by rubber tappers' wage indices as provided in Table 2.54.[58] By using these indices, cultivated assets in constant prices were obtained, as presented in Table 2.55.

---

[57] *Blue Book, Straits Settlements* provides information on minimum Indian rubber tappers' wage for the period 1913–38. For the year 1939, wage of 1938 was applied. Prior to 1913, no specific wage for rubber tapper was available. As an alternative option, the movement of wage rate for predial workers provided in *Blue Book, Straits Settlements* for the period 1900–14 was treated as a proxy of Indian rubber tappers' wages.

[58] Real wage indices of rubber tappers were derived by deflating nominal wage indices by the consumer price indices.

**Table 2.52:** Singapore: Rubber, Cultivated Assets, 1900–39 in Current Prices

(Straits $)

| | Estate | | | | | | | | | Smallholding | | | Total |
|---|---|---|---|---|---|---|---|---|---|---|---|---|---|
| | 1900–20 | | | 1921–30 | | | 1931–39 | | | 1900–39 | | | |
| | 1911 Price | Rubber Tappers' Earnings Index (1911 = 100) | Current Prices | 1924 Price | Rubber Tappers' Earnings Index (1924 = 100) | Current Prices | 1934 Price | Rubber Tappers' Earnings Index (1934 = 100) | Current Prices | 1924 Price | Rubber Tappers' Earnings Index (1924 = 100) | Current Prices | Current Prices |
| | [1] | [2] | [3] = [1] * [2] /100 | [1] | [2] | [3] = [1] * [2] /100 | [1] | [2] | [3] = [1] * [2] /100 | [1] | [2] | [3] = [1] * [2] /100 | |
| 1900 | — | 100.00 | — | | 50.00 | — | | 83.33 | — | — | 50.00 | — | — |
| 1901 | — | 100.00 | — | | 50.00 | — | | 83.33 | — | — | 50.00 | — | — |
| 1902 | — | 100.00 | — | | 50.00 | — | | 83.33 | — | — | 50.00 | — | — |
| 1903 | — | 100.00 | — | | 50.00 | — | | 83.33 | — | — | 50.00 | — | — |
| 1904 | 6,611 | 100.00 | 6,611 | | 50.00 | — | | 83.33 | — | — | 50.00 | — | 6,611 |
| 1905 | 89,822 | 100.00 | 89,822 | | 50.00 | — | | 83.33 | — | — | 50.00 | — | 89,822 |
| 1906 | 63,006 | 100.00 | 63,006 | | 50.00 | — | | 83.33 | — | — | 50.00 | — | 63,006 |
| 1907 | 271,891 | 100.00 | 271,891 | | 50.00 | — | | 83.33 | — | — | 50.00 | — | 271,891 |
| 1908 | 164,964 | 100.00 | 164,964 | | 50.00 | — | | 83.33 | — | — | 50.00 | — | 164,964 |
| 1909 | 155,202 | 100.00 | 155,202 | | 50.00 | — | | 83.33 | — | 175,009 | 50.00 | 87,504 | 242,706 |
| 1910 | 826,655 | 100.00 | 826,655 | | 50.00 | — | | 83.33 | — | 305,541 | 50.00 | 152,771 | 979,426 |
| 1911 | 866,253 | 100.00 | 866,253 | | 50.00 | — | | 83.33 | — | 263,335 | 50.00 | 131,668 | 997,921 |
| 1912 | 772,926 | 100.00 | 772,926 | | 50.00 | — | | 83.33 | — | 188,397 | 50.00 | 94,199 | 867,125 |
| 1913 | 534,974 | 150.00 | 802,461 | | 75.00 | — | | 125.00 | — | 111,584 | 75.00 | 83,688 | 886,149 |
| 1914 | 452,638 | 200.00 | 905,276 | | 100.00 | — | | 166.67 | — | 230,169 | 100.00 | 230,169 | 1,135,445 |
| 1915 | 439,901 | 200.00 | 879,801 | | 100.00 | — | | 166.67 | — | 92,031 | 100.00 | 92,031 | 971,832 |
| 1916 | 237,135 | 200.00 | 474,270 | | 100.00 | — | | 166.67 | — | 55,645 | 100.00 | 55,645 | 529,915 |
| 1917 | 723,109 | 200.00 | 1,446,218 | | 100.00 | — | | 166.67 | — | 273,975 | 100.00 | 273,975 | 1,720,193 |
| 1918 | 399,690 | 200.00 | 799,380 | | 100.00 | — | | 166.67 | — | 191,545 | 100.00 | 191,545 | 990,925 |
| 1919 | 524,016 | 320.00 | 1,676,853 | | 160.00 | — | | 266.67 | — | 255,994 | 160.00 | 409,591 | 2,086,444 |
| 1920 | 333,790 | 320.00 | 1,068,129 | | 160.00 | — | | 266.67 | — | 122,050 | 160.00 | 195,280 | 1,263,409 |
| 1921 | 305,203 | 320.00 | 976,650 | — | 160.00 | — | | 266.67 | — | 85,636 | 160.00 | 137,018 | 1,113,667 |
| 1922 | 292,308 | 200.00 | 584,616 | — | 100.00 | — | | 166.67 | — | 74,352 | 100.00 | 74,352 | 658,968 |
| 1923 | 119,063 | 200.00 | 238,127 | — | 100.00 | — | | 166.67 | — | 46,648 | 100.00 | 46,648 | 284,775 |
| 1924 | 75,911 | 200.00 | 151,823 | — | 100.00 | — | | 166.67 | — | 30,072 | 100.00 | 30,072 | 181,895 |
| 1925 | 3,836 | 200.00 | 7,673 | — | 100.00 | — | | 166.67 | — | 7,736 | 100.00 | 7,736 | 15,409 |
| 1926 | | 200.00 | — | — | 100.00 | — | | 166.67 | — | 1,456 | 100.00 | 1,456 | 1,456 |
| 1927 | | 200.00 | — | — | 100.00 | — | | 166.67 | — | — | 100.00 | — | — |
| 1928 | | 200.00 | — | — | 100.00 | — | | 166.67 | — | — | 100.00 | — | — |
| 1929 | | 200.00 | — | — | 100.00 | — | | 166.67 | — | — | 100.00 | — | — |
| 1930 | | 160.00 | — | — | 80.00 | — | | 133.33 | — | — | 80.00 | — | — |
| 1931 | | 140.00 | — | — | 70.00 | — | — | 116.67 | — | — | 70.00 | — | — |
| 1932 | | 100.00 | — | — | 50.00 | — | 405,495 | 83.33 | 337,913 | — | 50.00 | — | 337,913 |
| 1933 | | 112.00 | — | — | 56.00 | — | 121,420 | 93.33 | 113,325 | — | 56.00 | — | 113,325 |
| 1934 | | 120.00 | — | — | 60.00 | — | 295,935 | 100.00 | 295,935 | 505,610 | 60.00 | 303,366 | 599,301 |
| 1935 | | 140.00 | — | — | 70.00 | — | 243,376 | 116.67 | 283,939 | 98,874 | 70.00 | 69,212 | 353,151 |
| 1936 | | 140.00 | — | — | 70.00 | — | 144,565 | 116.67 | 168,660 | 62,480 | 70.00 | 43,736 | 212,396 |
| 1937 | | 160.00 | — | — | 80.00 | — | 132,446 | 133.33 | 176,594 | 62,480 | 80.00 | 49,984 | 226,578 |
| 1938 | | 160.00 | — | — | 80.00 | — | 51,805 | 133.33 | 69,073 | 119,040 | 80.00 | 95,232 | 164,305 |
| 1939 | | 160.00 | — | — | 80.00 | — | 46,128 | 133.33 | 61,504 | 76,364 | 80.00 | 61,091 | 122,595 |

## 2.4.5 *Change in Stock*

### 2.4.5.1 *Definition*

Stocks, or inventories, consist mainly of goods that have been purchased for intermediate consumption but not yet used, goods produced for sale but not yet sold (work in progress), and livestock being raised for slaughter. Government stocks of strategic materials, grains, and other goods of special importance to a country in time of crisis are also included. Work in progress on heavy machinery, ships, and similar items is included in stocks,

**Table 2.53:** Singapore: Coconuts, Cultivated Assets, 1900–39 in Current Prices

(Straits $)

| | Estate | | | | | | Smallholding | | | Total |
|---|---|---|---|---|---|---|---|---|---|---|
| | 1900–27 | | | 1928–39 | | | 1900–39 | | | |
| | 6 years to Maturity (1908 = 100) | | | 4 years to Maturity (1928 = 100) | | | 8 years to Maturity (1934 = 100) | | | |
| | 1908 Price | Rubber Tappers' Earnings Index (1908 = 100) | Current Prices | 1928 Price | Rubber Tappers' Earnings Index (1928 = 100) | Current Prices | 1932 Price | Rubber Tappers' Earnings Index (1932 = 100) | Current Prices | Current Prices |
| | [1] | [2] | [3] = [1]*[2] /100 | [1] | [2] | [3] = [1]*[2] /100 | [1] | [2] | [3] = [1]*[2] /100 | |
| 1900 | — | 100.00 | — | | 50.00 | — | — | 100.00 | — | — |
| 1901 | 58,786 | 100.00 | 58,786 | | 50.00 | — | 19,818 | 100.00 | 19,818 | 78,604 |
| 1902 | 40,984 | 100.00 | 40,984 | | 50.00 | — | 7,705 | 100.00 | 7,705 | 48,689 |
| 1903 | 25,617 | 100.00 | 25,617 | | 50.00 | — | 2,165 | 100.00 | 2,165 | 27,782 |
| 1904 | 163,623 | 100.00 | 163,623 | | 50.00 | — | 50,469 | 100.00 | 50,469 | 214,092 |
| 1905 | 145,526 | 100.00 | 145,526 | | 50.00 | — | 30,132 | 100.00 | 30,132 | 175,658 |
| 1906 | 92,583 | 100.00 | 92,583 | | 50.00 | — | 8,209 | 100.00 | 8,209 | 100,792 |
| 1907 | 322,917 | 100.00 | 322,917 | | 50.00 | — | 96,099 | 100.00 | 96,099 | 419,016 |
| 1908 | 155,129 | 100.00 | 155,129 | | 50.00 | — | 15,565 | 100.00 | 15,565 | 170,694 |
| 1909 | 184,640 | 100.00 | 184,640 | | 50.00 | — | 29,185 | 100.00 | 29,185 | 213,825 |
| 1910 | 106,746 | 100.00 | 106,746 | | 50.00 | — | 14,679 | 100.00 | 14,679 | 121,425 |
| 1911 | 364,899 | 100.00 | 364,899 | | 50.00 | — | 110,652 | 100.00 | 110,652 | 475,551 |
| 1912 | 188,635 | 100.00 | 188,635 | | 50.00 | — | 18,668 | 100.00 | 18,668 | 207,303 |
| 1913 | 100,830 | 150.00 | 151,245 | | 75.00 | — | 16,666 | 150.00 | 24,999 | 176,244 |
| 1914 | 89,050 | 200.00 | 178,100 | | 100.00 | — | 16,666 | 200.00 | 33,332 | 211,432 |
| 1915 | 76,570 | 200.00 | 153,140 | | 100.00 | — | 10,557 | 200.00 | 21,114 | 174,254 |
| 1916 | 76,570 | 200.00 | 153,140 | | 100.00 | — | 10,661 | 200.00 | 21,323 | 174,463 |
| 1917 | — | 200.00 | — | | 100.00 | — | 8,241 | 200.00 | 16,481 | 16,481 |
| 1918 | 35,462 | 200.00 | 70,924 | | 100.00 | — | 21,683 | 200.00 | 43,365 | 114,289 |
| 1919 | 132,648 | 320.00 | 424,474 | | 160.00 | — | 43,587 | 320.00 | 139,478 | 563,951 |
| 1920 | 56,265 | 320.00 | 180,048 | | 160.00 | — | 4,870 | 320.00 | 15,583 | 195,631 |
| 1921 | 47,260 | 320.00 | 151,232 | | 160.00 | — | 6,116 | 320.00 | 19,571 | 170,803 |
| 1922 | 42,250 | 200.00 | 84,500 | | 100.00 | — | 4,974 | 200.00 | 9,948 | 94,448 |
| 1923 | 42,250 | 200.00 | 84,500 | | 100.00 | — | 4,870 | 200.00 | 9,739 | 94,239 |
| 1924 | 32,565 | 200.00 | 65,130 | | 100.00 | — | 4,765 | 200.00 | 9,531 | 74,661 |
| 1925 | — | 200.00 | — | | 100.00 | — | 4,765 | 200.00 | 9,531 | 9,531 |
| 1926 | 2,856 | 200.00 | 5,712 | | 100.00 | — | 3,640 | 200.00 | 7,281 | 12,993 |
| 1927 | 1,080 | 200.00 | 2,160 | | 100.00 | — | 104 | 200.00 | 209 | 2,369 |
| 1928 | 900 | 200.00 | 1,800 | — | 100.00 | — | 104 | 200.00 | 209 | 2,009 |
| 1929 | 780 | 200.00 | 1,560 | — | 100.00 | — | — | 200.00 | — | 1,560 |
| 1930 | 780 | 160.00 | 1,248 | 581,184 | 80.00 | 464,947 | 20,888 | 160.00 | 33,420 | 499,616 |
| 1931 | 780 | 140.00 | 1,092 | 21,024 | 70.00 | 14,717 | 1,748 | 140.00 | 2,447 | 18,256 |
| 1932 | — | 100.00 | — | 182,464 | 50.00 | 91,232 | 8,296 | 100.00 | 8,296 | 99,528 |
| 1933 | | 112.00 | — | 26,864 | 56.00 | 15,044 | 2,296 | 112.00 | 2,572 | 17,615 |
| 1934 | | 120.00 | — | 26,864 | 60.00 | 16,118 | 2,296 | 120.00 | 2,755 | 18,874 |
| 1935 | | 140.00 | — | 26,864 | 70.00 | 18,805 | 53,354 | 140.00 | 74,696 | 93,501 |
| 1936 | | 140.00 | — | 5,840 | 70.00 | 4,088 | 6,569 | 140.00 | 9,197 | 13,285 |
| 1937 | | 160.00 | — | 5,840 | 80.00 | 4,672 | 6,569 | 160.00 | 10,511 | 15,183 |
| 1938 | | 160.00 | — | — | 80.00 | — | 4,821 | 160.00 | 7,714 | 7,714 |
| 1939 | | 160.00 | — | — | 80.00 | — | 4,821 | 160.00 | 7,714 | 7,714 |

but work in progress on construction is treated as gross fixed capital formation. The natural increase in standing crops and timber is not included in stocks, nor are new discoveries (or additions to proven reserves) of mineral resources, such as oil. In practice, problems may arise in drawing the line between the increase in

**Table 2.54:** Singapore: Indian Rubber Tapper's Wage Indices, 1900–39 (1914 = 100)

| Year | Index | Year | Index |
|---|---|---|---|
| 1900 | 50.00 | 1920 | 160.00 |
| 1901 | 50.00 | 1921 | 160.00 |
| 1902 | 50.00 | 1922 | 100.00 |
| 1903 | 50.00 | 1923 | 100.00 |
| 1904 | 50.00 | 1924 | 100.00 |
| 1905 | 50.00 | 1925 | 100.00 |
| 1906 | 50.00 | 1926 | 100.00 |
| 1907 | 50.00 | 1927 | 100.00 |
| 1908 | 50.00 | 1928 | 100.00 |
| 1909 | 50.00 | 1929 | 100.00 |
| 1910 | 50.00 | 1930 | 80.00 |
| 1911 | 50.00 | 1931 | 70.00 |
| 1912 | 50.00 | 1932 | 50.00 |
| 1913 | 75.00 | 1933 | 56.00 |
| 1914 | 100.00 | 1934 | 60.00 |
| 1915 | 100.00 | 1935 | 70.00 |
| 1916 | 100.00 | 1936 | 70.00 |
| 1917 | 100.00 | 1937 | 80.00 |
| 1918 | 100.00 | 1938 | 80.00 |
| 1919 | 160.00 | 1939 | 80.00 |

*Source*: Blue Book, Straits Settlements, 1900–38.

**Table 2.55:** Singapore: Cultivated Assets in 1914 Prices, 1900–39

(Straits $)

| 1900–39 (1914 = 100) | | | | | | | |
|---|---|---|---|---|---|---|---|
| 1900 | — | 1910 | 1,964,924 | 1920 | 1,958,281 | 1930 | 907,778 |
| 1901 | 131,963 | 1911 | 2,860,613 | 1921 | 1,396,065 | 1931 | 32,921 |
| 1902 | 84,863 | 1912 | 2,118,880 | 1922 | 1,175,007 | 1932 | 978,619 |
| 1903 | 48,990 | 1913 | 1,424,238 | 1923 | 575,530 | 1933 | 243,763 |
| 1904 | 389,060 | 1914 | 1,346,877 | 1924 | 387,926 | 1934 | 1,101,203 |
| 1905 | 475,762 | 1915 | 1,232,312 | 1925 | 38,539 | 1935 | 703,827 |
| 1906 | 289,807 | 1916 | 801,289 | 1926 | 23,011 | 1936 | 350,130 |
| 1907 | 1,224,631 | 1917 | 2,057,063 | 1927 | 3,725 | 1937 | 345,771 |
| 1908 | 602,615 | 1918 | 1,537,395 | 1928 | 3,136 | 1938 | 238,974 |
| 1909 | 800,500 | 1919 | 2,782,751 | 1929 | 2,379 | 1939 | 181,813 |

stocks and gross fixed capital formation for heavy machinery and ships that take a considerable time to complete. It often happens that the basic data supplied by producers make no distinction between finished and unfinished work.[59]

---

[59] Department of International Economic and Social Affairs, Statistical Office, United Nations (1986, 143).

What enters into gross capital formation is not total inventories, but the addition to inventories in the period of account. Since prices are likely to change over the course of the period, it is necessary to distinguish between the change in the value of inventories and the value of the physical change in them. It is the latter that is wanted, valued at purchasers' prices when acquired from other units and at producers' prices when produced by the unit owning the stocks. The valuation should, in principle, be at the prices current at the time the additions to stocks are made, and withdrawals from stocks for internal processing or for sale should similarly, in principle, be valued at the prices current at the time the withdrawal takes place. Work in progress, for which there is normally no market price, should be valued at explicit cost. In practice, however, it is almost never possible to follow these principles strictly. In devising alternative methods, the objective should be to ensure that what is being measured is the change in the physical quantity of stocks, measured at suitable fixed prices during the whole accounting period.

### 2.4.5.2 *Methodology for Estimates*

Currently, data on the value of stocks are collected in production censuses and surveys, and in special quarterly or annual surveys of stocks. The colonial government records, however, did not provide sufficient information to construct reliable estimates. Under these serious constraints of data unavailability, an observation was made to examine whether there is any statistical relationship between GDP growth rate and value of changes in stocks for the period 1960–2000.[60] For the period 1960–2000, correlations between these variables are 0.42334. The correlation of closest period 1960–69 was even higher, i.e., 0.77217. This correlation test somewhat portrays the fact that GDP growth rate has been positively correlated with the level of change in stock.

---

[60] Figures obtained from Department of Statistics, Singapore (1996) and Asian Development Bank (2001).

**Table 2.56:** Singapore: Change in Stocks as a Proportion to GDP, 1960–69.

| | GDP Growth Rate (%) | Weights on Changes in Stock to GDP (%) |
|---|---|---|
| 1960 | | 2 |
| 1961 | 8 | −1 |
| 1962 | 8 | 1 |
| 1963 | 10 | 1 |
| 1964 | −3 | −0 |
| 1965 | 9 | 1 |
| 1966 | 12 | 2 |
| 1967 | 12 | 2 |
| 1968 | 14 | 2 |
| 1969 | 15 | 2 |

*Source*: Department of Statistics, Singapore (1996, 56).

Subsequently, GDP growth rate and percentage contribution of changes in stock to GDP for the period 1960–69 were observed; as presented in Table 2.56, size of changes in stock to GDP varied ranging from −1 percent to 2 percent.

Using this observation, the following ranges of weights were assigned for the changes of stock to GDP in relation to GDP growth rate (See Table 2.57). Subsequently, similar ranging bands were assigned on the basis of the growth rate of estimated GDP (exclusive of change of stocks) for the periods 1900–39 and 1950–60, as presented in Table 2.58.

### 2.4.5.3 *Change in Stocks in 1914 Prices*

The deflation of change in stocks is complex as it requires an adjustment to remove stock appreciation in the accounting period as well. Stock appreciation is the change in the money value of stocks, in the accounting period, which is due to changes in price rather than changes in physical quantity of stocks. On the basis of this recognition, import unit value index was alternatively used as deflator. Admittedly, these arbitrary assignments of stock values are not entirely satisfactory from a

**Table 2.57:** Singapore: Weights Assigned for the Change of Stocks to GDP (%) in Relation to GDP Growth Rate

| GDP Growth Rate (%) | Weights on the Changes of Stock to GDP (%) |
|---|---|
| Less than −30% | −3.0 |
| −21 to −30 | −2.5 |
| −12 to −20 | −2.0 |
| −9 to −11 | −1.5 |
| −6 to −8 | −1 |
| −5 to +5 | 0 |
| 6　　8 | 1 |
| 9 to 11 | 1.5 |
| 12 to 20 | 2.0 |
| 20 to 30 | 2.5 |
| More than 30 | 3.0 |

**Table 2.58:** Singapore: Percentage Contributions of Change in Stocks to GDP, 1900–39 and 1950–60

|  |  |  |  |  |  |  |  |  |  |
|---|---|---|---|---|---|---|---|---|---|
| 1900 | 0.0 | 1910 | 1.5 | 1920 | 0.0 | 1930 | −2.0 | 1950 | 0.0 |
| 1901 | 1.5 | 1911 | −1.0 | 1921 | 2.5 | 1931 | −3.0 | 1951 | 2.0 |
| 1902 | 0.0 | 1912 | −1.5 | 1922 | 0.0 | 1932 | −2.0 | 1952 | −1.5 |
| 1903 | −1.5 | 1913 | 0.0 | 1923 | −1.5 | 1933 | 2.0 | 1953 | 2.5 |
| 1904 | 1.0 | 1914 | 1.5 | 1924 | −1.5 | 1934 | −1.0 | 1954 | 1.0 |
| 1905 | 2.0 | 1915 | 2.5 | 1925 | 2.0 | 1935 | 2.5 | 1955 | −1.0 |
| 1906 | 1.0 | 1916 | −1.5 | 1926 | 0.0 | 1936 | 0.0 | 1956 | 2.0 |
| 1907 | 0.0 | 1917 | 3.0 | 1927 | 0.0 | 1937 | 2.0 | 1957 | 0.0 |
| 1908 | 2.0 | 1918 | 2.0 | 1928 | 2.5 | 1938 | 0.0 | 1958 | 0.0 |
| 1909 | 0.0 | 1919 | 3.0 | 1929 | 2.5 | 1939 | 2.0 | 1959 | 0.0 |
|  |  |  |  |  |  |  |  | 1960 | 1.5 |

methodological point of view and further studies need to be made to obtain more refined figures.

## 2.5 Net Exports of Goods and Services

### 2.5.1 *Definition*

As presented in Table 2.59, Exports and Imports of Goods and Services defined in SNA68 include merchandize, transport and communication, insurance services, and miscellaneous goods

**Table 2.59:** Classification of Exports and Imports of Goods and Services.

| [A] Exports of Goods (1 + 2) | |
|---|---|
| 1 | Exports of merchandize, f.o.b |
| 2 | Adjustment of merchandize exports to change-of-ownership basis |
| [B] Exports of Services (3 + 4 + 5 + 6 + 7) | |
| 3 | Transport and communication |
| 4 | Insurance service charges |
| 5 | Other commodities |
| 6 | Direct purchases in the domestic market of nonresident households |
| 7 | Direct purchases in the domestic market of extraterritorial bodies (foreign embassies, international organizations, and foreign armed forces) |
| [A] + [B] Total Exports of Goods and Services | |

| [A] Imports of Goods (1 + 2) | |
|---|---|
| 1 | Imports of merchandize, c.i.f. |
| 1.1 | Imports of merchandize, f.o.b. |
| 1.2 | Transport services on merchandize imports |
| 1.3 | Insurance service charges on merchandize imports |
| 2 | Adjustment of merchandize imports to change-of-ownership basis |
| [B] Imports of Services (3 + 4 + 5 + 6 + 7) | |
| 3 | Other transport and communication |
| 4 | Other insurance service charges |
| 5 | Other commodities |
| 6 | Direct purchases abroad by government |
| 7 | Direct purchases abroad by resident households |
| [A] + [B] Total Exports of Goods and Services | |

*Source*: Department of International, Economic and Social Affairs, United Nations (1986, 148–149).

and services.[61] The definitions of merchandize trade used in SNA and in foreign trade statistics are similar in most respects. Merchandize exports are expressed in f.o.b. transaction values,[62] while Merchandize imports should be c.i.f. value.[63]

---

[61] It refers to the gross margin realized by resident merchants on goods purchased in another country and sold in a third country and reimbursements of the cost of home office services of parent companies by foreign branches and subsidiaries.

[62] In addition to the producer's value of commodities at the establishment of the exports, f.o.b. values include all costs of transporting the goods to the custom frontier of the exporting country, exports duties, and the cost of loading the goods onto the international carrier.

[63] Freight and insurance charges incurred after the merchandize has left the establishment of the exporters and until it reaches the customs frontier of the importer should be added to its f.o.b. value. Import duties and the cost of unloading the goods from the carrier are not included in the c.i.f. value.

Other than merchandize trade figures provided in foreign trade statistics, a number of items should be included as service trade. These are (1) fuel and stores sold or purchased abroad by ships and aircraft operated primarily in international waters by resident enterprises, and (2) repair work done as exports or imports of services. Additionally, direct purchases in the domestic market by nonresident households are included in exports of services, and direct purchases abroad by resident households are included as imports of services. SNA68 includes all purchases by extraterritorial bodies, such as foreign embassies, international organizations, or foreign armed forces, which are treated as exports of a country in which the purchases are made.

It is important to note that all transactions in goods and services between residents and nonresidents should, in principle, be recorded at the moment of which ownership of the goods passes between the buyer and the seller in the definition of national accounting. In other words, trade statistics as represented by the transaction of goods and services between the national geographical boundaries (i.e., across national custom frontiers) does not provide an actual picture of external trade in the national accounting sense.[64]

The export and import figures recorded for Singapore during the British colonial period in official publications essentially referred to imports and exports of goods which crossed the customs frontier. Since we were not able to identify the ownership of these goods, data in this series could not be used to provide specific figures for the exports and imports of goods and services in line with the national accounting framework. Therefore, only data on net exports of goods and services are presented in order

---

[64] Practically, it is difficult to quantify the difference between the value of goods that still remain in the country of exporter after the change in ownership has occurred and the value of goods that have crossed custom boundaries of a country without change in ownership. (Department of International Economic and Social Affairs, United Nations (1986, 147).

to overcome this inability to identify transactions involving change in ownership.

## 2.5.2 *Merchandize Trade in Current Prices*

### 2.5.2.1 *1900–27 Series*

As presented in Table 2.60, six different sources on merchandize trade were available during the period 1900–39. For the period 1900–27, the *Appendix to the Report on the Trade, Straits Settlements* provided information on Singapore's trade with the Rest of the World (ROW, exclusive of trade with the Malay states) and also Singapore's trade with the Malay States. However, this set of data series is no longer available after 1927.

This is mainly because the British colonial authority created British Malaya (Straits Settlements, Federated Malay States, and the five Unfederated Malay States) as one consolidated administrative entity from 1921 onward. The *Annual Report, Returns of Imports and Exports, British Malaya* provided fairly detailed information on trade, such as the quantity and value of imports/exports as well as the origin and destination of each item. Singapore was treated as a major entry/exit gate for British Malaya. Data recorded in the *Annual Report, the Foreign Trade of Malaya* partially provided trade figures on Singapore with the ROW (exclusive of trade with the Malay States). However, data on Singapore's trade with the Malay States became no longer available due to the termination of compiling trade data which treated Singapore as a separate entity.

### 2.5.2.2 *1928–39 and 1950–60 Series*

For the above time periods, the figures for merchandize trade of Singapore were available only from 1956 onward in the *Annual Report, Singapore's External Trade*. For the periods 1928–39 and 1950–55, no official data on total merchandize trade of Singapore were available. Given this scenario, estimates constructed by GW Huff for the missing years were used.

**Table 2.60:**  Singapore: Statistical Sources of Trade Statistics, 1900–39

| Year | Singapore as a Separate Entity (1) + (2) | | | | | | | | | | | | |
|---|---|---|---|---|---|---|---|---|---|---|---|---|---|
| | (1) Singapore's Trade with Rest of World (Exclusive of Trade with Malaya) | | | | | | | (2) Singapore's Trade with Malaya | | | | | |
| | 1899–1901 | 1902–07 | 1908–12 | 1900–19 | 1900–27 | 1921–37 | 1928–39 | 1899–1901 | 1902–19 | 1908–12 | 1900–19 | 1900–27 | 1928–39 |
| 1899 | | | | | | | | | | | | | |
| 1900 | STCOP UK | | | | | | | STCOP UK | | | | | |
| 1901 | | | | | | | | | | | | | |
| 1902 | | | | | | | | | | | | | |
| 1903 | | | | | | | | | | | | | |
| 1904 | | | | | | | | | | | | | |
| 1905 | | STCPP | | | | | | | | | | | |
| 1906 | | | | | | | | | | | | | |
| 1907 | | | | | | | | | | | | | |
| 1908 | | | | | | | | | | | | | |
| 1909 | | | | SSBB | | | | | | | SSBB | | |
| 1910 | | | STBCPP | | | | | | STCPP | STBCPP | | | |
| 1911 | | | | | | | | | | | | | |
| 1912 | | | | | | | | | | | | | |
| 1913 | | | | | ARTSS | | | | | | | ARTSS | |
| 1914 | | | | | | | | | | | | | |
| 1915 | | | | | | | | | | | | | |
| 1916 | | | | | | | | | | | | | |
| 1917 | | | | | | | | | | | | | |
| 1918 | | | | | | | | | | | | | |
| 1919 | | | | | | | | | | | | | |
| 1920 | | | | | | | | | | | | | |
| 1921 | | | | | | | | | | | | | |
| 1922 | | | | | | | | | | | | | |
| 1923 | | | | | | | | | | | | | |
| 1924 | | | | | | | | | | | | | |
| 1925 | | | | | | | | | | | | | |
| 1926 | | | | | | | | | | | | | |
| 1927 | | | | | | | | | | | | | |
| 1928 | | | | | | | | | | | | | |
| 1929 | | | | | | BM | | | | | | | Not Available |
| 1930 | | | | | | | | | | | | | |
| 1931 | | | | | | | | | | | | | |
| 1932 | | | | | | | | | | | | | |
| 1933 | | | | | | | | | | | | | |
| 1934 | | | | | | | FTM | | | | | | |
| 1935 | | | | | | | | | | | | | |
| 1936 | | | | | | | | | | | | | |
| 1937 | | | | | | | | | | | | | |
| 1938 | | | | | | | | | | | | | |
| 1939 | | | | | | | | | | | | | |

*Source*:

*Abbreviations*:

| | |
|---|---|
| STCOPUK | Statistical Tables Relating to the Colonial and Other Possessions of the United Kingdom. |
| STCPP | Statistical Tables Relating to the Colonial and Other Possessions and Protectorates. |
| STBCPP | Statistical Tables Relating to British Colonies, Possessions, and Protectorates. |
| SSBB | Blue Book, Straits Settlements. |
| ARTSS | Appendix to the Report on Trade, Straits Settlements. |
| BM | Returns of Foreign Imports and Exports, British Malaya. |
| FTM | Foreign Trade, Malaya. |

## 2.5.3 *Merchandize Trade and Its Adjustment*

By nature, a number of reasons can be listed for discrepancies in trade statistics, including, but not limited, to false invoicing of imports and exports, simple errors in counting and recording, time lags, and smuggling. In fact, sudden fluctuation of trade import and export value for several years seems quite impossible to explain when we aggregate the other components of GDP. Therefore, to check the reliability of trade figures, quantitative investigations were made by observing the net import value of selected major categories. Here, it is assumed that the quantity of net imports retained in the domestic market was fully consumed (exclusive of stock) by both resident and nonresident households at market prices. In this exercise, the net import value of manufactured textiles retained in Singapore was computed for the period 1900–27 using the *Appendix to the Report on Trade, Straits Settlements*. Subsequently, this data series was compared with private final consumption expenditure on clothing in the domestic market.

Generally, net import values on manufactured textiles were always higher than that of private final consumption expenditure on clothing. In addition, it was found that the total net import value of food and beverages was generally higher than that of private final consumption expenditure on these items saved for a couple of years. Using this observation, it was decided to adjust the import value of merchandize items accordingly. The resulting adjusted net exports in current prices for the periods 1900–39 and 1950–60 are presented in Table 2.61.

### 2.5.4 *Services Trade, 1900–39 and 1950–60*

#### 2.5.4.1 *Observation of Post-1960's Official Data*

In contrast to the merchandize trade which is based essentially on official records, no direct information is available on trade in services for the periods 1900–39 and 1950–60. Official figures on trade in services for Singapore can only be traced from the balance-of-payments accounts which became available beginning in 1960. The percentage contribution of services trade also changed over time. In 1960, the percentage contribution of service exports to

**Table 2.61:** Singapore: Merchandize Net Exports in Current Prices, 1900–39 and 1950–60

(Straits $ Millions)

| Merchandize Net Exports at Current Prices | | | | | |
|------|-------|------|--------|------|--------|
| 1900 | −28.3 | 1920 | −117.5 | 1950 | −247.7 |
| 1901 | −25.8 | 1921 | −77.7 | 1951 | −282.0 |
| 1902 | −26.9 | 1922 | −43.6 | 1952 | −550.4 |
| 1903 | −33.6 | 1923 | −63.2 | 1953 | −366.6 |
| 1904 | −34.7 | 1924 | −85.3 | 1954 | −339.3 |
| 1905 | −28.7 | 1925 | −87.3 | 1955 | −494.0 |
| 1906 | −24.4 | 1926 | −106.6 | 1956 | −500.4 |
| 1907 | −29.4 | 1927 | −137.6 | 1957 | −613.7 |
| 1908 | −25.1 | 1928 | −106.5 | 1958 | −599.7 |
| 1909 | −25.3 | 1929 | −64.9 | 1959 | −467.4 |
| 1910 | −24.4 | 1930 | −57.0 | 1960 | −600.6 |
| 1911 | −32.1 | 1931 | −64.2 | | |
| 1912 | −44.7 | 1932 | −57.8 | | |
| 1913 | −54.0 | 1933 | −16.7 | | |
| 1914 | −49.5 | 1934 | −36.8 | | |
| 1915 | −35.4 | 1935 | −28.8 | | |
| 1916 | −51.4 | 1936 | −44.0 | | |
| 1917 | −45.3 | 1937 | −45.1 | | |
| 1918 | −65.7 | 1938 | −74.0 | | |
| 1919 | −44.3 | 1939 | −61.9 | | |

total goods and services exported was 16.7 percent and its proportion increased to 24.5 percent by 1970. On the other hand, the percentage contribution of service imports (exclusive of freight and insurance) to total goods and services imported was negligible. In 1960, the figure was only 1.7 percent and its proportion increased slightly to 3.3 percent by 1970. The percentage contribution of merchandize trade has varied over time and its composition has been subject to change. Therefore, the conversion ratio method might not be favorable to identify the value of service trade for Singapore. Because of the deficiencies of available information on the service trade, two possible areas of estimates were deemed to be feasible, namely, (i) the trade of goods and services made in port and (ii) the nonresident consumption made in the domestic market. The following procedures were applied for their estimation for the periods 1900–39 and 1950–60.

### 2.5.4.2 *Exports of Bunker Coal and Petroleum to Foreign Ships*

It is assumed that a major portion of coal retained in Singapore (total imports less total exports of coal) was used for the supply of bunker coal to foreign ships. Trade information was derived from the *Statistical Tables Relating to the Colonial and Other Possessions of the United Kingdom* for the period 1900–01, *Statistical Tables Relating to the Colonial and Other Possessions and Protectorates* for the period 1902–07, and *Statistical Tables Relating to British Self-Governing Dominions, Crown Colonies, Possessions, and Protectorates* for the period 1908–12. No figures was available for the period 1913–21. Alternatively, the movement of revenue derived from wharfage, storage, and stevedorage was applied. Subsequently for the period 1922–39, *the Foreign Trade of Malaya* provided figures on bunker coal supplied to ships in Singapore and Penang, respectively. Unfortunately, a disaggregated figure for Singapore was not available. Therefore, the proportion for Singapore was estimated on the basis of the number of vessels that entered Singapore and Penang. After World War II, net import figures of coal were again not available. However, the outward movement of outward tonnage on coal ships from Singapore, which was provided for in the *Singapore Harbour Board Report (1963)*, was used as a proxy to estimate the figure on sales of coal.

Because of the technological innovation, some ships started to use petroleum. Singapore served as a supplier of petroleum. *The Foreign Trade of Malaya* provided data for the petroleum sold for ships entering Singapore for the period 1922–38. After World War II, no direct information was available. Alternatively, the movement of inward and outward tonnage on petroleum ships from Singapore, which was provided in the *Singapore Harbour Board Report (1963)*, was used as a proxy to estimate the figure on sales of petroleum to the ships.

### 2.5.4.3 *Sale of Water to Foreign Ships*

The *Annual Administration Report on Singapore Municipality* provided information on the sale of water to ships for the period 1918–39. The *Annual Administration Report of City Council, Singapore*, also provided specific revenue obtained from the sale of water to ships for the period 1950–59. No figures were available prior to 1918. Thus, an estimation procedure was applied to fill the gap for the period 1900–17. Because of the deficiencies of data, the movement of revenue derived from wharfage, storage, and stevedorage was applied to calculate water revenue during the said period.

### 2.5.4.4 *Revenue Collection Using on Services Provided by the Singapore Harbour Board*

The *Annual Report, Singapore Harbour Board* provided the revenue collected from services provided to foreign ships by docks and machine shops. Additionally, the *Singapore Harbour Board* collected revenue from services on wharfage, storage, and stevedorage. Statistical figures on the above-mentioned revenue were available for the periods 1910–36 and 1950–60. Prior to 1910, the movement of earnings from the sale of coal was applied as a proxy to estimate the revenue earned from wharfage, storage, and stevedorage.

### 2.5.4.5 *Revenue Collected by the Colony of Singapore*

The *Blue Book, Straits Settlements* provided figures on revenue from port and harbor dues in Singapore. The revenue collection was terminated by 1913.

### 2.5.4.6 *Private Final Consumption Expenditure by Nonresidents in the Domestic Market*

A large number of foreign ship passengers purchased goods and services in the territory of Singapore. Additionally, many diplomatic missions were located in Singapore. Most Western industrialized countries and Japan-stationed embassies or high commissions in Singapore, but the data on the actual number of people employed were not available. Most importantly, there was a massive number of immigrants, mainly from mainland China, who entered Singapore for a short period of time before departing to another part of British Malaya as well as other countries in the South East Asian region.

### 2.5.5 *External Trade of Goods and Services in 1914 Prices*

#### 2.5.5.1 *Construction of Import and Export Unit Value Indices, 1900–39 and 1950–60 (1914 = 100)*

In the economy of any country, there will always be a large variety of trading goods and services. From one period to the next, both the quantity and the price of these goods and services are subject to change due to the transition of market structure. Price indices of imports and exports attempt to isolate the effects of price changes on the value of these goods and services and measure the aggregate effect of these changes in a single number. For the construction of price indices, three different types of indicies can be constructed, namely, (i) the Laspeyres Price Index, (ii) Paasche Price Index, and (iii) Fisher Price Index. The most commonly used indices are the fixed weight indices where quantities are held constant for either some past period or the current period. The Laspeyres Index keeps the quantities ($Q$) fixed for some period in the past (0). In its simplest form, it is a ratio of what it costs today to purchase the same set of goods and services that were purchased in a specific previous period. The Paasche Price Index keeps the quantities fixed at their levels in the current period ($t$). In its simplest form, it is the ratio of what today's purchases cost compared to what they would have cost in the previous period.

Both these indices fail the time reversal, circularity, and factor reversal tests. There are classes of indices, called superlative indices, which pass the factor reversal test and have the property of being a closer approximation to the ideal consumer utility function than the Paasche or Laspeyres. These indices use weight information from two periods. The simplest of these indices is the Fisher Price Index, which is the geometric mean (square root) of the Laspeyres and Paasche index.

Fixed-base indices such as Laspeyres and Paasche have a common point of comparison to which all price measures are related. Chained indices use a current period as the point of reference and then link the index for this period to that of the previous period. When the comparison point is changed in fixed-base indices, the entire series must be recalculated using the aggregation weights of the new comparison point. External trade is usually covered through export and import price indices, which measure the change in prices of representative export and import transactions. When specific information from exporters and importers cannot be obtained, unit values (average prices for specific products) were used as a proxy for prices to compute indices. The use of chained Laspeyres price indices with annual weight updates is an appropriate measure of price change for National Accounting. Therefore, chained Laspeyres indices were used as an appropriate proxy for these estimates.[65] In the case of Singapore, the feature of import and export unit value indices was quite different from other countries. For example, in the case of neighboring country like Malaya, the export unit value indices could be constructed on the basis of a few major export commodities such as rubber and tin since the price movements of these few items can represent the pattern of total merchandize exports. On the other hand, the movement of import unit value indices of Malaya followed in tandem with that of the CPI, since Malaya mainly imported various consumer items because of the lack of a local food production and manufacturing base.

---

[65] Currently, Department of Statistics (Singapore) conducts compilation of export and import unit value indices using the Laspeyres formula (Department of Statistics, Singapore, 2008).

**Table 2.62:** Singapore: Import and Export Price Index for Goods and Services, 1960–95 (1990 = 100)

| | Exports of Goods and Services | Imports of Goods and Services | | Exports of Goods and Services | Imports of Goods and Services | | Exports of Goods and Services | Imports of Goods and Services | | Exports of Goods and Services | Imports of Goods and Services |
|---|---|---|---|---|---|---|---|---|---|---|---|
| 1960 | 52.5 | 53.4 | 1970 | 52.6 | 53.5 | 1980 | 113.1 | 116.1 | 1990 | 100.0 | 100.0 |
| 1961 | 52.5 | 53.4 | 1971 | 53.2 | 54.1 | 1981 | 116.9 | 119.7 | 1991 | 97.6 | 96.4 |
| 1962 | 52.5 | 53.4 | 1972 | 53.4 | 54.4 | 1982 | 116.6 | 117.2 | 1992 | 94.0 | 93.0 |
| 1963 | 52.4 | 53.3 | 1973 | 60.5 | 61.6 | 1983 | 111.0 | 111.2 | 1993 | 93.1 | 91.9 |
| 1964 | 53.3 | 54.2 | 1974 | 85.4 | 85.7 | 1984 | 104.9 | 106.2 | 1994 | 92.1 | 89.2 |
| 1965 | 53.0 | 53.9 | 1975 | 86.1 | 86.7 | 1985 | 103.3 | 105.1 | 1995 | 91.3 | 88.1 |
| 1966 | 50.7 | 51.6 | 1976 | 91.9 | 92.6 | 1986 | 89.5 | 91.1 | | | |
| 1967 | 51.0 | 51.9 | 1977 | 95.6 | 96.7 | 1987 | 96.3 | 98.7 | | | |
| 1968 | 48.2 | 49.0 | 1978 | 97.5 | 98.8 | 1988 | 97.9 | 99.4 | | | |
| 1969 | 50.2 | 51.1 | 1979 | 102.8 | 104.9 | 1989 | 99.3 | 99.9 | | | |

*Source*: Department of Statistics, Singapore (1996, 62–63).

Therefore, the level and movement of export and import unit value indices in Malaya varied differently throughout the period.

In the case of Singapore, however, the level and movement of export and import unit value indices was almost identical. As given in Table 2.62, the official import and export price indices of Singapore (1990 = 100) was fairly close to each other in the 1960s, 1970s, and 1980s, and subsequently even in the first half of the 1990s, the price indices did not deviate much. This phenomenon can be explained because Singapore served as an *entrepôt*. The bulk of the items imported into Singapore were re-exported to other parts of world. Using this observation, it would be safe to assume that this situation prevailed retrospectively during the periods 1900–39 and 1950–60. The nature of statistical data that was available necessitated the construction of import/export price indices for three different periods, namely, 1900–27, 1928–39, and 1950–60.

### 2.5.5.1.1 1900–27 Series

For this period, the *Appendix to the Report on the Trade, Straits Settlements* provided trade statistics of Singapore as an entity. Fortunately, this report provided value of merchandize imports and exports by class of commodities, namely, [A] live animals, food, drinks, and narcotics; [B] raw materials; and

[C] manufactured and partly manufactured articles. In the case of Class [B] and Class [C], further breakdown was made for [a] textile goods, [b] metal goods, and [c] others (See Table 2.63), and the price indices which represent each component were chosen and used for each class of commodities. Weights of each major class of commodities for imports/exports varied over time. In particular, weights on food, drinks, and narcotics have frequently changed. As presented in Table 2.64, import unit value indices made use of seven time intervals, namely, 1900–08, 1908–14, 1914–16, 1916–19, 1919–20, 1920–22, and 1922–27. Weights were chosen for import unit value indices for the years 1904, 1914, 1916, 1918, 1919, 1921, and 1923. In the case of export unit value indices, eight time intervals were determined, namely, 1900–08, 1908–14, 1914–16, 1916–19, 1919–20, 1920–22, 1922–25, and 1925–27. The weights chosen were for the years 1904, 1914, 1916, 1918, 1919, 1921, 1924, and 1927 (See Table 2.65). The various interval series were then chained at their overlapping years to generate a continuous import and export unit value index series with 1914 as the reference year by applying the conversion factors.

### 2.5.5.1.2  1928–39 and 1950–60 Series

The termination of the collection of trade figures whereby Singapore was treated as a separate entity in 1927 meant that the previous time series database were no longer available beginning in 1928. WG Huff's time series database on major export commodities of Singapore was instead used for the periods 1928–39 and 1950–60 (See Table 2.66).

Given that the information on import value and volume was rather weak, it was assumed that the export unit value indices would be a good proxy for the import unit value index, an assumption not altogether unreasonable as seen from the data provided in Table 2.62 for the years 1960–95. Using on the information on value and volume of exports of tin, rubber, petroleum, canned pineapples, and palm oil, the unit value of each

**Table 2.63:** Singapore: Price Indices by Class of Commodities, 1900–27 (1914 = 100)

| | A — Live Animals, Food, Drinks, and Narcotics | B — Raw Materials | | | C — Manufactured and Partly Manufactured Articles | | | |
| --- | --- | --- | --- | --- | --- | --- | --- | --- |
| | Total | [a] Textiles | [b] Metal | [c] Other | [a] Textiles | [b] Metal | [c] Other | |
| | Food and Beverage Indices | Clothing Indices | Tin Price Indices | Rubber Price Indices* | Clothing Indices | Tin Price Indices | UK M&E Indices | |
| 1900 | 81.97 | 78.94 | 88.74 | 100.07 | 78.94 | 88.74 | 101.96 | 1900 |
| 1901 | 82.91 | 84.45 | 78.81 | 120.10 | 84.45 | 78.81 | 96.81 | 1901 |
| 1902 | 85.51 | 86.79 | 80.13 | 141.52 | 86.79 | 80.13 | 92.72 | 1902 |
| 1903 | 85.51 | 92.79 | 84.11 | 126.54 | 92.79 | 84.11 | 90.72 | 1903 |
| 1904 | 87.28 | 90.19 | 84.11 | 97.25 | 90.19 | 84.11 | 90.72 | 1904 |
| 1905 | 90.18 | 87.98 | 94.70 | 92.44 | 87.98 | 94.70 | 90.72 | 1905 |
| 1906 | 87.80 | 84.42 | 119.87 | 101.20 | 84.42 | 119.87 | 90.72 | 1906 |
| 1907 | 85.69 | 82.99 | 114.57 | 81.52 | 82.99 | 114.57 | 93.77 | 1907 |
| 1908 | 87.02 | 86.31 | 88.08 | 80.32 | 86.31 | 88.08 | 96.81 | 1908 |
| 1909 | 85.83 | 76.42 | 89.40 | 99.55 | 76.42 | 89.40 | 93.77 | 1909 |
| 1910 | 87.09 | 84.38 | 102.65 | 121.51 | 84.38 | 102.65 | 93.77 | 1910 |
| 1911 | 102.81 | 84.03 | 127.15 | 104.44 | 84.03 | 127.15 | 96.81 | 1911 |
| 1912 | 105.84 | 83.07 | 138.41 | 106.75 | 83.07 | 138.41 | 100.91 | 1912 |
| 1913 | 105.09 | 99.53 | 133.77 | 97.26 | 99.53 | 133.77 | 105.00 | 1913 |
| 1914 | 100.00 | 100.00 | 100.00 | 100.00 | 100.00 | 100.00 | 100.00 | 1914 |
| 1915 | 104.73 | 138.32 | 108.61 | 109.11 | 138.32 | 108.61 | 127.47 | 1915 |
| 1916 | 106.47 | 161.28 | 120.53 | 124.54 | 161.28 | 120.53 | 151.94 | 1916 |
| 1917 | 115.77 | 144.02 | 157.62 | 122.72 | 144.02 | 157.62 | 195.72 | 1917 |
| 1918 | 139.48 | 189.80 | 218.54 | 97.27 | 189.80 | 218.54 | 215.15 | 1918 |
| 1919 | 183.87 | 229.60 | 170.86 | 90.02 | 229.60 | 170.86 | 251.79 | 1919 |
| 1920 | 243.98 | 291.60 | 196.03 | 80.92 | 291.60 | 196.03 | 253.37 | 1920 |
| 1921 | 167.96 | 237.20 | 109.27 | 34.76 | 237.20 | 109.27 | 178.82 | 1921 |
| 1922 | 144.20 | 182.80 | 105.96 | 33.85 | 182.80 | 105.96 | 135.31 | 1922 |
| 1923 | 144.28 | 163.60 | 133.77 | 55.70 | 163.60 | 133.77 | 128.42 | 1923 |
| 1924 | 144.61 | 157.10 | 164.90 | 50.48 | 157.10 | 164.90 | 130.83 | 1924 |
| 1925 | 149.58 | 158.10 | 172.85 | 127.51 | 158.10 | 172.85 | 130.41 | 1925 |
| 1926 | 158.49 | 157.50 | 192.72 | 86.38 | 157.50 | 192.72 | 127.79 | 1926 |
| 1927 | 154.85 | 155.40 | 191.39 | 67.06 | 155.40 | 191.39 | 130.10 | 1927 |

*Notes*: The following price indices were applied for the construction of weighted import and export unit value indices.

**[A] Live animals, food, drinks, and narcotics**: Weighted food and beverage price indices which are constructed in the CPI by major object of consumption for the private final consumption expenditure.

**[B] Raw materials:**

[1] Textiles: Weighted clothing price indices which are constructed in the CPI by major object of consumption for the private final consumption expenditure.

[2] Metal: Tin export price indices.

[3] Other: Rubber price indices.

**[C] Manufactured and Partly Manufactured Articles**:

[1] Textiles: Weighted clothing price indices.

[2] Metal: Tin price indices.

[3] Other: UK price indices of M&E.

*In the beginning of the twentieth century, rubber was not the major commodity item. Its importance emerged only in 1908 and drastic expansion was experienced only after 1910. Alternatively, rubber and other staple commodities weighted indices were applied for the period 1900–14.

*Source*:

**Table 2.64:** Singapore: Import Unit Value Indices, 1900–27 (1914 = 100)

| | | | | Weights | Base Year |
|---|---|---|---|---|---|
| **1900–1908** | A — Live Animals, Food, Drinks, and Narcotics | Total | Food and Beverage Indices | 0.4189 | 1904 |
| | B — Raw Materials | [a] Textiles | Clothing indices | 0.0096 | |
| | | [b] Metal | Tin price indices | 0.1720 | |
| | | [c] Other | Rubber and staple commodities weighted price indices | 0.2040 | |
| | C — Manufactured and Partly Manufactured Articles | [a] Textiles | Clothing indices | 0.0956 | |
| | | [b] Metal | Tin price indices | 0.0358 | |
| | | [c] Other | UK M&E indices | 0.0640 | |
| **1908–1914** | A — Live Animals, Food, Drinks, and Narcotics | Total | Food and Beverage Indices | 0.4585 | 1914 |
| | B — Raw Materials | [a] Textiles | Clothing indices | 0.0029 | |
| | | [b] Metal | Tin price indices | 0.1463 | |
| | | [c] Other | Rubber and other commodities weighted price indices | 0.2362 | |
| | C — Manufactured and Partly Manufactured Articles | [a] Textiles | Clothing indices | 0.0689 | |
| | | [b] Metal | Tin price indices | 0.0360 | |
| | | [c] Other | UK M&E indices | 0.0512 | |
| **1914–1916** | A — Live Animals, Food, Drinks, and Narcotics | Total | Food and Beverage Indices | 0.3555 | 1916 |
| | B — Raw Materials | [a] Textiles | Clothing indices | 0.0029 | |
| | | [b] Metal | Tin price indices | 0.1161 | |
| | | [c] Other | Rubber price indices | 0.3564 | |
| | C — Manufactured and Partly Manufactured Articles | [a] Textiles | Clothing indices | 0.0761 | |
| | | [b] Metal | Tin price indices | 0.0387 | |
| | | [c] Other | UK M&E indices | 0.0543 | |
| **1916–1919** | A — Live Animals, Food, Drinks, and Narcotics | Total | Food and Beverage indices | 0.3638 | 1918 |
| | B — Raw Materials | [a] Textiles | Clothing indices | 0.0013 | |
| | | [b] Metal | Tin price indices | 0.1206 | |
| | | [c] Other | Rubber price indices | 0.3516 | |
| | C — Manufactured and Partly Manufactured Articles | [a] Textiles | Clothing indices | 0.0797 | |
| | | [b] Metal | Tin price indices | 0.0257 | |
| | | [c] Other | UK M&E indices | 0.0574 | |
| **1919–1920** | A — Live Animals, Food, Drinks, and Narcotics | Total | Food and beverage Indices | 0.3167 | 1919 |
| | B — Raw Materials | [a] Textiles | Clothing indices | 0.0021 | |
| | | [b] Metal | Tin price indices | 0.0806 | |
| | | [c] Other | Rubber price indices | 0.4200 | |
| | C — Manufactured and Partly Manufactured Articles | [a] Textiles | Clothing indices | 0.0979 | |
| | | [b] Metal | Tin price indices | 0.0358 | |
| | | [c] Other | UK M&E indices | 0.0469 | |
| **1920–1922** | A — Live Animals, Food, Drinks, and Narcotics | Total | Food and Beverage Indices | 0.3950 | 1921 |
| | B — Raw Materials | [a] Textiles | Clothing indices | 0.0023 | |
| | | [b] Metal | Tin price indices | 0.0986 | |
| | | [c] Other | Rubber price indices | 0.2705 | |
| | C — Manufactured and Partly Manufactured Articles | [a] Textiles | Clothing indices | 0.1147 | |
| | | [b] Metal | Tin price indices | 0.0618 | |
| | | [c] Other | UK M&E indices | 0.0571 | |
| **1922–1927** | A — Live Animals, Food, Drinks, and Narcotics | Total | Food and Beverage Indices | 0.3187 | 1923 |
| | B — Raw Materials | [a] Textiles | Clothing indices | 0.0025 | |
| | | [b] Metal | Tin price indices | 0.0768 | |
| | | [c] Other | Rubber price indices | 0.4175 | |
| | C — Manufactured and Partly Manufactured Articles | [a] Textiles | Clothing indices | 0.0872 | |
| | | [b] Metal | Tin price indices | 0.0425 | |
| | | [c] Other | UK M&E indices | 0.0547 | |

**Table 2.65:** Singapore: Export Unit Value Indices, 1900–27 (1914 = 100)

| | | | | Weights | Base Year |
|---|---|---|---|---|---|
| 1900–1908 | A — Live Animals, Food, Drinks, and Narcotics | Total | Food and Beverage Indices | 0.4161 | 1904 |
| | B — Raw Materials | [a] Textiles | Clothing indices | 0.0104 | |
| | | [b] Metal | Tin price indices | 0.2096 | |
| | | [c] Other | Rubber and staple commodities weighted price indices | 0.2030 | |
| | C — Manufactured and Partly Manufactured Articles | [a] Textiles | Clothing indices | 0.1007 | |
| | | [b] Metal | Tin price indices | 0.0164 | |
| | | [c] Other | UK M&E indices | 0.0438 | |
| 1908–1914 | A — Live Animals, Food, Drinks, and Narcotics | Total | Food and Beverage Indices | 0.4224 | 1914 |
| | B — Raw Materials | [a] Textiles | Clothing indices | 0.0030 | |
| | | [b] Metal | Tin price indices | 0.1812 | |
| | | [c] Other | Rubber and staple commodities weighted price indices | 0.2659 | |
| | C — Manufactured and Partly Manufactured Articles | [a] Textiles | Clothing indices | 0.0657 | |
| | | [b] Metal | Tin price indices | 0.0228 | |
| | | [c] Other | UK M&E indices | 0.0389 | |
| 1914–1916 | A — Live Animals, Food, Drinks, and Narcotics | Total | Food and Beverage Indices | 0.3474 | 1916 |
| | B — Raw Materials | [a] Textiles | Clothing indices | 0.0030 | |
| | | [b] Metal | Tin price indices | 0.1396 | |
| | | [c] Other | Rubber price indices | 0.3771 | |
| | C — Manufactured and Partly Manufactured Articles | [a] Textiles | Clothing indices | 0.0654 | |
| | | [b] Metal | Tin price indices | 0.0270 | |
| | | [c] OtherU | UK M&E indices | 0.0406 | |
| 1916–1919 | A — Live Animals, Food, Drinks, and Narcotics | Total | Food and Beverage Indices | 0.3513 | 1918 |
| | B — Raw Materials | [a] Textiles | Clothing indices | 0.0015 | |
| | | [b] Metal | Tin price indices | 0.1533 | |
| | | [c] Other | Rubber price indices | 0.3569 | |
| | C — Manufactured and Partly Manufactured Articles | [a] Textiles | Clothing indices | 0.0703 | |
| | | [b] Metal | Tin price indices | 0.0196 | |
| | | [c] Other | UK M&E indices | 0.0470 | |
| 1919–1920 | A — Live Animals, Food, Drinks, and Narcotics | Total | Food and Beverage Indices | 0.2968 | 1919 |
| | B — Raw Materials | [a] Textiles | Clothing indices | 0.0021 | |
| | | [b] Metal | Tin price indices | 0.1022 | |
| | | [c] Other | Rubber price indices | 0.4619 | |
| | C — Manufactured and Partly Manufactured Articles | [a] Textiles | Clothing indices | 0.0826 | |
| | | [b] Metal | Tin price indices | 0.0164 | |
| | | [c] Other | UK M&E indices | 0.0381 | |
| 1920–1922 | A — Live Animals, Food, Drinks, and Narcotics | Total | Food and Beverage Indices | 0.4033 | 1921 |
| | B — Raw Materials | [a] Textiles | Clothing indices | 0.0021 | |
| | | [b] Metal | Tin price indices | 0.1008 | |
| | | [c] Other | Rubber price indices | 0.3214 | |
| | C — Manufactured and Partly Manufactured Articles | [a] Textiles | Clothing indices | 0.0889 | |
| | | [b] Metal | Tin price indices | 0.0322 | |
| | | [c] Other | UK M&E indices | 0.0513 | |
| 1922–1925 | A — Live Animals, Food, Drinks, and Narcotics | Total | Food and Beverage Indices | 0.2797 | 1924 |
| | B — Raw Materials | [a] Textiles | Clothing indices | 0.0008 | |
| | | [b] Metal | Tin price indices | 0.0017 | |
| | | [c] Other | Rubber price indices | 0.3711 | |
| | C — Manufactured and Partly Manufactured Articles | [a] Textiles | Clothing indices | 0.0709 | |
| | | [b] Metal | Tin price indices | 0.1620 | |
| | | [c] Other | UK M&E indices | 0.1137 | |
| 1925–1927 | A — Live Animals, Food, Drinks, and Narcotics | TotalF | Food and Beverage Indices | 0.2311 | 1927 |
| | B — Raw Materials | [a] Textiles | Clothing indices | 0.0001 | |
| | | [b] Metal | Tin price indices | 0.0015 | |
| | | [c] Other | Rubber price indices | 0.4001 | |
| | C — Manufactured and Partly Manufactured Articles | [a] Textiles | Clothing indices | 0.0643 | |
| | | [b] Metal | Tin price indices | 0.1468 | |
| | | [c] Other | UK M&E indices | 0.1137 | |

**Table 2.66:** Singapore: Export Value and Quantity by Major Commodity Goods, 1927–39 and 1949–60 (Based on figures by WG Huff)

| | Tin | | | Rubber | | | Petroleum | | | Canned Pineapples | | | Palm Oil | | | |
|---|---|---|---|---|---|---|---|---|---|---|---|---|---|---|---|---|
| | Value ($,000) | Volume (tons) | Unit Value | Value ($,000) | Volume (tons) | Unit Value | Value ($,000) | Volume (tons) | Unit Value | Value ($,000) | Volume (tons) | Unit Value | Value ($,000) | Volume (tons) | Unit Value | |
| 1927 | 91,929 | 37,634 | 2.44 | 271,354 | 200,307 | 1.35 | 73,659 | 466,257 | 0.16 | 7,494 | 36,259 | 0.21 | | | | 1927 |
| 1928 | 82,565 | 42,756 | 1.93 | 162,407 | 201,263 | 0.81 | **61,577** | **417,443** | **0.15** | 7,761 | 42,739 | 0.18 | | | | 1928 |
| 1929 | 76,560 | 43,352 | 1.77 | 183,592 | 253,875 | 0.72 | 49,494 | 368,629 | 0.13 | 8,735 | 55,352 | 0.16 | | | | 1929 |
| 1930 | 47,257 | 37,468 | 1.26 | 100,461 | 233,799 | 0.43 | **57,298** | **405,616** | **0.14** | 7,297 | 53,515 | 0.14 | | | | 1930 |
| 1931 | 29,800 | 29,784 | 1.00 | 49,937 | 220,545 | 0.23 | 65,101 | 442,603 | 0.15 | 6,545 | 54,620 | 0.12 | | | | 1931 |
| 1932 | 24,565 | 20,840 | 1.18 | 28,536 | 184,296 | 0.15 | 58,145 | 420,106 | 0.14 | 7,002 | 58,139 | 0.12 | | | | 1932 |
| 1933 | 51,208 | 30,913 | 1.66 | 45,451 | 230,352 | 0.20 | 42,285 | 394,082 | 0.11 | 5,382 | 51,769 | 0.10 | 1,031 | 9,202 | 0.11 | 1933 |
| 1934 | 45,333 | 23,550 | 1.92 | 124,045 | 315,990 | 0.39 | 44,649 | 453,958 | 0.10 | 5,971 | 57,166 | 0.10 | 1,034 | 12,603 | 0.08 | 1934 |
| 1935 | 52,725 | 27,999 | 1.88 | 112,379 | 258,579 | 0.43 | 50,911 | 511,457 | 0.10 | 6,644 | 60,481 | 0.11 | 2,528 | 18,045 | 0.14 | 1935 |
| 1936 | 63,457 | 37,511 | 1.69 | 131,428 | 218,697 | 0.60 | 42,416 | 480,939 | 0.09 | 7,099 | 64,243 | 0.11 | 3,066 | 21,478 | 0.14 | 1936 |
| 1937 | 77,692 | 38,150 | 2.04 | 206,172 | 285,933 | 0.72 | 54,047 | 627,518 | 0.09 | 6,988 | 65,197 | 0.11 | 4,834 | 28,344 | 0.17 | 1937 |
| 1938 | 39,082 | 24,784 | 1.58 | 120,511 | 225,751 | 0.53 | 54,924 | 742,949 | 0.07 | 6,372 | 64,382 | 0.10 | 4,063 | 33,111 | 0.12 | 1938 |
| 1939 | 69,527 | 36,044 | 1.93 | 178,765 | 259,238 | 0.69 | 52,561 | 681,242 | 0.08 | 8,869 | 74,050 | 0.12 | 3,472 | 36,061 | 0.10 | 1939 |
| 1949 | 120,591 | 23,935 | 5.04 | 381,691 | 484,848 | 0.79 | 121,621 | 1,522,957 | 0.08 | 5,551 | 7,115 | 0.78 | 24,407 | 35,004 | 0.70 | 1949 |
| 1950 | 207,190 | 35,855 | 5.78 | 1,405,274 | 655,025 | 2.15 | 160,677 | 1,906,991 | 0.08 | 11,049 | 13,173 | 0.84 | 22,243 | 34,475 | 0.65 | 1950 |
| 1951 | 261,457 | 29,399 | 8.89 | 2,518,844 | 750,221 | 3.36 | 201,701 | 1,880,855 | 0.11 | 15,714 | 15,761 | 1.00 | 26,434 | 31,192 | 0.85 | 1951 |
| 1952 | 217,429 | 27,013 | 8.05 | 915,895 | 555,343 | 1.65 | 307,796 | 2,358,420 | 0.13 | 11,625 | 10,913 | 1.07 | 30,302 | 31,865 | 0.95 | 1952 |
| 1953 | 172,292 | 26,853 | 6.42 | 750,764 | 506,480 | 1.48 | 341,584 | 2,613,622 | 0.13 | 17,797 | 16,264 | 1.09 | 17,710 | 26,174 | 0.68 | 1953 |
| 1954 | 195,912 | 33,263 | 5.89 | 785,088 | 555,297 | 1.41 | 350,556 | 2,732,430 | 0.13 | 23,461 | 19,890 | 1.18 | 15,822 | 23,645 | 0.67 | 1954 |
| 1955 | 202,192 | 33,322 | 6.07 | 1,399,635 | 604,152 | 2.32 | 371,097 | 3,115,858 | 0.12 | 27,172 | 25,898 | 1.05 | 17,810 | 27,153 | 0.66 | 1955 |
| 1956 | 138,657 | 21,330 | 6.50 | 1,216,551 | 596,600 | 2.04 | 446,236 | 2,936,508 | 0.15 | 29,048 | 28,333 | 1.03 | 20,737 | 28,996 | 0.72 | 1956 |
| 1957 | 133,562 | 20,843 | 6.41 | 1,171,094 | 617,198 | 1.90 | 444,964 | 3,005,649 | 0.15 | 31,229 | 34,837 | 0.90 | 16,516 | 22,094 | 0.75 | 1957 |
| 1958 | 48,337 | 7,884 | 6.13 | 1,045,556 | 650,204 | 1.61 | 370,308 | 2,459,169 | 0.15 | 31,145 | 38,754 | 0.80 | 17,730 | 27,867 | 0.64 | 1958 |
| 1959 | 4,448 | 677 | 6.57 | 1,533,074 | 722,580 | 2.12 | 371,657 | 2,494,965 | 0.15 | 26,586 | 36,599 | 0.73 | 19,078 | 26,026 | 0.73 | 1959 |
| 1960 | 5,161 | 775 | 6.66 | 1,426,513 | 598,378 | 2.38 | 379,209 | 2,687,573 | 0.14 | 25,243 | 35,937 | 0.70 | 23,811 | 33,767 | 0.71 | 1960 |

*Source:* Huff (1994, 372–385).

commodity was derived. During the period 1927–60 (excluding the years 1940–49), the criteria for the selection of intervals and their base years included the element of relative stability of the export share of commodities. Eleven intervals were set, namely, 1927–28, 1928–29, 1929–30, 1930–31, 1931–32, 1932–34, 1934–39, 1939–51, 1951–53, 1953–58, and 1958–60, and the commodity weights for the respective base years 1928, 1929, 1930, 1931, 1932, 1934, 1936, 1950, 1953, 1957, and 1959 were identified. These staple commodities–based export unit value indices, however, accounted only for 30–50 percent of total merchandize exports of Singapore. Thus, it was necessary to consider other trade items such as food, beverages and tobacco, clothing, and transport. Unfortunately, it was impossible to trace the specific unit value for many items. As an alternative, the CPI was introduced. Weights on CPI were obtained as residuals of major commodity exports to total merchandize exports (See Table 2.67).

By linking the two separate series of import and export unit value indices, a separate set of import and export unit value indices (1914 = 100) for the periods 1900–39 and 1950–60 was

**Table 2.67:** Singapore: Export Unit Value Index, 1927–39 and 1950–60 (1914 = 100)

| | Items | Weights of Export Items | Weights of Export Commodity Items and CPI | Base Year |
|---|---|---|---|---|
| 1927–28 | Tin | 0.2627 | | 1928 |
| | Rubber | 0.5167 | 0.4692 | |
| | Canned pineapples | 0.0247 | | |
| | Petroleum | 0.1959 | | |
| | CPI | | 0.5308 | |
| 1928–29 | Tin | 0.2405 | | 1929 |
| | Rubber | 0.5766 | 0.4611 | |
| | Canned pineapples | 0.0274 | | |
| | Petroleum | 0.1555 | | |
| | CPI | | 0.5389 | |
| 1929–30 | Tin | 0.2226 | | 1930 |
| | Rubber | 0.4732 | 0.4020 | |
| | Canned pineapples | 0.0344 | | |
| | Petroleum | 0.2699 | | |
| | CPI | | 0.5980 | |
| 1930–31 | Tin | 0.1969 | | 1931 |
| | Rubber | 0.3299 | 0.4619 | |
| | Canned pineapples | 0.0432 | | |
| | Petroleum | 0.4300 | | |
| | CPI | | 0.5381 | |
| 1931–32 | Tin | 0.2077 | | 1932 |
| | Rubber | 0.2413 | 0.4356 | |
| | Canned pineapples | 0.0592 | | |
| | Petroleum | 0.4917 | | |
| | CPI | | 0.5644 | |
| 1932–34 | Tin | 0.2118 | | 1934 |
| | Rubber | 0.5796 | 0.5428 | |
| | Petroleum | 0.2086 | | |
| | CPI | | 0.4572 | |
| 1934–39 | Tin | 0.2564 | | 1936 |
| | Rubber | 0.5311 | | |
| | Petroleum | 0.1714 | 0.5588 | |
| | Canned pineapples | 0.0287 | | |
| | Palm oil | 0.0124 | | |
| | CPI | | 0.4412 | |
| 1939, 1949–51 | Tin | 0.1147 | | 1950 |
| | Rubber | 0.7779 | | |
| | Petroleum | 0.0889 | 0.6023 | |
| | Canned pineapples | 0.0061 | | |
| | Palm oil | 0.0123 | | |
| | CPI | | 0.3977 | |
| 1951–53 | Tin | 0.1713 | | 1953 |
| | Rubber | 0.8225 | | |
| | Petroleum | 0.2624 | 0.4899 | |
| | Canned pineapples | 0.0133 | | |
| | Palm oil | 0.0191 | | |
| | CPI | | 0.5101 | |
| 1953–1958 | Tin | 0.0743 | | 1957 |
| | Rubber | 0.6516 | | |
| | Petroleum | 0.2476 | 0.5168 | |
| | Canned pineapples | 0.0174 | | |
| | Palm oil | 0.0092 | | |
| | CPI | | 0.4832 | |
| 1958–60 | Tin | 0.0023 | | 1959 |
| | Rubber | 0.7842 | | |
| | Petroleum | 0.1901 | 0.5682 | |
| | Canned pineapples | 0.0136 | | |
| | Palm oil | 0.0098 | | |
| | CPI | | 0.4318 | |

obtained. As seen from Table 2.68 and Fig. 2.1, both import and export unit value indices for the periods 1900–39 and 1950–60 (1914 = 100) moved very much in tandem, although the levels differed slightly.

**Table 2.68:** Singapore: Import Unit Value Indices and Export Unit Value Indices, 1900–39 and 1950–60 (1914 = 100)

| | Import Unit Value Indices | Export Unit Value Indices | | Import Unit Value Indices | Export Unit Value Indices | | Import Unit Value Indices | Export Unit Value Indices | | Import Unit Value Indices | Export Unit Value Indices | | Import Unit Value Indices | Export Unit Value Indices |
|---|---|---|---|---|---|---|---|---|---|---|---|---|---|---|
| 1900 | 87.68 | 87.24 | 1910 | 98.21 | 99.49 | 1920 | 189.99 | 177.60 | 1930 | 78.26 | 76.90 | 1950 | 235.24 | 231.13 |
| 1901 | 90.33 | 89.82 | 1911 | 105.98 | 106.68 | 1921 | 117.89 | 116.09 | 1931 | 64.84 | 63.70 | 1951 | 332.36 | 326.55 |
| 1902 | 96.03 | 95.60 | 1912 | 110.11 | 110.97 | 1922 | 100.81 | 99.74 | 1932 | 55.87 | 54.89 | 1952 | 273.39 | 263.69 |
| 1903 | 94.31 | 94.05 | 1913 | 108.07 | 108.47 | 1923 | 113.59 | 110.37 | 1933 | 53.14 | 55.47 | 1953 | 232.56 | 228.50 |
| 1904 | 88.83 | 88.58 | 1914 | 100.00 | 100.00 | 1924 | 119.72 | 113.46 | 1934 | 68.67 | 67.47 | 1954 | 226.04 | 222.09 |
| 1905 | 91.02 | 90.95 | 1915 | 110.78 | 110.24 | 1925 | 149.97 | 145.08 | 1935 | 69.73 | 68.51 | 1955 | 266.17 | 261.52 |
| 1906 | 96.64 | 96.99 | 1916 | 121.89 | 121.22 | 1926 | 137.37 | 132.91 | 1936 | 72.66 | 71.39 | 1956 | 258.56 | 254.04 |
| 1907 | 90.71 | 90.93 | 1917 | 131.16 | 131.05 | 1927 | 126.37 | 124.16 | 1937 | 80.37 | 78.97 | 1957 | 252.80 | 248.38 |
| 1908 | 86.08 | 85.79 | 1918 | 144.57 | 145.01 | 1928 | 103.98 | 102.16 | 1938 | 69.01 | 67.80 | 1958 | 243.88 | 239.61 |
| 1909 | 89.45 | 89.87 | 1919 | 150.70 | 154.34 | 1929 | 98.40 | 96.68 | 1939 | 76.98 | 75.63 | 1959 | 267.22 | 262.55 |
| | | | | | | | | | | | | 1960 | 273.29 | 268.51 |

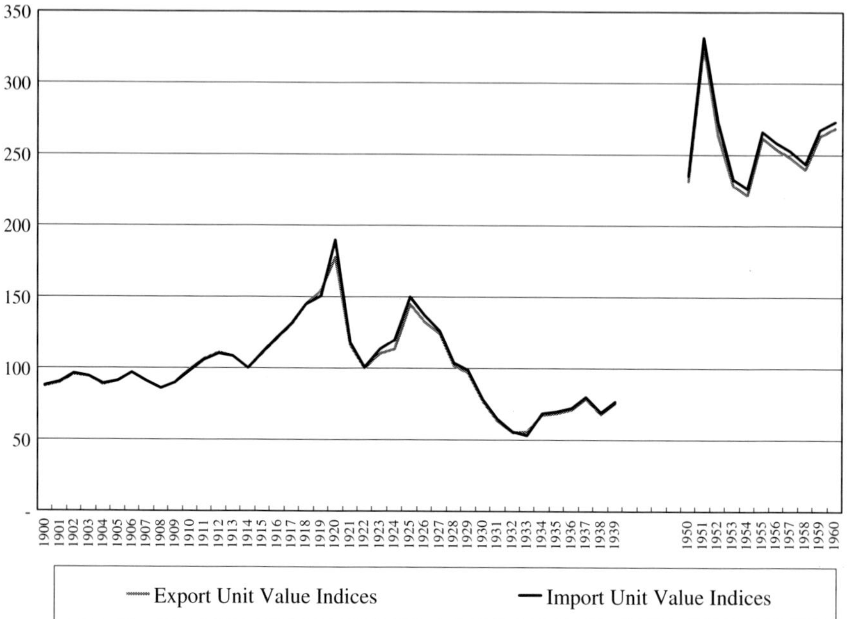


**Fig. 2.1:** Singapore: Import Unit Value Indices and Export Unit Value Indices, 1900–39 and 1950–60 (1914 = 100)

## 2.5.5.2 *Deflators for Port Services*

There were no price indices which could represent the price movement of port services, such as bunkering and water supply services, revenue from the services on port wharfage, storage and stevedorage, nor port harbor dues. Hence, as an alternative, the weighted price indices on fuel and communication of the United Kingdom were applied (See Table 2.69).

Table 2.70 provides the net exports of goods and services at current and constant prices for 1900–39 and 1950–60.

**Table 2.69:** Weighted Price Indices on Fuel and Communication of the United Kingdom, 1900–39 and 1950–60 (1914 = 100)

| 1900–39 and 1950–60 (1914 = 100) | | | | | | | | | |
|---|---|---|---|---|---|---|---|---|---|
| 1900 | 97.86 | 1910 | 93.96 | 1920 | 220.26 | 1930 | 167.88 | 1950 | 281.55 |
| 1901 | 95.60 | 1911 | 94.67 | 1921 | 230.35 | 1931 | 166.69 | 1951 | 302.80 |
| 1902 | 93.28 | 1912 | 103.97 | 1922 | 195.97 | 1932 | 164.75 | 1952 | 329.27 |
| 1903 | 92.99 | 1913 | 100.54 | 1923 | 180.89 | 1933 | 162.24 | 1953 | 343.68 |
| 1904 | 92.83 | 1914 | 100.00 | 1924 | 181.91 | 1934 | 160.69 | 1954 | 355.37 |
| 1905 | 92.51 | 1915 | 105.51 | 1925 | 179.01 | 1935 | 158.72 | 1955 | 372.86 |
| 1906 | 94.36 | 1916 | 119.94 | 1926 | 183.75 | 1936 | 160.82 | 1956 | 401.81 |
| 1907 | 98.48 | 1917 | 139.44 | 1927 | 174.33 | 1937 | 163.65 | 1957 | 422.72 |
| 1908 | 96.14 | 1918 | 165.28 | 1928 | 168.33 | 1938 | 165.03 | 1958 | 438.94 |
| 1909 | 94.93 | 1919 | 194.08 | 1929 | 169.10 | 1939 | 172.73 | 1959 | 442.61 |
| | | | | | | | | 1960 | 447.48 |

*Source*: Based on Feinstein (1972, T134–135).

**Table 2.70:** Singapore: Net Exports of Goods and Services at Current and Constant Prices, 1900–39 and 1950–60

(Straits $ Millions)

| | Current Prices | | | 1914 Prices |
|---|---|---|---|---|
| | Net Exports (Merchandize) | Net Exports (Services) | Net Exports of Goods and Services | Net Exports of Goods and Services |
| | [1] | [2] | [3] = [1] + [2] | [4] |
| 1900 | -28.3 | 23.1 | -5.2 | -6.1 |
| 1901 | -25.8 | 22.7 | -3.0 | -2.2 |
| 1902 | -26.9 | 20.9 | -6.0 | -4.0 |
| 1903 | -33.6 | 20.6 | -13.0 | -12.2 |
| 1904 | -34.7 | 21.1 | -13.6 | -15.1 |
| 1905 | -28.7 | 20.8 | -7.9 | -8.5 |
| 1906 | -24.4 | 20.6 | -3.8 | -3.4 |
| 1907 | -29.4 | 21.0 | -8.4 | -10.4 |
| 1908 | -25.1 | 22.7 | -2.4 | -4.0 |
| 1909 | -25.3 | 21.5 | -3.7 | -5.5 |
| 1910 | -24.4 | 22.5 | -1.9 | -3.1 |
| 1911 | -32.1 | 23.2 | -8.9 | -7.5 |
| 1912 | -44.7 | 24.5 | -20.2 | -18.2 |
| 1913 | -54.0 | 25.9 | -28.1 | -25.1 |
| 1914 | -49.5 | 27.2 | -22.4 | -22.4 |
| 1915 | -35.4 | 26.0 | -9.4 | -6.1 |
| 1916 | -51.4 | 27.6 | -23.8 | -16.5 |
| 1917 | -45.3 | 33.2 | -12.1 | -7.9 |
| 1918 | -65.7 | 39.0 | -26.7 | -20.2 |
| 1919 | -44.3 | 44.8 | 0.5 | -15.7 |
| 1920 | -117.5 | 65.8 | -51.6 | -5.4 |
| 1921 | -77.7 | 68.0 | -9.7 | -25.7 |
| 1922 | -43.6 | 54.7 | 11.0 | -6.3 |
| 1923 | -63.2 | 54.4 | -8.9 | -8.6 |
| 1924 | -85.3 | 55.4 | -29.9 | -11.2 |
| 1925 | -87.3 | 60.0 | -27.3 | -1.1 |
| 1926 | -106.6 | 66.7 | -40.0 | -16.6 |
| 1927 | -137.6 | 70.1 | -67.6 | -54.8 |
| 1928 | -106.5 | 72.7 | -33.8 | -46.0 |
| 1929 | -64.9 | 75.5 | 10.6 | -6.6 |
| 1930 | -57.0 | 70.5 | 13.5 | -15.0 |
| 1931 | -64.2 | 52.9 | -11.3 | -52.2 |
| 1932 | -57.8 | 46.3 | -11.5 | -58.5 |
| 1933 | -16.7 | 35.8 | 19.1 | -25.3 |
| 1934 | -36.8 | 36.1 | -0.7 | -16.0 |
| 1935 | -28.8 | 42.0 | 13.2 | 0.6 |
| 1936 | -44.0 | 44.0 | 0.0 | -16.5 |
| 1937 | -45.1 | 49.6 | 4.5 | -7.0 |
| 1938 | -74.0 | 54.7 | -19.3 | -56.2 |
| 1939 | -61.9 | 56.1 | -5.7 | -27.8 |
| 1950 | -247.7 | 214.4 | -33.4 | -18.7 |
| 1951 | -282.0 | 257.9 | -24.0 | 5.2 |
| 1952 | -550.4 | 292.2 | -258.3 | -88.1 |
| 1953 | -366.6 | 334.7 | -31.9 | -57.0 |
| 1954 | -339.3 | 343.1 | 3.8 | -45.4 |
| 1955 | -494.0 | 339.5 | -154.5 | -80.9 |
| 1956 | -500.4 | 386.3 | -114.1 | -79.1 |
| 1957 | -613.7 | 412.9 | -200.8 | -122.1 |
| 1958 | -599.7 | 422.4 | -177.3 | -125.4 |
| 1959 | -467.4 | 401.7 | -65.8 | -59.2 |
| 1960 | -600.6 | 462.0 | -138.6 | -90.2 |

**Chapter Three**

# The Result of GDP Estimates in Singapore and Overall Patterns of Growth for the Twentieth Century

## 3.1 Introduction

In Chapter 2, each component of GDP was constructed by employing various estimating techniques on the basis of the availability of historical statistical information to meet the modern definition as outlined in *A System of National Accounts (SNA) 1968*. By summing up each component, historical GDP estimates of Singapore were then constructed. This estimated GDP series, however, requires to be checked from various aspects to assess the reliability or validity of the estimate. After these processes, the historical GDP series (1900–39 and 1950–60) supplemented with the official GDP series 1960–2000 in both current and constant prices was then obtained, after which the pattern of economic growth in Singapore for the twentieth century was examined.

This chapter is organized as follows: Section 3.2 presents the result of GDP estimates of Singapore for the periods 1900–39 and 1950–60 in both current and 1914 prices. Using these derived time series, an attempt was made to assess the reliability of each component of GDP in Section 3.3. Subsequently, this derived series was extended to cover 100 years by supplementing it with the post-1960 statistical time series with a single base year

(1990 = 100) for conducting quantitative analysis of Singapore for the twentieth century, which appear in Chapters 4 and 5. Section 3.4 explains the overall pattern of growth for 100 years with respect to GDP growth and share of the various components of GDP.

## 3.2 Results of GDP Estimates

The results of GDP estimates and its components in both current and 1914 prices for the periods 1900–39 and 1950–60 are presented in Tables 3.1–3.2 and Figs. 3.1–3.4. The average annual growth rate of GDP for the periods 1900–39 and 1950–60 in current prices was 5.2% and 7.2% whereas this growth rate in 1914 prices was 4.5% and 4.8%, respectively. The average annual per-capita GDP growth rate for the same time periods was 2.2% and 2.4% in current prices and 1.5% and 0.03% in 1914 prices.

An examination of the yearly growth rates in GDP in current prices during the period under review, however, yielded years which experienced extremely high growth rates as in 1917 (41%), 1919 (38%), and 1928 (36%) and conversely extremely low growth rates well into the negative territory for the year 1931 (–38%). Similarly extremely high GDP growth rates in real terms were recorded for the years 1917 (29%), 1922 (23%), 1933 (46%), and 1953 (36%) whereas high negative rates were noted for 1916 (–20%), 1927 (–21%), 1931 (–43%), 1938 (–22%), and 1952 (–37%).

An analysis of the share of each component of Singapore's GDP showed certain notable features. First, the share of private final consumption expenditure (PFCE) was high. For the years 1903–04, 1912–14, 1916, and 1927, total PFCE recorded was higher than that of GDP in current prices.[66] This implied that

---

[66] Weight on private final consumption expenditure by resident households in Finland (1917) and Dutch (1844–46) exceeded the figure of GDP. Other than these countries, historical estimates of Korea experienced the weight of more than 90% for most of the 1910s. Therefore, this phenomenon is not merely recorded in Singapore.

**Table 3.1:** Singapore: Gross Domestic Product in Purchasers' Value in Current Prices, 1900–39 and 1950–60 (Straits $ in Millions)

| Year | Private Final Consumption Expenditure in the Domestic Market by Resident Households (PFCE) [1] | % of GDP | Growth rate (%) | Government Final Consumption Expenditure (GFCE) [2] | % of GDP | Growth rate (%) | Gross Capital Formation (GCF) [3] | % of GDP | Growth rate (%) | Net Exports of Goods and Services (NETEX) [4] | % of GDP | GDP at Market Prices (Current Prices) [5] = [1] + [2] + [3] + [4] | Growth rate (%) | Year |
|---|---|---|---|---|---|---|---|---|---|---|---|---|---|---|
| 1900 | 33.7 | 96 | | 2.2 | 6 | | 4.3 | 12 | | -5.2 | -15 | 35.1 | | 1900 |
| 1901 | 34.6 | 87 | 3 | 2.7 | 7 | 19 | 5.6 | 14 | 26 | -3.0 | -8 | 39.9 | 13 | 1901 |
| 1902 | 36.1 | 96 | 4 | 2.6 | 7 | -5 | 5.1 | 14 | -9 | -6.0 | -16 | 37.8 | -5 | 1902 |
| 1903 | 37.3 | 110 | 3 | 3.2 | 10 | 24 | 6.3 | 19 | 20 | -13.0 | -38 | 33.8 | -11 | 1903 |
| 1904 | 38.1 | 102 | 2 | 3.7 | 10 | 12 | 9.2 | 25 | 38 | -13.6 | -36 | 37.4 | 10 | 1904 |
| 1905 | 39.5 | 93 | 4 | 3.3 | 8 | -11 | 7.8 | 18 | -16 | -7.9 | -18 | 42.7 | 13 | 1905 |
| 1906 | 40.3 | 88 | 2 | 3.1 | 7 | -4 | 6.4 | 14 | -21 | -3.8 | -8 | 46.0 | 7 | 1906 |
| 1907 | 41.6 | 93 | 3 | 3.1 | 7 | -1 | 8.4 | 19 | 28 | -8.4 | -19 | 44.7 | -3 | 1907 |
| 1908 | 43.6 | 78 | 5 | 3.3 | 6 | 6 | 11.3 | 20 | 30 | -2.4 | -4 | 55.8 | 22 | 1908 |
| 1909 | 44.3 | 82 | 2 | 3.1 | 6 | -6 | 10.4 | 19 | -8 | -3.7 | -7 | 54.1 | -3 | 1909 |
| 1910 | 46.7 | 76 | 5 | 3.8 | 6 | 19 | 12.8 | 21 | 20 | -1.9 | -3 | 61.4 | 13 | 1910 |
| 1911 | 49.3 | 88 | 5 | 4.0 | 7 | 4 | 11.8 | 21 | -8 | -8.9 | -16 | 56.2 | -9 | 1911 |
| 1912 | 51.3 | 103 | 4 | 3.9 | 8 | -1 | 15.1 | 30 | 25 | -20.2 | -41 | 50.0 | -12 | 1912 |
| 1913 | 53.3 | 111 | 4 | 4.9 | 10 | 22 | 18.0 | 37 | 18 | -28.1 | -58 | 48.0 | -4 | 1913 |
| 1914 | 56.2 | 104 | 5 | 4.9 | 9 | 1 | 15.1 | 28 | -17 | -22.4 | -42 | 53.9 | 11 | 1914 |
| 1915 | 58.6 | 86 | 4 | 4.4 | 7 | -10 | 14.1 | 21 | -7 | -9.4 | -14 | 67.8 | 23 | 1915 |
| 1916 | 62.0 | 107 | 6 | 4.7 | 8 | 6 | 15.0 | 26 | 6 | -23.8 | -41 | 58.0 | -16 | 1916 |
| 1917 | 74.0 | 85 | 18 | 4.6 | 5 | -2 | 20.5 | 24 | 31 | -12.1 | -14 | 86.9 | 41 | 1917 |
| 1918 | 93.5 | 95 | 23 | 6.5 | 7 | 34 | 24.8 | 25 | 19 | -26.7 | -27 | 98.1 | 12 | 1918 |
| 1919 | 107.5 | 75 | 14 | 6.9 | 5 | 6 | 29.1 | 20 | 16 | 0.5 | 0 | 144.0 | 38 | 1919 |
| 1920 | 137.7 | 94 | 25 | 11.3 | 8 | 49 | 49.1 | 34 | 52 | -51.6 | -35 | 146.5 | 2 | 1920 |
| 1921 | 141.8 | 75 | 3 | 13.3 | 7 | 16 | 43.7 | 23 | -12 | -9.7 | -5 | 189.1 | 26 | 1921 |
| 1922 | 141.9 | 77 | 0 | 12.2 | 7 | -8 | 18.1 | 10 | -88 | 11.0 | 6 | 183.3 | -3 | 1922 |
| 1923 | 144.9 | 88 | 2 | 12.0 | 7 | -2 | 16.5 | 10 | -10 | -8.9 | -5 | 164.5 | -11 | 1923 |
| 1924 | 148.7 | 100 | 3 | 13.2 | 9 | 9 | 17.2 | 12 | 4 | -29.9 | -20 | 149.2 | -10 | 1924 |
| 1925 | 155.9 | 89 | 5 | 12.2 | 7 | -7 | 33.5 | 19 | 66 | -27.3 | -16 | 174.2 | 15 | 1925 |
| 1926 | 162.6 | 94 | 4 | 13.3 | 8 | 9 | 37.3 | 22 | 11 | -40.0 | -23 | 173.2 | -1 | 1926 |
| 1927 | 174.4 | 106 | 7 | 14.5 | 9 | 9 | 43.8 | 27 | 16 | -67.6 | -41 | 165.1 | -5 | 1927 |
| 1928 | 184.0 | 78 | 5 | 14.7 | 6 | 1 | 72.4 | 31 | 50 | -33.8 | -14 | 237.3 | 36 | 1928 |
| 1929 | 183.7 | 65 | 0 | 15.9 | 6 | 8 | 71.1 | 25 | -2 | 10.6 | 4 | 281.3 | 17 | 1929 |
| 1930 | 171.4 | 72 | -7 | 16.5 | 7 | 4 | 37.6 | 16 | -64 | 13.5 | 6 | 239.0 | -16 | 1930 |
| 1931 | 131.1 | 80 | -27 | 16.5 | 10 | 0 | 27.8 | 17 | -30 | -11.3 | -7 | 164.1 | -38 | 1931 |
| 1932 | 119.0 | 84 | -10 | 14.5 | 10 | -13 | 20.1 | 14 | -33 | -11.5 | -8 | 142.0 | -14 | 1932 |
| 1933 | 121.8 | 70 | 2 | 13.0 | 7 | -11 | 20.4 | 12 | 2 | 19.1 | 11 | 174.3 | 20 | 1933 |
| 1934 | 123.5 | 81 | 1 | 11.7 | 8 | -11 | 18.6 | 12 | -10 | -0.7 | 0 | 153.0 | -13 | 1934 |
| 1935 | 144.5 | 71 | 16 | 12.7 | 6 | 8 | 33.7 | 17 | 60 | 13.2 | 6 | 204.1 | 29 | 1935 |
| 1936 | 159.9 | 79 | 10 | 12.8 | 6 | 1 | 30.7 | 15 | -9 | 0.0 | 0 | 203.4 | 0 | 1936 |
| 1937 | 182.6 | 74 | 13 | 13.8 | 6 | 7 | 47.4 | 19 | 44 | 4.5 | 2 | 248.3 | 20 | 1937 |
| 1938 | 195.9 | 85 | 7 | 14.9 | 6 | 8 | 39.8 | 17 | -17 | -19.3 | -8 | 231.4 | -7 | 1938 |
| 1939 | 201.4 | 76 | 3 | 15.5 | 6 | 4 | 55.1 | 21 | 32 | -5.7 | -2 | 266.3 | 14 | 1939 |
| 1950 | 912.8 | 81 | | 74.4 | 7 | | 168.7 | 15 | | -33.4 | -3 | 1,122.5 | | 1950 |
| 1951 | 1,081.2 | 78 | 17 | 91.9 | 7 | 21 | 234.3 | 17 | 33 | -24.0 | -2 | 1,383.4 | 21 | 1951 |
| 1952 | 1,161.2 | 96 | 7 | 106.2 | 9 | 14 | 194.4 | 16 | -19 | -258.3 | -21 | 1,203.6 | -14 | 1952 |
| 1953 | 1,368.1 | 82 | 16 | 123.8 | 7 | 15 | 207.3 | 12 | 6 | -31.9 | -2 | 1,667.2 | 33 | 1953 |
| 1954 | 1,382.2 | 80 | 1 | 143.6 | 8 | 15 | 197.7 | 11 | -5 | 3.8 | 0 | 1,727.4 | 4 | 1954 |
| 1955 | 1,393.8 | 88 | 1 | 154.5 | 10 | 7 | 184.6 | 12 | -7 | -154.5 | -10 | 1,578.4 | -9 | 1955 |
| 1956 | 1,633.2 | 84 | 16 | 164.8 | 8 | 6 | 269.6 | 14 | 38 | -114.1 | -6 | 1,953.6 | 21 | 1956 |
| 1957 | 1,712.3 | 89 | 5 | 166.8 | 9 | 1 | 252.7 | 13 | -6 | -200.8 | -10 | 1,931.1 | -1 | 1957 |
| 1958 | 1,779.1 | 88 | 4 | 179.6 | 9 | 7 | 232.2 | 12 | -8 | -177.3 | -9 | 2,013.6 | 4 | 1958 |
| 1959 | 1,690.3 | 83 | -5 | 186.7 | 9 | 4 | 222.5 | 11 | -4 | -65.8 | -3 | 2,033.8 | 1 | 1959 |
| 1960 | 2,016.0 | 87 | 18 | 139.1 | 6 | -29 | 291.0 | 13 | 27 | -138.6 | -6 | 2,307.5 | 13 | 1960 |

| | PFCE | | GFCE | | GCF | | NETEX | | GDP | Per-capita GDP |
|---|---|---|---|---|---|---|---|---|---|---|
| | % of GDP | Growth rate (%) | % of GDP | Growth rate (%) | % of GDP | Growth rate (%) | % of GDP | Growth rate (%) | Growth rate (%) | Growth rate (%) |
| 1900–1939 | 87.2 | 4.6 | 7.2 | 5.0 | 19.9 | 6.5 | -14.4 | | 5.2 | 2.2 |
| 1900–1914 | 93.7 | 3.7 | 7.5 | 5.7 | 20.7 | 8.9 | -21.9 | | 3.1 | 0.2 |
| 1914–1939 | 83.4 | 5.1 | 7.1 | 4.6 | 19.4 | 5.2 | -9.9 | | 6.4 | 3.3 |
| 1950–1960 | 85.2 | 7.9 | 8.1 | 6.3 | 13.2 | 5.5 | -6.5 | | 7.2 | 2.4 |

**Table 3.2:** Singapore: Gross Domestic Product in Purchasers' Value in 1914 Prices, 1900–39 and 1950–60 (Straits $ in Millions)

| | Private Final Consumption Expenditure in the Domestic Market by Resident Households (PFCE) | | | Government Final Consumption Expenditure (GFCE) | | | Gross Capital Formation (GCF) | | | Net Exports of Goods and Services (NETEX) | | GDP at Market Prices (1914 Prices) | | |
|---|---|---|---|---|---|---|---|---|---|---|---|---|---|---|
| | [1] | % of GDP | Growth rate (%) | [2] | % of GDP | Growth rate (%) | [3] | % of GDP | Growth rate (%) | [4] | % of GDP | [5] = [1] + [2] + [3] + [4] | Growth rate (%) | |
| 1900 | 40.7 | 99 | | 2.7 | 7 | | 3.7 | 9 | | -6.1 | -15 | 41.1 | | 1900 |
| 1901 | 41.4 | 87 | 2 | 3.2 | 7 | 18 | 5.1 | 11 | 32 | -2.2 | -5 | 47.5 | 14 | 1901 |
| 1902 | 41.6 | 92 | 1 | 2.9 | 7 | -9 | 4.5 | 10 | -12 | -4.0 | -9 | 45.2 | -5 | 1902 |
| 1903 | 42.5 | 108 | 2 | 3.7 | 9 | 23 | 5.5 | 14 | 19 | -12.2 | -31 | 39.4 | -14 | 1903 |
| 1904 | 43.4 | 107 | 2 | 4.2 | 10 | 12 | 8.1 | 20 | 39 | -15.1 | -37 | 40.5 | 3 | 1904 |
| 1905 | 44.2 | 94 | 2 | 3.7 | 8 | -13 | 7.5 | 16 | -8 | -8.5 | -18 | 46.8 | 14 | 1905 |
| 1906 | 45.7 | 86 | 3 | 3.6 | 7 | -3 | 7.1 | 13 | -5 | -3.4 | -6 | 52.9 | 12 | 1906 |
| 1907 | 47.2 | 96 | 3 | 3.5 | 7 | -1 | 8.8 | 18 | 22 | -10.4 | -21 | 49.1 | -7 | 1907 |
| 1908 | 48.8 | 81 | 3 | 3.7 | 6 | 5 | 11.5 | 19 | 27 | -4.0 | -7 | 60.1 | 20 | 1908 |
| 1909 | 50.9 | 85 | 4 | 3.6 | 6 | -3 | 10.8 | 18 | -7 | -5.5 | -9 | 59.7 | -1 | 1909 |
| 1910 | 52.6 | 78 | 3 | 4.3 | 6 | 18 | 13.8 | 20 | 25 | -3.1 | -5 | 67.6 | 12 | 1910 |
| 1911 | 50.7 | 83 | -4 | 4.1 | 7 | -6 | 13.8 | 23 | 0 | -7.5 | -12 | 61.0 | -10 | 1911 |
| 1912 | 51.8 | 97 | 2 | 3.9 | 7 | -3 | 16.1 | 30 | 16 | -18.2 | -34 | 53.6 | -13 | 1912 |
| 1913 | 52.7 | 107 | 2 | 4.8 | 10 | 20 | 16.7 | 34 | 4 | -25.1 | -51 | 49.0 | -9 | 1913 |
| 1914 | 56.2 | 104 | 6 | 4.9 | 9 | 2 | 15.1 | 28 | -10 | -22.4 | -42 | 53.9 | 9 | 1914 |
| 1915 | 55.0 | 84 | -2 | 4.2 | 6 | -17 | 12.8 | 19 | -17 | -6.1 | -9 | 65.9 | 20 | 1915 |
| 1916 | 54.8 | 102 | 0 | 4.2 | 8 | 0 | 11.4 | 21 | -11 | -16.5 | -31 | 53.8 | -20 | 1916 |
| 1917 | 62.8 | 87 | 14 | 3.9 | 5 | -6 | 13.0 | 18 | 13 | -7.9 | -11 | 71.8 | 29 | 1917 |
| 1918 | 66.6 | 106 | 6 | 4.6 | 7 | 16 | 11.9 | 19 | -9 | -20.2 | -32 | 62.9 | -13 | 1918 |
| 1919 | 62.4 | 96 | -7 | 4.0 | 6 | -14 | 14.5 | 22 | 20 | -15.7 | -24 | 65.2 | 4 | 1919 |
| 1920 | 62.2 | 77 | 0 | 5.1 | 6 | 24 | 18.5 | 23 | 24 | -5.4 | -7 | 80.4 | 21 | 1920 |
| 1921 | 81.1 | 98 | 26 | 7.6 | 9 | 40 | 19.8 | 24 | 7 | -25.7 | -31 | 82.7 | 3 | 1921 |
| 1922 | 90.9 | 88 | 11 | 7.8 | 8 | 3 | 11.3 | 11 | -55 | -6.3 | -6 | 103.8 | 23 | 1922 |
| 1923 | 95.3 | 89 | 5 | 7.9 | 7 | 1 | 12.5 | 12 | 10 | -8.6 | -8 | 107.1 | 3 | 1923 |
| 1924 | 98.2 | 90 | 3 | 8.7 | 8 | 10 | 13.4 | 12 | 6 | -11.2 | -10 | 109.0 | 2 | 1924 |
| 1925 | 100.5 | 75 | 2 | 7.9 | 6 | -10 | 26.4 | 20 | 68 | -1.1 | -1 | 133.7 | 20 | 1925 |
| 1926 | 101.4 | 82 | 1 | 8.3 | 7 | 5 | 29.9 | 24 | 12 | -16.6 | -13 | 123.0 | -8 | 1926 |
| 1927 | 110.4 | 111 | 8 | 9.2 | 9 | 10 | 35.1 | 35 | 16 | -54.8 | -55 | 99.8 | -21 | 1927 |
| 1928 | 117.5 | 84 | 6 | 9.4 | 7 | 2 | 58.9 | 42 | 52 | -46.0 | -33 | 139.8 | 34 | 1928 |
| 1929 | 119.9 | 66 | 2 | 10.4 | 6 | 10 | 58.7 | 32 | 0 | -6.6 | -4 | 182.4 | 27 | 1929 |
| 1930 | 117.6 | 80 | -2 | 11.3 | 8 | 9 | 33.3 | 23 | -57 | -15.0 | -10 | 147.2 | -21 | 1930 |
| 1931 | 105.3 | 111 | -11 | 13.2 | 14 | 16 | 28.9 | 30 | -14 | -52.2 | -55 | 95.3 | -43 | 1931 |
| 1932 | 108.6 | 128 | 3 | 13.2 | 16 | 0 | 21.8 | 26 | -28 | -58.5 | -69 | 85.1 | -11 | 1932 |
| 1933 | 119.7 | 88 | 10 | 12.7 | 9 | -3 | 28.3 | 21 | 26 | -25.3 | -19 | 135.4 | 46 | 1933 |
| 1934 | 118.2 | 86 | -1 | 11.2 | 8 | -13 | 23.7 | 17 | -18 | -16.0 | -12 | 137.0 | 1 | 1934 |
| 1935 | 133.1 | 69 | 12 | 11.7 | 6 | 4 | 46.8 | 24 | 68 | 0.6 | 0 | 192.2 | 34 | 1935 |
| 1936 | 149.8 | 79 | 12 | 12.0 | 6 | 3 | 43.4 | 23 | -8 | -16.5 | -9 | 188.8 | -2 | 1936 |
| 1937 | 161.5 | 70 | 7 | 12.2 | 5 | 2 | 63.1 | 27 | 37 | -7.0 | -3 | 229.8 | 20 | 1937 |
| 1938 | 179.0 | 97 | 10 | 13.6 | 7 | 11 | 47.7 | 26 | -28 | -56.2 | -31 | 184.2 | -22 | 1938 |
| 1939 | 182.8 | 78 | 2 | 14.0 | 6 | 3 | 64.5 | 28 | 30 | -27.8 | -12 | 233.6 | 24 | 1939 |
| 1950 | 254.2 | 81 | | 20.7 | 7 | | 58.9 | 19 | | -18.7 | -6 | 315.2 | | 1950 |
| 1951 | 239.5 | 72 | -6 | 20.4 | 6 | -2 | 68.1 | 20 | 15 | 5.2 | 2 | 333.2 | 6 | 1951 |
| 1952 | 247.2 | 108 | 3 | 22.6 | 10 | 10 | 48.0 | 21 | -35 | -88.1 | -38 | 229.7 | -37 | 1952 |
| 1953 | 298.4 | 90 | 19 | 27.0 | 8 | 18 | 62.0 | 19 | 26 | -57.0 | -17 | 330.5 | 36 | 1953 |
| 1954 | 316.3 | 88 | 6 | 32.9 | 9 | 20 | 57.5 | 16 | -8 | -45.4 | -13 | 361.4 | 9 | 1954 |
| 1955 | 326.4 | 99 | 3 | 36.2 | 11 | 10 | 49.4 | 15 | -15 | -80.9 | -24 | 331.0 | -9 | 1955 |
| 1956 | 378.4 | 91 | 15 | 38.2 | 9 | 5 | 77.5 | 19 | 45 | -79.1 | -19 | 415.0 | 23 | 1956 |
| 1957 | 385.5 | 105 | 2 | 37.6 | 10 | -2 | 67.2 | 18 | -14 | -122.1 | -33 | 368.2 | -12 | 1957 |
| 1958 | 402.6 | 104 | 4 | 40.6 | 10 | 8 | 70.0 | 18 | 4 | -125.4 | -32 | 387.7 | 5 | 1958 |
| 1959 | 386.9 | 87 | -4 | 42.7 | 10 | 5 | 74.2 | 17 | 6 | -59.2 | -13 | 444.6 | 14 | 1959 |
| 1960 | 461.3 | 91 | 18 | 31.8 | 6 | -29 | 106.2 | 21 | 36 | -90.2 | -18 | 509.1 | 14 | 1960 |

| | PFCE | | GFCE | | GCF | | NETEX | | GDP | Per-capita GDP |
|---|---|---|---|---|---|---|---|---|---|---|
| | % of GDP | Growth rate (%) | % of GDP | Growth rate (%) | % of GDP | Growth rate (%) | % of GDP | Growth rate (%) | Growth rate (%) | Growth rate (%) |
| 1900–1939 | 90.7 | 3.9 | 7.6 | 4.2 | 21.6 | 7.3 | -19.9 | | 4.5 | 1.5 |
| 1900–1914 | 93.7 | 2.3 | 7.5 | 4.3 | 18.9 | 10.0 | -20.1 | | 1.9 | -1.0 |
| 1914–1939 | 88.9 | 4.7 | 7.7 | 4.2 | 23.2 | 5.8 | -19.7 | | 5.9 | 2.8 |
| 1950–1960 | 92.2 | 6.0 | 8.8 | 4.3 | 18.4 | 5.9 | -19.3 | | 4.8 | 0.03 |

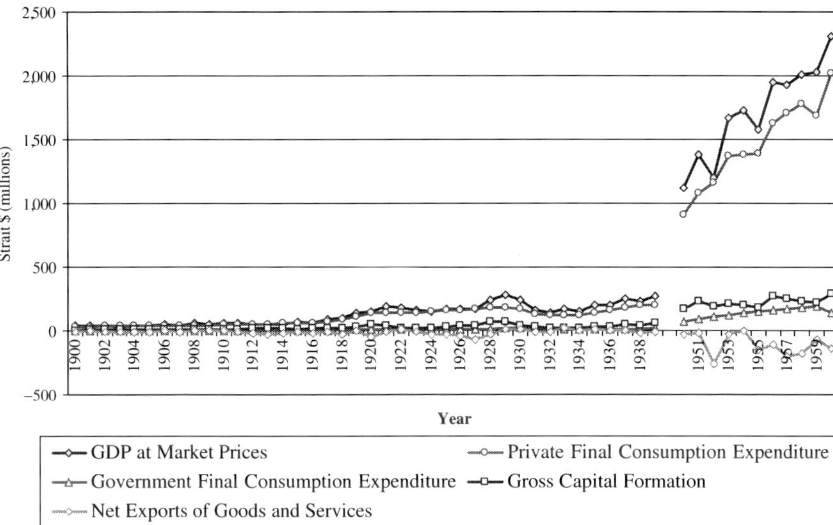

**Fig. 3.1:** Singapore: Gross Domestic Product in Purchasers' Value in Current Prices, 1900–39 and 1950–60 (Straits $ in millions)

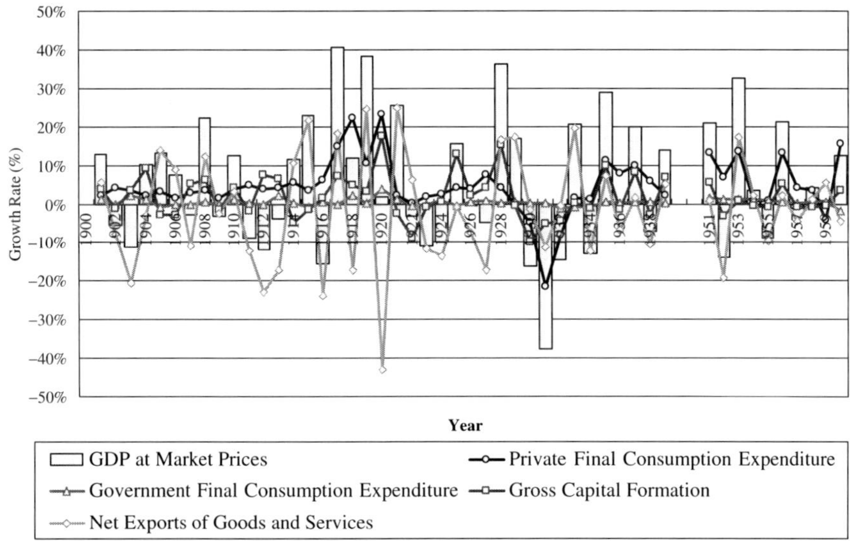

**Fig. 3.2:** Singapore: Annual Growth Rate of GDP and Its Components at Current Prices, 1900–39 and 1950–60

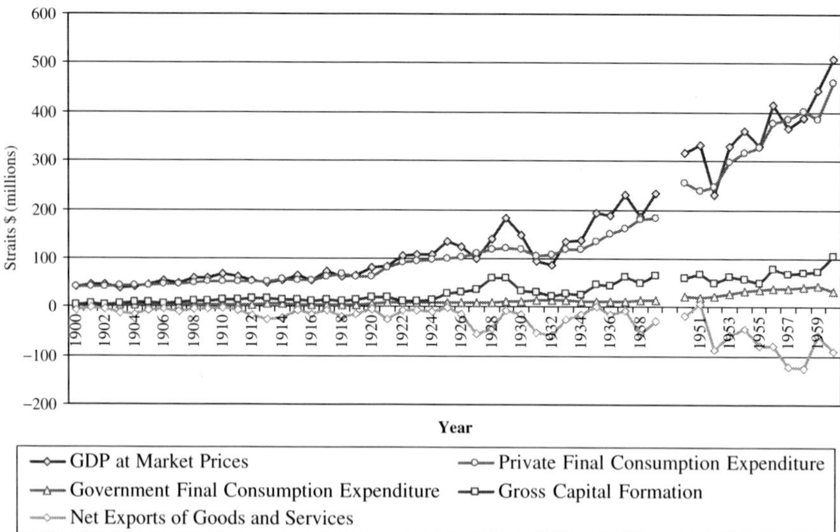

**Fig. 3.3:** Singapore: Gross Domestic Product in Purchasers' Value in 1914 Prices, 1900–39 and 1950–60 (Straits $ in millions)

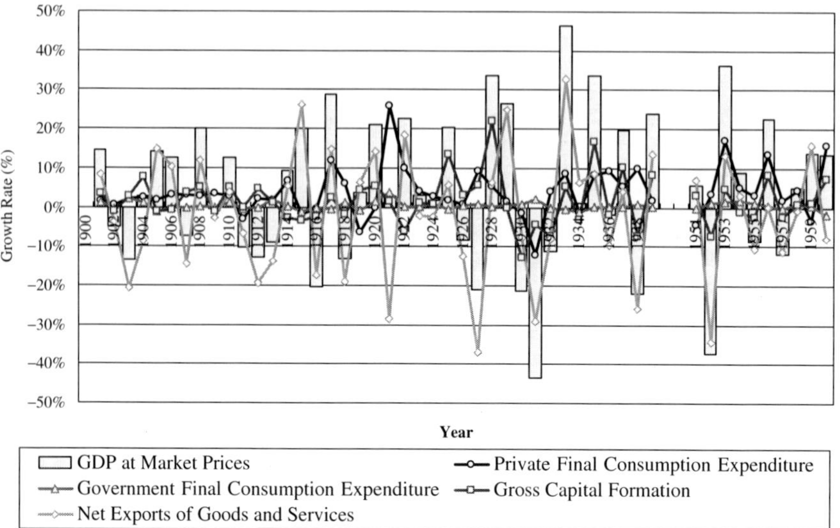

**Fig. 3.4:** Singapore: Annual Growth Rate of GDP and Its Components at 1914 Prices, 1900–39 and 1950–60

personal consumption expenditure by resident households in current terms exceeded the national income. Second, it is also important to note that the share of net exports of goods and services to GDP in current prices was in most years in the negative territory. Its share has fluctuated heavily from –58% in 1913 and to +11% in 1933 in current prices and from –69% in 1932 to +2% in 1951 in 1914 prices. Third, it was observed that the share of government final consumption expenditure remained stable in the range of 6% to 10% in current prices and 5% to 16% in 1914 prices during the period under review.

## 3.3 Assessment of GDP Estimates

In the field of historical GDP estimates, there are broadly three ways in which the reliability of the main aggregates can be assessed: (1) by comparison with other estimates; (2) by comparison from two or more different approaches (e.g., production and income approach in the case of GDP); and (3) by reference to the subjective evaluations of statistical personnel responsible for the compilation of the each component (Feinstein, 1972, 10). In the case of GDP estimates of Singapore, however, there are constraints in conducting these reliability checks. To begin with, there were no previous exercises, attempted in the construction of historical GDP estimates for Singapore. For the second method, up to today, no attempt has been made in constructing GDP estimates from the income and production approach. This is mainly because the statistical data are so much lacking that they do not permit the construction of GDP using these alternative approaches. In the case of income approach, the British colonial authority did not collect basic statistical information relating to income and profit earnings by various sectors. For the production approach, as described earlier, Singapore as a regional entrepôt had been primarily engaged in wholesale trade and services sector.[67] Therefore, estimates for value added by sector would be

---

[67] In 1960, 78% of GDP was service sector (Peebles, Gavin, and Peter Wilson, 1996, 5).

extremely difficult due to the deficiencies of data. The third method involves assessing the reliability of the GDP series, undertaken by the investigator responsible for the estimates and expressed in terms of reliability grades (Feinstein, 1972, 20). However, this assessment would be arbitrary because it is rare that we can set a correct margin of error. In view of these constraints, the following four alternative approaches were employed: First, this study examines if the estimates made bear any consistency with the official figures compiled by the Department of Statistics, Singapore, for the years after 1960. Second, a check of the level of GDP between the estimated figure and the available official figure released by the Department of Statistics, Singapore, for the years 1959–60 was made. Subsequently, the average annual growth rate and share of each component of GDP for the periods 1900–39 and 1950–2000 was also observed. Nelson and Plosser (1982) presented statistical evidence that there are nonstationary (difference stationary) in the macroeconomic time series for the United States. Similar tests were employed for Singapore to evaluate whether each component of the GDP figure was consistent with the overall data for the twentieth century as a whole.

Fourth, economic factors and events gleaned from official documents and records which contributed towards the upturns and downturns of each component of GDP for particular years were noted as supporting proof.

Finally, the historical GDP estimates from this exercise were compared with the figures available for other countries to compare the patterns, levels, and trends of these estimates.

### 3.3.1 *Consistency Check*

The first official GDP of Singapore was constructed by the Department of Statistics for the year 1960. Additionally, GDP estimates for the year 1959 were released by Goh Keng Swee (1995). As presented in Table 3.3, notably, estimates of GDP were fairly close with that of the figures from the above sources

**Table 3.3:** Singapore: Gross Domestic Product at Current Prices, 1959–60, (Straits $ in millions)

| Year | Official Figure | | Estimates by Sugimoto |
|---|---|---|---|
| 1959 | 1968 | [A] | 2034 |
| 1960 | 2150 | [B] | 2307 |

*Sources*:
[A] Goh Keng Swee (1995).
[B] Department of Statistics, Singapore (1996).

**Table 3.4:** Singapore: Average Annual Growth Rate of GDP and Its Components at Current and Constant Prices, 1900–2000

| | At Current Prices | | | | | At Constant Prices | | | | |
|---|---|---|---|---|---|---|---|---|---|---|
| | PFCE | GFCE | GCF | NETEX | GDP | PFCE | GFCE | GCF | NETEX | GDP |
| | | | | | | 1914 Prices | | | | |
| 1900–1910 | 3.3 | 5.4 | 10.8 | | 5.6 | 2.6 | 4.7 | 13.1 | | 5.0 |
| 1910–1920 | 10.8 | 10.9 | 13.5 | | 8.7 | 1.7 | 1.7 | 2.9 | | 1.7 |
| 1920–1930 | 2.2 | 3.8 | -2.7 | | 4.9 | 6.4 | 8.0 | 5.9 | | 6.0 |
| 1930–1939 | 1.8 | -0.7 | 4.3 | | 1.2 | 4.9 | 2.4 | 7.4 | | 5.1 |
| 1950–1960 | 7.9 | 6.3 | 5.5 | | 7.2 | 6.0 | 4.3 | 5.9 | | 4.8 |
| | | | | | | 1990 Prices | | | | |
| 1960–1970 | 7.1 | 14.6 | 22.2 | | 9.9 | 6.1 | 13.3 | 14.5 | | 8.8 |
| 1970–1980 | 11.9 | 12.6 | 16.4 | | 14.6 | 6.8 | 7.0 | 8.9 | | 8.6 |
| 1980–1990 | 8.7 | 10.2 | 7.4 | | 10.0 | 5.9 | 6.5 | 5.0 | | 7.0 |
| 1990–2000 | 7.3 | 9.0 | 7.2 | | 8.5 | 5.7 | 8.1 | 7.0 | | 7.2 |

despite the differing methodologies employed for their computation. Unfortunately, other than for these two years, only GNP estimates were available for the period 1956–60.

The average annual growth rate of each component of GDP for each decade for the periods 1900–39 and 1950–2000 in both current and constant prices is presented in Table 3.4. Generally, the GDP and its components showed relatively higher average annual growth rates during the second half of the twentieth century as compared with that of the pre–World War II period. It may be possible to conclude that the rapid and sustained growth of GDP of Singapore recorded in our estimate may find general acceptance for both the British Colonial period and the period of

**Table 3.5:** Singapore: Gross Domestic Product and Its Components at Current Prices, 1900–1970

| | Current Prices | | | | | |
|------|------|------|------|------|------|------|
| | PFCE | GFCE | GCF | NETEX | GDP | |
| 1900 | 96 | 6 | 12 | −15 | 100 | |
| 1905 | 93 | 8 | 18 | −18 | 100 | |
| 1910 | 76 | 6 | 21 | −3 | 100 | |
| 1915 | 86 | 7 | 21 | −14 | 100 | |
| 1920 | 94 | 8 | 34 | −35 | 100 | |
| 1925 | 89 | 7 | 19 | −16 | 100 | [A] |
| 1930 | 72 | 7 | 16 | 6 | 100 | |
| 1935 | 71 | 6 | 17 | 6 | 100 | |
| 1939 | 76 | 6 | 21 | −2 | 100 | |
| 1950 | 81 | 7 | 15 | −3 | 100 | |
| 1955 | 88 | 1 | 12 | −10 | 100 | |
| 1960 | 87 | 6 | 3 | −6 | 100 | |
| 1960 | 89 | 8 | 11 | −8 | 100 | |
| 1965 | 79 | 10 | 22 | −11 | 100 | [B] |
| 1970 | 68 | 12 | 39 | −18 | 100 | |

*Note*:
For the years 1960, 1965, and 1970, percentage share of statistical discrepancy to GDP was allocated under NETEX.

*Sources*:
[A] Sugimoto's Estimates.
[B] Department of Statistics, Singapore (1996).
Abbreviations:
PFCE = Private Final Consumption Expenditure by Resident Households.
GFCE = Government Final Consumption Expenditure.
GCF = Gross Capital Formation.
NETEX = Net Exports of Goods and Services.

self-government. It will also be noted that the share of each component of GDP of Singapore in both current and constant prices was also not significantly different from that of 1960s (See Table 3.5).

### 3.3.1.1 *Unit Root Test*

In addition to previous consistency checks on the historical GDP estimates, this section conducts unit root tests for checking the consistency of time-series data on GDP and its components. Relating to this, Nelson and Plosser (1982) presented statistical evidence that supports the hypothesis of a unit root in the macroeconomic time series for the United States which included GNP, employment, wages, prices, interest rate, and stock prices. Their study is widely recognized as an important literature in macroeconomics and econometrics. The presence or absence of unit roots, to put it simply, helps to identify some features of the underlying data-generating process of a series. If a series has no unit roots, it is characterized as stationary and therefore exhibits mean reversion in that it fluctuates around a constant long-run mean. Also the absence of unit roots implies that the series has a finite variance which does not depend on time and that the effects of shocks dissolve over time. Alternatively, if the series feature a unit root, they are better characterized as nonstationary processes that have no tendency to return to a long-run deterministic path.

Considered below are two alternative models used to represent GDP time series:

$$y_t = a + bt + e_t \tag{1}$$
$$y_t = a + y_{t-1} + e_t \tag{2}$$

where:

$y_t$   represents the natural logarithm of GDP at time $t$.
t   represents a time trend.
b   is a constant that gives the growth rate of variable.
e   is an error term with zero mean and finite variance.

The first specification implies that GDP equals the constant $a$ at time zero ($y_0 = a$) and growth over time at a constant rate $b$, with the error term explaining deviations from the trend in each year. In other words, the variable $y_t$ presents a stationary fluctuation around the time trend $a + b_t$. Therefore, the variable is described as *trend stationary* (TS), and stationarity is achieved by removing the time trend ("detrending"), i.e., regressing $y_t$ on $t$.

In short, for the first specification, the effects of a shock at time $t$ tend to zero over time, since the error term affects the outcome in the current period but has no persistent influence in succeeding time periods.

Model 2, on the other hand, specifies that GDP grows at rate $a$ from its previous value, with an error term playing a role every year. Despite the apparent similitude between the two models, they are indeed very different and lead to different implications in many respects. First, model 2 is nonstationary and cannot be made stationary through detrending. It will be noted that the first difference of the series is given by $a + e_t$, a stationary process. So, stationarity can be achieved by differencing, and the model is called *difference stationary* (DS). Model 2 is one of the simplest AR(1) processes, and can be described as a random walk with drift. The dependent variable displays a random fluctuation given by the error term $e_t$, in addition to the growth given by the drift term $a$. Contrary to model 1, however, there is no tendency for $y_t$ to return to a predetermined mean value, and its trajectory is given by an accumulation of disturbances. In other words, the error term affects not only what happens in the current period, but also what happens in all succeeding periods. To better visualize this point, we can - substitute repeatedly for the lagged $y_t$ value in equation (2) to get:

$$y_t = y_0 + a_t + \sum_{i=1}^{t} e_i \tag{3}$$

It is straightforward to see that the variance of $y_t$ without bound over time and that shocks to the system (captured by the error term) have a permanent effect on the series.

The study by Nelson and Plosser (1982) concludes that the evidence presented supports the DS representation of nonstationary (difference stationary) in economic time series. In other words, their study found that many fluctuations in

GDP and its components are permanent in the sense that there is no tendency for GDP to revert to trend line following a shock. Similar results were obtained amongst others by Sosa-Escudero (1997), Carrera, Feliz, and Panigo (1999), Noriega and Ramirez-Zamora (1999), Thornton (2001), and Rapach (2002).

Many studies begin by testing for unit root using augmented Dickey-Fuller's test (Dickey and Fuller, 1979, 1981) and Philips and Perron's test (Philips and Perron, 1988). To test the unit root property of the $\Delta$GDP $(Y)$ time series, the following regression equation (4) is used:

$$\Delta Y = \alpha_0 + \alpha_1 Y_{t-1} + \alpha_2 T + \sum_{j=1}^{p} \beta_j \Delta Y_{t-j} + \varepsilon_t \tag{4}$$

where $\Delta$ is the first-difference operator, $T$ is time trend, and $\varepsilon$ $t$ is assumed to be Gaussian white noise. The number of lags, $p$ in the dependent variable is chosen to ensure that the errors are white noise. The two most commonly used methods for the selection of lag length are Akaike Information Criteria (AIC) and Schwartz Info Criteria (SIC). This study employed the SIC approach which has been widely used in the literature for the selection of the optimal lag length. Unit root tests of this type are referred to as augmented Dickey-Fullers, (ADF) tests. The null hypothesis is that the series is nonstationary against the alternative hypothesis of stationarity. The ADF test is based on the estimated parameter $\alpha_1$ and its corresponding $t$-statistic. When $\alpha_1 = 0$, the time series $\beta_t$ is nonstationarity so that the standard asymptotic analysis cannot be used to obtain the distributions of the test statistics. A problem with the ADF test is that it involves the inclusion of extra difference terms in the testing equation. Alternatively, the Philips-Perron (PP) approach allows for the presence of unknown forms of autocorrelation and conditional heteroscedasticity in the error term, and is based on testing regression (1), except that $p = 0$. This method uses a nonparametric correction for serial correlation. The statistics are then transformed to remove the effects of serial correlation on the asymptotic distribution of the test statistics. For both tests, a $t$-statistic larger in absolute value than the critical value results in the rejection of the null hypothesis of a unit root in favor of the stationarity alternative.

Table 3.6 shows the result of unit root tests for GDP and its components of Singapore for the period 1960–2000 (1990 prices) on the basis of official data compiled from Department of Statistics, Singapore, and the ADB Key Indicators. For unit root tests, the ADF and PP approaches were conducted.

As observed from the results of unit root tests, time series of real GDP and its components are all integrated of order 1, I(1), since only its first difference and second difference are stationary. This result portrays that the null hypothesis of a unit root test cannot be rejected, indicating that Singapore's time series of GDP and its components are difference stationary for the period 1960–2000. These results are similar to those observed for other countries.

A similar exercise on unit root tests was made this time for the period 1900–39, using 1914 as the base year.[68] As observed in Table 3.7, the results of two different unit root tests for both 1900–39 and 1950–60 are all integrated of order 1. The results were similar to that of the data for the period 1960–2000 as seen earlier in Table 3.6. The result of these econometric tests bears out the fact that there are consistencies in the nature of long-term time-series data on Singapore for the entire twentieth century.

---

[68] For the period of 1950–60, no unit root test was conducted due to the shortage of number of observations.

**Table 3.6:** Singapore: The Results of Unit Root Tests of GDP and Its Components (1990 Prices), 1960–2000

*Augmented Dickey-Fuller Test*

| | Levels | Trend | Lags[1] | First Difference | Trend | Lags[1] | Second Difference | Trend | Lags[1] | Order |
|---|---|---|---|---|---|---|---|---|---|---|
| GDP | −2.744437 | Yes | 1 | −6.378192*** | Yes | 0 | −6.888162*** | Yes | 0 | I(1) |
| PFCE | −2.488435 | Yes | 0 | −5.425393*** | Yes | 0 | −6.647346*** | Yes | 1 | I(1) |
| GFCE | −1.522812 | Yes | 0 | −5.843068*** | Yes | 0 | −11.11444*** | Yes | 0 | I(1) |
| GCF | −1.594248 | Yes | 0 | −5.730494*** | Yes | 0 | −6.931361*** | Yes | 1 | I(1) |
| EXGS | 0.708007 | No | 0 | −5.547558*** | No | 0 | −9.954132*** | No | 0 | I(1) |
| IMGS | 0.497826 | No | 0 | −5.733827*** | No | 0 | −8.239051*** | No | 1 | I(1) |

*Phillips-Perron Test (Constant and no Trend)*

| | Levels | Trend | Band-Width[2] | First Difference | Trend | Band-Width[2] | Second Difference | Trend | Band-Width[2] | Order |
|---|---|---|---|---|---|---|---|---|---|---|
| GDP | −2.764241 | Yes | 1 | −9.279439*** | Yes | 2 | −25.52034*** | Yes | 3 | I(1) |
| PFCE | −2.224479 | Yes | 1 | −5.473416*** | Yes | 1 | −13.48829*** | Yes | 14 | I(1) |
| GFCE | −1.522812 | Yes | 2 | −5.834362*** | Yes | 2 | −36.67194*** | Yes | 3 | I(1) |
| GCF | −1.659389 | Yes | 0 | −5.730494*** | Yes | 1 | −18.60471*** | Yes | 10 | I(1) |
| EXGS | 0.668348 | No | 2 | −5.538378*** | No | 1 | −17.84169*** | No | 10 | I(1) |
| IMGS | 0.446229 | No | 2 | −5.724699*** | No | 2 | −12.62309*** | No | 2 | I(1) |

*Notes*:
1. All variables are natural logarithm figure; 2. Automatic selection of lag were determined by Schwartz Info Criterion; 3. Bandwidth was determined on the basis of the Newey-West using Bartlett kernel; 4. (***,**,*) denotes significance at the 1, 5, and 10% level, respectively.; 5. I(0) = stationary, I(1) = unit root.
Abbreviations: PFCE = Private Final Consumption Expenditure by Resident Households, GFCE = Government Final Consumption Expenditure, GCF = Gross Capital Formation, EXGS = Exports of Goods and Services, IMGS = Imports of Goods and Services.
*Source*:

**Table 3.7:** Singapore: The Results of Unit Root Tests of GDP and Its Components (1914 Prices), 1900–39

*Augmented Dickey-Fuller Test*

| | Levels | Trend | Lags[1] | First Difference | Trend | Lags[1] | Second Difference | Trend | Lags[1] | Order |
|---|---|---|---|---|---|---|---|---|---|---|
| GDP | −0.700543 | No | 0 | −6.913214*** | No | 0 | −6.811257*** | No | 2 | I(1) |
| PFCE | −2.651279 | Yes | 0 | −5.400934*** | No | 1 | −7.897427*** | Yes | 1 | I(1) |
| GFCE | −2.491583 | Yes | 0 | −6.537564*** | No | 0 | −8.267926*** | Yes | 0 | I(1) |
| GCF | −1.415085 | No | 0 | −6.813627*** | No | 0 | −11.92415*** | No | 0 | I(1) |
| EXGS | −1.804277 | Yes | 0 | −7.010903*** | No | 0 | −8.198379*** | Yes | 1 | I(1) |
| IMGS | −1.559027 | Yes | 0 | −6.288120*** | No | 0 | −7.964125*** | Yes | 1 | I(1) |

*Phillips-Perron Test*

| | Levels | Trend | Band-Width[2] | First Difference | Trend | Band-Width[2] | Second Difference | Trend | Band-Width[2] | Order |
|---|---|---|---|---|---|---|---|---|---|---|
| GDP | 0.126424 | No | 33 | −11.66003*** | No | 37 | −26.36706*** | No | 14 | I(1) |
| PFCE | −2.186524 | Yes | 5 | −4.984350*** | No | 5 | −16.82710*** | Yes | 20 | I(1) |
| GFCE | −2.540027 | Yes | 1 | −6.571247*** | No | 2 | −23.24026*** | Yes | 9 | I(1) |
| GCF | −3.059313 | Yes | 0 | −7.104991*** | No | 1 | −37.11039*** | Yes | 1 | I(1) |
| EXGS | −1.885684 | Yes | 3 | −6.967272*** | No | 3 | −15.69813*** | Yes | 3 | I(1) |
| IMGS | −1.850829 | Yes | 3 | −6.306713*** | No | 3 | −11.15228*** | Yes | 0 | I(1) |

*Notes:*

1. All variables are natural logarithm figure; 2. Automatic selection of lag were determined by Schwartz Info Criterion; 3. Bandwidth was determined on the basis of the Newey-West using Bartlett kernel; 4. (***,**,*) denotes significance at the 1, 5, and 10% level, respectively. 5. I(0) = stationary, I(1) = unit root.

Abbreviations: PFCE = Private Final Consumption Expenditure by Resident Households, GFCE = Government Final Consumption Expenditure, GCF = Gross Capital Formation, EXGS = Exports of Goods and Services, IMGS = Imports of Goods and Services.

*Source:* Authors's own calculations.

Similar unit root test was conducted for other Asian countries, namely, Japan, Taiwan, Korea, and Malaya, and all countries showed a similar result of unit root test.[69]

### 3.3.2 *Upturns and Downturns of Each Component of GDP, 1900–39 and 1950–60*

In the case of commodity-producing countries such as Malaya, for example, production or exports of major commodities such as rubber and tin may more or less portray the movement of real GDP. On the other hand, due to the deficiencies of influential major determinant variables, it is difficult to explain the movement of real GDP in the case of Singapore. Alternatively, a greater insight into the upturns and downturns of GDP of Singapore could possibly be gained by observing the movements of each component of GDP.

#### 3.3.2.1 *Private Final Consumption Expenditure in Current and 1914 Prices*

PFCE by resident households in the domestic market was the single largest component which represented on average 86.5%

---

[69] For unit root test, PP approach was tested. For all countries, real GDPs of Japan, Taiwan, Korea, and Malaya were integrated of order 1, I(1), *difference stationary*. Therefore, null hypotheses of unit root for all countries listed below were not rejected at 1% level.

| Country | Period | Base Year | Levels | Trend | Band-width$^2$ | First Difference | Trend | Band-width$^2$ | Second Difference | Trend | Band-width$^2$ | Order |
|---|---|---|---|---|---|---|---|---|---|---|---|---|
| Japan | 1903–38 | 1934–36 | –0.331987 | Yes | 1 | –5.593847[†††] | Yes | 1 | –16.33138[†††] | Yes | 10 | I(1) |
| Taiwan | 1903–38 | 1934–36 | –1.308562 | Yes | 4 | –8.309289[†††] | Yes | 1 | –16.18597[†††] | Yes | 4 | I(1) |
| Korea | 1911–38 | 1934–36 | –0.99868 | Yes | 3 | –5.329979[†††] | Yes | 2 | –23.55882[†††] | Yes | 9 | I(1) |
| Malaya | 1900–39 | 1914 | –2.979818 | Yes | 3 | –6.733598[†††] | Yes | 6 | –22.90363[†††] | Yes | 16 | I(1) |

1. Automatic selection of lag was determined by Schwartz Info Criterion.
2. Bandwidth was determined on the basis of the Newey-West using Bartlett kernel.
3. All variables are natural logarithm figure.
4. (†††, ††, †) denotes significance at the 1%, 5% and 10% level, respectively.
5. I(0) = stationary, I(1) = unit root.

and 85.7% of GDP for the two periods 1900–39 and 1950–60, respectively. In terms of growth rate, the average annual growth rate of PFCE in current prices was 4.6% and 7.9% for the periods 1900–39 and 1950–60, respectively, whereas in constant terms, the average annual growth rate was recorded at 3.9% and 6.0% for these two periods.

In per-capita terms, the PFCE of Singapore grew at an average annual rate of 1.4% and 2.8% in current terms, whereas in constant terms, they grew by 0.7% and 0.6%, respectively.

Annually, total and per-capita private final consumption expenditure in nominal or constant terms showed frequent fluctuations during the period. In current terms, PFCE grew remarkably for the period 1917–20, namely, 17.6% (1917), 23.4% (1918), 13.9% (1919), and 24.8% (1920), respectively. Their growth rate in real terms was, however, in the negative territory for the later years of this period, recording rates of 13.5% (1917), 5.9% (1918), –6.6% (1919), and –0.3% (1920) for the respective years. This could be attributed to the sharp increase in CPI by some 20.4% in 1919 and 25.0% in 1920. This increase was mainly fuelled by the sharp increase in the prices of nearly all major objects of consumption.

The sharp decline in the growth rates of PFCE in both current and constant terms for Singapore was experienced during the Great Depression years of 1930–32. In current terms, negative growth rates of –14.3% (1930), –29.7% (1931) and –12.2% (1932), were recorded for the respective years. In constant terms, negative growth was observed for the years 1930 (–9.4%) and 1931 (–13.7%). Singapore faced serious downturns as a result of the worldwide slump. In line with this, major export commodities such as rubber, tin, and petroleum experienced a drastic fall in their prices. The reasonableness of PFCE estimates in terms of major objects of consumption for Singapore is demonstrated in Table 3.8. This table provides the percentage share of PFCE for each major object of consumption in current prices for selected years. It would be comforting to note that the independently

**Table 3.8:** Singapore: Percentage Private Final Consumption Expenditure by Major Object of Consumption, Selected Years (Percent)

| | **Percentage Share of PFCE** | | | | | | |
|---|---|---|---|---|---|---|---|
| Major Object of Consumption | 1905 | 1918 | 1929 | 1955 | **1956*** | 1965 | 1980 |
| Food, Beverages, and Tobacco | 49.63 | 49.40 | 48.86 | 48.79 | 48.70 | 35.90 | 25.80 |
| Clothing | 8.70 | 11.70 | 8.60 | 9.60 | 10.20 | 9.10 | 8.20 |
| Rent | 4.70 | 4.10 | 9.90 | 10.10 | 10.60 | 8.50 | 9.00 |
| Miscellaneous | 36.97 | 34.83 | 32.55 | 31.51 | 30.50 | 46.56 | 57.04 |
| Total | 100.00 | 100.00 | 100.00 | 100.00 | 100.00 | 100.00 | 100.00 |

*Source*: For the years 1965 and 1980, the figures were derived from the Department of Statistics, Singapore (1983, 64–65).
*Estimates made by Benham (1959, 1).

arrived percentage shares of each major object of consumption for the selected years 1905, 1918, 1929, 1955, 1965, and 1980 are similar in pattern with Frederick Benham's estimate for the year 1956.

### 3.3.2.2 *Government Final Consumption Expenditure in Current and 1914 Prices*

As has been touched upon in Chapter 2, Section 2.3, the outputs of producers of government services were derived by the summation of (i) compensation of employees; (ii) intermediate consumption; and (iii) depreciation.[70] Average weights on compensation of employees and intermediate consumption were 55% and 45% for the period 1900–39 and 65% and 35% for the period 1950–60, respectively. This distribution is similar to that of the official figure; 66 % and 34 % in 1973. The output of government services

---

[70] In this estimate, the value of depreciation was estimated as 1% of aggregated figures of compensation of employees and intermediate consumption on the basis of an educated guess. Therefore, it hardly gave any significant impact to total government output.

generally experienced gradual increases throughout the period under review. Significant increases were recorded for the years 1918 (34%) and 1920 (49%). Both these expansions could be attributed to the British Colonial Government allocating huge temporary allowances to compensate for sudden price increases of consumer goods. The reduction of personal emoluments recorded in 1932–34 could be attributed to the retrenchment of government staff during the recession period.

### 3.3.2.3 *Gross Capital Formation in Current and 1914 Prices*

Unlike PFCE and GFCE, the level of GCF experienced frequent fluctuations. Additionally, the share of GCF against GDP was high on certain occasions. During the second decade of the twentieth century, when rubber and tin production was rapidly expanding in Malaya and the Netherland Indies, Singapore experienced large-scale capital formation. To consolidate its position as the foremost premier entrepôt in the region, massive capital formation was initiated by both the private and government sectors. Despite its small resident population, Singapore needed to undertake relatively large-scale infrastructure projects, such as port and aerodrome facilities, to meet regional and international demand. Unfortunately, it was difficult to quantify these activities since there was no specific information which could portray the movement of gross capital formation. The only available time-series data in our collection was capital formation figures which consists of construction (residential, nonresidential, and other constructions) and investment on machinery and equipment obtained from government financial statements contained in reports emanating from the Singapore Harbour Board, Colony of Singapore, and Singapore Municipality. Table 3.9 lists some major government capital formation pertaining to construction. The colonial government attempted to construct sophisticated harbor facilities. Modern port and harbor facilities which were constructed during the period 1908–20 were regarded as "second

**Table 3.9:** Singapore: Gross Capital Formation and Major Government Construction Projects, 1900–39 and 1950–60

| Year | GCF Current Prices | | Singapore Harbor Board | | | | Colony of Singapore | | Singapore Municipality |
| | Straits $ Millions | Growth Rate (%) | Singapore Harbor Works | Tanjong Pagar Main Wharf Reconstruction | New Graving Dock at Keppel Harbour | Singapore Harbor works | Singapore-Johore Railway | Construction of Govt. Office | Road, Street, and Bridges |
|---|---|---|---|---|---|---|---|---|---|
| 1900 | 4.3 | 0% | | | | | | | |
| 1901 | 4.6 | 7% | | | | | 0.7 | | |
| 1902 | 5.1 | 10% | | | | | 0.5 | | |
| 1903 | 7.0 | 30% | | | | | | | |
| 1904 | 8.6 | 21% | | | | | 0.1 | | |
| 1905 | 6.5 | −28% | | | | | 0.5 | | |
| 1906 | 5.7 | −14% | | | | | | | |
| 1907 | 8.4 | 39% | | | | | | | |
| 1908 | 9.4 | 11% | | | | | | | |
| 1909 | 10.4 | 10% | | 1.5 | | | | | |
| 1910 | 11.2 | 8% | | 1.0 | | | | | |
| 1911 | 12.6 | 12% | 2.0 | 0.2 | 1.1 | | | | |
| 1912 | 16.3 | 26% | 2.4 | 2.0 | 0.6 | | | | |
| 1913 | 18.2 | 11% | 2.8 | 1.3 | | | | | |
| 1914 | 13.1 | −33% | 1.1 | 1.8 | | | | | |
| 1915 | 12.1 | −8% | | 2.0 | | | | | |
| 1916 | 16.5 | 31% | | 2.2 | | | | | |
| 1917 | 14.0 | −16% | | | | | | | |
| 1918 | 25.8 | 61% | | 2.4 | | | | | |
| 1919 | 18.5 | −33% | | 2.5 | | | | | |
| 1920 | 49.8 | 99% | | | | 15.1 | | | |
| 1921 | 35.4 | −34% | | | | | | | |
| 1922 | 18.1 | −67% | | | | | | | |
| 1923 | 19.8 | 9% | | | | | | | |
| 1924 | 20.2 | 2% | | | | | | | |
| 1925 | 28.3 | 34% | | | | | | | 1.3 |
| 1926 | 37.3 | 28% | | | | | | 2.1 | 1.6 |
| 1927 | 43.8 | 16% | | | | | | 2.7 | 1.0 |
| 1928 | 50.3 | 14% | | | | | | 1.7 | 1.5 |
| 1929 | 58.7 | 15% | | | | | | 0.2 | 1.0 |
| 1930 | 43.6 | −30% | | | | | | | 1.1 |
| 1931 | 38.0 | −14% | | | | | | 0.3 | |
| 1932 | 25.1 | −41% | | | | | | | |
| 1933 | 15.3 | −50% | | | | | | | |
| 1934 | 25.6 | 52% | | | | | | 0.9 | |
| 1935 | 24.7 | −4% | | | | | | 1.1 | |
| 1936 | 29.6 | 18% | | | | | | 2.1 | |
| 1937 | 38.8 | 27% | | | | | | | |
| 1938 | 39.8 | 3% | | | | | | 0.7 | |
| 1939 | 47.0 | 17% | | | | | | | |
| 1950 | 180.0 | 0% | | | | | | | |
| 1951 | 186.6 | 4% | | | | | | | |
| 1952 | 224.8 | 19% | | | | | | | |
| 1953 | 125.9 | −58% | | | | | | | |
| 1954 | 171.9 | 31% | | | | | | | |
| 1955 | 208.4 | 19% | | | | | | | |
| 1956 | 202.2 | −3% | | | | | | | |
| 1957 | 252.7 | 22% | | | | | | | |
| 1958 | 222.2 | −13% | | | | | | | |
| 1959 | 222.5 | 0% | | | | | | | |
| 1960 | 233.9 | 5% | | | | | | | |

to no port out East."[71] This large-scale capital formation contributed greatly to ensure the economic development of Singapore as a regional entrepôt.

Another notable government capital formation was the construction of government office buildings undertaken by the authority of Colony of Singapore, whereas road, street, and bridge construction was initiated by the Singapore Municipality in the later half of the 1920s. These expenditures were incurred to meet the increasing demand for infrastructure as a result of socioeconomic development.

### 3.3.2.4 *Net Exports of Goods and Services in Current and 1914 Prices*

As observed in Tables 3.1 and 3.2 earlier, net exports of goods and services of Singapore were generally in the negative territory in both current and constant prices. This was purely because of the fact that Singapore did not have any significant domestic production base. Singapore imported various types of items from many parts of the world. A major portion of these imported items was then re-exported. Parts of the imports retained in the domestic market were eventually allocated for intermediate and final consumption expenditure, capital formation, and stocks.

One might wonder how Singapore, which experienced consistent negative net exports together with an income balance which was usually represented by an outflow, could be viable economically. This anomaly can be explained by observing the official balance of payments data of Singapore. As presented in Table 3.10, while the merchandize trade balance was regularly negative even after achieving self-governance, the combined invisible trade and capital and financial account (CFA) were positive largely due to inflows of foreign direct investment, generating an overall surplus and a steady accumulation of foreign exchange reserves.

---

[71] Huff (1994, 140).

**Table 3.10:**  Singapore: Balance of Payments, 1960–71

(Straits $ in Millions)

| Year | Merchandize Imports | Merchandize Exports | Merchandize Net Exports | Invisible Trade and Net Capital Inflows | Overall Balance |
|---|---|---|---|---|---|
| 1960 | 3497 | 2964 | −533 | 647 | 114 |
| 1961 | 3358 | 2750 | −608 | 623 | 15 |
| 1962 | 3431 | 2860 | −571 | 762 | 191 |
| 1963 | 3996 | 3291 | −705 | 785 | 80 |
| 1964 | 3252 | 2601 | −651 | 561 | −90 |
| 1965 | 3570 | 2810 | −760 | 728 | −32 |
| 1966 | 3825 | 3168 | −657 | 844 | 187 |
| 1967 | 4149 | 3239 | −910 | 1269 | 359 |
| 1968 | 4759 | 3589 | −1170 | 1718 | 548 |
| 1969 | 5863 | 4471 | −1392 | 1860 | 468 |
| 1970 | 7047 | 4428 | −2619 | 3080 | 461 |
| 1971 | 8090 | 5075 | −3015 | 3846 | 831 |

*Source*: Goh Keng Swee (1995, 12–13).

Therefore, the overall balance of payments of Singapore was consistently positive with a few exceptions. It can be posited that it was not implausible that the overall balance of payments during the pre-independence period behaved in a similar manner in the absence of statistical information on the capital account for the earlier years.

### 3.3.2.4.1 Exports of Goods and Services

As presented in Table 3.11, merchandize exports at current prices have increased from $185.8 million in 1900 to $435.9 million in 1939. Between 1950 and 60, it increased from $3.0 billion to $3.5 billion. The annual growth rate of exports, however, experienced frequent fluctuations.

Three major downturns of merchandize exports were experienced for the years 1920–21 (–55%), 1930–31 (–48%), 1937–38

**Table 3.11:** Singapore: Total Merchandize Exports and Exports of Major Commodities, 1900–39 and 1950–60

| Year | Total Merchandize Exports | | [1] Rubber | | | [2] Tin | | | [3] Petroleum | | | [4] = [1] + [2] + [3] | | Year |
|---|---|---|---|---|---|---|---|---|---|---|---|---|---|---|
| | Value ($,000) | Growth Rate (%) | Value ($,000) | Growth Rate (%) | % Share | Value ($,000) | Growth Rate (%) | % Share | Value ($,000) | Growth Rate (%) | % Share | Value ($,000) | % Share | |
| 1900 | 185,788 | | | | — | 34,505 | | 19 | 2,282 | | 1 | 36,787 | 20 | 1900 |
| 1901 | 194,810 | 5 | | — | | 36,896 | 7 | 19 | 2,238 | −2 | 1 | 39,134 | 20 | 1901 |
| 1902 | 209,278 | 7 | | — | | 38,592 | 4 | 18 | 1,543 | −37 | 1 | 40,135 | 19 | 1902 |
| 1903 | 211,524 | 1 | | — | | 41,782 | 8 | 20 | 3,422 | 80 | 2 | 45,204 | 21 | 1903 |
| 1904 | 199,956 | −6 | 26 | | 0 | 41,796 | 0 | 21 | 5,818 | 53 | 3 | 47,640 | 24 | 1904 |
| 1905 | 197,619 | −1 | 528 | 301 | 0 | 38,980 | −7 | 20 | 1,068 | −170 | 1 | 40,576 | 21 | 1905 |
| 1906 | 202,211 | 1 | ,648 | 114 | 1 | 46,333 | 17 | 23 | 833 | −25 | 1 | 48,814 | 24 | 1906 |
| 1907 | 001,830 | 2 | ,895 | 56 | 1 | 43,929 | −5 | 22 | 835 | 0 | 0 | 47,659 | 24 | 1907 |
| 1908 | 181,050 | −11 | 2,940 | 2 | 2 | 33,478 | −27 | 18 | 922 | 10 | 1 | 37,340 | 21 | 1908 |
| 1909 | 285,627 | 5 | ,438 | 62 | 3 | 32,038 | −4 | 17 | 925 | 0 | 0 | 38,401 | 21 | 1909 |
| 1910 | 219,520 | −7 | 9,838 | 59 | 4 | 34,669 | 8 | 16 | 854 | −8 | 0 | 45,361 | 21 | 1910 |
| 1911 | 226,768 | 3 | 12,435 | 23 | 5 | 41,373 | 18 | 18 | 473 | −59 | 0 | 54,281 | 24 | 1911 |
| 1912 | 241,814 | 6 | 10,270 | −19 | 4 | 47,879 | 15 | 20 | 724 | 43 | 0 | 58,873 | 24 | 1912 |
| 1913 | 256,154 | 6 | 13,961 | 31 | 5 | 55,875 | 15 | 22 | 621 | −15 | | 70,457 | 28 | 1913 |
| 1914 | 228,330 | −11 | 21,328 | 42 | 9 | 40,905 | −31 | 18 | 663 | 7 | 0 | 62,896 | 28 | 1914 |
| 1915 | 303,860 | 29 | 54,642 | 94 | 18 | 55,000 | 30 | 18 | 1,206 | 60 | 0 | 110,848 | 36 | 1915 |
| 1916 | 377,950 | 22 | 103,254 | 64 | 27 | 51,410 | −7 | 14 | 3,213 | 98 | 1 | 157,877 | 42 | 1916 |
| 1917 | 491,849 | 26 | 171,637 | 51 | 35 | 60,828 | 17 | 12 | 841 | −134 | 0 | 233,306 | 47 | 1917 |
| 1918 | 496,637 | 1 | 139,136 | −21 | 28 | 73,454 | 19 | 15 | 696 | −19 | 0 | 213,286 | 43 | 1918 |
| 1919 | 720,347 | 37 | 260,934 | 63 | 36 | 72,427 | −1 | 10 | 1,259 | 59 | 0 | 334,620 | 46 | 1919 |
| 1920 | 724,271 | 1 | 232,510 | −12 | 32 | 70,491 | −3 | 10 | 1,956 | 44 | 0 | 304,957 | 42 | 1920 |
| 1921 | 415,808 | −55 | 83,918 | −102 | 20 | 41,713 | −52 | 10 | 1,890 | −3 | 0 | 127,521 | 31 | 1921 |
| 1922 | 414,959 | 0 | 104,132 | 22 | 25 | 44,721 | 7 | 11 | 10,762 | 174 | 3 | 159,615 | 38 | 1922 |
| 1923 | 512,781 | 21 | 158,185 | 42 | 31 | 46,727 | 4 | 9 | 34,833 | 117 | 7 | 239,745 | 47 | 1923 |
| 1924 | 551,010 | 7 | 151,856 | −4 | 28 | 75,168 | 48 | 14 | 30,768 | −12 | 6 | 257,792 | 47 | 1924 |
| 1925 | 899,853 | 49 | 405,844 | 98 | 45 | 72,556 | −4 | 8 | 71,127 | 84 | 8 | 549,527 | 61 | 1925 |
| 1926 | 874,758 | −3 | 342,328 | −17 | 39 | 76,338 | 5 | 9 | 78,658 | 10 | 9 | 497,324 | 57 | 1926 |
| 1927 | 791,614 | −10 | 271,354 | −23 | 34 | 91,929 | 19 | 12 | 73,659 | −7 | 9 | 436,942 | 55 | 1927 |
| 1928 | 652,825 | −19 | 162,407 | −51 | 25 | 82,565 | −1 | 13 | | | — | 244,972 | 38 | 1928 |
| 1929 | 658,964 | 1 | 183,592 | 12 | 28 | 76,560 | −8 | 12 | 49,494 | | 8 | 309,646 | 47 | 1929 |
| 1930 | 526,016 | −23 | 100,461 | −60 | 19 | 47,257 | −48 | 9 | | | — | 147,718 | 28 | 1930 |
| 1931 | 326,419 | −48 | 49,937 | −70 | 15 | 29,800 | −46 | 9 | 65,101 | | 20 | 144,838 | 44 | 1931 |
| 1932 | 269,487 | −19 | 28,536 | −56 | 11 | 24,565 | −19 | 9 | 58,145 | −11 | 22 | 111,246 | 41 | 1932 |
| 1933 | 289,624 | 7 | 45,451 | 47 | 16 | 51,208 | 73 | 18 | 42,285 | −32 | 15 | 138,944 | 48 | 1933 |
| 1934 | 331,880 | 14 | 124,045 | 100 | 37 | 45,333 | −12 | 14 | 44,649 | 5 | 13 | 214,027 | 64 | 1934 |
| 1935 | 345,552 | 4 | 112,379 | −10 | 33 | 52,725 | 15 | 15 | 50,911 | 13 | 15 | 216,015 | 63 | 1935 |
| 1936 | 365,742 | 6 | 131,428 | 16 | 36 | 63,457 | 19 | 17 | 42,416 | −18 | 12 | 237,301 | 65 | 1936 |
| 1937 | 492,141 | 30 | 206,172 | 45 | 42 | 77,692 | 20 | 16 | 54,047 | 24 | 11 | 337,911 | 69 | 1937 |
| 1938 | 339,475 | −37 | 120,511 | −54 | 35 | 39,082 | −69 | 12 | 54,924 | 2 | 16 | 214,517 | 63 | 1938 |
| 1939 | 435,886 | 25 | 178,765 | 39 | 41 | 69,527 | 58 | 16 | 52,561 | −4 | 12 | 300,853 | 69 | 1939 |
| 1950 | 3,025,750 | | 1,405,274 | | 46 | 207,190 | | 7 | 160,677 | | 5 | 1,773,141 | 59 | 1950 |
| 1951 | 4,745,242 | 45 | 2,518,844 | 58 | 53 | 261,457 | 23 | 6 | 201,701 | 23 | 4 | 2,982,002 | 63 | 1951 |
| 1952 | 3,199,610 | −39 | 915,895 | −101 | 29 | 217,429 | −18 | 7 | 307,796 | 42 | 10 | 1,441,120 | 45 | 1952 |
| 1953 | 2,654,114 | −19 | 750,764 | −20 | 28 | 172,292 | −23 | 6 | 341,584 | 10 | 13 | 1,264,640 | 48 | 1953 |
| 1954 | 2,685,518 | 1 | 785,088 | 4 | 29 | 195,912 | 13 | 7 | 350,556 | 3 | 13 | 1,331,556 | 50 | 1954 |
| 1955 | 3,368,699 | 23 | 1,399,635 | 58 | 42 | 202,192 | 3 | 6 | 371,097 | 6 | 11 | 1,972,924 | 59 | 1955 |
| 1956 | 3,428,975 | 2 | 1,216,551 | −14 | 35 | 138,657 | −38 | 4 | 446,236 | 18 | 13 | 1,801,444 | 53 | 1956 |
| 1957 | 3,478,133 | 1 | 1,171,094 | −4 | 34 | 133,562 | −4 | 4 | 444,964 | 0 | 13 | 1,749,620 | 50 | 1957 |
| 1958 | 3,140,343 | −10 | 1,045,556 | −1 | 33 | 48,337 | −102 | 2 | 370,308 | −18 | 12 | 1,464,201 | 47 | 1958 |
| 1959 | 3,440,263 | 9 | 1,533,074 | 38 | 45 | 4,448 | −239 | 0 | 371,657 | 0 | 11 | 1,909,179 | 55 | 1959 |
| 1960 | 3,477,053 | 1 | 1,426,513 | −7 | 41 | 5,161 | 15 | 0 | 379,209 | 2 | 11 | 1,810,883 | 52 | 1960 |

▨ Not Available

(−37%), and 1951–52 (−39%). On the other hand, five booms were recorded for the years 1918–19 (37%), 1924–25 (49%), 1936–37 (30%), 1950–51 (45%), and 1954–55 (23%). These patterns of fluctuations in merchandize export growth of Singapore are inextricably linked to international economic conditions. A boom during World War I (1915–17); the immediate postwar buying euphoria and worldwide inflation in 1919; recession from mid-1920 to 1921; a sharp upswing in the mid-1920s; and the slump in the early 1930's, followed by a partial recovery in the form of a miniboom in 1937 were some of the extreme conditions during the period 1900–39. For the period 1950–60, drastic expansion was recorded for 1951 due to the Korean War.

Using Huff's estimates on export value of major export commodities, an attempt was made to provide supportive reasons, which led to these fluctuations. As presented in Table 3.10, rubber, tin, and petroleum were the three major commodities which can portray the movement of merchandize exports. In 1917, the three comprised 47% of Singapore's total exports. This proportion rose to 61% in 1925 because of further rapid increases in rubber exports and the sudden growth of petroleum trade. In 1955, these three commodities combined to account for some 59% of Singapore's exports though the share of tin had significantly decreased. Of these three commodities, the share of rubber to total merchandize exports in particular rapidly increased after 1914. The share of rubber varied from 5% (1913) to 45% (1925) and 53% (1951). In line with growing predominance of rubber exports, in relation to Singapore's total merchandize exports, it has inevitably influenced the level and resulting fluctuations of Singapore's total merchandize exports (See Fig. 3.5).

Worlds demand for rubber was basically strongly tied to the development of motorized transport. The automobile industry needed rubber mainly for the manufacturing of tyres. Between 1913 and 1930s, the United States annually imported one-half to three-quarters of worlds rubber production. Its automotive industry took three-quarters of these imports. Because of high export dependence on the United States and the demand and supply conditions for rubber, instability in the American economy had a powerful impact on Singapore. As presented in Table 3.12, total merchandize exports to United States which mainly comprised rubber, tin, and petroleum increased more than 10 times between 1911 and 1927. In the 1950s, however, the destination of Singapore's primary exports shifted from the United States to Europe because of the invention and widespread use of the cheaper synthetic rubber in United States paralleled

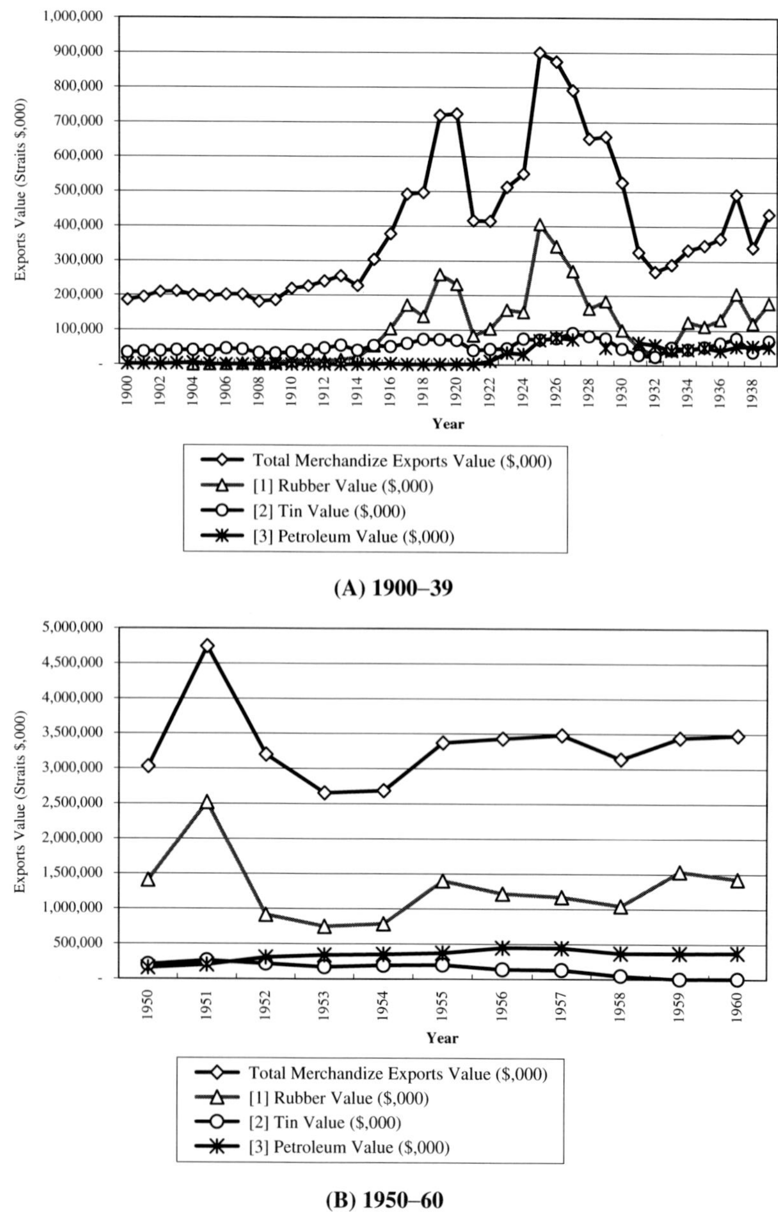



**(A) 1900–39**



**(B) 1950–60**

**Figure 3.5:**  Singapore: Merchandize Exports by Major Export Commodities.
*Source*: Figure arranged from Huff (1994).

**Table 3.12:** Singapore: Exports by Country and Region, 1911–13, 1925–27 and 1957–59 (Annual Average)

| | 1911–1913 | | 1925–1927 | | 1957–1959 | |
|---|---|---|---|---|---|---|
| | $'000 | % | $'000 | % | $'000 | % |
| **Southeast Asia** | 123,111 | 47.8% | 304,543 | 35.1% | 1,317,149 | 39.3% |
| Malaya (Peninsular Malaysia) | 58,485 | 22.7% | 148,631 | 17.1% | 694,688 | 20.7% |
| Netherland East Indies (Indonesia) | 39,358 | 15.3% | 102,041 | 11.8% | 244,642 | 7.3% |
| Siam (Thailand) | 9,666 | 3.8% | 22,405 | 2.6% | 82,283 | 2.5% |
| Indo-China (Vietnam) | 2,323 | 0.9% | 9,463 | 1.1% | 49,737 | 1.5% |
| British Borneo (Sarawak, North Borneo, and Brunei) | 6,182 | 2.4% | 14,102 | 1.6% | 164,467 | 4.9% |
| Burma | 5,467 | 2.1% | 5,900 | 0.7% | 23,937 | 0.7% |
| Philippine Islands and Sulu Archipelago | 1,630 | 0.6% | 2,000 | 0.2% | 57,395 | 1.7% |
| **Europe, North America, and Japan** | 105,916 | 41.1% | 470,440 | 54.2% | 1,381,892 | 41.2% |
| United Kingdom | 35,925 | 13.9% | 49,208 | 5.7% | 278,808 | 8.3% |
| Europe | 33,372 | 13.0% | 75,460 | 8.7% | 594,735 | 17.7% |
| United States | 31,188 | 12.1% | 316,768 | 36.5% | 253,309 | 7.6% |
| Canada | 638 | 0.2% | 2,378 | 0.3% | 46,226 | 1.4% |
| Japan | 4,793 | 1.9% | 26,626 | 3.1% | 208,814 | 6.2% |
| **Rest of World** | 28,597 | 11.1% | 93,295 | 10.7% | 653,872 | 19.5% |
| Hong Kong | 8,137 | 3.2% | 6,826 | 0.8% | 50,881 | 1.5% |
| China | 3,240 | 1.3% | 7,959 | 0.9% | 75,498 | 2.3% |
| India | 11,553 | 4.5% | 14,399 | 1.7% | 62,144 | 1.9% |
| Sri Lanka | 1,919 | 0.7% | 4,152 | 0.5% | 12,147 | 0.4% |
| Australia | 1,501 | 0.6% | 30,619 | 3.5% | 118,724 | 3.5% |
| Others | 2,246 | 0.9% | 29,339 | 3.4% | 334,477 | 10.0% |
| **Gross Exports (Inclusive of Coins and Bullions)** | 257,624 | 100.0% | 868,278 | 100.0% | 3,352,913 | 100.0% |

*Notes*:
1. The figures include treasure of bullion and specie.
2. Columns may not add to totals due to rounding.
*Source*: Huff (1994, 81 and 282–283).

by the emergence of a large demand of rubber in Europe, including Eastern Europe.

### 3.3.2.4.2 Imports of Goods and Services

As described earlier, the structure of imports by major object was similar to that of exports. Merchandize imports of Singapore have generally moved in tandem to that of merchandize exports, though the former was consistently higher than the latter. Apart from rubber, tin, petroleum, and other commodities, most of the major consumer and capital goods imported recorded higher values than exports since retained imports in the domestic market were finally distributed for either intermediate or final consumption, capital formation, and stocks. Singapore's pattern of imports from Asia has been substantially modified when Singapore developed as an entrepôt dealing essentially with the

**Table 3.13:** Singapore: Imports by Country and Region, 1911–13, 1925–27, and 1957–59 (Annual Average)

| | 1911–1913 | | 1925–1927 | | 1957–1959 | |
|---|---|---|---|---|---|---|
| | $'000 | % | $'000 | % | $'000 | % |
| **Southeast Asia** | 182,584 | 57.3% | 694,775 | 69.7% | 2,229,456 | 57.0% |
| Malaya (Peninsular Malaysia) | 64,565 | 20.3% | 203,537 | 20.4% | 742,144 | 19.0% |
| Netherland East Indies (Indonesia) | 56,577 | 17.8% | 344,747 | 34.6% | 1,066,791 | 27.3% |
| Siam (Thailand) | 30,329 | 9.5% | 72,565 | 7.3% | 142,220 | 3.6% |
| Indo-China (Vietnam) | 11,560 | 3.6% | 20,196 | 2.0% | 41,698 | 1.1% |
| British Borneo (Sarawak, North Borneo, and Brunei) | 5,431 | 1.7% | 40,087 | 4.0% | 200,837 | 5.1% |
| Burma | 12,430 | 3.9% | 12,336 | 1.2% | 33,496 | 0.9% |
| Philippine Islands, and Sulu Archipelago | 1,692 | 0.5% | 1,306 | 0.1% | 2,269 | 0.1% |
| **Europe, North America, and Japan** | 65,382 | 20.5% | 184,419 | 18.5% | 1,045,944 | 26.7% |
| United Kingdom | 34,656 | 10.9% | 89,396 | 9.0% | 390,957 | 10.0% |
| Europe | 16,183 | 5.1% | 35,860 | 3.6% | 270,696 | 6.9% |
| United States | 4,825 | 1.5% | 30,824 | 3.1% | 127,015 | 3.2% |
| Canada | 104 | 0.0% | 2,328 | 0.2% | 11,390 | 0.3% |
| Japan | 9,614 | 3.0% | 26,011 | 2.6% | 245,886 | 6.3% |
| **Rest of World** | 70,572 | 22.2% | 117,662 | 11.8% | 637,790 | 16.3% |
| Hong Kong | 25,909 | 8.1% | 27,180 | 2.7% | 86,295 | 2.2% |
| China | 8,395 | 2.6% | 32,233 | 3.2% | 135,122 | 3.5% |
| India | 19,934 | 6.3% | 30,821 | 3.1% | 66,395 | 1.7% |
| Sri Lanka | 621 | 0.2% | 798 | 0.1% | 2,430 | 0.1% |
| Australia | 10,781 | 3.4% | 13,481 | 1.4% | 112,726 | 2.9% |
| Others | 4,932 | 1.5% | 13,151 | 1.3% | 234,821 | 6.0% |
| Gross Imports (Inclusive of Coins and Bullions) | 318,538 | 100.0% | 996,856 | 100.0% | 3,913,191 | 100.0% |

*Notes*:
1. The figures include treasure of bullion and specie.
2. Columns may not add to totals due to rounding.
*Source*: Huff (1994, 81 and 282–283).

import and export of commodities such as rubber, tin, and petroleum. The city became more dependent on imports from its immediate hinterland of Malaya, Netherlands East Indies, and British Borneo, which were the main suppliers of these commodities which were re-exported to the West. As presented in Table 3.13, these three territories combined accounted for 39.8% (1911–13), 59.1% (1925–27) and 51.4% (1957–59) of total merchandize imports of Singapore. Other than these major commodities, Singapore imported food from elsewhere in Southeast Asia and manufactures from the Western countries for domestic consumption and re-exports.

### 3.3.3 *International Comparison*

#### 3.3.3.1 *Growth Rate of GDP and Its Components*

It might be of interest to make comparisons of GDP estimates of Singapore with that of other nations. For this purpose, six countries were chosen, on the basis of data availability, they being the United Kingdom, United States, Japan, Korea, Taiwan, and Finland. Figure 3.6 depicts the comparison of Singapore's annual growth rate of GDP with these selected countries for the period 1900–39 at current prices.[72] One outstanding feature arising from these comparisons was the volatility in the GDP growth rates of Singapore compared to the other countries during this period. Nevertheless, there was a common pattern amongst all countries reflected in the sharp dip in GDP growth rates during the period of World War I and the Great Depression years in the early 1930s. It would be noted that the growth of Singapore in the 1930s was very similar to that of Malaya and United States.[73]

Subsequently, annual growth rate of each component of GDP was observed (See Figs. 3.7–3.11). Unlike annual growth rate of GDP, annual growth rate of each component of GDP was somewhat not significantly different from that observed for the other selected countries.

In the case of PFCE, all selected countries recorded remarkably steep annual growth rate increase during the 1916–20 period. Subsequently, all selected countries experienced a continuous negative growth during the world depression in the early 1930s. Annual growth rate of GFCE recorded significant increases, particularly in the United Kingdom and Japan during the World War I period and the Japan-Russo War, respectively. Unlike these countries, Singapore did not experience wide fluctuations of government final consumption expenditure.

The percentage annual growth rate of GCF for the period 1900–39 experienced relatively frequent volatilities. During the early 1920s and 1930s, most of the countries experienced negative growth due to the world wide recessions. Interestingly, the

---

[72] Ideally, comparison would be made on the basis of the constant prices with the same base year. However, it is impossible to conduct this exercise since each country used different base years. Therefore, it was decided to use current price figures for international comparison.

[73] For the period 1929–39, correlations of GDP growth between (a) Singapore and Malaya and (b) Singapore and United States were 0.7187 and 0.5959, respectively.

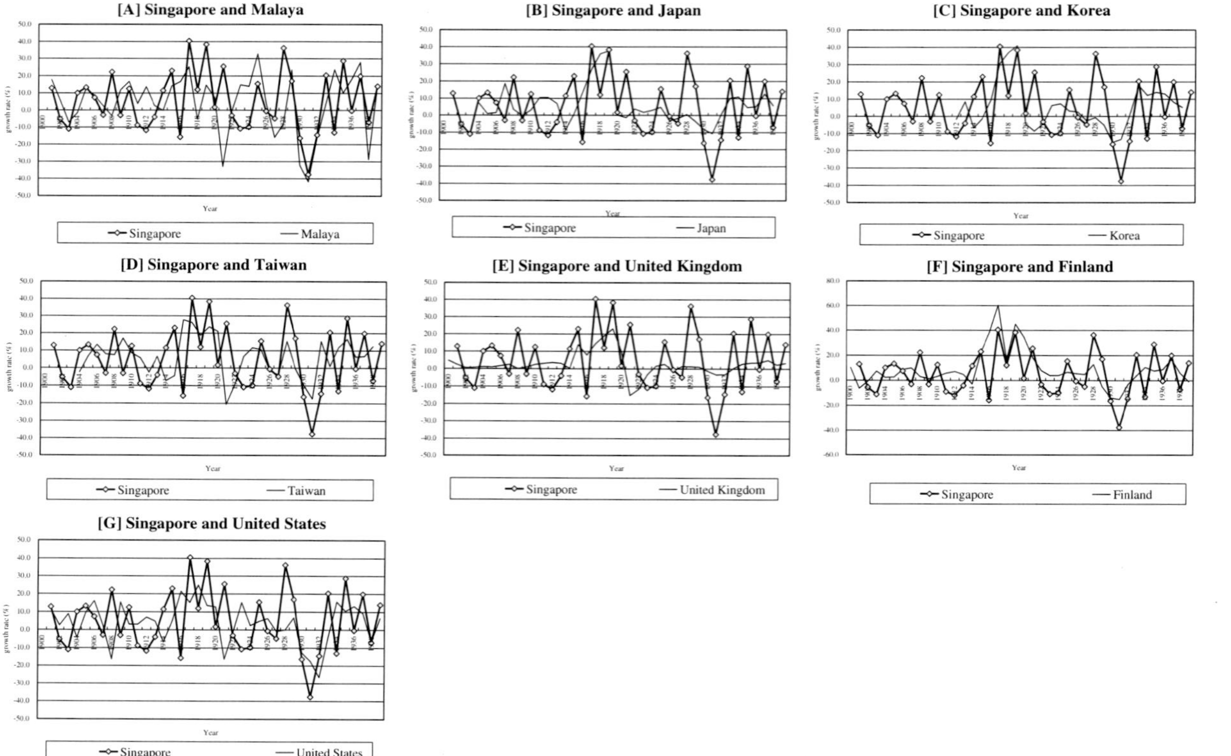


**Fig. 3.6:** Annual Growth Rates (%) of GDP of Singapore Against Selected Countries, 1900–39, at Current Prices

*Sources:* (Malaya) Nazrin, Raja (2002), (Japan, Korea, and Taiwan) Mizoguchi, Toshiyuki, and Umemura, Mataji (edit.) (1988), (UK) Feinstein, CH, (1974), (Finland) Hjerppe, Riitta (1996), (USA) Carter, Susan B (2006).

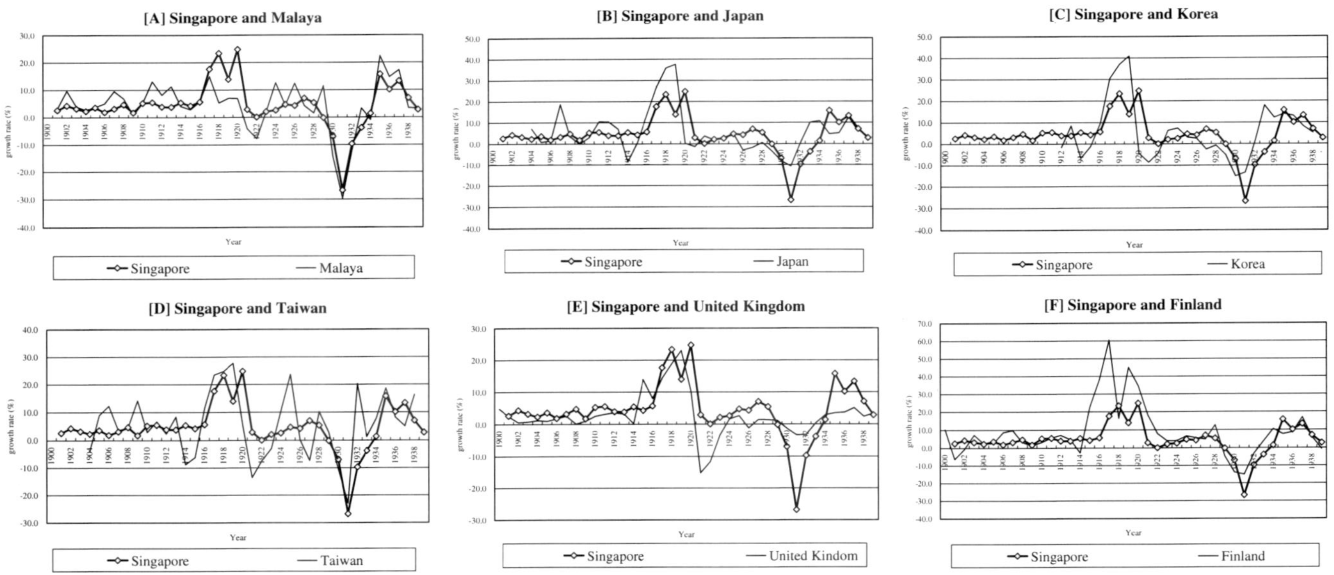

**Fig. 3.7:** Annual Growth Rates (%) of Private Final Consumption Expenditure by Resident Household (PFCE) of Singapore Against Selected Countries, 1900–39, at Current Prices

*Sources:* (Malaya) Nazrin, Raja (2006), (UK) Feinstein, CH, (1974), (Finland) Hjerppe, Riitta (1996), (Japan, Korea, and Taiwan) Mizoguchi, Toshiyuki, and Umemura, Mataji (edit.) (1988).

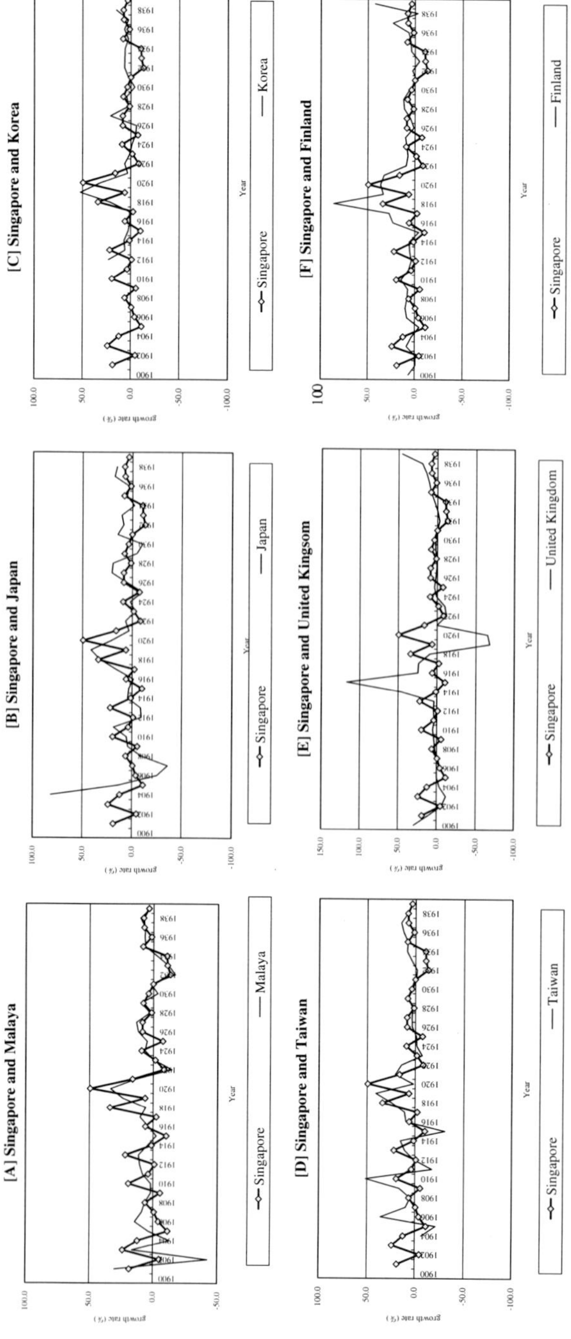


**Fig. 3.8:** Annual Growth Rates (%) of Government Final Consumption Expenditure (GFCE) of Singapore Against Selected Countries, 1900–39, at Current Prices

*Sources:* (Malaya) Nazrin, Raja (2002), (UK) Feinstein, CH, (1974), (Finland) Hjerppe, Riitta (1996), (Japan, Korea, and Taiwan) Mizoguchi, Toshiyuki, and Umemura, Mataji (edit.) (1988).

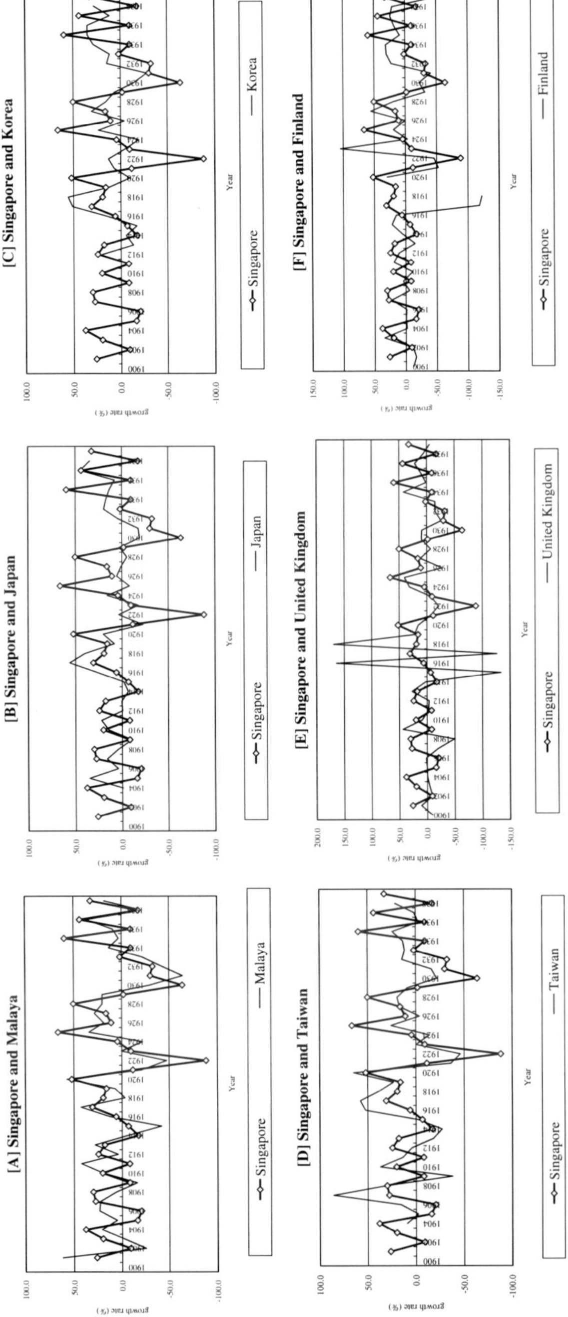


**Fig. 3.9:** Annual Growth Rates (%) of Gross Capital Formation (GCF) of Singapore Against Selected Countries, 1900–39 and 1950–60, at Current Prices

*Sources:* (Malaya) Nazrin, Raja (2002), (UK) Feinstein, CH, (1974), (Finland) Hjerppe, Riitta (1996), (Japan, Korea, and Taiwan) Mizoguchi, Toshiyuki, and Umemura, Mataji (edit.) (1988).

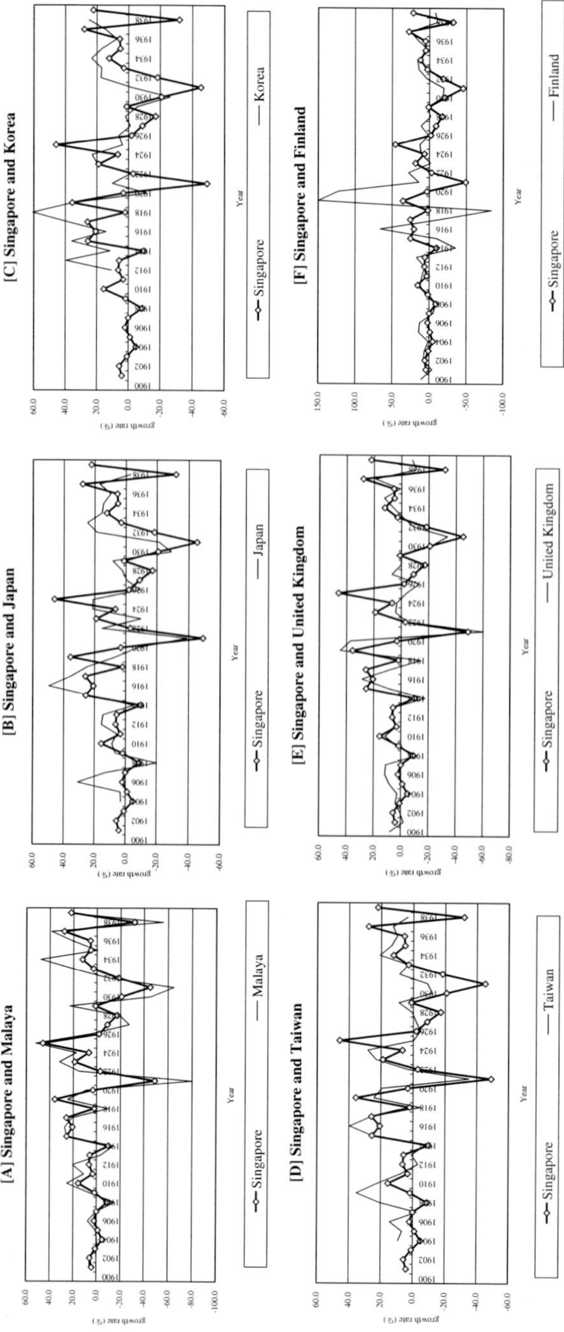


**Fig. 3.10:** Annual Growth Rates (%) of Exports of Goods and Services (EXGS) of Singapore Against Selected Countries, 1900–39 and 1950–60, at Current Prices

*Sources:* (Malaya) Nazrin, Raja (2002), (UK) Feinstein, CH, (1974), (Finland) Hjerppe, Riitta (1996), (Japan, Korea, and Taiwan) Mizoguchi, Toshiyuki, and Umemura, Mataji (edit.) (1988).

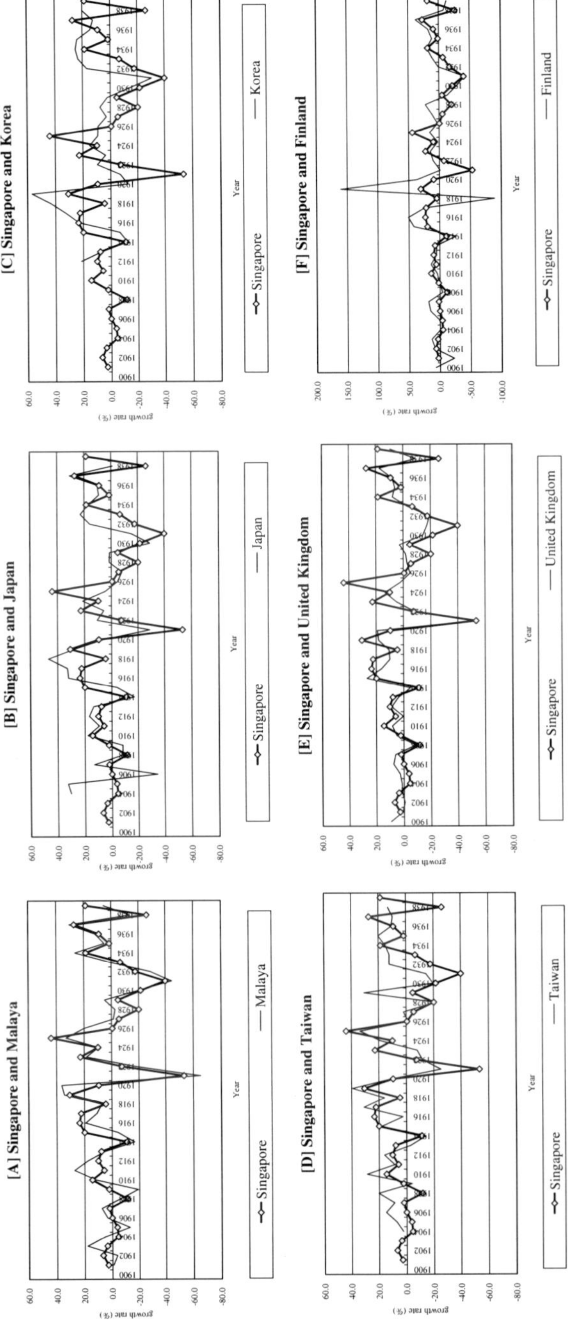


**Fig. 3.11:** Annual Growth Rates (%) of Imports of Goods and Services (IMGS) of Singapore Against Selected Countries, 1900–39 and 1950–60, at Current Prices

*Sources*: (Malaya) Nazrin, Raja (2002), (UK) Feinstein, CH, (1974), (Finland) Hjerppe, Riitta (1996), (Japan, Korea, and Taiwan) Mizoguchi, Toshiyuki, and Umemura, Mataji (edit.) (1988).

movement of Singapore was somewhat very similar to that of Malaya (See Fig. 3.9). Figures 3.10 and 3.11 portray the annual growth of both exports and imports of goods and services. As observed in the case of GCF, annual growth rates of both imports and exports of goods and services experienced similar patterns. Interestingly, Malaya, Japan, Taiwan, and Korea have all recorded similar patterns of growth during the period.

In addition to annual growth rate of GDP and its components, it is necessary to observe the difference in the percentage contribution of each GDP component to total GDP among the selected countries.

### 3.3.3.2 *Share of Each Component of GDP to GDP*

In terms of percentage share of each GDP component to total GDP, intercountry comparisons are presented in Table 3.14 and Figs. 3.12–3.15. In terms of share of PFCE and GCF to GDP, Singapore has experienced a relatively higher percentage share than that of the other countries. On the other hand, in terms of the share of GFCE, Singapore has shown to have relatively smaller percentage share than the other nations. One unique feature that does not escape notice in general is the continuous negative share of Singapore's net export of goods and services to GDP throughout the entire study period.[74] Singapore had extensive contacts with other nations and each of them served as a crucial port for their respective hinterland, undertaking certain essential distributive, financial, and transportation functions. This entrepôt background gave them certain initial advantages.

---

[74] It will be noted that the share of each component of GDP for Singapore has been relatively similar to that of the Dutch. Unfortunately, the share of each component of the Dutch GDP was available for the period 1814–1913 only.

**Table 3.14:** Percentage Share of Components of GDP to Total GDP for Selected Countries at Current Prices, 1900–60

| Private Final Consumption Expenditure by Resident Households | | | | | | | |
|---|---|---|---|---|---|---|---|
| | Singapore | Japan | Korea | Taiwan | UK | Finland | Dutch |
| 1900 | 96 | — | — | — | 84 | 85 | 84 |
| 1911 | 88 | 73 | 99 | 78 | 84 | 85 | 91 |
| 1926 | 94 | 78 | 92 | 72 | 87 | 81 | — |
| 1934 | 81 | 71 | 88 | 64 | 84 | 67 | — |
| 1950 | 81 | — | — | — | 73 | 65 | — |
| 1960 | 87 | — | — | — | 67 | 59 | — |

| Government Final Consumption Expenditure | | | | | | | |
|---|---|---|---|---|---|---|---|
| | Singapore | Japan | Korea | Taiwan | UK | Finland | Dutch |
| 1900 | 6 | — | — | — | 9 | 7 | 7 |
| 1911 | 7 | 9 | 3 | 6 | 8 | 9 | 6 |
| 1926 | 8 | 7 | 4 | 6 | 10 | 9 | — |
| 1934 | 8 | 12 | 6 | 7 | 10 | 11 | — |
| 1950 | 7 | — | — | — | 16 | 11 | — |
| 1960 | 6 | — | — | — | 16 | 13 | — |

| Gross Capital Formation | | | | | | | |
|---|---|---|---|---|---|---|---|
| | Singapore | Japan | Korea | Taiwan | UK | Finland | Dutch |
| 1900 | 12 | — | — | — | 10 | 16 | 13 |
| 1911 | 21 | 19 | 5 | 11 | 7 | 16 | 18 |
| 1926 | 22 | 18 | 5 | 13 | 10 | 10 | — |
| 1934 | 12 | 17 | 9 | 17 | 10 | 17 | — |
| 1950 | 15 | — | — | — | 12 | 22 | — |
| 1960 | 13 | — | — | — | 19 | 29 | — |

| Net Exports of Goods and Services | | | | | | | |
|---|---|---|---|---|---|---|---|
| | Singapore | Japan | KoreaT | aiwanU | KF | inland | Dutch |
| 1900 | −15 | 0 | 0 | 0 | −3 | −8 | −4 |
| 1911 | −16 | −1 | −7 | 5 | 1 | −9 | −16 |
| 1926 | −23 | −3 | 0 | 0 | −6 | 0 | — |
| 1934 | 0 | 0 | −3 | 12 | −4 | 5 | — |
| 1950 | −3 | 0 | 0 | 0 | −1 | 1 | — |
| 1960 | −6 | 0 | 0 | 0 | −2 | −1 | — |

*Sources*: (Japan, Korea, and Taiwan) Mizoguchi, Toshiyuki, and Umemura, Mataji (edit.) (1988), (UK) Feinstein (1974), (Finland) Hjerppe, Riitta (1996), (Dutch) J-P Smits, E Horlings and JL van Zanden (2000).

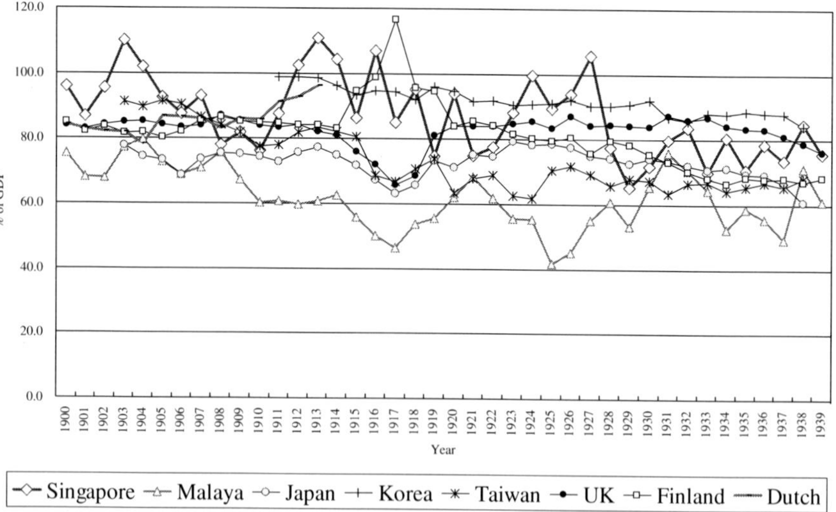


**Fig. 3.12:** Percentage Share of Private Final Consumption Expenditure in Gross Domestic Product in Current Prices, 1900–39, Singapore and Selected Countries

*Sources*: (Malaya) Nazrin, Raja (2002), (Japan, Korea, and Taiwan) Mizoguchi, Toshiyuki and Umemura, Mataji (edit.) (1988), (UK) Feinstein (1974), (Finland) Hjerppe, Riitta (1996), (Dutch) J-P Smits, E Horlings and JL van Zanden (2000).

But Singapore is almost totally lacking in natural resources. Its arable land can provide only a small portion of its food require-ments. Additionally, Singapore does not have her own rural hin-terlands in which a majority of their people still live and support themselves by subsistence or commercial agriculture. Nor do they have a domestic market large enough to serve as the initial base for industrialization. Hence, Singapore's very existence depended upon its ability to import, which, in turn, rested upon its capacity to earn the necessary foreign exchange by exporting goods and services to competitive regional and world markets.[75] The extreme

---

[75] As described on p. 146, while the merchandize trade balance was consistently negative, the combined invisible trade and capital and financial account (CFA) was positive largely due to the inflow of foreign direct investments.

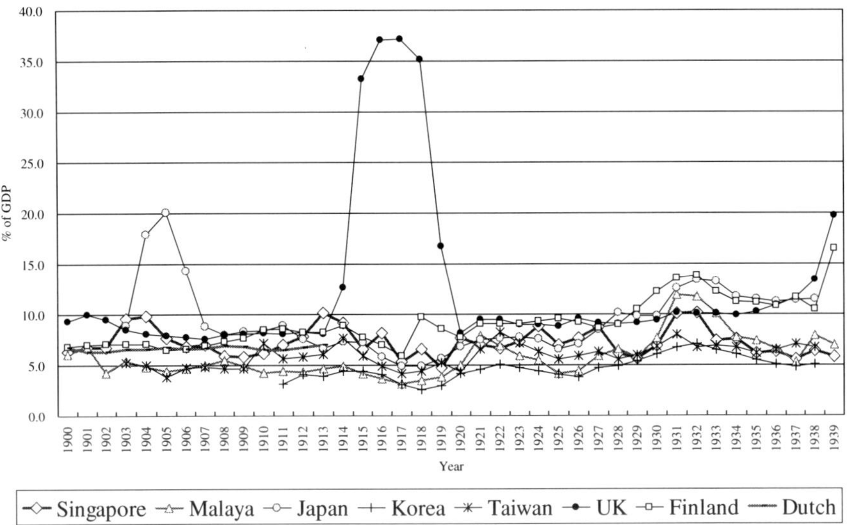


**Fig. 3.13:** Percentage Share of Government Final Consumption Expenditure in Gross Domestic Product in Current Prices, 1900–39, Singapore and Selected Countries

*Sources*: (Malaya) Nazrin, Raja (2002), (Japan, Korea, and Taiwan) Mizoguchi, Toshiyuki and Umemura, Mataji (edit.) (1988), (UK) Feinstein (1974), (Finland) Hjerppe, Riitta (1996), (Dutch) J-P Smits, E Horlings and JL van Zanden (2000).

dependence of Singapore on foreign trade, in consequence, led to it being extremely vulnerable against external economic shocks and consequently its impact on GDP (Peebles *et al.*, 2002).

## 3.4 Overall Pattern of Singapore's GDP during the Twentieth Century

### 3.4.1 *Transforming the Base Year from 1914 Prices to 1990 Prices for the Periods 1900–39 and 1950–60*

In order to conduct a quantitative investigation for this entire 100-year period, it becomes inevitable that a time-series data stretching over the twentieth century with one base year be constructed. In this exercise, the year 1990 was selected as base

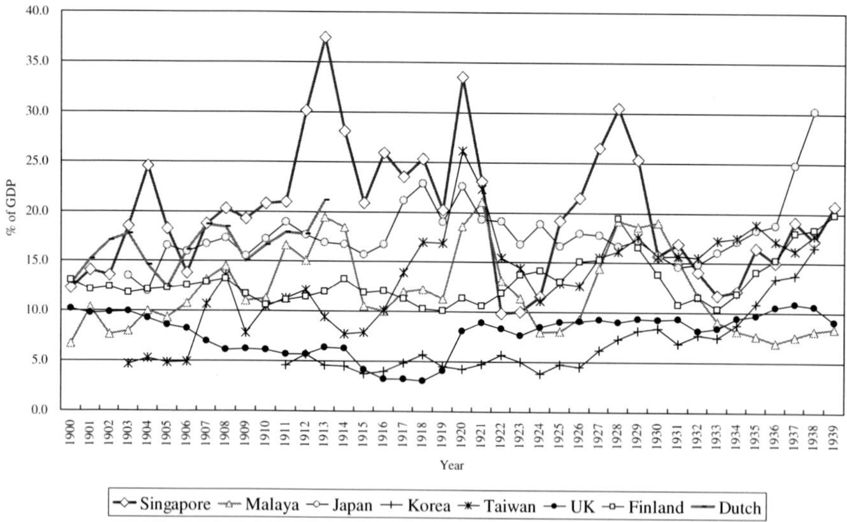


**Fig. 3.14:**   Percentage Share of Gross Capital Formation in Gross Domestic Product in Current Prices, 1900–39, Singapore and Selected Countries

*Sources*: (Malaya) Nazrin, Raja (2002), (Japan, Korea, and Taiwan) Mizoguchi, Toshiyuki and Umemura, Mataji (edit.) (1988), (UK) Feinstein (1974), (Finland) Hjerppe, Riitta (1996), (Dutch) J-P Smits, E Horlings and JL van Zanden (2000).

year for the entire twentieth century because of the availability of time-series data for the period 1960–95, provided in the *Singapore System of National Accounts 1995* and 1996–2000 in the *Asian Development Bank, Key Indicators of Developing Asian and Pacific Countries, 2001.* On the other hand, 1914 was selected as a base year for the periods 1900–39 and 1950–60 as discussed in Chapter 2. For purposes of conducting rebasing from 1914 to 1990 prices for the period, 1900–39 and 1950–60 from 1914 prices, the following formula was applied for re-scaling:

$$ {}^{x}E_{90} = {}^{x}E_{14} \times \frac{{}^{60}E_{90}}{{}^{60}E_{14}} $$

where ${}^{x}E_{y}$ is the estimate of year $x$ in base year $y$ prices.

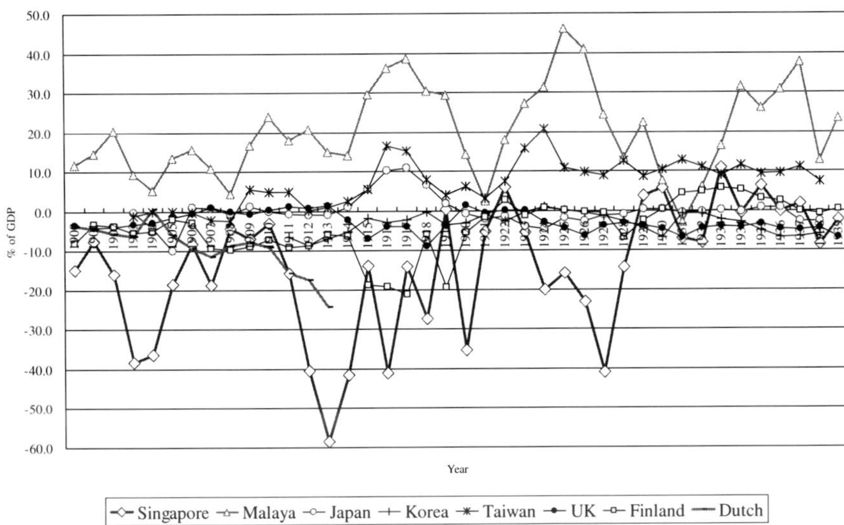


**Fig. 3.15:** Percentage Share of Net Exports of Goods and Services in Gross Domestic Product in Current Prices, 1900–39, Singapore and Selected Countries

*Sources*: (Malaya) Nazrin, Raja (2002), (Japan, Korea, and Taiwan) Mizoguchi, Toshiyuki and Umemura, Mataji (edit.) (1988), (UK) Feinstein (1974), (Finland) Hjerppe, Riitta (1996), (Dutch) J-P Smits, E Horlings and JL van Zanden (2000).

As presented in Chapter 2, PFCE and GFCE were deflated by CPI. On the other hand, other components of GDP were deflated differently. In the case of GCF, investment in cultivated assets, construction, transport, machinery and equipment, and change in stock was deflated by each deflator separately. Similar to this, merchandize trade and service trade were deflated by their respective deflators. Nevertheless, official database for the years 1960–2000 merely provides implicit deflators for each component of GDP. Under these constraints of availability of deflator, it was decided to apply the implicit deflators for GCF, EXGS, and IMGS (See Tables 3.15 and 3.16).

For the new series in 1990 prices, the growth rates of each component of GDP, namely, PFCE, GFCE, GCF, EXGS, and IMGS for the years 1900–39 and 1950–60 correspond to the 1914

**Table 3.15:** Conversion Ratio from 1914 Price to 1990 Price for the Period 1900–39 and 1950–60

| Private Final Consumption Expenditure (PFCE) | | |
|---|---|---|
| CPI (1914 = 100) for 1960 | [1] | 437.05 |
| Implicit Deflators for PFCE (1990 = 100) for 1960 | [2] | 40.93 |
| Conversion Ratio | [2]/[1] | 0.09 |
| **Government Final Consumption Expenditure (GFCE)** | | |
| CPI (1914 = 100) for 1960 | [1] | 437.05 |
| Implicit Deflators for GFCE (1990 = 100) for 1960 | [2] | 34.57 |
| Conversion Ratio | [2]/[1] | 0.08 |
| **Gross Capital Formation (GCF)** | | |
| Implicit Deflators for GCF (1914 = 100) for 1960 | [1] | 274.02 |
| Implicit Deflators for GCF (1990 = 100) for 1960 | [2] | 17.20 |
| Conversion Ratio | [2]/[1] | 0.06 |
| **Exports of Goods and Services (EXGS)** | | |
| Implicit Deflators for EXGS (1914 = 100) for 1960 | [1] | 280.99 |
| Implicit Deflators for EXGS (1914 = 100) for 1960 | [2] | 52.50 |
| Conversion Ratio | [2]/[1] | 0.19 |
| **Imports of Goods and Services (IMGS)** | | |
| Implicit Deflators for IMGS (1914 = 100) for 1960 | [1] | 273.29 |
| Implicit Deflators for IMGS (1914 = 100) for 1960 | [2] | 53.40 |
| Conversion Ratio | [2]/[1] | 0.20 |

constant price series. However, the growth rates of GDP components in 1990 prices are different from that of GDP series in 1914 prices. Similarly, as would be expected, the percentage share of each component of GDP in 1990 prices was different from 1914 prices.

For conducting the empirical investigation on the economic growth of Singapore for the twentieth century in Chapters 4 and 5, it is inevitable to use the time-series data on GDP and its components with a single base year.

### 3.4.2 *Overall Patterns of Growth for the Twentieth Century*

This section attempts to briefly re-examine the economic growth of Singapore during the entire twentieth century from the view points of GDP growth and share of each component of GDP against GDP.

**Table 3.16:** The Methodology for Deriving Deflators (1990 = 100) by Each Component of GDP, 1900–39 and 1950–2000

| | Private Final Consumption Expenditure [1] | | Government Final Consumption Expenditure [2] | | Gross Fixed Capital Formation [3] | | Exports of Goods and Services [4] | | Imports of Goods and Services [5] | | |
| --- | --- | --- | --- | --- | --- | --- | --- | --- | --- | --- | --- |
| | Implicit Deflator | | Implicit Deflator | | Implicit Deflator | | Implicit Deflator | | Implicit Deflator | | |
| | 1914=100 | 1990=100 | 1914=100 | 1990=100 | 1914=100 | 1990=100 | 1914=100 | 1990=100 | 1914=100 | 1990=100 | |
| 1900 | 82.73 | 7.75 | 82.73 | 6.54 | 116.56 | 7.32 | 87.73 | 16.39 | 87.68 | 17.13 | 1900 |
| 1901 | 83.57 | 7.83 | 83.57 | 6.61 | 110.20 | 6.92 | 89.91 | 16.80 | 90.33 | 17.65 | 1901 |
| 1902 | 86.73 | 8.12 | 86.73 | 6.86 | 113.57 | 7.13 | 95.11 | 17.77 | 96.03 | 18.76 | 1902 |
| 1903 | 87.79 | 8.22 | 87.79 | 6.94 | 114.49 | 7.19 | 93.73 | 17.51 | 94.31 | 18.43 | 1903 |
| 1904 | 87.89 | 8.23 | 87.89 | 6.95 | 113.54 | 7.13 | 88.77 | 16.58 | 88.83 | 17.36 | 1904 |
| 1905 | 89.51 | 8.38 | 89.51 | 7.08 | 104.70 | 6.57 | 90.96 | 16.99 | 91.02 | 17.79 | 1905 |
| 1906 | 88.13 | 8.25 | 88.13 | 6.97 | 89.66 | 5.63 | 96.43 | 18.02 | 96.64 | 18.88 | 1906 |
| 1907 | 88.04 | 8.25 | 88.04 | 6.96 | 95.33 | 5.98 | 91.14 | 17.03 | 90.71 | 17.72 | 1907 |
| 1908 | 89.25 | 8.36 | 89.25 | 7.06 | 98.45 | 6.18 | 86.52 | 16.16 | 86.08 | 16.82 | 1908 |
| 1909 | 87.13 | 8.16 | 87.13 | 6.89 | 96.88 | 6.08 | 89.98 | 16.81 | 89.45 | 17.48 | 1909 |
| 1910 | 88.78 | 8.31 | 88.78 | 7.02 | 92.50 | 5.81 | 98.67 | 18.44 | 98.21 | 19.19 | 1910 |
| 1911 | 97.35 | 9.12 | 97.35 | 7.70 | 85.57 | 5.37 | 105.61 | 19.73 | 105.98 | 20.71 | 1911 |
| 1912 | 99.03 | 9.27 | 99.03 | 7.83 | 93.52 | 5.87 | 110.02 | 20.56 | 110.11 | 21.51 | 1912 |
| 1913 | 101.09 | 9.47 | 101.09 | 8.00 | 107.89 | 6.77 | 107.72 | 20.13 | 108.07 | 21.12 | 1913 |
| 1914 | 100.00 | 9.37 | 100.00 | 7.91 | 100.00 | 6.28 | 100.00 | 18.68 | 100.00 | 19.54 | 1914 |
| 1915 | 106.54 | 9.98 | 106.54 | 8.43 | 110.90 | 6.96 | 109.89 | 20.53 | 110.78 | 21.65 | 1915 |
| 1916 | 113.14 | 10.60 | 113.14 | 8.95 | 132.20 | 8.30 | 120.81 | 22.57 | 121.89 | 23.82 | 1916 |
| 1917 | 117.78 | 11.03 | 117.78 | 9.32 | 157.39 | 9.88 | 130.73 | 24.42 | 131.16 | 25.63 | 1917 |
| 1918 | 140.43 | 13.15 | 140.43 | 11.11 | 208.19 | 13.07 | 145.25 | 27.14 | 144.57 | 28.25 | 1918 |
| 1919 | 172.28 | 16.14 | 172.28 | 13.63 | 200.33 | 12.58 | 155.62 | 29.08 | 150.70 | 29.45 | 1919 |
| 1920 | 221.30 | 20.73 | 221.30 | 17.50 | 265.74 | 16.68 | 180.53 | 33.73 | 189.99 | 37.12 | 1920 |
| 1921 | 174.82 | 16.37 | 174.82 | 13.83 | 221.32 | 13.90 | 123.13 | 23.01 | 117.89 | 23.04 | 1921 |
| 1922 | 156.16 | 14.62 | 156.16 | 12.35 | 159.71 | 10.03 | 104.67 | 19.56 | 100.81 | 19.70 | 1922 |
| 1923 | 152.11 | 14.25 | 152.11 | 12.03 | 131.57 | 8.26 | 113.76 | 21.26 | 113.59 | 22.20 | 1923 |
| 1924 | 151.49 | 14.19 | 151.49 | 11.98 | 128.88 | 8.09 | 116.57 | 21.78 | 119.72 | 23.39 | 1924 |
| 1925 | 155.07 | 14.52 | 155.07 | 12.26 | 126.57 | 7.95 | 146.06 | 27.29 | 149.97 | 29.30 | 1925 |
| 1926 | 160.33 | 15.02 | 160.33 | 12.68 | 124.82 | 7.84 | 134.90 | 25.20 | 137.37 | 26.84 | 1926 |
| 1927 | 158.00 | 14.80 | 158.00 | 12.50 | 124.90 | 7.84 | 126.62 | 23.66 | 126.37 | 24.69 | 1927 |
| 1928 | 156.66 | 14.67 | 156.66 | 12.39 | 122.86 | 7.71 | 106.02 | 19.81 | 103.98 | 20.32 | 1928 |
| 1929 | 153.27 | 14.35 | 153.27 | 12.12 | 121.01 | 7.60 | 100.75 | 18.82 | 98.40 | 19.23 | 1929 |
| 1930 | 145.73 | 13.65 | 145.73 | 11.53 | 112.92 | 7.09 | 81.73 | 15.27 | 78.26 | 15.29 | 1930 |
| 1931 | 124.49 | 11.66 | 124.49 | 9.85 | 96.28 | 6.04 | 68.93 | 12.88 | 64.84 | 12.67 | 1931 |
| 1932 | 109.58 | 10.26 | 109.58 | 8.67 | 92.19 | 5.79 | 59.87 | 11.19 | 55.87 | 10.92 | 1932 |
| 1933 | 101.76 | 9.53 | 101.76 | 8.05 | 72.27 | 4.54 | 59.05 | 11.03 | 53.14 | 10.38 | 1933 |
| 1934 | 104.44 | 9.78 | 104.44 | 8.26 | 78.53 | 4.93 | 70.66 | 13.20 | 68.67 | 13.42 | 1934 |
| 1935 | 108.53 | 10.16 | 108.53 | 8.58 | 71.99 | 4.52 | 72.11 | 13.47 | 69.73 | 13.62 | 1935 |
| 1936 | 106.70 | 9.99 | 106.70 | 8.44 | 70.60 | 4.43 | 74.85 | 13.98 | 72.66 | 14.20 | 1936 |
| 1937 | 113.08 | 10.59 | 113.08 | 8.94 | 75.11 | 4.72 | 81.90 | 15.30 | 80.37 | 15.70 | 1937 |
| 1938 | 109.42 | 10.25 | 109.42 | 8.65 | 83.49 | 5.24 | 72.60 | 13.56 | 69.01 | 13.48 | 1938 |
| 1939 | 110.16 | 10.32 | 110.16 | 8.71 | 85.39 | 5.36 | 79.51 | 14.85 | 76.98 | 15.04 | 1939 |
| 1950 | 359.02 | 33.62 | 359.02 | 28.40 | 286.27 | 17.97 | 236.01 | 44.10 | 235.24 | 45.97 | 1950 |
| 1951 | 451.51 | 42.29 | 451.51 | 35.71 | 343.94 | 21.59 | 329.63 | 61.59 | 332.36 | 64.94 | 1951 |
| 1952 | 469.80 | 44.00 | 469.80 | 37.16 | 405.01 | 25.43 | 272.03 | 50.83 | 273.39 | 53.42 | 1952 |
| 1953 | 458.41 | 42.93 | 458.41 | 36.26 | 334.21 | 20.98 | 240.67 | 44.97 | 232.56 | 45.44 | 1953 |
| 1954 | 436.94 | 40.92 | 436.94 | 34.56 | 343.77 | 21.58 | 234.26 | 43.77 | 226.04 | 44.17 | 1954 |
| 1955 | 427.08 | 40.00 | 427.08 | 33.78 | 374.11 | 23.49 | 270.61 | 50.56 | 266.17 | 52.01 | 1955 |
| 1956 | 431.66 | 40.43 | 431.66 | 34.14 | 347.89 | 21.84 | 264.83 | 49.48 | 258.56 | 50.52 | 1956 |
| 1957 | 444.20 | 41.60 | 444.20 | 35.13 | 375.85 | 23.60 | 260.01 | 48.58 | 252.80 | 49.40 | 1957 |
| 1958 | 441.93 | 41.39 | 441.93 | 34.95 | 331.93 | 20.84 | 253.01 | 47.27 | 243.88 | 47.65 | 1958 |
| 1959 | 436.87 | 40.91 | 436.87 | 34.55 | 299.91 | 18.83 | 273.82 | 51.16 | 267.22 | 52.22 | 1959 |
| 1960 | 437.05 | 40.93 | 437.05 | 34.57 | 274.02 | 17.20 | 280.99 | 52.50 | 273.29 | 53.40 | 1960 |
| 1961 | | 40.99 | | 36.15 | | 18.28 | | 52.50 | | 53.40 | 1961 |
| 1962 | | 41.10 | | 37.71 | | 23.39 | | 52.50 | | 53.40 | 1962 |
| 1963 | | 41.61 | | 37.78 | | 22.86 | | 52.40 | | 53.30 | 1963 |
| 1964 | | 42.09 | | 37.83 | | 26.46 | | 53.30 | | 54.20 | 1964 |
| 1965 | | 42.36 | | 37.85 | | 27.45 | | 53.00 | | 53.90 | 1965 |
| 1966 | | 43.20 | | 38.01 | | 29.04 | | 50.70 | | 51.60 | 1966 |
| 1967 | | 44.23 | | 38.17 | | 29.30 | | 51.00 | | 51.90 | 1967 |
| 1968 | | 44.78 | | 38.21 | | 31.09 | | 48.20 | | 49.00 | 1968 |
| 1969 | | 44.77 | | 38.70 | | 33.68 | | 50.20 | | 51.10 | 1969 |
| 1970 | | 45.35 | | 39.38 | | 37.19 | | 52.60 | | 53.50 | 1970 |
| 1971 | | 46.89 | | 41.83 | | 39.58 | | 53.20 | | 54.10 | 1971 |
| 1972 | | 48.10 | | 42.45 | | 44.43 | | 53.40 | | 54.40 | 1972 |
| 1973 | | 54.71 | | 45.43 | | 49.48 | | 60.50 | | 61.60 | 1973 |
| 1974 | | 61.46 | | 52.71 | | 58.30 | | 85.40 | | 85.70 | 1974 |
| 1975 | | 63.28 | | 56.23 | | 59.41 | | 86.10 | | 86.70 | 1975 |
| 1976 | | 63.68 | | 58.01 | | 62.43 | | 91.90 | | 92.60 | 1976 |
| 1977 | | 65.01 | | 59.14 | | 62.91 | | 95.60 | | 96.70 | 1977 |
| 1978 | | 66.71 | | 60.71 | | 65.13 | | 97.50 | | 98.80 | 1978 |
| 1979 | | 69.67 | | 63.14 | | 70.31 | | 102.80 | | 104.90 | 1979 |
| 1980 | | 75.46 | | 69.44 | | 79.10 | | 113.10 | | 116.10 | 1980 |
| 1981 | | 80.06 | | 75.18 | | 86.55 | | 116.90 | | 119.70 | 1981 |
| 1982 | | 66.09 | | 84.98 | | 87.06 | | 116.60 | | 117.20 | 1982 |
| 1983 | | 83.22 | | 86.74 | | 88.04 | | 111.00 | | 111.20 | 1983 |
| 1984 | | 85.86 | | 89.34 | | 88.83 | | 104.90 | | 106.20 | 1984 |
| 1985 | | 86.55 | | 108.54 | | 86.57 | | 103.30 | | 105.10 | 1985 |
| 1986 | | 86.90 | | 86.44 | | 84.60 | | 89.50 | | 91.10 | 1986 |
| 1987 | | 89.11 | | 86.45 | | 86.95 | | 96.30 | | 98.70 | 1987 |
| 1988 | | 92.55 | | 92.32 | | 94.93 | | 97.90 | | 99.40 | 1988 |
| 1989 | | 96.75 | | 98.48 | | 98.67 | | 99.30 | | 99.90 | 1989 |
| 1990 | | 100.00 | | 100.00 | | 100.00 | | 100.00 | | 100.00 | 1990 |
| 1991 | | 102.57 | | 100.66 | | 102.70 | | 97.60 | | 96.40 | 1991 |
| 1992 | | 104.95 | | 100.82 | | 104.88 | | 94.00 | | 93.00 | 1992 |
| 1993 | | 109.18 | | 101.56 | | 110.01 | | 93.10 | | 91.90 | 1993 |
| 1994 | | 14.10 | | 106.64 | | 109.34 | | 92.10 | | 89.20 | 1994 |
| 1995 | | 15.30 | | 107.02 | | 110.13 | | 91.30 | | 88.10 | 1995 |
| 1996 | | 14.35 | | 110.75 | | 107.79 | | 90.10 | | 86.80 | 1996 |
| 1997 | | 15.49 | | 111.63 | | 108.89 | | 89.00 | | 85.40 | 1997 |
| 1998 | | 14.22 | | 109.10 | | 106.67 | | 88.04 | | 84.47 | 1998 |
| 1999 | | 14.95 | | 104.57 | | 104.24 | | 88.23 | | 87.16 | 1999 |
| 2000 | | 16.33 | | 109.26 | | 101.19 | | 92.83 | | 90.41 | 2000 |

### 3.4.2.1 *Growth Rate of GDP and Its Component in the Twentieth Century*

Singapore's GDP growth rate has been high and remarkably consistent over a long time period, the size of economy being measured simply in terms of real domestic output. In 1939, real GDP (1990 prices) was 5.7 times its 1900 level. In 2000, real GDP increased tremendously such that it was 33.8 times its 1950 level. The annual average growth rate of GDP for the periods 1900–39 and 1950–2000 was 4.5% and 7.2% respectively, whereas the growth rate of real per-capita GDP for the same periods was 1.5% and 4.6%[76] (See Table 3.17 and Figs. 3.16 and 3.17). Both results

**Table 3.17:** Singapore: Average Annual Growth Rate of Each Component of GDP and Per-Capita GDP at 1990 Prices, 1900–2000

| | PFCE | GFCE | GCF | NETEX | GDP | | Per-capita GDP |
|---|---|---|---|---|---|---|---|
| 1900–10 | 2.6 | 4.7 | 13.1 | | 4.6 | 1900–10 | 1.8 |
| 1911–20 | 1.7 | 1.7 | 2.9 | | 2.2 | 1911–20 | -1.0 |
| 1921–30 | 6.4 | 8.0 | 5.9 | | 6.1 | 1921–30 | 2.8 |
| 1931–39 | 4.9 | 2.4 | 7.4 | | 5.0 | 1931–39 | 2.3 |
| 1950–60 | 6.0 | 4.3 | 5.9 | | 5.1 | 1950–60 | 0.3 |
| 1961–70 | 6.1 | 13.3 | 14.5 | | 8.8 | 1961–70 | 6.5 |
| 1971–80 | 6.8 | 7.0 | 8.9 | | 8.6 | 1971–80 | 7.1 |
| 1981–90 | 5.9 | 6.5 | 5.0 | | 7.0 | 1981–90 | 4.7 |
| 1991–2000 | 5.7 | 8.1 | 7.0 | | 7.2 | 1991–2000 | 4.5 |
| 1900–39 | 3.9 | 4.2 | 7.3 | | 4.5 | 1900–39 | 1.5 |
| 1950–2000 | 6.2 | 7.4 | 8.5 | | 7.2 | 1950–2000 | 4.6 |

*Source*:

*Abbreviations*:

PFCE = Private Final Consumption Expenditure by Resident Households.

GFCE = Government Final Consumption Expenditure.

GCF = Gross Capital Formation.

NETEX = Net Exports of Goods and Services.

---

[76] The annual average growth rate was calculated on the basis of the simple arithmetic average of yearly exponential growth rates.

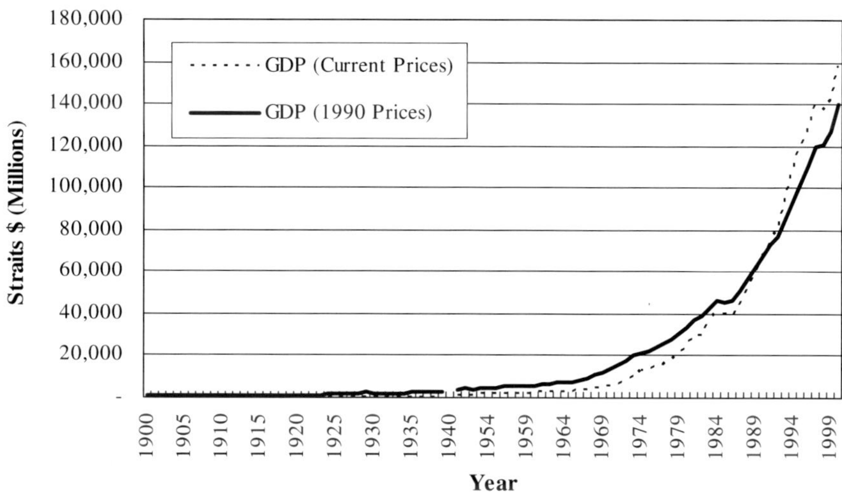

**Fig. 3.16:** Singapore: GDP at Current and Constant (1990 Prices), 1900–39 and 1950–2000

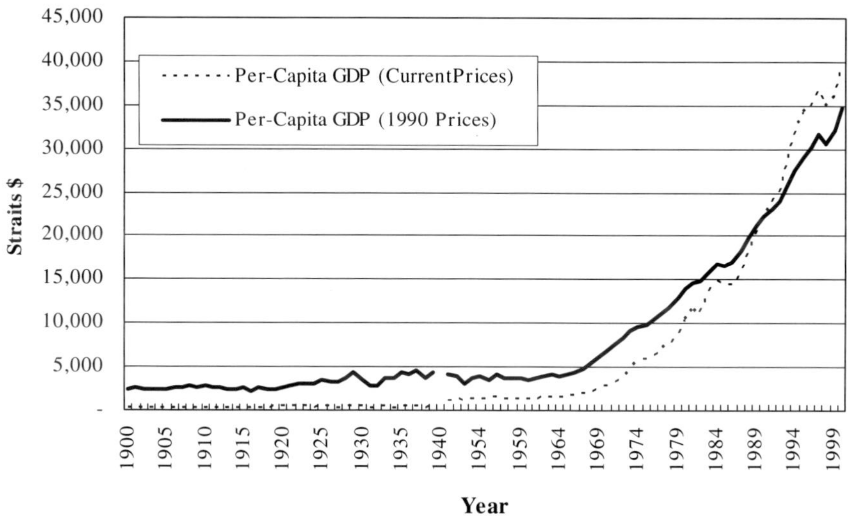

**Fig. 3.17:** Singapore: Per-Capita GDP at Current and Constant (1990), 1900–39 and 1950–2000

reinforce the historical fact that the overall growth rate of GDP during the post–World War II period was significantly higher than that of the pre–World War II period. Table 3.17 gives some indication of these growth rates for nine decades. The most rapid growth of real GDP and real per-capita GDP was recorded in the 1960s and 1970s. Subsequently, the growth rates were somewhat slightly lower after the 1980s. Each component of GDP also showed a similar phenomenon.

Table 3.18 depicts the annual growth rates of both real GDP and its components, and it can be seen that many fluctuations were observed during the British Colonial Period (up to 1957). Similarly, most of the negative growth rates for the twentieth century were recorded during the British Colonial Period for the years 1930–32, 1938, and 1952, namely, –21% (1930), –23% (1931), –7% (1932), –11% (1938), and –19% (1952). In fact, many countries faced a similar economic situation due to the world depression. On the other hand, high growth rates of more than 20% were recorded for the years 1933 (23%), 1935 (22%), 1953 (24%), and 1956 (21%). On the other hand, real GDP has recorded sustained and high growth rates during the period of self-government. For the years 1966–73, real GDP growth rates have constantly exceeded 10% exclusive of 1964 (–4%). During this period, huge and significant foreign direct investment (FDI) into Singapore was observed. For the period 1976–2000, real GDP growth rate was in the range of 6–11%, excluding the years 1985 (–2%) and 1998 (0.3%). During this period, Singapore's economy was boosted by the rapid expansion of the manufacturing and financial and business services (Peebles *et al.*, 2002, 95).

### 3.4.2.2 *Share of Each Component of GDP*

Table 3.19 shows the 10-yearly average share of each component of GDP for the periods 1900–39 and 1950–2000, whereas Table 3.20 and Fig. 3.18 present the annual share of each

**Table 3.18:** Singapore: Components of GDP, 1900–39 and 1950–2000 (1990 Prices)

| Year | Private Final Consumption Expenditure in The Domestic Market by Resident Households [1] Straits $ millions | % of GDP | % growth | Government Final Consumption Expenditure [2] Straits $ millions | % of GDP | % growth | Gross Capital Formation [3] Straits $ millions | % of GDP | % growth | Net Exports of Goods and Services [4] | % of GDP | Statistical Discrepancy Straits $ millions | % of GDP | GDP at Marktet Prices [5] = [1] + [2] + [3] + [4] | % growth | Year |
|---|---|---|---|---|---|---|---|---|---|---|---|---|---|---|---|---|
| 1900 | 434.7 | 79 | | 34.1 | 6 | | 59.2 | 11 | | 24.9 | 4 | | | 552.8 | | 1900 |
| 1901 | 441.8 | 73 | 2 | 40.6 | 7 | 18 | 81.4 | 13 | 32 | 45.3 | 7 | | | 609.1 | 10 | 1901 |
| 1902 | 444.5 | 75 | 1 | 37.3 | 6 | -9 | 72.2 | 12 | -12 | 36.5 | 6 | | | 590.5 | -3 | 1902 |
| 1903 | 453.4 | 78 | 2 | 46.8 | 8 | 23 | 87.3 | 15 | 19 | -4.5 | -1 | | | 582.9 | -1 | 1903 |
| 1904 | 463.4 | 74 | 2 | 52.8 | 8 | 12 | 128.6 | 21 | 39 | -18.9 | -3 | | | 625.9 | 7 | 1904 |
| 1905 | 471.5 | 73 | 2 | 46.2 | 7 | -13 | 118.7 | 18 | -8 | 12.8 | 2 | | | 649.3 | 4 | 1905 |
| 1906 | 487.9 | 71 | 3 | 45.1 | 7 | -3 | 112.9 | 17 | -5 | 36.7 | 5 | | | 682.7 | 5 | 1906 |
| 1907 | 504.1 | 73 | 3 | 44.8 | 6 | -1 | 140.1 | 20 | 22 | 4.0 | 1 | | | 692.9 | 1 | 1907 |
| 1908 | 521.1 | 66 | 3 | 47.0 | 6 | 5 | 183.1 | 23 | 27 | 34.9 | 4 | | | 786.1 | 13 | 1908 |
| 1909 | 543.1 | 69 | 4 | 45.5 | 6 | -3 | 171.4 | 22 | -7 | 25.6 | 3 | | | 785.7 | 0 | 1909 |
| 1910 | 561.7 | 64 | 3 | 54.3 | 6 | 18 | 219.8 | 25 | 25 | 41.6 | 5 | | | 877.3 | 11 | 1910 |
| 1911 | 541.0 | 65 | -4 | 51.3 | 6 | -6 | 219.2 | 26 | 0 | 16.9 | 2 | | | 828.5 | -6 | 1911 |
| 1912 | 552.8 | 67 | 2 | 49.9 | 6 | -3 | 256.3 | 31 | 16 | -36.3 | -4 | | | 822.7 | -1 | 1912 |
| 1913 | 562.5 | 68 | 2 | 60.8 | 7 | 20 | 265.5 | 32 | 4 | -67.2 | -8 | | | 821.6 | 0 | 1913 |
| 1914 | 600.0 | 71 | 6 | 62.3 | 7 | 2 | 241.0 | 28 | -10 | -54.6 | -6 | | | 848.7 | 3 | 1914 |
| 1915 | 587.6 | 67 | -2 | 52.7 | 6 | -17 | 203.1 | 23 | -17 | 39.3 | 4 | | | 882.7 | 4 | 1915 |
| 1916 | 585.4 | 72 | 0 | 52.7 | 6 | 0 | 181.1 | 22 | -11 | -6.0 | -1 | | | 813.3 | -8 | 1916 |
| 1917 | 670.8 | 68 | 14 | 49.4 | 5 | -6 | 207.1 | 21 | 13 | 53.7 | 5 | | | 981.1 | 19 | 1917 |
| 1918 | 710.8 | 75 | 6 | 58.2 | 6 | 16 | 190.0 | 20 | -9 | -17.0 | -2 | | | 941.9 | -4 | 1918 |
| 1919 | 666.1 | 68 | -7 | 50.5 | 5 | -14 | 231.5 | 24 | 20 | 34.8 | 4 | | | 982.9 | 4 | 1919 |
| 1920 | 664.5 | 61 | 0 | 64.5 | 6 | 24 | 294.2 | 27 | 24 | 75.0 | 7 | | | 1,098.2 | 11 | 1920 |
| 1921 | 865.9 | 70 | 26 | 96.0 | 8 | 40 | 314.8 | 25 | 7 | -39.5 | -3 | | | 1,237.2 | 12 | 1921 |
| 1922 | 970.3 | 73 | 11 | 98.8 | 7 | 3 | 180.8 | 14 | -55 | 73.2 | 6 | | | 1,323.0 | 7 | 1922 |
| 1923 | 1,017.2 | 73 | 5 | 99.8 | 7 | 1 | 199.5 | 14 | 10 | 73.1 | 5 | | | 1,389.7 | 5 | 1923 |
| 1924 | 1,048.2 | 73 | 3 | 109.8 | 8 | 10 | 212.9 | 15 | 6 | 64.6 | 4 | | | 1,435.5 | 3 | 1924 |
| 1925 | 1,073.2 | 62 | 2 | 99.6 | 6 | -10 | 421.0 | 24 | 68 | 148.6 | 9 | | | 1,742.3 | 19 | 1925 |
| 1926 | 1,083.0 | 62 | 1 | 104.9 | 6 | 5 | 475.7 | 27 | 12 | 78.7 | 5 | | | 1,742.3 | 0 | 1926 |
| 1927 | 1,178.5 | 68 | 8 | 115.9 | 7 | 10 | 558.7 | 32 | 16 | -121.1 | -7 | | | 1,731.9 | -1 | 1927 |
| 1928 | 1,254.2 | 56 | 6 | 118.4 | 5 | 2 | 938.8 | 42 | 52 | -74.9 | -3 | | | 2,236.5 | 26 | 1928 |
| 1929 | 1,280.0 | 52 | 2 | 131.0 | 5 | 10 | 935.6 | 38 | 0 | 137.3 | 6 | | | 2,483.9 | 10 | 1929 |
| 1930 | 1,256.0 | 62 | -2 | 143.0 | 7 | 9 | 530.0 | 26 | -57 | 94.2 | 5 | | | 2,023.2 | -21 | 1930 |
| 1931 | 1,124.8 | 70 | -11 | 167.4 | 10 | 16 | 459.9 | 28 | -14 | -137.9 | -9 | | | 1,614.3 | -23 | 1931 |
| 1932 | 1,159.8 | 77 | 3 | 166.9 | 11 | 0 | 346.7 | 23 | -28 | -175.5 | -12 | | | 1,497.9 | -7 | 1932 |
| 1933 | 1,277.8 | 68 | 10 | 161.1 | 9 | -3 | 450.6 | 24 | 26 | -0.4 | 0 | | | 1,889.1 | 23 | 1933 |
| 1934 | 1,262.3 | 69 | -1 | 141.3 | 8 | -13 | 376.7 | 21 | -18 | 40.0 | 2 | | | 1,820.3 | -4 | 1934 |
| 1935 | 1,421.7 | 58 | 12 | 147.5 | 6 | 4 | 745.7 | 31 | 68 | 128.9 | 5 | | | 2,443.8 | 29 | 1935 |
| 1936 | 1,599.7 | 64 | 12 | 152.2 | 6 | 3 | 691.6 | 28 | -8 | 44.2 | 2 | | | 2,487.6 | 2 | 1936 |
| 1937 | 1,724.0 | 57 | 7 | 154.5 | 5 | 2 | 1,004.9 | 33 | 37 | 119.5 | 4 | | | 3,002.9 | 19 | 1937 |
| 1938 | 1,911.6 | 71 | 10 | 172.5 | 6 | 11 | 760.2 | 28 | -28 | -160.5 | -6 | | | 2,683.9 | -11 | 1938 |
| 1939 | 1,952.4 | 62 | 2 | 177.5 | 6 | 3 | 1,027.6 | 33 | 30 | 2.9 | 0 | | | 3,160.4 | 16 | 1939 |
| 1950 | 2,714.7 | 66 | | 262.2 | 6 | | 938.5 | 23 | | 226.2 | 5 | | | 4,141.7 | | 1950 |
| 1951 | 2,556.9 | 60 | -6 | 257.4 | 6 | -2 | 1,085.2 | 25 | 15 | 382.6 | 9 | | | 4,282.1 | 3 | 1951 |
| 1952 | 2,639.3 | 75 | 3 | 285.8 | 8 | 10 | 764.4 | 22 | -35 | -149.8 | -4 | | | 3,539.7 | -19 | 1952 |
| 1953 | 3,186.6 | 71 | 19 | 341.4 | 8 | 18 | 987.8 | 22 | 26 | -0.5 | 0 | | | 4,515.3 | 24 | 1953 |
| 1954 | 3,377.8 | 71 | 6 | 415.6 | 9 | 20 | 916.0 | 19 | -8 | 71.0 | 1 | | | 4,780.4 | 6 | 1954 |
| 1955 | 3,484.8 | 75 | 3 | 457.3 | 10 | 10 | 786.1 | 17 | -15 | -92.7 | -2 | | | 4,635.4 | -3 | 1955 |
| 1956 | 4,040.0 | 71 | 15 | 482.8 | 8 | 5 | 1,234.4 | 22 | 45 | -66.9 | -1 | | | 5,690.3 | 21 | 1956 |
| 1957 | 4,116.0 | 76 | 2 | 474.8 | 9 | -2 | 1,071.0 | 20 | -14 | -274.0 | -5 | | | 5,387.7 | -5 | 1957 |
| 1958 | 4,298.7 | 77 | 4 | 513.7 | 9 | 8 | 1,114.2 | 20 | 4 | -311.8 | -6 | | | 5,614.9 | 4 | 1958 |
| 1959 | 4,131.3 | 70 | -4 | 540.2 | 9 | 5 | 1,181.9 | 20 | 6 | 25.9 | 0 | | | 5,879.3 | 5 | 1959 |
| 1960 | 4,694.4 | 80 | 13 | 467.2 | 8 | -15 | 1,421.2 | 24 | 18 | -448.2 | -8 | -243 | -4 | 5,891.7 | 0 | 1960 |
| 1961 | 5,145.0 | 80 | 9 | 573.1 | 9 | 20 | 1,475.9 | 23 | 4 | -548.2 | -9 | -251 | -4 | 6,394.7 | 8 | 1961 |
| 1962 | 5,340.5 | 78 | 4 | 627.1 | 9 | 9 | 1,672.2 | 24 | 12 | -404.0 | -6 | -390 | -6 | 6,846.3 | 7 | 1962 |
| 1963 | 5,591.5 | 74 | 5 | 729.7 | 10 | 15 | 2,130.9 | 28 | 24 | -671.1 | -9 | -218 | -3 | 7,562.8 | 10 | 1963 |
| 1964 | 5,317.5 | 73 | -5 | 743.5 | 10 | 2 | 2,049.1 | 28 | -4 | -480.1 | -7 | -393 | -5 | 7,237.1 | -4 | 1964 |
| 1965 | 5,524.9 | 72 | 4 | 813.2 | 11 | 9 | 2,359.6 | 31 | 14 | -541.7 | -7 | -438 | -6 | 7,718.2 | 6 | 1965 |
| 1966 | 5,917.1 | 69 | 7 | 924.5 | 11 | 13 | 2,511.4 | 29 | 6 | -389.5 | -5 | -428 | -5 | 8,535.2 | 10 | 1966 |
| 1967 | 6,449.7 | 67 | 9 | 1,004.5 | 10 | 8 | 2,837.3 | 29 | 12 | -462.3 | -5 | -182 | -2 | 9,647.3 | 12 | 1967 |
| 1968 | 7,101.1 | 64 | 10 | 1,174.6 | 11 | 16 | 3,458.1 | 31 | 20 | -382.2 | -3 | -329 | -3 | 11,023.0 | 13 | 1968 |
| 1969 | 7,683.4 | 61 | 8 | 1,446.6 | 12 | 21 | 4,267.2 | 34 | 21 | -811.8 | -6 | -88 | -1 | 12,497.2 | 13 | 1969 |
| 1970 | 8,643.7 | 61 | 12 | 1,758.3 | 12 | 20 | 6,034.6 | 43 | 35 | -1,961.0 | -14 | -298 | -2 | 14,177.2 | 13 | 1970 |
| 1971 | 9,663.7 | 61 | 11 | 2,058.0 | 13 | 16 | 7,018.4 | 44 | 15 | -2,473.2 | -16 | -312 | -2 | 15,955.0 | 12 | 1971 |
| 1972 | 10,543.1 | 58 | 9 | 2,332.5 | 13 | 13 | 7,635.9 | 42 | 8 | -2,228.0 | -12 | -200 | -1 | 18,083.4 | 13 | 1972 |
| 1973 | 11,589.3 | 58 | 9 | 2,460.5 | 12 | 5 | 8,175.4 | 41 | 7 | -1,312.1 | -7 | -795 | -4 | 20,118.6 | 11 | 1973 |
| 1974 | 12,459.9 | 58 | 7 | 2,463.1 | 11 | 0 | 9,794.2 | 46 | 18 | -2,306.2 | -11 | -933 | -4 | 21,478.5 | 7 | 1974 |
| 1975 | 12,833.7 | 57 | 3 | 2,530.7 | 11 | 3 | 9,040.2 | 40 | -8 | -1,470.5 | -7 | -605 | -3 | 22,329.0 | 4 | 1975 |
| 1976 | 13,514.7 | 56 | 5 | 2,657.3 | 11 | 5 | 9,581.0 | 40 | 6 | -1,112.0 | -5 | -707 | -3 | 23,933.9 | 7 | 1976 |
| 1977 | 14,258.0 | 55 | 5 | 2,902.3 | 11 | 9 | 9,217.8 | 36 | -4 | -97.5 | 0 | -490 | -2 | 25,791.1 | 7 | 1977 |
| 1978 | 15,213.4 | 54 | 6 | 3,236.3 | 12 | 11 | 10,682.3 | 38 | 15 | -471.7 | -2 | -654 | -2 | 28,006.1 | 8 | 1978 |
| 1979 | 16,141.4 | 53 | 6 | 3,220.6 | 11 | 0 | 12,657.8 | 41 | 17 | -515.9 | -2 | -890 | -3 | 30,613.7 | 9 | 1979 |
| 1980 | 17,109.6 | 51 | 6 | 3,524.6 | 10 | 9 | 14,699.8 | 44 | 15 | -522.0 | -2 | -1,230 | -4 | 33,581.6 | 9 | 1980 |
| 1981 | 17,897.8 | 49 | 5 | 3,709.4 | 10 | 5 | 15,697.9 | 43 | 7 | -54.5 | 0 | -444 | -1 | 36,807.0 | 9 | 1981 |
| 1982 | 18,584.8 | 47 | 4 | 4,201.4 | 11 | 12 | 17,985.3 | 46 | 14 | -925.7 | -2 | -509 | -1 | 39,337.2 | 7 | 1982 |
| 1983 | 19,469.7 | 46 | 5 | 4,606.0 | 11 | 9 | 19,985.6 | 47 | 11 | -513.9 | -1 | -993 | -2 | 42,554.7 | 8 | 1983 |
| 1984 | 20,463.4 | 44 | 5 | 4,846.5 | 11 | 5 | 21,858.5 | 47 | 9 | -228.5 | 0 | -848 | -2 | 46,091.7 | 8 | 1984 |
| 1985 | 20,280.9 | 45 | -1 | 6,033.2 | 13 | 22 | 19,118.4 | 42 | -13 | 197.0 | 0 | -285 | -1 | 45,344.9 | -2 | 1985 |
| 1986 | 21,179.9 | 46 | 4 | 6,096.6 | 13 | 1 | 17,395.6 | 38 | -9 | 1,481.7 | 3 | 234 | 1 | 46,388.0 | 2 | 1986 |
| 1987 | 23,227.1 | 46 | 9 | 6,147.9 | 12 | 1 | 18,745.1 | 37 | 7 | 2,549.0 | 5 | 231 | 0 | 50,899.9 | 9 | 1987 |
| 1988 | 26,353.3 | 46 | 13 | 5,780.9 | 10 | -6 | 18,256.2 | 32 | -3 | 6,036.3 | 11 | 394 | 1 | 56,821.1 | 11 | 1988 |
| 1989 | 28,594.8 | 46 | 8 | 6,106.4 | 10 | 5 | 20,640.0 | 33 | 12 | 6,647.5 | 11 | 300 | 0 | 62,288.8 | 9 | 1989 |
| 1990 | 30,762.0 | 45 | 7 | 6,779.7 | 10 | 10 | 24,348.8 | 36 | 17 | 5,988.4 | 9 | 0 | 0 | 67,878.9 | 9 | 1990 |
| 1991 | 32,560.0 | 45 | 6 | 7,387.1 | 10 | 9 | 25,070.8 | 34 | 3 | 7,908.8 | 11 | -66 | 0 | 72,860.9 | 7 | 1991 |
| 1992 | 34,716.6 | 45 | 6 | 7,564.5 | 10 | 2 | 27,759.1 | 36 | 10 | 7,670.8 | 10 | -317 | 0 | 77,393.8 | 6 | 1992 |
| 1993 | 38,472.1 | 45 | 10 | 8,461.3 | 10 | 11 | 32,289.6 | 38 | 15 | 7,008.7 | 8 | -759 | -1 | 85,473.2 | 10 | 1993 |
| 1994 | 40,567.6 | 43 | 5 | 8,467.2 | 9 | 0 | 32,367.7 | 34 | 0 | 13,591.9 | 14 | -931 | -1 | 94,063.6 | 10 | 1994 |
| 1995 | 42,630.1 | 42 | 5 | 9,525.4 | 9 | 12 | 35,712.2 | 35 | 10 | 15,981.4 | 16 | -1,550 | -2 | 102,299.1 | 8 | 1995 |
| 1996 | 46,122.1 | 42 | 8 | 11,022.5 | 10 | 15 | 44,098.1 | 40 | 21 | 11,168.4 | 10 | -1,712 | -2 | 110,699.2 | 8 | 1996 |
| 1997 | 48,884.3 | 41 | 6 | 11,806.3 | 10 | 7 | 50,201.2 | 42 | 13 | 11,663.9 | 10 | -2,416 | -2 | 120,140.2 | 8 | 1997 |
| 1998 | 47,451.6 | 39 | -3 | 12,746.8 | 11 | 8 | 41,994.9 | 35 | -18 | 20,327.7 | 17 | -2,314 | -2 | 120,206.9 | 0 | 1998 |
| 1999 | 49,961.6 | 39 | 5 | 13,378.0 | 11 | 5 | 44,225.6 | 35 | 5 | 22,243.3 | 17 | -2,559 | -2 | 127,250.0 | 6 | 1999 |
| 2000 | 54,641.1 | 39 | 9 | 15,212.6 | 11 | 13 | 49,191.1 | 35 | 11 | 23,449.0 | 17 | -2,654 | -2 | 139,839.5 | 9 | 2000 |

*Sources*: Figures for the periods, 1900–39 and 1950–59 are estimated by the author, whereas the figures for 1960–2000 are obtained from official publication of the Department of Statistics, Singapore (1996) and Asian Development Bank (2001).

**Table 3.19:** Singapore: Annual Average Share of Each Component to GDP at Current Prices, 1900–39 and 1950–2000

|  | PFCE | GFCE | GCF | NETEX |
|---|---|---|---|---|
| 1900–10 | 90.9 | 7.2 | 17.7 | −15.7 |
| 1911–20 | 94.8 | 7.3 | 26.6 | −28.7 |
| 1921–30 | 84.7 | 7.2 | 19.0 | −11.0 |
| 1931–39 | 77.2 | 7.3 | 16.3 | −0.7 |
| 1950–60 | 85.2 | 8.1 | 13.2 | −6.5 |
| 1961–70 | 78.6 | 10.3 | 22.3 | −11.9 |
| 1971–80 | 59.1 | 10.8 | 41.2 | −10.7 |
| 1981–90 | 45.5 | 11.6 | 41.5 | 1.2 |
| 1991–2000 | 41.9 | 9.5 | 34.5 | 15.2 |
| 1900–39 | 87.3 | 7.2 | 19.9 | −14.4 |
| 1950–2000 | 63.0 | 10.0 | 29.9 | -2.9 |

*Note*: Figures might not add to 100 because of the statistical discrepancy.

*Sources*: Figures for the periods 1900–39 and 1950–59 are estimated by the author, whereas the figures for 1960–2000 are obtained from official publication of the Department of Statistics, Singapore (1996) and Asian Development Bank (2001).

Abbreviations:

PFCE = Private Final Consumption Expenditure by Resident Households, GFCE = Government Final Consumption Expenditure, GCF = Gross Capital Formation, NETEX = Net Exports of Goods and Services.

component of GDP at current prices in Singapore for the same period.

For the periods 1900–39 and 1950–60, the 10-yearly average share of each component of GDP was relatively stable though the annual data generally displayed significant yearly changes.

In contrast to the British Colonial Period, structural changes were observed after the attainment of independence in 1965. In particular, PFCE showed drastic falls from about 89% of GDP in the 1960 to around 40% at the end of the twentieth century.

On the other hand, the share of GFCE to GDP remained fairly constant. The annual share of GCF to GDP, however, has gradually increased after independence from 20% to 40% within the 20-year period (1971–90) though it declined slightly during the 1990s. The most remarkable change was observed in the net exports of goods and services. Net exports were in the negative

**Table 3.20:** Singapore: Components of GDP, 1900–39 and 1950–2000 (Current Prices)

| | Private Final Consumption Expenditure in The Domestic Market by Resident Households [1] | | | Government Final Consumption Expenditure [2] | | | Gross Capital Formation [3] | | | Net Exports of Goods and Services [4] | | Statistical Discrepancy [4] | | GDP at Market Prices | | |
|---|---|---|---|---|---|---|---|---|---|---|---|---|---|---|---|---|
| | Straits $ millions | % of GDP | % growth | Straits $ millions | % of GDP | % growth | Straits $ millions | % of GDP | % growth | Straits $ millions | % of GDP | Straits $ millions | % of GDP | [5]=[1]+[2]+[3]+[4] | % growth | |
| 1900 | 33.7 | 96 | | 2.2 | 6 | | 4.3 | 12 | | -5.2 | -15 | | | 35.1 | | 1900 |
| 1901 | 34.6 | 87 | 3 | 2.7 | 7 | 19 | 5.6 | 14 | 26 | -3.0 | -8 | | | 39.9 | 13 | 1901 |
| 1902 | 36.1 | 96 | 4 | 2.6 | 7 | -5 | 5.1 | 14 | -9 | -6.0 | -16 | | | 37.8 | -5 | 1902 |
| 1903 | 37.3 | 110 | 3 | 3.2 | 10 | 24 | 6.3 | 19 | 20 | -13.0 | -38 | | | 33.8 | -11 | 1903 |
| 1904 | 38.1 | 102 | 2 | 3.7 | 10 | 12 | 9.2 | 25 | 38 | -13.6 | -36 | | | 37.4 | 10 | 1904 |
| 1905 | 39.5 | 93 | 4 | 3.3 | 8 | -11 | 7.8 | 18 | -16 | -7.9 | -18 | | | 42.7 | 13 | 1905 |
| 1906 | 40.3 | 88 | 2 | 3.1 | 7 | -4 | 6.4 | 14 | -21 | -3.8 | -8 | | | 46.0 | 7 | 1906 |
| 1907 | 41.6 | 93 | 3 | 3.1 | 7 | -1 | 8.4 | 19 | 28 | -8.4 | -19 | | | 44.7 | -3 | 1907 |
| 1908 | 43.6 | 78 | 5 | 3.3 | 6 | 6 | 11.3 | 20 | 30 | -2.4 | -4 | | | 55.8 | 22 | 1908 |
| 1909 | 44.3 | 82 | 2 | 3.1 | 6 | -6 | 10.4 | 19 | -8 | -3.7 | -7 | | | 54.1 | -3 | 1909 |
| 1910 | 46.7 | 76 | 5 | 3.8 | 6 | 19 | 12.8 | 21 | 20 | -1.9 | -3 | | | 61.4 | 13 | 1910 |
| 1911 | 49.3 | 88 | 5 | 4.0 | 7 | 4 | 11.8 | 21 | -8 | -8.9 | -16 | | | 56.2 | -9 | 1911 |
| 1912 | 51.3 | 103 | 4 | 3.9 | 8 | -1 | 15.1 | 30 | 25 | -20.2 | -41 | | | 50.0 | -12 | 1912 |
| 1913 | 53.3 | 111 | 4 | 4.9 | 10 | 22 | 18.0 | 37 | 18 | -28.1 | -58 | | | 48.0 | -4 | 1913 |
| 1914 | 56.2 | 104 | 5 | 4.9 | 9 | 1 | 15.1 | 28 | -17 | -22.4 | -42 | | | 53.9 | 11 | 1914 |
| 1915 | 58.6 | 86 | 4 | 4.4 | 7 | -10 | 14.1 | 21 | -7 | -9.4 | -14 | | | 67.8 | 23 | 1915 |
| 1916 | 62.0 | 107 | 6 | 4.7 | 8 | 6 | 15.0 | 26 | 6 | -23.8 | -41 | | | 58.0 | -16 | 1916 |
| 1917 | 74.0 | 85 | 18 | 4.6 | 5 | -2 | 20.5 | 24 | 31 | -12.1 | -14 | | | 86.9 | 41 | 1917 |
| 1918 | 93.5 | 95 | 23 | 6.5 | 7 | 34 | 24.8 | 25 | 19 | -26.7 | -27 | | | 98.1 | 12 | 1918 |
| 1919 | 107.5 | 75 | 14 | 6.9 | 5 | 6 | 29.1 | 20 | 16 | 0.5 | 0 | | | 144.0 | 38 | 1919 |
| 1920 | 137.7 | 94 | 25 | 11.3 | 8 | 49 | 49.1 | 34 | 52 | -51.6 | -35 | | | 146.5 | 2 | 1920 |
| 1921 | 141.8 | 75 | 3 | 13.3 | 7 | 16 | 43.7 | 23 | -12 | -9.7 | -5 | | | 189.1 | 26 | 1921 |
| 1922 | 141.9 | 77 | 0 | 12.2 | 7 | -8 | 18.1 | 10 | -88 | 11.0 | 6 | | | 183.3 | -3 | 1922 |
| 1923 | 144.9 | 88 | 2 | 12.0 | 7 | -2 | 16.5 | 10 | -10 | -8.9 | -5 | | | 164.5 | -11 | 1923 |
| 1924 | 148.7 | 100 | 3 | 13.2 | 9 | 9 | 17.2 | 12 | 4 | -29.9 | -20 | | | 149.2 | -10 | 1924 |
| 1925 | 155.9 | 89 | 5 | 12.2 | 7 | -7 | 33.5 | 19 | 66 | -27.3 | -16 | | | 174.2 | 15 | 1925 |
| 1926 | 162.6 | 94 | 4 | 13.3 | 8 | 9 | 37.3 | 22 | 11 | -40.0 | -23 | | | 173.2 | -1 | 1926 |
| 1927 | 174.4 | 106 | 7 | 14.5 | 9 | 9 | 43.8 | 27 | 16 | -67.6 | -41 | | | 165.1 | -5 | 1927 |
| 1928 | 184.0 | 78 | 5 | 14.7 | 6 | 1 | 72.4 | 31 | 50 | -33.8 | -14 | | | 237.3 | 36 | 1928 |
| 1929 | 183.7 | 65 | 0 | 15.9 | 6 | 8 | 71.1 | 25 | -2 | 10.6 | 4 | | | 281.3 | 17 | 1929 |
| 1930 | 171.4 | 72 | -7 | 16.5 | 7 | 4 | 37.6 | 16 | -64 | 13.5 | 6 | | | 239.0 | -16 | 1930 |
| 1931 | 131.1 | 80 | -27 | 16.5 | 10 | 0 | 27.8 | 17 | -30 | -11.3 | -7 | | | 164.1 | -38 | 1931 |
| 1932 | 119.0 | 84 | -10 | 14.5 | 10 | -13 | 20.1 | 14 | -33 | -11.5 | -8 | | | 142.0 | -14 | 1932 |
| 1933 | 121.8 | 70 | 2 | 13.0 | 7 | -11 | 20.4 | 12 | 2 | 19.1 | 11 | | | 174.3 | 20 | 1933 |
| 1934 | 123.5 | 81 | 1 | 11.7 | 8 | -11 | 18.6 | 12 | -10 | -0.7 | 0 | | | 153.0 | -13 | 1934 |
| 1935 | 144.5 | 71 | 16 | 12.7 | 6 | 8 | 33.7 | 17 | 60 | 13.2 | 6 | | | 204.1 | 29 | 1935 |
| 1936 | 159.9 | 79 | 10 | 12.8 | 6 | 1 | 30.7 | 15 | -9 | 0.0 | 0 | | | 203.4 | 0 | 1936 |
| 1937 | 182.6 | 74 | 13 | 13.8 | 6 | 7 | 47.4 | 19 | 44 | 4.5 | 2 | | | 248.3 | 20 | 1937 |
| 1938 | 195.9 | 85 | 7 | 14.9 | 6 | 8 | 39.8 | 17 | -17 | -19.3 | -8 | | | 231.4 | -7 | 1938 |
| 1939 | 201.4 | 76 | 3 | 15.5 | 6 | 4 | 55.1 | 21 | 32 | -5.7 | -2 | | | 266.3 | 14 | 1939 |
| 1950 | 912.8 | 81 | | 74.4 | 7 | | 168.7 | 15 | | -33.4 | -3 | | | 1,122.5 | | 1950 |
| 1951 | 1,081.2 | 78 | 17 | 91.9 | 7 | 21 | 234.3 | 17 | 33 | -24.0 | -2 | | | 1,383.4 | 21 | 1951 |
| 1952 | 1,161.2 | 96 | 7 | 106.2 | 9 | 14 | 194.4 | 16 | -19 | -258.3 | -21 | | | 1,203.6 | -14 | 1952 |
| 1953 | 1,368.1 | 82 | 16 | 123.8 | 7 | 15 | 207.3 | 12 | 6 | -31.9 | -2 | | | 1,667.2 | 33 | 1953 |
| 1954 | 1,382.2 | 80 | 1 | 143.6 | 8 | 15 | 197.7 | 11 | -5 | 3.8 | 0 | | | 1,727.4 | 4 | 1954 |
| 1955 | 1,393.8 | 88 | 1 | 154.5 | 10 | 7 | 184.6 | 12 | -7 | -154.5 | -10 | | | 1,578.4 | -9 | 1955 |
| 1956 | 1,633.2 | 84 | 16 | 164.8 | 8 | 6 | 269.6 | 14 | 38 | -114.1 | -6 | | | 1,953.6 | 21 | 1956 |
| 1957 | 1,712.3 | 89 | 5 | 166.8 | 9 | 1 | 252.7 | 13 | -6 | -200.8 | -10 | | | 1,931.1 | -1 | 1957 |
| 1958 | 1,779.1 | 88 | 4 | 179.6 | 9 | 7 | 232.2 | 12 | -8 | -177.3 | -9 | | | 2,013.6 | 4 | 1958 |
| 1959 | 1,690.3 | 83 | -5 | 186.7 | 9 | 4 | 222.5 | 11 | -4 | -65.8 | -3 | | | 2,033.8 | 1 | 1959 |
| 1960 | 1,921.5 | 89 | 13 | 161.5 | 8 | -14 | 244.5 | 11 | 9 | -300.9 | -14 | 123.0 | 6 | 2,149.6 | 6 | 1960 |
| 1961 | 2,108.8 | 91 | 9 | 207.2 | 9 | 25 | 269.8 | 12 | 10 | -351.0 | -15 | 94.3 | 4 | 2,329.1 | 8 | 1961 |
| 1962 | 2,195.1 | 87 | 4 | 236.5 | 9 | 13 | 391.2 | 16 | 37 | -276.9 | -11 | -32.2 | -1 | 2,513.7 | 8 | 1962 |
| 1963 | 2,326.6 | 83 | 6 | 275.7 | 10 | 15 | 487.1 | 17 | 22 | -426.9 | -15 | 127.4 | 5 | 2,789.9 | 10 | 1963 |
| 1964 | 2,238.2 | 82 | -4 | 281.3 | 10 | 2 | 542.2 | 20 | 11 | -318.7 | -12 | -28.4 | -1 | 2,714.6 | -3 | 1964 |
| 1965 | 2,340.6 | 79 | 4 | 307.8 | 10 | 9 | 647.7 | 22 | 18 | -356.3 | -12 | 16.4 | 1 | 2,956.2 | 9 | 1965 |
| 1966 | 2,556.2 | 77 | 9 | 351.4 | 11 | 13 | 729.4 | 22 | 12 | -273.7 | -8 | -40.6 | -1 | 3,322.7 | 12 | 1966 |
| 1967 | 2,852.6 | 76 | 11 | 383.4 | 10 | 9 | 831.2 | 22 | 13 | -315.9 | -8 | -2.8 | 0 | 3,748.5 | 12 | 1967 |
| 1968 | 3,179.7 | 74 | 11 | 448.8 | 10 | 16 | 1,075.2 | 25 | 26 | -283.6 | -7 | -105.1 | -2 | 4,315.0 | 14 | 1968 |
| 1969 | 3,439.7 | 69 | 8 | 559.9 | 11 | 22 | 1,437.4 | 29 | 29 | -532.4 | -11 | 115.3 | 2 | 5,019.9 | 15 | 1969 |
| 1970 | 3,919.6 | 68 | 13 | 692.5 | 12 | 21 | 2,244.5 | 39 | 45 | -1,179.1 | -20 | 127.4 | 2 | 5,804.9 | 15 | 1970 |
| 1971 | 4,531.5 | 66 | 15 | 860.8 | 13 | 22 | 2,778.1 | 41 | 21 | -1,484.2 | -22 | 154.3 | 2 | 6,840.5 | 16 | 1971 |
| 1972 | 5,071.2 | 62 | 11 | 990.2 | 12 | 14 | 3,392.7 | 41 | 20 | -1,378.2 | -17 | 119.1 | 1 | 8,195.0 | 18 | 1972 |
| 1973 | 6,340.1 | 62 | 22 | 1,117.7 | 11 | 12 | 4,045.2 | 39 | 18 | -1,041.0 | -10 | -205.1 | -2 | 10,256.9 | 22 | 1973 |
| 1974 | 7,657.6 | 61 | 19 | 1,298.4 | 10 | 15 | 5,709.8 | 45 | 34 | -2,043.9 | -16 | -11.8 | 0 | 12,610.1 | 21 | 1974 |
| 1975 | 8,120.7 | 60 | 6 | 1,423.0 | 11 | 9 | 5,370.4 | 40 | -6 | -1,416.4 | -11 | -54.7 | 0 | 13,443.0 | 6 | 1975 |
| 1976 | 8,605.9 | 59 | 6 | 1,541.5 | 11 | 8 | 5,981.7 | 41 | 11 | -1,199.4 | -8 | -278.8 | -2 | 14,650.9 | 9 | 1976 |
| 1977 | 9,268.6 | 58 | 7 | 1,716.3 | 11 | 11 | 5,799.1 | 36 | -3 | -424.2 | -3 | -320.8 | -2 | 16,039.0 | 9 | 1977 |
| 1978 | 10,149.1 | 57 | 9 | 1,964.7 | 11 | 14 | 6,957.4 | 39 | 18 | -897.6 | -5 | -343.2 | -2 | 17,830.4 | 11 | 1978 |
| 1979 | 11,245.2 | 55 | 10 | 2,033.6 | 10 | 3 | 8,899.9 | 43 | 25 | -1,445.1 | -7 | -210.6 | -1 | 20,523.0 | 14 | 1979 |
| 1980 | 12,911.3 | 51 | 14 | 2,447.4 | 10 | 19 | 11,627.6 | 46 | 27 | -2,215.8 | -9 | 320.2 | 1 | 25,090.7 | 20 | 1980 |
| 1981 | 14,329.3 | 49 | 10 | 2,788.6 | 10 | 13 | 13,587.0 | 46 | | -1,633.5 | -6 | 268.0 | 1 | 29,339.4 | 16 | 1981 |
| 1982 | 12,282.5 | 41 | -15 | 3,570.4 | 12 | 25 | 15,658.8 | 53 | 14 | -1,440.6 | -5 | -401.2 | -1 | 29,669.9 | 1 | 1982 |
| 1983 | 16,202.1 | 44 | 28 | 3,995.3 | 11 | 11 | 17,595.8 | 48 | 12 | -663.8 | -2 | -396.6 | -1 | 36,732.8 | 21 | 1983 |
| 1984 | 17,569.5 | 44 | 8 | 4,330.0 | 11 | 8 | 19,417.3 | 48 | 10 | -1,113.0 | -3 | 158.9 | 0 | 40,362.7 | 9 | 1984 |
| 1985 | 17,552.9 | 44 | 0 | 6,548.5 | 16 | 41 | 16,551.2 | 41 | -16 | -945.7 | -2 | 216.6 | 1 | 39,923.5 | -1 | 1985 |
| 1986 | 18,404.5 | 47 | 5 | 5,270.2 | 13 | -22 | 14,716.6 | 37 | -12 | 143.1 | 0 | 729.5 | 2 | 39,263.9 | -2 | 1986 |
| 1987 | 20,697.4 | 48 | 12 | 5,314.6 | 12 | 1 | 16,298.7 | 37 | 10 | 589.1 | 1 | 669.5 | 2 | 43,569.3 | 10 | 1987 |
| 1988 | 24,389.7 | 47 | 16 | 5,336.9 | 10 | 0 | 17,329.8 | 34 | 6 | 4,526.7 | 9 | 58.7 | 0 | 51,641.8 | 17 | 1988 |
| 1989 | 27,664.2 | 47 | 13 | 6,013.3 | 10 | 12 | 20,364.9 | 34 | 16 | 5,969.5 | 10 | -668.4 | -1 | 59,343.5 | 14 | 1989 |
| 1990 | 30,762.0 | 45 | 11 | 6,779.7 | 10 | 12 | 24,348.8 | 36 | 18 | 5,988.4 | 9 | 0.0 | 0 | 67,878.9 | 13 | 1990 |
| 1991 | 33,398.3 | 44 | 8 | 7,435.8 | 10 | 9 | 25,746.6 | 34 | 6 | 9,293.1 | 12 | -552.9 | -1 | 75,320.9 | 10 | 1991 |
| 1992 | 36,436.3 | 45 | 9 | 7,626.6 | 9 | 3 | 29,112.6 | 36 | 12 | 8,587.9 | 11 | -765.9 | -1 | 80,997.5 | 7 | 1992 |
| 1993 | 42,004.7 | 45 | 14 | 8,593.4 | 9 | 12 | 35,520.6 | 38 | 20 | 8,556.2 | 9 | -416.2 | 0 | 94,258.7 | 15 | 1993 |
| 1994 | 46,288.1 | 43 | 10 | 9,029.1 | 8 | 5 | 35,389.7 | 33 | 0 | 18,342.0 | 17 | -824.9 | -1 | 108,224.0 | 14 | 1994 |
| 1995 | 49,152.2 | 41 | 6 | 10,194.2 | 8 | 12 | 39,328.3 | 33 | 11 | 21,792.9 | 18 | 161.2 | 0 | 120,628.8 | 11 | 1995 |
| 1996 | 52,741.3 | 41 | 7 | 12,207.6 | 10 | 18 | 47,531.4 | 37 | 19 | 17,553.4 | 14 | -1,832.7 | -1 | 128,201.0 | 6 | 1996 |
| 1997 | 56,456.3 | 40 | 7 | 13,179.6 | 9 | 8 | 54,663.9 | 39 | 14 | 18,753.5 | 13 | -2,825.8 | -2 | 140,227.5 | 9 | 1997 |
| 1998 | 54,197.6 | 39 | -4 | 13,907.2 | 10 | 5 | 44,796.7 | 33 | -20 | 27,289.4 | 20 | -2,726.7 | -2 | 137,464.2 | -2 | 1998 |
| 1999 | 57,429.2 | 40 | 6 | 13,989.1 | 10 | 1 | 46,098.6 | 32 | 3 | 27,479.9 | 19 | -2,886.0 | -2 | 142,110.8 | 3 | 1999 |
| 2000 | 63,564.9 | 40 | 10 | 16,620.7 | 10 | 17 | 49,776.4 | 31 | 8 | 29,363.5 | 18 | -283.7 | 0 | 159,041.8 | 11 | 2000 |

*Sources*: Figures for the periods 1900–39 and 1950–59 are estimated by the author, whereas the figures for 1960–2000 are obtained from official publication of the Department of Statistics, Singapore (1996) and Asian Development Bank (2001).

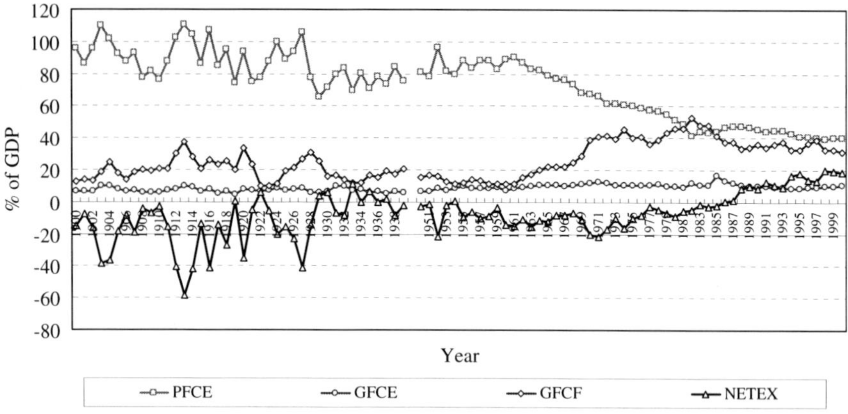

**Fig. 3.18:** Singapore: Share of Each Component of GDP to GDP at Current Prices, 1900–39 and 1950–2000

Abbreviations:

PFCE   Private Final Consumption Expenditure by Resident Households.

GFCE   Government Final Consumption Expenditure.

GCF    Gross Capital Formation.

NETEX  Net Exports of Goods and Services.

territory up to 1985. This situation dramatically reversed after 1985 when net exports began to predominate in the positive territory. By 2000, the share of net exports of goods and services was close to 20% of GDP.

There are a number of plausible explanatory factors for this incredible change which occurred during the last four decades in the structure of GDP. A large fall of PFCE can be explained by the remarkable increase in GDS over this long period[77] (Peebles *et al.*, 2002, 78 and Ghesquiere, 2007, 165). This increase of saving rate can be attributed to "forced saving" due

---

[77] Disposable income is equal to income (output) plus net transfers less taxes. Disposable income, in turn, is allocated to consumption and saving. Therefore, increases of the weight on saving will lead the fall of share of PFCE against GDP.

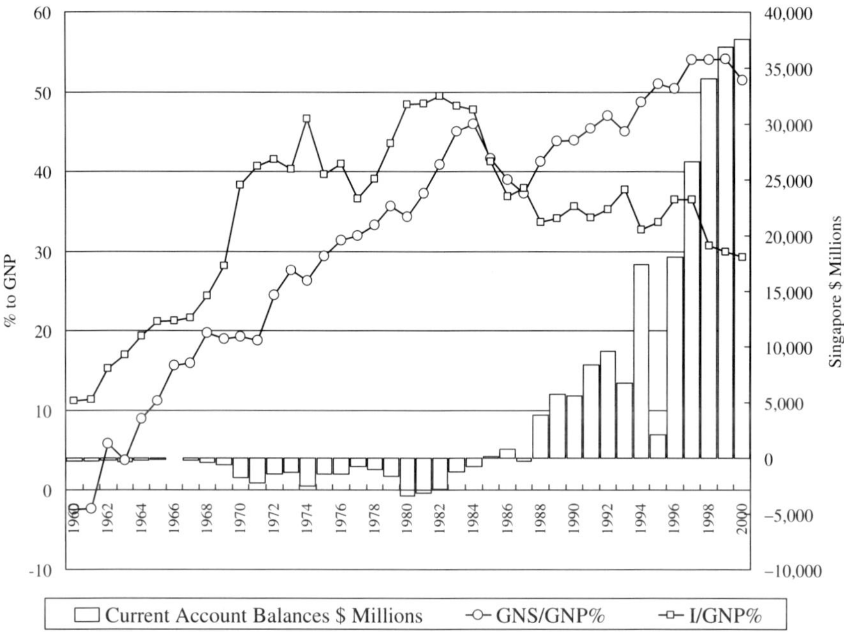


**Fig. 3.19:** Singapore: Saving and Investment as Ratio of GNP and Current Account Balance, 1960–2000

*Source*: Figure was created based on Table released by Peebles, Gavin and Wilson, Peter (2002, 274–275).

to the compulsory public provident fund system, the Central Provident Fund (CPF).[78]

As presented in Fig. 3.19, increases in savings naturally lead to the increase in financing domestic investments and

---

[78] The Central Provident Fund (CPF) was established by law in 1953 under the colonial administration and started operations in July 1955. It was initially intended as a fully funded pension plan for civil servants but has been expanded in coverage and scope immensely under the PAP government and has become an important part of social and economic policy and has been used for macro economic purposes. Employers and employees both contribute to the member's

lending abroad. The continuous reduction of the share of PFCE has led to a parallel increase in the share of GCF. This structure, however, experienced significant changes in 1985. Since then, gross national savings have exceeded domestic investments and this has led to large positive current account balances.[79]

account at rates that have changed significantly over time. All employees are required to be members, whereas permanent residents can be members. The self-employed can contribute to this fund. The scheme implies no transfers between economic classes and is not redistributive or aimed at reducing income inequality. It does not guarantee any minimum pension on retirement.

[79] The excess of saving over investment $(S - I)$ in the private sector is equal to the government budget deficit (Government purchases of goods and services $(G)$ plus government transfer payments $(TR)$ minus government revenue $(TA)$) plus the trade surplus (NEXGS); $S - I = (G + TR - TA) + NEXGS$. In the case of Singapore, the government budget has been in the surplus situation for many years. Thus, it is inevitable to conclude that when savings exceed investments, net exports of goods and services would be in the positive territory.

# Chapter Four

# Economic Instability and Economic Growth in Singapore in the Twentieth Century

## 4.1 Introduction

It will be recalled that the methodology employed for the construction of GDP estimates for the Colony of Singapore for the periods 1900–39 and 1950–60 was described in detail in Chapter 2. Subsequently in Chapter 3, the overall patterns of GDP of Singapore were investigated. The availability of this long-term economic database stretching over the last 100 years,[80] covering the British colonial era and the more recent period of self-government, enabled us to undertake a long-term quantitative economic analysis of Singapore.

This chapter is devoted to examining economic instability and its impact on the economic growth of Singapore during the twentieth century. In this study, economic instability is *defined* as the short-term fluctuations of real GDP after adjusting for trend (Dawe, 1996; Nazrin, 2000). As observed in Chapter 3, the salient feature of Singapore's economy is its high degree of openness to international trade. Singapore is often described as a 'very open re-export economy' because of to her heavy reliance on imported intermediate inputs as well as entrepôt exports (Huff, 1994;

---

[80] This study does not include 1940–49 due to the absence of historical GDP estimates.

Lloyd *et al.*, 1986; Peebles *et al.*, 1996 and 2002). Basically, this nature of Singapore's heavy dependence on the international economic environment remains essentially unchanged until today. Given this scenario, Singapore has been extraordinarily vulnerable to external shocks, whether it be a slowdown in export growth, a sharp exodus of short-term capital, a change in world interest rates, or an increase in imported inflation (Peebles and Wilson, 2002, 175).

Nevertheless, Singapore has experienced two major changes in the twentieth century: The first involved the shifting of trade dependence from the re-export of primary commodities to the exports of domestic manufactured goods. The second invovled, macroeconomic management which was dictated by the principle of *laissez-faire* under the British colonial administration and shifted to government-interventionist fiscal and monetary policies during the era of self-government (Huff, 1994).

Against this historical backdrop, this chapter focuses on answering three basic questions relating to the issue of economic instability and its concomitant effect on economic growth. The first attempt seeks to examine the pattern of volatility of real GDP and its components over the century. The second attempt is to identify the explanatory variables which could statistically explain the sources of real GDP volatility. The third attempt examines the effect of export instability and other relevant explanatory variables on the economic growth of Singapore. For all of the above questions, attention was focused particularly on whether there were any notable similarities or differences in the relationship between economic instability and economic growth for the two periods, namely, the British colonial era and the period of self-government.

This chapter is organized as follows: Section 4.2 conducts a literature review on the studies relating to (i) the extent of volatility of GDP and its components; (ii) the source of real GDP volatility; (iii) the effect of export instability on economic growth; and (iv) the studies on Singapore relating to this topic. Section 4.3 outlines the definition of economic instability and examines the extent of economic instability of Singapore's real GDP and its components, namely, private final consumption expenditure, government final consumption expenditure, gross capital formation, exports of goods and services, and imports of goods and services. Section 4.4 conducts two types of econometric tests, namely, the sources of output volatility and the effect of export instability on economic growth. On the basis of the results of econometric tests, international comparisons would be made in Section 4.5. Finally, Section 4.6 provides some concluding remarks.

## 4.2 Literature Review

### 4.2.1 *Declining Degree of Real GDP Volatility*

To date, many studies have been conducted touching on the issues of economic instability using the various empirical econometric tests with different time-series framework undertaken for both developed and developing countries. One of the academic questions relating to this subject was the declining degree of real GDP volatility over time. Christina Romer (1986, 1989), Sheffrin (1988), and Balke and Gordon (1989) observed the fact that real GDP volatility in the United States after World War II has been smaller than that prior to World War I and discussed that a diminution of volatility was the reflection of institutional developments and the successful application of macromanagement policies. With regard to this, Backus and Kehoe, (1992) compared output volatility prior to World War I (the prewar period 1870–1914), between the wars (the interwar period 1919–39), and the period immediately after World War II (1945–88) by using available long-term statistical data of 10 countries, namely, Australia, Canada, Denmark, Germany, Italy, Japan, Norway, Sweden, United Kingdom, and United States. This study also found that real GDP volatilities during the pre–World War I period were generally larger than those of the post–World War II period, the extent of the differences varying across countries. The changes in real GDP variability over time are that the interwar era experienced much larger fluctuations than the other two periods, although the extent of this higher volatility again varies from country to country. High volatilities were experienced during a brief depression in the early 1920s and the Great Depressions of the 1930s which wrought havoc to the world economy during these years.

Similar exercises were conducted by Bergman *et al.* (1998) and Basu *et al.* (1999) by extending the number of samples from 10 to 13 countries (Canada, Denmark, Finland, France, Germany, Italy, Japan, Netherlands, Norway, Spain, Sweden, United Kingdom, and United States). The time periods were decided on the basis of the four distinct international monetary regimes, namely, the classical gold standard period (1870–1914), the interwar period (1919–39), the Bretton Woods era (1945–71), and the floating exchange rate era (1970's to present). Their empirical tests find convergence with the observations made in the works of Backus and Patrick, J (1992). Volatility was considerably higher during the interwar years than during the pre–World War I and the post–World War II periods (See Fig. 4.1).

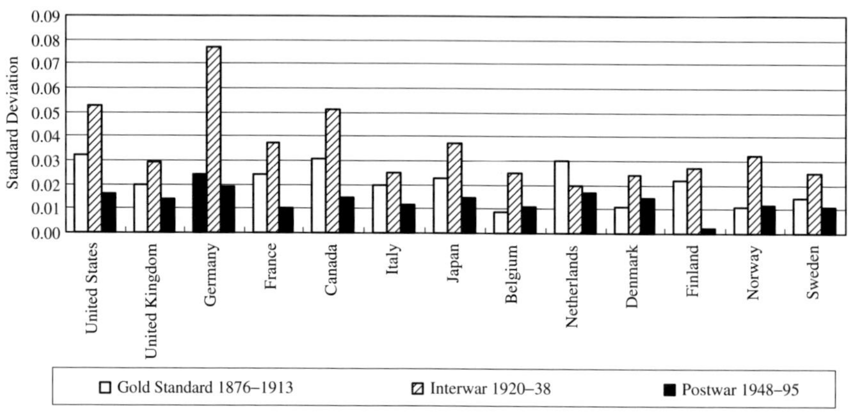


**Fig. 4.1:** Standard Deviations of Output (Real GDP) Volatility during Different Monetary Regimes

*Source*: Bergman *et al.* (1998).

In addition to real GDP volatilities, Backus *et al.* (1992) examined volatilities of expenditure components: consumption, gross investment, government spending, and net exports. Some stylized facts were observed: First, consumption expenditures have approximately the same standard deviation as output. Second, government spending exhibits little regularities with its volatility relative to output ranging from 0.81 in interwar Sweden to 8.72 in interwar Britain to 9.49 in prewar Japan.[81] Third, volatilities of investment (gross capital formation) have generally varied, with the level of standard deviation being two to four times larger than the output. Fourth, volatilities of net exports[82] varied across the countries (See Fig. 4.2).

In addition to standard deviations of volatility, Backus and Kehoe (1992) examined the cross-correlations between volatilities of each major component and real GDP. As presented in Fig. 4.3, cross-correlation between fluctuations in consumption and real GDP ranges from 0.41 in prewar United Kingdom to 0.91 in the prewar United States. Similarly, cross-correlations between investment volatility and are GDP are also relatively high. On the other hand, cross-correlations between government spending and real GDP, however, exhibit some irregularity. Of the 18 estimated cross-correlations, 10 are positive and 8 are negative. In the case of net exports, in two-thirds of the cases, the cross-correlations were negative and often strongly so. In the remaining cases, the cross-correlations were generally small.

In contrast to above studies, no similar long-term period empirical exercises were available for developing countries because of the dearth of long-term time-series data which stretch over the entire twentieth century. This study hopes to bridge the

---

[81] This large difference was partly due to the expansion of military spending during the Russo-Japanese War.

[82] Volatilities of net exports were measured as the ratio of current value net exports to nominal output.

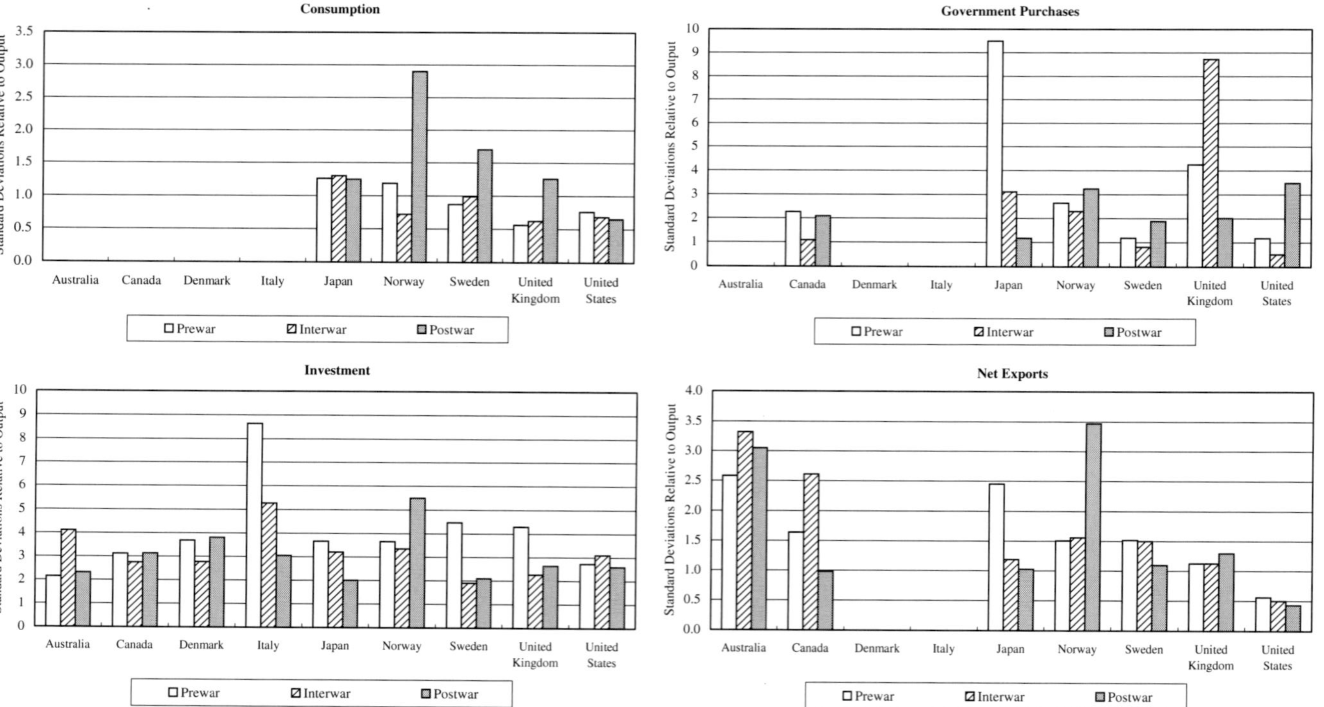


**Fig. 4.2:** Standard Deviations of Volatilities of Major Components of GDP Relative to Output (Real GDP) for Prewar, Interwar, and Postwar Period

*Source*: Backus and Kehoe (1992, 875).

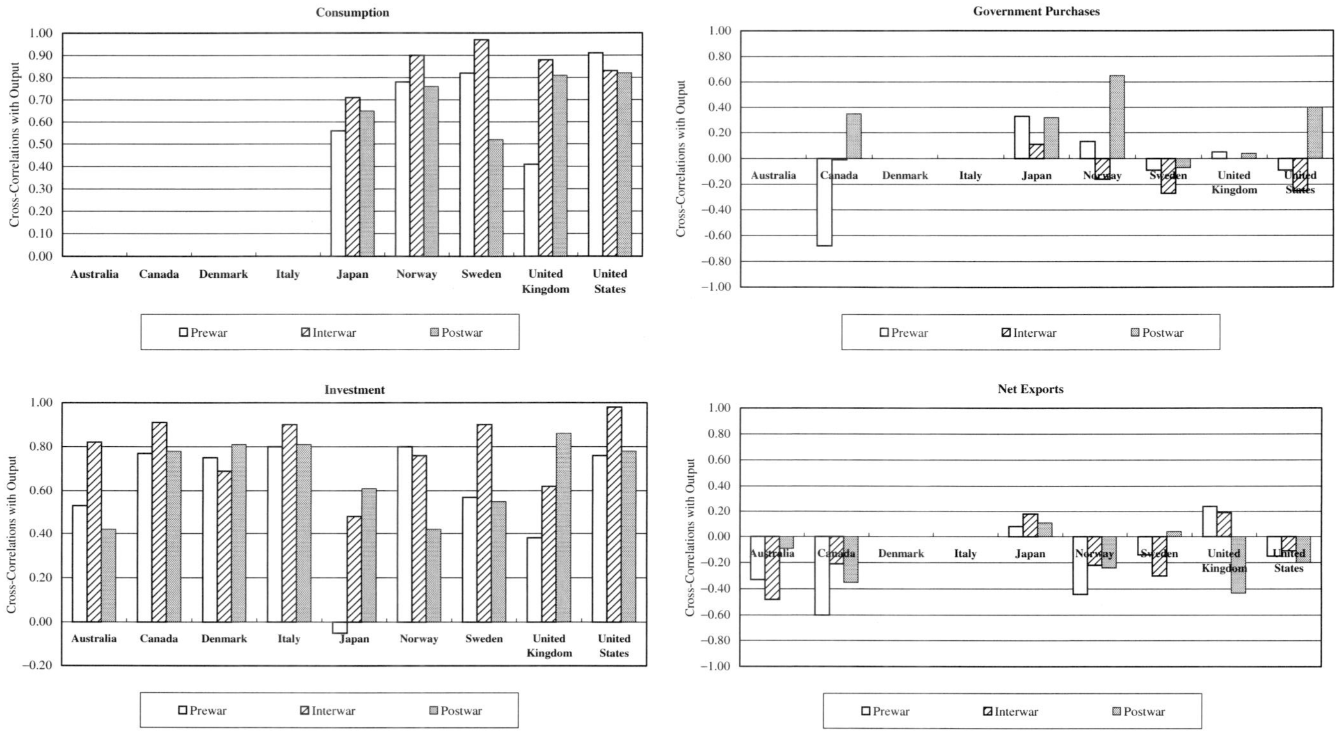

**Fig. 4.3:** Cross-Correlations between Volatilities of Each Major Component and Output (Real GDP)

*Source*: Backus and Kehoe (1992, 875).

**Table 4.1:** Standard Deviations of Annual Real GDP Growth (GDP % Growth Volatility)

|  | 1954–73 | 1974–83 | 1984–93 | 1994–2003 |
|---|---|---|---|---|
| World | 4.3 | 5.3 | 4.3 | 3.0 |
| United States | 2.5 | 2.8 | 1.9 | 1.2 |
| Germany | 2.4 | 2.0 | 1.9 | 1.0 |
| France | 1.2 | 1.4 | 1.6 | 1.2 |
| Italy | 1.5 | 2.7 | 1.4 | 0.9 |
| United Kingdom | 1.8 | 2.2 | 2.0 | 0.8 |
| Japan | 2.4 | 1.9 | 2.0 | 1.5 |

*Source*: Singh and Fagernäs (2006, 3).

gap by providing a case study of a developing country like Singapore (See Section 4.3). Empirical tests on the output volatility after World War II have been more widely examined for both developed and developing countries. Blanchard and Simon (2001) measured output volatility in United States, United Kingdom, Canada, France, Germany, Italy, and Japan since the first quarter of 1952. It was noted that volatility increased from the late 1960s to the mid-1980s, and this was followed by a sharp decline since the second half of the 1980s for all six countries. A similar pattern was observed from the exercise conducted by Singh and Fagernäs (2006) as presented in Table 4.1.

Most of the trend decrease in output volatility can be traced to a decrease in the volatility of consumption and investment. In contrast to regularities found in developed countries, a similar exercise applied for developing countries yielded different results. A study by Agénor, McDermott, and Prasad (2000) found that output volatilities of developing countries[83] were, on average, much higher than the level typically observed in industrial countries for the period 1978 (first quarter) to 1995 (fourth quarter).

---

[83] The countries are Chile, Colombia, India, South Korea, Malaysia, Mexico, Nigeria, Philippines, Tunisia, Turkey, and Uruguay.

**Table 4.2:**  Real GDP Growth Volatility (Standard Deviations and Mean of Growth)

|  |  | 1960–71 | 1972–81 | 1982–91 | 1992–2004 | 1992–2004 |
|---|---|---|---|---|---|---|
| South Asia | St.Dev | 2.6 | 3.6 | 1.8 | 1.3 | |
| | Mean | 4.0 | 3.6 | 5.2 | 5.7 | |
| East Asia and Pacific | St.Dev | 7.4 | 2.0 | 1.5 | 2.5 | 1.7 |
| | Mean | 4.9 | 6.5 | 7.7 | 7.9 | 8.6 |
| Latin America and Caribbean | St.Dev | 1.8 | 2.2 | 2.4 | 2.2 | |
| | Mean | 5.4 | 5.1 | 1.6 | 2.8 | |
| Middle East and North Africa | St.Dev | | 5.5 | 3.3 | 1.1 | |
| | Mean | | 3.8 | 3.7 | 3.8 | |
| Sub-Saharan Africa | St.Dev | 2.0 | 1.9 | 1.5 | 1.7 | |
| | Mean | 5.1 | 3.2 | 1.7 | 2.9 | |

*Source*: Arranged from Singh and Fagernäs (2006, 5, 7, and 9).

Similarly, studies by De Ferranti *et al.* (2000) and Singh and Fagernäs (2006) show that there are also significant geographical differences in output volatility among developing countries for the period 1960–2004. As presented in Table 4.2, evidence suggests that volatility has declined over the last two decades in South Asia and less so in the East Asia region as a whole. Among the latter country group, volatility has clearly declined for China, but whether this is the case for the other countries is not clear. To the best of my knowledge, there are, unfortunately, no previous studies which dealt with the issue of economic instability during the British Colonial Period and the period of self-government. This was plausibly due to the absence of long-term time-series economic data. This study, therefore, represents the first of its kind devoted specifically to examining the extent of instability of GDP and its components for Singapore during the twentieth century.

### 4.2.2 *The Source of Real GDP Volatilities*

As observed above, most of the developed/OECD countries experienced similar patterns of output volatilities in the long-term perspective. On the other hand, the results for developing countries were rather mixed. With regard to this, many studies have attempted to seek the possible explanatory factors (source) for the decline of real GDP volatility mainly in developed countries. Cecchetti, Stephen *et al.* (2006) surveyed the evidence and competing explanations and found support for the view in decline in the degree of volatility in the post–World War II period because of a number of reasons, namely, (i) improved inventory management policies (Kahn, *et al.*, 2002, Kent, Christopher *et al.*, 2005, McConnell *et al.*, 2000, McConnell, Mosser *et al.*, 1999), (ii) better monetary policy (e.g. inflation control) (Clarida, Gali, and Gertler, 2000; Blanchard and Simon, 2001; Martin and Rowthorn, 2004, and Kent, Christopher *et al.*, 2005), (iii) financial innovation in risk sharing (Dynan, *et al.*, 2006), (iv) increased international commercial openness (Barrell *et al.*, 2004, and (v) luck in the form of smaller shocks (Ahmed *et al.*, 2004 and Stock *et al.*, 1988, 1999). The first four factors emphasized the government's role in reducing the adverse effects on the economy arising from exogenous shocks. The fifth factor, however, may have led to a decline in the magnitude of the shocks globally over this period, regardless of any effect from the first four factors. On the basis of this this hypothesis, Cecchetti *et al.* (2006) conducted output volatility panel regression tests which showed that financial development, as measured by the importance of bank lending, is linked to real economic stability. Beyond the importance of financial development, this study provided evidence in favors of the view that improved inventory control policies played an important role in bringing about more stable growth. Furthermore, increased commercial openness, measured by the ratio of imports plus exports to GDP, does not appear to be associated with more stable growth.

In the case of developing countries, Singh *et al.* (2006) conducted econometric analysis of India, where real GDP volatility has declined over the past two decades. In their analysis of real GDP volatility, the following factors were regarded as possible explanatory variables: trade openness (*(imports + exports) as a share of GDP(%)*), private financial development (*private-sector credit as a share of GDP(%), private capital flows as a share of GDP(%))*, government macroeconomic management (*change in CPI, gross fiscal deficit as a share of GDP(%)*), external shocks (*terms of trade, percentage change*), the structure of the economy (e.g., *share of agriculture in GDP(%)*), GDP growth rate in the past year, and past experiences of real GDP volatility. Their regression results show that the move away from agriculture has stabilized the economy while increased financial depth and more favorable developments in terms of trade have had a similar effect.

In this study of Singapore, similar econometric tests would be applied. Unfortunately, the availability of statistical information on private-sector credit and share of gross value added of each sector of GDP are not generally available. Therefore, econometric tests based on only those variables for which data were available were made and are described in Section 4.4.

### 4.2.3 *The Effect of Economic Instability to Economic Growth*

#### 4.2.3.1 *Export Instability*

How economic instability affects economic growth has been an issue of research, initiated by the work of Ramey *et al.* (1994), who found that countries with large fluctuations in growth rates were inclined to have lower average growth rates. Many studies were conducted to identify the determinant variables relating to this issue, their focus being particularly with the effect of export instability on economic growth for both developed and developing nations. These studies found all three possible kinds of relationships between export instability and economic growth, namely, positive, negative, and no relationship.

Studies by McBean (1966) and Knudsen *et al.* (1975) found a positive relationship between the two variables. Their study argues that uncertainty of export earnings can lead to reduction in consumption and, in turn, an increase in savings and investments, and thus economic growth. The conventional measure of export instability, on the other hand, leads to an opposite conclusion that export instability has a negative impact on economic growth (Abraha, 2004; Dawe, 1996; Dupasquier and Patrick, 2006; Feder, 1984; Glezakos, 1973; Knudsen, 1975; Lim David, 1974, 1976; Moran, 1983; Ozler *et al.*, 1988; Rangarajan *et al.*, 1976; Sinha, 1999 and Voivodas, 1974).

A study by Sinha (1999) examined the relationship between export instability and investment and economic growth in nine Asian countries using time-series data (around 1950–97). A negative relationship between export instability and economic growth was found in the case of Japan, Malaysia, the Philippines, and Sri Lanka, whereas on the other hand, a positive relationship was found for South Korea, Myanmar, Pakistan, and Thailand. India, however, displayed mixed results. In the case of domestic investments, economic growth in most cases was found to be positively associated with it.

The results from previous studies on export instability and economic growth rate are very far from conclusive. However, what is clear is the tendency that export instability is higher for developing countries than for developed countries (Mullor Sebastian, 1988). The work by Love (1977, 1987, and 1992) is one of the few studies which examines the causal relationship between export instability and income instability. His time-series analysis found that developing countries which rely on the export of primary goods, which are subject to more fluctuations, experienced greater export instability than those countries relying primarily on the exports of industrial goods.

In the case of Singapore, Wilson (1994) investigated the export earnings instability of Singapore for the years 1957–88 measured over two separate time periods: 1957–71 and 1972–88. He found that the pattern of the export instability index of the latter period was even higher than that of the first period. Nevertheless, no specific study on Singapore has yet been made to cover the entire twentieth century. Therefore, this study attempts to fill the gap in reviewing the long-term patterns of economic instability in a typically small, open economy like that of Singapore.

Apart from "export instability," other explanatory variables were also examined and are described in the ensuing pages.

### 4.2.3.2 *Annual Growth Rate of Exports as a Proportion of GDP*

Westphal *et al.* (1985) and Pack *et al.* (1986) examined the relationship between the annual growth rate of exports as a proportion of GDP and the economic growth for Korea. Their study emphasizes that a high rate of growth of exports is an important source of economic growth. An export-oriented economy forces it to compete worldwide and to produce products that are competitive in quality and price. A growing export share provides the country with the foreign exchange to pay for its imports, particularly of capital goods that serve as an engine for further economic growth.

### 4.2.3.3 *Terms-of-Trade Volatility*

The study by Blattman *et al.* (2004) suggests that volatility in the terms-of-trade was damaging to economic growth particularly in the commodity producing colonies on the basis the experiences from 1870 to 1939 and assessed its impact on the economic performance of the sovereign industrialized countries and the primary–product producing colonies. Similarly, a study by Mendoza (1994 and 1995) which included 40 industrial and developing countries also showed that terms-of-trade volatility adversely affected economic growth. Similar results were derived from the empirical test on developing countries (Bleaney *et al.*, 2001, Turnovsky *et al.*, 2003).

### 4.2.3.4 *Share of Investment to GDP*

De Long and Summers (1991) focused on equipment investment as potentially a key factor in growth in a post–World War II cross-section of economies spanning the range from the poorest to the richest using data from the United Nations International Comparison Project. This study found that countries with high equipment investment grew extremely rapidly, even controlling for a number of other factors. This association suggested a causal relationship: rapid growth went with high equipment investment, no matter whether high investment was a consequence of high saving or of a low relative equipment prices. Subsequently, De Long *et al.* (1992) documented a statistically significant and robust cross-country partial correlation between the growth rate of GDP per worker and the equipment investment/GDP ratio.

### 4.2.3.5 *Annual Growth Rate of Government Final Consumption Expenditure as a Proportion of GDP*

The annual growth rate of the ratio of real government final consumption expenditure to real GDP was also tested as one of the possible determinant variables to economic growth. Relating to this, Barro (1991) has argued that higher growth rate of government final consumption spending lowers real GDP growth through the distorting effects resulting from taxation or government expenditure programs. The results he obtained from a cross-sectional study of 98 countries for 1965–85 affirms this proposition.

### 4.2.3.6 *Population Growth*

Neoclassical growth theory states that the steady-state growth rate of output equals the sum of the growth rate of the labor force and the growth rate of exogenous technological change. On the other hand, if a high population growth rate increases the dependency ratio, it will serve to retard economic growth (Simon, 1986). It could also be argued that a cheap labor supply discourages automation and other productivity-enhancing measures.

### 4.2.3.7 *Gross Domestic Product Per Capita with Time Lag*

Neoclassical growth theory predicts that in the transition to the steady state, countries with lower capital–labor ratios and hence lower output per capita will grow at a faster rate as a result of diminishing returns. Therefore, the lower the level of GDP per capita, the higher the potential for rapid growth.

Nazrin (2000) had conducted regression analysis by using above-mentioned explanatory variables for Malaya/Malaysia for the time periods 1895–1939 and 1947–97. His regression results found that the coefficient of export instability for both the periods was negative and statistically significant while coefficient became smaller in the second period. This implies that the problem of export instability becomes less as the structure of the economy changed. Additionally, he pointed out that the role of government macroeconomic management in offsetting the effect of instability also had a lot to do with the reduced impact on economic growth. This study of Singapore also attempts to test export instability over the periods 1900–39 and 1950–2000.

### 4.2.4 *Studies on Singapore Relating to This Issue*

Sachs and Warner (1995) identified Singapore as one of the most open economies in the world. Nevertheless, "open economies" which refer to the degree of integration with other countries, are different from the "dependence" on trade. Unlike other countries, in fact, Singapore's economy "depends" heavily on trading activities. In 2000, approximate figures of GDP in billions of dollars are presented as follows:

$$\text{GDP} = \text{PFCE} + \text{GFCE} + \text{GCF} + (\text{EX-IM})$$
$$160 = 64 + 17 + 50 + 29$$

This standard way of presenting the account of net exports do not seem as crucial as some elements of domestic demand.

However, we can rewrite this underlying relationship in terms of demand and supply as follows:

$$\text{Demand} = \text{Supply}$$
$$EX + C + G + I = GDP + IM$$
$$287 + 64 + 17 + 50 = 160 + 258$$

It can be seen that export demand is 4.5 times the amount of domestic private consumption and 5.7 times the amount of investments. For the period 1992–2000, for example, changes in the external demand (exports) accounted for over three-quarters of the changes in real total demand, whereas changes in domestic demand accounted only for less than a quarter (Peebles *et al.*, 2002, 175).

A similar exercise was conducted for the twentieth century to examine whether these relationships still held good. As presented in Table 4.3, changes in external demand (exports) accounted for 71.5% and 67.6% of the changes in real total

**Table 4.3:** Singapore: The Contribution of Domestic and External Demand to Growth in Total Demand, 1900–2000 (1990 Prices)

| | Aggregate Demand | Private Final Consumption Expenditure | Government Final Consumption Expenditure | Gross Capital Formation | Domestic Demand | External Demand |
|---|---|---|---|---|---|---|
| *Average Exponential Growth Rate (%)* | | | | | | |
| 1900–39 | 3.3 | 3.9 | 4.2 | 7.3 | 4.6 | **2.4** |
| 1950–2000 | 7.4 | 5.9 | 7.9 | 8.0 | 6.8 | **7.8** |
| *Average Composition (%)* | | | | | | |
| 1900–39 | 100.0 | 24.7 | 2.4 | 9.1 | 36.2 | **63.8** |
| 1950–2000 | 100.0 | 23.9 | 4.3 | 14.1 | 42.3 | **57.7** |
| *Contribution to Growth in Total Demand (%)* | | | | | | |
| 1900–39 | 3.3 | 1.0 | 0.1 | 0.9 | 1.8 | **1.5** |
| 1950–2000 | 7.4 | 1.4 | 0.4 | 1.3 | 3.0 | **4.4** |
| *Percentage Contribution to Growth in Total Demand* | | | | | | |
| 1900–39 | 100.0 | -1.4 | 2.7 | 27.6 | 27.9 | **72.1** |
| 1950–2000 | 100.0 | 14.9 | 1.2 | 16.4 | 32.4 | **67.6** |

*Note*: Figure was constructed on the basis of the statistical database presented in Chapter 3. All variables are 1990 prices

demand (1990 prices) for the prewar and postwar periods, respectively. In fact, throughout the twentieth century, Singapore's total demand was heavily determined by the changes in external demand.

This is not surprising since Singapore's share of external demand remain bigger than its domestic demand. This situation is different from that of other economies such as Japan and United States where domestic demand is the prime mover in total demand. This implies that any unforeseen shock in external demand may cause a serious impact on Singapore's change in total demand itself.

However, Singapore's economy has experienced a major structural shift in relation to economic volatility as a result of two major factors: First, there was the shift of trade dependence from primary commodity re-export to exports of domestic manufactured goods. Second, macroeconomic management which was dictated by the principle of *laissez-faire* under British colonial administration had shifted to government-interventionist fiscal and monetary policies in the era of self-government (Huff, 1994). It is important to investigate whether these shifts have in any way affected or impacted on economic instability.

Table 4.4 shows percentage contributions of three major export commodities from Singapore, namely, tin, rubber, and petroleum as against total merchandize exports for the year 1900–70. In the early twentieth century, tin accounted for the

**Table 4.4:** Singapore: Tin, Rubber and Petroleum Export Quantity Indices and Percentage Contributions to Merchandize Exports, 1900–70

| | Export Quantity (1920 = 100) | | | Percentage Contribution to Merchandize Exports | | | |
|---|---|---|---|---|---|---|---|
| | Tin | Rubber | Petroleum | Tin | Rubber | Petroleum | Total |
| 1910 | 82.6 | 0.7 | 221.0 | 15.8 | 4.5 | 0.4 | 20.7 |
| 1920 | 100.0 | 100.0 | 100.0 | 9.7 | 32.1 | 0.3 | 42.1 |
| 1930 | 128.5 | 161.4 | 5,720.5 | 9.0 | 19.1 | 10.9 | 39.0 |
| 1939 | 73.4 | 143.5 | 11,529.3 | 16.0 | 41.0 | 12.1 | 69.0 |
| 1950 | 70.9 | 308.2 | 23,633.7 | 6.8 | 46.4 | 5.3 | 58.6 |
| 1960 | 2.0 | 459.3 | 38,717.6 | 0.1 | 41.0 | 10.9 | 52.1 |
| 1970 | 0.2 | 600.7 | 178,387.2 | 0.0 | 24.4 | 17.2 | 41.7 |

*Source*: Extracted from Huff (1994, 372–385).

bulk of total merchandize exports. This structure, however, experienced some major transitions after the emergence of rubber in early 1910s and petroleum in the 1920s. By 1920, these three major export commodities accounted for about 42% of total merchandize exports and their share further increased to 69% in 1939. In the post–World War II period, the importance of tin dropped significantly. This is mainly because all major smelting work in Singapore ceased when the Straits Trading Company transferred its operation to larger smelters located in Butterworth (Penang).

The changes in the export structure brought with it severe fluctuations in annual export values, volume, and percentage contribution to total merchandize exports of these three major export commodities (See Fig. 4.4). These rapid fluctuations were strongly related to the change in the external demand for these commodities. The market price of these commodities has experienced rapid fluctuations (See Fig. 4.5). In particular, rubber price experienced very large fluctuations throughout the period despite the implementation of several rubber regulation schemes aimed at bringing stability in its price during the 1920s and 1930s.

Table 4.5 shows the standard deviations of price and export volume of these three major export commodities. In the case of

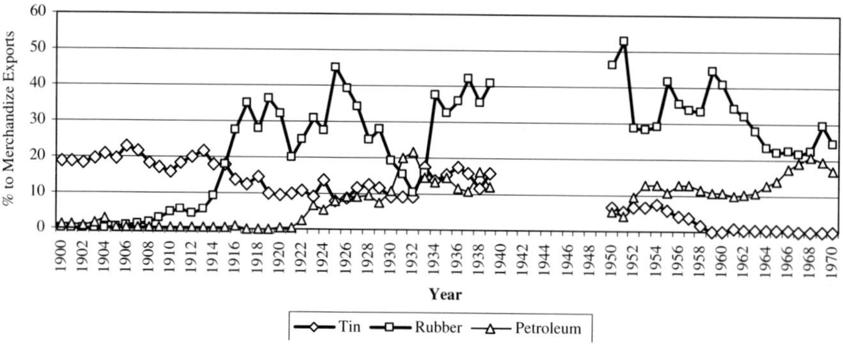


**Fig. 4.4:** Singapore: Percentage Contributions of Tin, Rubber, and Petroleum to Merchandize Exports, 1900–70

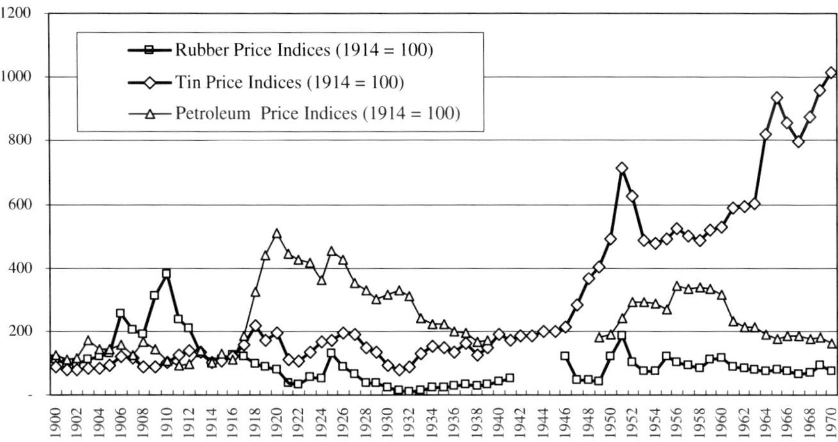


**Fig. 4.5:** Singapore: Export Unit Value Indices (1914 = 100) of Rubber, Tin, and Petroleum, 1900–70

**Table 4.5:** Singapore: Standard Deviation of Prices and Export Volume of Rubber, Tin, and Petroleum, 1900–70

| | Tin | | Rubber | | Petroleum | |
|---|---|---|---|---|---|---|
| | **Price** | **Quantity** | **Price** | **Quantity** | **Price** | **Quantity** |
| 1900–18 | 0.264 | 0.105 | 0.430 | 2.577 | 0.288 | 0.653 |
| 1919–39 | 0.256 | 0.191 | 0.703 | 0.283 | 0.349 | 1.672 |
| 1950–70 | 0.265 | 2.163 | 0.255 | 0.190 | 0.259 | 0.556 |

*Source*: Calculated based on Huff, WG (1994).

tin, standard deviations of price were relatively stable over time although export quantity had fallen significantly. In the case of rubber, high standard deviations on price were recorded during the interwar period. On the other hand, export quantity of petroleum had experienced high standard deviations for the same period.

With independence from the British in 1959, the ruling People's Action Party (PAP) ushered in the process of industrialization to diversify away from the *"entrepôt base"* which inevitably placed constraints in the form of employment and, more importantly to avoid high export earnings instability. For the period 1960–65, an import substitution policy was initiated on the basis of the expected integration with the Federation of Malaya.

Upon the inclusion of Singapore under the Federation of Malaysia in 1963, fiscal concession was given to 'pioneer' industries for the establishment of a viable industrial sector. However, when Singapore left the Federation of Malaysia in 1965, trade policies were entirely changed from inward to outward orientation. Because of the limited size of the domestic market and dearth of natural resources, the import substitution policy was no longer valid for Singapore. The focus in trade policy therefore switched toward the promotion of labor-intensive exports and the attraction of foreign investments. In 1967 when the British government announced its intention to phase out its military bases in the Republic by 1971, nearly one-fifth of Singapore's GDP[84] was at stake. This triggered the rapid development of export-oriented and labor-intensive industries. In 1968, the Economic Development Board, as part of the trade promotion exercise, was reorganized and tax incentives were given to encourage export promotion and foreign investment participation. The new strategy of export promotion combined with a lack of indigenous industrial entrepreneurs made the attraction of foreign investment a top priority.

The shift in the policy toward industrialization introduced in the 1960s initially focused upon low-skill-intensive exports of textiles and garments and simple electrical goods but moved toward capital-intensive petrol refining in the 1970s and to the manufacture of more sophisticated electronic goods in the 1970s and 1980s. Although petroleum refining and bunkering for ships and aircraft increased in importance in 1970s and 1980s, in value-added terms their contribution declined to 9.4% by 2000.

---

[84] Lee Kuan Yew (2000, 49).

**Table 4.6:** Singapore: Dependence on Trade 1970–2000

| | **Total Exports** | **Total** | **Oil Exports** | **Domestic Exports** | **Entrepôt Exports** |
|---|---|---|---|---|---|
| | | **Domestic Exports** | | | |
| **Singapore $ (Billions)** | | | | | |
| 1970 | 82 | 32 | 19 | 13 | 50 |
| 1975 | 95 | 56 | 19 | 37 | 39 |
| 1980 | 171 | 107 | 59 | 48 | 64 |
| 1985 | 129 | 84 | 42 | 42 | 45 |
| 1990 | 141 | 93 | 26 | 67 | 48 |
| 1995 | 141 | 83 | 12 | 71 | 58 |
| 2000 | 149 | 85 | 14 | 71 | 64 |
| **Distribution (%)** | | | | | |
| 1970 | 100.0 | 39.0 | 23.2 | 15.9 | 61.0 |
| 1975 | 100.0 | 58.9 | 20.0 | 38.9 | 41.1 |
| 1980 | 100.0 | 62.6 | 34.5 | 28.1 | 37.4 |
| 1985 | 100.0 | 65.1 | 32.6 | 32.6 | 34.9 |
| 1990 | 100.0 | 66.0 | 18.4 | 47.5 | 34.0 |
| 1995 | 100.0 | 58.9 | 8.5 | 50.4 | 41.1 |
| 2000 | 100.0 | 57.0 | 9.4 | 47.7 | 43.0 |

*Source*: Based on Wilson *et al.* (2005).

As presented in Table 4.6, a major expansion of domestic exports was observed beginning in 1975. In other words, the importance of the entrepôt trade to the economy measured by its contribution to GDP, seems to have hit a nadir in the mid-1970s (Krause *et al.*, 1987, 65).

In summary, it can be said that there was a significant shift of the trade structure, from a high concentration of exports of primary commodities to an expansion of exports comprising mainly domestically manufactured goods. The impact of this structural change was significant from the viewpoint of a spillover effect.

## 4.3 The Extent of Economic Instability in Singapore

### 4.3.1 *Definition and Measurement of Output Volatilities*

This section first clarifies the definition of economic instability and investigates the most suitable measurement of economic instability in this exercise. The representation of economic time-series data consists of the trend component and a cyclical component. The trend component of an economic time series is assumed to be characterized by a slow and smooth change over time. The cyclical component, on the contrary, is commonly characterized by recurrent large swings in the macroeconomic variables over relatively short periods of time. In the case of GDP, the study of movements in the trend or secular component has been long viewed as falling within the realm of growth theory. A cyclical fluctuation was a familiar topic of interest in the field of business cycle theory. Theories of growth have been concerned with examining the determinant variables in the long-run trends; for example, traditional one-sector neoclassical models have focused on factors such as capital accumulation, population growth, and technological change. Theories of business cycle, on the other hand, seek to answer the question of why economies go through cycles of recession and recovery, or boom and bust. Any theory of the business cycle makes two sorts of claims: what shocks are most important in disturbing the economy and what economic structure is necessary for propagating these shocks (Basu *et al.*, 1999).

In the case of economic instability, the attention was given to examine the movements in the cyclical component of real GDP. Therefore, in this study, economic instability is defined as the short-run fluctuations of real GDP after adjusting for trend. It is measured by taking the absolute deviation of real GDP from its long-run trend.

Unfortunately, there is no concrete method of identifying long-run trend (Nazrin, 2000; Singh *et al.*, 2006; Wilson, 1994).

In the final analysis, the choice of creation of trend is rather judgmental. A working definition of economic fluctuation of time series was filtered by the Hodrick-Prescott method, which removes trend movements from the data.[85] The choice of this method is mainly because many previous studies have applied it for empirical tests[86] (e.g., Agénor, *et al.*, 2000; Backus *et al.*, 1992; Blattman, Christopher *et al.*, 2004).

### 4.3.2 *Economic Instability of GDP and Its Components*

As described in the literature review, one of the major questions in all historical accounts of the evolution of the economic instability is whether the level of volatility increases or decreases over time. One simple way to look at economic volatility is to check the standard deviation of variables (Basu *et al.*, 1999). Figure 4.6 and Table 4.7 provide the degree of instability on log of real GDP and its components which was derived by the Hodrick-Prescott method. Determining periodical frame is an important step because the result would be different depending

---

[85] The Hodrick-Prescott filter, described by Hodrick *et al.* (1980) and Kydland *et al.* (1982), defines a trend $\{\tau_t\}$ for a series $\{y_t\}$ as the solution to the problem

$$\min_{(\tau_i)} \sum_{t=1}^{T} (y_t - \tau)^2 + \mu \sum_{t=2}^{T-1} [(\tau_{t+1} - \tau_t) - (\tau_t - \tau_{t-1})]^2$$

Fluctuations are defined as deviations from trend, $y_t - \tau_t$. We use $\mu = 100$ in all tables concerning fluctuations of variables. A procedure for computing the trend was made based on Eview 4.1.

[86] Bergman, Michael, Michael, and Jonung, (1998) apply the Baxter-King (1995) band-pass filter to extract all variations of a variable at business cycle frequencies. Love (1992) and Sinha (1999) define the measure of export instability as the absolute value of the deviations of actual exports from a 5 year moving average of exports. Singh and Fagernäs (2006) applied the 3 year moving average. Wilson (1994) selected the autocorrelation-corrected exponential regression model.

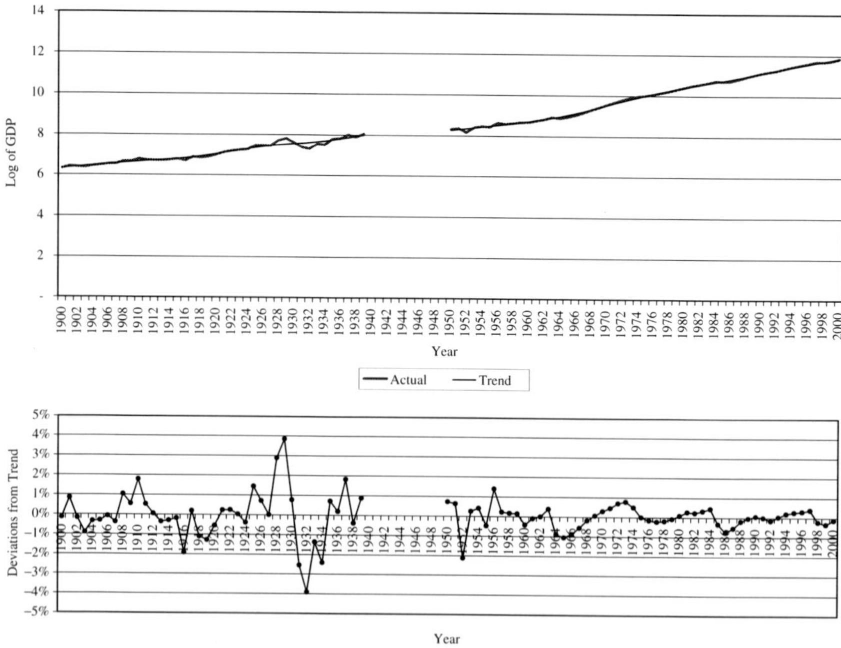

**Fig. 4.6:** Singapore: Trend GDP, Actual GDP, and Percentage Deviation of GDP from Trend, 1900–2000 (Trend Obtained Using HP Filter)

**Table 4.7:** Singapore: A Comparison of the Standard Deviation of the GDP Series Using Hodrick-Prescott Methods

| Period | Hodrick-Prescott |
|---|---|
| 1900–13 | 4.7 |
| 1914–39 | 12.4 |
| 1950–74 | 6.4 |
| 1975–2000 | 3.2 |

on the selection of the period. Alternatively, periodical frame for the pre–World War II was determined on the basis of the long-term international historical exercises led by Bergman *et al.* (1998) and Basu *et al.* (1999), namely, the Pre–World War I period (1900–13) and the interwar Period (1914–39). For the post–World War II period (1950–2000), two subperiods were set, namely, 1950–74 and 1975–2000, based on the historical fact that Singapore's economy had experienced a transformation from entrepôt trade involving the export of primary commodities to the one that increasingly depended on the export of domestically manufactured goods.

Using these unit root test, now we examine the degree of volatility. From the long-term perspective, the degree of real GDP instability for the period of interwar years (1914–39) was among the highest as compared with the other three periods. During the pre–World War I period, the standard deviations of real GDP instability was much smaller than that of the interwar period and even slightly smaller than that of first phase of postwar period (1950–74). The standard deviation of real GDP instability for the last period (1975–2000) was among the lowest in the twentieth century. The small standard deviation of real GDP for pre–World War I vis-à-vis that of interwar period observed for Singapore was consonant to that observed in other studies of industrialized countries. Singapore's standard deviation of pre–World War I period being even smaller than post–World War II periods, however, dissimilar to that observed in most of the industrialized countries. One plausible reason for the low standard deviation prior to World War I period for Singapore was the fact that role played by the export of primary commodities such as rubber, which was in its infancy then, was not significant yet in terms of its weight against Singapore's total trade.

Subsequently, the extent of economic instability for GDP and its components, namely, private final consumption expenditure (Fig. 4.7), government final consumption expenditure (Fig. 4.8), gross capital formation (Fig. 4.9), exports of goods and services (Fig. 4.10),[87] and imports of goods and services (Fig. 4.11) were

---

[87] The time-series figures on imports and exports of goods and services for the period 1960–2000 were not provided in the official statistical reports by the

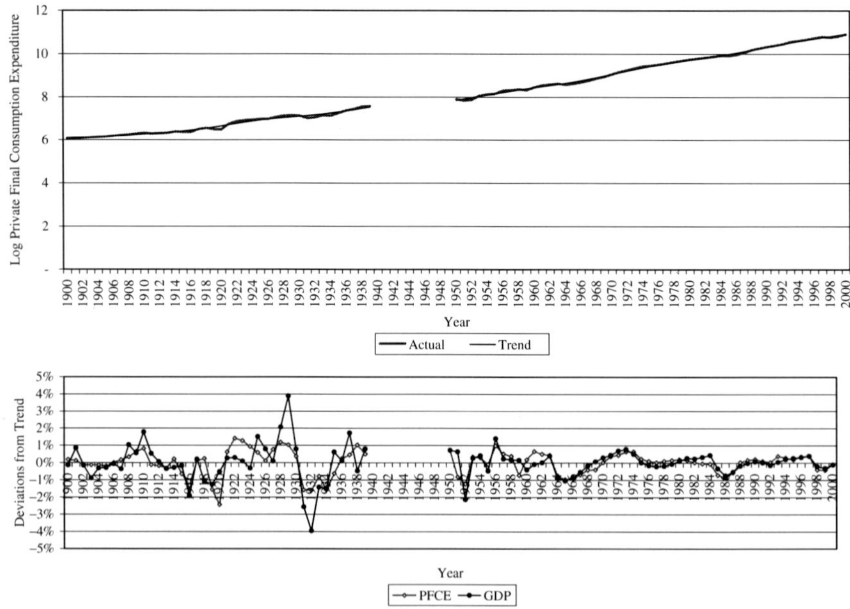



**Fig. 4.7:** Singapore: Private Final Consumption Expenditure, Trend, Actual and Percentage Deviation from Trend, 1900–2000 (1990 Prices)

Department of Statistics, Singapore. However, the figures for both imports and exports of goods and services in current prices (Singapore Dollars) were provided in the Penn-World Table Version 6.1. (Alan, Heston, *et al.* 2002). The figures on net exports on goods and services which are derived from Penn-World Table Version 6.1 were almost identical with official time-series figures provided by Department of Statistics, Singapore. On the basis of this observation, the figures provided in Penn-World Table Version 6.1 were deemed to be acceptable. Imports and exports of goods and services in 1990 prices were deflated by implicit export and import unit value indices of goods and services (1990 = 100). These derived net exports of goods and services figures in 1990 prices for the period 1960–2000 were, however, different from that given in official publications. In this exercise, we aimed to identify the trend and deviations from trend. Therefore, this derived figure was then used for conducting this specific analysis.

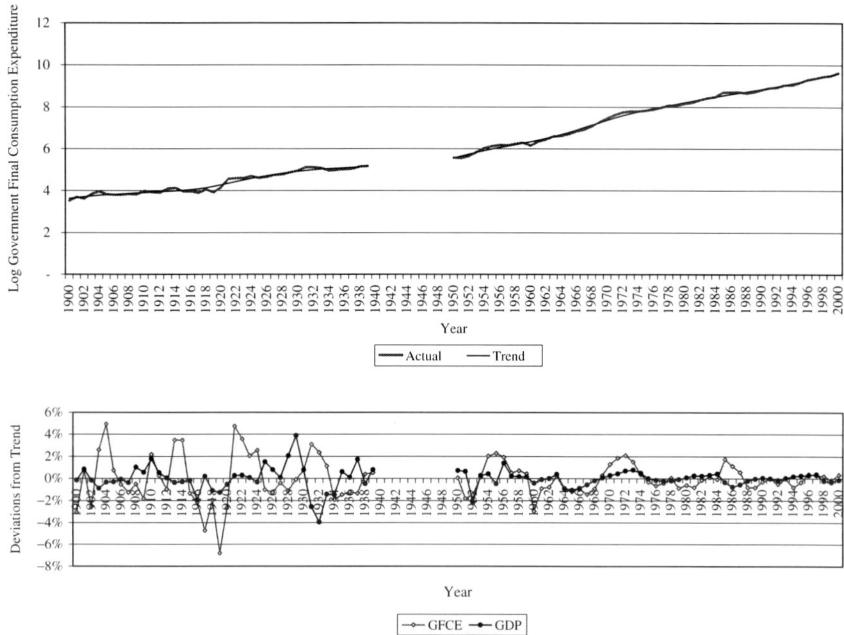

**Fig. 4.8:** Singapore: Government Final Consumption Expenditure, Trend, Actual and Percentage Deviation from Trend, 1900–2000 (1990 Prices)

*Source*: Computed from data contained in Chapter 3.

tested. Each of these variables was transformed to logarithms before filtering. Each graphical presentation is divided into two panels: The upper panel plots the actual and estimated trend values of the variable. The lower panel shows the percentage deviation of the cyclical component of the variable from its long-run trend. For comparison, the percentage deviation of the cyclical component of GDP from its long-run trend is also plotted in the lower panel of each diagram. The lower panel of each diagram shows that the degree of economic instability of each component of GDP was different from that of GDP. Generally, the degree of instability of PFCE was similar and its range was smaller than that of GDP. On the other hand, the degree of instability for GFCE and GCF were relatively larger than that of GDP. It is

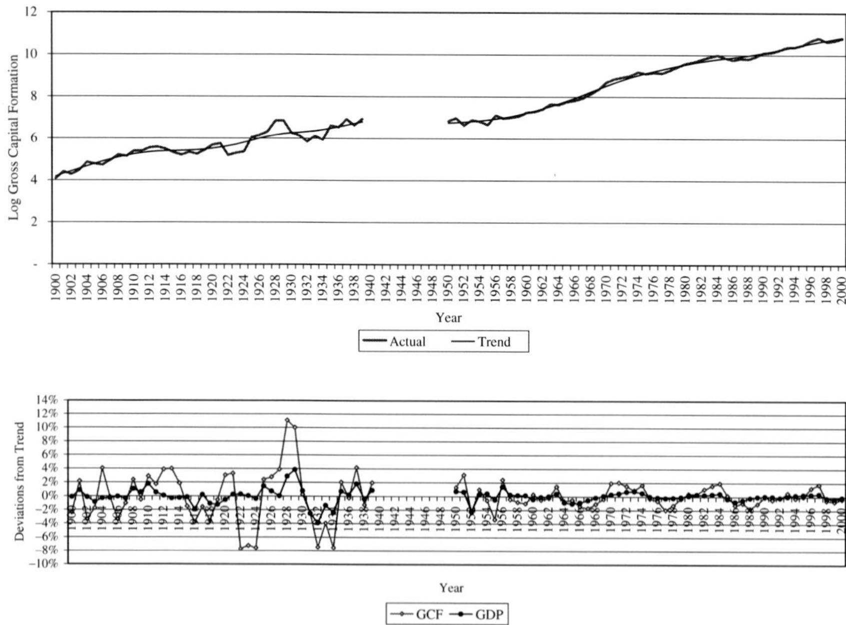



**Fig. 4.9:** Singapore: Gross Capital Formation, Trend, Actual and Percentage Deviation from Trend, 1900–2000 (1990 Prices)

*Source*: Computed from data contained in Chapter 3.

important to note here that deviations of GFCE from the HP filtered trend somewhat moved in the direction opposite to that of GDP during the World Depression Period (1930–32) and the short-term economic recession period (1985–86). The degree of instability for GCF, EXGS, and IMGS, however, showed similar direction to that of GDP. Generally, the degree of instability was similar to that of GDP. During periods of economic boom and recession, however, the degree of instability was more volatile as compared with that of GDP.

Table 4.8 shows the instability indicators of each component of GDP which is derived from the standard deviation of the cyclical fluctuations from trend. As mentioned above, one of the objectives of this study is to compare the degree of economic instability between the pre–World War II and post–World War II

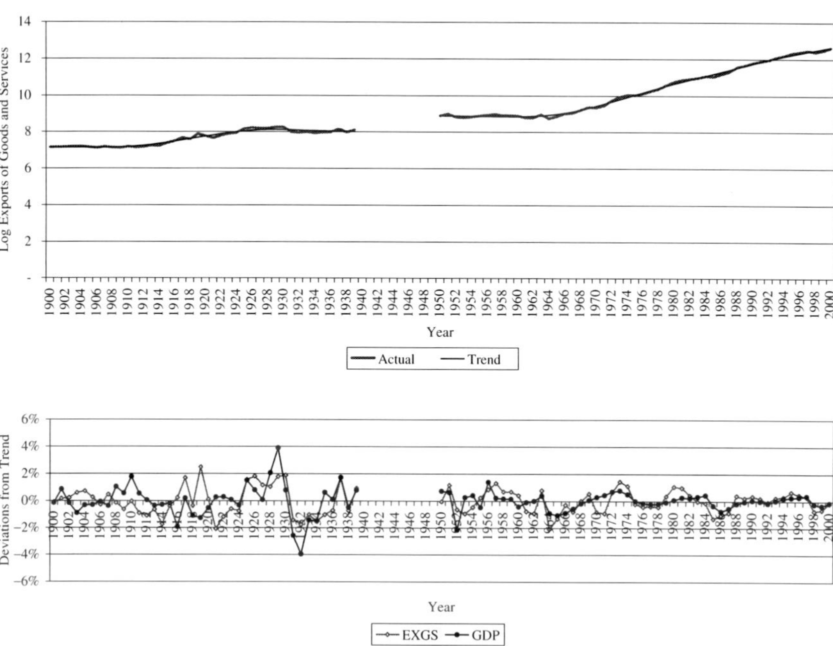

**Fig. 4.10:** Singapore: Exports of Goods and Services, Trend, Actual and Percentage Deviation from Trend, 1900–2000 (1990 Prices)

*Source*: Computed from data contained in Chapter 3.

periods. The following observations can be made: The highest instability for all components of GDP was recorded during the interwar period, whereas the petroleum swung the other way with the lowest degree of instability being observed during the last quarter of the twentieth century (1975–2000) for GDP, GFCE, and GCF. On the other hand, the degree of instability for PFCE, EXGS, and IMGS was recorded at its lowest in the pre–World War I period. Another important observation was that GDP and its components experienced an increase in the economic instability during the interwar period (1914–39) compared to the pre–World War I period (1900–13). Subsequently, the degree of instability has constantly dampened in the third quarter (1950–74) and fourth quarter (1975–2000) of the twentieth century.

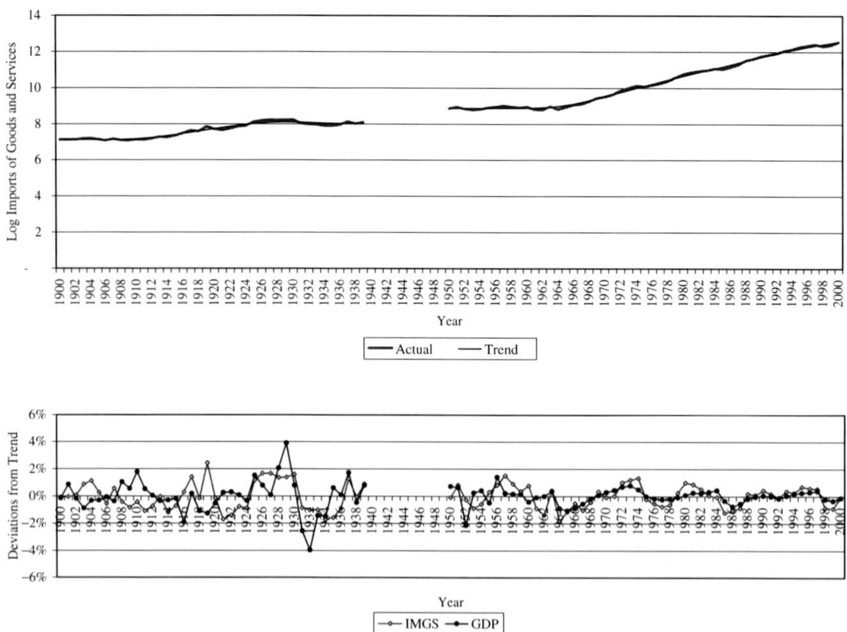

**Fig. 4.11:** Singapore: Imports of Goods and Services, Trend, Actual and Percentage Deviation from Trend, 1900–2000 (1990 Prices)

*Source*: Computed from data contained in Chapter 3.

Table 4.9 shows instability indicators of each component of GDP in relation to that of GDP. It was found that the relative instability indicator of private final consumption spending was less volatile than GDP before the war, but surprisingly more volatile than GDP for the period 1975–2000. The other components of GDP experienced greater instability in the British Colonial Period. Among these, gross domestic capital formation showed the highest volatility. Throughout the period, the relative instability indicator of gross capital formation to GDP was generally three times higher. There was a reduction in import and export instability as the century progressed.

In addition to the two above observations, Table 4.10 provides the results of cross-correlations between volatilities of each

**Table 4.8:** Singapore: Instability Indicators of GDP and the Aggregate Demand Components, 1900–2000, at 1990 Prices and Relative Instability Indicators of the Each Component of GDP (1914–39 = 100)

| Period | GDP | Private Final Consumption Expenditure | Government Final Consumption Expenditure | Gross Capital Formation | Exports of Goods and Services | Imports of Goods and Services |
|---|---|---|---|---|---|---|
| 1900–13 | 4.7 | 2.1 | 8.8 | 13.3 | 4.0 | 4.6 |
| 1914–39 | 12.4 | 7.5 | 11.5 | 30.5 | 11.0 | 10.1 |
| 1950–74 | 6.4 | 5.5 | 9.3 | 12.0 | 8.5 | 8.3 |
| 1975–2000 | 3.2 | 3.4 | 5.4 | 10.2 | 6.8 | 7.2 |

**Relative Instability Indicators of the Each Component of GDP (1914–39 = 100)**

| Period | GDP | Private Final Consumption Expenditure | Government Final Consumption Expenditure | Gross Capital Formation | Exports of Goods and Services | Imports of Goods and Services |
|---|---|---|---|---|---|---|
| 1900–13 | 37.7 | 28.0 | 76.5 | 43.7 | 36.8 | 45.5 |
| 1914–39 | 100.0 | 100.0 | 100.0 | 100.0 | 100.0 | 100.0 |
| 1950–74 | 52.1 | 73.4 | 80.3 | 39.2 | 77.4 | 82.3 |
| 1975–2000 | 25.7 | 45.1 | 46.3 | 33.5 | 61.6 | 71.3 |

**Table 4.9:** Singapore: Relative Instability Indicators of the Aggregate Demand Components, 1900–2000, at 1990 Prices

| Period | GDP | Private Final Consumption Expenditure | Government Final Consumption Expenditure | Gross Capital Formation | Exports of Goods and Services | Imports of Goods and Services |
|---|---|---|---|---|---|---|
| 1900–13 | 100.0 | 44.9 | 189.1 | 285.5 | 86.4 | 98.5 |
| 1914–39 | 100.0 | 60.5 | 93.3 | 246.7 | 88.7 | 81.7 |
| 1950–74 | 100.0 | 85.3 | 143.8 | 185.9 | 131.8 | 129.1 |
| 1975–2000 | 100.0 | 106.2 | 168.4 | 321.8 | 212.7 | 226.9 |

*Source*: Computed from data contained in Table 4.9.

**Table 4.10:** Singapore: Cross-Correlations between Volatilities of Each Component of GDP and GDP, 1900–2000, at 1990 Prices

| Period | GDP | Private Final Consumption Expenditure | Government Final Consumption Expenditure | Gross Capital Formation | Net Exports of Goods and Services |
|---|---|---|---|---|---|
| 1900–13 | 1.00 | 0.75 | −0.08 | 0.36 | 0.59 |
| 1914–39 | 1.00 | 0.68 | −0.11 | 0.78 | 0.50 |
| 1950–74 | 1.00 | 0.76 | 0.60 | 0.74 | −0.24 |
| 1975–2000 | 1.00 | 0.75 | −0.37 | 0.77 | −0.27 |

*Note*: Volatility of net exports of goods and services was measured without converting to natural logarithm term because of the fact that original net exports of goods and services were minus (−) for most of the twentieth century.

component of GDP and GDP itself for selected time periods. PFCE and GDP showed relatively strong (0.70) and positive cross-correlations for the period. A similar phenomenon was observed between GCF and GDP save for the period 1900–13. In the case of GFCE, cross-correlations of volatility have been weak and negative throughout the period, with the exception for the period 1950–74 which recorded a positive relationship (0.60). On the other hand, cross-correlations of volatilities between net exports and GDP were somewhat different. Prior to World War II, correlations for this component were positive, but during the later half of the twentieth century, a reverse situation was observed with these correlation values being in the negative territory.

## 4.4 Econometric Tests

### 4.4.1 *Explanation of Real GDP Volatilities*

#### 4.4.1.1 *Explanatory Variables*

As seen earlier, Singapore has experienced a decline of real GDP volatility over time. This section is devoted to empirically investigate what economic variables caused the decline of real GDP volatilities. In this exercise, five types of hypotheses were experimented on the basis of the empirical exercise made by Singh *et al.,* (2006). First, it has been argued that improvement of government's ability help to reduce the volatility of output due to the greater knowledge of the economy by policy makers and their ability to anticipate how to cope with economic shocks. Government budget deficit as a share of GDP is used to reflect the government's policy choices. Second, it is often argued somewhat counterintuitively that trade openness should not lead to greater, but to lower, volatility. Third, the role of shocks such as changes in terms of trade with respect to output volatility will also be considered. Fourth, the real GDP growth rate in the previous year may itself affect volatility of the current year. It is significant to see how GDP growth rate is associated with real GDP volatility. Fifth, past experiences of volatility itself have caused volatility in the subsequent period. On the basis on these premises, the following independent variables (Table 4.11) have been selected for this exercise.

The volatility of real GDP growth over the period was measured using the standard deviation. However, for the purposes of econometric time-series analysis, an annual measure is required

**Table 4.11:** Explanatory Variables for Regression

| Dependent Variable: Volatility of Real GDP Growth (%) | |
| --- | --- |
| **Independent Variables** | |
| SBY(–1) | Government fiscal deficit as a share of GDP (%) with 1-year time lag |
| Trade/GDP(–1) | Changes in trade (imports of goods and services + exports of goods and services) as a share of GDP (%) with 1-year time lag |
| TOT(–1) | Terms of trade, percentage change with 1-year time lag |
| GDP%(–1) | Percentage growth of real GDP with 1-year time lag |
| VOL(–1) | Volatility of real GDP with 1-year time lag |

(Singh *et al.* 2006, 17). The precise volatility measure used in this regression test is based on the recursive estimation used in the following equation:

$$y_t = \alpha + \beta_1 y_{t-1} + \beta_2 y_{t-2} + \gamma_t + \varepsilon_t$$

where $y_t$ is real GDP growth and $t$ represents time.

Time-series data on terms of trade were derived by using export and import unit value indices, the construction of which were described in Chapters 2 and 3.

Before turning to the econometric regression analysis, it is necessary to conduct unit root test to examine whether dependent and explanatory variables are trend stationary or difference stationary. As applied above, two types of unit root tests, namely, ADF and PP tests, were conducted for the periods 1900–39 and 1950–2000, respectively. The results (Table 4.12 [A]–[E]) show that the time series of [A] growth rate of real GDP, [B] volatility of GDP, [C] share of Government deficit to GDP (1900–39), [D] share of trade to GDP, and [E] annual percentage change of terms of trade are all integrated of order 0, I(0), therefore, regarded as trend stationary. [C] Share of government deficit to GDP (%) for the period 1950–2000 (ADF test) is, however, integrated of order 1, I(1), since only its first and second differences are stationary. This means that the null hypothesis of a unit root test cannot be rejected. Nevertheless, the PP test showed integrated of order 0, I(0). As discussed above, the result of PP test should be given priority over the results from the ADF test. The time-series regression will then include only stationary variables.

### 4.4.1.2 *Regression Results*

The selection of the period for this regression analysis was made on the basis of the historical experience that Singapore has undergone in terms of two types of different administration in the twentieth century, namely, the period of British colonial,

**Table 4.12:** Results of Unit Root Tests (1990 Prices)

[A] Results of Unit Root Tests on Growth of Gross Domestic Product (%)

| | Period | Levels | trend | lags[1] | First Difference | trend | lags[1] | Second Difference | trend | lags[1] | Order |
|---|---|---|---|---|---|---|---|---|---|---|---|
| ADF | 1900-1939 | -6.731829*** | Yes | 0 | -11.01591*** | Yes | 0 | -4.990693*** | Yes | 6 | I(0) |
| | 1950-2000 | -6.236542*** | Yes | 0 | -12.07564*** | Yes | 0 | -5.776294*** | Yes | 5 | I(0) |

| | Period | Levels | trend | Bandwidth[2] | First Difference | trend | Bandwidth[2] | Second Difference | trend | Bandwidth[2] | Order |
|---|---|---|---|---|---|---|---|---|---|---|---|
| PP | 1900-1939 | -7.637953*** | Yes | 9 | -30.44674*** | Yes | 20 | -43.66058*** | Yes | 13 | I(0) |
| | 1950-2000 | -6.223109*** | Yes | 3 | -14.62394*** | Yes | 5 | -27.74062*** | Yes | 7 | I(0) |

[B] Results of Unit Root Tests on Volatility of Real GDP growth (%)

| | Period | Levels | trend | lags[1] | First Difference | trend | lags[1] | Second Difference | trend | lags[1] | Order |
|---|---|---|---|---|---|---|---|---|---|---|---|
| ADF | 1900-1939 | -5.679102*** | Yes | 0 | -10.73193*** | Yes | 0 | -7.594588*** | Yes | 2 | I(0) |
| | 1950-2000 | -8.207704*** | Yes | 0 | -12.65713*** | Yes | 0 | -5.407161*** | Yes | 5 | I(0) |

| | Period | Levels | trend | Bandwidth[2] | First Difference | trend | Bandwidth[2] | Second Difference | trend | Bandwidth[2] | Order |
|---|---|---|---|---|---|---|---|---|---|---|---|
| PP | 1900-1939 | -5.69661*** | Yes | 9 | -32.2365*** | Yes | 30 | -43.7771*** | Yes | 13 | I(0) |
| | 1950-2000 | -7.94207*** | Yes | 3 | -34.8525*** | Yes | 21 | -40.6237*** | Yes | 18 | I(0) |

[C] Results of Unit Root Tests on Share of Government Deficit to GDP

| | Period | Levels | trend | lags[1] | First Difference | trend | lags[1] | Second Difference | trend | lags[1] | Order |
|---|---|---|---|---|---|---|---|---|---|---|---|
| ADF | 1900-1939 | -5.590361*** | Yes | 0 | -9.830936*** | Yes | 0 | -6.292093*** | Yes | 4 | I(0) |
| | 1950-2000 | -2.513268 | Yes | 3 | -13.79304*** | Yes | 0 | -11.06508*** | Yes | 1 | I(1) |

| | Period | Levels | trend | Bandwidth[2] | First Difference | trend | Bandwidth[2] | Second Difference | trend | Bandwidth[2] | Order |
|---|---|---|---|---|---|---|---|---|---|---|---|
| PP | 1900-1939 | -5.573827*** | Yes | 3 | -32.00959*** | Yes | 37 | -59.46962*** | Yes | 33 | I(0) |
| | 1950-2000 | -3.446567* | Yes | 3 | -13.2647*** | Yes | 2 | -21.67567*** | Yes | 0 | I(0) |

[D] Results of Unit Root Tests on Share of Trade to GDP

| | Period | Levels | trend | lags[1] | First Difference | trend | lags[1] | Second Difference | trend | lags[1] | Order |
|---|---|---|---|---|---|---|---|---|---|---|---|
| ADF | 1900-1939 | -6.213849*** | Yes | 0 | -7.860096*** | Yes | 1 | -8.80479*** | Yes | 2 | I(0) |
| | 1950-2000 | -7.990837*** | Yes | 0 | -9.750357*** | Yes | 1 | -13.38367*** | Yes | 1 | I(0) |

| | Period | Levels | trend | Bandwidth[2] | First Difference | trend | Bandwidth[2] | Second Difference | trend | Bandwidth[2] | Order |
|---|---|---|---|---|---|---|---|---|---|---|---|
| PP | 1900-1939 | -6.406631*** | Yes | 5 | -33.03873*** | Yes | 35 | -47.65318*** | Yes | 35 | I(0) |
| | 1950-2000 | -7.990837*** | Yes | 0 | -20.17221*** | Yes | 6 | -24.87343*** | Yes | 3 | I(0) |

[E] Results of Unit Root Tests on Terms of Trade (TOT)

| | Period | Levels | trend | lags[1] | First Difference | trend | lags[1] | Second Difference | trend | lags[1] | Order |
|---|---|---|---|---|---|---|---|---|---|---|---|
| ADF | 1900-1939 | -9.095181*** | Yes | 0 | -8.51861*** | Yes | 1 | -5.678672*** | Yes | 4 | I(0) |
| | 1950-2000 | -7.101295*** | Yes | 0 | -10.73563*** | Yes | 1 | -5.969188*** | Yes | 7 | I(0) |

| | Period | Levels | trend | Bandwidth[2] | First Difference | trend | Bandwidth[2] | Second Difference | trend | Bandwidth[2] | Order |
|---|---|---|---|---|---|---|---|---|---|---|---|
| PP | 1900-1939 | -10.97895*** | Yes | 6 | -52.44527*** | Yes | 28 | -28.0582*** | Yes | 3 | I(0) |
| | 1950-2000 | -7.253854*** | Yes | 5 | -27.05399*** | Yes | 32 | -32.20052*** | Yes | 41 | I(0) |

*Notes*:

1. Automatic selection of lag was determined by Schwartz Info Criterion.
2. Bandwidth was determined on the basis of the Newey-West using Bartlett kernel.
(***, **, *) denotes significance at the 1%, 5% and 10% level respectively.
I(0) = stationary, I(1) = unit root.

government, and self-government after the independence (1965). Because of the dearth of time-series data of 1940s, it was not possible to set the two different periods. Alternatively, three different periods of 1900–39, 1950–2000, and 1965–2000 were tested for regression analysis. The first two periods were selected to see whether there were any significant similarities or differences. The selection of the third period (1965–2000) was, however, set to see whether there were any similar features as compared with previous period.

Table 4.13 shows the results of the regression analysis for the three specific periods, with volatility of real GDP being used as dependent variable. From these regression results, one feature

**Table 4.13:** Singapore: Source of Real GDP Volatility by Specific Periods
Dependent Variable = Real GDP Volatility

| | 1900–39 | 1950–2000 | 1965–2000 |
|---|---|---|---|
| **Explanatory Variables** | [1] | [2] | [5] |
| Constant | −0.08 | 4.63 | 12.16 |
| | (−0.03) | (1.43) | (2.49)** |
| VOL(−1) | −0.06 | 0.58 | 1.86 |
| | (−0.13) | (1.26) | (3.07)*** |
| GDP%(−1) | 0.08 | −0.61 | −1.41 |
| | (0.19) | (−1.41) | (−2.37)** |
| SBY(−1) | −0.23 | −0.04 | 0.16 |
| | (−0.57) | (−0.29) | (1.64) |
| TOT(−1) | −0.47 | −0.12 | 0.10 |
| | (−0.68) | (−0.18) | (0.15) |
| TRADE/GDP(−1) | 0.70 | 0.36 | −0.65 |
| | (0.41) | (0.24) | (−0.35) |
| $R^2$ | 0.04247 | 0.05179 | 0.38581 |
| Standard Error of Regression | 11.12 | 4.38 | 2.83 |
| *F*-statistic | F(6.37) | F(6.48) | F(6.36) |
| | 0.275016 | 0.458811 | 3.768934 |
| | [0.9233] | [0.8045] | [0.0091] |
| Durbin-Watson | 1.8919# | 1.5341# | 1.8041# |

*Notes*:
(1) (***, **, *) significant at 1%, 5% and 10% level, respectively.
(2) Figures in ( ) refer to the *t*-statistics.
(3) Figures in [ ] refer to the marginal significance level.
(4) (#) null hypothesis of existence of serial correlation is rejected at 1% significant level.

was identified in Singapore's economy. Contrary to findings made in studies for other countries, the coefficient of explanatory variables such as the share of government budget deficit to GDP, percentage changes of terms of trade, and share of trade (exports and imports of goods and services) to GDP are not consistent by period and statistically not significant for all the periods. For the years 1965–2000, the coefficient of previous year's volatility of real GDP growth and 1-year lagged real GDP growth were statistically significant at 1% and 5% levels, respectively, but negligible. In short, these regression results reveal that there are no plausible explanatory variables which can statistically explain the sources of output growth volatility in Singapore for both during the British Colonial Period and in the period of self-government.

### 4.4.2 *The Effect of Economic Instability on Economic Growth*

#### 4.4.2.1 *Explanatory Variables*

Regression tests were run with the growth rate of real GDP per capita as the dependent variable. The primary interest of this regression exercise was to study the effect of export instability on economic growth. In line with the works of Kormendi and Meguire (1985), Dawe (1993), and Nazrin (2000), other plausible explanatory variables were also included in the effect to improve the specification of the model and increase the explanatory power of the regression (See Table 4.14). The final choice of explanatory variables, however, was ultimately governed by the practical consideration of data availability. Generally, the explanatory variables selected were very similar to that as used in the study by Nazrin (2000). Data for the 1900–39 and 1950–59 periods represent my own estimates, whereas those for the more recent years were obtained from official publication releases entitled *System of National Account 1995 Singapore* and *Asian Development Bank, Key Indicators 2001.*

**Table 4.14:** Explanatory Variables for Regression

Dependent Variable: Real Per-Capita GDP Growth (%)

Independent Variables

| | |
|---|---|
| MACHIN | Change in share of investment on machinery and equipment to GDP |
| CONSTRUC | Change in share of investment on construction to GDP |
| POP | Population growth (%) |
| GDPC | GDP per-capita |
| EXIN | Export instability indicator |
| GREXSHAR | Growth rate of exports as a proportion of GDP |
| GCSHAR | Growth rate of government final consumption expenditure as a proportion of GDP |

As described above, before turning to econometric regression analysis, unit root tests (Augmented Dickey Fuller test and Phillips-Perron test) have been applied for both dependent and independent variables (See Table 4.15). ADF and PP unit root test results showed that the time series appear to be stationary in their levels for (A) real per-capita GDP growth, (C) CON-STRUC, (F) EXIN, (G) GREXSHAR, and (H) GCSHAR, i.e., they are all integrated of order 0, I(0). On the other hand, unit root test on MACHIN POP and GDPC were stationary in first differences rather than in levels. Therefore, MACHIN, POP, and GDPC are *difference stationary* and integrated of order 1. The time-series regression should include only stationary variables. Therefore, alternatively, first difference of MACHIN, POP, and GDPC are applied for the regression.

### 4.4.2.2 *Regression Results*

The estimating time span was from 1900 to 2000 covering three periods, namely, 1900–39, 1950–2000, and 1975–2000. The first two periods were identified to see the overall picture of the pre–World War II period vis-à-vis the post–World War II era.

## Table 4.15: Results of Unit Root Tests (1990 Prices)

**[A] Results of Unit Root Tests on Real Per-capita GDP growth (%)**

| | Period | Levels | trend | lags[1] | First Difference | trend | lags[1] | Second Difference | trend | lags[1] | Order |
|---|---|---|---|---|---|---|---|---|---|---|---|
| ADF | 1900-1939 | -7.537025*** | Yes | 0 | -6.975864*** | Yes | 2 | -5.148174*** | Yes | 7 | I(0) |
| | 1950-2000 | -7.727637*** | Yes | 0 | -5.015317*** | Yes | 2 | -6.112558*** | Yes | 5 | I(0) |

| | Period | Levels | trend | Bandwidth[2] | First Difference | trend | Bandwidth[2] | Second Difference | trend | Bandwidth[2] | Order |
|---|---|---|---|---|---|---|---|---|---|---|---|
| PP | 1900-1939 | -18.62838*** | Yes | 37 | -31.28876*** | Yes | 15 | -40.69998*** | Yes | 12 | I(0) |
| | 1950-2000 | -7.68677*** | Yes | 4 | -15.80769*** | Yes | 1 | -23.3652*** | Yes | 1 | I(0) |

**[B] Results of Unit Root Tests on MACHIN**

| | Period | Levels | trend | lags[1] | First Difference | trend | lags[1] | Second Difference | trend | lags[1] | Order |
|---|---|---|---|---|---|---|---|---|---|---|---|
| ADF | 1900-1939 | -3.144064 | Yes | 0 | -7.25663*** | Yes | 0 | -8.101325*** | Yes | 1 | I(1) |
| | 1950-2000 | -1.494534 | Yes | 0 | -6.618517*** | Yes | 0 | -11.90124*** | Yes | 0 | I(1) |

| | Period | Levels | trend | Bandwidth[2] | First Difference | trend | Bandwidth[2] | Second Difference | trend | Bandwidth[2] | Order |
|---|---|---|---|---|---|---|---|---|---|---|---|
| PP | 1900-1939 | -3.127443 | Yes | 2 | -7.42359*** | Yes | 12 | -23.10612*** | Yes | 10 | I(1) |
| | 1950-2000 | -1.729622 | Yes | 3 | -6.61815*** | Yes | 3 | -20.33456*** | Yes | 7 | I(1) |

**[C] Results of Unit Root Tests on CONSTRUC**

| | Period | Levels | trend | lags[1] | First Difference | trend | lags[1] | Second Difference | trend | lags[1] | Order |
|---|---|---|---|---|---|---|---|---|---|---|---|
| ADF | 1900-1939 | -3.264208* | Yes | 0 | -6.562041*** | Yes | 3 | -7.091812*** | Yes | 2 | I(0) |
| | 1950-2000 | -3.763358** | Yes | 2 | -6.011241*** | Yes | 0 | -11.13506*** | Yes | 0 | I(0) |

| | Period | Levels | trend | Bandwidth[2] | First Difference | trend | Bandwidth[2] | Second Difference | trend | Bandwidth[2] | Order |
|---|---|---|---|---|---|---|---|---|---|---|---|
| PP | 1900-1939 | -3.206648* | Yes | 4 | -8.097467*** | Yes | 3 | -26.10839*** | Yes | 14 | I(0) |
| | 1950-2000 | -2.642867 | Yes | 0 | -5.994391*** | Yes | 6 | -23.48653*** | Yes | 12 | I(1) |

**[D] Results of Unit Root Tests on Population Growth**

| | Period | Levels | trend | lags[1] | First Difference | trend | lags[1] | Second Difference | trend | lags[1] | Order |
|---|---|---|---|---|---|---|---|---|---|---|---|
| ADF | 1900-1939 | -6.475748*** | Yes | 7 | -5.422539*** | Yes | 3 | -4.726867*** | Yes | 3 | I(0) |
| | 1950-2000 | -2.794071 | Yes | 0 | -7.451214*** | Yes | 0 | -5.91752*** | Yes | 6 | I(1) |

| | Period | Levels | trend | Bandwidth[2] | First Difference | trend | Bandwidth[2] | Second Difference | trend | Bandwidth[2] | Order |
|---|---|---|---|---|---|---|---|---|---|---|---|
| PP | 1900-1939 | -3.07816 | Yes | 3 | -4.985655*** | Yes | 3 | -8.249593*** | Yes | 4 | I(1) |
| | 1950-2000 | -2.794071 | Yes | 0 | -8.699432*** | Yes | 6 | -20.42238*** | Yes | 11 | I(1) |

**[E] Results of Unit Root Tests on GDPC**

| | Period | Levels | trend | lags[1] | First Difference | trend | lags[1] | Second Difference | trend | lags[1] | Order |
|---|---|---|---|---|---|---|---|---|---|---|---|
| ADF | 1900-1939 | -3.263372* | Yes | 0 | -5.633005*** | Yes | 0 | -7.365134*** | Yes | 2 | I(0) |
| | 1950-2000 | -0.654696 | Yes | 0 | -6.204539*** | Yes | 0 | -6.119545*** | Yes | 4 | I(1) |

| | Period | Levels | trend | Bandwidth[2] | First Difference | trend | Bandwidth[2] | Second Difference | trend | Bandwidth[2] | Order |
|---|---|---|---|---|---|---|---|---|---|---|---|
| PP | 1900-1939 | -3.167221 | Yes | 5 | -20.17437*** | Yes | 2 | -30.77797*** | Yes | 14 | I(1) |
| | 1950-2000 | -0.374226 | Yes | 11 | -7.490135*** | Yes | 9 | -16.75087*** | Yes | 18 | I(1) |

**[F] Results of Unit Root Tests on EXIN**

| | Period | Levels | trend | lags[1] | First Difference | trend | lags[1] | Second Difference | trend | lags[1] | Order |
|---|---|---|---|---|---|---|---|---|---|---|---|
| ADF | 1900-1939 | -4.043342*** | Yes | 0 | -8.311278*** | Yes | 0 | -6.585082*** | Yes | 2 | I(0) |
| | 1950-2000 | -4.293947*** | Yes | 0 | -7.844368*** | Yes | 1 | -9.004968*** | Yes | 1 | I(0) |

| | Period | Levels | trend | Bandwidth[2] | First Difference | trend | Bandwidth[2] | Second Difference | trend | Bandwidth[2] | Order |
|---|---|---|---|---|---|---|---|---|---|---|---|
| PP | 1900-1939 | -4.029493*** | Yes | 1 | -8.550944*** | Yes | 36 | -23.75345*** | Yes | 6 | I(0) |
| | 1950-2000 | -4.27237*** | Yes | 3 | -10.40277*** | Yes | 47 | -21.30501*** | Yes | 9 | I(0) |

**[G] Results of Unit Root Tests on GREXSHAR**

| | Period | Levels | trend | lags[1] | First Difference | trend | lags[1] | Second Difference | trend | lags[1] | Order |
|---|---|---|---|---|---|---|---|---|---|---|---|
| ADF | 1900-1939 | -5.989855*** | Yes | 0 | -9.9088*** | Yes | 1 | -6.854212*** | Yes | 2 | I(0) |
| | 1950-2000 | -7.265695*** | Yes | 0 | -9.15986*** | Yes | 1 | -11.77748*** | Yes | 1 | I(0) |

| | Period | Levels | trend | Bandwidth[2] | First Difference | trend | Bandwidth[2] | Second Difference | trend | Bandwidth[2] | Order |
|---|---|---|---|---|---|---|---|---|---|---|---|
| PP | 1900-1939 | -5.987733*** | Yes | 2 | -35.99585*** | Yes | 36 | -64.53198*** | Yes | 35 | I(0) |
| | 1950-2000 | -7.27847*** | Yes | 2 | -45.85592*** | Yes | 47 | -24.87374*** | Yes | 11 | I(0) |

**[H] Results of Unit Root Tests on GCSHAR**

| | Period | Levels | trend | lags[1] | First Difference | trend | lags[1] | Second Difference | trend | lags[1] | Order |
|---|---|---|---|---|---|---|---|---|---|---|---|
| ADF | 1900-1939 | -6.148656*** | Yes | 0 | -6.949908*** | Yes | 1 | -6.953464*** | Yes | 2 | I(0) |
| | 1950-2000 | -7.364163*** | Yes | 0 | -8.393242*** | Yes | 1 | -6.99744*** | Yes | 3 | I(0) |

| | Period | Levels | trend | Bandwidth[2] | First Difference | trend | Bandwidth[2] | Second Difference | trend | Bandwidth[2] | Order |
|---|---|---|---|---|---|---|---|---|---|---|---|
| PP | 1900-1939 | -6.148953*** | Yes | 2 | -37.27765*** | Yes | 36 | -66.66384*** | Yes | 35 | I(0) |
| | 1950-2000 | -7.398835*** | Yes | 3 | -47.19874*** | Yes | 47 | -28.69676*** | Yes | 14 | I(0) |

*Notes*:

1 Automatic selection of lag based on the Schwartz Info Criterion.

2 Bandwidth was determined based on the Newey-West using Bartlett kernel.

(***,**,*) denotes significance at the 1%, 5% and 10% level respectively.

I(0) = stationary, I(1) = unit root.

Additionally, one specific period of 1975–2000 was studied to empirically test the effect of changes in the export structure shifting from the dominance of entrepôt-based primary commodity export to the export of domestic manufactured goods since the middle of 1970s. In this exercise, the export instability index measured by 1-year time lags was applied.[88]

The results of regression tests are presented in Table 4.16. Importantly, the coefficient of export instability of 1-year time lag was negative and statistically significant at the 5% level for the period 1900–39 and 10% level for the periods 1950–2000 and 1975–2000. The coefficient of export instability for the period 1900–39 was –37.81. This negative coefficient figure, however, reduced slightly to the level of –28.16 for the period 1950–2000. It is crucial to note here that negative coefficient on export instability for the period 1975–2000 has even scaled down to –10.07. The result of this econometric regression test has clearly found the phenomenon that the effect of export instability to real per-capita GDP growth became smaller once Singapore trade structure experienced diversification to the export of manufactured goods.

The rate of growth in the export ratio to GDP shows a small negative coefficient of –0.001 for the period 1900–39, but not significant. Subsequently, for the period 1950–2000, the coefficient of this variable turned positive (0.001), but statistically not significant. For the period 1975–2000, the coefficient has slightly increased up to the level of 0.004 and is statistically significant for this period at the 1% level. This regression result shows that a high rate of growth of exports was not an important source of real economic growth.

---

[88] Several time lags were attempted for regression test such as 2 to 3 years time lags and combinations of 1- and 2-year lags. However, all regression results were insignificant. Additionally, the explanatory variables of D(MACHIN), D(POP), and D(GDPC)(–1) were omitted in this regression analysis on the ground that inclusion of these variable would lead to weak $F$-statistics results and apart from serial correlation.

**Table 4.16:** Singapore: Regression Results with the Rate of Growth of Real GDP Per Capita as the Dependent Variable, 1900–39, 1950–2000, and 1975–2000

| | Estimation Period | | |
| --- | --- | --- | --- |
| | **1900–39** | **1950–2000** | **1975–2000** |
| **Explanatory Variables** | **[1]** | **[2]** | **[4]** |
| CONSTANT | 7.92 | 4.50 | 5.92 |
| | (1.31) | (4.87)*** | (14.12)*** |
| CONSTRUC | −0.35 | | |
| | (−1.00) | | |
| EXIN (−1) | −37.81 | −28.16 | −10.07 |
| | (−1.89)* | (−2.30)** | (−2.03)** |
| GREXSHAR | −0.001 | 0.001 | 0.004 |
| | (−0.57) | (1.56) | (4.65)*** |
| GCSHAR | 0.0001 | 0.001 | 0.007 |
| | (0.54) | (1.27) | (4.30)*** |
| $R^2$ | 0.1617 | 0.1670 | 0.6695 |
| Standard Error of Regression | 10.5555 | 6.4614 | 1.751 |
| *F*-statistic | 1.6391 | 3.0747 | 14.8536 |
| | F(5.38) = 0.1871 | F(4.49) = 0.0368 | F(4.26) = 0.0000 |
| Durbin-Watson | 2.3511# | 2.1032# | 1.8674# |

*Source*:

*Notes*:

(1) (***, **, *) significant at 1%, 5%, and 10% level, respectively.

(2) Figures in ( ) refer to the *t*-statistics.

(3) Figures in [ ] refer to the marginal significance level.

(4) (#) null hypothesis of existence of serial correlation is rejected at 1 percent significant level.

In the case of coefficient of change with respect to the share of government final consumption expenditure to GDP, a small positive coefficient of 0.0001, though statistically not significant, was recorded for the period 1900–39. During the entire post–World War II period in the twentienth century, the coefficient became slightly higher, i.e., to 0.001 for the period 1950–2000.

For the period 1975–2000, the coefficient, in fact, increased from 0.001 to 0.007 and was statistically significant at 1% level. It goes without saying that the coefficient of this explanatory variable was very small and even negligible. This regression result implies that the high growth rate of government final consumption expenditure did not have any significant impact on the real per-capita GDP growth. This result differed from that obtained by a study by Barro (1991).

Using on the above results, it may be possible to draw several observations on the effect of economic instability on economic growth in Singapore for the twentieth century as follows.

First, the regression results show that export instability negatively impacted on the economic growth for both periods. Nevertheless, the negative coefficient value for the export instability became remarkably small for the post–World War II period because of the diversification of trade items, namely, the relative reduction on exports of primary commodities and expansion of exports of domestically produced manufactured items particularly after middle of 1970s.

Other than export instability, remarkable changes were identified between pre–World War II and the period thereafter. In the case of 1975–2000, the coefficient of annual growth rate of exports and government final consumption expenditure as a proportion of GDP were positive and statistically significant, though the coefficients were very small and negligible.

## 4.5 International Comparison

On the basis of the long-term observations of economic instability of Singapore and related econometric tests, this study found some unique features of Singapore's economic performance in the twentieth century in comparison with other countries.

First, the extent of real GDP volatilities observed for Singapore was similar to that experienced by developed countries. Standard deviations of interwar period were among the highest during the twentieth century. Nevertheless, the extent of economic instability of real GDP during the pre–World War I period was much smaller than that of the interwar period and even slightly smaller than that of first phase of postwar period (1950–74). This picture was somewhat dissimilar to that observed in most of the industrialized countries. One plausible reason for the low standard deviation prior to World War I period for Singapore was the fact that the role played by the export of primary commodities such as rubber, which was in its infancy then, was not significant yet in terms of its weight against Singapore's total trade.

On the contrary, output volatilities of other developing countries such as the Latin American countries during the post 1960 period have increased and the economic growth rates were rather unimpressive. On the other hand, there has been little change in Africa.

The similarities with industrialized nations can be explained by the fact that Singapore's economy was strongly dependent on the economic conditions of developed countries which were the major destinations of Singapore's major export commodities, such as rubber, tin, and petroleum. With respect to the relative economic instability indicators of each component to GDP, the phenomenon observed for PFCE, GFCE, and GCF in Singapore was again very similar to that of industrialized nations.[89]

In terms of cross-correlations between volatilities of each component of GDP and GDP in Singapore, PFCE and GCF recorded relatively constant and high cross-correlations over the period. Similar phenomenons were observed in industrialized countries. In the case of GFCE, cross-correlations between government spending and real GDP, however, exhibit some irregularity. In the case of Singapore, exclusive of first phase of post–World War II

---

[89] The study of Backus and Kehoe (1992) did not provide the standard deviations of volatilities of export and imports of goods and services relative to real GDP. Instead, standard deviations of volatilities of net exports of goods and services relative to real GDP were presented. However, my study could not obtain the volatility indicator because of the problem of deriving figures in natural logarithm term.

period, cross-correlation was negative and weak. In the case of net exports, in two-thirds of the cases, the cross-correlations were negative and often strongly so. In Singapore, cross-correlations of net exports during the pre–World War II period were somewhat positive, but turned to be negative in the latter half of the twentieth century.

Nevertheless, economic instability indicators of exports and imports of goods and services experienced a significant difference as compared with other developed nations. Singapore's figures remained high throughout the twentieth century whereas many industrialized nations experienced significant reductions. A study on India by Singh and Fagernäs (2006) showed that output volatility is persistent as it depends positively and significantly on previous volatility. Additionally, higher growth (lagged) is associated with more volatility. A similar phenomenon was experienced by Singapore.

In the case of India, government macroeconomic management which impacts on budget deficit is statistically not significant. In the case of Singapore, a similar phenomenon was observed.

As explained above, this study on the effect of economic instability to economic growth applied a similar econometric exercise as used by Nazrin (2000) for Malaya/Malaysia. Regression results of both Malaya and Singapore showed negative effects of export instability toward economic growth. This result is not surprising in the sense that both economies were strongly reliant on the exports of primary commodities in the early half of the century. In line with the diversification of the economic structure, the negative coefficient values have declined for both Singapore and Malaya/Malaysia.

## 4.6 Concluding Remarks

This chapter examines the extent, causes, and consequences of economic instability in Singapore during the twentieth century. Not unlike industrialized nations, the degree of economic instability experienced by Singapore has dampened in the post–World

War II period as compared with that of the pre–World War II years. Most notably, the highest real GDP instability was recorded during the interwar period though other periods also recorded a certain degree of real GDP volatility. Among GDP components, a relative instability indicator of private final consumption expenditure was found to be less volatile than that of GDP. On the other hand, the relative instability indicator of gross capital formation to GDP was almost three times. When we look at the relative instability indicator of each component, PFCE, GFCE, and GCF showed significant reduction of instability particularly during the last quarter of the twentieth century. Nevertheless, the degree of instability of exports and imports of goods and services did not change overtime. In fact, instability of trade export earnings has the most significant impact on real GDP growth. The instability of the export sector has, in turn, been influenced by the extreme volatility of export commodities during the British Colonial Era. Nevertheless, diversification of trade in Singapore was initiated during the period of self-government since the mid-1970s. This study attempts to undertake two kinds of empirical tests, namely, sources of output volatility and the effect of export instability on economic growth. The following features were observed from this empirical exercise: First, contrary to findings made in other studies, the major sources of output volatilities were not determined by explanatory variables such as share of government deficit to GDP, changes in trade as a share of GDP (%), and changes in terms of trade with 1-year time lag were not statistically significant. Second, export instability was seen to reduce economic growth for both periods. The coefficient of export instability has reduced over time. Importantly, the negative coefficient on export instability for the period 1975–2000 has even scaled down significantly. The result of this econometric regression test has clearly found the phenomenon that the effect of export instability to real per-capita GDP growth became smaller once Singapore's trade structure experienced diversification moving away from exports of primary commodities to the export of manufactured goods.

# Chapter Five

# Government Fiscal Behavior and Economic Growth in Singapore in the Twentieth Century

## 5.1 Introduction

In Chapter Four, we examined the relationship between economic instability and economic growth of Singapore in the twentieth century on the basis of the fact that her economic structure was characterized by an open economy and vulnerable to external shocks.

Another characteristic found in the economic growth in Singapore was with regard to the government's nature of fiscal behavior. The share of government expenditure to GDP remained small during the twentieth century.[90] The average share of real total general government expenditure to GDP (1990 prices) in Singapore for the periods 1900–39 and 1950–2000 was 17.0% and 18.0%, respectively, whereas that of industrialized nations generally recorded a share of over 40% since the 1980s.

The objective of this chapter is to understand the long-term pattern of government finance structure and empirically investigate the relationship between the government's fiscal behavior and economic growth in Singapore in the twentieth century. This

---

[90] This study does not include 1940–49 because of the absence of historical GDP estimates.

research is driven by the hypothesis that the government's finance behavior in relation to the economic growth in Singapore might have experienced a significant shift because of the administrative changes brought about in the process of transition from British colonial rule to one of self-government.

In Chapter Four, two types of econometric tests were conducted relating to the issues of extent, source, and consequence of economic instability. In regression tests, the government's fiscal behavior was selected as one of the explanatory variables. First, the share of government budget surplus to GDP was tested as to whether this was a possible source of real output volatility. Second, the effect of annual growth rate of government final consumption expenditure as a proportion of GDP growth on real per-capita GDP growth was tested to examine whether a higher growth rate of GFCE lowers real GDP growth through the distorting effects resulting from taxation or government expenditure programs. The results of both these empirical tests, however, were statistically not significant for the British colonial period as well as for the period of self-government.

This chapter investigates in depth the relationship between the government's fiscal behavior and the economic growth in Singapore. First, this chapter attempts to identify the characteristics of the colonial government's fiscal behavior as against that during the period of self-government in terms of budgetary process, revenue raising, expenditure allocation, and budget deficit/surplus management. Second, this study aims to conduct empirical econometric tests using time-series data stretching over the better part of the twentieth century. The validity of Wagner's law was tested to establish whether the government's fiscal behavior obeys Wagner's law or endogenously responds to the macroeconomic situation. Attention was focused on any notable similarities or differences that existed between the period of British colonial rule and the years of self-government. To undertake this econometric exercise, the conventional three-step approach needs to be employed: First, stationarity of the respective time series on government expenditure, GDP, and relevant variables is assessed using the unit root tests. Second, the hypothesis of a long-run relationship between the government expenditure and the real GDP is tested using the Johansen maximum likelihood technique. Third, the Granger causality test is used to examine the short-run direction of causality between the GDP and the government expenditure in the context of Wagner's law.

The structure of this chapter is arranged as follows: Section 5.2 outlines the literature review on (i) the characteristics of colonial government's finance behavior and (ii) previous econometric tests on government's finance behavior to economic growth. Section 5.3 provides the historical transition of government's finance behavior in Singapore in terms of revenue raising, expenditure allocation, and budget surplus/deficit management. Special attention was given to clarify the notable similarities or differences between the colonial period and the period of self-government. In Section 5.4, the framework and methodologies for econometric tests are described in general. Section 5.5 presents the econometric results and analyses. Finally, Section 5.6 provides some concluding remarks.

## 5.2 Literature Review

### 5.2.1 *Features of Colonial Government's Finance Behavior*

#### 5.2.1.1 *Small Size of the Government*

Historically, changes in government expenditure levels were largely fashioned by the changes in attitudes towards the role of the state in the economy. The study by Tanzi and Schuknecht (2000) elaborated the major transitions of government's involvement in the economy in industrialized countries during the twentieth century and found that growth in government expenditure has been a general phenomenon despite the considerable institutional differences. Tanzi and Schuknecht (2000) pointed out that the role of the state in the economy has experienced four major transitions in the twentieth century, namely, (i) the period up to World War I, (ii) the interwar period, (iii) the period until 1980, and (iv) the period after 1980.

Initially, the *laissez-faire* attitude occupied a position of predominance while the role of government in economic life was minimal. In fact, the onset of the World War I brought about considerable increases of government expenditure in the form of war expenses. Subsequently, the Great Depression periods in the late 1920s and early 1930s experienced worldwide were regarded as a monumental failure of the market economy and this had led to the expansion of government involvement in the nation's economy. The most notable expansion of government involvement in the economy was recorded for the years 1960 and 1980. As presented in Table 5.1, the percentage share of real general government expenditure to real GDP for selected years generally showed rapid growth for the period 1960–80 and remained relatively stable. In the 1980s, skepticism about the proper role of the state in allocation of resources, stabilization, and income distribution emerged (Buchanan, 1975; Premchand, 1983). Some critics also started to question the practical implementation of these

**Table 5.1:** Percentage Share of Real General Government Expenditure to Real GDP for Selected Years, 1870–1996 (1990 Prices)

| | Late 19th Century about 1870 | Pre World War I | Post World War I | Pre–World War II | Post–World War II | | | |
|---|---|---|---|---|---|---|---|---|
| | 1870 | 1913 | 1920 | 1937 | 1960 | 1980 | 1990 | 1996 |
| Australia | 18.3 | 16.5 | 19.3 | 14.8 | 21.2 | 34.1 | 34.9 | 35.9 |
| Austria | 1 0.5 | 17.0 | 14.7 | 20.6 | 35.7 | 48.1 | 38.6 | 51.6 |
| Canada | — | — | 16.7 | 25.0 | 28.6 | 38.8 | 46.0 | 44.7 |
| France | 12.6 | 17.0 | 27.6 | 29.0 | 34.6 | 46.1 | 49.8 | 55.0 |
| Germany | 10.0 | 14.8 | 25.0 | 34.1 | 32.4 | 47.9 | 45.1 | 49.1 |
| Italy | 13.7 | 17.1 | 30.1 | 31.1 | 30.1 | 42.1 | 53.4 | 52.7 |
| Japan | 8.8 | 8.3 | 14.8 | 25.4 | 17.5 | 32.0 | 31.3 | 35.9 |
| New Zealand | — | — | 24.6 | 25.3 | 26.9 | 38.1 | 41.3 | 34.7 |
| Norway | 5.9 | 9.3 | 16.0 | 11.8 | 29.9 | 43.8 | 54.9 | 49.2 |
| Sweden | 5.7 | 10.4 | 10.9 | 16.5 | 31.0 | 60.1 | 59.1 | 64.2 |
| Switzerland | 16.5 | 14.0 | 17.0 | 24.1 | 17.2 | 32.8 | 33.5 | 39.4 |
| United Kingdom | 9.4 | 12.7 | 26.2 | 30.0 | 32.2 | 43.0 | 39.9 | 43.0 |
| United States | 7.3 | 7.5 | 12.1 | 19.7 | 27.0 | 31.4 | 32.8 | 32.4 |
| Average | 10.8 | 13.1 | 19.6 | 23.8 | 28.0 | 41.9 | 43.0 | 45.0 |
| Singapore | | 22.7 | 22.2 | 18.8 | 10.7 | 25.2 | 19.2 | 21.8 |

*Source*: Tanzi and Schuknecht (2000, 6–7) and Sugimoto (2008).

policies. As deficits and public debt rose, many economists argued that the government had grown much beyond its justified role, undermining economic incentives, property rights, and economic freedom.

The 1990s have seen much interest in budgetary institutions and fiscal rules to prioritize and improve the efficiency of public spending and to make the government **live within its means**. Many countries, especially the industrial countries, have introduced important reforms that have helped to make fiscal policy sounder. The government began to focus on public spending on essential tasks and provided basic services in the most cost-effective ways. Unlike the previous period, these approaches are in fact aimed at reducing the size of public spending. Nevertheless, as presented in Table 5.1, few countries managed to reduce the government expenditure share to GDP. This implies that reduction of government expenditure is not an easy task as compared with its expansion.

Unlike statements of Tanzi and Schuknecht (2000), the share of real general government expenditure to real GDP in Singapore remained small and stable over time as compared with industrialized countries, as presented in Table 5.1. Historically, one major difference between Singapore and other industrialized countries was that Singapore was formerly governed by the British colonial authority. In fact, the foundation of revenue raising, expenditure allocation, and budget management was established and implemented by the colonial authority. The small share of government expenditure to GDP should also be treated as one of the features of the colonial government's fiscal behavior in Singapore. While the characteristic of the small share of government expenditure to GDP continued during the period of self-government, the underlying principle of government fiscal behavior underwent a substantial change. During the period of self-government's the budgetary process and actual implementation of government fiscal behavior were determined in line with its owns needs as opposed to the interest of the colonial government, which paid more attention to the benefits of the home country (Britain). One may be interested to know whether there are any common features in the government's fiscal behavior during the two periods, i.e., the British colonial period and the period of self-government.

In the following sections, this study highlights the two key terms which explain the features of colonial government's fiscal behavior, namely, "creation of a balanced budget structure (5.2.1.2)" and "weakness of colonial government's macroeconomic management (5.2.1.3)."

### 5.2.1.2 *Creation of a Balanced Budget Structure*

One of the characteristics of fiscal principle of the colony was to self-support and have a balanced budget, i.e., "living within means," such that there was no need for the exchequer of the home country to subsidize the colony (Tan, 1997). There are many criteria in assessing whether the budgetary performance achieved the objectives of this fiscal philosophy. The most important one is the actual surplus/deficit of the financial budgets.

Huff (2003b) has compiled the balance of government finance in Burma, Indochina, Thailand, British Malaya, Indonesia, and Philippines and elaborated that the colonial authorities of Southeast Asian countries generally favored balanced budgets. Although external shocks sometimes precluded budget balance, it, however, remained sufficiently near zero.

In the case of Hong Kong, for example, the philosophy and management of fiscal system was governed by the financial procedures stipulated in the colonial regulations. These financial procedures controlled the scope and scale of public expenditure and the financial reporting system of the colony (Tan, 1997).

Sugimoto (1997 and 2007a) examined the British colonial financial administration in the state of Johore for the period 1910–40. This study established that during the 35-period of British colonial administration, the central concern was the creation and accumulation of budget surpluses and its allocation to government portfolio financial investments in the British

Empire. For the period 1914–40, total accumulated government financial assets had increased from $2 million to $41 million and almost the entire assets were allocated for portfolio government financial investment. It was almost double the total annual government expenditure.

In fact, this government finance structure was strongly linked to the financial situation of the government of the United Kingdom. It will be noted that the United Kingdom faced serious government debt after World War I, which, in part, could be attributed to the expansion of government expenditure and also to the problems arising from budget management.

For the year 1913, the percentage of gross public debt to GDP in the United Kingdom was at 30.4%. However, the share to GDP dramatically increased to 132% and 188.1% in 1920 and 1937, respectively (Tanzi *et al.*, 2000, 65).

This does not mean that all colonies could afford to maintain the "living within means" fiscal principle. In fact, many colonies faced serious government finance deficit as a result of a weak revenue base compounded with the demand for extra-ordinary expenditure such as defense (Da Costa, 2007). For example, British India borrowed quite heavily to finance its expenditure, both in the London money market and in India. These borrowings peaked at the time of the World Wars (Roy, 2000, 229). Nevertheless, the colonial government authority always aimed to maintain a balanced budget. In line with this, the colonial countries by nature needed to conduct prudent government finance management. How did they realize such financial management? In fact, it was strongly related to the budgetary process. In any country, there are at least two stages before the actual implementation of government finance administration: First stage is the formulation phase, which involves making advance estimates of revenue and expenditure. This is entirely the responsibility of the executive arm of the government. The second stage involves seeking legislative approval to the executive's proposals. In most cases, the parliament has been entrusted with matters relating to taxation vis-à-vis tax decisions and spending policies. This being the case, the crucial causal force for determining the budget was the voter under democratic parliamentary systems which stimulated citizens participation in their choice of government. The budgetary process during the colonial period, however, differed from that practised during the period of self-government. In practice, the colonial budget was institutionalized to meet the needs and interests of the suzerain power. For example, the budgetary system of the Colony of Straits Settlements was formulated by the Treasury of the Colony of Straits Settlements at the first stage phase. Subsequently, authorization of the budget was discussed by the legislative council members and executive council members who were appointed by the governor (See Table 5.2).

The legal power of the governor, the advisory role of the two councils, and the ultimate control of the colonial office in London was essentially the setup applied for the colonies. On the other hand, the colonial authority did not permit resident participation in the formulation of the budget. Generally, raising revenue is

**Table 5.2:** Members of Legislative Council and Executive Council

| Members of Legislative Council | Members of Executive Council |
| --- | --- |
| Governor as president | Governor as president |
| Ex-officio members (11) | General officer commanding the |
| Official members (2) | Troops, Malaya (1) |
| Elected unofficial members | The colonial secretary, Penang, |
| (2 since 1924) | Malacca (2) Resident councilor, |
| 11 Nominated unofficial | Penang, Malacca (2) |
| members (11) | Attorney-general (1) |
| (Nominated unofficial members | Treasurer (1) |
| are subject to the confirmation | Official member (2) |
| or disallowance of His Majesty | Unofficial member (3) |
| the King) | |

( ) number of people.
*Sources*: Malayan Year Book (1939) and Mills, LA (1942).

politically sensitive but spending money is favorable for everyone.[91]

### 5.2.1.3 *Weakness of the Colonial Government Macroeconomic Management*

It is crucial to examine whether the colonial government planned and effectively implemented the macroeconomic management of the economy. As described previously, the emergence of the role of government became clearer with the onset of the Great Depression in the end of 1920s. In the case of Western industrialized countries, as mentioned above, the government's role in macroeconomic management became active during the Great Depression periods. It was market failure that clearly justified the government's intervention. For example, the United States introduced major public expenditure programs with the New Deal, and other governments authorized higher spending on the unemployed and on public works partly to create employment. In fact, the Depression was transmitted from the advanced industrial economies to

---

[91] Nevertheless, constitutional theory and actual practice was incongruent. In reality, the Governor was a limited monarch (Mills, 1942). His policy was influenced by local public opinion and the press, and one of his most cherished ambitions was that he shall not provide ammunition for any questions in the House of Commons in Britain. In other words, the Governor has to plan and implement the budget to meet the request of the colonial office in the United Kingdom by observing response from the local populace. After World War II, the situation changed slightly. The first election for the Legislative Council was held in 1948. The Legislative Council comprised nine elected unofficial members, four nominated unofficial members, five nominated officials, and four ex-officials. Nevertheless, the electorate numbered only 22,000 since voting was confined to only registered voters and registration was voluntary and not mandatory. It was a far cry from the budgetary system established in Western countries. After the formation of self-government, authorization of budget changed due to the creation of a democratic parliamentary system. Regular parliamentary elections chose the political party and led to increasing power and say of the citizens.

Southeast Asia through a sharp fall in demand for many of the region's major primary commodities such as rubber and tin which were exported to Western countries. Singapore was one of the few economies which underwent a macroeconomic shock, which was more severe than that experienced by other countries (Huff, 2001, 293).

In this regard, it is significant to see whether the colonial government authority had effectively implemented macroeconomic management. In order to fulfill the four major objectives of macroeconomic management, namely, (i) full employment, (ii) low inflation, (iii) a high, but sustainable, rate of economic growth, and (iv) keeping the balance of payments in equilibrium, there are two instruments of macroeconomic policy, namely, fiscal policy and monetary policy. Fiscal policy comprises government spending and taxation and is frequently used for countercyclical adjustment, aiming to automatically stabilize demand by increasing government expenditure. On the other hand, monetary policy is the process by which the government, central bank, or monetary authority manages the supply of money or by trading in the foreign exchange market. Generally monetary policy can be referred to as either being an expansionary policy or a contractionary policy. Expansionary policy is traditionally used to combat unemployment in a recession by lowering interest rates, whereas contractionary policy has the goal of raising interest rates to combat inflation.

To the best of my knowledge, there is no literature which systematically analyses the effect of the colonial government's macroeconomic management behavior on the nation's economy. It is partially because of the deficiencies of historical economic indicators. Nevertheless, there are some previous literatures explaining the government involvement in the nation's economy during the Great Depression period.

Huff (2001) conducted a study on the impact of the Great Depression periods to the colonial economy, particularly highlighting the issue of massive increases of unemployed labor during the period and elaborated on the implications of the colonial government's macroeconomic management behavior in British Malaya. He stressed that the British colonial authority had no intention of undertaking "purely relief works" to provide employment during the Great Depression Period. In fact, little new public works expenditure materialized: in 1931, two-thirds of the planned Straits Settlements expenditure of $15.2 million on extraordinary public works was to meet existing commitments. Instead of creating new job opportunities, the British colonial authority resorted to repatriation to regulate the size of the workforce (Huff, 2001; Kratoska, 2000).

Booth, Anne (2002) also pointed out that most Southeast Asian colonies ran considerable budget deficits in the early 1930's. This hardly reflected a conversion to Keynesian economics on the part of colonial officials, but rather an inability to reduce expenditures in the face of rapidly falling revenues.

In terms of monetary policy, the colonial currency board system can be viewed as minimal government involvement. Because colonial currency boards offer no scope for government regulation or intervention, they are the antithesis of a central bank (Huff, 2003a, 127; Roy, 2000, 233). In other words, colonial monetary policy was particularly inadequate in the task of stabilization of prices and outputs (Roy, 2000, 237). Before World War II, money supply in the Colony of Straits Settlements consisted chiefly of base money, M0, issued by currency boards. During the period, base money supply changed principally in response to changes in the current account of the balance of payments.

The fact that exchange rate policies were formulated largely in the interests of the metropolitan powers in the early decades of the twentieth century is hardly surprising (Booth, 1990). Exchange rate policies were used to promote tight economic links between the colonies and the metropolitan power, especially to encourage the import of industrial products from the sovereign's economy.

### 5.2.1.4 *Summary*

On the basis of the literature review, it might be possible to summarize the main features of the colonial government's financial behavior as follows: First, the major objective of the colonial government was the establishment of a self-sufficient budget structure so as not to depend on the home country. To ensure this principle was met budgetary process was handled by the people who represented the interests of the home country. Second, the colonial government did not implement as effectively macroeconomic management as was done in Western countries. The colonial government only passively reacted against the unforeseen economic changes taking place. Relating to this issue, this study will examine the relationship between the colonial government's fiscal behavior and economic growth in Section 5.4. Additionally, this study conducts the empirical econometric analysis.

### 5.2.2 *Previous Econometric Test on Government Expenditure and Economic Growth*

Subsequently, this study conducts a literature review on the empirical analysis relating to the relationship between government expenditure and economic activities. Over the past three decades, numerous empirical studies have been undertaken to seek the relationship between government expenditure and economic growth. The main interest of researchers was confined to two areas, namely, element(s) of government expenditure and relative size of the government expenditure to GDP. Table 5.3 provides a summary of the empirical investigations conducted to date.

As can be seen, the results obtained differed by country/region, analytical method employed, and periods chosen for the study. These differences in results obtained were partially due to the differences in the set of conditioning variables and initial conditions across studies, leading to a lack of consensus in the results (Levine *et al.*, 1992), and in part due to the ignorance of

**Table 5.3:** Summary of Selected Empirical Studies on Government Expenditure and Economic Growth

| Author(s) | Sample | Method | Explanatory Variable(s) | Results |
|---|---|---|---|---|
| Haque, ME and Osborn, DR (2007) | Panel of 30 LDCs (1970s and 1980s) | 3SLS | • Government capital expenditure/GDP<br>• Government current expenditure/GDP<br>• At the sectoral level, government investment and total expenditures in education | • Positively and significantly correlated with growth<br>• Insignificant<br>• Only outlays that are significantly associated with growth |
| Kneller *et al.* (1998) | Panel 22 OECD (1970–95) | OLS, GLS | • Investment/GDP, other and (non) productive expenditures, other and (non) distortionary taxes | • Productive expenditure enhances growth, but non-productive spending does not |
| Devarajan and Vinaya (1993) | Panel of 14 developed countries (1970–90) | OLS, 5-year moving average | • Various functional types of expenditure (health, education, transport, etc.) | • Health, transport, and communication have significant positive effect; education and defense a negative impact |

*(Continued)*

**Table 5.3:** *(Continued)*

| Author(s) | Sample | Method | Explanatory Variable(s) | Results |
|---|---|---|---|---|
| Ahsan, SM, Kwan, ACC, and Shani, BS (1996) | Time series Canada (1953–1988) | OLS, GLS | • Share of real total government expenditure/GDP<br>• Real total government expenditure | • Positive significant |
| Lin, SAY (1994) | Panel of 62 countries (1960–85) | OLS, 2, 3SLS | • Share of investment, government expenditure in GDP, growth rate of labor force; exports, foreign direct investment share in GDP | • Mixed results. Nonproductive Spending insignificant impact on ADC, but significant positive on LDC. |
| Barro (1991) | Cross-section (98 countries) (1960–85) | OLS | • Government final consumption expenditure | • Government consumption expenditure has a significant negative effect |
| Alexander, WR (1990) | 13 countries (OECD) panel (1959–84) | OLS | • Government consumption expenditure, gross fixed capital formation, deficits, and exports | • Growth of government spending, and inflation have significant negative impact on growth |
| Landau, D (1983), (1986) | Panel of 27 LDCs | OLS | • Various types of government expenditure | • Government consumption expenditure has a negative impact |
| Kormendi and Meguire (1985) | Panel of 47 countries | OLS | • Government final consumption expenditure | • Government consumption has no significant effect |

the implication of government budget constraint for their regression (Helms, 1985; Kneller *et al.*, 1999a, 1999b; Mofidi *et al.*, 1990).

Many studies were conducted on the basis of the "cross-section" or "panel-pooled data." The defect of such empirical studies, however, is the statistical constraint that "cross-sectional analysis can identify correlation but not causation between variables" (Hsieh *et al.*, 1994; Wing, Yuk, 2005). In view of this, time-series analysis is crucial to determine the flow(s) of causality.

In 1893, Adolph Wagner put forward his well-known proposition that there is a positive relationship between economic activities and government expenditure (Henrekon, 1993). It is one of the economic theories that emphasizes economic growth as the fundamental determinant of government sector growth. Empirical tests of this law have yielded results that differ considerably from one country to another (See Table 5.4).

Wagner and Weber (1977) tested the hypothesis for 34 countries over the period 1950–72. The study by Abizadeh and Gray (1985) covered 55 countries over the period 1963–79 and their findings support the proposition in the cases of wealthier nations, but not for the poorest countries. Ram's study (1986, 1987) covering the period 1960–80 encompassing 115 countries found limited support to Wagner's hypothesis. Afxentiou and Serletis (1996) examined six European countries (France, Italy, Germany, Belgium, the Netherlands, and Luxemburg) over the period 1961–91 and found no evidence supporting Wagner's hypothesis for the countries studied. Ansari *et al.* (1997) studied three African countries, namely, Ghana, Kenya, and South Africa and found little evidence supporting Wagner's hypothesis. Wahab (2004) in his study intended to disentangle the effects of accelerating and decelerating economic growth in government expenditure for OECD, EU, and G7 countries for the period 1950–2000. He found evidence that lends support to Wagner's law for EU countries only. However, his findings suggested that for all countries in general, government expenditure increased less than proportionately with accelerating economic growth and

**Table 5.4:** Summary of Selected Empirical Studies on Granger Causality Test

| Author(s) | Sample | Variable | Direction of Causality | Variable |
|---|---|---|---|---|
| Compartive studies (post–WWII period) | | | | |
| Ram, Rati (1986, 1987) | 115 Countries (1960–80) | R TGE/Real GDP | → | Real GDP |
| Hsiah and Lai (1994) | G7 Countries | RTGE/Real GDP | No uniform causality | Per-capita real GDP |
| Ansari, MI, Gordon, DV and Akuamoah, C (1997) | Ghana (1961–88) | RTGE | ← | RGDP |
| | Kenya (1964–89) | RTGE | ~ | RGDP |
| | South Africa (1957–90) | RTGE | → | RGDP |
| Ghali, KH (1999) | All OECD (1970.1Q – 1994.3Q) | RTGE/real GDP | → | Real GDP |
| Kolluri *et al.* (2000) | G7 (1960–93) | Three different categories of government spending | ~ | Real GDP |
| | UK (1960–93) | | ← | Real GDP |
| Tsangyao Chang (2002) | South Korea (1954–96) Taiwan (1951–96) Thailand (1951–95) Japan (1952–95) USA (1951–96) UK (1951–96) | Five versions of Wagner's law (Found the validity of Wagner's law exception of Thailand) | | |
| Wahab (2004) | OECD, EU and G7 (1950–2000) | RTGE | ← | Real GDP |

(*Continued*)

**Table 5.4:**  *(Continued)*

| Author(s) | Sample | Variable | Direction of Causality | Variable |
|---|---|---|---|---|
| Specific country studies (post–WWII period) | | | | |
| Gupta (1967), Bird (1971), Ahsan *et al.* (1989), and Biswal *et al.* (1999) | Canada (1950–95) | Total government current expenditure | ← | Real GDP |
| | | Government fixed capital formation | ↔ | Real GDP |
| Tan (2003) | Malaysia (end of 1980s–1997) | RTGE | → | Real GDP |
| | | ROG | → | Real GDP |
| | | RDG | → | Real GDP |
| Pluta (1979), Sun (1997), and Huang (2006) | Taiwan (1979–2002) | RTGE | ~ | Real GDP |
| Demirbas, S (1999) | Turkey (1950–90) | RTPE | ~ | Real GNP |
| Halicioğlu (2003) | | RTPCE | ~ | Real GNP |
| Courakis, AS, Moura-Roque, F, and Tridimas, G (1993) | Greece, and Portugal (1958–85) | Various components of expenditure | ~ | Real GDP |
| | | Defense expenditure | | |

*(Continued)*

**Table 5.4:** *(Continued)*

| Author(s) | Sample | Variable | Direction of Causality | Variable |
|---|---|---|---|---|
| Karavitis, Nicholas (1987) | Greece (1950–80) | Various components of expenditure | ← | Real GDP |
| Chletsos, M, and Kollias, C (1997) | Greece (1958–93) | | ↔ | Per-capita real GDP |
| Singh, B, and Sahni, BS (1984) | India (1950–81) | RTGE and various components of public expenditure | ~ | GNI |
| Nagarajan and Spears (1990), Murthy (1993), Ashworth (1994), and Hayo, B (1994) | Mexico (various periods) | RTGE and various components of public expenditure | ← | Real GDP |
| Ganti and Kalluri (1978), Vatter and Walker (1986), and Yousefi and Abizadeh (1992) | USA (various periods) | RTGE and various components of public expenditure | ← | Real GDP |
| Gyles (1991) | UK | RTGE and various components of public expenditure | ↔ | Real GDP |

*(Continued)*

**Table 5.4:** *(Continued)*

| Author(s) | Sample | Variable | Direction of Causality | Variable |
|---|---|---|---|---|
| Historical studies (inclusive of Pre–WWII period) | | | | |
| Thornton, John (1999) | Denmark, Germany, Italy, Norway, Sweden, UK (mid-19th century to 1913) | Unidirectional causality ran mainly from income to government expenditure. Considerable support for Wagner's law | | |
| Wing Yuk (2005) | UK (1830–1993) | RTGE | → | Real GDP |
| Oxley, Les (1994) | UK (1870–1913) | RTGE | ← | Real GDP |
| | | R TGE/real GDP | → | Real GDP |
| | | Volume of exports | → | Real GDP |
| Islam, Anisul, M (2001) | USA (1929–96) | Relative size of TGE | ← | Per-capita real income |
| Mann, Arthur J (1980) | Mexico (1925–76) | Six different versions of Wagner's principle | Mixed result | Real GDP Per-capita real GDP |

*Notes*: ← (→) indicates direction of causality running from the variable on the right (left) to the one on the left (right).

↔ indicates both directions of causality.

~ indicates absence of causality.

*Abbreviations*:

  RDG = Real Government Development Expenditure, ROG = Real Operating Government Expenditure.

  RTGE = Real Total Government Expenditure, RTPE = Real Total Public Expenditure.

RTPCE = Real Total Public Consumption Expenditure.

decreased more than proportionately with decelerating economic growth.

The study by Kolluri *et al.* (2000), which focused on the relationship between economic growth and certain components of public expenditure of the G7 countries for the period 1960–93, yielded results to the contrary. Wagner's Law was confirmed for all seven countries; i.e., there were signs of long-run equilibrium relationships between different categories of government spending and economic growth. For the United Kingdom, in particular, Wagner's law was confirmed for all three categories of government expenditure as indicated by the positive signs displayed for the coefficients.

Besides these works, there are many country-specific studies. Gupta (1967), Bird (1971), Ahsan *et al.* (1996) and Biswal *et al.* (1999) studied Wagner's law for Canada. Mann (1980), Nagarajan *et al.* (1990), Murthy (1993), Ashworth (1994), and Hayo (1994) examined the validity of Wagner's law for Mexico. Ganti *et al.* (1978), Vatter *et al.* (1986), and Yousefi *et al.* (1992) studied the applicability of this law for the United States; Pluta (1979) and Sun (1997) for Taiwan; Khan (1990) for Pakistan; Gyles (1991) for the United Kingdom; Henrekson (1993) for Sweden; Hondroyiannis and Papapetrou (1995) for Greece; Nomura (1995) for Japan; Tan (2003) for Malaysia, and Singh (1996) for India. In general, country-specific studies, with few exceptions, have found support for Wagner's proposition.

Most of the works focused on the post–World War II period. However, there are a number of studies which tested the validity of Wagner's law for the period prior to World War II, such as the United Kingdom (Oxley, 1994; Wing Yuk, 2005), the United States (Islam, 2001), and Mexico (Mann, Arthur J, 1980). The results obtained differed from country to country, very much influenced by government expenditure and the periods chosen for the study.

To the best of my knowledge, there is no study which examines the validity of Wagner's law between the pre–World War II period and the post–World War II period. In the case of Singapore, there was no empirical exercise made on the applicability of

Wagner's law. As described in Section 5.2.1, studies on Singapore government's finance behavior have mostly concentrated on the pattern of government revenue and expenditure and hardly gave any attention to the relationship between government expenditure and economic growth. Unlike other previous country-specific studies, this chapter focuses on seeking out any notable similarities or differences that existed during the two periods, namely, the period of British colonial rule and the period of self-government, in respect of the government's finance behavior in relation to economic growth.

## 5.3 Historical Transitions of the Government's Finance Behavior of Singapore in the Twentieth Century

This section briefly observes the long-term structural changes of revenue raising, expenditure allocation, and budget management of Singapore in the twentieth century.

### 5.3.1 *Government Revenue*

#### 5.3.1.1 *Growth of Government Revenue*

Figure 5.1 provides a chart on Singapore's general government revenue at current prices for the twentieth century.[92] Prior to World War II, government revenue experienced fluctuations over time. The most rapid revenue growth of 53% was recorded in

---

[92] Revenue is composed of heterogeneous elements. Accordingly, the elements are classified according to different characteristics depending on the type of revenue, namely, (i) taxes, (ii) social contribution, (iii) grants, and (iv) other revenue (IMF, 2001, 47). In this study, government revenue refers to revenue collected from Colony of Singapore, Municipality of Singapore/City Council of Singapore for the periods 1900–39 and 1950–60. Revenue from trading department was not included in this definition. After 1960, revenue credited to the Consolidated Revenue Account was used.

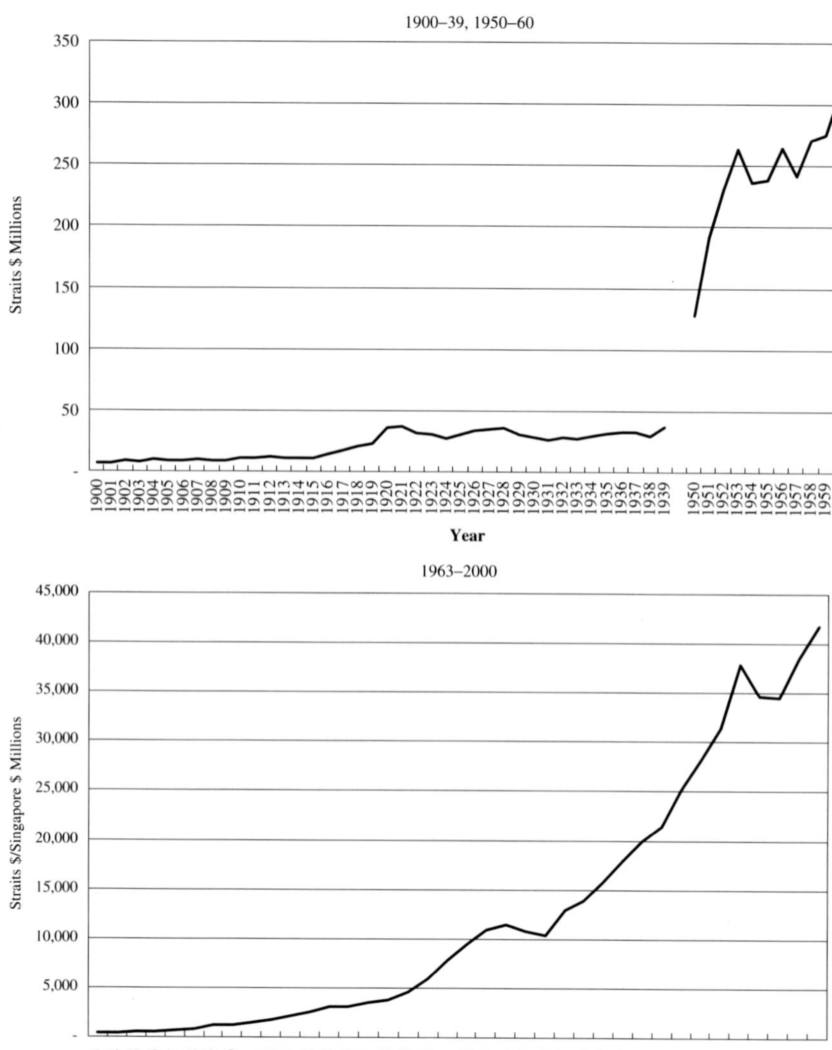


**Fig. 5.1:** Singapore: General Government Revenue at Current Prices, 1900–39 and 1950–2000

*Sources*:

| | |
|---|---|
| 1900–39, 1950–60: | Constructed by Author. |
| 1960–81: | Department of Statistics, Singapore (1983). |
| 1982: | Estimated by Author. |
| 1983–2000: | Asia Development Bank (2001 and 2005). |

1920. It was due to the introduction of income tax as a temporary measure to compensate for the deficiencies of revenue-raising capacity. After the termination of this implementation in 1922, the total revenue collection fell by 16% despite revenue being raised from other sources having improved.

Another reduction of revenue was observed in 1929. It was solely due to the reduction of revenue collection from the sales of opium.

Clear distinctions of the size of revenue can be observed between the prewar and postwar periods. It is partially due to inflation but mainly due to the implementation of income tax in 1947. After the formation of self-government, revenue earning has experienced a steep increase over time. However, a notable reduction of revenue was recorded during the recession period, namely, 1985–86 and 1997–98.

### 5.3.1.2 *Changes in Revenue Structure*

According to the study by Tanzi *et al.* (2000) on revenue structure, the revenue composition in Western industrialized countries experienced considerable changes over the century. Initially, indirect taxes were the most crucial revenue source. Nevertheless, narrow tax bases prevented the revenue-raising capacity. After World War II, income tax and social security contributions have become the most crucial revenue categories, comprising almost two-thirds of the total government revenue. By 1960, this ratio between direct and indirect tax revenue still prevailed. Additionally, social security contributions started to become an important revenue source. For the period 1960–2000, revenue increases were largely derived from direct taxes and social security contributions. In most of the Western countries, personal income taxes came to be seen as the best and fairest taxes. Personal income taxes were ideal instruments because they could be progressive and thus contribute to the objective of income redistribution. These direct taxes are more in conformity with the ability-to-pay principle and are more befitting of a modern community, because they are generally levied at progressive rates (Goode, 1984, 89).

Unlike industrialized countries, the revenue structure of developing countries depends upon customs (export and import duties) and excise duties, poll tax, commodity taxes, and other indirect taxes for its sources of revenue. These indirect taxes are regressive in nature and the tax burden falls heavily and unevenly on the poor (Goode, 1984). A developed country relies more on income tax, profit tax, property tax, estate duties, inheritance tax, and other direct taxes for its revenue.

### 5.3.1.3 *British Colonial Period (1900–39 and 1950–59)*

The British colonial government in Singapore formed three levels of government bodies, namely, the Colony of Singapore, the Municipality/City Council, and the Rural Board. As presented in Table 5.5, the Colony of Singapore accounts for between 72.1% and 90.0% of total revenue, whereas the Municipality/City Council and the Rural Board contributed about 8.5–27.9% and 0.8–2.0%, respectively.

With elected self-government for all internal matters under the 1959 Constitution, the ruling People's Action Party abolished the City Council and the Rural Board on the ground that Singapore was too small to afford such differentiation in roles (Lee, 1974, 68–69).

The British colonial authority needed to identify potential revenue sources for Singapore which became part of its colonies in the early nineteenth century. Unlike other British colonial territories which relied on export duties, Singapore as a free port relied heavily on trade for its economic activities. Under these circumstances, the British colonial authority could not impose any export duties as their revenue source. Alternatively, the colonial authority needed to rely on the revenue collection from the sales of opium/chandu (Emerson, 1969; Lim, 1967; Trocki, 1990). As can be seen from Table 5.5, more than half of the entire revenue came from this single revenue source during the 1900–20s.

**Table 5.5:** Singapore: Revenue by Major Sources at the Level of Colony of Singapore, Municipality/City Council of Singapore, and Rural Board at Current Prices, 1900–39 (Percentage)

**Percentage of Total by Level**

| | 1907 | 1915 | 1920 | 1928 | 1933 | 1938 | 1952 | 1956 |
|---|---|---|---|---|---|---|---|---|
| Colony of Singapore | 72.1 | 77.8 | 84.4 | 72.9 | 74.7 | 72.7 | 90.0 | 85.9 |
| Municipality/City Council of Singapore | 27.9 | 20.5 | 14.8 | 26.0 | 23.9 | 25.3 | 8.5 | 12.4 |
| Rural Board | | 1.7 | 0.8 | 1.1 | 1.4 | 2.0 | 1.5 | 1.7 |
| Total | 100.0 | 100.0 | 100.0 | 100.0 | 100.0 | 100.0 | 100.0 | 100.0 |

**Percentage Composition of Revenue at Each Level**

| | 1907 | 1915 | 1920 | 1928 | 1933 | 1938 | 1952 | 1956 |
|---|---|---|---|---|---|---|---|---|
| **Colony of Singapore** | | | | | | | | |
| Sales of opium[2] | 49.2 | 61.3 | 44.4 | 35.1 | 20.4 | 18.3 | | |
| Sales of liquor | 12.1 | 10.8 | 6.9 | 10.6 | 8.1 | 10.9 | 6.7 | 9.2 |
| Import duty | 12.1 | 10.8 | 10.7 | 21.8 | 21.8 | 26.6 | 26.5 | 26.4 |
| Stamp duty | 4.7 | 5.5 | 5.6 | 8.7 | 5.7 | 13.6 | 0.8 | 0.9 |
| Income tax | | | 14.2 | | | | 34.6 | 29.6 |
| Interest on investment and loan[3] | 0.0 | 2.1 | 1.3 | 3.9 | 16.8 | 14.2 | 1.8 | 1.8 |
| Others[1] | 21.9 | 9.5 | 16.8 | 19.8 | 27.2 | 16.4 | 29.6 | 32.1 |
| Total | 100.0 | 100.0 | 100.0 | 100.0 | 100.0 | 100.0 | 100.0 | 100.0 |
| **Municipality / City Council of Singapore** | | | | | | | | |
| Rates | 47.9 | 62.7 | 55.2 | 61.9 | 55.3 | 52.9 | 61.5 | 71.1 |
| Taxes | 7.9 | 9.0 | 23.1 | 9.7 | 8.8 | 11.6 | 1.9 | 1.2 |
| Licences | 1.4 | 2.7 | 0.7 | 0.5 | 4.3 | 3.0 | 6.7 | 5.2 |
| Fees | 3.1 | 3.7 | 4.5 | 8.7 | 12.7 | 12.0 | 23.0 | 16.2 |
| Miscellaneous | 3.7 | 7.8 | 4.7 | 10.9 | 8.7 | 11.0 | 2.3 | 1.5 |
| Reimbursements | 4.3 | 1.6 | 3.8 | 3.1 | 5.0 | 4.1 | 0.0 | 0.0 |
| Rents | 31.7 | 12.4 | 8.0 | 5.3 | 5.1 | 5.3 | 4.5 | 4.9 |
| Total | 100.0 | 100.0 | 100.0 | 100.0 | 100.0 | 100.0 | 100.0 | 100.0 |
| **Rural Board [4]** | | | | | | | | |
| Revenue proper | | 35.4 | 77.0 | 87.7 | 69.0 | 58.6 | NA | NA |
| Government contribution | | 64.6 | 23.0 | 12.3 | 31.0 | 41.4 | NA | NA |
| Total | | 100.0 | 100.0 | 100.0 | 100.0 | 100.0 | 100.0 | 100.0 |

*Notes:*

(1) Others in the Colony of Singapore include fees of courts, rents of government property, land sales, postage stamps and others, overpayments recovered, motor cars and drivers' licenses etc.

(2) Net revenue earning from the sales of opium was available for Straits Settlements as a whole for the period 1911–30. The distribution for Singapore for that period was derived using the average distribution for the period 1931–39.

(3) Interest obtained from the Opium Revenue Replacement Fund for the period 1933–39 was also presented for Straits Settlements as a whole. The distribution for Singapore was calculated on the basis of the size of revenue earning from the sales of opium for the relevant years.

(4) The Rural Board was established in 1908.

*Sources*: Blue Book, Straits Settlements, various series; Financial Statement of Colony of Singapore, various series; Annual, Administration Report of the Singapore Municipality, various series; Annual Administration Report of the City Council of Singapore, various series.

Nevertheless, its reliance on opium sales as a revenue source reduced gradually over the period. The revenue from opium was paid into the "Opium Revenue Replacement Fund" for each year and the money invested in securities abroad. More importantly, the British colonial authority ceased to depend on opium revenue by abolishing the opium sales immediately after the end of World War II.

Import duties increasing became an important revenue source over time. Import duties that were imposed were that on petrol (1909) followed by tobacco (1916), which became a crucial duty item. By the 1930s, the revenue derived from import duties already exceeded that derived from the sales of opium. This expansion was achieved through the increases of the rate of duty.[93] To overcome this serious, weak foundation of revenue sources, the British colonial administration introduced income tax during the period 1920–23. As no similar tax was imposed in the Federated Malay States and Unfederated Malay States, commercial interests in the Straits Settlements argued against the discriminatory treatment. The law was finally repealed (Lee, 1974, 81).

It is important to note that interest from government financial investment such as the Opium Revenue Replacement Fund, Sterling Security Fund, and other loans had brought considerable stable revenue for the Colony of Singapore.

After World War II, money collected in the way of import duties represented the most important revenue source coinciding with the abolishment of revenue collection from the sales of opium. Nevertheless, the government could not expect any further increase in the size of revenue. Under such circumstances,

---

[93] For instance, duty of petroleum with a flash point of 73° Fahrenheit was 5 cents per gallon when it was first imposed in 1909, and this was increased to 10 cents in 1925 and raised further to 35 cents per gallon in 1931. The duty of tobacco was 60 cents per pound before August 9, 1921, raised to 80 cents after that date, raised further to $1.00 per pound in 1925 and raised further still to $1.10 in 1932 (Lim, 1967, 256).

the income tax bill was finally introduced in 1947. "The Income Tax Ordinance of Singapore" was modeled after that of the United Kingdom. Comparatively speaking, the government imposed a relatively moderate progressive tax rate in Singapore (Edwards, 1970).

As Singapore was a free-enterprise and open economy, too progressive a rate would hinder people's incentive to work, save, and invest. The company income tax was applied to limited companies, public and private, but not to unincorporated firms such as sole proprietors and partnerships because the profit of the latter is accrued to the proprietors or partners and the personal income tax is applied to them accordingly. The company income tax was at the flat rate of 40% on "taxable profit." The revenue structure, in fact, has changed rapidly within a relatively short historical time frame.

In the case of the Municipality, increasing urbanization of Singapore led to increases in revenue through the rates it levied on property and the services an urban center needed. The construction of respective revenue sources remained became relatively stable over time. The Rural Board, which existed under the Municipal ordinance, with powers similar to the Municipality/City Council, similarly derived its revenue from the levying of rates.

### 5.3.1.4 *Self-Government Period (1959–2000)*

After the formation of self-government, income tax comprising company and individual taxes remained the most crucial revenue sources for Singapore as presented in Table 5.6. The size of revenue from income tax accounted for more or less half of the total taxes by 1975. In line with the expansion of income taxes, revenue from selling, leasing, and renting of government assets such as land, facilities, and motorvehicle-related taxes also showed increases. On the other hand, the percentage contribution of revenue from custom and excise duties had gradually decreased.

In 1985, the government of Singapore set up an economic committee to identify new directions for its future economic

**Table 5.6:** Singapore: Revenue by Major Sources at Current Prices, 1960–2000 (Percentage)

| | 1960 | 1965 | 1970 | 1975 | 1980 | 1985 | 1990 | 1995 | 2000 |
|---|---|---|---|---|---|---|---|---|---|
| Income tax | 24.4 | 20.7 | 20.8 | 36.0 | 33.2 | 28.1 | 37.5 | 35.4 | 43.2 |
| Import duty and excise | 33.1 | 29.8 | 23.6 | 12.9 | 11.7 | 9.2 | 10.0 | 6.4 | 5.7 |
| Property tax | 3.2 | 12.2 | 9.0 | 9.8 | 9.7 | 11.1 | 8.5 | 6.6 | 4.8 |
| Motor vehicle taxes | 2.3 | 5.5 | 4.9 | 4.8 | 8.5 | 6.4 | 10.2 | 7.3 | 7.0 |
| Stamp duty | 1.3 | 1.2 | 1.9 | 1.5 | 2.8 | 2.9 | 5.0 | 5.5 | 4.4 |
| Goods and services tax | | | | | | | | 6.6 | 7.2 |
| Others | 8.0 | 6.9 | 10.6 | 5.1 | 5.5 | 5.6 | 9.3 | 10.3 | 9.0 |
| Non-tax revenue | 27.7 | 23.7 | 29.2 | 29.9 | 28.6 | 36.6 | 19.6 | 21.8 | 18.7 |
| Total | 100.0 | 100.0 | 100.0 | 100.0 | 100.0 | 100.0 | 100.0 | 100.0 | 100.0 |

*Notes*:

(1) Others include tax on betting, estate duty, other transfer receipt, and other nontransfer receipt.

(2) Nontax revenue includes sales of goods and services from current operations, reimbursements for services and sales of lands, and interest and dividends received.

*Sources*:

1951 and 1956: Financial Statements of Colony of Singapore and Lee Soo Ann (1974, 83).

1960–1995: Low, (1998, 111).

2000: Year Book of Statistics, Singapore, Various Series.

prosperity. The committee report submitted in 1986 suggested a new tax system. First, suggestion was made to reduce corporate and personal income taxes from 40% to 30% and subsequently 25%. It was mainly because Singapore government would like to attract foreign investment and foreign talents. Additionally, income tax has a detrimental effort on savings and enterprise. In response to this suggestion, the highest scale of company income tax rate and individual tax rate was brought down to 33%. Additionally, the reduction of property tax to 16% was implemented in 1990.

Second, the committee recommended structural tax system from direct to indirect taxes as the main source of revenue. This is because the reduction in income tax revenue has to be compensated by an increase in other revenue. Option is laid on the introduction of indirect taxation on goods and services (GST).

Needless to say, GST is inherently regressive in nature since everybody pays the same tax rate regardless of the income level. However, it was rationalized on the ground that broad-based goods and service tax would not create disincentive to corporations (regarding profitability) and individuals (with regard to savings). Finally, on April 1, 1994, the government introduced the GST (Lim, 2004, 257).

Other than tax revenue, it must be highlighted that the proportion of nontax revenue is relatively high in Singapore as compared with other countries. A few key items account for the difference between Singapore and other countries. First, revenue from the lease of land is substantial, at about 7% of the GDP, since the government owns more than 80% of the land in Singapore. Second, prudent investment of the large accumulated stock of government assets has provided a substantial income stream to the government, estimated at about 5% of GDP (Ghesquiere, 2007, 57).

In short, the government's finance structure underwent a substantial transformation, from relying on traditional revenue sources such as revenue from the sale of opium during the colonial period to more diversified and modern revenue sources during the period of self-government. Most notable among the changes was the shifting of the tax burden unevenly from the low-income group to all income group levels on the basis of the ability-to-pay principle, which is more befitting of a modern community, because they are generally levied at progressive rates. However, it is important to note the consistency of both the colonial government and the self-government in constantly paying attention to create a revenue system which provided incentives to foreign investors.

### 5.3.2 Government Expenditure

#### 5.3.2.1 Growth of Government Expenditure

In the twentieth century, Singapore has experienced a long-term real GDP growth rate (1990 prices) of 4.5% and 7.2% for the

**Table 5.7:** Singapore: Trend of Government Expenditures (Period annual Averages), 1900–2000 (1990 Prices)

| | Average % growth | | | | | | | | Share of TGE to GDP (%) | Share of GFCE to GDP (%) | Share of GFCF to GDP (%) |
|---|---|---|---|---|---|---|---|---|---|---|---|
| | Real GDP | Per-Capita Real GDP | Real TGE | Per-Capita Real TGE | Real GFCE | Per-Capita Real GFCE | Real GFCF | Per-Capita Real GFCF | | | |
| 1900–1910 | 4.6 | 1.8 | 4.1 | 1.3 | 5.5 | 1.9 | 5.8 | 2.8 | 13.8 | 6.6 | 1.6 |
| 1911–1920 | 2.2 | −1.0 | 11.7 | 8.2 | 2.7 | -1.5 | 31.9 | 27.8 | 15.1 | 6.0 | 1.8 |
| 1921–1930 | 6.1 | 2.8 | 10.1 | 6.5 | 9.3 | 4.6 | 24.5 | 20.4 | 17.5 | 6.6 | 2.6 |
| 1931–1939 | 5.0 | 2.3 | 6.8 | 4.0 | 2.7 | -0.2 | 3.7 | 0.9 | 21.5 | 7.3 | 3.1 |
| 1950–1960 | 5.1 | 0.3 | 6.8 | 1.8 | 6.4 | -0.5 | 10.5 | 5.3 | 12.5 | 8.6 | 5.4 |
| 1961–1970 | 8.8 | 6.5 | 15.6 | 12.9 | 14.4 | 10.9 | 18.0 | 15.2 | 17.5 | 10.4 | 7.7 |
| 1971–1980 | 8.6 | 7.1 | 9.4 | 7.7 | 7.3 | 5.4 | 12.5 | 10.8 | 20.7 | 11.6 | 9.4 |
| 1981–1990 | 7.0 | 4.7 | 5.9 | 3.4 | 7.7 | 4.2 | 4.9 | 2.4 | 22.6 | 11.3 | 11.6 |
| 1991–2000 | 7.2 | 4.5 | 7.6 | 4.7 | 8.5 | 5.3 | 9.9 | 6.9 | 16.7 | 10.0 | 7.6 |
| 1900–1939 | 4.5 | 1.5 | 8.2 | 5.0 | 5.1 | 1.2 | 16.8 | 13.3 | 17.0 | 6.6 | 2.0 |
| 1950–2000 | 7.2 | 4.6 | 9.1 | 6.1 | 8.9 | 5.1 | 11.2 | 8.1 | 18.0 | 10.4 | 8.4 |

*Sources*:

[1900–39 and 1950–59] Sugimoto (2008), [1960–1995] Department of Statistics, Singapore (1996).

[1995–2000] Asian Development Bank (2001).

*Abbreviations*:

TGC = Total Government Expenditure, GFCE = Government Final Consumption Expenditure.

GFCF = Government Fixed Capital Formation.

periods 1900–39 and 1950–2000, respectively. In real per-capita terms, a moderate growth rate of 1.5% was recorded for the period 1900–39. On the other hand, a higher growth rate of 4.6% was attained for the period 1950–2000. Hence, there are intertemporal differences in terms of real growth rate between these two distinct periods. As presented in Table 5.7, the most remarkable growth in terms of real GDP and per-capita real GDP was recorded during 1921–30 in the pre–World War II period and 1960–80 in the postwar period. A similar phenomenon was observed in terms of real total government expenditure, government final consumption expenditure, and government fixed capital formation. It will not escape the notice that Government Fixed Capital Formation (GFCF) showed the highest average growth during the period 1910–30.

The average growth was even higher than that in the post-Independence period. It was mainly because of the government's efforts to undertake major infrastructure projects in order to ensure it maintained its eminent position as the regional trading center.

In terms of share of real government expenditure to GDP, GFCE generally remained stable for the entire century exclusive of the 1960s. On the other hand, the share of GFCF to GDP showed a gradual expansion from 1921 onward reaching its peak (11.6%) during the 1981–90 period, after which it declined to 7.6% during the next decade. In terms of size of real government expenditure to GDP, real total government expenditure of Singapore for the years 1900–39 and 1950–2000 was 17.0% and 18.0%, respectively; this was remarkably low compared with other industrialized nations as can be seen from the data shown on page xxx. Both GFCE and GFCF also have experienced gradual increases of their shares of GDP until 1990, after which a slight reduction was experienced.

### 5.3.2.2 *Changes in the Composition of Government Expenditure*

As described above, government spending was initially mostly limited to the maintenance of law and order, external security, and provision of limited government services and investments. However, over the subsequent decades, government expenditure increased significantly. In the case of OECD countries, notable increases were observed in the area of social expenditure.[94] As presented in Table 5.8, the share of government expenditure on law, order and defence, education, health, and pensions to GDP gradually increased over the period. This was mainly due to the increasing government obligations, or, seen from another side, of

---

[94] This category includes education, health, pensions, unemployment benefits, and other transfer programs.

**Table 5.8:** Percentage Share of Government Social Expenditure to GDP (Average of OECD Countries*)

| Type of Expenditure | About 1870 | About 1910 | 1913 | About 1930 | 1937 | 1960 | 1980 | 1993 | 1996 |
|---|---|---|---|---|---|---|---|---|---|
| Law, order, and defence expenditure | | | | | | | | 4.1 | 3.7 |
| Education | 0.6 | | 1.3 | | 2.1 | 3.5 | 5.8 | 6.1 | |
| Health | | 0.3 | | 0.4 | | 2.4 | 5.8 | 6.4 | |
| Pensions | | | 0.4 | | 1.9 | 4.5 | 8.4 | 9.6 | |
| Unemployment | | | | | 1.3 | 0.3 | 0.9 | 1.6 | 2.7 |

*Notes*:

Law, order, and defence expenditure covers the police forces, intelligence services, prisons and other correctional facilities, the judicial system, and ministries of internal affairs.

(*) refers to Australia. Austria, Belgium, Canada, France, Germany, Ireland, Italy, Japan, Netherlands, New Zealand, Norway, Spain, Sweden, Switzerland, United Kingdom, and United States.

*Sources*:

Law, order, and defence expenditure: OECD (2007, 195).

Education, health, pensions, unemployment: Constructed based on Tanzi and Schuknecht (2000, 34, 38, 41 and 43).

citizens' entitlements in the social area (Tanzi *et al.*, 2000, 32). Particularly, expenditure on education has been regarded as a function of economic growth and equity, social stability, and democratic values.

It is interesting to observe whether Singapore experienced a similar pattern of government expenditure. Table 5.9 provides share of government expenditure on (i) defence, justice, and police; (ii) education; (iii) health; and (iv) social security and welfare against GDP in Singapore for the twentieth century. Several observations can be drawn. First, the government expenditure on defence, justice, and police remained high throughout the twentieth century despite some fluctuations observed in the pre–World War II period. Unlike other categories of government expenditure, defence expenditure makes

**Table 5.9:** Singapore: Percentage Share of Expenditure to GDP by Major Objects at Current Prices (%) Selected Years

| | Defence, Justice, and Police | Education | Health | Social Security and Welfare |
|---|---|---|---|---|
| 1900 | 1.2 | 0.3 | 0.5 | 0.3 |
| 1905 | 1.1 | 0.2 | 0.7 | 0.4 |
| 1910 | 3.1 | 0.2 | 0.5 | 0.3 |
| 1915 | 5.5 | 0.2 | 0.5 | 0.3 |
| 1920 | 3.3 | 0.2 | 0.4 | 0.3 |
| 1925 | 3.1 | 0.3 | 0.5 | 0.2 |
| 1930 | 2.9 | 0.4 | 0.6 | 0.2 |
| 1935 | 3.2 | 0.5 | 0.6 | 0.2 |
| 1952 | 1.2 | 1.3 | 0.7 | 0.7 |
| 1955 | 2.6 | 2.7 | 1.8 | 1.0 |
| 1960 | 1.6 | 2.7 | 1.5 | 1.0 |
| 1964 | 0.1 | 3.9 | 2.4 | 1.8 |
| 1970 | 5.7 | 5.4 | 1.4 | 1.0 |
| 1975 | 5.5 | 4.8 | 1.1 | 0.9 |
| 1980 | 5.2 | 4.1 | 0.9 | 0.9 |
| 1983 | 4.2 | 4.9 | 1.4 | 0.3 |
| 1990 | 5.1 | 4.3 | 1.0 | 0.5 |
| 1995 | 4.7 | 3.1 | 1.2 | 0.8 |
| 2000 | 4.8 | 4.0 | 1.0 | 0.7 |

*Sources*:

| | |
|---|---|
| 1900–39: | Constructed by Author. |
| 1950–60: | Lee Soo Ann (1974). |
| 1965–80: | Department of Statistics, Singapore (1983). |
| 1985–2000: | Asian Development Bank (2001 and 2005). |

little or no direct contribution to the economic development (Lim, 2004, 241). However, this expenditure was considered essential to maintain peace and order in Singapore. In 1964, expenditure for this category experienced a sudden drop due to the historical fact that Singapore became a part of the Federation of Malaysia, which bore to undertake expenditure for this purpose. After the attainment of independence in 1965, the percentage share of defence remained high as during the pre-1963 period. This implies that government expenditure on defence was one of the indispensable areas for the establishment of internal and external security of Singapore.

Second, share of government expenditure on both education and health to GDP was recorded at very low levels throughout the pre–World War II period. These categories can be interpreted as contributing to investment in human and social capital and are priority areas for the government. In this sense, it is clear that the British colonial authority did not pay as much attention to these expenditure categories. The postwar period saw the share of government expenditure on education increase steadily over the years. However, government expenditure on health remained small even during the period of self-government period. In fact, the share of health expenditure in Singapore was much lower than that of other OECD countries. This is because the healthcare system of Singapore differed from those in the United States and Western Europe. The goal is to provide quality healthcare for all Singaporeans at minimal cost to society by relying on a combination of public and private service delivery, but without a national health insurance system. Nonetheless, Singapore's healthcare system was ranked among the most successful in the world in terms of cost-effectiveness and community health results (Ghesquiere, 2007, 67, 69).

Third, not unlike health expenditure, government outlays for social security and welfare were very low throughout the century. It amounted, on average, to less than 1% of GDP in 1990–2001, compared with 13% in the typical OECD country. In Singapore, old-age security is seen as being primarily the responsibility of the individual and family, followed by the community through charity, with the state acting only as a last resort.[95] There is no formal unemployment insurance scheme. Indirectly, individuals out of work have to rely primarily on accumulated savings or

---

[95] Public pensions are limited to holders of political positions, the judiciary, and top civil servants and military officers (Ghesquiere, 2007, 53).

family support.[96] Relating to this, the Central Provident Fund, which was put in place in 1955, played significant role. This compulsory savings scheme has relieved the budget for much of the social security expenditure.

In short, the share of government expenditure to GDP during both the British colonial government and the period of self-government remained small. In particular, share of government expenditure on social welfare (exclusive of education) did not show any expansion, whereas those of other OECD countries experienced continuous increases over the period. It is, however, essential to note that there are notable differences in the management of government expenditure between the British colonial period and the period of self-government. The British colonial government, as argued above, always aimed to create a balanced or even a surplus budget structure so as not to burden the colonial home government. Thus, the priority was not to foster the improvement of the quality of government services and their effectiveness. On the other hand, self-government consciously limited the growth of expenditure by focusing on quality service and competitiveness. In the process of budgeting, every government department is required to specify its output and set performance targets as part of the annual budgetary process. These targets are monitored and form the basis for evaluating the performance of the departments. By doing so, the driving force of budgeting is shifted from resource requirements to output performance.

### 5.3.3 *Budget Surplus/Deficit and Financial Assets*

Putting together the revenue and expenditure side of the government sector and added to it that for the statutory boards

---

[96] If these are absent, the government provdes a social safety net as a last resort, but this is subject to stringent means-testing. Government resists introducing entitlement programs, emphasizing instead retraining and incentives that foster job creation (Ghesquiere, 2007, 54).

to arrive at the overall balance for the government sector. Figure 5.2 shows the overall budget surplus/deficit of Singapore for the twentieth century.[97] Prior to 1920, the balance of surplus/deficit was relatively negligible, except for a couple of years (1911 and 1919). However, substantial deficits were recorded since 1925. During the Great Depression years of the 1930s and the years thereafter, Singapore recorded continuous budget deficits. This picture was somewhat different from the other Malay states (Sugimoto, 1997 and 2007a), which relied on revenue source from export duties. The reduction of revenue collected from the sale of opium/chandu had a major contributory effect on the decline of revenue-raising capacity in Singapore and this led to the emergence of budget deficit despite attempts by the colonial government to seek alternative revenue sources in the form of import duties, amongst the major being import duty from petrol. In line with this, it cannot be denied that the British colonial government in Singapore could no longer maintain a balanced budget since the 1920s. This issue, however, need to be examined from the wider scope. From the viewpoint of the British colonial authority, Singapore somewhat functioned as a part of British Malaya. As described before, the Federated Malay States, Johore, and Kedah had recorded continuous government budget surplus. This is mainly because those states could receive export duties which were imposed on primary commodities such as rubber and tin. Instead, Singapore has served as entrepot. During the period, the Colony of Straits Settlements issued loans and it was purchased by other wealthy states of British Malaya.[98]

---

[97] Because of the lack of information on statutory boards, figures prior to 1960 only refer to the Colony and Municipality/City Council.

[98] For example, The Straits Settlements' 7% Loan was issued on April 26, 1921, at the amount of $20,216,300 and wholly purchased by colonial governments of the territories of British Malaya, namely, the Federated Malay States Government ($15,000,000), Johore Government ($800,000), Singapore Municipality ($3,500,000), and Penang Municipality ($916,300) (Annual Report, Colony of Straits Settlements, 1921, 12–13).

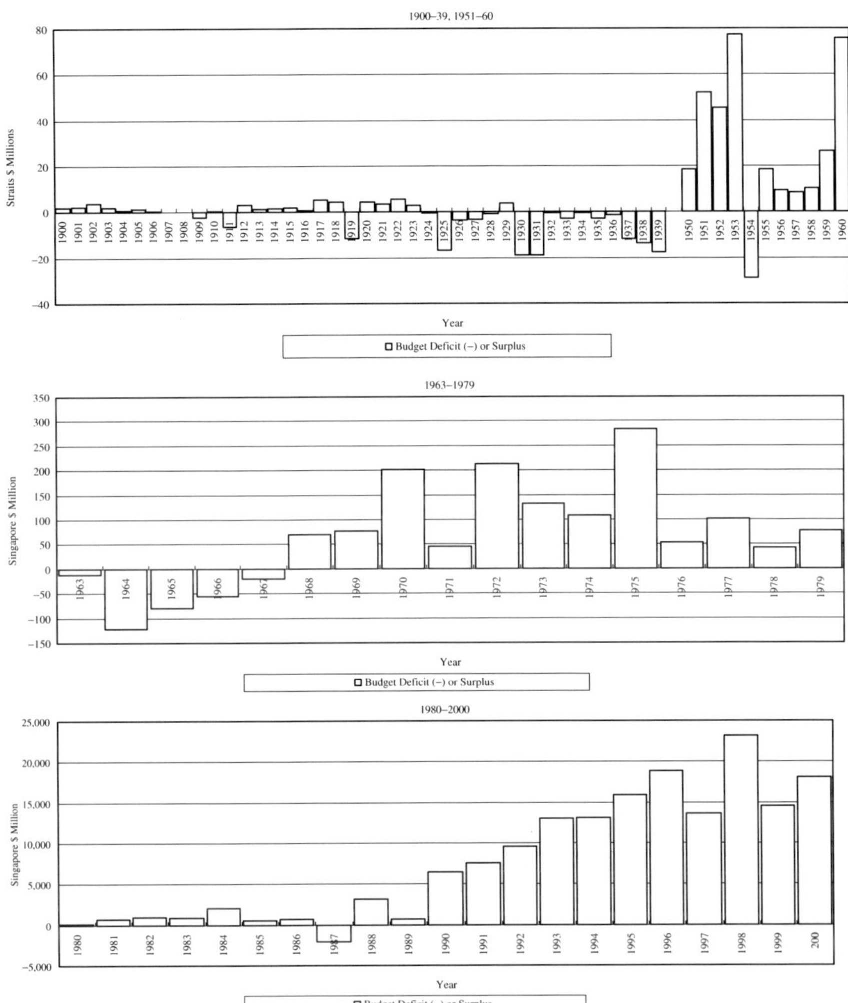


**Fig. 5.2:** Singapore: Budget Deficit (−)/Surplus at Current Prices, 1900–1939, 1950–79 and 1980–2000

*Note*: (1) Total Revenue = Total Revenue + Grant (2) Total Expenditure = Total Expenditure + Lending Minus Repayments.

*Sources*: [1900–39, 1950–60] Sugimoto (2008), [1960–2000] IMF Government Finance Statistics, Various Series.

In this regard, Singapore has played a functional role. However, in the immediate post–World War II period Singapore recorded continuous budget surpluses over time. Lee Soo Ann (1974) found that the British colonial budget management paid special attention to achieving budget surpluses for the period 1948–60. In fact, there were significant differences between the budget estimated and the actual expenditure and revenue figures. Naturally, this led to the accumulation of budget surpluses and substantial amounts were allocated for foreign asset holdings.[99]

This major transition was realized mainly because of the introduction of income tax and its steady expansion as a major revenue source. Excluding the early years of the 1960s and the year 1987, the government's prudent budgetary practices resulted in budget surpluses which have grown larger especially over the period 1990–2000. According to the Jang and Nakabayashi (2005), the government budget surplus amounted to on average 10.6% of GDP during the 1990–2001 period, whereas a typical OECD country for the same period recorded a budget deficit to the tune of –3.6%.

### 5.3.4 *Summary*

Using the above observations, summarized below are the following main features of government finance of Singapore: First, the implementation of various measures by the government to raise revenue and allocate expenditure had undergone major structural changes between the prewar and postwar periods. In the prewar period, revenue collection was almost entirely based on the sales of opium/chandu since its free port status precluded imposition of export duties, a privilege enjoyed by the Malay States of British Malaya. For several years, the British colonial government attempted to introduce income tax

---

[99] A similar phenomenon was observed in the Malayan state of Johore prior to World War II (Sugimoto, 1997, 2007a).

but failed to do so due to strong objections from its residents. Initially, Singapore managed to sufficiently obtain revenue to meet the size of its expenditure. Nevertheless, over the years, the Colony of Singapore faced a situation of budget deficits since the 1920s as a result of increases in government expenditure.

The structure of government finance in Singapore changed significantly after World War II because of the introduction of income tax and complete abolition of revenue derived from the sales of opium/chandu by the British colonial authority. Within a short period of time, the size of revenue from income tax experienced an increase and this was matched by increases in government expenditure. In terms of budget management, the balance of government finance constantly showed a surplus since the 1950s. Importantly, this structure remained unchanged even after the attainment of independence and its absolute amount of budget surplus increased over time, particularly so in the last two decades.

Second, it is possible to say that the government expenditure behavior was basically conservative and prudent throughout the period despite the differing underlying motives during the prewar and postwar periods. In the prewar period, one of the major concerns of British colonial authority was to attain a balanced budget or even budget surplus with a conservative spending tendency. In fact, large amounts of accumulated government budget surpluses were funneled to the British homeland and other British colonies in the form of portfolio financial investment. This principle, however, could not be sustained since the mid-1920s mainly because of the complete absence of earnings from export duty and partially because of the relative reduction of the revenue earnings from the sales of opium. However, the situation reverted to the original status in the postwar period. The British colonial government was again able to successfully obtain budget surpluses for most of the years after the introduction of income tax. After the formation of self-government, not only have budgetary surpluses been chronic but they have grown larger and larger over the years. By conventional wisdom, this budget operation should raise hackles of crowding-out and contractionary effects. Nevertheless, these effects have been obviated in part by the government recycling funds back into the economy. One way was been means of direct investment especially in the productive economic infrastructure projects as well as in field of education, training, and health. Additionally, outside the domestic economy, investments by the state in global assets and activities brought in more investment income as well as secured a wider portfolio of investments. The point is that surpluses were productively used rather than lockedup to cause potential adverse deflationary effects (Low, 1998, 148).

Third, using the above the observation, it is possible to draw a hypothesis that the government's finance behavior under British colonial rule (particularly, prior to WWII period) could not afford to focus on the economic growth of Singapore. Maintaining the principle of "free port status" caused weakness in the revenue-raising capacity. Under this serious constraint, government expenditure allocation must be highly constrained in order to maintain a balanced budget. Consequently, the British colonial government's fiscal behavior was somewhat different from the type of government involvement experienced in the developed countries since the end of 1920s, as described by Tanzi *et al.* (2000). In fact, as pointed out by Booth (2002) on the experiences in the Netherland Indies, the British colonial government's policy in Singapore also hardly reflected a conversion to Keynesian economics, but rather was a manifestation of its inability to allocate expenditures in the face of rapidly falling revenues.

On the other hand, the self-government period was one which was geared for the economic growth of Singapore. It is crucial to note here that the Singapore government implemented efficient government intervention by maintaining the principle of a small-sized government, though most of the developed countries experienced a rapid expansion in the share of government expenditure to GDP during the period of the 1960s–1970s. In developed countries, growing skepticism of excessive government intervention emerged in the 1980s because of the rising fiscal deficit and public debt. Governments of the developed countries reformed their policy regimes toward less state involvement and consequently led to cuts in public expenditure. However, many developed countries faced difficulties because the past commitments and resistance of groups with strong entitlements on public spending (Tanzi *et al.*, 2000, 20). In this sense, the principle of a small-sized government in Singapore established during the British colonial period spilled over to the period of self-government.

In the following section, this study conducts econometric tests to examine the statistical relationship between the government's fiscal behavior and the economic growth of Singapore in the twentieth century and clarify whether we can find any notable differences between these two distinct periods.

## 5.4 Econometric Test

### 5.4.1 *Testing Methodology*

In 1893, Adolph Wagner offered a model of the determination of public expenditure in which it was stated that public expenditure growth was a natural consequence of economic growth. Later, his views were formulated as a law, often referred to as "Wagner's law." His main contribution in this field was that he tried to establish generalizations about public expenditures, not from postulates about the logic of choice, but rather by direct inference from historical evidence (Demirbas, 1999; Halicioğlu, 2003; Henrekson, 1993). The interpretation of Wagner's law, however, seems to be more controversial in a sense that several versions of the law have been introduced and tested empirically since the 1960s. The most common functional forms of Wagner's law cited in the literature are given below:

$$\ln \text{TGE}_t = \alpha + \beta \ln Y_t + \varepsilon_t \ ,..., \quad (1) \ \text{Peacock-Wiseman (P-W)}$$
$$(1961, 1968)$$
$$\ln \text{GFCE}_t = \alpha + \beta \ln Y_t + \varepsilon \ ,..., \quad (2) \ \text{Pryor (1968)}$$

$$\text{In GFCF}_t = \alpha + \beta \ln Y_t + \varepsilon_t \ ,..., \quad (3)$$
$$\ln (\text{TGE/Y})_t = \alpha + \beta \ln Y_t + \varepsilon_t \ ,..., \quad (4) \text{ Mann (1980)}$$
$$\ln (\text{GFCE/Y})_t = \alpha + \beta \ln Y_t + \varepsilon_t \ ,..., \quad (5)$$
$$\ln (\text{GFCF/Y})_t = \alpha + \beta \ln Y_t + \varepsilon_t \ ,..., \quad (6)$$
$$(\text{B/Y})_t = \alpha + \beta Y_t + \varepsilon_t \quad ,..., \quad (7)$$

where TGE, GFCE, GFCF, and B refer to real total government expenditure, real government final consumption expenditure, real government fixed capital formation, and government overall budget surplus, respectively. The notation Y refers to real GDP. The first version comprising equation (1) was originally employed by Peacock and Wiseman (1961, 1968), Musgrave (1969), Goffiman and Mahar (1971), and Chang (2002) and Huang *et al.* (2006). This is the simplest of all the versions of Wagner's hypothesis and has been widely used in many studies concerning total government expenditure. The second version (equation (2)) was used by Pryor (1969). Similarly, this study was with regard to government fixed capital formation.

Equations (1) through (3) may be perceived as the level version, whereas equations (4)–(6) are the relative versions of Wagner's law. Versions (4)–(6) represent the Musgrave and Mann's idea that Wagner's law is interpreted as postulating a rising share of government expenditure to GDP. Similar to versions (1)–(3), Wagner's hypothesis is validated if the elasticity of the government expenditure as a share of GDP exceeds unity.[100]

In addition to the six versions mentioned above, this study tests the share of overall government budget surplus to GDP as in equation (7). This test is especially relevant since both the British colonial government and the self-government after independence paid particular attention to balancing budgets.

This study decides to empirically investigate all versions of Wagner's law for Singapore for the periods 1900–39 and 1950–2000.

---

[100] In fact, ambiguity exists as to whether the law refers to the relative share of government in an economy or merely to the absolute size of the government (Islam, 2001).

Proceeding to test Wagner's law relating to the statistical properties of data, it is necessary to go through the following three steps: In Step 1, it is necessary to investigate the stationarity properties of the data, in particular whether it is *trend stationarity* (TS) or *difference stationarity* (DS), and the order of integration of the data. In this regard, it is necessary to examine the time-series properties of the variables because of the implicit assumption that the data were stationary. However, recent developments in time-series analysis found that most macroeconomic time series have a unit root (a stochastic trend) and this property is described as difference stationarity so that the first difference of a time-series is stationary (Nelson *et al.*, 1982). Hence, for stage 1, the nonstationary property of the series must be examined first.

To test the stationarity of the time-series data, augmented Dickey-Fuller (ADF) test and the Philipps-Perron (PP) regression test are attempted.[101] If the variables are found to be nonstationary in their levels, then one needs to apply the cointegration test, discussed below. In other words, the cointegration test is carried out only on the first-difference stationary variables.

Once unit root was confirmed for a data series, the question is whether there exists some long-run equilibrium relationship among variables. Step 2 tests this issue which is reffered to as cointegration in most of the literature works. The concept of cointegration was first introduced by Granger (1981). From the statistical point of view, a long-term relationship means that the variables move together over time so that short-term disturbances from the long-term trend are corrected (Manning *et al.*, 1993). A lack of cointegration suggests that such variables have no long-run relationship: in principal, they can wander

---

[101] The equation and methodology for both ADF and PP tests were described earlier in detail in Chapters 3 and 4. Therefore, description regarding this is not discussed in this chapter to avoid duplicity.

arbitrarily far away from each other (Dickey *et al.*, 1991).[102] If cointegration exists between the two variables, there can be no systematic divergence between the variables from some long-run equilibrium relationship. In other words, cointegration constitutes a sufficient condition for causality. Hence if variables are cointegrated, then either unidirectional or bidirectional causal relationship must exist between them.

Cointegration tests in this study are conducted using the method developed by Johansen (1988) and Johansen and Juselius (1990). This procedure is regarded as the most reliable test for cointegration and avoids the problems with the Engle and Granger's (1987) two-step procedure, as shown by Kremers *et al.* (1992) and Gonzola (1994). Johansen method applies the maximal likelihood procedure to determine the presence of cointegrating vectors in nonstationary time series.

Following Johansen (1988) and Johansen and Juselius (1990), a two-dimensional (2 × 1) vector autoregressive model with Gaussian errors can be expressed by

$$Y_t = A_1 Y_{t-1} + A_2 Y_{t-2} + ,..., + A_k Y_{t-k} + \mu + \varepsilon_t$$
$$t = 1, 2 ,..., T,$$

where $Y_t$ = is real GDP and government expenditure] and $\varepsilon_t$ is i.i.d. N(0, $\Sigma$). By taking first-differencing on the vector level, the model in error correction form is

$$\Delta Y_t = \Gamma_1 \Delta Y_{t-1} + \Gamma_2 \Delta Y_{t-2} + \cdots + \Gamma_{k-1} \Delta Y_{t-k+1} - \Pi Y_{t-1} + \mu + \varepsilon_t,$$

where

$$\Gamma_i = -I + A_1 + A_2 + \cdots + A_i,$$

---

[102] Many early researchers who looked at Wagner's law ignored the stationarity requirement of the variables. However, the standard regression techniques are invalid when applied to nonstationary variables.

For $i = 1, 2, ..., k - 1$, $\Pi = I - A_1 - A_2 - \cdots - A_k$. The $\Pi$ matrix conveys information about the long-run relationship between $Y_t$ variables (real GDP and government expenditure), and the rank of $\Pi$ is the number of linearly independent and stationary linear combination of real GDP and government spending. Thus, testing for cointegration involves testing for the rank of $\Pi$ matrix $r$ by examining whether the Eigenvalues of $\Pi$ are significantly different from zero. Three possible conditions exist: (a) the $\Pi$ matrix has full column rank, implying that the $Y_t$ was stationary in level to begin with; (b) the $\Pi$ matrix has zero rank, in which case the system is a traditional first-differenced VAR; and (c) the $\Pi$ matrix has rank $r$ such that $0 < r < 2$, implying that there exist $r$ linear combinations of $Y_t$ that are stationary or cointegrated. If condition (c) prevails, then $\Pi$ can be decomposed into two $2 \times r$ matrices, $\alpha$ and $\beta$, such that $\Pi = \alpha\beta'$. The vectors of $\beta$ represent the $r$ linear cointegrating relationships such that $\beta'Y_t$ is stationary. By testing the significance of the $\beta$ coefficients, whether the variables entering the cointegrating relationship significantly will be known. The loading matrix $\alpha$ represents the error-correction parameters which can be interpreted as speed of adjustment parameters.

Johansen (1988) and Johansen and Juselius (1990) propose two test statistics for testing the number of cointegrating vectors (or the rank of $\Pi$): the trace (Tr) and the maximum Eigenvalue (L-max) statistics. The likelihood ratio statistic for the trace test is

$$\text{Tr} = -T \sum_{i=r+1}^{p-2} \ln(1 - \hat{\lambda}_i), \qquad \text{where } \hat{\lambda}_r+1, ..., \hat{\lambda}_p,$$

are the estimated $p - r$ smallest Eigenvalues. The null hypothesis to be tested is that there are at most $r$ cointegrating vectors. That is, the number of cointegrating vectors is less than or equal to $r$, where $r$ is 0 or 1 (in this study). In each case, the null hypothesis is tested against the general alternative. Alternatively, the L-max statistic is

$$\text{L-max} = -T \ln(1 - \hat{\lambda}_{r+1}).$$

In this test, the null hypothesis of $r$ cointegrating vectors is tested against the alternative of $r + 1$ cointegrating vectors. Thus, the null hypothesis $r = 0$ is tested against the alternative that $r = 1$, $r = 1$ against the alternative $r = 2$, and so forth. It is well known that the cointegration tests are very sensitive to the choice of lag length. Here, the Schwartz criterion (SC) is used to select the number of lags required in the cointegration test. The SC is defined as follows:

$$SC = \ln\left(\frac{y'M_1 y}{T}\right) + \frac{K_1 \ln T}{T},$$

where $M_1 = I - X_1(X_1'X_1)^{-1} X_1'$, and $T$ is the sample size. Here, $K_1$ is chosen so as to numerically minimize $SC$ above.

Finally, Step 3 carries out Granger-type causality tests augmented with the error-correction term derived from the appropriate cointegrating relationship, as identified in Step 2. Engle and Granger (1987) show that if two nonstationary variables are cointegrated, then a vector autoregression in the first differences is misspecified. Therefore it is necessary to conduct cointegration test before running the causality test.

An appropriate formulation for such a Granger-Type causality test is presented in equations below:

$$\Delta \ln G_t = \alpha_o + \sum_{i=1}^{n} \alpha_{1i} \, \Delta \ln G_{t-i} + \sum_{i=1}^{n} \alpha_{2i} \, \Delta \ln Y_{t-i} + \alpha_3 z_{t-1} + \eta_{0t}$$

$$\Delta \ln Y_t = \beta_0 + \sum_{i=1}^{n} \beta_{1i} \, \Delta \ln G_{t-i} + \sum_{i=1}^{n} \beta_{2i} \, \Delta \ln Y_{t-i} + \beta_3 z_{t-1} + \eta_{0t},$$

where $\Delta$ is the difference operator and $z$ is the estimated cointegrating vector. $Y$ can be said to Granger cause $G$ if $\alpha_3$ is statistically significant. Similarly, statistical significance of $\beta_3$ would imply $G$ Granger causing $Y$. Bidirectional causality arises when both the parameters are statistically significant. Hence, Wagner's law would be validated if $Y$ Granger causes $G$.

In case of noncointegration between the variables, the standard Granger causality approach may be relied on to study their lead-lag relationships that involve the specification of the following vector autoregression (VAR) model:

$$\Delta \ln G_1 = \alpha_0 + \sum_{i=1}^{n} \alpha_{1i} \, \Delta \ln G_{t-i} + \sum_{i=1}^{n} \alpha_{2i} \, \Delta \ln Y_{t-i} + \eta_{0t},$$

$$\Delta \ln Y_t = \beta_0 + \sum_{i=1}^{n} \beta_{1i} \, \Delta \ln G_{t-i} + \sum_{i=1}^{n} \beta_{2i} \, \Delta \ln Y_{t-i} + \eta_{0t}.$$

$Y$ would be said to Granger cause $G$ if $\alpha_{2i}$'s are jointly significantly different from zero, while the converse holds if $\beta_{1i}$'s have such joint significance. Bidirectional causality appears if both the conditions are established.

### 5.4.2 *Data*

For conducting this empirical analysis, various time-series data are required. For consistency purposes, the time-series data which stretch over the twentieth century were all standardized in 1990 prices.

In the case of GDP and GFCE, the figures presented in Chapter Three were used. Figures on GFCF were estimated using official publications such as the *Blue Book, Straits Settlements, Financial Statement, Straits Settlements* and *Administration Report on Singapore Municipality* for the period 1900–39. For the period 1950–60, *Financial Statement, Colony of Singapore, Financial Statement, State of Singapore* and *Administration Report on Singapore City Council* were used. Nevertheless, figures provided in the government expenditure account were not detailed enough, a case in point being that of public works. If the works were contracted out to the private contractors, it is necessary to take into account the additional, not declared, value for the computation. On the other hand, in cases where public works are internally implemented, we should take this given figure as own fixed capital formation. (Please see App Fig. 1.) Because of absence of detailed accounts, this figure has been treated as government fixed capital formation.

For deflating purposes, this government fixed capital formation was classified into fixed capital formation, comprising (a) construction and (b) machinery and equipment and transport. These respective figures were then firstly deflated to 1914 prices by using the price indices of cement for construction and the UK price indices on machinery and plant in the case of the latter.

Subsequently, the official publications entitled *Singapore System of National Account 1995* and *Yearbook of Statistics, Singapore* were used to obtain the information on government fixed capital formation for the period 1960–2000. Implicit deflators of government fixed capital formation (1990 = 100) for the 1960–2000 were then connected with the implicit deflators for the periods 1900–39 and 1950–60 to obtain the long-term deflators which stretched over the entire twentieth century.

In the case of total government expenditure for the periods 1900–39 and 1950–60, the same sources stated above were again used. For deriving the constant prices (1914 prices), total government expenditure was then deflated by the major classification of expenditure, namely, (i) personal emoluments, (ii) intermediate consumption expenditure, (iii) fixed capital formation pertaining to construction, (iv) fixed capital formation on machinery, equipment, and transport, and (v) transfer and others. Each component of government expenditure was deflated respectively as follows. All the above items were deflated by CPI with the exception of (iv), which used the UK price indices on machinery and plant. Subsequently, data on total government expenditure for the period 1960–2000 in current and 1990 prices were compiled from the *Singapore System of National Accounts 1995*, *Yearbook of Statistics, Singapore* and *IMF International Financial Statistics*, 2006. For the conversion of 1914 prices to

1990 prices for the periods 1900–39 and 1950–1960, a methodology similar to that as described earlier was employed.

## 5.5 Empirical Results

### 5.5.1 *Unit Root Test*

Because cointegration test requires the use of nonstationary variables and error-correction equations require the use of stationary variables, each data series is first examined for the probable order of difference stationarity. Table 5.10 reports the result of nonstationary tests for real GDP (LY), real total government expenditure (LTGE), real government final consumption expenditure (LGFCE), real government fixed capital formation (LGFCF), the share of real total government expenditure to real GDP (LSTGY), the share of real government final consumption expenditure to real GDP (LSGFCEY), real total government fixed capital formation to real GDP (LSGFCFY), and share of government budget deficit surplus to current GDP (SBY) for the following specified periods, namely, 1900–39 and 1950–2000, using ADF and PP tests.

For the period 1900–39, the ADF test showed mixed results. The variables for LY, LTG, LGFCE, LGCF, and LSGFCEY were nonstationarity (unit root) in levels but stationary in first differences; i.e., they are integrated of order one (I(1)). On the other hand, nonstationarity for the level can be rejected for LSTGY, LGFCFY, and SBY. Thus, those variables were integrated of order zero (I(0)). In the case of PP test, the nonstationarity of LSGFCEY at the level can be rejected at the significance level of 5%. Using these results, integrated of order one, I(1), was assigned for LY, LTG, LGFCE, and LGFCF, for the period 1900–39. For the period 1950–2000, in turn, all variables were nonstationary at all levels. In contrast, when the data are differenced, nonstationarity can be rejected for all data series. This unit root test (ADF and PP tests) indicates that all the data series for the period 1950–2000 are integrated of order 1, (I (1)).

## 5.5.2 *Cointegration Tests*

Since a difference stationary on relevant variables has been identified for both periods, the next question seeks to answer whether there are any long-run equilibrium relationships between real government expenditure and real GDP growth. Regarding the Johansen method, a VAR model was first fitted to the data to

**Table 5.10:**   Unit Root Test ADF and PP Tests for Stationary

**1900–39**

ADF Test (Constant and Trend)

|  | Levels | Lags[1] | First Difference | Lags[1] | Second Difference | Lags[1] | Order |
|---|---|---|---|---|---|---|---|
| [A] LY | −2.78374 | 0 | −6.731818*** | 0 | −11.01584*** | 0 | I(1) |
| [B] LTG | −3.814653** | 0 | −8.033059*** | 0 | −4.987201*** | 4 | I(0) |
| [C] LGFCE | −2.469285 | 0 | −6.470095*** | 0 | −8.205939*** | 1 | I(1) |
| [D] LGCF | −3.770553** | 0 | −9.052408*** | 0 | −5.09191*** | 6 | I(0) |
| [E] LSTGY | −3.837329** | 0 | −5.047314*** | 3 | −4.902809*** | 6 | I(0) |
| [F] LSGFCEY | −3.141115 | 0 | −6.386649*** | 0 | −4.648197*** | 9 | I(1) |
| [G] LSGCFY | −4.126179** | 0 | −8.909765*** | 0 | −5.641769*** | 6 | I(0) |
| [H] SBY | −5.590353*** | 0 | −9.830936*** | 0 | −6.292099*** | 4 | I(0) |

ADF Test (Constant)

|  | Levels | lags[1] | First Difference | lags[1] | Second Difference | lags[1] | Order |
|---|---|---|---|---|---|---|---|
| [A] LY | −0.15100 | 0 | −6.755893*** | 0 | −11.18046*** | 0 | I(1) |
| [B] LTG | −1.130992 | 0 | −8.138393*** | 0 | −5.025721*** | 4 | I(1) |
| [C] LGFCE | −0.746311 | 0 | −6.556167*** | 0 | −8.306657*** | 1 | I(1) |
| [D] LGCF | −2.383191 | 0 | −9.178221*** | 0 | −5.205502*** | 6 | I(1) |
| [E] LSTGY | −3.250663** | 0 | −7.137025*** | 0 | −4.974354*** | 5 | I(0) |
| [F] LSGFCEY | −3.205802** | 0 | −6.464899*** | 0 | −5.711237*** | 9 | I(0) |
| [G] LSGCFY | −3.807094*** | 0 | −9.03616*** | 0 | −5.752735*** | 6 | I(0) |
| [H] SBY | −4.391307*** | 0 | −9.969996*** | 0 | −6.35749*** | 4 | I(0) |

PP Test (Constant and Trend)

|  | Levels | Bandwidth[2] | First Difference | Bandwidth[2] | Second Difference | Bandwidth[2] | Order |
|---|---|---|---|---|---|---|---|
| [A] LY | −2.838095 | 3 | −7.637926*** | 9 | −30.44664*** | 20 | I(1) |
| [B] LTG | −3.789503** | 3 | −20.02938*** | 37 | −35.446*** | 17 | I(0) |
| [C] LGFCE | −2.524723 | 2 | −6.501746*** | 2 | −22.99899*** | 9 | I(1) |
| [D] LGCF | −3.742731** | 2 | −15.79308*** | 20 | −50.31967*** | 26 | I(0) |
| [E] LSTGY | −3.497332** | 8 | −18.2599*** | 37 | −30.76099*** | 17 | I(0) |
| [F] LSGFCEY | −3.300951* | 2 | −7.111945*** | 6 | −27.57471*** | 20 | I(0) |
| [G] LSGCFY | −4.093705** | 1 | −22.361*** | 37 | −43.7105*** | 21 | I(0) |
| [H] SBY | −5.573819*** | 3 | −32.00957*** | 37 | −59.46965*** | 33 | I(0) |

PP Test (Constant)

|  | Levels | Bandwidth[2] | First Difference | Bandwidth[2] | Second Difference | Bandwidth[2] | Order |
|---|---|---|---|---|---|---|---|
| [A] LY | 0.605039 | 11 | −7.335052*** | 8 | −30.98098*** | 20 | I(1) |
| [B] LTG | −0.902239 | 26 | −17.1768*** | 32 | −36.08674*** | 17 | I(1) |
| [C] LGFCE | −0.728743 | 1 | −6.591153*** | 2 | −21.88664*** | 10 | I(1) |
| [D] LGCF | −2.383191 | 0 | −15.54101*** | 20 | −20.54456*** | 3 | I(1) |
| [E] LSTGY | −3.10222** | 7 | −13.63349*** | 37 | −31.28533*** | 17 | I(0) |
| [F] LSGFCEY | −3.362399** | 2 | −22.8611*** | 6 | −28.11533*** | 20 | I(0) |
| [G] LSGCFY | −3.780956*** | 2 | −22.79482*** | 37 | −44.16968*** | 21 | I(0) |
| [H] SBY | −4.332332*** | 1 | −32.58154*** | 37 | −59.35003*** | 35 | I(0) |

*(Continued)*

**Table 5.10:**   *(Continued)*

**1950–2000**

ADF Test (Constant and Trend)

| | Levels | Lags[1] | First Difference | Lags[1] | Second Difference | Lags[1] | Order |
|---|---|---|---|---|---|---|---|
| [A] LY | –3.078195 | 1 | –8.407613*** | 0 | –5.038208*** | 3 | I(1) |
| [B] LTG | –1.298083 | 0 | –6.997054*** | 0 | –13.03122*** | 0 | I(1) |
| [C] LGFCE | –1.724503 | 0 | –6.260416*** | 0 | –11.24465*** | 0 | I(1) |
| [D] LGCF | –2.659453 | 0 | –10.77978*** | 0 | –16.45091*** | 0 | I(1) |
| [E] LSTGY | –1.251329 | 1 | –9.328335*** | 0 | –14.74253*** | 0 | I(1) |
| [F] LSGFCEY | –2.914305 | 0 | –8.253654*** | 0 | –13.96485*** | 0 | I(1) |
| [G] LSGCFY | –2.701623 | 0 | –10.58573*** | 0 | –16.45671*** | 0 | I(1) |
| [H]SBY | –2.579934 | 3 | –13.81956*** | 0 | –11.18855*** | 1 | I(1) |

ADF Test (Constant)

| | Levels | Lags[1] | First Difference | Lags[1] | Second Difference | Lags[1] | Order |
|---|---|---|---|---|---|---|---|
| [A] LY | 0.753408 | 1 | –8.344712*** | 0 | –14.64466*** | 0 | I(1) |
| [B] LTG | –1.458986 | 0 | –6.971704*** | 0 | –13.18521*** | 0 | I(1) |
| [C] LGFCE | –0.694785 | 0 | –6.238491*** | 0 | –11.38402*** | 0 | I(1) |
| [D] LGCF | –1.785802 | 0 | –10.65997*** | 0 | –16.63653*** | 0 | I(1) |
| [E] LSTGY | –1.605284 | 1 | –9.324743*** | 0 | –14.9659*** | 0 | I(1) |
| [F] LSGFCEY | –2.305553 | 6 | –7.965965*** | 0 | –14.06737*** | 0 | I(1) |
| [G] LSGCFY | –2.724488* | 0 | –10.46779*** | 0 | –16.64528*** | 0 | I(0) |
| [H]SBY | –0.652582 | 1 | –13.70274*** | 0 | –11.24676*** | 1 | I(1) |

PP Test (Constant and Trend)

| | Levels | Bandwidth[2] | First Difference | Bandwidth[2] | Second Difference | Bandwidth[2] | Order |
|---|---|---|---|---|---|---|---|
| [A] LY | –3.227707* | 4 | –8.382089*** | 4 | –15.47021*** | 1 | I(0) |
| [B] LTG | –1.326666 | 1 | –6.995509*** | 2 | –45.31031*** | 36 | I(1) |
| [C] LGFCE | –1.845273 | 1 | –6.260416*** | 0 | –33.05377*** | 31 | I(1) |
| [D] LGCF | –2.552074 | 4 | –13.64865*** | 8 | –54.50292*** | 18 | I(1) |
| [E] LSTGY | –2.374247 | 1 | –9.169686*** | 3 | –53.19499*** | 31 | I(1) |
| [F] LSGFCEY | –2.914305 | 0 | –8.214355*** | 1 | –37.5317*** | 28 | I(1) |
| [G] LSGCFY | –2.600917 | 5 | –11.55729*** | 6 | –50.39451*** | 17 | I(1) |
| [H]SBY | –3.467982* | 3 | –13.17839*** | 2 | –21.78444*** | 0 | I(0) |

PP Test (Constant)

| | Levels | Bandwidth[2] | First Difference | Bandwidth[2] | Second Difference | Bandwidth[2] | Order |
|---|---|---|---|---|---|---|---|
| [A] LY | 0.818733 | 4 | –8.318235*** | 4 | –14.64466*** | 0 | I(1) |
| [B] LTG | –1.450364 | 3 | –6.968625*** | 2 | –16.07731*** | 3 | I(1) |
| [C] LGFCE | –0.677723 | 3 | –6.238491*** | 0 | –13.44321*** | 3 | I(1) |
| [D] LGCF | –1.958535 | 3 | –11.01277*** | 5 | –55.21298*** | 18 | I(1) |
| [E] LSTGY | –2.878653* | 1 | –9.065948*** | 2 | –19.63955*** | 3 | I(0) |
| [F] LSGFCEY | –3.186071** | 0 | –7.94208*** | 1 | –29.23749*** | 20 | I(0) |
| [G] LSGCFY | –2.687726* | 11 | –10.48893*** | 4 | –50.93432*** | 17 | I(0) |
| [H]SBY | –1.806544 | 3 | –12.70184*** | 5 | –22.0251*** | 0 | I(1) |

*Notes*:

1. Automatic selection of lag based on the Schwartz Info Criterion.

2. Bandwidth was determined based on the Newey-West using Bartlett kernel.

All variables are in natural logs exclusive of share of budget deficit to GDP.

(***,**,*) denotes significance at the 1%, 5%, and 10% level, respectively.

I(0) = stationary, I(1) = unit root.

find an appropriate lag structure. The SC likelihood ratio test suggest two lags for most of the VAR models examined for different versions of Wagner's hypothesis models based on the specified periods 1900–39 and 1950–2000.

As presented in Table 5.11, the results of Max-Eigen test and Trace test show that the null hypotheses of no cointegration between (1) LTG and LYSBY and (2) LGFCE and LY were rejected at 5% levels of significance, respectively, for the period 1900–39. For the rest of the versions, the null hypothesis of no cointegration cannot be rejected. For the period 1950–2000, the results of Max-Eigen test and Trace test presented that the null hypotheses of no cointegration between SBY and LY (7) can be rejected at 1% level of significance, respectively. Other than these versions, the null hypothesis of no cointegration was not rejected.

### 5.5.3 *Granger Causality Tests*

After obtaining the results from the cointegration tests, the procedure adopted is as follows. When the variables are not cointegrated, the causality tests are conducted by running the standard Granger regressions (as indicated on p. xxx without the error correction terms). However, if the cointegration hypothesis is not rejected, the standard Granger regressions are misspecified. Thus, error-correction models (as indicated on p. xxx) can be applied to these time series for determining Granger causality.

The difficulty in fitting these models revolves around determining the appropriate lag lengths. Both lags are frequently chosen to have the same value, and lag lengths of 1, 2, 3, and 4 are usually used. There are several criteria to determine "optimum" lag lengths, such as Akaike's information criterion, Akaike's FPE, and Schwarz criterion. Following Afxentiou and Serletis (1992), this study has chosen four different commonly chosen lag lengths of 1, 2, 3, and 4. The null hypothesis of noncausality is tested using F-statistics. The results of F-tests for the periods 1900–39 and 1950–2000 are furnished in Table 5.12.

In the tests, causality is hypothesized to run from $Y$ to the dependent variable, which takes three different forms; TGE, GFCE, and GFCF for the period 1900–39, and seven different forms; TGE, GFCE, GFCF, STGY SGFCEY, SGFCFY, and SBY

**Table 5.11:** Johansen Maximum Likelihood Procedure Cointegration LR Test Based on the Max-Eigen Test and Trace Test of the Stochastic Matrix, 1900–39 and 1950–2000

| | | | | | 1900–39 | | | |
|---|---|---|---|---|---|---|---|---|
| | Eigenvalues $(\lambda)$ | Max-Eigen Test $(\lambda_{max})$ | Critical Value $(\lambda_{max})$ (5%) | Critical Value $(\lambda_{max})$ (1%) | The Trace Test $(\lambda_{trace})$ | Critical Value $(\lambda_{trace})$ (5%) | Critical Value $(\lambda_{trace})$ (1%) |
| **(1) LTG and LY (Var lag = 2)** | | | | | | | |
| $H_0$:$r = 0$ | 0.356107 | 16.24* | 14.07 | 18.63 | 16.53* | 15.41 | 20.04 |
| $H_0$:$r \leq 1$ | 0.006578 | 0.24 | 3.76 | 6.65 | 0.24 | 3.76 | 6.65 |
| **(2) LGFCE and LY (Var lag = 2)** | | | | | | | |
| $H_0$:$r = 0$ | 0.342847 | 15.53* | 14.07 | 18.63 | 15.53* | 15.41 | 20.04 |
| $H_0$:$r \leq 1$ | 0.0000014 | 0.0001 | 3.76 | 6.65 | 0.0001 | 3.76 | 6.65 |
| **(3) LGFCF and LY (Var lag = 2)** | | | | | | | |
| $H_0$:$r = 0$ | 0.180713 | 7.37 | 14.07 | 18.63 | 7.42 | 15.41 | 20.04 |
| $H_0$:$r \leq 1$ | 0.001134 | 0.04 | 3.76 | 6.65 | 0.04 | 3.76 | 6.65 |

*(Continued)*

**Table 5.11:** *(Continued)*

**1950–2000**

| | Eigenvalues ($\lambda$) | Max-Eigen Test ($\lambda_{max}$) | Critical Value ($\lambda_{max}$) (5%) | Critical Value ($\lambda_{max}$) (1%) | The Trace Test ($\lambda_{trace}$) | Critical Value ($\lambda_{trace}$) (5%) | Critical Value ($\lambda_{trace}$) (1%) |
|---|---|---|---|---|---|---|---|
| **(1) LTG and LY (Var lag = 2)** | | | | | | | |
| $H_0:r = 0$ | 0.130486 | 6.57 | 14.07 | 18.63 | 6.60 | 15.41 | 20.04 |
| $H_0:r \leq 1$ | 0.000628 | 0.03 | 3.76 | 6.65 | 0.03 | 3.76 | 6.65 |
| **(2) LGFCE and LY (Var lag = 2)** | | | | | | | |
| $H_0:r = 0$ | 0.208156 | 11.20 | 14.07 | 18.63 | 11.27 | 15.41 | 20.04 |
| $H_0:r \leq 1$ | 0.001325 | 0.06 | 3.76 | 6.65 | 0.06 | 3.76 | 6.65 |
| **(3) LGFCF and LY (Var lag = 2)** | | | | | | | |
| $H_0:r = 0$ | 0.149644 | 7.62 | 14.07 | 18.63 | 8.03 | 15.41 | 20.04 |
| $H_0:r \leq 1$ | 0.008777 | 0.41 | 3.76 | 6.65 | 0.41 | 3.76 | 6.65 |
| **(4) LSTGY and LY (VAR lag = 2)** | | | | | | | |
| $H_0:r = 0$ | 0.130486 | 6.57 | 14.07 | 18.63 | 6.60 | 15.41 | 20.04 |
| $H_0:r \leq 1$ | 0.000628 | 0.03 | 3.76 | 6.65 | 0.03 | 3.76 | 6.65 |

*(Continued)*

**Table 5.11:** *(Continued)*

| | | | 1950–2000 | | | |
|---|---|---|---|---|---|---|
| Eigenvalues $(\lambda)$ | Max-Eigen Test $(\lambda_{max})$ | Critical Value $(\lambda_{max})$ (5%) | Critical Value $(\lambda_{max})$ (1%) | The Trace Test $(\lambda_{trace})$ | Critical Value $(\lambda_{trace})$ (5%) | Critical Value $(\lambda_{trace})$ (1%) |
| **(5) LSGFCEY and LY (Var lag = 2)** | | | | | | |
| $H_0$;$r = 0$    0.208156 | 11.20 | 14.07 | 18.63 | 6.60 | 15.41 | 20.04 |
| $H_0$;$r \leq 1$    0.001325 | 0.06 | 3.76 | 6.65 | 0.03 | 3.76 | 6.65 |
| **(6) LSGFCFY and LY (Var lag = 2)** | | | | | | |
| $H_0$;$r = 0$    0.149644 | 7.62 | 14.07 | 18.63 | 8.03 | 15.41 | 20.04 |
| $H_0$;$r \leq 1$    0.008777 | 0.41 | 3.76 | 6.65 | 0.41 | 3.76 | 6.65 |
| **(7) SBY and LY (Var lag = 2)** | | | | | | |
| $H_0$;$r = 0$    0.540674 | 14.18* | 14.07 | 18.63 | 14.29 | 15.41 | 20.04 |
| $H_0$;$r \leq 1$    0.200965 | 0.11 | 3.76 | 6.65 | 0.11 | 3.76 | 6.65 |

*Notes:* $(\lambda_{max})$ is the maximal Eigenvalue test statistic for at most $r$ cointegrating vectors against the alternative of $r + 1$ cointegrating vectors; $(\lambda_{trace})$ is the stochastic matrix trace test for at most $r$ cointegrating vectors.
* indicates significance at the 95% level.

**Table 5.12:** The Results of Granger Causality Tests, 1900–39 and 1950–2000

| | | 1900–39 | | | | |
|---|---|---|---|---|---|---|
| | | **F-Values** | | | | |
| | | **1 Lag** | **2 Lags** | **3 Lags** | **4 Lags** | **Direction(s)** |
| 1 | LY does not Granger cause LTG | 8.24 | 4.06 | 2.86 | 1.31 | LY→LTG |
| | LTG does not Granger cause LY | 3.40 | 2.90 | 2.64 | 1.51 | |
| 2 | LY does not Granger cause LGFCE | 8.36 | 5.03 | 3.69 | 3.70 | LY→LGFCE |
| | LGFCE does not Granger cause LY | 1.88 | 0.87 | 1.14 | 1.12 | |
| 3 | LY does not Granger cause LGFCF | 11.11 | 3.78 | 2.26 | 1.23 | LY→LGCF |
| | LGFCF does not Granger cause LY | 0.88 | 0.40 | 0.39 | 0.41 | |
| 4 | LY does not Granger cause LSTGY | 3.17 | 2.40 | 1.84 | 1.08 | LY~LSTGY |
| | LSTGY does not Granger cause LY | 3.41 | 2.90 | 2.64 | 1.51 | |
| 5 | LY does not Granger cause LSGFCEY | 0.00 | 0.03 | 0.41 | 2.42 | LY~LGFCEY |
| | LSGFCEY does not Granger cause LY | 1.89 | 0.88 | 1.15 | 1.12 | |
| 6 | LY does not Granger cause LSGFCFY | 3.41 | 1.60 | 1.09 | 0.58 | LY~LGFCFY |
| | LSGFCFY does not Granger cause LY | 0.89 | 0.40 | 0.39 | 0.42 | |
| 7 | Y does not Granger cause SBY | 10.53 | 5.69 | 3.92 | 3.23 | Y→SBY |
| | SBY does not Granger cause Y | 0.18 | 0.68 | 0.65 | 0.11 | |

(*Continued*)

**Table 5.12:**   (Continued)

| | | 1950–2000 | | | | |
| | | F-Values | | | | |
| | | 1 Lag | 2 Lags | 3 Lags | 4 Lags | Direction(s) |
|---|---|---|---|---|---|---|
| 1 | LY does not Granger cause LTG | 2.07 | 2.99 | 1.73 | 2.64 | |
| | LTG does not Granger cause LY | 4.33 | 0.72 | 1.93 | 3.69 | LY←LTG |
| 2 | LY does not Granger cause LGFCE | 0.34 | 1.16 | 2.37 | 1.77 | |
| | LGFCE does not Granger cause LY | 9.23 | 5.44 | 0.64 | 1.43 | LY←LGFCE |
| 3 | LY does not Granger cause LGFCF | 3.36 | 0.34 | 0.67 | 1.09 | LY~LGFCF |
| | LGFCF does not Granger cause LY | 2.02 | 1.61 | 2.65 | 1.47 | |
| 4 | LY does not Granger cause LSTGY | 0.02 | 2.44 | 1.38 | 1.08 | |
| | LSTGY does not Granger cause LY | 4.33 | 0.72 | 1.93 | 3.69 | LY←LSTGY |
| 5 | LY does not Granger cause LSGFCEY | 0.10 | 1.73 | 2.49 | 1.12 | |
| | LSGFCEY does not Granger cause LY | 9.23 | 5.44 | 0.93 | 1.43 | LY←LSGCY |
| 6 | LY does not Granger cause LSGFCFY | 0.84 | 0.05 | 0.46 | 0.83 | LY~LSGFCEY |
| | LSGFCFY does not Granger cause LY | 2.02 | 1.61 | 2.65 | 1.47 | |
| 7 | Y does not Granger cause SBY | 17.95 | 7.08 | 8.19 | 6.25 | Y→SBY |
| | SBY does not Granger cause Y | 0.09 | 0.17 | 0.94 | 1.01 | |

*Notes:*
→ indicates direction of causality running from the variable on the left to the one on the right.
← indicates the reverse.
~ indicates absence of causality
The related F-critical values at 5% significance level are 4.11, 3.30, 2.92, and 2.73, respectively.

for the period 1950–2000, respectively. In other words, the hypothesis that the change in GDP causes a change in government expenditure requires that the reverse is not true.

In respect of the prewar period, the growth of real GDP caused the growth of total government expenditure, government final consumption expenditure, government fixed capital formation, and share of government deficit to GDP. These results indicate that unidirectional causality ran mainly from economic growth to various components of government expenditure (TGE, GFCE, and GFCF), but not vice versa — results consistent with Wagner's hypothesis. In the case of postwar period, however, the direction has reversed. Causality is observed from various components and types of government expenditure to GDP. The growth of total government expenditure, government final consumption expenditure, share of total government expenditure to GDP, and share of government final consumption expenditure to GDP was found to cause the growth of real GDP.

## 5.6 Concluding Remarks

This study examines the relationship between the government's fiscal behavior and the economic growth of Singapore for the twentieth century. This research is driven by the hypothesis that the government's finance behavior in Singapore has experienced a significant shift due to the administrative changes from British colonial rule to that of self-government. First, this study conducts literature review and seeks the characteristics of the colonial government's finance behavior. Unlike self-government, the general principle of the government's finance behavior during the colonial period was the establishment of a balanced budget system so as not to create a financial burden to the colonial master's home country. To achieve this objective, the budgetary process was authorized by the people who represented the interests of the home country. Under these circumstances, the colonial government only undertook passive measures and did not implement any significant fiscal policy for economic growth.

Subsequently, the long-term transition of the government's fiscal behavior from the viewpoint of revenue raising, expenditure allocation, and budget management is examined. Significant changes in the government's finance behavior were observed between the pre– and post–World War II periods because of the abolishment of revenue from the sales of chandu and introduction of income tax. Within a short period of time, the size of revenue had experienced increases. Similarly, government expenditure also increased. Nevertheless, government expenditure management in Singapore has been conservative and prudent for the entire twentieth century. This is mainly due to the fact that during both periods the aim was to obtain a budget surplus, the proceeds of which were invested overseas in the form of portfolio financial investment though the motives differed between the colonial and postcolonial periods.

On the basis of this recognition, focus was given to identify whether any notable differences and similarities exist in the relationship between real government expenditure total government expenditure (TGE), government consumption expenditure (GFCE), government fixed capital formation (GFCF) share of TGE, GFCE and GFCF to GDP, and share of government budget balance to GDP, (SBY) in terms of direction and magnitude. For analytical purposes, two econometric techniques of cointegration and Granger causality test were initiated. Cointegration test result provided the existence of long-run equilibrium between (1) real GDP and real total government expenditure (equation 1) and (2) government final consumption expenditure and real GDP (equation 2) in prewar Singapore, while postwar Singapore recorded the cointegration of share of government budget balance to GDP and real GDP (equation 7). Hence a sufficient condition for causality was proved. However, the result of cointegration test could not establish any consistencies between the pre– and post–World War II periods. Subsequently, Granger causality test results suggest a different picture. In respect of the prewar period, the growth of real GDP caused the growth of TGE, GFCE, and GFCF. Similar phenomenon was observed for share of real total government expenditure and share of real total government capital formation. Additionally, the share of government budget surpluses to real GDP also depicted a similar direction. Generally, this result somewhat appeared to obey Wagner's law. Thus, it was economic growth that nurtured the expansion of government expenditure in the prewar period.

On the other hand, in the case of the post-war period, the direction and magnitude was the reverse. The growth of total government expenditure, government final consumption expenditure, share of total government expenditure to GDP, and share of government final consumption expenditure to GDP was found to cause the growth of real GDP. The policy of the post-Independence government of Singapore was to foster high economic growth to facilitate meeting its socioeconomic redistribution objectives. This may be based on the conviction that increasing government expenditure could help sustain economic growth. The need to spend to enhance the underlying productive capacity of the economy and preserve the sense of economic well-being of its population was also being constantly borne in mind.

# Chapter Six

# Conclusion

This study provides the estimates of the gross domestic product (GDP) of Singapore for the periods 1900–39 and 1950–60, in both current and constant prices. Subsequently, time-series data stretching over the twentieth century with one base year (1990 prices) were constructed for the purpose of econometric analysis.[103] On the basis of this historical GDP series and relevant time-series data, two types of empirical investigations on the long-term economic growth of Singapore were made, namely, (i) economic instability and economic growth and (ii) government fiscal behavior and economic growth.

This chapter firstly reviews the significance of the construction of historical GDP estimates as a new branch of research of the economic history of Singapore. It also describes the major findings on the overall patterns of Singapore's GDP and related empirical investigations on the long-term economic growth of Singapore. Lastly, limitations of this study and the area of future research area are outlined.

## 6.1 Significance of the Construction of Historical GDP Estimates of Singapore

Research on the long-term economic growth of Singapore has been hampered until now by the absence of long-term statistical

---

[103] Time-series data on GDP and its components for both prewar and postwar series were constructed on the basis of the concept and definitions of System of National Account, 1968.

series on national accounts prior to 1956. This explains why the existing literature on the economic development of Singapore prior to independence has been confined merely to studies on specific sectors. This phenomenon is not merely observed for Singapore. In fact, most of the former colonies in Asia and Africa faced a similar predicament.

In Western industrialized nations, however, the field of the construction of historical GDP estimates has been regarded as one of the dynamic branches of economic history. In fact, the construction of historical GDP estimates was closely associated with the creation and development of *The System of National Accounts* (SNA). Historical statistical data were scrutinized and recompiled in the form of national accounts and their validity was tested.

This existing research gap between developed and developing countries could mainly be attributed to the lack of statistical information in the case of the latter. More important, the absence of local experts who could initiate these types of exercises was another major obstacle as commented by Simon Kuznets. The emergence of interest for the construction of historical economic statistics in Asian countries began in the mid-1990s. In this regard, the Hitotsubashi University in Japan initiated the Asian Historical Statistic Project (ASHSTAT). Another research project by HRH Raja Dr Nazrin Shah in 1998 focused on the construction of historical GDP estimates of Malaya for the period 1900–39. This research project of Malaya has, in the process, immensely helped in the construction of a similar series for Singapore, which was a part of British Malaya during the British colonial period.

On the basis of the constraints of data availability during the period under study, it was decided to apply the expenditure approach rather than production and income approaches to obtain GDP estimates of Singapore. Various creative methodologies were applied but always consciously conforming, as closely as possible, to the definitions as outlined in *The System of National Accounts* (SNA) *1968*. The construction of historical

GDP estimates series of Singapore has in some measure helped to fill the existing research gap in quantifying the long-term economic growth of Singapore.

## 6.2 Major Findings

### 6.2.1 *Overall Patterns of Singapore's GDP for the Twentieth Century*

The estimate of long-term historical GDP series helped in the overview of the economic performance of Singapore. In constant terms (1990 prices), the annual average growth rates of GDP for the periods 1900–1939 and 1950–2000 were 4.4% and 7.2%, whereas growth rates of real per-capita GDP for similar periods were 1.4% and 4.6%, respectively. Both the results reinforce the historical fact that the overall growth rate of GDP during the post–World War II period was significantly higher than that of the pre–World War II period. Most notable negative growth rates during the twentieth century were recorded during the world economic depression years of 1930–31, namely –21% and –23%, respectively. In the pre-independence period (1900–39, 1950–64), the share of each component of GDP was relatively stable over time though there were occasional fluctuations. In contrast to this period, long-term structural changes were observed after the attainment of independence in 1965. In particular, private final consumption expenditure by resident households (PFCE) showed drastic falls from about 74% of GDP in the 1960s to around 40% at the end of the twentieth century.

A large fall of PFCE can be explained by the remarkable increase in gross domestic savings (GDS) over this long period (Peebles *et al.*, 2002, 78). This increase of the savings rate can be attributed to "forced savings" because the compulsory public contribution system in the form of the Central Provident Fund (CPF). Increases in savings provided the source for financing domestic investments as well as lending abroad. On the other hand, the share of government final consumption expenditure

(GFCE) to GDP remained fairly constant over the period. Generally, the share of gross capital formation (GCF) has gradually increased after independence, registering an increase from 20% to 40% within the 20-year period (1971–90). Thereafter, the share of GCF, however, has somewhat declined slightly to around 35% during the post-1990 period.

The most remarkable change was observed in the net exports of goods and services. From the beginning the twentieth century until the 1970s the figures on net exports of goods and services were negative, i.e., imports of goods and services exceeded exports for these years. However, from 1985 onward, these figures on the net exports of goods and services began to turn positive with exports of goods and services exceeding imports of goods and services over the next 15 years. Healthy current account balances were the result of gross national savings exceeding domestic investments.

### 6.2.2 *Economic Instability and Economic Growth in Singapore in the Twentieth Century*

This study adopts a historical perspective in examining the relationship between economic instability and economic growth of Singapore in the twentieth century. As has been observed, one unique characteristic of Singapore's economic structure is its high degree of openness to international trade. Inevitably, this economic structure which strongly relied on the external economic environment led to economic instability. In this study, economic instability is defined as the short-term fluctuations of real GDP after adjusting for trend. This study attempts to deal with three questions: First, the focus of the study was to ascertain whether the degree of output volatility had dampened over time. The second was to seek the explanatory variables which could statistically explain real GDP volatility. The third aims to seek the effect of economic instability on economic growth.

Relating to the first question above, GDP and its components experienced increases in economic instability from the pre–World War I period (1900–13) to the interwar period (1914–39). Subsequently, the degree of instability has constantly dampened in the third (1950–74) and fourth quarters (1975–2000) of the twentieth century. Nevertheless, the degree of instability of exports and imports of goods and services has not fallen as compared with other components of GDP. With regard to the second question, possible explanatory variables of sources of real GDP volatility were empirically tested. Contrary to findings made in other studies, the major sources of output volatilities were not determined by explanatory variables, such as share of government deficit to GDP, changes in trade as a share of GDP (%), and changes in terms of trade with 1-year time lag were not statistically significant. Relating to the third question of the effect of economic instability to economic growth, econometric tests found that export instability had a negative effect on economic growth during both the prewar and postwar periods. However, it became less of a problem in the latter half of the twentieth century as the structure of the economy became more diversified. Other than export instability, the coefficients of annual growth rate of exports as a proportion of GDP and annual growth rate of government final consumption expenditure as a proportion of GDP for the 1975–2000 turned positive and were statistically significant at 1% and 5% levels, respectively. However, the coefficient was very small and negligible.

### 6.2.3 *Government Fiscal Behavior and Economic Growth in Singapore in the Twentieth Century*

This study examines the issue of government fiscal behavior and economic growth of Singapore in the twentieth century. This research is driven by the hypothesis that government fiscal behavior in relation to economic growth in Singapore might have experienced a significant shift due to the administrative changes brought about in the process of transition from British colonial rule to one of self-government. First, this study examines the nature the of colonial government's fiscal behavior from the viewpoint of budgetary process, revenue raising, expenditure allocation and budget balance management, and the observation of long-term government fiscal behavior by extending the information to cover the rest of the twentieth century. Significant changes in government fiscal behavior were observed between the pre– and post–World War II periods because of the abolishment of revenue from the sale of opium and the subsequent introduction of income tax. This transition impacted on the revenue-raising capacity as well as the size of government expenditure. Nevertheless, both the British colonial government and the self-government after independence attempted to establish a balanced or even a budget surplus structure. The proceeds of government budget surplus were invested overseas in the form of portfolio financial investment though the motives differed between the colonial and postcolonial periods. Subsequently, in the same chapter, the validity of Wagner's law was tested. The hypothesis of a long-run equilibrium relationship between various government expenditure components and real GDP was tested using Johansen maximum likelihood technique. For the period 1900–39, long-term equilibrium relationships were found for (i) real GDP and total government expenditure, (ii) real GDP and government final consumption expenditure, and (iii) real GDP and government fixed capital formation for the period 1900–39. For the period 1950–2000, long-term equilibrium relationship was found between real GDP and share of budget surplus to GDP. The above results showed that there were no consistencies in terms of long-run equilibrium relationship between various government expenditure components and real GDP in the pre– and post–World War II periods.

Subsequently, the Granger causality test was conducted between GDP and various government expenditure components. The results suggest a different picture between pre– and post–World War II periods. In respect of the prewar period, the growth of real GDP caused the growth of total government expenditure, government final consumption expenditure and gross fixed capital formation. A similar phenomenon was observed for share of overall balance of budget to GDP. Generally, this result somewhat appeared to obey Wagner's law. Thus, it was economic growth that nurtured the expansion of government expenditure in the prewar period. On the other hand, in the case of the postwar period, the direction was the reverse. The growth of total government expenditure, government final consumption expenditure, share of total government expenditure to GDP, and share of government final consumption expenditure to GDP was found to cause the growth of real GDP. The policy of the post-Independence government of Singapore was to foster high economic growth to facilitate meeting its socioeconomic redistribution objectives. This may be based on the conviction that increasing government expenditure could help sustain economic growth.

## 6.3 Limitations of this Study and Future Research Areas

Confidence in the results obtained from a study can be reinforced if alternative approaches used yield results which are close and not too dissimilar. One major handicap of this study is that the alternative approaches, mainly the production and income methods in the construction of GDP estimates, cannot be undertaken simply because of the absence of statistical information required for their estimation. Unlike other agriculture-based countries, the major economic activities in Singapore were wholesale and retail trade. Thus, it was impossible to trace various types of relevant statistical information to conduct these estimates on the basis of the available British colonial data series. Under these constraints, historical GDP estimates of Singapore were confined to using only the expenditure approach and no other estimates were available for comparative purposes.

Notwithstanding the above constraints, the methodologies used in this study were tested for their reliability from the viewpoint of annual growth and share of each component of GDP.

Consistency check was done for data generated by this study with official figures available for certain overlapping years in particular 1959 and 1960. Additionally, the estimation procedures used in the study yielded results that were in conformity with economic events as contained in the official documents and records. Finally, the historical GDP estimates of Singapore were compared with the figures available for other countries for checks on patterns, levels, and trends and were found to be reasonable.

Future research in this area can include studies which cover several other aspects not covered in this study. First, the construction of historical GDP estimates can be undertaken for Singapore by extending the period of estimates of GDP to cover the earlier period 1870–1900. During this period, statistical data on government finance and trade were fortunately available with Singapore being treated as a separate entity and not treated as part of the Colony of Straits Settlements. It is significant to examine the economic performance of Singapore before the emergence of rubber as a major export commodity. Second, collection of supportive descriptive and quantitative information would be helpful to improve the reliability of historical GDP estimates. Third, it might be useful to construct estimates of purchasing power parity (PPP) converters for the expenditure side of the GDP of Singapore vis-à-vis other countries such as Japan, the United Kingdom, and the United States for the pre–World War II period.[104] These efforts will help to identify the level of real per-capita GDP of Singapore in relation to other countries. Fourth, it is important to conduct other empirical investigations in relation

---

[104] The estimation of purchasing power parity (PPP) converters for expenditure-side GDP of Singapore to common comparable unit (CCU) with proper base year requires a detailed matching of prices for many goods and services in private consumption, capital formation, and government expenditure. In the case of Asia, studies by Fukao, Kyoji, *et al.* (2006) and Fukao Kyoji and Ma (2006) provided estimates of PPP converters for Japan, Korea, Taiwan, and China with base year of 1933–34.

to the long-term economic growth of Singapore. One of the potential research areas is to conduct econometric modeling of Singapore during the British colonial period, as a followup to the study initiated by Abeysinghe *et al.* (2007) for the period 1960–2000. Finally, it might be interesting to know whether the methodology employed for the construction of historical GDP estimates of Singapore could be replicated for other former British colonies in Asia and Africa.

# Appendices

# Appendix 1

# Singapore: Cost-of-Living Indices by Major Object of Consumption and Consumption Standard, 1899–1914

No official cost-of-living indices were available throughout this period. Therefore, information on market prices and import unit value index was used to estimate the price indices for the period 1899–1914. The same classification of consumption standards and major objects of consumption item was used for the period 1914–39. The following estimating procedures were applied for each major object of consumption.

## 1 Food Price Indices

Information on annual average of market price of food items is available in the *Blue Book, Straits Settlements* for the period 1899–1914. Twelve (12) food items were available throughout the period. Each market price was then converted into price indices (1914 = 100). Unfortunately, weights within food items for the year 1914 were not available. In view of this, the weights reported in the per-capita private final consumption expenditure on food in 1949 as published in the *Annual Report of Labour Department, Colony of Singapore, 1949* were compared and evaluated with the one derived for the Malay and Chinese labor standard (1936) and Indian labor standards (1933). These three sources provided us a guideline in arriving at what were deemed to be the most likely weights of the food items, the results of which are presented in Appendix Table 1 below.

## 2 Tobacco/Tobacco and Beverages Price Indices

Statistical information on imports unit value of tobacco in Singapore for the years 1899–1912 was available in the *Statistical Tables Relating to the Colonial and Other Possessions of The United Kingdom* for the period 1900–01, the *Statistical Tables Relating to the Colonial and Other Possessions and Protectorates* for the period 1902–07, and the *Statistical Tables Relating to British Self-Governing Dominions, Crown Colonies, Possessions and Protectorates* for the period 1908–12. Subsequently, the import unit value indices derived from the *Annual Report on Report of Trade and Customs, Federated Malay States* series were alternatively applied for the period 1913–14. Tobacco and beverages price indices for the European Standard were constructed using a two-step procedure. At first, the price indices of beverages were constructed on the basis of the simple arithmetic average of market price indices of wine, brandy, and beer provided in the *Blue Book, Straits Settlements*. Subsequently, weights of tobacco and beverages were taken to be 0.85 and 0.15, respectively, on the basis of the European Standard as presented in the survey of Household Expenditure of Singapore (1930).

## 3 Clothing Price Indices

No market or import unit value of clothing was available throughout the period. Nevertheless, Singapore's import unit value of textiles comprising dyed, cotton yarn, gray cotton yarn, raw bleached cotton, and silk piece goods was used for the period 1899–1912 on the basis of the *Statistical Tables Relating to the Colonial and Other Possessions of The Uunited Kingdom* for the period 1900–01, *Statistical Tables Relating to the Colonial and Other Possessions and Protectorates* for the period 1902–07, and *Statistical Tables Relating to British Self-Governing Dominions,*

**Appendix Table 1:** The Assigned Weights of Food by Item for the Construction of Food Price Indices for All Standards

|  | Items | Quantity | Weights for 1914 (%) |
|---|---|---|---|
| 1 | Rice, white | per 133.3 lbs | 35.00 |
| 2 | Sugar, white | per kati | 2.00 |
| 3 | Salt | per kati | 2.00 |
| 4 | Beef | per lb | 4.50 |
| 5 | Mutton | per lb | 4.50 |
| 6 | Pork | per kati | 4.50 |
| 7 | Fish | per kati | 4.50 |
| 8 | Wheaten flour | per barrel of 196 lbs | 2.00 |
| 9 | Milk | per quart | 3.00 |
| 10 | Tea | per lb | 1.00 |
| 11 | Coffee | per 133.3 lbs | 1.00 |
| 12 | Others food index | | 36.00 |
| | | | 100.00 |

*Crown Colonies, Possessions and Protectorates* for the period 1908–12. Price indices (1914 = 100) were then computed by using a simple arithmetic average. Because of the lack of figures for the period 1913–14, import unit values of cotton piece goods for FMS were used for the period 1912–14 and linked with that of Singapore, on the basis of the conversion ratio of 1.10 in 1912.

## 4 Rent Price Indices

For the period 1908–14, the report created by the *Commissions Appointed by the Excellency the Governor of the Straits Settlements and the High Commissioner of the Federated Malay States* (1919) was used to compute the rent price indices for the European Standard. For the years 1900–07, however, no specific data were available to estimate the price movements of rent of dwellings. There is no other option but to apply the average growth rate of rental prices for the Asiatic and European Standards for the period 1900–07 on the basis of the average growth rate of 1908–14. The Asiatic Standard was then taken to represent the movement of rent for all labor standards. Owing to the weakness of the underlying data, the computation of these indices is inevitably subject to errors.

## 5  Servant Price Indices

The movement of the wage index of nonagricultural workers was found to move in tandem with the Singapore's cost-of-living index on servants from 1920 to 38. Taking into account this close relationship in the movement of these two indices, it was assumed that this relationship would also hold good for the period 1900–13 and the servants price index was calculated accordingly.

## 6  Club Price Indices

The price index for expenditure on clubs was based on the simple arithmetic average prices of "food" and "tobacco and beverages" consumed by those of the European Standard.

# Appendix 2

# Singapore: Cost-of-Living Indices by Major Object of Consumption and Consumption Standard, 1914–39

The publication *Average Prices, Declared Trade Values, Exchange, Currency and Cost-of-Living, Malaya, 1939* presented a continuous series of Singapore's cost-of-living indices (1914 = 100) for the period 1914 and 1918–38 for the European, Eurasian, and Asiatic Clerical Standards for various consumption categories such as food, beverages and tobacco, clothing, and rental. In addition, indices on servants and transport were available for the Eurasian and European Standards, whereas the clubbing index for the European Standard only. However, official data on cost-of-living index for the labor standard were not available. In view of this, the cost-of-living index of the Asiatic Clerical Standard was applied to the Chinese, Malay, and Indian labor standards. The following computation procedures were undertaken to establish the price indices for the missing years of 1915–17 and 1939 for each major object of consumption.

## 1 Food Price Indices for the Period 1915–17 and 1939

### 1.1 *Asiatic Standard*

For the construction of weighted food price indices for the Asiatic Standard, the following steps were taken: First, information on

313

the full-meat diet of Malay and Chinese labor standards in 1936 and that of Indian laborer's specimen monthly budget in 1933 was gathered to identify the appropriate weights for each food item for each labor standard. Second, unit market price series for each expenditure item for each standard was then constructed for the period 1914–39 on the basis of the market price data provided in the *Blue Book, Straits Settlements*. The unit market price series was then converted to an index with base year 1914 = 100. Third, using the weights on food items and the relevant price index of each labor standard, the weighted price index for each labor standard was then derived for the period 1914–39. The overall price index was then calculated by taking into account the base weights (1914) of private final consumption expenditure on food for each of the labor standards. This derived price index on food for the year 1918 stood at 155.72, whereas the cost-of-living index on food for the Asiatic Clerical Standard was recorded at 140.40 for the year 1918 using 1914 = 100. In light of this, the price index estimate on food required some minor adjustments. To bring it in line with the given cost-of-living index of food, an adjustment factor of 0.9016 (140.40/155.72) was applied for the period 1915–17. The food price index for the year 1939 was derived by applying the movement of the food prices which had been constructed.

## 1.2 *European and Eurasian Clerical Standards*

Data on the food index for European and Eurasian standards are available in respect of 1914 and 1918–38. Hence to fill the 1915–17 and 1939 gaps in the data, it is postulated that some relationship exists between the food index for the European and Eurasian Standards and the food index for Asiatic Clerical Standard for which data are available throughout 1914–39. The ordinary least squares estimate of the relationship over the period 1918–38 is as follows:

$$\ln \text{EPSFt} = 2.4317 + 0.54119 \ln \text{ASFt} - 0.015457\ \text{T}$$
$$\quad\quad (5.5175) \quad\quad\quad (6.6167) \quad (-4.3191)$$

$$R^2 = 0.9093$$

where     ln = Natural logarithm

      EPSF = Food index for European and Eurasian Standards

      ASF = Food index for Asiatic Clerical Standard

      T = Time trend

and figure in parentheses refer to the t-statistics.

The above-estimated equation could explain about 91% of the movements in the food index for European and Eurasian Standards and the estimated coefficients are all highly statistically significant.

The 1915–17 and 1939 figures of the food index for the European and Eurasian Standards were then derived by substituting the figures of the index for Asiatic Clerical Standard and the value of the time trend variable for the corresponding years in the above-estimated equation and then taking the anti-logs of such derived figures.

## 2 Price Indices of "Tobacco" and "Beverages and Tobacco" for the Period 1915–17 and 1939

### 2.1 *Tobacco Price Indices for the Asiatic and Eurasian Standards, 1915–17*

The price indices for tobacco were based on the import unit value of tobacco. The import unit value was then converted into price indices with the 1914 as base year. The price movements based on the import unit value were then compared with the price movements as recorded by Singapore's cost-of-living indices for tobacco for the period 1914–1918. It was noted that the import unit value index showed a price increase of 32.8% from 1914 to 1918, whereas the Singapore cost-of-living index showed a price increase of 74.3% for the same period. In other words, the import unit value index for 1918 was only 76.2% of the Singapore cost-of-living index. Using this observation, it is felt that the underestimation for the years 1915, 1916, and 1917 would also be of the same magnitude and thereafter applied a conversion factor (0.762) to ensure that the import unit value price indices were in line with the Singapore cost-of-living index for tobacco for the period 1915–17. The Singapore cost-of-living index for tobacco for the year 1938 was available, but not for 1939. The movement of tobacco price from 1938 to 1939 was solely based on the price movement of "unmanufactured tobacco" from 1938 to 1939.

## 2.2 *Beverages and Tobacco Price Indices for European Standard*

The methodology adopted to determine the tobacco price indices for the European Standard was similar to that for the Asiatic and Eurasian Standards. It was noted that there were no separate tobacco indices for the European Standard. Indices were available only for beverages and tobacco. Therefore, a beverages and tobacco index was constructed for the European Standard. The weights for expenditure on beverages (85%) and tobacco (15%) were based on the European Standard as contained in the survey of Household Expenditure of Singapore (1930). The price index for beverages for 1914–18 was based on the simple arithmetic average of the import unit value of brandy, gin, whisky, and wine, and for the years 1938, and on beer and ale, brandy, and whisky for 1939. The weighted indices of beverages and tobacco were then computed. For the period 1914–18, the Singapore cost-of-living indices showed that there was a 74.8% increase in price from 1914 to 1918, whereas the import unit value index showed a price increase of 114.46%. In other words, the indices computed based on the import unit value overstated the Singapore cost-of-living indices increase by 22.7% for the year 1918. The 1915, 1916, and 1917 data were adjusted accordingly on the basis of the import unit value indices. For the price increase from 1938 to 1939, the weighted (tobacco and beverages) import unit value price indices were applied.

# 3 Price Indices of Clothing for the Period 1915–17 and 1939

Detailed statistics on prices of clothing (c.i.f. values or market prices) were not available during this period. The only information available was the import unit value of "sarongs and selendangs" and "woolen cloth." It was not possible to assign the appropriate weights for each of these items. It was necessary to obtain detailed information on a number of clothing items to assign the proper weights for each of the items. The latter information was also not available. Therefore, there is no other option but to take the simple arithmetic average of the two groups of commodities to determine the price movements of clothing. This approach is rather crude in nature and is, therefore, subject to errors. It is noted that the price index from 1914 to 1918 had risen from 100.00 to 129.13 on the basis of the import unit value index, whereas the Singapore cost-of-living index for clothing showed that the price index had risen from 100.00 in 1914 to 189.80 in 1918. This meant that the import unit value index for 1918 was only 68% of the Singapore cost-of-living index in 1918. Using this observation, it was felt that the underestimation for the years 1915, 1916, and 1917 would be of the same magnitude and thereafter applied an adjustment factor of 0.68 to ensure that the import unit value indices were in line with the Singapore cost-of-living indices for clothing for the period 1915–17. The Singapore cost-of-living indices for clothing for all standards were identical from 1918–30. From 1931 and thereafter, the European Standard prices on clothing differed from the price movements of clothing of all other standards. However, the price movement of clothing for all standards (except the European Standard from 1931 and thereafter) continued to be identical throughout the period 1918–38. The estimates for clothing for the year 1939 were based on the simple arithmetic average of the import unit value of silk piece goods, woolen cloth, cotton piece goods (dyed and other), and cotton sarong. There was an 8.7% increase in cloth prices from 1938 to 1939. This price increase was then applied to the

Singapore cost-of-living price indices for 1938 to arrive at the clothing price indices of the respective standards.

## 4 Price Indices of Rental of Dwellings, 1915–17 and 1939

### 4.1 *Asiatic and All Labor Standards*

There were no comprehensive housing censuses prior to World War I. No data were available on the total number of dwellings by types of units (e.g., bungalows, semi-detached, etc.). Only scanty data were available on rental values of dwellings from 1908 to 19 in Singapore in the urban areas. Information on the rental values in Singapore was available, ranging from $25 to $60 per month for 26 housing units. Using these data, it was assumed that the movements of the rental values of these types of units would provide a fairly reliable movement in the price of rentals of dwellings of the Asiatic and all labor standards in Malaya. These data were used to compute the rental of dwelling indices from 1908 to 19 (1914 = 100). Figures on the Asiatic rental value indices of dwellings were available from the Singapore cost-of-living indices for the years 1918 and 1919. A comparison was made with the Singapore rental price indices (cost-of-living) with that of the data computed using the 26 sample dwellings from the *Commissions Appointed by the Excellency the Governor of the Straits Settlements and the High Commissioner of the Federated Malay States* (1919). The results are presented in Appendix Table 2.

**Appendix Table 2:** Price Indices on Rent for Asiatic Standard

|  | 1918 | 1919 |
|---|---|---|
| Bucknill report | 117.40 | 130.60 |
| Singapore cost-of-living indices (rental of dwellings) | 120.00 | 130.00 |

The fact that the 1918 and 1919 rental indices from the two sources of data are almost identical or close to each other provides us the confidence that the indices computed from the 26 housing units will also provide a fairly reasonable estimate of the rental value of dwellings from 1908 to 17. Consequently, it was decided that for the Asiatic Clerical and all labor standards, the rental indices computed in this manner would be used in the computation of the cost-of-living indices for Singapore.

## 4.2 *European Standard*

*Commissions Appointed by the Excellency the Governor of the Straits Settlements and the High Commissioner of the Federated Malay States* (1919) listed down the rental value price indices of 23 units of dwellings whose rentals ranged from S$65 a month to S$170. Using the data set from the Bucknill report, it was noted that for the years 1918 and 1919, when compared with the Singapore cost-of-living indices on rentals, the estimates based on the 23 units of dwellings from the "Bucknill Report" far exceeded the Singapore cost-of-living rental indices. This being the case, it was decided that an alternative approach needs to be taken to identify and compute the rental of dwelling indices that would conform to the 1918 and 1919 cost-of-living indices. The seven selected housing units provided us a series in which the 1918 and 1919 data conformed to the 1918 and 1919 cost-of-living indices data on rentals of dwellings in Singapore. It was felt that this series for some reason or other provided us a probable estimate for the years 1908–17 for the European Standard.

## 4.3 *Price of Rental Value Indices for the Year 1939 for the Different Standards*

The cost-of-living indices on rent by standards were not available for the year 1939. Surrogate data had to be used to estimate the rent by standards for the year 1939. It was felt that the change in the assessment values from 1938 to 1939 as contained in *Average Prices, Declared Trade Values, Exchange and Currency, Malaya, 1939* report would provide a reasonable estimate of the changes in the rental values (price) from 1938 to 1939. For the European Standard, the average of group III (rental price range: $100–$350) was selected, whereas that for the Eurasians, Asiatic Clerical, and all labor standards, the average of Group I (rental price range: less than $49) was taken.

## 5 Servant Price Indices for Asiatic, Eurasian, and European Standards

Data for the servant price indices for the period 1915–17 and 1939 are rather weak. An attempt was made to establish whether there was a relationship between the Singapore cost-of-living price indices of servants to that of nominal wage indices of non-agriculture (trades and Indian factory labor) and agriculture (Indian rubber estate tappers) workers. It was noted that from 1920 to 1929 the nominal wage rate of nonagriculture workers and that of Singapore cost-of-living indices for servants remained rather stable though the levels differed. In general, the nominal wage of nonagriculture workers by and large moved in the same direction as the Singapore cost-of-living indices of servants from 1920 to 1938. Taking into account the stable relationship of movements of nonagricultural worker's wage indices to the Singapore cost-of-living indices of servants, particularly 1900–29, the relationship of 1918 indices of nonagriculture workers to that of Singapore cost-of-living indices of servants was applied for the period 1915–17. The estimates done in this manner are admittedly subject to errors. It was noted that the nominal wage rate indices of nonagriculture workers in 1937 and 1938 remained relatively stable. The Singapore cost-of-living indices of servants also remained relatively stable in 1937 and 1938. The price indices in 1939 for nonagricultural workers continued to remain as in 1937 and 1938 and it is therefore felt that the Singapore cost-of-living servant indices would also remain the same in 1939 as in 1938.

## 6 Transport Price Indices for Asiatic, Eurasian, and European Standards

Per-capita transport and traveling allowances price indices (Straits Settlements) for the European Standard were computed on the basis of the UK travel and vehicle consumer price index for the period 1900–17 (Prest, 1954, 135). Surprisingly, the price index for this item was generally stable from 1900 to 1916. Notable price increases were observed in 1917, 1918, and 1919, as compared to 1914. It was then assumed that the transport price index of the United Kingdom would more or less portray the movements of transport price indices of the European Standard. However, for the year 1917, I would assume that the UK indices overstate the actual price indices and therefore an adjustment factor had to be introduced to smooth the price increase from 1917 to 1918. The price index of Singapore for transport for 1918–38 remained status quo. The 1939 price indices were estimated on the basis of the wholesale prices of petrol (London Chamber of Commerce Journal).

## 7 Price Indices of Clubs for European Standard for the Period 1915–17 and 1939

The price indices for expenditure in clubs were based on the simple arithmetic average of "food" and "beverages and tobacco" consumed by the European Standard. It was noted that the "club" price index based on the import unit value showed a price increase of 55.65% from 1914 to 1918, whereas the Singapore cost-of-living index showed a price increase of 34% for the same period. In other words, the import unit value index for 1918 overstated the price increase by 16.2%. Using this observation, it was felt that the overestimation for the years 1915–17 would also be of the same magnitude and consequently applied an adjustment factor of 1.162 to ensure that the import unit value price indices were in line with the Singapore cost-of-living indices for "clubbing" for the period 1915–17. The Singapore cost-of-living index for "clubbing" for the year 1938 was available but not for 1939. The price index for "clubbing" was solely based on the simple arithmetic average price movements of "food" and "beverages and tobacco" from 1938 to 1939.

# Appendix 3

# Singapore: Cost-of-Living Indices by Major Object of Consumption and Consumption Standard, 1939 and 1947–60

The monthly statistical bulletin, *Federation of Malaya* provided the cost-of-living indices by major object of consumption for the labor standards with the base year of 1947 and 1959 and other standards (Chinese, Indian, and Eurasian Clerical Standards, Malay Clerical Standard, and European Standard) with the base year 1939 and 1947, respectively. For the labor standards, price data by major object of consumption were not available for the reference years 1939 and 1948, whereas that for the other standards they were not available for the year 1947. The missing year data for each of the consumer standards were computed in the following manner.

The price data for Chinese and Indian labor standards for the year 1948 were based on the given price movements by each major object of consumption of the Chinese, Indian, and Eurasian Standards from 1948 to 1949. The price indices for the same year, Malay labor standard on the other hand, were based on the price movements of each major object of consumption of the Malay clerical grades standard from 1948 to 1949.

The price movements by major object of consumption for the year 1947 for all other consumption standards were computed as follows:

[a]  The Chinese, Indian, and Eurasian Clerical Standard price index was based on the price movements of each major object of consumption of the Chinese labor standard from 1947 to 1948.

[b]  The Malay clerical grades standard price index was based on the price movement of each major object of consumption of the Malay labor standard from 1947 to 1948.

[c]  The European Standard price index was based on the price movement of each major object of consumption of the Chinese labor standard from 1947 to 1948.

The price index of transport and servants for the year 1947 for the "Chinese, Indian, and Eurasian Clerical" and "European" Standards was based on the price movements of petrol prices and nonagricultural wage indices from 1947 to 1948. These estimates are, therefore, subject to large errors.

In the case of European Standard, the price index for clubbing for the year 1947 was based on the simple arithmetic average of "food and beverages" and "tobacco." The price indices for the Chinese and Indian labor standards in 1939 were based on the derived price movements of the Chinese, Indian, and Eurasian Clerical Standard from 1939 to 1947, whereas that of the Malay labour standard was based on the price movements of the Malay clerical grades standard for the same period. The different base years data were then linked to derive price indices for the entire period 1939–60 with 1949 as the base year.

## Appendix Table 3: Singapore: Computation of Consumer Price Indices by Major Object of Consumption (1914 = 100), 1899–1914

| Food and Groceries | 1914 Weight | 1899 Price Index (1914 = 100) | 1899 Weighted Index | 1900 Price Index (1914 = 100) | 1900 Weighted Index | 1901 Price Index (1914 = 100) | 1901 Weighted Index | 1902 Price Index (1914 = 100) | 1902 Weighted Index | 1903 Price Index (1914 = 100) | 1903 Weighted Index |
|---|---|---|---|---|---|---|---|---|---|---|---|
| Chinese Labor Standard | 0.479 | 81.12 | 38.88 | 81.97 | 39.28 | 82.91 | 39.73 | 85.51 | 40.98 | 85.51 | 40.98 |
| Malay Labor Standard | 0.130 | 81.12 | 10.55 | 81.97 | 10.65 | 82.91 | 10.78 | 85.51 | 11.11 | 85.51 | 11.11 |
| Indian Labor Standard | 0.058 | 81.12 | 4.73 | 81.97 | 4.78 | 82.91 | 4.84 | 85.51 | 4.99 | 85.51 | 4.99 |
| Asiatic Clerical Standard | 0.095 | 81.12 | 7.73 | 81.97 | 7.82 | 82.91 | 7.90 | 85.51 | 8.15 | 85.51 | 8.15 |
| Eurasian Clerical Standard | 0.012 | 81.12 | 0.99 | 81.97 | 1.00 | 82.91 | 1.01 | 85.51 | 1.04 | 85.51 | 1.04 |
| European Standard | 0.225 | 81.12 | 18.25 | 81.97 | 18.44 | 82.91 | 18.65 | 85.51 | 19.23 | 85.51 | 19.23 |
| | 1.000 | | *81.12* | | *81.97* | | *82.91* | | *85.51* | | *85.51* |

| Tobacco | 1914 Weight | 1899 Price Index (1914 = 100) | 1899 Weighted Index | 1900 Price Index (1914 = 100) | 1900 Weighted Index | 1901 Price Index (1914 = 100) | 1901 Weighted Index | 1902 Price Index (1914 = 100) | 1902 Weighted Index | 1903 Price Index (1914 = 100) | 1903 Weighted Index |
|---|---|---|---|---|---|---|---|---|---|---|---|
| Chinese Labor Standard | 0.304 | 68.18 | 20.70 | 71.97 | 21.85 | 68.67 | 20.85 | 76.48 | 23.22 | 85.38 | 25.92 |
| Malay Labor Standard | 0.107 | 68.18 | 7.32 | 71.97 | 7.72 | 68.67 | 7.37 | 76.48 | 8.21 | 85.38 | 9.16 |
| Indian Labor Standard | 0.064 | 68.18 | 4.35 | 71.97 | 4.59 | 68.67 | 4.38 | 76.48 | 4.88 | 85.38 | 5.45 |
| Asiatic Clerical Standard | 0.035 | 68.18 | 2.41 | 71.97 | 2.54 | 68.67 | 2.43 | 76.48 | 2.70 | 85.38 | 3.02 |
| Eurasian Clerical Standard | 0.004 | 68.18 | 0.27 | 71.97 | 0.29 | 68.67 | 0.28 | 76.48 | 0.31 | 85.38 | 0.34 |
| European Standard | 0.486 | 95.23 | 46.27 | 95.80 | 46.54 | 95.30 | 46.30 | 96.47 | 46.87 | 97.81 | 47.52 |
| | 1.000 | | *81.32* | | *83.55* | | *81.61* | | *86.19* | | *91.42* |

| Clothing | 1914 Weight | 1899 Price Index (1914 = 100) | 1899 Weighted Index | 1900 Price Index (1914 = 100) | 1900 Weighted Index | 1901 Price Index (1914 = 100) | 1901 Weighted Index | 1902 Price Index (1914 = 100) | 1902 Weighted Index | 1903 Price Index (1914 = 100) | 1903 Weighted Index |
|---|---|---|---|---|---|---|---|---|---|---|---|
| Chinese Labor Standard | 0.289 | 76.31 | 22.04 | 78.94 | 22.81 | 84.45 | 24.40 | 86.79 | 25.07 | 92.79 | 26.81 |
| Malay Labor Standard | 0.083 | 76.31 | 6.31 | 78.94 | 6.53 | 84.45 | 6.98 | 86.79 | 7.18 | 92.79 | 7.67 |
| Indian Labor Standard | 0.028 | 76.31 | 2.10 | 78.94 | 2.17 | 84.45 | 2.33 | 86.79 | 2.39 | 92.79 | 2.55 |
| Asiatic Clerical Standard | 0.081 | 76.31 | 6.19 | 78.94 | 6.40 | 84.45 | 6.85 | 86.79 | 7.04 | 92.79 | 7.53 |
| Eurasian Clerical Standard | 0.009 | 76.31 | 0.70 | 78.94 | 0.73 | 84.45 | 0.78 | 86.79 | 0.80 | 92.79 | 0.86 |
| European Standard | 0.511 | 76.31 | 38.96 | 78.94 | 40.30 | 84.45 | 43.11 | 86.79 | 44.31 | 92.79 | 47.37 |
| | 1.000 | | *76.31* | | *78.94* | | *84.45* | | *86.79* | | *92.79* |

| Rent | 1914 Weight | 1899 Price Index (1914 = 100) | 1899 Weighted Index | 1900 Price Index (1914 = 100) | 1900 Weighted Index | 1901 Price Index (1914 = 100) | 1901 Weighted Index | 1902 Price Index (1914 = 100) | 1902 Weighted Index | 1903 Price Index (1914 = 100) | 1903 Weighted Index |
|---|---|---|---|---|---|---|---|---|---|---|---|
| Chinese Labor Standard | 0.181 | 69.37 | 12.58 | 71.08 | 12.89 | 72.84 | 13.21 | 74.63 | 13.53 | 76.48 | 13.87 |
| Malay Labor Standard | 0.041 | 69.37 | 2.81 | 71.08 | 2.88 | 72.84 | 2.95 | 74.63 | 3.03 | 76.48 | 3.10 |
| Indian Labor Standard | 0.028 | 69.37 | 1.97 | 71.08 | 2.02 | 72.84 | 2.07 | 74.63 | 2.12 | 76.48 | 2.18 |
| Asiatic Clerical Standard | 0.165 | 69.37 | 11.41 | 71.08 | 11.70 | 72.84 | 11.98 | 74.63 | 12.28 | 76.48 | 12.58 |
| Eurasian Clerical Standard | 0.019 | 69.37 | 1.30 | 71.08 | 1.33 | 72.84 | 1.36 | 74.63 | 1.40 | 76.48 | 1.43 |
| European Standard | 0.566 | 79.35 | 44.95 | 80.58 | 45.64 | 81.84 | 46.35 | 83.11 | 47.07 | 84.40 | 47.81 |
| | 1.000 | | *75.02* | | *76.46* | | *77.93* | | *79.43* | | *80.96* |

| Servant | 1914 Weight | 1899 Price Index (1914 = 100) | 1899 Weighted Index | 1900 Price Index (1914 = 100) | 1900 Weighted Index | 1901 Price Index (1914 = 100) | 1901 Weighted Index | 1902 Price Index (1914 = 100) | 1902 Weighted Index | 1903 Price Index (1914 = 100) | 1903 Weighted Index |
|---|---|---|---|---|---|---|---|---|---|---|---|
| Asiatic Clerical Standard | 0.051 | 69.64 | 3.53 | 75.00 | 3.80 | 73.21 | 3.71 | 82.14 | 4.16 | 82.14 | 4.16 |
| Eurasian Clerical Standard | 0.006 | 69.64 | 0.40 | 75.00 | 0.43 | 73.21 | 0.42 | 82.14 | 0.47 | 82.14 | 0.47 |
| European Standard | 0.944 | 69.64 | 65.71 | 75.00 | 70.77 | 73.21 | 69.08 | 82.14 | 77.51 | 82.14 | 77.51 |
| | 1.000 | | *69.64* | | *75.00* | | *73.21* | | *82.14* | | *82.14* |

| Transport | 1914 Weight | 1899 Price Index (1914 = 100) | 1899 Weighted Index | 1900 Price Index (1914 = 100) | 1900 Weighted Index | 1901 Price Index (1914 = 100) | 1901 Weighted Index | 1902 Price Index (1914 = 100) | 1902 Weighted Index | 1903 Price Index (1914 = 100) | 1903 Weighted Index |
|---|---|---|---|---|---|---|---|---|---|---|---|
| Asiatic Clerical Standard | 0.165 | 109.66 | 18.08 | 107.87 | 17.78 | 107.44 | 17.71 | 107.23 | 17.67 | 107.34 | 17.69 |
| Eurasian Clerical Standard | 0.019 | 109.66 | 2.05 | 107.87 | 2.02 | 107.44 | 2.01 | 107.23 | 2.01 | 107.34 | 2.01 |
| European Standard | 0.816 | 109.66 | 89.53 | 107.87 | 88.07 | 107.44 | 87.72 | 107.23 | 87.54 | 107.34 | 87.63 |
| | 1.000 | | *109.66* | | *107.87* | | *107.44* | | *107.23* | | *107.34* |

| Club | 1914 Weight | 1899 Price Index (1914 = 100) | 1899 Weighted Index | 1900 Price Index (1914 = 100) | 1900 Weighted Index | 1901 Price Index (1914 = 100) | 1901 Weighted Index | 1902 Price Index (1914 = 100) | 1902 Weighted Index | 1903 Price Index (1914 = 100) | 1903 Weighted Index |
|---|---|---|---|---|---|---|---|---|---|---|---|
| European Standard | 1.000 | 88.18 | 88.18 | 88.88 | 88.88 | 89.10 | 89.10 | 90.99 | 90.99 | 91.66 | 91.66 |
| | | | *88.18* | | *88.88* | | *89.10* | | *90.99* | | *91.66* |

| | 1914 Weight | 1899 Price Index (1914 = 100) | 1899 Weighted Index | 1900 Price Index (1914 = 100) | 1900 Weighted Index | 1901 Price Index (1914 = 100) | 1901 Weighted Index | 1902 Price Index (1914 = 100) | 1902 Weighted Index | 1903 Price Index (1914 = 100) | 1903 Weighted Index |
|---|---|---|---|---|---|---|---|---|---|---|---|
| Food | 0.5429 | 81.12 | 44.04 | 81.97 | 44.50 | 82.91 | 45.01 | 85.51 | 46.42 | 85.51 | 46.42 |
| Tobacco | 0.0561 | 81.32 | 4.56 | 83.55 | 4.69 | 81.61 | 4.58 | 86.19 | 4.83 | 91.42 | 5.13 |
| Clothing | 0.1082 | 76.31 | 8.26 | 78.94 | 8.54 | 84.45 | 9.14 | 86.79 | 9.39 | 92.79 | 10.04 |
| Rent | 0.0594 | 75.02 | 4.46 | 76.46 | 4.54 | 77.93 | 4.63 | 79.43 | 4.72 | 80.96 | 4.81 |
| Servant | 0.1218 | 69.64 | 8.48 | 75.00 | 9.13 | 73.21 | 8.91 | 82.14 | 10.00 | 82.14 | 10.00 |
| Transport | 0.0739 | 109.66 | 8.11 | 107.87 | 7.98 | 107.44 | 7.94 | 107.23 | 7.93 | 107.34 | 7.94 |
| Club | 0.0377 | 88.18 | 3.33 | 88.88 | 3.35 | 89.10 | 3.36 | 90.99 | 3.43 | 91.66 | 3.46 |
| | 1.0000 | | *81.23* | | *82.73* | | *83.57* | | *86.73* | | *87.79* |

*(Continued)*

## Appendix Table 3: (*Continued*)

| Food and Groceries | 1914 Weight | 1904 Price Index (1914 = 100) | 1904 Weighted Index | 1905 Price Index (1914 = 100) | 1905 Weighted Index | 1906 Price Index (1914 = 100) | 1906 Weighted Index | 1907 Price Index (1914 = 100) | 1907 Weighted Index | 1908 Price Index (1914 = 100) | 1908 Weighted Index |
|---|---|---|---|---|---|---|---|---|---|---|---|
| Chinese Labor Standard | 0.479 | 87.28 | 41.83 | 90.18 | 43.21 | 87.80 | 42.07 | 85.69 | 41.06 | 87.02 | 41.70 |
| Malay Labor Standard | 0.130 | 87.28 | 11.35 | 90.18 | 11.72 | 87.80 | 11.41 | 85.69 | 11.14 | 87.02 | 11.31 |
| Indian Labor Standard | 0.058 | 87.28 | 5.09 | 90.18 | 5.26 | 87.80 | 5.12 | 85.69 | 5.00 | 87.02 | 5.08 |
| Asiatic Clerical Standard | 0.095 | 87.28 | 8.32 | 90.18 | 8.60 | 87.80 | 8.37 | 85.69 | 8.17 | 87.02 | 8.30 |
| Eurasian Clerical Standard | 0.012 | 87.28 | 1.06 | 90.18 | 1.10 | 87.80 | 1.07 | 85.69 | 1.04 | 87.02 | 1.06 |
| European Standard | 0.225 | 87.28 | 19.63 | 90.18 | 20.28 | 87.80 | 19.75 | 85.69 | 19.27 | 87.02 | 19.57 |
| | 1.000 | | *87.28* | | *90.18* | | *87.80* | | *85.69* | | *87.02* |

| Tobacco | 1914 Weight | 1904 Price Index (1914 = 100) | 1904 Weighted Index | 1905 Price Index (1914 = 100) | 1905 Weighted Index | 1906 Price Index (1914 = 100) | 1906 Weighted Index | 1907 Price Index (1914 = 100) | 1907 Weighted Index | 1908 Price Index (1914 = 100) | 1908 Weighted Index |
|---|---|---|---|---|---|---|---|---|---|---|---|
| Chinese Labor Standard | 0.304 | 77.75 | 23.61 | 81.96 | 24.89 | 76.51 | 23.23 | 82.79 | 25.14 | 83.64 | 25.40 |
| Malay Labor Standard | 0.107 | 77.75 | 8.34 | 81.96 | 8.80 | 76.51 | 8.21 | 82.79 | 8.89 | 83.64 | 8.98 |
| Indian Labor Standard | 0.064 | 77.75 | 4.96 | 81.96 | 5.23 | 76.51 | 4.88 | 82.79 | 5.29 | 83.64 | 5.34 |
| Asiatic Clerical Standard | 0.035 | 77.75 | 2.75 | 81.96 | 2.90 | 76.51 | 2.70 | 82.79 | 2.93 | 83.64 | 2.96 |
| Eurasian Clerical Standard | 0.004 | 77.75 | 0.31 | 81.96 | 0.33 | 76.51 | 0.31 | 82.79 | 0.33 | 83.64 | 0.34 |
| European Standard | 0.486 | 96.66 | 46.96 | 97.29 | 47.27 | 96.48 | 46.87 | 97.42 | 47.33 | 97.55 | 47.39 |
| | 1.000 | | *86.94* | | *89.41* | | *86.21* | | *89.90* | | *90.40* |

| Clothing | 1914 Weight | 1904 Price Index (1914 = 100) | 1904 Weighted Index | 1905 Price Index (1914 = 100) | 1905 Weighted Index | 1906 Price Index (1914 = 100) | 1906 Weighted Index | 1907 Price Index (1914 = 100) | 1907 Weighted Index | 1908 Price Index (1914 = 100) | 1908 Weighted Index |
|---|---|---|---|---|---|---|---|---|---|---|---|
| Chinese Labor Standard | 0.289 | 90.19 | 26.06 | 87.98 | 25.42 | 84.42 | 24.39 | 82.99 | 23.98 | 86.31 | 24.93 |
| Malay Labor Standard | 0.083 | 90.19 | 7.46 | 87.98 | 7.28 | 84.42 | 6.98 | 82.99 | 6.86 | 86.31 | 7.14 |
| Indian Labor Standard | 0.028 | 90.19 | 2.48 | 87.98 | 2.42 | 84.42 | 2.32 | 82.99 | 2.29 | 86.31 | 2.38 |
| Asiatic Clerical Standard | 0.081 | 90.19 | 7.32 | 87.98 | 7.14 | 84.42 | 6.85 | 82.99 | 6.73 | 86.31 | 7.00 |
| Eurasian Clerical Standard | 0.009 | 90.19 | 0.83 | 87.98 | 0.81 | 84.42 | 0.78 | 82.99 | 0.77 | 86.31 | 0.80 |
| European Standard | 0.511 | 90.19 | 46.05 | 87.98 | 44.92 | 84.42 | 43.10 | 82.99 | 42.37 | 86.31 | 44.06 |
| | 1.000 | | *90.19* | | *87.98* | | *84.42* | | *82.99* | | *86.31* |

| Rent | 1914 Weight | 1904 Price Index (1914 = 100) | 1904 Weighted Index | 1905 Price Index (1914 = 100) | 1905 Weighted Index | 1906 Price Index (1914 = 100) | 1906 Weighted Index | 1907 Price Index (1914 = 100) | 1907 Weighted Index | 1908 Price Index (1914 = 100) | 1908 Weighted Index |
|---|---|---|---|---|---|---|---|---|---|---|---|
| Chinese Labor Standard | 0.181 | 78.36 | 14.21 | 80.30 | 14.56 | 82.28 | 14.92 | 84.31 | 15.29 | 86.39 | 15.66 |
| Malay Labor Standard | 0.041 | 78.36 | 3.18 | 80.30 | 3.26 | 82.28 | 3.34 | 84.31 | 3.42 | 86.39 | 3.50 |
| Indian Labor Standard | 0.028 | 78.36 | 2.23 | 80.30 | 2.29 | 82.28 | 2.34 | 84.31 | 2.40 | 86.39 | 2.46 |
| Asiatic Clerical Standard | 0.165 | 78.36 | 12.89 | 80.30 | 13.21 | 82.28 | 13.54 | 84.31 | 13.87 | 86.39 | 14.21 |
| Eurasian Clerical Standard | 0.019 | 78.36 | 1.47 | 80.30 | 1.50 | 82.28 | 1.54 | 84.31 | 1.58 | 86.39 | 1.62 |
| European Standard | 0.566 | 85.71 | 48.55 | 87.04 | 49.30 | 88.40 | 50.07 | 89.77 | 50.85 | 91.16 | 51.64 |
| | 1.000 | | *82.53* | | *84.12* | | *85.74* | | *87.40* | | *89.09* |

| Servant | 1914 Weight | 1904 Price Index (1914 = 100) | 1904 Weighted Index | 1905 Price Index (1914 = 100) | 1905 Weighted Index | 1906 Price Index (1914 = 100) | 1906 Weighted Index | 1907 Price Index (1914 = 100) | 1907 Weighted Index | 1908 Price Index (1914 = 100) | 1908 Weighted Index |
|---|---|---|---|---|---|---|---|---|---|---|---|
| Asiatic Clerical Standard | 0.051 | 78.57 | 3.98 | 78.57 | 3.98 | 82.14 | 4.16 | 91.07 | 4.62 | 91.07 | 4.62 |
| Eurasian Clerical Standard | 0.006 | 78.57 | 0.45 | 78.57 | 0.45 | 82.14 | 0.47 | 91.07 | 0.52 | 91.07 | 0.52 |
| European Standard | 0.944 | 78.57 | 74.14 | 78.57 | 74.14 | 82.14 | 77.51 | 91.07 | 85.93 | 91.07 | 85.93 |
| | 1.000 | | *78.57* | | *78.57* | | *82.14* | | *91.07* | | *91.07* |

| Transport | 1914 Weight | 1904 Price Index (1914 = 100) | 1904 Weighted Index | 1905 Price Index (1914 = 100) | 1905 Weighted Index | 1906 Price Index (1914 = 100) | 1906 Weighted Index | 1907 Price Index (1914 = 100) | 1907 Weighted Index | 1908 Price Index (1914 = 100) | 1908 Weighted Index |
|---|---|---|---|---|---|---|---|---|---|---|---|
| Asiatic Clerical Standard | 0.165 | 107.23 | 17.67 | 107.12 | 17.66 | 107.23 | 17.67 | 105.07 | 17.32 | 104.64 | 17.25 |
| Eurasian Clerical Standard | 0.019 | 107.23 | 2.01 | 107.12 | 2.01 | 107.23 | 2.01 | 105.07 | 1.97 | 104.64 | 1.96 |
| European Standard | 0.816 | 107.23 | 87.54 | 107.12 | 87.46 | 107.23 | 87.54 | 105.07 | 85.78 | 104.64 | 85.43 |
| | 1.000 | | *107.23* | | *107.12* | | *107.23* | | *105.07* | | *104.64* |

| Club | 1914 Weight | 1904 Price Index (1914 = 100) | 1904 Weighted Index | 1905 Price Index (1914 = 100) | 1905 Weighted Index | 1906 Price Index (1914 = 100) | 1906 Weighted Index | 1907 Price Index (1914 = 100) | 1907 Weighted Index | 1908 Price Index (1914 = 100) | 1908 Weighted Index |
|---|---|---|---|---|---|---|---|---|---|---|---|
| European Standard | 1.000 | 91.97 | 91.97 | 93.74 | 93.74 | 92.14 | 92.14 | 91.55 | 91.55 | 92.28 | 92.28 |
| | | | *91.97* | | *93.74* | | *92.14* | | *91.55* | | *92.28* |

| | 1914 Weight | 1904 Price Index (1914 = 100) | 1904 Weighted Index | 1905 Price Index (1914 = 100) | 1905 Weighted Index | 1906 Price Index (1914 = 100) | 1906 Weighted Index | 1907 Price Index (1914 = 100) | 1907 Weighted Index | 1908 Price Index (1914 = 100) | 1908 Weighted Index |
|---|---|---|---|---|---|---|---|---|---|---|---|
| Food | 0.5429 | 87.28 | 47.39 | 90.18 | 48.96 | 87.80 | 47.67 | 85.69 | 46.52 | 87.02 | 47.24 |
| Tobacco | 0.0561 | 86.94 | 4.88 | 89.41 | 5.02 | 86.21 | 4.84 | 89.90 | 5.04 | 90.40 | 5.07 |
| Clothing | 0.1082 | 90.19 | 9.76 | 87.98 | 9.52 | 84.42 | 9.13 | 82.99 | 8.98 | 86.31 | 9.34 |
| Rent | 0.0594 | 82.53 | 4.90 | 84.12 | 5.00 | 85.74 | 5.09 | 87.40 | 5.19 | 89.09 | 5.29 |
| Servant | 0.1218 | 78.57 | 9.57 | 78.57 | 9.57 | 82.14 | 10.00 | 91.07 | 11.09 | 91.07 | 11.09 |
| Transport | 0.0739 | 107.23 | 7.93 | 107.12 | 7.92 | 107.23 | 7.93 | 105.07 | 7.77 | 104.64 | 7.74 |
| Club | 0.0377 | 91.97 | 3.47 | 93.74 | 3.54 | 92.14 | 3.48 | 91.55 | 3.45 | 92.28 | 3.48 |
| | 1.0000 | | **87.89** | | **89.51** | | **88.13** | | **88.04** | | **89.25** |

(*Continued*)

## Appendix Table 3:   (Continued)

**Food and Groceries**

| | 1914 Weight | 1909 Price Index (1914 = 100) | 1909 Weighted Index | 1910 Price Index (1914 = 100) | 1910 Weighted Index | 1911 Price Index (1914 = 100) | 1911 Weighted Index | 1912 Price Index (1914 = 100) | 1912 Weighted Index | 1913 Price Index (1914 = 100) | 1913 Weighted Index |
|---|---|---|---|---|---|---|---|---|---|---|---|
| Chinese Labor Standard | 0.479 | 85.83 | 41.13 | 87.09 | 41.74 | 102.81 | 49.27 | 105.84 | 50.72 | 105.09 | 50.36 |
| Malay Labor Standard | 0.130 | 85.83 | 11.16 | 87.09 | 11.32 | 102.81 | 13.36 | 105.84 | 13.76 | 105.09 | 13.66 |
| Indian Labor Standard | 0.058 | 85.83 | 5.01 | 87.09 | 5.08 | 102.81 | 6.00 | 105.84 | 6.17 | 105.09 | 6.13 |
| Asiatic Clerical Standard | 0.095 | 85.83 | 8.18 | 87.09 | 8.30 | 102.81 | 9.80 | 105.84 | 10.09 | 105.09 | 10.02 |
| Eurasian Clerical Standard | 0.012 | 85.83 | 1.05 | 87.09 | 1.06 | 102.81 | 1.25 | 105.84 | 1.29 | 105.09 | 1.28 |
| European Standard | 0.225 | 85.83 | 19.31 | 87.09 | 19.59 | 102.81 | 23.12 | 105.84 | 23.80 | 105.09 | 23.64 |
| | 1.000 | | *85.83* | | *87.09* | | *102.81* | | *105.84* | | *105.09* |

**Tobacco**

| | 1914 Weight | 1909 Price Index (1914 = 100) | 1909 Weighted Index | 1910 Price Index (1914 = 100) | 1910 Weighted Index | 1911 Price Index (1914 = 100) | 1911 Weighted Index | 1912 Price Index (1914 = 100) | 1912 Weighted Index | 1913 Price Index (1914 = 100) | 1913 Weighted Index |
|---|---|---|---|---|---|---|---|---|---|---|---|
| Chinese Labor Standard | 0.304 | 79.39 | 24.11 | 83.12 | 25.24 | 79.72 | 24.21 | 80.65 | 24.49 | 98.50 | 29.91 |
| Malay Labor Standard | 0.107 | 79.39 | 8.52 | 83.12 | 8.92 | 79.72 | 8.56 | 80.65 | 8.66 | 98.50 | 10.57 |
| Indian Labor Standard | 0.064 | 79.39 | 5.07 | 83.12 | 5.31 | 79.72 | 5.09 | 80.65 | 5.15 | 98.50 | 6.29 |
| Asiatic Clerical Standard | 0.035 | 79.39 | 2.81 | 83.12 | 2.94 | 79.72 | 2.82 | 80.65 | 2.85 | 98.50 | 3.48 |
| Eurasian Clerical Standard | 0.004 | 79.39 | 0.32 | 83.12 | 0.33 | 79.72 | 0.32 | 80.65 | 0.32 | 98.50 | 0.40 |
| European Standard | 0.486 | 96.91 | 47.08 | 97.47 | 47.35 | 96.96 | 47.11 | 97.10 | 47.17 | 99.77 | 48.48 |
| | 1.000 | | *87.90* | | *90.09* | | *88.10* | | *88.64* | | *99.12* |

**Clothing**

| | 1914 Weight | 1909 Price Index (1914 = 100) | 1909 Weighted Index | 1910 Price Index (1914 = 100) | 1910 Weighted Index | 1911 Price Index (1914 = 100) | 1911 Weighted Index | 1912 Price Index (1914 = 100) | 1912 Weighted Index | 1913 Price Index (1914 = 100) | 1913 Weighted Index |
|---|---|---|---|---|---|---|---|---|---|---|---|
| Chinese Labor Standard | 0.289 | 76.42 | 22.08 | 84.38 | 24.38 | 84.03 | 24.28 | 83.07 | 24.00 | 99.53 | 28.75 |
| Malay Labor Standard | 0.083 | 76.42 | 6.32 | 84.38 | 6.98 | 84.03 | 6.95 | 83.07 | 6.87 | 99.53 | 8.23 |
| Indian Labor Standard | 0.028 | 76.42 | 2.10 | 84.38 | 2.32 | 84.03 | 2.31 | 83.07 | 2.29 | 99.53 | 2.74 |
| Asiatic Clerical Standard | 0.081 | 76.42 | 6.20 | 84.38 | 6.84 | 84.03 | 6.82 | 83.07 | 6.74 | 99.53 | 8.07 |
| Eurasian Clerical Standard | 0.009 | 76.42 | 0.70 | 84.38 | 0.78 | 84.03 | 0.77 | 83.07 | 0.77 | 99.53 | 0.92 |
| European Standard | 0.511 | 76.42 | 39.02 | 84.38 | 43.08 | 84.03 | 42.90 | 83.07 | 42.41 | 99.53 | 50.81 |
| | 1.000 | | *76.42* | | *84.38* | | *84.03* | | *83.07* | | *99.53* |

**Rent**

| | 1914 Weight | 1909 Price Index (1914 = 100) | 1909 Weighted Index | 1910 Price Index (1914 = 100) | 1910 Weighted Index | 1911 Price Index (1914 = 100) | 1911 Weighted Index | 1912 Price Index (1914 = 100) | 1912 Weighted Index | 1913 Price Index (1914 = 100) | 1913 Weighted Index |
|---|---|---|---|---|---|---|---|---|---|---|---|
| Chinese Labor Standard | 0.181 | 85.66 | 15.53 | 84.93 | 15.40 | 85.66 | 15.53 | 86.39 | 15.66 | 96.23 | 17.45 |
| Malay Labor Standard | 0.041 | 85.66 | 3.48 | 84.93 | 3.45 | 85.66 | 3.48 | 86.39 | 3.50 | 96.23 | 3.90 |
| Indian Labor Standard | 0.028 | 85.66 | 2.44 | 84.93 | 2.42 | 85.66 | 2.44 | 86.39 | 2.46 | 96.23 | 2.74 |
| Asiatic Clerical Standard | 0.165 | 85.66 | 14.09 | 84.93 | 13.97 | 85.66 | 14.09 | 86.39 | 14.21 | 96.23 | 15.83 |
| Eurasian Clerical Standard | 0.019 | 85.66 | 1.60 | 84.93 | 1.59 | 85.66 | 1.60 | 86.39 | 1.62 | 96.23 | 1.80 |
| European Standard | 0.566 | 86.91 | 49.23 | 86.91 | 49.23 | 84.05 | 47.61 | 84.73 | 47.99 | 86.75 | 49.14 |
| | 1.000 | | *86.37* | | *86.05* | | *84.75* | | *85.45* | | *90.86* |

**Servant**

| | 1914 Weight | 1909 Price Index (1914 = 100) | 1909 Weighted Index | 1910 Price Index (1914 = 100) | 1910 Weighted Index | 1911 Price Index (1914 = 100) | 1911 Weighted Index | 1912 Price Index (1914 = 100) | 1912 Weighted Index | 1913 Price Index (1914 = 100) | 1913 Weighted Index |
|---|---|---|---|---|---|---|---|---|---|---|---|
| Asiatic Clerical Standard | 0.051 | 91.07 | 4.62 | 91.07 | 4.62 | 91.07 | 4.62 | 91.07 | 4.62 | 91.07 | 4.62 |
| Eurasian Clerical Standard | 0.006 | 91.07 | 0.52 | 91.07 | 0.52 | 91.07 | 0.52 | 91.07 | 0.52 | 91.07 | 0.52 |
| European Standard | 0.944 | 91.07 | 85.93 | 91.07 | 85.93 | 91.07 | 85.93 | 91.07 | 85.93 | 91.07 | 85.93 |
| | 1.000 | | *91.07* | | *91.07* | | *91.07* | | *91.07* | | *91.07* |

**Transport**

| | 1914 Weight | 1909 Price Index (1914 = 100) | 1909 Weighted Index | 1910 Price Index (1914 = 100) | 1910 Weighted Index | 1911 Price Index (1914 = 100) | 1911 Weighted Index | 1912 Price Index (1914 = 100) | 1912 Weighted Index | 1913 Price Index (1914 = 100) | 1913 Weighted Index |
|---|---|---|---|---|---|---|---|---|---|---|---|
| Asiatic Clerical Standard | 0.165 | 103.67 | 17.09 | 103.24 | 17.02 | 102.91 | 16.96 | 103.02 | 16.98 | 99.46 | 16.39 |
| Eurasian Clerical Standard | 0.019 | 103.67 | 1.94 | 103.24 | 1.93 | 102.91 | 1.93 | 103.02 | 1.93 | 99.46 | 1.86 |
| European Standard | 0.816 | 103.67 | 84.64 | 103.24 | 84.29 | 102.91 | 84.02 | 103.02 | 84.11 | 99.46 | 81.20 |
| | 1.000 | | *103.67* | | *103.24* | | *102.91* | | *103.02* | | *99.46* |

**Club**

| | 1914 Weight | 1909 Price Index (1914 = 100) | 1909 Weighted Index | 1910 Price Index (1914 = 100) | 1910 Weighted Index | 1911 Price Index (1914 = 100) | 1911 Weighted Index | 1912 Price Index (1914 = 100) | 1912 Weighted Index | 1913 Price Index (1914 = 100) | 1913 Weighted Index |
|---|---|---|---|---|---|---|---|---|---|---|---|
| European Standard | 1.000 | 91.37 | 91.37 | 92.28 | 92.28 | 99.88 | 99.88 | 101.47 | 101.47 | 102.43 | 102.43 |
| | | | *91.37* | | *92.28* | | *99.88* | | *101.47* | | *102.43* |

| | 1914 Weight | 1909 Price Index (1914 = 100) | 1909 Weighted Index | 1910 Price Index (1914 = 100) | 1910 Weighted Index | 1911 Price Index (1914 = 100) | 1911 Weighted Index | 1912 Price Index (1914 = 100) | 1912 Weighted Index | 1913 Price Index (1914 = 100) | 1913 Weighted Index |
|---|---|---|---|---|---|---|---|---|---|---|---|
| Food | 0.5429 | 85.83 | 46.60 | 87.09 | 47.28 | 102.81 | 55.82 | 105.84 | 57.46 | 105.09 | 57.05 |
| Tobacco | 0.0561 | 87.90 | 4.93 | 90.09 | 5.05 | 88.10 | 4.94 | 88.64 | 4.97 | 99.12 | 5.56 |
| Clothing | 0.1082 | 76.42 | 8.27 | 84.38 | 9.13 | 84.03 | 9.09 | 83.07 | 8.99 | 99.53 | 10.77 |
| Rent | 0.0594 | 86.37 | 5.13 | 86.05 | 5.11 | 84.75 | 5.03 | 85.45 | 5.08 | 90.86 | 5.40 |
| Servant | 0.1218 | 91.07 | 11.09 | 91.07 | 11.09 | 91.07 | 11.09 | 91.07 | 11.09 | 91.07 | 11.09 |
| Transport | 0.0739 | 103.67 | 7.66 | 103.24 | 7.63 | 102.91 | 7.61 | 103.02 | 7.62 | 99.46 | 7.35 |
| Club | 0.0377 | 91.37 | 3.45 | 92.28 | 3.48 | 99.88 | 3.77 | 101.47 | 3.83 | 102.43 | 3.86 |
| | 1.0000 | | **87.13** | | **88.78** | | **97.35** | | **99.03** | | **101.09** |

**Appendix Table 4:** Singapore: Computation of Consumer Price Indices by Major Object of Consumption (1914 = 100), 1914–39

**Food**

| | | 1914 | 1915 | | 1916 | | 1917 | | 1918 | | 1919 | | 1920 | |
|---|---|---|---|---|---|---|---|---|---|---|---|---|---|---|
| | Weight | Price Index (1914 = 100) | Price Index (1914 = 100) | Weighted Index | Price Index (1914 = 100) | Weighted Index | Price Index (1914 = 100) | Weighted Index | Price Index (1914 = 100) | Weighted Index | Price Index (1914 = 100) | Weighted Index | Price Index (1914 = 100) | Weighted Index |
| Chinese Labor Standard | 0.479 | 100.00 | 96.60 | 46.29 | 98.98 | 47.43 | 109.53 | 52.49 | 140.40 | 67.28 | 191.20 | 91.63 | 253.20 | 121.34 |
| Malay Labor Standard | 0.130 | 100.00 | 96.60 | 12.56 | 98.98 | 12.87 | 109.53 | 14.24 | 140.40 | 18.25 | 191.20 | 24.85 | 253.20 | 32.91 |
| Indian Labor Standard | 0.058 | 100.00 | 96.60 | 5.64 | 98.98 | 5.77 | 109.53 | 6.39 | 140.40 | 8.19 | 191.20 | 11.15 | 253.20 | 14.77 |
| Asiatic Clerical Standard | 0.095 | 100.00 | 96.60 | 9.21 | 98.98 | 9.44 | 109.53 | 10.44 | 140.40 | 13.39 | 191.20 | 18.23 | 253.20 | 24.14 |
| Eurasian Clerical Standard | 0.012 | 100.00 | 130.89 | 1.60 | 130.59 | 1.59 | 135.83 | 1.66 | 136.50 | 1.66 | 160.30 | 1.95 | 214.30 | 2.61 |
| European Standard | 0.225 | 100.00 | 130.89 | 29.44 | 130.59 | 29.37 | 135.83 | 30.55 | 136.50 | 30.70 | 160.30 | 36.05 | 214.30 | 48.20 |
| | 1.000 | 100.00 | | 104.73 | | 106.47 | | 115.77 | | 139.48 | | 183.87 | | 243.98 |

**Beverage and Tobacco**

| | | 1914 | 1915 | | 1916 | | 1917 | | 1918 | | 1919 | | 1920 | |
|---|---|---|---|---|---|---|---|---|---|---|---|---|---|---|
| | Weight | Price Index (1914 = 100) | Price Index (1914 = 100) | Weighted Index | Price Index (1914 = 100) | Weighted Index | Price Index (1914 = 100) | Weighted Index | Price Index (1914 = 100) | Weighted Index | Price Index (1914 = 100) | Weighted Index | Price Index (1914 = 100) | Weighted Index |
| Chinese Labor Standard | 0.304 | 100.00 | 105.44 | 32.02 | 165.69 | 50.31 | 131.26 | 39.86 | 174.30 | 52.92 | 200.00 | 60.73 | 257.10 | 78.06 |
| Malay Labor Standard | 0.107 | 100.00 | 105.44 | 11.32 | 165.69 | 17.78 | 131.26 | 14.09 | 174.30 | 18.71 | 200.00 | 21.47 | 257.10 | 27.59 |
| Indian Labor Standard | 0.064 | 100.00 | 105.44 | 6.73 | 165.69 | 10.58 | 131.26 | 8.38 | 174.30 | 11.13 | 200.00 | 12.77 | 257.10 | 16.41 |
| Asiatic Clerical Standard | 0.035 | 100.00 | 105.44 | 3.73 | 165.69 | 5.86 | 131.26 | 4.64 | 174.30 | 6.16 | 200.00 | 7.07 | 257.10 | 9.09 |
| Eurasian Clerical Standard | 0.004 | 100.00 | 105.44 | 0.42 | 165.69 | 0.67 | 131.26 | 0.53 | 174.30 | 0.70 | 200.00 | 0.80 | 257.10 | 1.03 |
| European Standard | 0.486 | 100.00 | 77.42 | 37.61 | 104.40 | 50.72 | 124.22 | 60.35 | 174.80 | 84.93 | 204.10 | 99.16 | 214.70 | 104.31 |
| | 1.000 | 100.00 | | 91.83 | | 135.91 | | 127.84 | | 174.54 | | 201.99 | | 236.50 |

**Clothing**

| | | 1914 | 1915 | | 1916 | | 1917 | | 1918 | | 1919 | | 1920 | |
|---|---|---|---|---|---|---|---|---|---|---|---|---|---|---|
| | Weight | Price Index (1914 = 100) | Price Index (1914 = 100) | Weighted Index | Price Index (1914 = 100) | Weighted Index | Price Index (1914 = 100) | Weighted Index | Price Index (1914 = 100) | Weighted Index | Price Index (1914 = 100) | Weighted Index | Price Index (1914 = 100) | Weighted Index |
| Chinese Labor Standard | 0.289 | 100.00 | 138.32 | 39.96 | 161.28 | 46.59 | 144.02 | 41.61 | 189.80 | 54.83 | 229.60 | 66.33 | 291.60 | 84.24 |
| Malay Labor Standard | 0.083 | 100.00 | 138.32 | 11.44 | 161.28 | 13.34 | 144.02 | 11.91 | 189.80 | 15.70 | 229.60 | 18.99 | 291.60 | 24.12 |
| Indian Labor Standard | 0.028 | 100.00 | 138.32 | 3.81 | 161.28 | 4.44 | 144.02 | 3.97 | 189.80 | 5.23 | 229.60 | 6.32 | 291.60 | 8.03 |
| Asiatic Clerical Standard | 0.081 | 100.00 | 138.32 | 11.22 | 161.28 | 13.08 | 144.02 | 11.68 | 189.80 | 15.40 | 229.60 | 18.62 | 291.60 | 23.65 |
| Eurasian Clerical Standard | 0.009 | 100.00 | 138.32 | 1.27 | 161.28 | 1.49 | 144.02 | 1.33 | 189.80 | 1.75 | 229.60 | 2.12 | 291.60 | 2.69 |
| European Standard | 0.511 | 100.00 | 138.32 | 70.61 | 161.28 | 82.34 | 144.02 | 73.52 | 189.80 | 96.90 | 229.60 | 117.22 | 291.60 | 148.87 |
| | 1.000 | 100.00 | | 138.32 | | 161.28 | | 144.02 | | 189.80 | | 229.60 | | 291.60 |

**Rent**

| | | 1914 | 1915 | | 1916 | | 1917 | | 1918 | | 1919 | | 1920 | |
|---|---|---|---|---|---|---|---|---|---|---|---|---|---|---|
| | Weight | Price Index (1914 = 100) | Price Index (1914 = 100) | Weighted Index | Price Index (1914 = 100) | Weighted Index | Price Index (1914 = 100) | Weighted Index | Price Index (1914 = 100) | Weighted Index | Price Index (1914 = 100) | Weighted Index | Price Index (1914 = 100) | Weighted Index |
| Chinese Labor Standard | 0.181 | 100.00 | 103.23 | 18.72 | 106.15 | 19.25 | 107.53 | 19.50 | 120.00 | 21.76 | 130.00 | 23.57 | 150.00 | 27.20 |
| Malay Labor Standard | 0.041 | 100.00 | 103.23 | 4.19 | 106.15 | 4.31 | 107.53 | 4.36 | 120.00 | 4.87 | 130.00 | 5.27 | 150.00 | 6.09 |
| Indian Labor Standard | 0.028 | 100.00 | 103.23 | 2.94 | 106.15 | 3.02 | 107.53 | 3.06 | 120.00 | 3.42 | 130.00 | 3.70 | 150.00 | 4.27 |
| Asiatic Clerical Standard | 0.165 | 100.00 | 103.23 | 16.98 | 106.15 | 17.46 | 107.53 | 17.69 | 120.00 | 19.74 | 130.00 | 21.39 | 150.00 | 24.68 |
| Eurasian Clerical Standard | 0.019 | 100.00 | 103.23 | 1.93 | 106.15 | 1.98 | 107.53 | 2.01 | 120.00 | 2.24 | 130.00 | 2.43 | 150.00 | 2.80 |
| European Standard | 0.566 | 100.00 | 98.02 | 55.52 | 99.61 | 56.42 | 98.27 | 55.66 | 110.00 | 62.31 | 121.00 | 68.54 | 169.00 | 95.73 |
| | 1.000 | 100.00 | | 100.28 | | 102.44 | | 102.29 | | 114.34 | | 124.90 | | 160.76 |

**Servant**

| | | 1914 | 1915 | | 1916 | | 1917 | | 1918 | | 1919 | | 1920 | |
|---|---|---|---|---|---|---|---|---|---|---|---|---|---|---|
| | Weight | Price Index (1914 = 100) | Price Index (1914 = 100) | Weighted Index | Price Index (1914 = 100) | Weighted Index | Price Index (1914 = 100) | Weighted Index | Price Index (1914 = 100) | Weighted Index | Price Index (1914 = 100) | Weighted Index | Price Index (1914 = 100) | Weighted Index |
| Asiatic Clerical Standard | 0.051 | 100.00 | 103.82 | 5.26 | 103.82 | 5.26 | 113.09 | 5.73 | 116.80 | 5.92 | 116.80 | 5.92 | 155.50 | 7.88 |
| Eurasian Clerical Standard | 0.006 | 100.00 | 103.82 | 0.60 | 103.82 | 0.60 | 113.09 | 0.65 | 116.80 | 0.67 | 116.80 | 0.67 | 155.50 | 0.90 |
| European Standard | 0.944 | 100.00 | 103.82 | 97.96 | 103.82 | 97.96 | 113.09 | 106.71 | 116.80 | 110.21 | 116.80 | 110.21 | 155.50 | 146.72 |
| | 1.000 | 100.00 | | 103.82 | | 103.82 | | 113.09 | | 116.80 | | 116.80 | | 155.50 |

**Transport**

| | | 1914 | 1915 | | 1916 | | 1917 | | 1918 | | 1919 | | 1920 | |
|---|---|---|---|---|---|---|---|---|---|---|---|---|---|---|
| | Weight | Price Index (1914 = 100) | Price Index (1914 = 100) | Weighted Index | Price Index (1914 = 100) | Weighted Index | Price Index (1914 = 100) | Weighted Index | Price Index (1914 = 100) | Weighted Index | Price Index (1914 = 100) | Weighted Index | Price Index (1914 = 100) | Weighted Index |
| Asiatic Clerical Standard | 0.165 | 100.00 | 101.83 | 16.79 | 103.13 | 17.00 | 108.64 | 17.91 | 112.50 | 18.54 | 122.90 | 20.26 | 126.80 | 20.90 |
| Eurasian Clerical Standard | 0.019 | 100.00 | 101.83 | 1.91 | 103.13 | 1.93 | 108.64 | 2.03 | 112.50 | 2.11 | 122.90 | 2.30 | 126.80 | 2.38 |
| European Standard | 0.816 | 100.00 | 101.83 | 83.14 | 103.13 | 84.20 | 108.64 | 88.70 | 112.50 | 91.85 | 122.90 | 100.34 | 126.80 | 103.52 |
| | 1.000 | 100.00 | | 101.83 | | 103.13 | | 108.64 | | 112.50 | | 122.90 | | 126.80 |

**Club**

| | | 1914 | 1915 | | 1916 | | 1917 | | 1918 | | 1919 | | 1920 | |
|---|---|---|---|---|---|---|---|---|---|---|---|---|---|---|
| | Weight | Price Index (1914 = 100) | Price Index (1914 = 100) | Weighted Index | Price Index (1914 = 100) | Weighted Index | Price Index (1914 = 100) | Weighted Index | Price Index (1914 = 100) | Weighted Index | Price Index (1914 = 100) | Weighted Index | Price Index (1914 = 100) | Weighted Index |
| European Standard | 1.000 | 100.00 | 91.31 | 91.31 | 103.77 | 103.77 | 113.88 | 113.88 | 134.00 | 134.00 | 147.40 | 147.40 | 163.50 | 163.50 |
| | 1.000 | 100.00 | | 91.31 | | 103.77 | | 113.88 | | 134.00 | | 147.40 | | 163.50 |

| | | 1914 | 1915 | | 1916 | | 1917 | | 1918 | | 1919 | | 1920 | |
|---|---|---|---|---|---|---|---|---|---|---|---|---|---|---|
| | Weight | Price Index (1914 = 100) | Price Index (1914 = 100) | Weighted Index | Price Index (1914 = 100) | Weighted Index | Price Index (1914 = 100) | Weighted Index | Price Index (1914 = 100) | Weighted Index | Price Index (1914 = 100) | Weighted Index | Price Index (1914 = 100) | Weighted Index |
| Food | 0.543 | 100.00 | 104.73 | 56.86 | 106.47 | 57.81 | 115.77 | 62.85 | 139.48 | 75.72 | 183.87 | 99.83 | 243.98 | 132.46 |
| Beverage and Tobacco | 0.056 | 100.00 | 91.83 | 5.15 | 135.91 | 7.62 | 127.84 | 7.17 | 174.54 | 9.79 | 201.99 | 11.33 | 236.50 | 13.27 |
| Clothing | 0.108 | 100.00 | 138.32 | 14.96 | 161.28 | 17.45 | 144.02 | 15.58 | 189.80 | 20.53 | 229.60 | 24.84 | 291.60 | 31.55 |
| Rent | 0.059 | 100.00 | 100.28 | 5.96 | 102.44 | 6.09 | 102.29 | 6.08 | 114.34 | 6.79 | 124.90 | 7.42 | 160.76 | 9.55 |
| Servant | 0.122 | 100.00 | 103.82 | 12.64 | 103.82 | 12.64 | 113.09 | 13.77 | 116.80 | 14.22 | 116.80 | 14.22 | 155.50 | 18.93 |
| Transport | 0.074 | 100.00 | 101.83 | 7.53 | 103.13 | 7.62 | 108.64 | 8.03 | 112.50 | 8.32 | 122.90 | 9.09 | 126.80 | 9.37 |
| Club | 0.038 | 100.00 | 91.31 | 3.44 | 103.77 | 3.91 | 113.88 | 4.30 | 134.00 | 5.05 | 147.40 | 5.56 | 163.50 | 6.17 |
| | 1.000 | 100.00 | | 106.54 | | 113.14 | | 117.78 | | 140.43 | | 172.28 | | 221.30 |

(*Continued*)

## Appendix Table 4:  *(Continued)*

| Food | 1914 Weight | 1914 Price Index (1914 = 100) | 1921 Price Index (1914 = 100) | 1921 Weighted Index | 1922 Price Index (1914 = 100) | 1922 Weighted Index | 1923 Price Index (1914 = 100) | 1923 Weighted Index | 1924 Price Index (1914 = 100) | 1924 Weighted Index | 1925 Price Index (1914 = 100) | 1925 Weighted Index | 1926 Price Index (1914 = 100) | 1926 Weighted Index |
|---|---|---|---|---|---|---|---|---|---|---|---|---|---|---|
| Chinese Labor Standard | 0.479 | 100.00 | 167.70 | 80.36 | 145.50 | 69.73 | 145.30 | 69.63 | 146.10 | 70.01 | 151.50 | 72.60 | 160.20 | 76.77 |
| Malay Labor Standard | 0.130 | 100.00 | 167.70 | 21.80 | 145.50 | 18.91 | 145.30 | 18.89 | 146.10 | 18.99 | 151.50 | 19.69 | 160.20 | 20.82 |
| Indian Labor Standard | 0.058 | 100.00 | 167.70 | 9.78 | 145.50 | 8.49 | 145.30 | 8.48 | 146.10 | 8.52 | 151.50 | 8.84 | 160.20 | 9.35 |
| Asiatic Clerical Standard | 0.095 | 100.00 | 167.70 | 15.99 | 145.50 | 13.87 | 145.30 | 13.85 | 146.10 | 13.93 | 151.50 | 14.45 | 160.20 | 15.27 |
| Eurasian Clerical Standard | 0.012 | 100.00 | 168.80 | 2.06 | 140.00 | 1.71 | 141.00 | 1.72 | 139.80 | 1.70 | 143.40 | 1.75 | 153.00 | 1.86 |
| European Standard | 0.225 | 100.00 | 168.80 | 37.97 | 140.00 | 31.49 | 141.00 | 31.71 | 139.80 | 31.44 | 143.40 | 32.25 | 153.00 | 34.41 |
|  | 1.000 | 100.00 |  | **167.96** |  | **144.20** |  | **144.28** |  | **144.61** |  | **149.58** |  | **158.49** |

| Beverage and Tobacco | 1914 Weight | 1914 Price Index (1914 = 100) | 1921 Price Index (1914 = 100) | 1921 Weighted Index | 1922 Price Index (1914 = 100) | 1922 Weighted Index | 1923 Price Index (1914 = 100) | 1923 Weighted Index | 1924 Price Index (1914 = 100) | 1924 Weighted Index | 1925 Price Index (1914 = 100) | 1925 Weighted Index | 1926 Price Index (1914 = 100) | 1926 Weighted Index |
|---|---|---|---|---|---|---|---|---|---|---|---|---|---|---|
| Chinese Labor Standard | 0.304 | 100.00 | 242.90 | 73.75 | 242.90 | 73.75 | 200.00 | 60.73 | 185.70 | 56.38 | 185.70 | 56.38 | 194.20 | 58.97 |
| Malay Labor Standard | 0.107 | 100.00 | 242.90 | 26.07 | 242.90 | 26.07 | 200.00 | 21.47 | 185.70 | 19.93 | 185.70 | 19.93 | 194.20 | 20.84 |
| Indian Labor Standard | 0.064 | 100.00 | 242.90 | 15.51 | 242.90 | 15.51 | 200.00 | 12.77 | 185.70 | 11.85 | 185.70 | 11.85 | 194.20 | 12.40 |
| Asiatic Clerical Standard | 0.035 | 100.00 | 242.90 | 8.58 | 242.90 | 8.58 | 200.00 | 7.07 | 185.70 | 6.56 | 185.70 | 6.56 | 194.20 | 6.86 |
| Eurasian Clerical Standard | 0.004 | 100.00 | 242.90 | 0.98 | 242.90 | 0.98 | 200.00 | 0.80 | 185.70 | 0.75 | 185.70 | 0.75 | 194.20 | 0.78 |
| European Standard | 0.486 | 100.00 | 231.20 | 112.33 | 223.70 | 108.68 | 203.20 | 98.72 | 192.10 | 93.33 | 186.70 | 90.71 | 181.30 | 88.08 |
|  | 1.000 | 100.00 |  | **237.22** |  | **233.57** |  | **201.55** |  | **188.81** |  | **186.19** |  | **187.93** |

| Clothing | 1914 Weight | 1914 Price Index (1914 = 100) | 1921 Price Index (1914 = 100) | 1921 Weighted Index | 1922 Price Index (1914 = 100) | 1922 Weighted Index | 1923 Price Index (1914 = 100) | 1923 Weighted Index | 1924 Price Index (1914 = 100) | 1924 Weighted Index | 1925 Price Index (1914 = 100) | 1925 Weighted Index | 1926 Price Index (1914 = 100) | 1926 Weighted Index |
|---|---|---|---|---|---|---|---|---|---|---|---|---|---|---|
| Chinese Labor Standard | 0.289 | 100.00 | 237.20 | 68.53 | 182.80 | 52.81 | 163.60 | 47.26 | 157.10 | 45.39 | 158.10 | 45.68 | 157.50 | 45.50 |
| Malay Labor Standard | 0.083 | 100.00 | 237.20 | 19.62 | 182.80 | 15.12 | 163.60 | 13.53 | 157.10 | 12.99 | 158.10 | 13.08 | 157.50 | 13.03 |
| Indian Labor Standard | 0.028 | 100.00 | 237.20 | 6.53 | 182.80 | 5.03 | 163.60 | 4.50 | 157.10 | 4.33 | 158.10 | 4.35 | 157.50 | 4.34 |
| Asiatic Clerical Standard | 0.081 | 100.00 | 237.20 | 19.24 | 182.80 | 14.83 | 163.60 | 13.27 | 157.10 | 12.74 | 158.10 | 12.82 | 157.50 | 12.78 |
| Eurasian Clerical Standard | 0.009 | 100.00 | 237.20 | 2.19 | 182.80 | 1.68 | 163.60 | 1.51 | 157.10 | 1.45 | 158.10 | 1.46 | 157.50 | 1.45 |
| European Standard | 0.511 | 100.00 | 237.20 | 121.10 | 182.80 | 93.32 | 163.60 | 83.52 | 157.10 | 80.20 | 158.10 | 80.71 | 157.50 | 80.41 |
|  | 1.000 | 100.00 |  | **237.20** |  | **182.80** |  | **163.60** |  | **157.10** |  | **158.10** |  | **157.50** |

| Rent | 1914 Weight | 1914 Price Index (1914 = 100) | 1921 Price Index (1914 = 100) | 1921 Weighted Index | 1922 Price Index (1914 = 100) | 1922 Weighted Index | 1923 Price Index (1914 = 100) | 1923 Weighted Index | 1924 Price Index (1914 = 100) | 1924 Weighted Index | 1925 Price Index (1914 = 100) | 1925 Weighted Index | 1926 Price Index (1914 = 100) | 1926 Weighted Index |
|---|---|---|---|---|---|---|---|---|---|---|---|---|---|---|
| Chinese Labor Standard | 0.181 | 100.00 | 154.00 | 27.92 | 181.00 | 32.82 | 217.00 | 39.34 | 230.00 | 41.70 | 242.00 | 43.88 | 257.00 | 46.60 |
| Malay Labor Standard | 0.041 | 100.00 | 154.00 | 6.25 | 181.00 | 7.34 | 217.00 | 8.80 | 230.00 | 9.33 | 242.00 | 9.82 | 257.00 | 10.43 |
| Indian Labor Standard | 0.028 | 100.00 | 154.00 | 4.38 | 181.00 | 5.15 | 217.00 | 6.18 | 230.00 | 6.55 | 242.00 | 6.89 | 257.00 | 7.32 |
| Asiatic Clerical Standard | 0.165 | 100.00 | 154.00 | 25.34 | 181.00 | 29.78 | 217.00 | 35.70 | 230.00 | 37.84 | 242.00 | 39.82 | 257.00 | 42.28 |
| Eurasian Clerical Standard | 0.019 | 100.00 | 154.00 | 2.88 | 181.00 | 3.38 | 217.00 | 4.06 | 230.00 | 4.30 | 242.00 | 4.52 | 257.00 | 4.81 |
| European Standard | 0.566 | 100.00 | 179.00 | 101.39 | 191.00 | 108.19 | 204.00 | 115.55 | 208.00 | 117.82 | 213.00 | 120.65 | 220.00 | 124.61 |
|  | 1.000 | 100.00 |  | **168.16** |  | **186.66** |  | **209.64** |  | **217.54** |  | **225.57** |  | **236.04** |

| Servant | 1914 Weight | 1914 Price Index (1914 = 100) | 1921 Price Index (1914 = 100) | 1921 Weighted Index | 1922 Price Index (1914 = 100) | 1922 Weighted Index | 1923 Price Index (1914 = 100) | 1923 Weighted Index | 1924 Price Index (1914 = 100) | 1924 Weighted Index | 1925 Price Index (1914 = 100) | 1925 Weighted Index | 1926 Price Index (1914 = 100) | 1926 Weighted Index |
|---|---|---|---|---|---|---|---|---|---|---|---|---|---|---|
| Asiatic Clerical Standard | 0.051 | 100.00 | 155.50 | 7.88 | 155.50 | 7.88 | 155.50 | 7.88 | 155.50 | 7.88 | 155.50 | 7.88 | 155.50 | 7.88 |
| Eurasian Clerical Standard | 0.006 | 100.00 | 155.50 | 0.90 | 155.50 | 0.90 | 155.50 | 0.90 | 155.50 | 0.90 | 155.50 | 0.90 | 155.50 | 0.90 |
| European Standard | 0.944 | 100.00 | 155.50 | 146.72 | 155.50 | 146.72 | 155.50 | 146.72 | 155.50 | 146.72 | 155.50 | 146.72 | 155.50 | 146.72 |
|  | 1.000 | 100.00 |  | **155.50** |  | **155.50** |  | **155.50** |  | **155.50** |  | **155.50** |  | **155.50** |

| Transport | 1914 Weight | 1914 Price Index (1914 = 100) | 1921 Price Index (1914 = 100) | 1921 Weighted Index | 1922 Price Index (1914 = 100) | 1922 Weighted Index | 1923 Price Index (1914 = 100) | 1923 Weighted Index | 1924 Price Index (1914 = 100) | 1924 Weighted Index | 1925 Price Index (1914 = 100) | 1925 Weighted Index | 1926 Price Index (1914 = 100) | 1926 Weighted Index |
|---|---|---|---|---|---|---|---|---|---|---|---|---|---|---|
| Asiatic Clerical Standard | 0.165 | 100.00 | 122.80 | 20.24 | 112.00 | 18.46 | 94.80 | 15.63 | 99.40 | 16.38 | 105.30 | 17.36 | 103.50 | 17.06 |
| Eurasian Clerical Standard | 0.019 | 100.00 | 122.80 | 2.30 | 112.00 | 2.10 | 94.80 | 1.78 | 99.40 | 1.86 | 105.30 | 1.97 | 103.50 | 1.94 |
| European Standard | 0.816 | 100.00 | 122.80 | 100.26 | 112.00 | 91.44 | 94.80 | 77.40 | 99.40 | 81.15 | 105.30 | 85.97 | 103.50 | 84.50 |
|  | 1.000 | 100.00 |  | **122.80** |  | **112.00** |  | **94.80** |  | **99.40** |  | **105.30** |  | **103.50** |

| Club | 1914 Weight | 1914 Price Index (1914 = 100) | 1921 Price Index (1914 = 100) | 1921 Weighted Index | 1922 Price Index (1914 = 100) | 1922 Weighted Index | 1923 Price Index (1914 = 100) | 1923 Weighted Index | 1924 Price Index (1914 = 100) | 1924 Weighted Index | 1925 Price Index (1914 = 100) | 1925 Weighted Index | 1926 Price Index (1914 = 100) | 1926 Weighted Index |
|---|---|---|---|---|---|---|---|---|---|---|---|---|---|---|
| European Standard | 1.000 | 100.00 | 176.70 | 176.70 | 177.40 | 177.40 | 169.20 | 169.20 | 164.10 | 164.10 | 164.20 | 164.20 | 161.70 | 161.70 |
|  | 1.000 | 100.00 |  | **176.70** |  | **177.40** |  | **169.20** |  | **164.10** |  | **164.20** |  | **161.70** |

|  | 1914 Weight | 1914 Price Index (1914 = 100) | 1921 Price Index (1914 = 100) | 1921 Weighted Index | 1922 Price Index (1914 = 100) | 1922 Weighted Index | 1923 Price Index (1914 = 100) | 1923 Weighted Index | 1924 Price Index (1914 = 100) | 1924 Weighted Index | 1925 Price Index (1914 = 100) | 1925 Weighted Index | 1926 Price Index (1914 = 100) | 1926 Weighted Index |
|---|---|---|---|---|---|---|---|---|---|---|---|---|---|---|
| Food | 0.543 | 100.00 | 167.96 | 91.19 | 144.20 | 78.29 | 144.28 | 78.33 | 144.61 | 78.51 | 149.58 | 81.21 | 158.49 | 86.05 |
| Beverage and Tobacco | 0.056 | 100.00 | 237.22 | 13.31 | 233.57 | 13.10 | 201.55 | 11.31 | 188.81 | 10.59 | 186.19 | 10.44 | 187.93 | 10.54 |
| Clothing | 0.108 | 100.00 | 237.20 | 25.66 | 182.80 | 19.78 | 163.60 | 17.70 | 157.10 | 17.00 | 158.10 | 17.10 | 157.50 | 17.04 |
| Rent | 0.059 | 100.00 | 168.16 | 9.99 | 186.66 | 11.09 | 209.64 | 12.45 | 217.54 | 12.92 | 225.57 | 13.40 | 236.04 | 14.02 |
| Servant | 0.122 | 100.00 | 155.50 | 18.93 | 155.50 | 18.93 | 155.50 | 18.93 | 155.50 | 18.93 | 155.50 | 18.93 | 155.50 | 18.93 |
| Transport | 0.074 | 100.00 | 122.80 | 9.08 | 112.00 | 8.28 | 94.80 | 7.01 | 99.40 | 7.35 | 105.30 | 7.78 | 103.50 | 7.65 |
| Club | 0.038 | 100.00 | 176.70 | 6.66 | 177.40 | 6.69 | 169.20 | 6.38 | 164.10 | 6.19 | 164.20 | 6.19 | 161.70 | 6.10 |
|  | 1.000 | 100.00 |  | **174.82** |  | **156.16** |  | **152.11** |  | **151.49** |  | **155.07** |  | **160.33** |

*(Continued)*

## Appendix Table 4: *(Continued)*

| Food | 1914 Weight | 1914 Price Index (1914 = 100) | 1927 Price Index (1914 = 100) | 1927 Weighted Index | 1928 Price Index (1914 = 100) | 1928 Weighted Index | 1929 Price Index (1914 = 100) | 1929 Weighted Index | 1930 Price Index (1914 = 100) | 1930 Weighted Index | 1931 Price Index (1914 = 100) | 1931 Weighted Index | 1932 Price Index (1914 = 100) | 1932 Weighted Index |
|---|---|---|---|---|---|---|---|---|---|---|---|---|---|---|
| Chinese Labor Standard | 0.479 | 100.00 | 154.80 | 74.18 | 151.20 | 72.46 | 149.70 | 71.74 | 140.20 | 67.19 | 103.00 | 49.36 | 86.50 | 41.45 |
| Malay Labor Standard | 0.130 | 100.00 | 154.80 | 20.12 | 151.20 | 19.65 | 149.70 | 19.46 | 140.20 | 18.22 | 103.00 | 13.39 | 86.50 | 11.24 |
| Indian Labor Standard | 0.058 | 100.00 | 154.80 | 9.03 | 151.20 | 8.82 | 149.70 | 8.73 | 140.20 | 8.18 | 103.00 | 6.01 | 86.50 | 5.05 |
| Asiatic Clerical Standard | 0.095 | 100.00 | 154.80 | 14.76 | 151.20 | 14.42 | 149.70 | 14.27 | 140.20 | 13.37 | 103.00 | 9.82 | 86.50 | 8.25 |
| Eurasian Clerical Standard | 0.012 | 100.00 | 155.00 | 1.89 | 149.40 | 1.82 | 141.40 | 1.72 | 132.00 | 1.61 | 109.70 | 1.34 | 97.80 | 1.19 |
| European Standard | 0.225 | 100.00 | 155.00 | 34.86 | 149.40 | 33.60 | 141.40 | 31.80 | 132.00 | 29.69 | 109.70 | 24.67 | 97.80 | 22.00 |
| | 1.000 | 100.00 | | 154.85 | | 150.77 | | 147.73 | | 138.26 | | 104.59 | | 89.18 |

| Beverage and Tobacco | 1914 Weight | 1914 Price Index (1914 = 100) | 1927 Price Index (1914 = 100) | 1927 Weighted Index | 1928 Price Index (1914 = 100) | 1928 Weighted Index | 1929 Price Index (1914 = 100) | 1929 Weighted Index | 1930 Price Index (1914 = 100) | 1930 Weighted Index | 1931 Price Index (1914 = 100) | 1931 Weighted Index | 1932 Price Index (1914 = 100) | 1932 Weighted Index |
|---|---|---|---|---|---|---|---|---|---|---|---|---|---|---|
| Chinese Labor Standard | 0.304 | 100.00 | 185.70 | 56.38 | 185.70 | 56.38 | 185.70 | 56.38 | 171.40 | 52.04 | 171.40 | 52.04 | 165.70 | 50.31 |
| Malay Labor Standard | 0.107 | 100.00 | 185.70 | 19.93 | 185.70 | 19.93 | 185.70 | 19.93 | 171.40 | 18.40 | 171.40 | 18.40 | 165.70 | 17.78 |
| Indian Labor Standard | 0.064 | 100.00 | 185.70 | 11.85 | 185.70 | 11.85 | 185.70 | 11.85 | 171.40 | 10.94 | 171.40 | 10.94 | 165.70 | 10.58 |
| Asiatic Clerical Standard | 0.035 | 100.00 | 185.70 | 6.56 | 185.70 | 6.56 | 185.70 | 6.56 | 171.40 | 6.06 | 171.40 | 6.06 | 165.70 | 5.86 |
| Eurasian Clerical Standard | 0.004 | 100.00 | 185.70 | 0.75 | 185.70 | 0.75 | 185.70 | 0.75 | 171.40 | 0.69 | 171.40 | 0.69 | 165.70 | 0.67 |
| European Standard | 0.486 | 100.00 | 176.00 | 85.51 | 176.30 | 85.66 | 167.00 | 81.14 | 168.70 | 81.96 | 178.40 | 86.68 | 172.00 | 83.57 |
| | 1.000 | 100.00 | | 180.99 | | 181.13 | | 176.61 | | 170.09 | | 174.80 | | 168.76 |

| Clothing | 1914 Weight | 1914 Price Index (1914 = 100) | 1927 Price Index (1914 = 100) | 1927 Weighted Index | 1928 Price Index (1914 = 100) | 1928 Weighted Index | 1929 Price Index (1914 = 100) | 1929 Weighted Index | 1930 Price Index (1914 = 100) | 1930 Weighted Index | 1931 Price Index (1914 = 100) | 1931 Weighted Index | 1932 Price Index (1914 = 100) | 1932 Weighted Index |
|---|---|---|---|---|---|---|---|---|---|---|---|---|---|---|
| Chinese Labor Standard | 0.289 | 100.00 | 155.40 | 44.90 | 151.90 | 43.88 | 141.00 | 40.74 | 139.80 | 40.39 | 133.20 | 38.48 | 110.00 | 31.78 |
| Malay Labor Standard | 0.083 | 100.00 | 155.40 | 12.85 | 151.90 | 12.56 | 141.00 | 11.66 | 139.80 | 11.56 | 133.20 | 11.02 | 110.00 | 9.10 |
| Indian Labor Standard | 0.028 | 100.00 | 155.40 | 4.28 | 151.90 | 4.18 | 141.00 | 3.88 | 139.80 | 3.85 | 133.20 | 3.67 | 110.00 | 3.03 |
| Asiatic Clerical Standard | 0.081 | 100.00 | 155.40 | 12.61 | 151.90 | 12.32 | 141.00 | 11.44 | 139.80 | 11.34 | 133.20 | 10.80 | 110.00 | 8.92 |
| Eurasian Clerical Standard | 0.009 | 100.00 | 155.40 | 1.43 | 151.90 | 1.40 | 141.00 | 1.30 | 139.80 | 1.29 | 133.20 | 1.23 | 110.00 | 1.01 |
| European Standard | 0.511 | 100.00 | 155.40 | 79.33 | 151.90 | 77.55 | 141.00 | 71.98 | 139.80 | 71.37 | 139.80 | 71.37 | 132.30 | 67.54 |
| | 1.000 | 100.00 | | 155.40 | | 151.90 | | 141.00 | | 139.80 | | 136.57 | | 121.38 |

| Rent | 1914 Weight | 1914 Price Index (1914 = 100) | 1927 Price Index (1914 = 100) | 1927 Weighted Index | 1928 Price Index (1914 = 100) | 1928 Weighted Index | 1929 Price Index (1914 = 100) | 1929 Weighted Index | 1930 Price Index (1914 = 100) | 1930 Weighted Index | 1931 Price Index (1914 = 100) | 1931 Weighted Index | 1932 Price Index (1914 = 100) | 1932 Weighted Index |
|---|---|---|---|---|---|---|---|---|---|---|---|---|---|---|
| Chinese Labor Standard | 0.181 | 100.00 | 284.00 | 51.49 | 312.00 | 56.57 | 314.50 | 57.02 | 289.70 | 52.53 | 247.40 | 44.86 | 200.40 | 36.33 |
| Malay Labor Standard | 0.041 | 100.00 | 284.00 | 11.52 | 312.00 | 12.66 | 314.50 | 12.76 | 289.70 | 11.75 | 247.40 | 10.04 | 200.40 | 8.13 |
| Indian Labor Standard | 0.028 | 100.00 | 284.00 | 8.09 | 312.00 | 8.88 | 314.50 | 8.95 | 289.70 | 8.25 | 247.40 | 7.04 | 200.40 | 5.71 |
| Asiatic Clerical Standard | 0.165 | 100.00 | 284.00 | 46.73 | 312.00 | 51.33 | 314.50 | 51.75 | 289.70 | 47.66 | 247.40 | 40.71 | 200.40 | 32.97 |
| Eurasian Clerical Standard | 0.019 | 100.00 | 284.00 | 5.31 | 312.00 | 5.83 | 314.50 | 5.88 | 289.70 | 5.42 | 247.40 | 4.63 | 200.40 | 3.75 |
| European Standard | 0.566 | 100.00 | 230.00 | 130.28 | 248.00 | 140.47 | 249.00 | 141.04 | 229.50 | 129.99 | 201.60 | 114.19 | 166.50 | 94.31 |
| | 1.000 | 100.00 | | 253.41 | | 275.75 | | 277.40 | | 255.60 | | 221.46 | | 181.20 |

| Servant | 1914 Weight | 1914 Price Index (1914 = 100) | 1927 Price Index (1914 = 100) | 1927 Weighted Index | 1928 Price Index (1914 = 100) | 1928 Weighted Index | 1929 Price Index (1914 = 100) | 1929 Weighted Index | 1930 Price Index (1914 = 100) | 1930 Weighted Index | 1931 Price Index (1914 = 100) | 1931 Weighted Index | 1932 Price Index (1914 = 100) | 1932 Weighted Index |
|---|---|---|---|---|---|---|---|---|---|---|---|---|---|---|
| Asiatic Clerical Standard | 0.051 | 100.00 | 155.50 | 7.88 | 155.50 | 7.88 | 155.50 | 7.88 | 152.90 | 7.75 | 138.00 | 7.00 | 124.70 | 6.32 |
| Eurasian Clerical Standard | 0.006 | 100.00 | 155.50 | 0.90 | 155.50 | 0.90 | 155.50 | 0.90 | 152.90 | 0.88 | 138.00 | 0.79 | 124.70 | 0.72 |
| European Standard | 0.944 | 100.00 | 155.50 | 146.72 | 155.50 | 146.72 | 155.50 | 146.72 | 152.90 | 144.27 | 138.00 | 130.21 | 124.70 | 117.66 |
| | 1.000 | 100.00 | | 155.50 | | 155.50 | | 155.50 | | 152.90 | | 138.00 | | 124.70 |

| Transport | 1914 Weight | 1914 Price Index (1914 = 100) | 1927 Price Index (1914 = 100) | 1927 Weighted Index | 1928 Price Index (1914 = 100) | 1928 Weighted Index | 1929 Price Index (1914 = 100) | 1929 Weighted Index | 1930 Price Index (1914 = 100) | 1930 Weighted Index | 1931 Price Index (1914 = 100) | 1931 Weighted Index | 1932 Price Index (1914 = 100) | 1932 Weighted Index |
|---|---|---|---|---|---|---|---|---|---|---|---|---|---|---|
| Asiatic Clerical Standard | 0.165 | 100.00 | 94.20 | 15.53 | 93.10 | 15.35 | 89.70 | 14.79 | 85.50 | 14.09 | 96.20 | 15.86 | 89.00 | 14.67 |
| Eurasian Clerical Standard | 0.019 | 100.00 | 94.20 | 1.76 | 93.10 | 1.74 | 89.70 | 1.68 | 85.50 | 1.60 | 96.20 | 1.80 | 89.00 | 1.67 |
| European Standard | 0.816 | 100.00 | 94.20 | 76.91 | 93.10 | 76.01 | 89.70 | 73.23 | 85.50 | 69.81 | 96.20 | 78.54 | 89.00 | 72.66 |
| | 1.000 | 100.00 | | 94.20 | | 93.10 | | 89.70 | | 85.50 | | 96.20 | | 89.00 |

| Club | 1914 Weight | 1914 Price Index (1914 = 100) | 1927 Price Index (1914 = 100) | 1927 Weighted Index | 1928 Price Index (1914 = 100) | 1928 Weighted Index | 1929 Price Index (1914 = 100) | 1929 Weighted Index | 1930 Price Index (1914 = 100) | 1930 Weighted Index | 1931 Price Index (1914 = 100) | 1931 Weighted Index | 1932 Price Index (1914 = 100) | 1932 Weighted Index |
|---|---|---|---|---|---|---|---|---|---|---|---|---|---|---|
| European Standard | 1.000 | 100.00 | 159.50 | 159.50 | 159.50 | 159.50 | 155.30 | 155.30 | 156.10 | 156.10 | 160.50 | 160.50 | 160.10 | 160.10 |
| | 1.000 | 100.00 | | 159.50 | | 159.50 | | 155.30 | | 156.10 | | 160.50 | | 160.10 |

| | 1914 Weight | 1914 Price Index (1914 = 100) | 1927 Price Index (1914 = 100) | 1927 Weighted Index | 1928 Price Index (1914 = 100) | 1928 Weighted Index | 1929 Price Index (1914 = 100) | 1929 Weighted Index | 1930 Price Index (1914 = 100) | 1930 Weighted Index | 1931 Price Index (1914 = 100) | 1931 Weighted Index | 1932 Price Index (1914 = 100) | 1932 Weighted Index |
|---|---|---|---|---|---|---|---|---|---|---|---|---|---|---|
| Food | 0.543 | 100.00 | 154.85 | 84.07 | 150.77 | 81.86 | 147.73 | 80.21 | 138.26 | 75.06 | 104.59 | 56.78 | 89.18 | 48.42 |
| Beverage and Tobacco | 0.056 | 100.00 | 180.99 | 10.15 | 181.13 | 10.16 | 176.61 | 9.91 | 170.09 | 9.54 | 174.80 | 9.81 | 168.76 | 9.47 |
| Clothing | 0.108 | 100.00 | 155.40 | 16.81 | 151.90 | 16.43 | 141.00 | 15.25 | 139.80 | 15.12 | 136.57 | 14.78 | 121.38 | 13.13 |
| Rent | 0.059 | 100.00 | 253.41 | 15.05 | 275.75 | 16.38 | 277.40 | 16.48 | 255.60 | 15.18 | 221.46 | 13.15 | 181.20 | 10.76 |
| Servant | 0.122 | 100.00 | 155.50 | 18.93 | 155.50 | 18.93 | 155.50 | 18.93 | 152.90 | 18.62 | 138.00 | 16.80 | 124.70 | 15.18 |
| Transport | 0.074 | 100.00 | 94.20 | 6.96 | 93.10 | 6.88 | 89.70 | 6.63 | 85.50 | 6.32 | 96.20 | 7.11 | 89.00 | 6.58 |
| Club | 0.038 | 100.00 | 159.50 | 6.02 | 159.50 | 6.02 | 155.30 | 5.86 | 156.10 | 5.89 | 160.50 | 6.05 | 160.10 | 6.04 |
| | 1.000 | 100.00 | | 158.00 | | 156.66 | | 153.27 | | 145.73 | | 124.49 | | 109.58 |

*(Continued)*

# Appendix Table 4:   (*Continued*)

| Food | 1914 Weight | 1914 Price Index (1914 = 100) | 1933 Price Index (1914 = 100) | 1933 Weighted Index | 1934 Price Index (1914 = 100) | 1934 Weighted Index | 1935 Price Index (1914 = 100) | 1935 Weighted Index | 1936 Price Index (1914 = 100) | 1936 Weighted Index | 1937 Price Index (1914 = 100) | 1937 Weighted Index | 1938 Price Index (1914 = 100) | 1938 Weighted Index | 1939 Price Index (1914 = 100) | 1939 Weighted Index |
|---|---|---|---|---|---|---|---|---|---|---|---|---|---|---|---|---|
| Chinese Labor Standard | 0.479 | 100.00 | 78.80 | 37.76 | 83.40 | 39.97 | 93.90 | 45.00 | 91.00 | 43.61 | 101.50 | 48.64 | 93.70 | 44.90 | 92.83 | 44.48 |
| Malay Labor Standard | 0.130 | 100.00 | 78.80 | 10.24 | 83.40 | 10.84 | 93.90 | 12.21 | 91.00 | 11.83 | 101.50 | 13.19 | 93.70 | 12.18 | 92.83 | 12.07 |
| Indian Labor Standard | 0.058 | 100.00 | 78.80 | 4.60 | 83.40 | 4.87 | 93.90 | 5.48 | 91.00 | 5.31 | 101.50 | 5.92 | 93.70 | 5.47 | 92.83 | 5.42 |
| Asiatic Clerical Standard | 0.095 | 100.00 | 78.80 | 7.51 | 83.40 | 7.95 | 93.90 | 8.95 | 91.00 | 8.68 | 101.50 | 9.68 | 93.70 | 8.93 | 92.83 | 8.85 |
| Eurasian Clerical Standard | 0.012 | 100.00 | 93.80 | 1.14 | 96.10 | 1.17 | 97.20 | 1.18 | 96.10 | 1.17 | 102.60 | 1.25 | 96.20 | 1.17 | 88.53 | 1.08 |
| European Standard | 0.225 | 100.00 | 93.80 | 21.10 | 96.10 | 21.61 | 97.20 | 21.86 | 96.10 | 21.61 | 102.60 | 23.08 | 96.20 | 21.64 | 88.53 | 19.91 |
| | 1.000 | 100.00 | | 82.36 | | 86.41 | | 94.68 | | 92.21 | | 101.76 | | 94.29 | | 91.81 |

| Beverage and Tobacco | 1914 Weight | 1914 Price Index (1914 = 100) | 1933 Price Index (1914 = 100) | 1933 Weighted Index | 1934 Price Index (1914 = 100) | 1934 Weighted Index | 1935 Price Index (1914 = 100) | 1935 Weighted Index | 1936 Price Index (1914 = 100) | 1936 Weighted Index | 1937 Price Index (1914 = 100) | 1937 Weighted Index | 1938 Price Index (1914 = 100) | 1938 Weighted Index | 1939 Price Index (1914 = 100) | 1939 Weighted Index |
|---|---|---|---|---|---|---|---|---|---|---|---|---|---|---|---|---|
| Chinese Labor Standard | 0.304 | 100.00 | 142.90 | 43.39 | 142.90 | 43.39 | 128.60 | 39.05 | 128.60 | 39.05 | 128.60 | 39.05 | 128.60 | 39.05 | 144.68 | 43.93 |
| Malay Labor Standard | 0.107 | 100.00 | 142.90 | 15.34 | 142.90 | 15.34 | 128.60 | 13.80 | 128.60 | 13.80 | 128.60 | 13.80 | 128.60 | 13.80 | 144.68 | 15.53 |
| Indian Labor Standard | 0.064 | 100.00 | 142.90 | 9.12 | 142.90 | 9.12 | 128.60 | 8.21 | 128.60 | 8.21 | 128.60 | 8.21 | 128.60 | 8.21 | 144.68 | 9.24 |
| Asiatic Clerical Standard | 0.035 | 100.00 | 142.90 | 5.05 | 142.90 | 5.05 | 128.60 | 4.54 | 128.60 | 4.54 | 128.60 | 4.54 | 128.60 | 4.54 | 144.68 | 5.11 |
| Eurasian Clerical Standard | 0.004 | 100.00 | 142.90 | 0.57 | 142.90 | 0.57 | 128.60 | 0.52 | 128.60 | 0.52 | 128.60 | 0.52 | 128.60 | 0.52 | 144.68 | 0.58 |
| European Standard | 0.486 | 100.00 | 168.00 | 81.62 | 170.50 | 82.84 | 166.50 | 80.89 | 165.90 | 80.60 | 165.90 | 80.60 | 164.20 | 79.78 | 164.07 | 79.71 |
| | 1.000 | 100.00 | | 155.09 | | 156.31 | | 147.01 | | 146.72 | | 146.72 | | 145.90 | | 154.10 |

| Clothing | 1914 Weight | 1914 Price Index (1914 = 100) | 1933 Price Index (1914 = 100) | 1933 Weighted Index | 1934 Price Index (1914 = 100) | 1934 Weighted Index | 1935 Price Index (1914 = 100) | 1935 Weighted Index | 1936 Price Index (1914 = 100) | 1936 Weighted Index | 1937 Price Index (1914 = 100) | 1937 Weighted Index | 1938 Price Index (1914 = 100) | 1938 Weighted Index | 1939 Price Index (1914 = 100) | 1939 Weighted Index |
|---|---|---|---|---|---|---|---|---|---|---|---|---|---|---|---|---|
| Chinese Labor Standard | 0.289 | 100.00 | 106.90 | 30.88 | 99.50 | 28.75 | 99.70 | 28.80 | 98.30 | 28.40 | 105.80 | 30.57 | 108.10 | 31.23 | 117.50 | 33.95 |
| Malay Labor Standard | 0.083 | 100.00 | 106.90 | 8.84 | 99.50 | 8.23 | 99.70 | 8.25 | 98.30 | 8.13 | 105.80 | 8.75 | 108.10 | 8.94 | 117.50 | 9.72 |
| Indian Labor Standard | 0.028 | 100.00 | 106.90 | 2.94 | 99.50 | 2.74 | 99.70 | 2.75 | 98.30 | 2.71 | 105.80 | 2.91 | 108.10 | 2.98 | 117.50 | 3.24 |
| Asiatic Clerical Standard | 0.081 | 100.00 | 106.90 | 8.67 | 99.50 | 8.07 | 99.70 | 8.09 | 98.30 | 7.97 | 105.80 | 8.58 | 108.10 | 8.77 | 117.50 | 9.53 |
| Eurasian Clerical Standard | 0.009 | 100.00 | 106.90 | 0.99 | 99.50 | 0.92 | 99.70 | 0.92 | 98.30 | 0.91 | 105.80 | 0.98 | 108.10 | 1.00 | 117.50 | 1.08 |
| European Standard | 0.511 | 100.00 | 124.10 | 63.36 | 121.60 | 62.08 | 119.50 | 61.01 | 119.50 | 61.01 | 119.50 | 61.01 | 119.50 | 61.01 | 129.90 | 66.31 |
| | 1.000 | 100.00 | | 115.68 | | 110.78 | | 109.81 | | 109.12 | | 112.79 | | 113.92 | | 123.83 |

| Rent | 1914 Weight | 1914 Price Index (1914 = 100) | 1933 Price Index (1914 = 100) | 1933 Weighted Index | 1934 Price Index (1914 = 100) | 1934 Weighted Index | 1935 Price Index (1914 = 100) | 1935 Weighted Index | 1936 Price Index (1914 = 100) | 1936 Weighted Index | 1937 Price Index (1914 = 100) | 1937 Weighted Index | 1938 Price Index (1914 = 100) | 1938 Weighted Index | 1939 Price Index (1914 = 100) | 1939 Weighted Index |
|---|---|---|---|---|---|---|---|---|---|---|---|---|---|---|---|---|
| Chinese Labor Standard | 0.181 | 100.00 | 175.60 | 31.84 | 175.60 | 31.84 | 175.60 | 31.84 | 175.60 | 31.84 | 177.70 | 32.22 | 188.90 | 34.25 | 207.65 | 37.65 |
| Malay Labor Standard | 0.041 | 100.00 | 175.60 | 7.12 | 175.60 | 7.12 | 175.60 | 7.12 | 175.60 | 7.12 | 177.70 | 7.21 | 188.90 | 7.66 | 207.65 | 8.42 |
| Indian Labor Standard | 0.028 | 100.00 | 175.60 | 5.00 | 175.60 | 5.00 | 175.60 | 5.00 | 175.60 | 5.00 | 177.70 | 5.06 | 188.90 | 5.38 | 207.65 | 5.91 |
| Asiatic Clerical Standard | 0.165 | 100.00 | 175.60 | 28.89 | 175.60 | 28.89 | 175.60 | 28.89 | 175.60 | 28.89 | 177.70 | 29.24 | 188.90 | 31.08 | 207.65 | 34.16 |
| Eurasian Clerical Standard | 0.019 | 100.00 | 175.60 | 3.28 | 175.60 | 3.28 | 175.60 | 3.28 | 175.60 | 3.28 | 177.70 | 3.32 | 188.90 | 3.53 | 207.65 | 3.88 |
| European Standard | 0.566 | 100.00 | 146.40 | 82.92 | 146.40 | 82.92 | 146.40 | 82.92 | 146.40 | 82.92 | 149.60 | 84.74 | 154.80 | 87.68 | 162.83 | 92.23 |
| | 1.000 | 100.00 | | 159.06 | | 159.06 | | 159.06 | | 159.06 | | 161.78 | | 169.58 | | 182.26 |

| Servant | 1914 Weight | 1914 Price Index (1914 = 100) | 1933 Price Index (1914 = 100) | 1933 Weighted Index | 1934 Price Index (1914 = 100) | 1934 Weighted Index | 1935 Price Index (1914 = 100) | 1935 Weighted Index | 1936 Price Index (1914 = 100) | 1936 Weighted Index | 1937 Price Index (1914 = 100) | 1937 Weighted Index | 1938 Price Index (1914 = 100) | 1938 Weighted Index | 1939 Price Index (1914 = 100) | 1939 Weighted Index |
|---|---|---|---|---|---|---|---|---|---|---|---|---|---|---|---|---|
| Asiatic Clerical Standard | 0.051 | 100.00 | 115.80 | 5.87 | 123.70 | 6.27 | 127.40 | 6.46 | 125.70 | 6.37 | 130.00 | 6.59 | 128.20 | 6.50 | 128.20 | 6.50 |
| Eurasian Clerical Standard | 0.006 | 100.00 | 115.80 | 0.67 | 123.70 | 0.71 | 127.40 | 0.73 | 125.70 | 0.72 | 130.00 | 0.75 | 128.20 | 0.74 | 128.20 | 0.74 |
| European Standard | 0.944 | 100.00 | 115.80 | 109.26 | 123.70 | 116.72 | 127.40 | 120.21 | 125.70 | 118.60 | 130.00 | 122.66 | 128.20 | 120.96 | 128.20 | 120.96 |
| | 1.000 | 100.00 | | 115.80 | | 123.70 | | 127.40 | | 125.70 | | 130.00 | | 128.20 | | 128.20 |

| Transport | 1914 Weight | 1914 Price Index (1914 = 100) | 1933 Price Index (1914 = 100) | 1933 Weighted Index | 1934 Price Index (1914 = 100) | 1934 Weighted Index | 1935 Price Index (1914 = 100) | 1935 Weighted Index | 1936 Price Index (1914 = 100) | 1936 Weighted Index | 1937 Price Index (1914 = 100) | 1937 Weighted Index | 1938 Price Index (1914 = 100) | 1938 Weighted Index | 1939 Price Index (1914 = 100) | 1939 Weighted Index |
|---|---|---|---|---|---|---|---|---|---|---|---|---|---|---|---|---|
| Asiatic Clerical Standard | 0.165 | 100.00 | 85.40 | 14.08 | 84.50 | 13.93 | 82.40 | 13.58 | 80.00 | 13.19 | 81.40 | 13.42 | 81.50 | 13.43 | 82.18 | 13.55 |
| Eurasian Clerical Standard | 0.019 | 100.00 | 85.40 | 1.60 | 84.50 | 1.58 | 82.40 | 1.54 | 80.00 | 1.50 | 81.40 | 1.52 | 81.50 | 1.53 | 82.18 | 1.54 |
| European Standard | 0.816 | 100.00 | 85.40 | 69.72 | 84.50 | 68.99 | 82.40 | 67.27 | 80.00 | 65.31 | 81.40 | 66.46 | 81.50 | 66.54 | 82.18 | 67.09 |
| | 1.000 | 100.00 | | 85.40 | | 84.50 | | 82.40 | | 80.00 | | 81.40 | | 81.50 | | 82.18 |

| Club | 1914 Weight | 1914 Price Index (1914 = 100) | 1933 Price Index (1914 = 100) | 1933 Weighted Index | 1934 Price Index (1914 = 100) | 1934 Weighted Index | 1935 Price Index (1914 = 100) | 1935 Weighted Index | 1936 Price Index (1914 = 100) | 1936 Weighted Index | 1937 Price Index (1914 = 100) | 1937 Weighted Index | 1938 Price Index (1914 = 100) | 1938 Weighted Index | 1939 Price Index (1914 = 100) | 1939 Weighted Index |
|---|---|---|---|---|---|---|---|---|---|---|---|---|---|---|---|---|
| European Standard | 1.000 | 100.00 | 158.40 | 158.40 | 159.50 | 159.50 | 157.70 | 157.70 | 157.40 | 157.40 | 157.70 | 157.70 | 159.40 | 159.40 | 152.87 | 152.87 |
| | 1.000 | 100.00 | | 158.40 | | 159.50 | | 157.70 | | 157.40 | | 157.70 | | 159.40 | | 152.87 |

| | 1914 Weight | 1914 Price Index (1914 = 100) | 1933 Price Index (1914 = 100) | 1933 Weighted Index | 1934 Price Index (1914 = 100) | 1934 Weighted Index | 1935 Price Index (1914 = 100) | 1935 Weighted Index | 1936 Price Index (1914 = 100) | 1936 Weighted Index | 1937 Price Index (1914 = 100) | 1937 Weighted Index | 1938 Price Index (1914 = 100) | 1938 Weighted Index | 1939 Price Index (1914 = 100) | 1939 Weighted Index |
|---|---|---|---|---|---|---|---|---|---|---|---|---|---|---|---|---|
| Food | 0.543 | 100.00 | 82.36 | 44.71 | 86.41 | 46.91 | 94.68 | 51.40 | 92.21 | 50.06 | 101.76 | 55.25 | 94.29 | 51.19 | 91.81 | 49.84 |
| Beverage and Tobacco | 0.056 | 100.00 | 155.09 | 8.70 | 156.31 | 8.77 | 147.01 | 8.25 | 146.72 | 8.23 | 146.72 | 8.23 | 145.90 | 8.18 | 154.10 | 8.64 |
| Clothing | 0.108 | 100.00 | 115.68 | 12.52 | 110.78 | 11.99 | 109.81 | 11.88 | 109.12 | 11.81 | 112.79 | 12.20 | 113.92 | 12.32 | 123.83 | 13.40 |
| Rent | 0.059 | 100.00 | 159.06 | 9.45 | 159.06 | 9.45 | 159.06 | 9.45 | 159.06 | 9.45 | 161.78 | 9.61 | 169.58 | 10.07 | 182.26 | 10.83 |
| Servant | 0.122 | 100.00 | 115.80 | 14.10 | 123.70 | 15.06 | 127.40 | 15.51 | 125.70 | 15.31 | 130.00 | 15.83 | 128.20 | 15.61 | 128.20 | 15.61 |
| Transport | 0.074 | 100.00 | 85.40 | 6.31 | 84.50 | 6.25 | 82.40 | 6.09 | 80.00 | 5.91 | 81.40 | 6.02 | 81.50 | 6.03 | 82.18 | 6.08 |
| Club | 0.038 | 100.00 | 158.40 | 5.97 | 159.50 | 6.02 | 157.70 | 5.95 | 157.40 | 5.94 | 157.70 | 5.95 | 159.40 | 6.01 | 152.87 | 5.77 |
| | 1.000 | 100.00 | | 101.76 | | 104.44 | | 108.53 | | 106.70 | | 113.08 | | 109.42 | | 110.16 |

## Appendix Table 5: Singapore: Computation of Consumer Price Indices by Major Object of Consumption (1949 = 100), 1939 and 1947–60

### Food

| Food | 1949 Weight | 1939 Price Index (1949 = 100) | 1939 Weighted Index | 1947 Price Index (1949 = 100) | 1947 Weighted Index | 1948 Price Index (1949 = 100) | 1948 Weighted Index | 1949 Price Index (1949 = 100) | 1949 Weighted Index | 1950 Price Index (1949 = 100) | 1950 Weighted Index |
|---|---|---|---|---|---|---|---|---|---|---|---|
| Chinese Labor Standard | 0.5188 | 26.39 | 13.69 | 120.48 | 62.50 | 107.65 | 55.85 | 100.00 | 51.88 | 104.82 | 54.38 |
| Malay Labor Standard | 0.0657 | 24.63 | 1.62 | 104.17 | 6.84 | 109.61 | 7.20 | 100.00 | 6.57 | 109.38 | 7.18 |
| Indian Labor Standard | 0.0990 | 23.05 | 2.28 | 105.26 | 10.42 | 107.65 | 10.66 | 100.00 | 9.90 | 106.32 | 10.53 |
| Chinese, Indian, and Eurasian Clerical | 0.1277 | 26.39 | 3.37 | 120.48 | 15.39 | 107.65 | 13.75 | 100.00 | 12.77 | 112.66 | 14.39 |
| Malay Clerical Grades Standard | 0.0150 | 24.63 | 0.37 | 104.17 | 1.56 | 109.61 | 1.64 | 100.00 | 1.50 | 111.33 | 1.67 |
| European Standard | 0.1738 | 34.13 | 5.93 | 116.88 | 20.32 | 104.44 | 18.15 | 100.00 | 17.38 | 108.53 | 18.86 |
| | 1.0000 | | 27.26 | | 117.03 | | 107.25 | | 100.00 | | 107.01 |

### Tobacco

| Tobacco | 1949 Weight | 1939 Price Index (1949 = 100) | 1939 Weighted Index | 1947 Price Index (1949 = 100) | 1947 Weighted Index | 1948 Price Index (1949 = 100) | 1948 Weighted Index | 1949 Price Index (1949 = 100) | 1949 Weighted Index | 1950 Price Index (1949 = 100) | 1950 Weighted Index |
|---|---|---|---|---|---|---|---|---|---|---|---|
| Chinese Labor Standard | 0.2879 | 37.74 | 10.86 | 116.28 | 33.48 | 94.72 | 27.27 | 100.00 | 28.79 | 104.65 | 30.13 |
| Malay Labor Standard | 0.0475 | 37.45 | 1.78 | 102.04 | 4.85 | 94.01 | 4.46 | 100.00 | 4.75 | 118.37 | 5.62 |
| Indian Labor Standard | 0.0513 | 42.68 | 2.19 | 116.28 | 5.96 | 94.72 | 4.86 | 100.00 | 5.13 | 104.65 | 5.36 |
| Chinese, Indian, and Eurasian Clerical | 0.0390 | 37.74 | 1.47 | 116.28 | 4.53 | 94.72 | 3.69 | 100.00 | 3.90 | 112.45 | 4.38 |
| Malay Clerical Grades Standard | 0.0044 | 37.45 | 0.16 | 102.04 | 0.45 | 94.01 | 0.41 | 100.00 | 0.44 | 111.61 | 0.49 |
| European Standard | 0.5700 | 35.84 | 20.43 | 121.00 | 68.98 | 98.57 | 56.19 | 100.00 | 57.00 | 106.09 | 60.48 |
| | 1.0000 | | 36.90 | | 118.23 | | 96.87 | | 100.00 | | 106.46 |

### Clothing

| Clothing | 1949 Weight | 1939 Price Index (1949 = 100) | 1939 Weighted Index | 1947 Price Index (1949 = 100) | 1947 Weighted Index | 1948 Price Index (1949 = 100) | 1948 Weighted Index | 1949 Price Index (1949 = 100) | 1949 Weighted Index | 1950 Price Index (1949 = 100) | 1950 Weighted Index |
|---|---|---|---|---|---|---|---|---|---|---|---|
| Chinese Labor Standard | 0.3104 | 32.05 | 9.95 | 163.93 | 50.89 | 101.28 | 31.44 | 100.00 | 31.04 | 111.48 | 34.60 |
| Malay Labor Standard | 0.0415 | 17.77 | 0.74 | 99.01 | 4.11 | 55.09 | 2.28 | 100.00 | 4.15 | 107.92 | 4.48 |
| Indian Labor Standard | 0.0300 | 34.91 | 1.05 | 178.57 | 5.36 | 101.28 | 3.04 | 100.00 | 3.00 | 103.57 | 3.11 |
| Chinese, Indian, and Eurasian Clerical | 0.0694 | 32.05 | 2.22 | 163.93 | 11.37 | 101.28 | 7.03 | 100.00 | 6.94 | 99.68 | 6.91 |
| Malay Clerical Grades Standard | 0.0083 | 32.05 | 0.27 | 178.57 | 1.49 | 99.36 | 0.83 | 100.00 | 0.83 | 99.68 | 0.83 |
| European Standard | 0.5404 | 32.57 | 17.60 | 163.44 | 88.32 | 100.98 | 54.57 | 100.00 | 54.04 | 105.21 | 56.86 |
| | 1.0000 | | 31.83 | | 161.54 | | 99.19 | | 100.00 | | 106.79 |

### Rent

| Rent | 1949 Weight | 1939 Price Index (1949 = 100) | 1939 Weighted Index | 1947 Price Index (1949 = 100) | 1947 Weighted Index | 1948 Price Index (1949 = 100) | 1948 Weighted Index | 1949 Price Index (1949 = 100) | 1949 Weighted Index | 1950 Price Index (1949 = 100) | 1950 Weighted Index |
|---|---|---|---|---|---|---|---|---|---|---|---|
| Chinese Labor Standard | 0.2483 | 31.69 | 7.87 | 107.53 | 26.70 | 90.00 | 22.35 | 100.00 | 24.83 | 103.23 | 25.63 |
| Malay Labor Standard | 0.0259 | 32.03 | 0.83 | 107.53 | 2.79 | 99.36 | 2.58 | 100.00 | 2.59 | 103.23 | 2.68 |
| Indian Labor Standard | 0.0363 | 31.69 | 1.15 | 107.53 | 3.91 | 90.00 | 3.27 | 100.00 | 3.63 | 103.23 | 3.75 |
| Chinese, Indian, and Eurasian Clerical | 0.1139 | 31.69 | 3.61 | 107.53 | 12.25 | 90.00 | 10.25 | 100.00 | 11.39 | 103.23 | 11.76 |
| Malay Clerical Grades Standard | 0.0127 | 31.69 | 0.40 | 107.53 | 1.36 | 90.00 | 1.14 | 100.00 | 1.27 | 103.23 | 1.31 |
| European Standard | 0.5629 | 38.79 | 21.84 | 107.53 | 60.53 | 90.00 | 50.66 | 100.00 | 56.29 | 103.23 | 58.10 |
| | 1.0000 | | 35.70 | | 107.53 | | 90.24 | | 100.00 | | 103.23 |

### Servant

| Servant | 1949 Weight | 1939 Price Index (1949 = 100) | 1939 Weighted Index | 1947 Price Index (1949 = 100) | 1947 Weighted Index | 1948 Price Index (1949 = 100) | 1948 Weighted Index | 1949 Price Index (1949 = 100) | 1949 Weighted Index | 1950 Price Index (1949 = 100) | 1950 Weighted Index |
|---|---|---|---|---|---|---|---|---|---|---|---|
| Chinese, Indian, and Eurasian Clerical | 0.1457 | 34.36 | 5.01 | 116.60 | 16.98 | 97.59 | 14.22 | 100.00 | 14.57 | 104.81 | 15.27 |
| Malay Clerical Grades Standard | 0.0162 | 34.72 | 0.56 | 116.57 | 1.89 | 97.57 | 1.58 | 100.00 | 1.62 | 105.21 | 1.70 |
| European Standard | 0.8382 | 40.82 | 34.21 | 113.13 | 94.82 | 94.69 | 79.37 | 100.00 | 83.82 | 103.67 | 86.89 |
| | 1.0000 | | 39.78 | | 113.70 | | 95.16 | | 100.00 | | 103.86 |

### Transport

| Transport | 1949 Weight | 1939 Price Index (1949 = 100) | 1939 Weighted Index | 1947 Price Index (1949 = 100) | 1947 Weighted Index | 1948 Price Index (1949 = 100) | 1948 Weighted Index | 1949 Price Index (1949 = 100) | 1949 Weighted Index | 1950 Price Index (1949 = 100) | 1950 Weighted Index |
|---|---|---|---|---|---|---|---|---|---|---|---|
| Chinese, Indian, and Eurasian Clerical | 0.2422 | 51.28 | 12.42 | 123.76 | 29.97 | 103.59 | 25.09 | 100.00 | 24.22 | 105.13 | 25.46 |
| Malay Clerical Grades Standard | 0.0304 | 51.28 | 1.56 | 123.15 | 3.75 | 103.08 | 3.14 | 100.00 | 3.04 | 105.13 | 3.20 |
| European Standard | 0.7274 | 55.87 | 40.64 | 119.47 | 86.91 | 100.00 | 72.74 | 100.00 | 72.74 | 102.79 | 74.77 |
| | 1.0000 | | 54.62 | | 120.62 | | 100.96 | | 100.00 | | 103.43 |

### Club

| Club | 1949 Weight | 1939 Price Index (1949 = 100) | 1939 Weighted Index | 1947 Price Index (1949 = 100) | 1947 Weighted Index | 1948 Price Index (1949 = 100) | 1948 Weighted Index | 1949 Price Index (1949 = 100) | 1949 Weighted Index | 1950 Price Index (1949 = 100) | 1950 Weighted Index |
|---|---|---|---|---|---|---|---|---|---|---|---|
| European Standard | 1.0000 | 34.97 | 34.97 | 96.92 | 96.92 | 101.57 | 101.57 | 100.00 | 100.00 | 107.34 | 107.34 |
| | 0.3558 | | 34.97 | | 96.92 | | 101.57 | | 100.00 | | 107.34 |

### Summary

| | 1949 Weight | 1939 Price Index (1949 = 100) | 1939 Weighted Index | 1947 Price Index (1949 = 100) | 1947 Weighted Index | 1948 Price Index (1949 = 100) | 1948 Weighted Index | 1949 Price Index (1949 = 100) | 1949 Weighted Index | 1950 Price Index (1949 = 100) | 1950 Weighted Index |
|---|---|---|---|---|---|---|---|---|---|---|---|
| Food | 0.49011243 | 27.26 | 13.36 | 117.03 | 57.36 | 107.25 | 52.56 | 100.00 | 49.01 | 107.01 | 52.45 |
| Tobacco | 0.09010465 | 36.90 | 3.32 | 118.23 | 10.65 | 96.87 | 8.73 | 100.00 | 9.01 | 106.46 | 9.59 |
| Clothing | 0.12456521 | 31.83 | 3.96 | 161.54 | 20.12 | 99.19 | 12.36 | 100.00 | 12.46 | 106.79 | 13.30 |
| Rent | 0.09482084 | 35.70 | 3.38 | 107.53 | 10.20 | 90.24 | 8.56 | 100.00 | 9.48 | 103.23 | 9.79 |
| Servant | 0.12216267 | 39.78 | 4.86 | 113.70 | 13.89 | 95.16 | 11.63 | 100.00 | 12.22 | 103.86 | 12.69 |
| Transport | 0.04617403 | 54.62 | 2.52 | 120.62 | 5.57 | 100.96 | 4.66 | 100.00 | 4.62 | 103.43 | 4.78 |
| Club | 0.03206017 | 34.97 | 1.12 | 96.92 | 3.11 | 101.57 | 3.26 | 100.00 | 3.21 | 107.34 | 3.44 |
| | 1.00000 | | 32.54 | | 120.90 | | 101.75 | | 100.00 | | 106.04 |

(*Continued*)

## Appendix Table 5: *(Continued)*

**Food**

| | 1949 | 1951 | | 1952 | | 1953 | | 1954 | | 1955 | |
|---|---|---|---|---|---|---|---|---|---|---|---|
| Food | Weight | Price Index (1949 = 100) | Weighted Index | Price Index (1949 = 100) | Weighted Index | Price Index (1949 = 100) | Weighted Index | Price Index (1949 = 100) | Weighted Index | Price Index (1949 = 100) | Weighted Index |
| Chinese Labor Standard | 0.5188 | 144.58 | 75.00 | 153.01 | 79.38 | 143.37 | 74.38 | 128.92 | 66.88 | 122.89 | 63.75 |
| Malay Labor Standard | 0.0657 | 141.67 | 9.30 | 144.79 | 9.51 | 140.63 | 9.23 | 127.08 | 8.34 | 122.92 | 8.07 |
| Indian Labor Standard | 0.0990 | 141.05 | 13.97 | 146.32 | 14.49 | 140.00 | 13.86 | 126.32 | 12.51 | 121.05 | 11.99 |
| Chinese, Indian, and Eurasian Clerical | 0.1277 | 143.27 | 18.30 | 146.44 | 18.70 | 141.42 | 18.06 | 126.91 | 16.21 | 119.79 | 15.30 |
| Malay Clerical Grades Standard | 0.0150 | 140.89 | 2.11 | 143.84 | 2.16 | 139.66 | 2.09 | 124.38 | 1.87 | 116.26 | 1.74 |
| European Standard | 0.1738 | 137.54 | 23.91 | 143.00 | 24.86 | 138.57 | 24.08 | 131.40 | 22.84 | 130.38 | 22.66 |
| | 1.0000 | | 142.59 | | 149.09 | | 141.72 | | 128.65 | | 123.52 |

**Tobacco**

| | 1949 | 1951 | | 1952 | | 1953 | | 1954 | | 1955 | |
|---|---|---|---|---|---|---|---|---|---|---|---|
| Tobacco | Weight | Price Index (1949 = 100) | Weighted Index | Price Index (1949 = 100) | Weighted Index | Price Index (1949 = 100) | Weighted Index | Price Index (1949 = 100) | Weighted Index | Price Index (1949 = 100) | Weighted Index |
| Chinese Labor Standard | 0.2879 | 136.05 | 39.17 | 137.21 | 39.50 | 139.53 | 40.17 | 146.51 | 42.18 | 145.35 | 41.85 |
| Malay Labor Standard | 0.0475 | 131.63 | 6.25 | 131.63 | 6.25 | 136.73 | 6.49 | 145.92 | 6.93 | 143.88 | 6.83 |
| Indian Labor Standard | 0.0513 | 136.05 | 6.97 | 137.21 | 7.03 | 139.53 | 7.15 | 146.51 | 7.51 | 145.35 | 7.45 |
| Chinese, Indian, and Eurasian Clerical | 0.0390 | 119.25 | 4.65 | 119.62 | 4.66 | 123.77 | 4.82 | 133.58 | 5.21 | 134.72 | 5.25 |
| Malay Clerical Grades Standard | 0.0044 | 118.35 | 0.52 | 118.73 | 0.52 | 122.85 | 0.54 | 132.58 | 0.58 | 133.71 | 0.58 |
| European Standard | 0.5700 | 111.83 | 63.74 | 114.34 | 65.17 | 115.41 | 65.79 | 118.28 | 67.42 | 118.28 | 67.42 |
| | 1.0000 | | 121.30 | | 123.14 | | 124.96 | | 129.83 | | 129.38 |

**Clothing**

| | 1949 | 1951 | | 1952 | | 1953 | | 1954 | | 1955 | |
|---|---|---|---|---|---|---|---|---|---|---|---|
| Clothing | Weight | Price Index (1949 = 100) | Weighted Index | Price Index (1949 = 100) | Weighted Index | Price Index (1949 = 100) | Weighted Index | Price Index (1949 = 100) | Weighted Index | Price Index (1949 = 100) | Weighted Index |
| Chinese Labor Standard | 0.3104 | 154.10 | 47.83 | 149.18 | 46.31 | 137.70 | 42.74 | 122.95 | 38.16 | 118.03 | 36.64 |
| Malay Labor Standard | 0.0415 | 148.51 | 6.16 | 144.55 | 5.99 | 129.70 | 5.38 | 116.83 | 4.84 | 113.86 | 4.72 |
| Indian Labor Standard | 0.0300 | 148.21 | 4.45 | 146.43 | 4.40 | 135.71 | 4.08 | 121.43 | 3.65 | 116.07 | 3.49 |
| Chinese, Indian, and Eurasian Clerical | 0.0694 | 117.63 | 8.16 | 111.22 | 7.71 | 98.72 | 6.85 | 94.87 | 6.58 | 93.91 | 6.51 |
| Malay Clerical Grades Standard | 0.0083 | 117.63 | 0.98 | 111.22 | 0.93 | 98.72 | 0.82 | 94.87 | 0.79 | 93.91 | 0.78 |
| European Standard | 0.5404 | 125.08 | 67.59 | 123.78 | 66.89 | 114.01 | 61.61 | 113.36 | 61.26 | 112.38 | 60.73 |
| | 1.0000 | | 135.18 | | 132.23 | | 121.48 | | 115.28 | | 112.87 |

**Rent**

| | 1949 | 1951 | | 1952 | | 1953 | | 1954 | | 1955 | |
|---|---|---|---|---|---|---|---|---|---|---|---|
| Rent | Weight | Price Index (1949 = 100) | Weighted Index | Price Index (1949 = 100) | Weighted Index | Price Index (1949 = 100) | Weighted Index | Price Index (1949 = 100) | Weighted Index | Price Index (1949 = 100) | Weighted Index |
| Chinese Labor Standard | 0.2483 | 125.81 | 31.24 | 133.33 | 33.11 | 140.86 | 34.97 | 144.09 | 35.78 | 141.94 | 35.24 |
| Malay Labor Standard | 0.0259 | 125.81 | 3.26 | 133.33 | 3.46 | 140.86 | 3.65 | 144.09 | 3.74 | 141.94 | 3.68 |
| Indian Labor Standard | 0.0363 | 125.81 | 4.57 | 133.33 | 4.84 | 140.86 | 5.12 | 144.09 | 5.23 | 141.94 | 5.16 |
| Chinese, Indian, and Eurasian Clerical | 0.1139 | 125.81 | 14.33 | 133.33 | 15.19 | 140.86 | 16.05 | 144.09 | 16.41 | 141.94 | 16.17 |
| Malay Clerical Grades Standard | 0.0127 | 125.81 | 1.59 | 133.33 | 1.69 | 140.86 | 1.78 | 144.09 | 1.82 | 141.94 | 1.80 |
| European Standard | 0.5629 | 125.81 | 70.81 | 133.33 | 75.05 | 140.86 | 79.29 | 144.09 | 81.10 | 141.94 | 79.89 |
| | 1.0000 | | 125.81 | | 133.33 | | 140.86 | | 144.09 | | 141.94 |

**Servant**

| | 1949 | 1951 | | 1952 | | 1953 | | 1954 | | 1955 | |
|---|---|---|---|---|---|---|---|---|---|---|---|
| Servant | Weight | Price Index (1949 = 100) | Weighted Index | Price Index (1949 = 100) | Weighted Index | Price Index (1949 = 100) | Weighted Index | Price Index (1949 = 100) | Weighted Index | Price Index (1949 = 100) | Weighted Index |
| Chinese, Indian, and Eurasian Clerical | 0.1457 | 127.84 | 18.62 | 146.39 | 21.32 | 154.98 | 22.57 | 154.98 | 22.57 | 154.30 | 22.47 |
| Malay Clerical Grades Standard | 0.0162 | 128.13 | 2.07 | 146.88 | 2.38 | 159.03 | 2.57 | 155.56 | 2.52 | 154.86 | 2.51 |
| European Standard | 0.8382 | 116.33 | 97.50 | 128.57 | 107.76 | 135.92 | 113.92 | 138.37 | 115.97 | 139.59 | 117.00 |
| | 1.0000 | | 118.19 | | 131.46 | | 139.07 | | 141.07 | | 141.98 |

**Transport**

| | 1949 | 1951 | | 1952 | | 1953 | | 1954 | | 1955 | |
|---|---|---|---|---|---|---|---|---|---|---|---|
| Transport | Weight | Price Index (1949 = 100) | Weighted Index | Price Index (1949 = 100) | Weighted Index | Price Index (1949 = 100) | Weighted Index | Price Index (1949 = 100) | Weighted Index | Price Index (1949 = 100) | Weighted Index |
| Chinese, Indian, and Eurasian Clerical | 0.2422 | 129.23 | 31.30 | 122.56 | 29.68 | 109.74 | 26.58 | 106.67 | 25.83 | 109.23 | 26.45 |
| Malay Clerical Grades Standard | 0.0304 | 129.23 | 3.93 | 122.56 | 3.73 | 109.74 | 3.34 | 106.67 | 3.24 | 109.23 | 3.32 |
| European Standard | 0.7274 | 110.06 | 80.06 | 111.17 | 80.87 | 111.17 | 80.87 | 110.06 | 80.06 | 110.61 | 80.46 |
| | 1.0000 | | 115.28 | | 114.28 | | 110.78 | | 109.13 | | 110.24 |

**Club**

| | 1949 | 1951 | | 1952 | | 1953 | | 1954 | | 1955 | |
|---|---|---|---|---|---|---|---|---|---|---|---|
| Club | Weight | Price Index (1949 = 100) | Weighted Index | Price Index (1949 = 100) | Weighted Index | Price Index (1949 = 100) | Weighted Index | Price Index (1949 = 100) | Weighted Index | Price Index (1949 = 100) | Weighted Index |
| European Standard | 1.0000 | 125.00 | 125.00 | 129.02 | 129.02 | 127.27 | 127.27 | 125.00 | 125.00 | 124.48 | 124.48 |
| | 0.3558 | | 125.00 | | 129.02 | | 127.27 | | 125.00 | | 124.48 |

| | 1949 | 1951 | | 1952 | | 1953 | | 1954 | | 1955 | |
|---|---|---|---|---|---|---|---|---|---|---|---|
| | Weight | Price Index (1949 = 100) | Weighted Index | Price Index (1949 = 100) | Weighted Index | Price Index (1949 = 100) | Weighted Index | Price Index (1949 = 100) | Weighted Index | Price Index (1949 = 100) | Weighted Index |
| Food | 0.49011243 | 142.59 | 69.89 | 149.09 | 73.07 | 141.72 | 69.46 | 128.65 | 63.05 | 123.52 | 60.54 |
| Tobacco | 0.09010465 | 121.30 | 10.93 | 123.14 | 11.10 | 124.96 | 11.26 | 129.83 | 11.70 | 129.38 | 11.66 |
| Clothing | 0.12456521 | 135.18 | 16.84 | 132.23 | 16.47 | 121.48 | 15.13 | 115.28 | 14.36 | 112.87 | 14.06 |
| Rent | 0.09482084 | 125.81 | 11.93 | 133.33 | 12.64 | 140.86 | 13.36 | 144.09 | 13.66 | 141.94 | 13.46 |
| Servant | 0.12216267 | 118.19 | 14.44 | 131.46 | 16.06 | 139.07 | 16.99 | 141.07 | 17.23 | 141.98 | 17.34 |
| Transport | 0.04617403 | 115.28 | 5.32 | 114.28 | 5.28 | 110.78 | 5.12 | 109.13 | 5.04 | 110.24 | 5.09 |
| Club | 0.03206017 | 125.00 | 4.01 | 129.02 | 4.14 | 127.27 | 4.08 | 125.00 | 4.01 | 124.48 | 3.99 |
| | 1.00000 | | 133.35 | | 138.75 | | 135.39 | | 129.05 | | 126.14 |

*(Continued)*

# Appendix Table 5:   (*Continued*)

| Food | 1949 Weight | 1956 Price Index (1949 = 100) | 1956 Weighted Index | 1957 Price Index (1949 = 100) | 1957 Weighted Index | 1958 Price Index (1949 = 100) | 1958 Weighted Index | 1959 Price Index (1949 = 100) | 1959 Weighted Index | 1960 Price Index (1949 = 100) | 1960 Weighted Index |
|---|---|---|---|---|---|---|---|---|---|---|---|
| Chinese Labor Standard | 0.5188 | 122.89 | 63.75 | 128.92 | 66.88 | 126.51 | 65.63 | 121.69 | 63.13 | 121.69 | 63.13 |
| Malay Labor Standard | 0.0657 | 123.96 | 8.14 | 130.21 | 8.55 | 128.13 | 8.41 | 123.96 | 8.14 | 122.72 | 8.06 |
| Indian Labor Standard | 0.0990 | 124.21 | 12.30 | 131.58 | 13.03 | 127.37 | 12.61 | 123.16 | 12.20 | 121.93 | 12.07 |
| Chinese, Indian, and Eurasian Clerical | 0.1277 | 119.26 | 15.23 | 122.96 | 15.71 | 120.58 | 15.40 | 118.73 | 15.17 | 118.73 | 15.17 |
| Malay Clerical Grades Standard | 0.0150 | 116.75 | 1.75 | 120.94 | 1.81 | 118.97 | 1.78 | 116.50 | 1.75 | 116.50 | 1.75 |
| European Standard | 0.1738 | 132.76 | 23.08 | 136.52 | 23.73 | 137.20 | 23.85 | 139.25 | 24.20 | 139.25 | 24.20 |
| | 1.0000 | | **124.25** | | **129.70** | | **127.69** | | **124.58** | | **124.38** |

| Tobacco | 1949 Weight | 1956 Price Index (1949 = 100) | 1956 Weighted Index | 1957 Price Index (1949 = 100) | 1957 Weighted Index | 1958 Price Index (1949 = 100) | 1958 Weighted Index | 1959 Price Index (1949 = 100) | 1959 Weighted Index | 1960 Price Index (1949 = 100) | 1960 Weighted Index |
|---|---|---|---|---|---|---|---|---|---|---|---|
| Chinese Labor Standard | 0.2879 | 146.51 | 42.18 | 151.16 | 43.52 | 150.00 | 43.18 | 147.67 | 42.52 | 147.67 | 42.52 |
| Malay Labor Standard | 0.0475 | 144.90 | 6.88 | 145.92 | 6.93 | 145.92 | 6.93 | 144.90 | 6.88 | 143.45 | 6.81 |
| Indian Labor Standard | 0.0513 | 146.51 | 7.51 | 151.16 | 7.75 | 150.00 | 7.69 | 147.67 | 7.57 | 147.67 | 7.57 |
| Chinese, Indian, and Eurasian Clerical | 0.0390 | 134.72 | 5.25 | 135.09 | 5.26 | 135.85 | 5.29 | 135.85 | 5.29 | 135.85 | 5.29 |
| Malay Clerical Grades Standard | 0.0044 | 133.71 | 0.58 | 133.71 | 0.58 | 134.08 | 0.58 | 134.83 | 0.59 | 134.83 | 0.59 |
| European Standard | 0.5700 | 118.28 | 67.42 | 118.64 | 67.63 | 119.35 | 68.04 | 119.71 | 68.24 | 119.71 | 68.24 |
| | 1.0000 | | **129.83** | | **131.67** | | **131.72** | | **131.09** | | **131.02** |

| Clothing | 1949 Weight | 1956 Price Index (1949 = 100) | 1956 Weighted Index | 1957 Price Index (1949 = 100) | 1957 Weighted Index | 1958 Price Index (1949 = 100) | 1958 Weighted Index | 1959 Price Index (1949 = 100) | 1959 Weighted Index | 1960 Price Index (1949 = 100) | 1960 Weighted Index |
|---|---|---|---|---|---|---|---|---|---|---|---|
| Chinese Labor Standard | 0.3104 | 116.39 | 36.13 | 116.39 | 36.13 | 113.11 | 35.11 | 108.20 | 33.58 | 109.28 | 33.92 |
| Malay Labor Standard | 0.0415 | 116.83 | 4.84 | 120.79 | 5.01 | 116.83 | 4.84 | 110.89 | 4.60 | 113.11 | 4.69 |
| Indian Labor Standard | 0.0300 | 119.64 | 3.59 | 132.14 | 3.97 | 128.57 | 3.86 | 128.57 | 3.86 | 131.14 | 3.94 |
| Chinese, Indian, and Eurasian Clerical | 0.0694 | 94.23 | 6.54 | 95.83 | 6.65 | 96.79 | 6.71 | 97.44 | 6.76 | 97.44 | 6.76 |
| Malay Clerical Grades Standard | 0.0083 | 93.91 | 0.78 | 95.83 | 0.80 | 96.79 | 0.81 | 97.44 | 0.81 | 97.44 | 0.81 |
| European Standard | 0.5404 | 112.38 | 60.73 | 114.33 | 61.79 | 115.96 | 62.67 | 115.64 | 62.49 | 115.64 | 62.49 |
| | 1.0000 | | **112.61** | | **114.34** | | **114.00** | | **112.10** | | **112.61** |

| Rent | 1949 Weight | 1956 Price Index (1949 = 100) | 1956 Weighted Index | 1957 Price Index (1949 = 100) | 1957 Weighted Index | 1958 Price Index (1949 = 100) | 1958 Weighted Index | 1959 Price Index (1949 = 100) | 1959 Weighted Index | 1960 Price Index (1949 = 100) | 1960 Weighted Index |
|---|---|---|---|---|---|---|---|---|---|---|---|
| Chinese Labor Standard | 0.2483 | 150.54 | 37.38 | 154.84 | 38.44 | 158.06 | 39.25 | 160.22 | 39.78 | 160.22 | 39.78 |
| Malay Labor Standard | 0.0259 | 150.54 | 3.90 | 154.84 | 4.01 | 158.06 | 4.10 | 160.22 | 4.15 | 160.22 | 4.15 |
| Indian Labor Standard | 0.0363 | 150.54 | 5.47 | 154.84 | 5.62 | 158.06 | 5.74 | 160.22 | 5.82 | 160.22 | 5.82 |
| Chinese, Indian, and Eurasian Clerical | 0.1139 | 150.54 | 17.15 | 154.84 | 17.64 | 158.06 | 18.01 | 160.22 | 18.25 | 160.22 | 18.25 |
| Malay Clerical Grades Standard | 0.0127 | 150.54 | 1.91 | 154.84 | 1.96 | 158.06 | 2.00 | 160.22 | 2.03 | 160.22 | 2.03 |
| European Standard | 0.5629 | 150.54 | 84.74 | 154.84 | 87.16 | 158.06 | 88.97 | 160.22 | 90.18 | 160.22 | 90.18 |
| | 1.0000 | | **150.54** | | **154.84** | | **158.06** | | **160.22** | | **160.22** |

| Servant | 1949 Weight | 1956 Price Index (1949 = 100) | 1956 Weighted Index | 1957 Price Index (1949 = 100) | 1957 Weighted Index | 1958 Price Index (1949 = 100) | 1958 Weighted Index | 1959 Price Index (1949 = 100) | 1959 Weighted Index | 1960 Price Index (1949 = 100) | 1960 Weighted Index |
|---|---|---|---|---|---|---|---|---|---|---|---|
| Chinese, Indian, and Eurasian Clerical | 0.1457 | 154.98 | 22.57 | 154.98 | 22.57 | 154.98 | 22.57 | 154.98 | 22.57 | 154.98 | 22.57 |
| Malay Clerical Grades Standard | 0.0162 | 155.56 | 2.52 | 155.56 | 2.52 | 155.56 | 2.52 | 155.56 | 2.52 | 155.56 | 2.52 |
| European Standard | 0.8382 | 140.00 | 117.34 | 140.00 | 117.34 | 140.00 | 117.34 | 140.00 | 117.34 | 140.00 | 117.34 |
| | 1.0000 | | **142.43** | | **142.43** | | **142.43** | | **142.43** | | **142.43** |

| Transport | 1949 Weight | 1956 Price Index (1949 = 100) | 1956 Weighted Index | 1957 Price Index (1949 = 100) | 1957 Weighted Index | 1958 Price Index (1949 = 100) | 1958 Weighted Index | 1959 Price Index (1949 = 100) | 1959 Weighted Index | 1960 Price Index (1949 = 100) | 1960 Weighted Index |
|---|---|---|---|---|---|---|---|---|---|---|---|
| Chinese, Indian, and Eurasian Clerical | 0.2422 | 107.69 | 26.08 | 108.21 | 26.20 | 108.72 | 26.33 | 107.69 | 26.08 | 108.77 | 26.34 |
| Malay Clerical Grades Standard | 0.0304 | 107.69 | 3.28 | 108.21 | 3.29 | 108.72 | 3.31 | 107.69 | 3.28 | 108.77 | 3.31 |
| European Standard | 0.7274 | 113.41 | 82.49 | 118.44 | 86.15 | 118.99 | 86.56 | 121.79 | 88.59 | 123.01 | 89.47 |
| | 1.0000 | | **111.85** | | **115.65** | | **116.19** | | **117.95** | | **119.12** |

| Club | 1949 Weight | 1956 Price Index (1949 = 100) | 1956 Weighted Index | 1957 Price Index (1949 = 100) | 1957 Weighted Index | 1958 Price Index (1949 = 100) | 1958 Weighted Index | 1959 Price Index (1949 = 100) | 1959 Weighted Index | 1960 Price Index (1949 = 100) | 1960 Weighted Index |
|---|---|---|---|---|---|---|---|---|---|---|---|
| European Standard | 1.0000 | 125.70 | 125.70 | 127.80 | 127.80 | 128.50 | 128.50 | 129.72 | 129.72 | 131.02 | 131.02 |
| | 0.3558 | | **125.70** | | **127.80** | | **128.50** | | **129.72** | | **131.02** |

| | 1949 Weight | 1956 Price Index (1949 = 100) | 1956 Weighted Index | 1957 Price Index (1949 = 100) | 1957 Weighted Index | 1958 Price Index (1949 = 100) | 1958 Weighted Index | 1959 Price Index (1949 = 100) | 1959 Weighted Index | 1960 Price Index (1949 = 100) | 1960 Weighted Index |
|---|---|---|---|---|---|---|---|---|---|---|---|
| Food | 0.49011243 | 124.25 | 60.90 | 129.70 | 63.57 | 127.69 | 62.58 | 124.58 | 61.06 | 124.38 | 60.96 |
| Tobacco | 0.09010465 | 129.83 | 11.70 | 131.67 | 11.86 | 131.72 | 11.87 | 131.09 | 11.81 | 131.02 | 11.81 |
| Clothing | 0.12456521 | 112.61 | 14.03 | 114.34 | 14.24 | 114.00 | 14.20 | 112.10 | 13.96 | 112.61 | 14.03 |
| Rent | 0.09482084 | 150.54 | 14.27 | 154.84 | 14.68 | 158.06 | 14.99 | 160.22 | 15.19 | 160.22 | 15.19 |
| Servant | 0.12216267 | 142.43 | 17.40 | 142.43 | 17.40 | 142.43 | 17.40 | 142.43 | 17.40 | 142.43 | 17.40 |
| Transport | 0.04617403 | 111.85 | 5.16 | 115.65 | 5.34 | 116.19 | 5.37 | 117.95 | 5.45 | 119.12 | 5.50 |
| Club | 0.03206017 | 125.70 | 4.03 | 127.80 | 4.10 | 128.50 | 4.12 | 129.72 | 4.16 | 131.02 | 4.20 |
| | 1.00000 | | **127.49** | | **131.20** | | **130.52** | | **129.03** | | **129.08** |

## Appendix Table 6: Singapore: Computation of PFCE in the Domestic Market, 1900–39 and 1948–60, European Standard — Food in Current and 1914 Prices (Straits $)

| Year | Annual Per-Capita Private Final Consumption Expenditure in Real Terms (1914 Prices) (Straits $) | Weighted Real Wage Indices of Agriculture and Nonagriculture Sectors (1914 = 100) | Changes in Real Wages (%) | Changes in Real Consumption (%) | Real Per-Capita Private Final Consumption Expenditure Based on Real Wages and Income Elasticities of Demand (1914 Prices) (Straits $) | European Population Standard (Numbers) | Total Real Private Final Consumption Expenditure on Food in the Domestic Market (1914 Prices) (Straits $) | Food Price Indices (1914 = 100) | Total Private Final Consumption Expenditure on Food in the Domestic Market (Current Prices) (Straits $) |
|---|---|---|---|---|---|---|---|---|---|
| | Step 4 | Step 5 | Step 6 | Step 7 | | Step 8 | Step 9 | Step 10 | Step 11 |
| | [1] | [2] | [3] | [4] | [5] | [6] | [7] = [5] x [6] | [8] | [9] = [7] x [8] / 100 |
| 1899 | | 116.03 | | | 397.96 | 13,667 | 5,439,107 | 81.12 | 4,412,406 |
| 1900 | | 113.92 | −1.81% | −1.27% | 392.91 | 13,566 | 5,330,194 | 81.97 | 4,369,042 |
| 1901 | | 112.77 | −1.01% | −0.71% | 390.14 | 13,911 | 5,427,068 | 82.91 | 4,499,325 |
| 1902 | | 108.67 | −3.64% | −2.55% | 380.20 | 14,310 | 5,440,909 | 85.51 | 4,652,316 |
| 1903 | | 107.35 | −1.21% | −0.85% | 376.97 | 14,720 | 5,548,916 | 85.51 | 4,744,669 |
| 1904 | | 107.24 | −0.11% | −0.07% | 376.69 | 15,141 | 5,703,397 | 87.28 | 4,977,968 |
| 1905 | | 105.29 | −1.82% | −1.27% | 371.91 | 15,575 | 5,792,605 | 90.18 | 5,223,634 |
| 1906 | | 106.94 | 1.56% | 1.09% | 375.97 | 16,023 | 6,024,044 | 87.80 | 5,289,017 |
| 1907 | | 107.05 | 0.10% | 0.07% | 376.24 | 16,483 | 6,201,579 | 85.69 | 5,313,974 |
| 1908 | | 107.87 | 0.77% | 0.54% | 378.27 | 16,958 | 6,414,603 | 87.02 | 5,582,067 |
| 1909 | | 110.50 | 2.44% | 1.71% | 384.73 | 17,445 | 6,711,682 | 85.83 | 5,760,682 |
| 1910 | | 108.44 | −1.86% | −1.30% | 379.72 | 17,946 | 6,814,297 | 87.09 | 5,934,800 |
| 1911 | | 98.90 | −8.80% | −6.16% | 356.32 | 18,503 | 6,592,851 | 102.81 | 6,778,183 |
| 1912 | | 97.22 | −1.70% | −1.19% | 352.09 | 19,118 | 6,731,180 | 105.84 | 7,124,071 |
| 1913 | | 95.24 | −2.04% | −1.43% | 347.07 | 19,750 | 6,854,720 | 105.09 | 7,203,681 |
| 1914 | | 100.00 | 5.00% | 3.50% | 359.21 | 20,400 | 7,327,950 | 100.00 | 7,327,950 |
| 1915 | | 93.86 | −6.14% | −4.30% | 343.76 | 21,069 | 7,242,660 | 104.73 | 7,585,155 |
| 1916 | | 88.38 | −5.83% | −4.08% | 329.73 | 21,756 | 7,173,622 | 106.47 | 7,638,020 |
| 1917 | | 100.72 | 13.95% | 9.77% | 361.94 | 22,464 | 8,130,391 | 115.77 | 9,412,300 |
| 1918 | | 104.36 | 3.61% | 2.53% | 371.09 | 23,192 | 8,606,305 | 139.48 | 12,003,667 |
| 1919 | | 92.87 | −11.01% | −7.70% | 342.50 | 23,941 | 8,199,725 | 183.87 | 15,077,106 |
| 1920 | | 89.13 | −4.03% | −2.82% | 332.84 | 24,711 | 8,224,894 | 243.98 | 20,066,803 |
| 1921 | | 112.82 | 26.58% | 18.61% | 394.78 | 27,757 | 10,957,825 | 167.96 | 18,404,853 |
| 1922 | | 123.66 | 9.60% | 6.72% | 421.32 | 29,018 | 12,225,691 | 144.20 | 17,628,945 |
| 1923 | | 126.94 | 2.66% | 1.86% | 429.16 | 30,082 | 12,909,727 | 144.28 | 18,626,209 |
| 1924 | | 127.47 | 0.41% | 0.29% | 430.40 | 31,165 | 13,413,301 | 144.61 | 19,396,465 |
| 1925 | | 124.53 | −2.31% | −1.62% | 423.44 | 32,515 | 13,768,225 | 149.58 | 20,594,430 |
| 1926 | | 120.44 | −3.28% | −2.30% | 413.71 | 33,811 | 13,987,688 | 158.49 | 22,169,479 |
| 1927 | | 127.57 | 5.93% | 4.15% | 430.87 | 35,143 | 15,141,927 | 154.85 | 23,446,884 |
| 1928 | | 131.90 | 3.39% | 2.38% | 441.10 | 36,493 | 16,097,336 | 150.77 | 24,270,469 |
| 1929 | | 131.51 | −0.30% | −0.21% | 440.19 | 37,864 | 16,667,209 | 147.73 | 24,622,799 |
| 1930 | 434.85 | 129.23 | −1.73% | −1.21% | 434.85 | 37,403 | 16,264,686 | 138.26 | 22,486,856 |
| 1931 | | 115.38 | −10.72% | −7.50% | 402.22 | 36,586 | 14,715,907 | 104.59 | 15,391,167 |
| 1932 | | 122.09 | 5.82% | 4.07% | 418.60 | 35,489 | 14,855,891 | 89.18 | 13,248,386 |
| 1933 | | 136.87 | 12.10% | 8.47% | 454.06 | 33,443 | 15,185,011 | 82.36 | 12,505,866 |
| 1934 | | 130.38 | −4.74% | −3.32% | 439.00 | 34,140 | 14,987,527 | 86.41 | 12,950,916 |
| 1935 | | 137.02 | 5.09% | 3.56% | 454.65 | 37,200 | 16,913,087 | 94.68 | 16,013,727 |
| 1936 | | 148.89 | 8.66% | 6.06% | 482.21 | 39,206 | 18,905,496 | 92.21 | 17,432,618 |
| 1937 | | 150.08 | 0.80% | 0.56% | 484.91 | 42,347 | 20,534,128 | 101.76 | 20,895,697 |
| 1938 | | 155.10 | 3.35% | 2.34% | 496.27 | 46,152 | 22,904,054 | 94.29 | 21,596,868 |
| 1939 | | 154.06 | −0.67% | −0.47% | 493.94 | 47,292 | 23,359,018 | 91.81 | 21,445,527 |

| Year | Annual Per-Capita Private Final Consumption Expenditure in Real Terms (1914 Prices) (Straits $) | Weighted Real Wage Indices of Agriculture and Non-agriculture Sectors (1914 = 100) | Changes in Real Wages (%) | Changes in Real Consumption (%) | Real Per-Capita Private Final Consumption Expenditure Based on Real Wages and Income Elasticities of Demand (1914 Prices) (Straits $) | European Population Standard (Numbers) | Total Real Private Final Consumption Expenditure on Food in the Domestic Market (1914 Prices) (Straits $) | Food Price Indices (1914 = 100) | Total Private Final Consumption Expenditure on Food in the Domestic Market (Current Prices) (Straits $) |
|---|---|---|---|---|---|---|---|---|---|
| | Step 4 | Step 5 | Step 6 | Step 7 | | Step 8 | Step 9 | Step 10 | Step 11 |
| | [1] | [2] | [3] | [4] | [5] | [6] | [7] = [5] x [6] | [8] | [9] = [7] x [8] / 100 |
| 1947 | | 164.71 | | | 324.32 | 56,289 | 18,255,364 | 394.16 | 71,954,987 |
| 1948 | 344.90 | 179.65 | 9.067% | 6.347% | 344.90 | 57,648 | 19,882,898 | 361.21 | 71,818,963 |
| 1949 | | 220.02 | 22.473% | 15.731% | 399.16 | 58,722 | 23,439,406 | 336.79 | 78,941,707 |
| 1950 | | 203.15 | −7.666% | −5.366% | 377.74 | 61,326 | 23,165,302 | 360.41 | 83,489,050 |
| 1951 | | 181.26 | −10.776% | −7.543% | 349.25 | 64,086 | 22,381,866 | 480.24 | 107,486,516 |
| 1952 | | 176.19 | −2.797% | −1.958% | 342.41 | 67,620 | 23,153,681 | 502.13 | 116,261,314 |
| 1953 | | 206.53 | 17.217% | 12.052% | 383.68 | 71,508 | 27,435,948 | 477.30 | 130,950,539 |
| 1954 | | 208.97 | 1.183% | 0.828% | 386.85 | 74,892 | 28,972,205 | 433.27 | 125,527,001 |
| 1955 | | 204.74 | −2.023% | −1.416% | 381.38 | 78,330 | 29,873,146 | 415.99 | 124,269,457 |
| 1956 | | 230.57 | 12.617% | 8.832% | 415.06 | 82,296 | 34,157,654 | 418.47 | 142,939,681 |
| 1957 | | 215.81 | −6.401% | −4.481% | 396.46 | 86,756 | 34,395,185 | 436.83 | 150,249,636 |
| 1958 | | 215.37 | −0.205% | −0.144% | 395.89 | 90,840 | 35,962,661 | 430.04 | 154,652,705 |
| 1959 | | 194.19 | −9.837% | −6.886% | 368.63 | 94,776 | 34,937,265 | 419.57 | 146,586,615 |
| 1960 | | 230.48 | 18.691% | 13.084% | 416.86 | 98,046 | 40,871,439 | 418.89 | 171,204,779 |

*(Continued)*

**Appendix Table 6:** Singapore: Computation of PFCE in the Domestic Market, 1900–39 and 1948–60, Eurasian Standard [1899–1939] Chinese, Indian, and Eurasian Clerical Standard [1947–1960] — Food in Current and 1914 Prices (Straits $)

| Year | Annual Per-Capita Private Final Consumption Expenditure in Real Terms (1914 Prices) (Straits $) | Weighted Real Wage Indices of Agriculture and Non-agriculture Sectors (1914 = 100) | Changes in Real Wages (%) | Changes in Real Consumption (%) | Real Per-Capita Private Final Consumption Expenditure Based on Real Wages and Income Elasticities of Demand (1914 Prices) (Straits $) | Eurasian Population Standard (Numbers) | Total Real Private Final Consumption Expenditure on Food in the Domestic Market (1914 Prices) (Straits $) | Food Price Indices (1914 = 100) | Total Private Final Consumption Expenditure on Food in the Domestic Market (Current Prices) (Straits $) |
|---|---|---|---|---|---|---|---|---|---|
| | Step 4 | Step 5 | Step 6 | Step 7 | | Step 8 | Step 9 | Step 10 | Step 11 |
| | [1] | [2] | [3] | [4] | [5] | [6] | [7] = [5] x [6] | [8] | [9] = [7] x [8] / 100 |
| 1899 | | 116.03 | | | 129.40 | 2,278 | 294,754 | 81.12 | 239,115 |
| 1900 | | 113.92 | −1.814% | −1.270% | 127.75 | 2,261 | 288,852 | 81.97 | 236,765 |
| 1901 | | 112.77 | −1.008% | −0.705% | 126.85 | 2,318 | 294,102 | 82.91 | 243,826 |
| 1902 | | 108.67 | −3.637% | −2.546% | 123.62 | 2,385 | 294,852 | 85.51 | 252,117 |
| 1903 | | 107.35 | −1.214% | −0.850% | 122.57 | 2,453 | 300,705 | 85.51 | 257,121 |
| 1904 | | 107.24 | −0.106% | −0.074% | 122.48 | 2,523 | 309,076 | 87.28 | 269,764 |
| 1905 | | 105.29 | −1.816% | −1.271% | 120.93 | 2,596 | 313,911 | 90.18 | 283,077 |
| 1906 | | 106.94 | 1.562% | 1.094% | 122.25 | 2,670 | 326,453 | 87.80 | 286,620 |
| 1907 | | 107.05 | 0.102% | 0.071% | 122.33 | 2,747 | 336,074 | 85.69 | 287,973 |
| 1908 | | 107.87 | 0.772% | 0.541% | 123.00 | 2,826 | 347,618 | 87.02 | 302,501 |
| 1909 | | 110.50 | 2.437% | 1.706% | 125.09 | 2,908 | 363,717 | 85.83 | 312,181 |
| 1910 | | 108.44 | −1.861% | −1.303% | 123.46 | 2,991 | 369,278 | 87.09 | 321,616 |
| 1911 | | 98.90 | −8.802% | −6.162% | 115.86 | 3,084 | 357,277 | 102.81 | 367,321 |
| 1912 | | 97.22 | −1.696% | −1.187% | 114.48 | 3,186 | 364,774 | 105.84 | 386,065 |
| 1913 | | 95.24 | −2.036% | −1.425% | 112.85 | 3,292 | 371,468 | 105.09 | 390,379 |
| 1914 | | 100.00 | 4.995% | 3.497% | 116.80 | 3,400 | 397,113 | 100.00 | 397,113 |
| 1915 | | 93.86 | −6.142% | −4.299% | 111.77 | 3,511 | 392,491 | 104.73 | 411,052 |
| 1916 | | 88.38 | −5.833% | −4.083% | 107.21 | 3,626 | 388,750 | 106.47 | 413,917 |
| 1917 | | 100.72 | 13.954% | 9.768% | 117.68 | 3,744 | 440,599 | 115.77 | 510,068 |
| 1918 | | 104.36 | 3.614% | 2.530% | 120.66 | 3,865 | 466,390 | 139.48 | 650,498 |
| 1919 | | 92.87 | −11.007% | −7.705% | 111.36 | 3,990 | 444,356 | 183.87 | 817,053 |
| 1920 | | 89.13 | −4.028% | −2.819% | 108.22 | 4,118 | 445,720 | 243.98 | 1,087,453 |
| 1921 | | 112.82 | 26.583% | 18.608% | 128.36 | 4,270 | 548,144 | 167.96 | 920,667 |
| 1922 | | 123.66 | 9.603% | 6.722% | 136.99 | 4,464 | 611,566 | 144.20 | 881,853 |
| 1923 | | 126.94 | 2.658% | 1.861% | 139.54 | 4,628 | 645,784 | 144.28 | 931,739 |
| 1924 | | 127.47 | 0.412% | 0.288% | 139.94 | 4,795 | 670,974 | 144.61 | 970,270 |
| 1925 | | 124.53 | −2.308% | −1.615% | 137.68 | 5,002 | 688,728 | 149.58 | 1,030,196 |
| 1926 | | 120.44 | −3.285% | −2.299% | 134.52 | 5,202 | 699,707 | 158.49 | 1,108,985 |
| 1927 | | 127.57 | 5.925% | 4.148% | 140.10 | 5,407 | 757,445 | 154.85 | 1,172,884 |
| 1928 | | 131.90 | 3.394% | 2.376% | 143.43 | 5,614 | 805,238 | 150.77 | 1,214,082 |
| 1929 | | 131.51 | −0.296% | −0.208% | 143.13 | 5,825 | 833,744 | 147.73 | 1,231,707 |
| 1930 | 141.39 | 129.23 | −1.734% | −1.214% | 141.39 | 5,754 | 813,609 | 138.26 | 1,124,861 |
| 1931 | | 115.38 | −10.717% | −7.502% | 130.78 | 2,814 | 368,067 | 104.59 | 384,956 |
| 1932 | | 122.09 | 5.817% | 4.072% | 136.11 | 2,730 | 371,568 | 89.18 | 331,362 |
| 1933 | | 136.87 | 12.102% | 8.471% | 147.64 | 2,573 | 379,800 | 82.36 | 312,791 |
| 1934 | | 130.38 | −4.738% | −3.316% | 142.74 | 2,626 | 374,861 | 86.41 | 323,922 |
| 1935 | | 137.02 | 5.092% | 3.564% | 147.83 | 2,862 | 423,022 | 94.68 | 400,528 |
| 1936 | | 148.89 | 8.661% | 6.062% | 156.79 | 3,016 | 472,855 | 92.21 | 436,016 |
| 1937 | | 150.08 | 0.798% | 0.558% | 157.67 | 3,257 | 513,590 | 101.76 | 522,633 |
| 1938 | | 155.10 | 3.348% | 2.343% | 161.36 | 3,550 | 572,865 | 94.29 | 540,170 |
| 1939 | | 154.06 | −0.672% | −0.470% | 160.60 | 3,638 | 584,244 | 91.81 | 536,385 |

| Year | Annual Per-Capita Private Final Consumption Expenditure in Real Terms (1914 Prices) (Straits $) | Weighted Real Wage Indices of Agriculture and Non-agriculture Sectors (1914 = 100) | Changes in Real Wages (%) | Changes in Real Consumption (%) | Real Per-Capita Private Final Consumption Expenditure Based on Real Wages and Income Elasticities of Demand (1914 Prices) (Straits $) | Chinese, Indian, and Eurasian Clerical Population Standard (Numbers) | Total Real Private Final Consumption Expenditure on Food in the Domestic Market (1914 Prices) (Straits $) | Food Price Indices (1914 = 100) | Total Private Final Consumption Expenditure on Food in the Domestic Market (Current Prices) (Straits $) |
|---|---|---|---|---|---|---|---|---|---|
| | Step 4 | Step 5 | Step 6 | Step 7 | | Step 8 | Step 9 | Step 10 | Step 11 |
| | [1] | [2] | [3] | [4] | [5] | [6] | [7] = [5] x [6] | [8] | [9] = [7] x [8] / 100 |
| 1947 | | 164.71 | | | 109.19 | 14,072 | 1,536,486 | 394.16 | 6,056,184 |
| 1948 | 116.12 | 179.65 | 9.067% | 6.347% | 116.12 | 14,412 | 1,673,470 | 361.21 | 6,044,736 |
| 1949 | | 220.02 | 22.473% | 15.731% | 134.38 | 14,681 | 1,972,808 | 336.79 | 6,644,231 |
| 1950 | | 203.15 | −7.666% | −5.366% | 127.17 | 15,332 | 1,949,738 | 360.41 | 7,026,964 |
| 1951 | | 181.26 | −10.776% | −7.543% | 117.58 | 16,022 | 1,883,799 | 480.24 | 9,046,742 |
| 1952 | | 176.19 | −2.797% | −1.958% | 115.28 | 16,905 | 1,948,759 | 502.13 | 9,785,284 |
| 1953 | | 206.53 | 17.217% | 12.052% | 129.17 | 17,877 | 2,309,182 | 477.30 | 11,021,621 |
| 1954 | | 208.97 | 1.183% | 0.828% | 130.24 | 18,723 | 2,438,483 | 433.27 | 10,565,142 |
| 1955 | | 204.74 | −2.023% | −1.416% | 128.40 | 19,583 | 2,514,312 | 415.99 | 10,459,300 |
| 1956 | | 230.57 | 12.617% | 8.832% | 139.74 | 20,574 | 2,874,923 | 418.47 | 12,030,703 |
| 1957 | | 215.81 | −6.401% | −4.481% | 133.47 | 14,459 | 1,929,943 | 436.83 | 8,430,637 |
| 1958 | | 215.37 | −0.205% | −0.144% | 133.28 | 15,140 | 2,017,896 | 430.04 | 8,677,697 |
| 1959 | | 194.19 | −9.837% | −6.886% | 124.10 | 15,796 | 1,960,360 | 419.57 | 8,225,101 |
| 1960 | | 230.48 | 18.691% | 13.084% | 140.34 | 16,341 | 2,293,332 | 418.89 | 9,606,448 |

*(Continued)*

# Appendix Table 6: Singapore: Computation of PFCE in the Domestic Market, 1900–39 and 1948–60, Asiatic Clerical Standard [1899–1939] Malay Clerical Standard [1947–1960] — Food in Current and 1914 Prices (Straits $)

| Year | Annual Per-Capita Private Final Consumption Expenditure in Real Terms (1914 Prices) (Straits $) | Weighted Real Wage Indices of Agriculture and Non-agriculture Sectors (1914 = 100) | Changes in Real Wages (%) | Changes in Real Consumption (%) | Real Per-Capita Private Final Consumption Expenditure Based on Real Wages and Income Elasticities of Demand (1914 Prices) (Straits $) | Asiatic Clerical Population Standard (Numbers) | Total Real Private Final Consumption Expenditure on Food in the Domestic Market (1914 Prices) (Straits $) | Food Price Indices (1914 = 100) | Total Private Final Consumption Expenditure on Food in the Domestic Market (Current Prices) (Straits $) |
|---|---|---|---|---|---|---|---|---|---|
| | Step 4 | Step 5 | Step 6 | Step 7 | | Step 8 | Step 9 | Step 10 | Step 11 |
| | [1] | [2] | [3] | [4] | [5] | [6] | [7] = [5] x [6] | [8] | [9] = [7] x [8] / 100 |
| 1899 | | 116.03 | | | 122.17 | 19,362 | 2,365,451 | 81.12 | 1,918,941 |
| 1900 | | 113.92 | -1.814% | -1.270% | 120.62 | 19,219 | 2,318,085 | 81.97 | 1,900,083 |
| 1901 | | 112.77 | -1.008% | -0.705% | 119.77 | 19,707 | 2,360,215 | 82.91 | 1,956,742 |
| 1902 | | 108.67 | -3.637% | -2.546% | 116.72 | 20,273 | 2,366,234 | 85.51 | 2,023,278 |
| 1903 | | 107.35 | -1.214% | -0.850% | 115.73 | 20,853 | 2,413,206 | 85.51 | 2,063,442 |
| 1904 | | 107.24 | -0.106% | -0.074% | 115.64 | 21,449 | 2,480,389 | 87.28 | 2,164,903 |
| 1905 | | 105.29 | -1.816% | -1.271% | 114.17 | 22,065 | 2,519,186 | 90.18 | 2,271,742 |
| 1906 | | 106.94 | 1.562% | 1.094% | 115.42 | 22,699 | 2,619,838 | 87.80 | 2,300,177 |
| 1907 | | 107.05 | 0.102% | 0.071% | 115.50 | 23,351 | 2,697,047 | 85.69 | 2,311,031 |
| 1908 | | 107.87 | 0.772% | 0.541% | 116.13 | 24,023 | 2,789,691 | 87.02 | 2,427,624 |
| 1909 | | 110.50 | 2.437% | 1.706% | 118.11 | 24,714 | 2,918,889 | 85.83 | 2,505,303 |
| 1910 | | 108.44 | -1.861% | -1.303% | 116.57 | 25,423 | 2,963,516 | 87.09 | 2,581,026 |
| 1911 | | 98.90 | -8.802% | -6.162% | 109.39 | 27,137 | 2,968,406 | 102.81 | 3,051,851 |
| 1912 | | 97.22 | -1.696% | -1.187% | 108.09 | 28,039 | 3,030,688 | 105.84 | 3,207,586 |
| 1913 | | 95.24 | -2.036% | -1.425% | 106.55 | 28,967 | 3,086,311 | 105.09 | 3,243,430 |
| 1914 | | 100.00 | 4.995% | 3.497% | 110.27 | 29,920 | 3,299,381 | 100.00 | 3,299,381 |
| 1915 | | 93.86 | -6.142% | -4.299% | 105.53 | 30,901 | 3,260,980 | 104.73 | 3,415,187 |
| 1916 | | 88.38 | -5.833% | -4.083% | 101.22 | 31,909 | 3,229,896 | 106.47 | 3,438,989 |
| 1917 | | 100.72 | 13.954% | 9.768% | 111.11 | 32,947 | 3,660,677 | 115.77 | 4,237,852 |
| 1918 | | 104.36 | 3.614% | 2.530% | 113.92 | 34,015 | 3,874,956 | 139.48 | 5,404,605 |
| 1919 | | 92.87 | -11.007% | -7.705% | 105.14 | 35,113 | 3,691,895 | 183.87 | 6,788,409 |
| 1920 | | 89.13 | -4.028% | -2.819% | 102.18 | 36,243 | 3,703,227 | 243.98 | 9,035,001 |
| 1921 | | 112.82 | 26.583% | 18.608% | 121.19 | 46,973 | 5,692,752 | 167.96 | 9,561,594 |
| 1922 | | 123.66 | 9.603% | 6.722% | 129.34 | 49,107 | 6,351,428 | 144.20 | 9,158,498 |
| 1923 | | 126.94 | 2.658% | 1.861% | 131.75 | 50,907 | 6,706,794 | 144.28 | 9,676,592 |
| 1924 | | 127.47 | 0.412% | 0.288% | 132.13 | 52,741 | 6,968,408 | 144.61 | 10,076,751 |
| 1925 | | 124.53 | -2.308% | -1.615% | 129.99 | 55,025 | 7,152,797 | 149.58 | 10,699,112 |
| 1926 | | 120.44 | -3.285% | -2.299% | 127.00 | 57,218 | 7,266,811 | 158.49 | 11,517,373 |
| 1927 | | 127.57 | 5.925% | 4.148% | 132.27 | 59,473 | 7,866,456 | 154.85 | 12,181,004 |
| 1928 | | 131.90 | 3.394% | 2.376% | 135.41 | 61,758 | 8,362,805 | 150.77 | 12,608,868 |
| 1929 | | 131.51 | -0.296% | -0.208% | 135.13 | 64,077 | 8,658,862 | 147.73 | 12,791,909 |
| 1930 | 133.49 | 129.23 | -1.734% | -1.214% | 133.49 | 63,298 | 8,449,746 | 138.26 | 11,682,255 |
| 1931 | | 115.38 | -10.717% | -7.502% | 123.48 | 61,915 | 7,645,132 | 104.59 | 7,995,939 |
| 1932 | | 122.09 | 5.817% | 4.072% | 128.51 | 60,059 | 7,717,856 | 89.18 | 6,882,733 |
| 1933 | | 136.87 | 12.102% | 8.471% | 139.39 | 56,595 | 7,888,838 | 82.36 | 6,496,983 |
| 1934 | | 130.38 | -4.738% | -3.316% | 134.77 | 57,775 | 7,786,242 | 86.41 | 6,728,193 |
| 1935 | | 137.02 | 5.092% | 3.564% | 139.57 | 62,954 | 8,786,599 | 94.68 | 8,319,369 |
| 1936 | | 148.89 | 8.661% | 6.062% | 148.03 | 66,348 | 9,821,685 | 92.21 | 9,056,503 |
| 1937 | | 150.08 | 0.798% | 0.558% | 148.86 | 71,663 | 10,667,783 | 101.76 | 10,855,624 |
| 1938 | | 155.10 | 3.348% | 2.343% | 152.35 | 78,104 | 11,898,996 | 94.29 | 11,219,893 |
| 1939 | | 154.06 | -0.672% | -0.470% | 151.63 | 80,032 | 12,135,356 | 91.81 | 11,141,269 |

| Year | Annual Per-Capita Private Final Consumption Expenditure in Real Terms (1914 Prices) (Straits $) | Weighted Real Wage Indices of Agriculture and Non-agriculture Sectors (1914 = 100) | Changes in Real Wages (%) | Changes in Real Consumption (%) | Real Per-Capita Private Final Consumption Expenditure Based on Real Wages and Income Elasticities of Demand (1914 Prices) (Straits $) | Malay Clerical Population Standard (Numbers) | Total Real Private Final Consumption Expenditure on Food in the Domestic Market (1914 Prices) (Straits $) | Food Price Indices (1914 = 100) | Total Private Final Consumption Expenditure on Food in the Domestic Market (Current Prices) (Straits $) |
|---|---|---|---|---|---|---|---|---|---|
| | Step 4 | Step 5 | Step 6 | Step 7 | | Step 8 | Step 9 | Step 10 | Step 11 |
| | [1] | [2] | [3] | [4] | [5] | [6] | [7] = [5] x [6] | [8] | [9] = [7] x [8] / 100 |
| 1947 | | 164.71 | | | 117.49 | 126,649 | 14,880,415 | 394.16 | 58,652,354 |
| 1948 | 124.95 | 179.65 | 9.067% | 6.347% | 124.95 | 129,708 | 16,207,060 | 361.21 | 58,541,478 |
| 1949 | | 220.02 | 22.473% | 15.731% | 144.61 | 132,125 | 19,106,061 | 336.79 | 64,347,408 |
| 1950 | | 203.15 | -7.666% | -5.366% | 136.85 | 137,984 | 18,882,632 | 360.41 | 68,054,065 |
| 1951 | | 181.26 | -10.776% | -7.543% | 126.52 | 144,194 | 18,244,033 | 480.24 | 87,615,014 |
| 1952 | | 176.19 | -2.797% | -1.958% | 124.05 | 152,145 | 18,873,159 | 502.13 | 94,767,577 |
| 1953 | | 206.53 | 17.217% | 12.052% | 139.00 | 160,893 | 22,363,745 | 477.30 | 106,741,141 |
| 1954 | | 208.97 | 1.183% | 0.828% | 140.15 | 168,507 | 23,615,987 | 433.27 | 102,320,276 |
| 1955 | | 204.74 | -2.023% | -1.416% | 138.16 | 176,243 | 24,350,367 | 415.99 | 101,295,220 |
| 1956 | | 230.57 | 12.617% | 8.832% | 150.37 | 185,166 | 27,842,779 | 418.47 | 116,513,798 |
| 1957 | | 215.81 | -6.401% | -4.481% | 143.63 | 267,497 | 38,420,248 | 436.83 | 167,832,451 |
| 1958 | | 215.37 | -0.205% | -0.144% | 143.42 | 280,090 | 40,171,155 | 430.04 | 172,750,785 |
| 1959 | | 194.19 | -9.837% | -6.886% | 133.55 | 292,226 | 39,025,764 | 419.57 | 163,740,769 |
| 1960 | | 230.48 | 18.691% | 13.084% | 151.02 | 302,309 | 45,654,378 | 418.89 | 191,239,850 |

(*Continued*)

## Appendix Table 6: Singapore: Computation of PFCE in the Domestic Market, 1900–39 and 1948–60, Chinese Labor Standard — Food in Current and 1914 Prices (Straits $)

| Year | Annual Per-Capita Private Final Consumption Expenditure in Real Terms (1914 Prices) (Straits $) | Weighted Real Wage Indices of Agriculture and Non-agriculture Sectors (1914 = 100) | Changes in Real Wages (%) | Changes in Real Consumption (%) | Real Per-Capita Private Final Consumption Expenditure Based on Real Wages and Income Elasticities of Demand (1914 Prices) (Straits $) | Chinese Labor Population Standard (Numbers) | Total Real Private Final Consumption Expenditure on Food in the Domestic Market (1914 Prices) (Straits $) | Food Price Indices (1914 = 100) | Total Private Final Consumption Expenditure on Food in the Domestic Market (Current Prices) (Straits $) |
|---|---|---|---|---|---|---|---|---|---|
| | Step 4 | Step 5 | Step 6 | Step 7 | | Step 8 | Step 9 | Step 10 | Step 11 |
| | [1] | [2] | [3] | [4] | [5] | [6] | [7] = [5] x [6] | [8] | [9] = [7] x [8] / 100 |
| 1899 | | 116.03 | | | 78.77 | 135,535 | 10,676,299 | 81.12 | 8,661,010 |
| 1900 | | 113.92 | −1.814% | −1.270% | 77.77 | 134,530 | 10,462,517 | 81.97 | 8,575,892 |
| 1901 | | 112.77 | −1.008% | −0.705% | 77.22 | 137,948 | 10,652,668 | 82.91 | 8,831,623 |
| 1902 | | 108.67 | −3.637% | −2.546% | 75.26 | 141,912 | 10,679,836 | 85.51 | 9,131,925 |
| 1903 | | 107.35 | −1.214% | −0.850% | 74.62 | 145,970 | 10,891,840 | 85.51 | 9,313,202 |
| 1904 | | 107.24 | −0.106% | −0.074% | 74.56 | 150,145 | 11,195,067 | 87.28 | 9,771,141 |
| 1905 | | 105.29 | −1.816% | −1.271% | 73.61 | 154,457 | 11,370,172 | 90.18 | 10,253,353 |
| 1906 | | 106.94 | 1.562% | 1.094% | 74.42 | 158,890 | 11,824,459 | 87.80 | 10,381,691 |
| 1907 | | 107.05 | 0.102% | 0.071% | 74.47 | 163,456 | 12,172,938 | 85.69 | 10,430,678 |
| 1908 | | 107.87 | 0.772% | 0.541% | 74.87 | 168,162 | 12,591,079 | 87.02 | 10,956,913 |
| 1909 | | 110.50 | 2.437% | 1.706% | 76.15 | 172,999 | 13,174,207 | 85.83 | 11,307,512 |
| 1910 | | 108.44 | −1.861% | −1.303% | 75.16 | 177,962 | 13,375,628 | 87.09 | 11,649,283 |
| 1911 | | 98.90 | −8.802% | −6.162% | 70.53 | 185,643 | 13,093,203 | 102.81 | 13,461,266 |
| 1912 | | 97.22 | −1.696% | −1.187% | 69.69 | 191,815 | 13,367,921 | 105.84 | 14,148,191 |
| 1913 | | 95.24 | −2.036% | −1.425% | 68.70 | 198,160 | 13,613,267 | 105.09 | 14,306,294 |
| 1914 | | 100.00 | 4.995% | 3.497% | 71.10 | 204,683 | 14,553,088 | 100.00 | 14,553,088 |
| 1915 | | 93.86 | −6.142% | −4.299% | 68.04 | 211,389 | 14,383,705 | 104.73 | 15,063,889 |
| 1916 | | 88.38 | −5.833% | −4.083% | 65.27 | 218,286 | 14,246,597 | 106.47 | 15,168,877 |
| 1917 | | 100.72 | 13.954% | 9.768% | 71.64 | 225,385 | 16,146,711 | 115.77 | 18,692,545 |
| 1918 | | 104.36 | 3.614% | 2.530% | 73.45 | 232,691 | 17,091,862 | 139.48 | 23,838,921 |
| 1919 | | 92.87 | −11.007% | −7.705% | 67.79 | 240,206 | 16,284,408 | 183.87 | 29,942,678 |
| 1920 | | 89.13 | −4.028% | −2.819% | 65.88 | 247,933 | 16,334,393 | 243.98 | 39,852,067 |
| 1921 | | 112.82 | 26.583% | 18.608% | 78.14 | 258,351 | 20,188,023 | 167.96 | 33,907,970 |
| 1922 | | 123.66 | 9.603% | 6.722% | 83.39 | 270,088 | 22,523,862 | 144.20 | 32,478,485 |
| 1923 | | 126.94 | 2.658% | 1.861% | 84.95 | 279,989 | 23,784,087 | 144.28 | 34,315,783 |
| 1924 | | 127.47 | 0.412% | 0.288% | 85.19 | 290,074 | 24,711,841 | 144.61 | 35,734,856 |
| 1925 | | 124.53 | −2.308% | −1.615% | 83.82 | 302,638 | 25,365,732 | 149.58 | 37,941,912 |
| 1926 | | 120.44 | −3.285% | −2.299% | 81.89 | 314,698 | 25,770,056 | 158.49 | 40,843,686 |
| 1927 | | 127.57 | 5.925% | 4.148% | 85.28 | 327,100 | 27,896,556 | 154.85 | 43,197,098 |
| 1928 | | 131.90 | 3.394% | 2.376% | 87.31 | 339,668 | 29,656,743 | 150.77 | 44,714,421 |
| 1929 | | 131.51 | −0.296% | −0.208% | 87.13 | 352,424 | 30,706,641 | 147.73 | 45,363,531 |
| 1930 | | 129.23 | −1.734% | −1.214% | 86.07 | 348,138 | 29,965,058 | 138.26 | 41,428,401 |
| 1931 | | 115.38 | −10.717% | −7.502% | 79.62 | 354,606 | 28,232,001 | 104.59 | 29,527,465 |
| 1932 | | 122.09 | 5.817% | 4.072% | 82.86 | 343,972 | 28,500,555 | 89.18 | 25,416,607 |
| 1933 | | 136.87 | 12.102% | 8.471% | 89.88 | 324,135 | 29,131,961 | 82.36 | 23,992,107 |
| 1934 | | 130.38 | −4.738% | −3.316% | 86.90 | 330,894 | 28,753,094 | 86.41 | 24,845,921 |
| 1935 | | 137.02 | 5.092% | 3.564% | 89.99 | 360,555 | 32,447,220 | 94.68 | 30,721,827 |
| 1936 | 95.45 | 148.89 | 8.661% | 6.062% | 95.45 | 379,993 | 36,269,593 | 92.21 | 33,443,923 |
| 1937 | | 150.08 | 0.798% | 0.558% | 95.98 | 410,436 | 39,394,071 | 101.76 | 40,087,730 |
| 1938 | | 155.10 | 3.348% | 2.343% | 98.23 | 447,323 | 43,940,700 | 94.29 | 41,432,906 |
| 1939 | | 154.06 | −0.672% | −0.470% | 97.77 | 458,365 | 44,813,534 | 91.81 | 41,142,562 |

| Year | Annual Per-Capita Private Final Consumption Expenditure in Real Terms (1914 Prices) (Straits $) | Weighted Real Wage Indices of Agriculture and Non-agriculture Sectors (1914 = 100) | Changes in Real Wages (%) | Changes in Real Consumption (%) | Real Per-Capita Private Final Consumption Expenditure Based on Real Wages and Income Elasticities of Demand (1914 Prices) (Straits $) | Chinese Labor Population Standard (Numbers) | Total Real Private Final Consumption Expenditure on Food in the Domestic Market (1914 Prices) (Straits $) | Food Price Indices (1914 = 100) | Total Private Final Consumption Expenditure on Food in the Domestic Market (Current Prices) (Straits $) |
|---|---|---|---|---|---|---|---|---|---|
| | Step 4 | Step 5 | Step 6 | Step 7 | | Step 8 | Step 9 | Step 10 | Step 11 |
| | [1] | [2] | [3] | [4] | [5] | [6] | [7] = [5] x [6] | [8] | [9] = [7] x [8] / 100 |
| 1947 | | 164.71 | | | 85.89 | 562,886 | 48,347,790 | 394.16 | 190,566,709 |
| 1948 | | 179.65 | 9.067% | 6.347% | 91.34 | 576,480 | 52,658,176 | 361.21 | 190,206,461 |
| 1949 | 105.71 | 220.02 | 22.473% | 15.731% | 105.71 | 587,220 | 62,077,288 | 336.79 | 209,070,446 |
| 1950 | | 203.15 | −7.666% | −5.366% | 100.04 | 613,260 | 61,351,347 | 360.41 | 221,113,702 |
| 1951 | | 181.26 | −10.776% | −7.543% | 92.50 | 640,860 | 59,276,484 | 480.24 | 284,668,964 |
| 1952 | | 176.19 | −2.797% | −1.958% | 90.68 | 676,200 | 61,320,570 | 502.13 | 307,908,275 |
| 1953 | | 206.53 | 17.217% | 12.052% | 101.61 | 715,080 | 72,661,792 | 477.30 | 346,811,448 |
| 1954 | | 208.97 | 1.183% | 0.828% | 102.45 | 748,920 | 76,730,440 | 433.27 | 332,447,666 |
| 1955 | | 204.74 | −2.023% | −1.416% | 101.00 | 783,300 | 79,116,505 | 415.99 | 329,117,168 |
| 1956 | | 230.57 | 12.617% | 8.832% | 109.92 | 822,960 | 90,463,664 | 418.47 | 378,563,678 |
| 1957 | | 215.81 | −6.401% | −4.481% | 105.00 | 788,031 | 82,742,576 | 436.83 | 361,447,159 |
| 1958 | | 215.37 | −0.205% | −0.144% | 104.85 | 825,130 | 86,513,364 | 430.04 | 372,039,375 |
| 1959 | | 194.19 | −9.837% | −6.886% | 97.63 | 860,882 | 84,046,628 | 419.57 | 352,635,234 |
| 1960 | | 230.48 | 18.691% | 13.084% | 110.40 | 890,585 | 98,322,138 | 418.89 | 411,857,778 |

(*Continued*)

## Appendix Table 6: Singapore: Computation of PFCE in the Domestic Market, 1900–39 and 1948–60, Malay Labor Standard — Food in Current and 1914 Prices (Straits $)

| Year | Annual Per-Capita Private Final Consumption Expenditure in Real Terms (1914 Prices) (Straits $) | Weighted Real Wage Indices of Agriculture and Non-agriculture Sectors (1914 = 100) | Changes in Real Wages (%) | Changes in Real Consumption (%) | Real Per-Capita Private Final Consumption Expenditure Based on Real Wages and Income Elasticities of Demand (1914 Prices) (Straits $) | Malay Labor Population Standard (Numbers) | Total Real Private Final Consumption Expenditure on Food in the Domestic Market (1914 Prices) (Straits $) | Food Price Indices (1914 = 100) | Total Private Final Consumption Expenditure on Food in the Domestic Market (Current Prices) (Straits $) |
|---|---|---|---|---|---|---|---|---|---|
| | Step 4 | Step 5 | Step 6 | Step 7 | | Step 8 | Step 9 | Step 10 | Step 11 |
| | [1] | [2] | [3] | [4] | [5] | [6] | [7] = [5] x [6] | [8] | [9] = [7] x [8] / 100 |
| 1899 | | 116.03 | | | 75.66 | 41,002 | 3,102,431 | 81.12 | 2,516,807 |
| 1900 | | 113.92 | −1.814% | −1.270% | 74.70 | 40,698 | 3,040,308 | 81.97 | 2,492,072 |
| 1901 | | 112.77 | −1.008% | −0.705% | 74.18 | 41,732 | 3,095,564 | 82.91 | 2,566,385 |
| 1902 | | 108.67 | −3.637% | −2.546% | 72.29 | 42,931 | 3,103,458 | 85.51 | 2,653,650 |
| 1903 | | 107.35 | −1.214% | −0.850% | 71.67 | 44,159 | 3,165,065 | 85.51 | 2,706,328 |
| 1904 | | 107.24 | −0.106% | −0.074% | 71.62 | 45,422 | 3,253,180 | 87.28 | 2,839,400 |
| 1905 | | 105.29 | −1.816% | −1.271% | 70.71 | 46,726 | 3,304,063 | 90.18 | 2,979,527 |
| 1906 | | 106.94 | 1.562% | 1.094% | 71.48 | 48,068 | 3,436,075 | 87.80 | 3,016,820 |
| 1907 | | 107.05 | 0.102% | 0.071% | 71.54 | 49,449 | 3,537,340 | 85.69 | 3,031,056 |
| 1908 | | 107.87 | 0.772% | 0.541% | 71.92 | 50,873 | 3,658,847 | 87.02 | 3,183,974 |
| 1909 | | 110.50 | 2.437% | 1.706% | 73.15 | 52,336 | 3,828,299 | 85.83 | 3,285,855 |
| 1910 | | 108.44 | −1.861% | −1.303% | 72.20 | 53,837 | 3,886,830 | 87.09 | 3,385,171 |
| 1911 | | 98.90 | −8.802% | −6.162% | 67.75 | 52,424 | 3,551,601 | 102.81 | 3,651,440 |
| 1912 | | 97.22 | −1.696% | −1.187% | 66.94 | 54,167 | 3,626,119 | 105.84 | 3,837,772 |
| 1913 | | 95.24 | −2.036% | −1.425% | 65.99 | 55,959 | 3,692,671 | 105.09 | 3,880,658 |
| 1914 | | 100.00 | 4.995% | 3.497% | 68.30 | 57,801 | 3,947,602 | 100.00 | 3,947,602 |
| 1915 | | 93.86 | −6.142% | −4.299% | 65.36 | 59,695 | 3,901,656 | 104.73 | 4,086,160 |
| 1916 | | 88.38 | −5.833% | −4.083% | 62.69 | 61,642 | 3,864,465 | 106.47 | 4,114,638 |
| 1917 | | 100.72 | 13.954% | 9.768% | 68.82 | 63,647 | 4,379,881 | 115.77 | 5,070,452 |
| 1918 | | 104.36 | 3.614% | 2.530% | 70.56 | 65,710 | 4,636,258 | 139.48 | 6,466,434 |
| 1919 | | 92.87 | −11.007% | −7.705% | 65.12 | 67,832 | 4,417,232 | 183.87 | 8,122,110 |
| 1920 | | 89.13 | −4.028% | −2.819% | 63.28 | 70,014 | 4,430,791 | 243.98 | 10,810,085 |
| 1921 | | 112.82 | 26.583% | 18.608% | 75.06 | 55,513 | 4,166,847 | 167.96 | 6,998,671 |
| 1922 | | 123.66 | 9.603% | 6.722% | 80.11 | 58,035 | 4,648,969 | 144.20 | 6,703,623 |
| 1923 | | 126.94 | 2.658% | 1.861% | 81.60 | 60,163 | 4,909,082 | 144.28 | 7,082,845 |
| 1924 | | 127.47 | 0.412% | 0.288% | 81.83 | 62,330 | 5,100,572 | 144.61 | 7,375,744 |
| 1925 | | 124.53 | −2.308% | −1.615% | 80.51 | 65,030 | 5,235,537 | 149.58 | 7,831,285 |
| 1926 | | 120.44 | −3.285% | −2.299% | 78.66 | 67,621 | 5,318,990 | 158.49 | 8,430,216 |
| 1927 | | 127.57 | 5.925% | 4.148% | 81.92 | 70,286 | 5,757,904 | 154.85 | 8,915,965 |
| 1928 | | 131.90 | 3.394% | 2.376% | 83.87 | 72,986 | 6,121,210 | 150.77 | 9,229,144 |
| 1929 | | 131.51 | −0.296% | −0.208% | 83.69 | 75,727 | 6,337,911 | 147.73 | 9,363,121 |
| 1930 | | 129.23 | −1.734% | −1.214% | 82.68 | 74,807 | 6,184,846 | 138.26 | 8,550,903 |
| 1931 | | 115.38 | −10.717% | −7.502% | 76.48 | 56,287 | 4,304,542 | 104.59 | 4,502,062 |
| 1932 | | 122.09 | 5.817% | 4.072% | 79.59 | 54,599 | 4,345,488 | 89.18 | 3,875,278 |
| 1933 | | 136.87 | 12.102% | 8.471% | 86.33 | 51,450 | 4,441,759 | 82.36 | 3,658,084 |
| 1934 | | 130.38 | −4.738% | −3.316% | 83.47 | 52,523 | 4,383,993 | 86.41 | 3,788,265 |
| 1935 | | 137.02 | 5.092% | 3.564% | 86.44 | 57,231 | 4,947,238 | 94.68 | 4,684,166 |
| 1936 | 91.68 | 148.89 | 8.661% | 6.062% | 91.68 | 60,316 | 5,530,036 | 92.21 | 5,099,205 |
| 1937 | | 150.08 | 0.798% | 0.558% | 92.20 | 65,149 | 6,006,426 | 101.76 | 6,112,188 |
| 1938 | | 155.10 | 3.348% | 2.343% | 94.36 | 71,004 | 6,699,652 | 94.29 | 6,317,288 |
| 1939 | | 154.06 | −0.672% | −0.470% | 93.91 | 72,756 | 6,832,733 | 91.81 | 6,273,019 |

| Year | Annual Per-Capita Private Final Consumption Expenditure in Real Terms (1914 Prices) (Straits $) | Weighted Real Wage Indices of Agriculture and Non-agriculture Sectors (1914 = 100) | Changes in Real Wages (%) | Changes in Real Consumption (%) | Real Per-Capita Private Final Consumption Expenditure Based on Real Wages and Income Elasticities of Demand (1914 Prices) (Straits $) | Malay Labor Population Standard (Numbers) | Total Real Private Final Consumption Expenditure on Food in the Domestic Market (1914 Prices) (Straits $) | Food Price Indices (1914 = 100) | Total Private Final Consumption Expenditure on Food in the Domestic Market (Current Prices) (Straits $) |
|---|---|---|---|---|---|---|---|---|---|
| | Step 4 | Step 5 | Step 6 | Step 7 | | Step 8 | Step 9 | Step 10 | Step 11 |
| | [1] | [2] | [3] | [4] | [5] | [6] | [7] = [5] x [6] | [8] | [9] = [7] x [8] / 100 |
| 1947 | | 164.71 | | | 72.48 | 84,433 | 6,119,372 | 394.16 | 24,119,997 |
| 1948 | | 179.65 | 9.067% | 6.347% | 77.08 | 86,472 | 6,664,937 | 361.21 | 24,074,400 |
| 1949 | 89.20 | 220.02 | 22.473% | 15.731% | 89.20 | 88,083 | 7,857,112 | 336.79 | 26,462,012 |
| 1950 | | 203.15 | −7.666% | −5.366% | 84.41 | 91,989 | 7,765,230 | 360.41 | 27,986,325 |
| 1951 | | 181.26 | −10.776% | −7.543% | 78.05 | 96,129 | 7,502,615 | 480.24 | 36,030,503 |
| 1952 | | 176.19 | −2.797% | −1.958% | 76.52 | 101,430 | 7,761,334 | 502.13 | 38,971,899 |
| 1953 | | 206.53 | 17.217% | 12.052% | 85.74 | 107,262 | 9,196,791 | 477.30 | 43,895,867 |
| 1954 | | 208.97 | 1.183% | 0.828% | 86.45 | 112,338 | 9,711,759 | 433.27 | 42,077,846 |
| 1955 | | 204.74 | −2.023% | −1.416% | 85.23 | 117,495 | 10,013,763 | 415.99 | 41,656,305 |
| 1956 | | 230.57 | 12.617% | 8.832% | 92.75 | 123,444 | 11,449,971 | 418.47 | 47,914,742 |
| 1957 | | 215.81 | −6.401% | −4.481% | 88.60 | 144,593 | 12,810,660 | 436.83 | 55,961,232 |
| 1958 | | 215.37 | −0.205% | −0.144% | 88.47 | 151,400 | 13,394,474 | 430.04 | 57,601,177 |
| 1959 | | 194.19 | −9.837% | −6.886% | 82.38 | 157,960 | 13,012,560 | 419.57 | 54,596,921 |
| 1960 | | 230.48 | 18.691% | 13.084% | 93.16 | 163,410 | 15,222,773 | 418.89 | 63,766,080 |

*(Continued)*

**Appendix Table 6:** Singapore: Computation of PFCE in the Domestic Market, 1900–39 and 1948–60, Indian Labor Standard — Food in Current and 1914 Prices (Straits $)

| Year | Annual Per-Capita Private Final Consumption Expenditure in Real Terms (1914 Prices) (Straits $) | Weighted Real Wage Indices of Agriculture and Non-agriculture Sectors (1914 = 100) | Changes in Real Wages (%) | Changes in Real Consumption (%) | Real Per-Capita Private Final Consumption Expenditure Based on Real Wages and Income Elasticities of Demand (1914 Prices) (Straits $) | Indian Labor Population Standard (Numbers) | Total Real Private Final Consumption Expenditure on Food in the Domestic Market (1914 Prices) (Straits $) | Food Price Indices (1914 = 100) | Total Private Final Consumption Expenditure on Food in the Domestic Market (Current Prices) (Straits $) |
| --- | --- | --- | --- | --- | --- | --- | --- | --- | --- |
| | Step 4 | Step 5 | Step 6 | Step 7 | | Step 8 | Step 9 | Step 10 | Step 11 |
| | [1] | [2] | [3] | [4] | [5] | [6] | [7] = [5] x [6] | [8] | [9] = [7] x [8] / 100 |
| 1899 | | 116.03 | | | 84.91 | 15,945 | 1,353,955 | 81.12 | 1,098,379 |
| 1900 | | 113.92 | −1.814% | −1.270% | 83.83 | 15,827 | 1,326,844 | 81.97 | 1,087,584 |
| 1901 | | 112.77 | −1.008% | −0.705% | 83.24 | 16,229 | 1,350,958 | 82.91 | 1,120,016 |
| 1902 | | 108.67 | −3.637% | −2.546% | 81.12 | 16,696 | 1,354,404 | 85.51 | 1,158,099 |
| 1903 | | 107.35 | −1.214% | −0.850% | 80.43 | 17,173 | 1,381,290 | 85.51 | 1,181,089 |
| 1904 | | 107.24 | −0.106% | −0.074% | 80.37 | 17,664 | 1,419,745 | 87.28 | 1,239,164 |
| 1905 | | 105.29 | −1.816% | −1.271% | 79.35 | 18,171 | 1,441,951 | 90.18 | 1,300,318 |
| 1906 | | 106.94 | 1.562% | 1.094% | 80.22 | 18,693 | 1,499,563 | 87.80 | 1,316,593 |
| 1907 | | 107.05 | 0.102% | 0.071% | 80.28 | 19,230 | 1,543,757 | 85.69 | 1,322,806 |
| 1908 | | 107.87 | 0.772% | 0.541% | 80.71 | 19,784 | 1,596,785 | 87.02 | 1,389,542 |
| 1909 | | 110.50 | 2.437% | 1.706% | 82.09 | 20,353 | 1,670,737 | 85.83 | 1,434,005 |
| 1910 | | 108.44 | −1.861% | −1.303% | 81.02 | 20,937 | 1,696,281 | 87.09 | 1,477,348 |
| 1911 | | 98.90 | −8.802% | −6.162% | 76.03 | 21,586 | 1,641,156 | 102.81 | 1,687,291 |
| 1912 | | 97.22 | −1.696% | −1.187% | 75.12 | 22,304 | 1,675,590 | 105.84 | 1,773,393 |
| 1913 | | 95.24 | −2.036% | −1.425% | 74.05 | 23,042 | 1,706,343 | 105.09 | 1,793,210 |
| 1914 | | 100.00 | 4.995% | 3.497% | 76.64 | 23,800 | 1,824,144 | 100.00 | 1,824,144 |
| 1915 | | 93.86 | −6.142% | −4.299% | 73.35 | 24,580 | 1,802,913 | 104.73 | 1,888,170 |
| 1916 | | 88.38 | −5.833% | −4.083% | 70.35 | 25,382 | 1,785,727 | 106.47 | 1,901,330 |
| 1917 | | 100.72 | 13.954% | 9.768% | 77.23 | 26,208 | 2,023,895 | 115.77 | 2,343,001 |
| 1918 | | 104.36 | 3.614% | 2.530% | 79.18 | 27,057 | 2,142,365 | 139.48 | 2,988,069 |
| 1919 | | 92.87 | −11.007% | −7.705% | 73.08 | 27,931 | 2,041,155 | 183.87 | 3,753,139 |
| 1920 | | 89.13 | −4.028% | −2.819% | 71.02 | 28,829 | 2,047,420 | 243.98 | 4,995,223 |
| 1921 | | 112.82 | 26.583% | 18.608% | 84.23 | 34,162 | 2,877,603 | 167.96 | 4,833,245 |
| 1922 | | 123.66 | 9.603% | 6.722% | 89.90 | 35,714 | 3,210,554 | 144.20 | 4,629,487 |
| 1923 | | 126.94 | 2.658% | 1.861% | 91.57 | 37,023 | 3,390,186 | 144.28 | 4,891,375 |
| 1924 | | 127.47 | 0.412% | 0.288% | 91.83 | 38,357 | 3,522,428 | 144.61 | 5,093,650 |
| 1925 | | 124.53 | −2.308% | −1.615% | 90.35 | 40,018 | 3,615,634 | 149.58 | 5,408,244 |
| 1926 | | 120.44 | −3.285% | −2.299% | 88.27 | 41,613 | 3,673,266 | 158.49 | 5,821,863 |
| 1927 | | 127.57 | 5.925% | 4.148% | 91.93 | 43,253 | 3,976,378 | 154.85 | 6,157,319 |
| 1928 | | 131.90 | 3.394% | 2.376% | 94.12 | 44,915 | 4,227,275 | 150.77 | 6,373,598 |
| 1929 | | 131.51 | −0.296% | −0.208% | 93.92 | 46,602 | 4,376,928 | 147.73 | 6,466,122 |
| 1930 | | 129.23 | −1.734% | −1.214% | 92.78 | 46,035 | 4,271,222 | 138.26 | 5,905,208 |
| 1931 | | 115.38 | −10.717% | −7.502% | 85.82 | 50,658 | 4,347,565 | 104.59 | 4,547,059 |
| 1932 | | 122.09 | 5.817% | 4.072% | 89.32 | 49,139 | 4,388,921 | 89.18 | 3,914,011 |
| 1933 | 96.88 | 136.87 | 12.102% | 8.471% | 96.88 | 46,305 | 4,486,154 | 82.36 | 3,694,646 |
| 1934 | | 130.38 | −4.738% | −3.316% | 93.67 | 47,271 | 4,427,810 | 86.41 | 3,826,128 |
| 1935 | | 137.02 | 5.092% | 3.564% | 97.01 | 51,508 | 4,996,684 | 94.68 | 4,730,984 |
| 1936 | | 148.89 | 8.661% | 6.062% | 102.89 | 54,285 | 5,585,307 | 92.21 | 5,150,171 |
| 1937 | | 150.08 | 0.798% | 0.558% | 103.46 | 58,634 | 6,066,459 | 101.76 | 6,173,279 |
| 1938 | | 155.10 | 3.348% | 2.343% | 105.89 | 63,903 | 6,766,614 | 94.29 | 6,380,428 |
| 1939 | | 154.06 | −0.672% | −0.470% | 105.39 | 65,481 | 6,901,025 | 91.81 | 6,335,717 |

| Year | Annual Per-Capita Private Final Consumption Expenditure in Real Terms (1914 Prices) (Straits $) | Weighted Real Wage Indices of Agriculture and Non-agriculture Sectors (1914 = 100) | Changes in Real Wages (%) | Changes in Real Consumption (%) | Real Per-Capita Private Final Consumption Expenditure Based on Real Wages and Income Elasticities of Demand (1914 Prices) (Straits $) | Indian Labor Population Standard (Numbers) | Total Real Private Final Consumption Expenditure on Food in the Domestic Market (1914 Prices) (Straits $) | Food Price Indices (1914 = 100) | Total Private Final Consumption Expenditure on Food in the Domestic Market (Current Prices) (Straits $) |
| --- | --- | --- | --- | --- | --- | --- | --- | --- | --- |
| | Step 4 | Step 5 | Step 6 | Step 7 | | Step 8 | Step 9 | Step 10 | Step 11 |
| | [1] | [2] | [3] | [4] | [5] | [6] | [7] = [5] x [6] | [8] | [9] = [7] x [8] / 100 |
| 1947 | | 164.71 | | | 98.37 | 93,814 | 9,228,276 | 394.16 | 36,373,992 |
| 1948 | | 179.65 | 9.067% | 6.347% | 104.61 | 96,080 | 10,051,011 | 361.21 | 36,305,230 |
| 1949 | 121.07 | 220.02 | 22.473% | 15.731% | 121.07 | 97,870 | 11,848,863 | 336.79 | 39,905,851 |
| 1950 | | 203.15 | −7.666% | −5.366% | 114.57 | 102,210 | 11,710,300 | 360.41 | 42,204,580 |
| 1951 | | 181.26 | −10.776% | −7.543% | 105.93 | 106,810 | 11,314,265 | 480.24 | 54,335,548 |
| 1952 | | 176.19 | −2.797% | −1.958% | 103.85 | 112,700 | 11,704,426 | 502.13 | 58,771,299 |
| 1953 | | 206.53 | 17.217% | 12.052% | 116.37 | 119,180 | 13,869,156 | 477.30 | 66,196,855 |
| 1954 | | 208.97 | 1.183% | 0.828% | 117.33 | 124,820 | 14,645,750 | 433.27 | 63,455,200 |
| 1955 | | 204.74 | −2.023% | −1.416% | 115.67 | 130,550 | 15,101,185 | 415.99 | 62,819,499 |
| 1956 | | 230.57 | 12.617% | 8.832% | 125.89 | 137,160 | 17,267,048 | 418.47 | 72,257,490 |
| 1957 | | 215.81 | −6.401% | −4.481% | 120.25 | 144,593 | 17,387,123 | 436.83 | 75,952,748 |
| 1958 | | 215.37 | −0.205% | −0.144% | 120.08 | 151,400 | 18,179,498 | 430.04 | 78,178,545 |
| 1959 | | 194.19 | −9.837% | −6.886% | 111.81 | 157,960 | 17,661,150 | 419.57 | 74,101,053 |
| 1960 | | 230.48 | 18.691% | 13.084% | 126.44 | 163,410 | 20,660,936 | 418.89 | 86,545,791 |

(*Continued*)

## Appendix Table 6: Singapore: Computation of PFCE in the Domestic Market, 1900–39 and 1948–60, European Standard — Beverages and Tobacco in Current and 1914 Prices (Straits $)

| Year | Annual Per-Capita Private Final Consumption Expenditure in Real Terms (1914 Prices) (Straits $) | Weighted Real Wage Indices of Agriculture and Non-agriculture Sectors (1914 = 100) | Changes in Real Wages (%) | Changes in Real Consumption (%) | Real Per-Capita Private Final Consumption Expenditure Based on Real Wages and Income Elasticities of Demand (1914 Prices) (Straits $) | European Population Standard (Numbers) | Total Real Private Final Consumption Expenditure on Beverage and Tobacco in the Domestic Market (1914 Prices) (Straits $) | Beverage and Tobacco Price Indices (1914 = 100) | Total Private Final Consumption Expenditure on Beverages and Tobacco in the Domestic Market (Current Prices) (Straits $) |
|---|---|---|---|---|---|---|---|---|---|
| | Step 4 | Step 5 | Step 6 | Step 7 | | Step 8 | Step 9 | Step 10 | Step 11 |
| | [1] | [2] | [3] | [4] | [5] | [6] | [7] = [5] x [6] | [8] | [9] = [7] x [8] / 100 |
| 1899 | | 116.03 | | | 90.52 | 13,667 | 1,237,123 | 81.32 | 1,006,048 |
| 1900 | | 113.92 | −1.814% | −1.814% | 88.87 | 13,566 | 1,205,668 | 83.55 | 1,007,297 |
| 1901 | | 112.77 | −1.008% | −1.008% | 87.98 | 13,911 | 1,223,844 | 81.61 | 998,791 |
| 1902 | | 108.67 | −3.637% | −3.637% | 84.78 | 14,310 | 1,213,228 | 86.19 | 1,045,724 |
| 1903 | | 107.35 | −1.214% | −1.214% | 83.75 | 14,720 | 1,232,766 | 91.42 | 1,126,968 |
| 1904 | | 107.24 | −0.106% | −0.106% | 83.66 | 15,141 | 1,266,683 | 86.94 | 1,101,209 |
| 1905 | | 105.29 | −1.816% | −1.816% | 82.14 | 15,575 | 1,279,398 | 89.41 | 1,143,900 |
| 1906 | | 106.94 | 1.562% | 1.562% | 83.43 | 16,023 | 1,336,684 | 86.21 | 1,152,353 |
| 1907 | | 107.05 | 0.102% | 0.102% | 83.51 | 16,483 | 1,376,497 | 89.90 | 1,237,471 |
| 1908 | | 107.87 | 0.772% | 0.772% | 84.15 | 16,958 | 1,427,061 | 90.40 | 1,289,998 |
| 1909 | | 110.50 | 2.437% | 2.437% | 86.21 | 17,445 | 1,503,887 | 87.90 | 1,321,965 |
| 1910 | | 108.44 | −1.861% | −1.861% | 84.60 | 17,946 | 1,518,242 | 90.09 | 1,367,792 |
| 1911 | | 98.90 | −8.802% | −8.802% | 77.15 | 18,503 | 1,427,567 | 88.10 | 1,257,645 |
| 1912 | | 97.22 | −1.696% | −1.696% | 75.85 | 19,118 | 1,450,015 | 88.64 | 1,285,291 |
| 1913 | | 95.24 | −2.036% | −2.036% | 74.30 | 19,750 | 1,467,479 | 99.12 | 1,454,517 |
| 1914 | | 100.00 | 4.995% | 4.995% | 78.01 | 20,400 | 1,591,505 | 100.00 | 1,591,505 |
| 1915 | | 93.86 | −6.142% | −6.142% | 73.22 | 21,069 | 1,542,697 | 91.83 | 1,416,584 |
| 1916 | | 88.38 | −5.833% | −5.833% | 68.95 | 21,756 | 1,500,116 | 135.91 | 2,038,877 |
| 1917 | | 100.72 | 13.954% | 13.954% | 78.57 | 22,464 | 1,765,031 | 127.84 | 2,256,424 |
| 1918 | | 104.36 | 3.614% | 3.614% | 81.41 | 23,192 | 1,888,105 | 174.54 | 3,295,554 |
| 1919 | | 92.87 | −11.007% | −11.007% | 72.45 | 23,941 | 1,734,547 | 201.99 | 3,503,645 |
| 1920 | | 89.13 | −4.028% | −4.028% | 69.53 | 24,711 | 1,718,239 | 236.50 | 4,063,634 |
| 1921 | | 112.82 | 26.583% | 26.583% | 88.02 | 27,757 | 2,443,086 | 237.22 | 5,795,380 |
| 1922 | | 123.66 | 9.603% | 9.603% | 96.47 | 29,018 | 2,799,341 | 233.57 | 6,538,468 |
| 1923 | | 126.94 | 2.658% | 2.658% | 99.03 | 30,082 | 2,979,109 | 201.55 | 6,004,534 |
| 1924 | | 127.47 | 0.412% | 0.412% | 99.44 | 31,165 | 3,099,131 | 188.81 | 5,851,452 |
| 1925 | | 124.53 | −2.308% | −2.308% | 97.15 | 32,515 | 3,158,753 | 186.19 | 5,881,150 |
| 1926 | | 120.44 | −3.285% | −3.285% | 93.96 | 33,811 | 3,176,734 | 187.93 | 5,970,117 |
| 1927 | | 127.57 | 5.925% | 5.925% | 99.52 | 35,143 | 3,497,568 | 180.99 | 6,330,153 |
| 1928 | | 131.90 | 3.394% | 3.394% | 102.90 | 36,493 | 3,755,238 | 181.13 | 6,801,976 |
| 1929 | | 131.51 | −0.296% | −0.296% | 102.60 | 37,864 | 3,884,714 | 176.61 | 6,860,973 |
| 1930 | 100.82 | 129.23 | −1.734% | −1.734% | 100.82 | 37,403 | 3,770,935 | 170.09 | 6,413,916 |
| 1931 | | 115.38 | −10.717% | −10.717% | 90.01 | 36,586 | 3,293,262 | 174.80 | 5,756,654 |
| 1932 | | 122.09 | 5.817% | 5.817% | 95.25 | 35,489 | 3,380,337 | 168.76 | 5,704,685 |
| 1933 | | 136.87 | 12.102% | 12.102% | 106.78 | 33,443 | 3,570,870 | 155.09 | 5,538,235 |
| 1934 | | 130.38 | −4.738% | −4.738% | 101.72 | 34,140 | 3,472,617 | 156.31 | 5,428,029 |
| 1935 | | 137.02 | 5.092% | 5.092% | 106.90 | 37,200 | 3,976,569 | 147.01 | 5,846,102 |
| 1936 | | 148.89 | 8.661% | 8.661% | 116.15 | 39,206 | 4,553,910 | 146.72 | 6,681,596 |
| 1937 | | 150.08 | 0.798% | 0.798% | 117.08 | 42,347 | 4,957,979 | 146.72 | 7,274,456 |
| 1938 | | 155.10 | 3.348% | 3.348% | 121.00 | 46,152 | 5,584,471 | 145.90 | 8,147,533 |
| 1939 | | 154.06 | −0.672% | −0.672% | 120.19 | 47,292 | 5,683,862 | 154.10 | 8,758,684 |

| Year | Annual Per-Capita Private Final Consumption Expenditure in Real Terms (1914 Prices) (Straits $) | Weighted Real Wage Indices of Agriculture and Non-agriculture Sectors (1914 = 100) | Changes in Real Wages (%) | Changes in Real Consumption (%) | Real Per-Capita Private Final Consumption Expenditure Based on Real Wages and Income Elasticities of Demand (1914 Prices) (Straits $) | European Population Standard (Numbers) | Total Real Private Final Consumption Expenditure on Beverage and Tobacco in the Domestic Market (1914 Prices) (Straits $) | Beverage and Tobacco Price Indices (1914 = 100) | Total Private Final Consumption Expenditure on Beverages and Tobacco in the Domestic Market (Current Prices) (Straits $) |
|---|---|---|---|---|---|---|---|---|---|
| | Step 4 | Step 5 | Step 6 | Step 7 | | Step 8 | Step 9 | Step 10 | Step 11 |
| | [1] | [2] | [3] | [4] | [5] | [6] | [7] = [5] x [6] | [8] | [9] = [7] x [8] / 100 |
| 1947 | | 164.71 | | | 160.64 | 56,289 | 9,042,300 | 493.82 | 44,652,793 |
| 1948 | 175.21 | 179.65 | 9.067% | 9.067% | 175.21 | 57,648 | 10,100,362 | 404.61 | 40,866,858 |
| 1949 | | 220.02 | 22.473% | 22.473% | 214.58 | 58,722 | 12,600,687 | 417.66 | 52,628,319 |
| 1950 | | 203.15 | −7.666% | −7.666% | 198.13 | 61,326 | 12,150,708 | 444.64 | 54,026,729 |
| 1951 | | 181.26 | −10.776% | −10.776% | 176.78 | 64,086 | 11,329,303 | 506.62 | 57,396,914 |
| 1952 | | 176.19 | −2.797% | −2.797% | 171.84 | 67,620 | 11,619,665 | 514.31 | 59,761,353 |
| 1953 | | 206.53 | 17.217% | 17.217% | 201.42 | 71,508 | 14,403,412 | 521.93 | 75,175,582 |
| 1954 | | 208.97 | 1.183% | 1.183% | 203.81 | 74,892 | 15,263,446 | 542.23 | 82,763,618 |
| 1955 | | 204.74 | −2.023% | −2.023% | 199.68 | 78,330 | 15,641,213 | 540.39 | 84,523,091 |
| 1956 | | 230.57 | 12.617% | 12.617% | 224.88 | 82,296 | 18,506,546 | 542.24 | 100,349,254 |
| 1957 | | 215.81 | −6.401% | −6.401% | 210.48 | 86,756 | 18,260,581 | 549.94 | 100,422,640 |
| 1958 | | 215.37 | −0.205% | −0.205% | 210.05 | 90,840 | 19,080,983 | 550.13 | 104,970,472 |
| 1959 | | 194.19 | −9.837% | −9.837% | 189.39 | 94,776 | 17,949,441 | 547.50 | 98,273,495 |
| 1960 | | 230.48 | 18.691% | 18.691% | 224.79 | 98,046 | 22,039,388 | 547.21 | 120,602,695 |

*(Continued)*

**Appendix Table 6:** Singapore: Computation of PFCE in the Domestic Market, 1900–39 and 1948–60, Eurasian Standard [1899–1939] Chinese, Indian, and Eurasian Clerical Standard [1947–1960] — Beverages and Tobacco in Current and 1914 Prices (Straits $).

| Year | Annual Per-Capita Private Final Consumption Expenditure in Real Terms (1914 Prices) (Straits $) | Weighted Real Wage Indices of Agriculture and Non-agriculture Sectors (1914 = 100) | Changes in Real Wages (%) | Changes in Real Consumption (%) | Real Per-Capita Private Final Consumption Expenditure Based on Real Wages and Income Elasticities of Demand (1914 Prices) (Straits $) | Eurasian Population Standard (Numbers) | Total Real Private Final Consumption Expenditure on Beverage and Tobacco in the Domestic Market (1914 Prices) (Straits $) | Beverage and Tobacco Price Indices (1914 = 100) | Total Private Final Consumption Expenditure on Beverages and Tobacco in the Domestic Market (Current Prices) (Straits $) |
|---|---|---|---|---|---|---|---|---|---|
| | Step 4 | Step 5 | Step 6 | Step 7 | | Step 8 | Step 9 | Step 10 | Step 11 |
| | [1] | [2] | [3] | [4] | [5] | [6] | [7] = [5] x [6] | [8] | [9] = [7] x [8] / 100 |
| 1899 | | 116.03 | | | 4.56 | 2,278 | 10,389 | 81.32 | 8,448 |
| 1900 | | 113.92 | −1.814% | −1.814% | 4.48 | 2,261 | 10,125 | 83.55 | 8,459 |
| 1901 | | 112.77 | −1.008% | −1.008% | 4.43 | 2,318 | 10,277 | 81.61 | 8,387 |
| 1902 | | 108.67 | −3.637% | −3.637% | 4.27 | 2,385 | 10,188 | 86.19 | 8,781 |
| 1903 | | 107.35 | −1.214% | −1.214% | 4.22 | 2,453 | 10,352 | 91.42 | 9,464 |
| 1904 | | 107.24 | −0.106% | −0.106% | 4.22 | 2,523 | 10,637 | 86.94 | 9,247 |
| 1905 | | 105.29 | −1.816% | −1.816% | 4.14 | 2,596 | 10,744 | 89.41 | 9,606 |
| 1906 | | 106.94 | 1.562% | 1.562% | 4.20 | 2,670 | 11,225 | 86.21 | 9,677 |
| 1907 | | 107.05 | 0.102% | 0.102% | 4.21 | 2,747 | 11,559 | 89.90 | 10,392 |
| 1908 | | 107.87 | 0.772% | 0.772% | 4.24 | 2,826 | 11,984 | 90.40 | 10,833 |
| 1909 | | 110.50 | 2.437% | 2.437% | 4.34 | 2,908 | 12,629 | 87.90 | 11,101 |
| 1910 | | 108.44 | −1.861% | −1.861% | 4.26 | 2,991 | 12,749 | 90.09 | 11,486 |
| 1911 | | 98.90 | −8.802% | −8.802% | 3.89 | 3,084 | 11,988 | 88.10 | 10,561 |
| 1912 | | 97.22 | −1.696% | −1.696% | 3.82 | 3,186 | 12,176 | 88.64 | 10,793 |
| 1913 | | 95.24 | −2.036% | −2.036% | 3.74 | 3,292 | 12,323 | 99.12 | 12,214 |
| 1914 | | 100.00 | 4.995% | 4.995% | 3.93 | 3,400 | 13,365 | 100.00 | 13,365 |
| 1915 | | 93.86 | −6.142% | −6.142% | 3.69 | 3,511 | 12,955 | 91.83 | 11,896 |
| 1916 | | 88.38 | −5.833% | −5.833% | 3.47 | 3,626 | 12,597 | 135.91 | 17,121 |
| 1917 | | 100.72 | 13.954% | 13.954% | 3.96 | 3,744 | 14,822 | 127.84 | 18,948 |
| 1918 | | 104.36 | 3.614% | 3.614% | 4.10 | 3,865 | 15,855 | 174.54 | 27,674 |
| 1919 | | 92.87 | −11.007% | −11.007% | 3.65 | 3,990 | 14,566 | 201.99 | 29,422 |
| 1920 | | 89.13 | −4.028% | −4.028% | 3.50 | 4,118 | 14,429 | 236.50 | 34,124 |
| 1921 | | 112.82 | 26.583% | 26.583% | 4.43 | 4,270 | 18,938 | 237.22 | 44,923 |
| 1922 | | 123.66 | 9.603% | 9.603% | 4.86 | 4,464 | 21,699 | 233.57 | 50,683 |
| 1923 | | 126.94 | 2.658% | 2.658% | 4.99 | 4,628 | 23,093 | 201.55 | 46,544 |
| 1924 | | 127.47 | 0.412% | 0.412% | 5.01 | 4,795 | 24,023 | 188.81 | 45,358 |
| 1925 | | 124.53 | −2.308% | −2.308% | 4.89 | 5,002 | 24,485 | 186.19 | 45,588 |
| 1926 | | 120.44 | −3.285% | −3.285% | 4.73 | 5,202 | 24,625 | 187.93 | 46,277 |
| 1927 | | 127.57 | 5.925% | 5.925% | 5.01 | 5,407 | 27,111 | 180.99 | 49,068 |
| 1928 | | 131.90 | 3.394% | 3.394% | 5.18 | 5,614 | 29,109 | 181.13 | 52,726 |
| 1929 | | 131.51 | −0.296% | −0.296% | 5.17 | 5,825 | 30,112 | 176.61 | 53,183 |
| 1930 | 5.08 | 129.23 | −1.734% | −1.734% | 5.08 | 5,754 | 29,230 | 170.09 | 49,718 |
| 1931 | | 115.38 | −10.717% | −10.717% | 4.54 | 2,814 | 12,764 | 174.80 | 22,311 |
| 1932 | | 122.09 | 5.817% | 5.817% | 4.80 | 2,730 | 13,101 | 168.76 | 22,110 |
| 1933 | | 136.87 | 12.102% | 12.102% | 5.38 | 2,573 | 13,840 | 155.09 | 21,465 |
| 1934 | | 130.38 | −4.738% | −4.738% | 5.13 | 2,626 | 13,459 | 156.31 | 21,038 |
| 1935 | | 137.02 | 5.092% | 5.092% | 5.39 | 2,862 | 15,412 | 147.01 | 22,658 |
| 1936 | | 148.89 | 8.661% | 8.661% | 5.85 | 3,016 | 17,650 | 146.72 | 25,896 |
| 1937 | | 150.08 | 0.798% | 0.798% | 5.90 | 3,257 | 19,216 | 146.72 | 28,194 |
| 1938 | | 155.10 | 3.348% | 3.348% | 6.10 | 3,550 | 21,644 | 145.90 | 31,578 |
| 1939 | | 154.06 | −0.672% | −0.672% | 6.06 | 3,638 | 22,029 | 154.10 | 33,947 |

| Year | Annual Per-Capita Private Final Consumption Expenditure in Real Terms (1914 Prices) (Straits $) | Weighted Real Wage Indices of Agriculture and Non-agriculture Sectors (1914 = 100) | Changes in Real Wages (%) | Changes in Real Consumption (%) | Real Per-Capita Private Final Consumption Expenditure Based on Real Wages and Income Elasticities of Demand (1914 Prices) (Straits $) | Chinese, Indian and Eurasian Clerical Population Standard (Numbers) | Total Real Private Final Consumption Expenditure on Beverage and Tobacco in the Domestic Market (1914 Prices) (Straits $) | Beverage and Tobacco Price Indices (1914 = 100) | Total Private Final Consumption Expenditure on Beverages and Tobacco in the Domestic Market (Current Prices) (Straits $) |
|---|---|---|---|---|---|---|---|---|---|
| | Step 4 | Step 5 | Step 6 | Step 7 | | Step 8 | Step 9 | Step 10 | Step 11 |
| | [1] | [2] | [3] | [4] | [5] | [6] | [7] = [5] x [6] | [8] | [9] = [7] x [8] / 100 |
| 1947 | | 164.71 | | | 4.69 | 14,072 | 66,009 | 493.82 | 325,966 |
| 1948 | 5.12 | 179.65 | 9.067% | 9.067% | 5.12 | 14,412 | 73,733 | 404.61 | 298,328 |
| 1949 | | 220.02 | 22.473% | 22.473% | 6.27 | 14,681 | 91,985 | 417.66 | 384,187 |
| 1950 | | 203.15 | −7.666% | −7.666% | 5.79 | 15,332 | 88,700 | 444.64 | 394,396 |
| 1951 | | 181.26 | −10.776% | −10.776% | 5.16 | 16,022 | 82,704 | 506.62 | 418,998 |
| 1952 | | 176.19 | −2.797% | −2.797% | 5.02 | 16,905 | 84,824 | 514.31 | 436,258 |
| 1953 | | 206.53 | 17.217% | 17.217% | 5.88 | 17,877 | 105,145 | 521.93 | 548,782 |
| 1954 | | 208.97 | 1.183% | 1.183% | 5.95 | 18,723 | 111,423 | 542.23 | 604,175 |
| 1955 | | 204.74 | −2.023% | −2.023% | 5.83 | 19,583 | 114,181 | 540.39 | 617,019 |
| 1956 | | 230.57 | 12.617% | 12.617% | 6.57 | 20,574 | 135,098 | 542.24 | 732,550 |
| 1957 | | 215.81 | −6.401% | −6.401% | 6.15 | 14,459 | 88,868 | 549.94 | 488,724 |
| 1958 | | 215.37 | −0.205% | −0.205% | 6.13 | 15,140 | 92,861 | 550.13 | 510,857 |
| 1959 | | 194.19 | −9.837% | −9.837% | 5.53 | 15,796 | 87,354 | 547.50 | 478,265 |
| 1960 | | 230.48 | 18.691% | 18.691% | 6.56 | 16,341 | 107,258 | 547.21 | 586,934 |

(*Continued*)

## Appendix Table 6: Singapore: Computation of PFCE in the Domestic Market, 1900–39 and 1948–60, Asiatic Clerical Standard [1899–1939] Malay, Clerical Standard [1947–1960] — Beverages and Tobacco in Current and 1914 Prices (Straits $)

| Year | Annual Per-Capita Private Final Consumption Expenditure in Real Terms (1914 Prices) (Straits $) | Weighted Real Wage Indices of Agriculture and Non-agriculture Sectors (1914 = 100) | Changes in Real Wages (%) | Changes in Real Consumption (%) | Real Per-Capita Private Final Consumption Expenditure Based on Real Wages and Income Elasticities of Demand (1914 Prices) (Straits $) | Asiatic Clerical Population Standard (Numbers) | Total Real Private Final Consumption Expenditure on Beverage and Tobacco in the Domestic Market (1914 Prices) (Straits $) | Beverage and Tobacco Price Indices (1914 = 100) | Total Private Final Consumption Expenditure on Beverages and Tobacco in the Domestic Market (Current Prices) (Straits $) |
|---|---|---|---|---|---|---|---|---|---|
| | Step 4 | Step 5 | Step 6 | Step 7 | | Step 8 | Step 9 | Step 10 | Step 11 |
| | [1] | [2] | [3] | [4] | [5] | [6] | [7]= [5] x [6] | [8] | [9]= [7] x [8] / 100 |
| 1899 | | 116.03 | | | 4.56 | 19,362 | 88,304 | 81.32 | 71,810 |
| 1900 | | 113.92 | –1.814% | –1.814% | 4.48 | 19,219 | 86,059 | 83.55 | 71,899 |
| 1901 | | 112.77 | –1.008% | –1.008% | 4.43 | 19,707 | 87,356 | 81.61 | 71,292 |
| 1902 | | 108.67 | –3.637% | –3.637% | 4.27 | 20,273 | 86,598 | 86.19 | 74,642 |
| 1903 | | 107.35 | –1.214% | –1.214% | 4.22 | 20,853 | 87,993 | 91.42 | 80,441 |
| 1904 | | 107.24 | –0.106% | –0.106% | 4.22 | 21,449 | 90,414 | 86.94 | 78,603 |
| 1905 | | 105.29 | –1.816% | –1.816% | 4.14 | 22,065 | 91,322 | 89.41 | 81,650 |
| 1906 | | 106.94 | 1.562% | 1.562% | 4.20 | 22,699 | 95,411 | 86.21 | 82,253 |
| 1907 | | 107.05 | 0.102% | 0.102% | 4.21 | 23,351 | 98,252 | 89.90 | 88,329 |
| 1908 | | 107.87 | 0.772% | 0.772% | 4.24 | 24,023 | 101,862 | 90.40 | 92,078 |
| 1909 | | 110.50 | 2.437% | 2.437% | 4.34 | 24,714 | 107,345 | 87.90 | 94,360 |
| 1910 | | 108.44 | –1.861% | –1.861% | 4.26 | 25,423 | 108,370 | 90.09 | 97,631 |
| 1911 | | 98.90 | –8.802% | –8.802% | 3.89 | 27,137 | 105,494 | 88.10 | 92,937 |
| 1912 | | 97.22 | –1.696% | –1.696% | 3.82 | 28,039 | 107,153 | 88.64 | 94,980 |
| 1913 | | 95.24 | –2.036% | –2.036% | 3.74 | 28,967 | 108,444 | 99.12 | 107,486 |
| 1914 | | 100.00 | 4.995% | 4.995% | 3.93 | 29,920 | 117,609 | 100.00 | 117,609 |
| 1915 | | 93.86 | –6.142% | –6.142% | 3.69 | 30,901 | 114,002 | 91.83 | 104,682 |
| 1916 | | 88.38 | –5.833% | –5.833% | 3.47 | 31,909 | 110,855 | 135.91 | 150,669 |
| 1917 | | 100.72 | 13.954% | 13.954% | 3.96 | 32,947 | 130,432 | 127.84 | 166,745 |
| 1918 | | 104.36 | 3.614% | 3.614% | 4.10 | 34,015 | 139,527 | 174.54 | 243,534 |
| 1919 | | 92.87 | –11.007% | –11.007% | 3.65 | 35,113 | 128,179 | 201.99 | 258,912 |
| 1920 | | 89.13 | –4.028% | –4.028% | 3.50 | 36,243 | 126,974 | 236.50 | 300,294 |
| 1921 | | 112.82 | 26.583% | 26.583% | 4.43 | 46,973 | 208,314 | 237.22 | 494,153 |
| 1922 | | 123.66 | 9.603% | 9.603% | 4.86 | 49,107 | 238,691 | 233.57 | 557,514 |
| 1923 | | 126.94 | 2.658% | 2.658% | 4.99 | 50,907 | 254,019 | 201.55 | 511,987 |
| 1924 | | 127.47 | 0.412% | 0.412% | 5.01 | 52,741 | 264,253 | 188.81 | 498,934 |
| 1925 | | 124.53 | –2.308% | –2.308% | 4.89 | 55,025 | 269,336 | 186.19 | 501,466 |
| 1926 | | 120.44 | –3.285% | –3.285% | 4.73 | 57,218 | 270,870 | 187.93 | 509,052 |
| 1927 | | 127.57 | 5.925% | 5.925% | 5.01 | 59,473 | 298,226 | 180.99 | 539,751 |
| 1928 | | 131.90 | 3.394% | 3.394% | 5.18 | 61,758 | 320,197 | 181.13 | 579,982 |
| 1929 | | 131.51 | –0.296% | –0.296% | 5.17 | 64,077 | 331,237 | 176.61 | 585,013 |
| 1930 | 5.08 | 129.23 | –1.734% | –1.734% | 5.08 | 63,298 | 321,535 | 170.09 | 546,894 |
| 1931 | | 115.38 | –10.717% | –10.717% | 4.54 | 61,915 | 280,806 | 174.80 | 490,851 |
| 1932 | | 122.09 | 5.817% | 5.817% | 4.80 | 60,059 | 288,230 | 168.76 | 486,420 |
| 1933 | | 136.87 | 12.102% | 12.102% | 5.38 | 56,595 | 304,476 | 155.09 | 472,227 |
| 1934 | | 130.38 | –4.738% | –4.738% | 5.13 | 57,775 | 296,099 | 156.31 | 462,830 |
| 1935 | | 137.02 | 5.092% | 5.092% | 5.39 | 62,954 | 339,069 | 147.01 | 498,478 |
| 1936 | | 148.89 | 8.661% | 8.661% | 5.85 | 66,348 | 388,297 | 146.72 | 569,718 |
| 1937 | | 150.08 | 0.798% | 0.798% | 5.90 | 71,663 | 422,751 | 146.72 | 620,269 |
| 1938 | | 155.10 | 3.348% | 3.348% | 6.10 | 78,104 | 476,170 | 145.90 | 694,713 |
| 1939 | | 154.06 | –0.672% | –0.672% | 6.06 | 80,032 | 484,644 | 154.10 | 746,824 |

| Year | Annual Per-Capita Private Final Consumption Expenditure in Real Terms (1914 Prices) (Straits $) | Weighted Real Wage Indices of Agriculture and Non-agriculture Sectors (1914 = 100) | Changes in Real Wages (%) | Changes in Real Consumption (%) | Real Per-Capita Private Final Consumption Expenditure Based on Real Wages and Income Elasticities of Demand (1914 Prices) (Straits $) | Malay Clerical Population Standard (Numbers) | Total Real Private Final Consumption Expenditure on Beverage and Tobacco in the Domestic Market (1914 Prices) (Straits $) | Beverage and Tobacco Price Indices (1914 = 100) | Total Private Final Consumption Expenditure on Beverages and Tobacco in the Domestic Market (Current Prices) (Straits $) |
|---|---|---|---|---|---|---|---|---|---|
| | Step 4 | Step 5 | Step 6 | Step 7 | | Step 8 | Step 9 | Step 10 | Step 11 |
| | [1] | [2] | [3] | [4] | [5] | [6] | [7] = [5] x [6] | [8] | [9] = [7] x [8] / 100 |
| 1947 | | 164.71 | | | 4.69 | 126,649 | 594,080 | 493.82 | 2,933,692 |
| 1948 | 5.12 | 179.65 | 9.067% | 9.067% | 5.12 | 129,708 | 663,595 | 404.61 | 2,684,956 |
| 1949 | | 220.02 | 22.473% | 22.473% | 6.27 | 132,125 | 827,866 | 417.66 | 3,457,684 |
| 1950 | | 203.15 | –7.666% | –7.666% | 5.79 | 137,984 | 798,302 | 444.64 | 3,549,560 |
| 1951 | | 181.26 | –10.776% | –10.776% | 5.16 | 144,194 | 744,336 | 506.62 | 3,770,982 |
| 1952 | | 176.19 | –2.797% | –2.797% | 5.02 | 152,145 | 763,413 | 514.31 | 3,926,325 |
| 1953 | | 206.53 | 17.217% | 17.217% | 5.88 | 160,893 | 946,305 | 521.93 | 4,939,041 |
| 1954 | | 208.97 | 1.183% | 1.183% | 5.95 | 168,507 | 1,002,810 | 542.23 | 5,437,576 |
| 1955 | | 204.74 | –2.023% | –2.023% | 5.83 | 176,243 | 1,027,629 | 540.39 | 5,553,173 |
| 1956 | | 230.57 | 12.617% | 12.617% | 6.57 | 185,166 | 1,215,881 | 542.24 | 6,592,953 |
| 1957 | | 215.81 | –6.401% | –6.401% | 6.15 | 267,497 | 1,644,063 | 549.94 | 9,041,395 |
| 1958 | | 215.37 | –0.205% | –0.205% | 6.13 | 280,090 | 1,717,926 | 550.13 | 9,450,852 |
| 1959 | | 194.19 | –9.837% | –9.837% | 5.53 | 292,226 | 1,616,050 | 547.50 | 8,847,900 |
| 1960 | | 230.48 | 18.691% | 18.691% | 6.56 | 302,309 | 1,984,282 | 547.21 | 10,858,275 |

*(Continued)*

**Appendix Table 6:** Singapore: Computation of PFCE in the Domestic Market, 1900–39 and 1948–60, Chinese Labor Standard — Beverages and Tobacco in Current and 1914 Prices (Straits $)

| Year | Annual Per-Capita Private Final Consumption Expenditure in Real Terms (1914 Prices) (Straits $) | Weighted Real Wage Indices of Agriculture and Non-agriculture Sectors (1914 = 100) | Changes in Real Wages (%) | Changes in Real Consumption (%) | Real Per-Capita Private Final Consumption Expenditure Based on Real Wages and Income Elasticities of Demand (1914 Prices) (Straits $) | Chinese Labor Population Standard (Numbers) | Total Real Private Final Consumption Expenditure on Beverage and Tobacco in the Domestic Market (1914 Prices) (Straits $) | Beverage and Tobacco Price Indices (1914 = 100) | Total Private Final Consumption Expenditure on Beverages and Tobacco in the Domestic Market (Current Prices) (Straits $) |
|---|---|---|---|---|---|---|---|---|---|
| | Step 4 | Step 5 | Step 6 | Step 7 | | Step 8 | Step 9 | Step 10 | Step 11 |
| | [1] | [2] | [3] | [4] | [5] | [6] | [7] = [5] x [6] | [8] | [9] = [7] x [8] / 100 |
| 1899 | | 116.03 | | | 4.68 | 135,535 | 634,748 | 81.32 | 516,187 |
| 1900 | | 113.92 | −1.814% | −1.088% | 4.63 | 134,530 | 623,181 | 83.55 | 520,648 |
| 1901 | | 112.77 | −1.008% | −0.605% | 4.60 | 137,948 | 635,151 | 81.61 | 518,353 |
| 1902 | | 108.67 | −3.637% | −2.182% | 4.50 | 141,912 | 639,147 | 86.19 | 550,904 |
| 1903 | | 107.35 | −1.214% | −0.728% | 4.47 | 145,970 | 652,633 | 91.42 | 596,623 |
| 1904 | | 107.24 | −0.106% | −0.064% | 4.47 | 150,145 | 670,873 | 86.94 | 583,233 |
| 1905 | | 105.29 | −1.816% | −1.089% | 4.42 | 154,457 | 682,620 | 89.41 | 610,325 |
| 1906 | | 106.94 | 1.562% | 0.937% | 4.46 | 158,890 | 708,796 | 86.21 | 611,052 |
| 1907 | | 107.05 | 0.102% | 0.061% | 4.46 | 163,456 | 729,611 | 89.90 | 655,920 |
| 1908 | | 107.87 | 0.772% | 0.463% | 4.48 | 168,162 | 754,094 | 90.40 | 681,666 |
| 1909 | | 110.50 | 2.437% | 1.462% | 4.55 | 172,999 | 787,127 | 87.90 | 691,910 |
| 1910 | | 108.44 | −1.861% | −1.117% | 4.50 | 177,962 | 800,668 | 90.09 | 721,326 |
| 1911 | | 98.90 | −8.802% | −5.281% | 4.26 | 185,643 | 791,114 | 88.10 | 696,949 |
| 1912 | | 97.22 | −1.696% | −1.017% | 4.22 | 191,815 | 809,099 | 88.64 | 717,184 |
| 1913 | | 95.24 | −2.036% | −1.221% | 4.17 | 198,160 | 825,651 | 99.12 | 818,358 |
| 1914 | | 100.00 | 4.995% | 2.997% | 4.29 | 204,683 | 878,391 | 100.00 | 878,391 |
| 1915 | | 93.86 | −6.142% | −3.685% | 4.13 | 211,389 | 873,739 | 91.83 | 802,313 |
| 1916 | | 88.38 | −5.833% | −3.500% | 3.99 | 218,286 | 870,673 | 135.91 | 1,183,372 |
| 1917 | | 100.72 | 13.954% | 8.372% | 4.32 | 225,385 | 974,253 | 127.84 | 1,245,490 |
| 1918 | | 104.36 | 3.614% | 2.168% | 4.42 | 232,691 | 1,027,646 | 174.54 | 1,793,684 |
| 1919 | | 92.87 | −11.007% | −6.604% | 4.12 | 240,206 | 990,775 | 201.99 | 2,001,285 |
| 1920 | | 89.13 | −4.028% | −2.417% | 4.03 | 247,933 | 997,935 | 236.50 | 2,360,115 |
| 1921 | | 112.82 | 26.583% | 15.950% | 4.67 | 258,351 | 1,205,725 | 237.22 | 2,860,168 |
| 1922 | | 123.66 | 9.603% | 5.762% | 4.94 | 270,088 | 1,333,129 | 233.57 | 3,113,811 |
| 1923 | | 126.94 | 2.658% | 1.595% | 5.01 | 279,989 | 1,404,044 | 201.55 | 2,829,917 |
| 1924 | | 127.47 | 0.412% | 0.247% | 5.03 | 290,074 | 1,458,213 | 188.81 | 2,753,243 |
| 1925 | | 124.53 | −2.308% | −1.385% | 4.96 | 302,638 | 1,500,309 | 186.19 | 2,793,363 |
| 1926 | | 120.44 | −3.285% | −1.971% | 4.86 | 314,698 | 1,529,348 | 187.93 | 2,874,142 |
| 1927 | | 127.57 | 5.925% | 3.555% | 5.03 | 327,100 | 1,646,128 | 180.99 | 2,979,282 |
| 1928 | | 131.90 | 3.394% | 2.037% | 5.13 | 339,668 | 1,744,191 | 181.13 | 3,159,306 |
| 1929 | | 131.51 | −0.296% | −0.178% | 5.13 | 352,424 | 1,806,475 | 176.61 | 3,190,499 |
| 1930 | | 129.23 | −1.734% | −1.040% | 5.07 | 348,138 | 1,765,942 | 170.09 | 3,003,659 |
| 1931 | | 115.38 | −10.717% | −6.430% | 4.75 | 354,606 | 1,683,084 | 174.80 | 2,942,047 |
| 1932 | | 122.09 | 5.817% | 3.490% | 4.91 | 343,972 | 1,689,597 | 168.76 | 2,851,379 |
| 1933 | | 136.87 | 12.102% | 7.261% | 5.27 | 324,135 | 1,707,761 | 155.09 | 2,648,650 |
| 1934 | | 130.38 | −4.738% | −2.843% | 5.12 | 330,894 | 1,693,811 | 156.31 | 2,647,587 |
| 1935 | | 137.02 | 5.092% | 3.055% | 5.28 | 360,555 | 1,902,031 | 147.01 | 2,796,246 |
| 1936 | 5.55 | 148.89 | 8.661% | 5.196% | 5.55 | 379,993 | 2,108,734 | 146.72 | 3,093,981 |
| 1937 | | 150.08 | 0.798% | 0.479% | 5.58 | 410,436 | 2,288,577 | 146.72 | 3,357,850 |
| 1938 | | 155.10 | 3.348% | 2.009% | 5.69 | 447,323 | 2,544,360 | 145.90 | 3,712,126 |
| 1939 | | 154.06 | −0.672% | −0.403% | 5.67 | 458,365 | 2,596,653 | 154.10 | 4,001,375 |

| Year | Annual Per-Capita Private Final Consumption Expenditure in Real Terms (1914 Prices) (Straits $) | Weighted Real Wage Indices of Agriculture and Non-agriculture Sectors (1914 = 100) | Changes in Real Wages (%) | Changes in Real Consumption (%) | Real Per-Capita Private Final Consumption Expenditure Based on Real Wages and Income Elasticities of Demand (1914 Prices) (Straits $) | Chinese Labor Population Standard (Numbers) | Total Real Private Final Consumption Expenditure on Beverage and Tobacco in the Domestic Market (1914 Prices) (Straits $) | Beverage and Tobacco Price Indices (1914 = 100) | Total Private Final Consumption Expenditure on Beverages and Tobacco in the Domestic Market (Current Prices) (Straits $) |
|---|---|---|---|---|---|---|---|---|---|
| | Step 4 | Step 5 | Step 6 | Step 7 | | Step 8 | Step 9 | Step 10 | Step 11 |
| | [1] | [2] | [3] | [4] | [5] | [6] | | [8] | |
| 1947 | | 164.71 | | | 6.51 | 562,886 | 3,664,934 | 493.82 | 18,098,222 |
| 1948 | | 179.65 | 9.067% | 9.067% | 7.10 | 576,480 | 4,093,777 | 404.61 | 16,563,744 |
| 1949 | 8.70 | 220.02 | 22.473% | 22.473% | 8.70 | 587,220 | 5,107,184 | 417.66 | 21,330,782 |
| 1950 | | 203.15 | −7.666% | −7.666% | 8.03 | 613,260 | 4,924,803 | 444.64 | 21,897,571 |
| 1951 | | 181.26 | −10.776% | −10.776% | 7.17 | 640,860 | 4,591,879 | 506.62 | 23,263,541 |
| 1952 | | 176.19 | −2.797% | −2.797% | 6.96 | 676,200 | 4,709,566 | 514.31 | 24,221,871 |
| 1953 | | 206.53 | 17.217% | 17.217% | 8.16 | 715,080 | 5,837,846 | 521.93 | 30,469,411 |
| 1954 | | 208.97 | 1.183% | 1.183% | 8.26 | 748,920 | 6,186,426 | 542.23 | 33,544,918 |
| 1955 | | 204.74 | −2.023% | −2.023% | 8.09 | 783,300 | 6,339,539 | 540.39 | 34,258,050 |
| 1956 | | 230.57 | 12.617% | 12.617% | 9.11 | 822,960 | 7,500,887 | 542.24 | 40,672,552 |
| 1957 | | 215.81 | −6.401% | −6.401% | 8.53 | 788,031 | 6,722,752 | 549.94 | 36,971,252 |
| 1958 | | 215.37 | −0.205% | −0.205% | 8.51 | 825,130 | 7,024,789 | 550.13 | 38,645,566 |
| 1959 | | 194.19 | −9.837% | −9.837% | 7.68 | 860,882 | 6,608,204 | 547.50 | 36,180,030 |
| 1960 | | 230.48 | 18.691% | 18.691% | 9.11 | 890,585 | 8,113,945 | 547.21 | 44,400,671 |

(*Continued*)

## Appendix Table 6: Singapore: Computation of PFCE in the Domestic Market, 1900–39 and 1948–60, Malay Labor Standard — Beverages and Tobacco in Current and 1914 Prices (Straits $)

| Year | Annual Per-Capita Private Final Consumption Expenditure in Real Terms (1914 Prices) (Straits $) | Weighted Real Wage Indices of Agriculture and Non-agriculture Sectors (1914 = 100) | Changes in Real Wages (%) | Changes in Real Consumption (%) | Real Per-Capita Private Final Consumption Expenditure Based on Real Wages and Income Elasticities of Demand (1914 Prices) (Straits $) | Malay Labor Population Standard (Numbers) | Total Real Private Final Consumption Expenditure on Beverage and Tobacco in the Domestic Market (1914 Prices) (Straits $) | Beverage and Tobacco Price Indices (1914 = 100) | Total Private Final Consumption Expenditure on Beverages and Tobacco in the Domestic Market (Current Prices) (Straits $) |
|---|---|---|---|---|---|---|---|---|---|
| | Step 4 | Step 5 | Step 6 | Step 7 | | Step 8 | Step 9 | Step 10 | Step 11 |
| | [1] | [2] | [3] | [4] | [5] | [6] | [7] = [5] x [6] | [8] | [9] = [7] x [8] / 100 |
| 1899 | | 116.03 | | | 5.86 | 41,002 | 240,359 | 81.32 | 195,464 |
| 1900 | | 113.92 | −1.814% | −1.088% | 5.80 | 40,698 | 235,979 | 83.55 | 197,153 |
| 1901 | | 112.77 | −1.008% | −0.605% | 5.76 | 41,732 | 240,512 | 81.61 | 196,284 |
| 1902 | | 108.67 | −3.637% | −2.182% | 5.64 | 42,931 | 242,025 | 86.19 | 208,610 |
| 1903 | | 107.35 | −1.214% | −0.728% | 5.60 | 44,159 | 247,132 | 91.42 | 225,922 |
| 1904 | | 107.24 | −0.106% | −0.064% | 5.59 | 45,422 | 254,039 | 86.94 | 220,852 |
| 1905 | | 105.29 | −1.816% | −1.089% | 5.53 | 46,726 | 258,487 | 89.41 | 231,111 |
| 1906 | | 106.94 | 1.562% | 0.937% | 5.58 | 48,068 | 268,399 | 86.21 | 231,386 |
| 1907 | | 107.05 | 0.102% | 0.061% | 5.59 | 49,449 | 276,281 | 89.90 | 248,376 |
| 1908 | | 107.87 | 0.772% | 0.463% | 5.61 | 50,873 | 285,552 | 90.40 | 258,126 |
| 1909 | | 110.50 | 2.437% | 1.462% | 5.70 | 52,336 | 298,060 | 87.90 | 262,005 |
| 1910 | | 108.44 | −1.861% | −1.117% | 5.63 | 53,837 | 303,188 | 90.09 | 273,144 |
| 1911 | | 98.90 | −8.802% | −5.281% | 5.33 | 52,424 | 279,638 | 88.10 | 246,353 |
| 1912 | | 97.22 | −1.696% | −1.017% | 5.28 | 54,167 | 285,995 | 88.64 | 253,505 |
| 1913 | | 95.24 | −2.036% | −1.221% | 5.22 | 55,959 | 291,845 | 99.12 | 289,267 |
| 1914 | | 100.00 | 4.995% | 2.997% | 5.37 | 57,801 | 310,488 | 100.00 | 310,488 |
| 1915 | | 93.86 | −6.142% | −3.685% | 5.17 | 59,695 | 308,843 | 91.83 | 283,596 |
| 1916 | | 88.38 | −5.833% | −3.500% | 4.99 | 61,642 | 307,760 | 135.91 | 418,290 |
| 1917 | | 100.72 | 13.954% | 8.372% | 5.41 | 63,647 | 344,372 | 127.84 | 440,247 |
| 1918 | | 104.36 | 3.614% | 2.168% | 5.53 | 65,710 | 363,245 | 174.54 | 634,019 |
| 1919 | | 92.87 | −11.007% | −6.604% | 5.16 | 67,832 | 350,212 | 201.99 | 707,401 |
| 1920 | | 89.13 | −4.028% | −2.417% | 5.04 | 70,014 | 352,743 | 236.50 | 834,237 |
| 1921 | | 112.82 | 26.583% | 15.950% | 5.84 | 55,513 | 324,295 | 237.22 | 769,279 |
| 1922 | | 123.66 | 9.603% | 5.762% | 6.18 | 58,035 | 358,562 | 233.57 | 837,499 |
| 1923 | | 126.94 | 2.658% | 1.595% | 6.28 | 60,163 | 377,635 | 201.55 | 761,142 |
| 1924 | | 127.47 | 0.412% | 0.247% | 6.29 | 62,330 | 392,205 | 188.81 | 740,520 |
| 1925 | | 124.53 | −2.308% | −1.385% | 6.21 | 65,030 | 403,527 | 186.19 | 751,310 |
| 1926 | | 120.44 | −3.285% | −1.971% | 6.08 | 67,621 | 411,338 | 187.93 | 773,037 |
| 1927 | | 127.57 | 5.925% | 3.555% | 6.30 | 70,286 | 442,747 | 180.99 | 801,316 |
| 1928 | | 131.90 | 3.394% | 2.037% | 6.43 | 72,986 | 469,122 | 181.13 | 849,736 |
| 1929 | | 131.51 | −0.296% | −0.178% | 6.42 | 75,727 | 485,874 | 176.61 | 858,125 |
| 1930 | | 129.23 | −1.734% | −1.040% | 6.35 | 74,807 | 474,972 | 170.09 | 807,872 |
| 1931 | | 115.38 | −10.717% | −6.430% | 5.94 | 56,287 | 334,402 | 174.80 | 584,539 |
| 1932 | | 122.09 | 5.817% | 3.490% | 6.15 | 54,599 | 335,696 | 168.76 | 566,524 |
| 1933 | | 136.87 | 12.102% | 7.261% | 6.59 | 51,450 | 339,305 | 155.09 | 526,245 |
| 1934 | | 130.38 | −4.738% | −2.843% | 6.41 | 52,523 | 336,534 | 156.31 | 526,034 |
| 1935 | | 137.02 | 5.092% | 3.055% | 6.60 | 57,231 | 377,904 | 147.01 | 555,570 |
| 1936 | 6.95 | 148.89 | 8.661% | 5.196% | 6.95 | 60,316 | 418,972 | 146.72 | 614,725 |
| 1937 | | 150.08 | 0.798% | 0.479% | 6.98 | 65,149 | 454,704 | 146.72 | 667,152 |
| 1938 | | 155.10 | 3.348% | 2.009% | 7.12 | 71,004 | 505,524 | 145.90 | 737,541 |
| 1939 | | 154.06 | −0.672% | −0.403% | 7.09 | 72,756 | 515,914 | 154.10 | 795,010 |

| Year | Annual Per-Capita Private Final Consumption Expenditure in Real Terms (1914 Prices) (Straits $) | Weighted Real Wage Indices of Agriculture and Non-agriculture Sectors (1914 = 100) | Changes in Real Wages (%) | Changes in Real Consumption (%) | Real Per-Capita Private Final Consumption Expenditure Based on Real Wages and Income Elasticities of Demand (1914 Prices) (Straits $) | Malay Labor Population Standard (Numbers) | Total Real Private Final Consumption Expenditure on Beverage and Tobacco in the Domestic Market (1914 Prices) (Straits $) | Beverage and Tobacco Price Indices (1914 = 100) | Total Private Final Consumption Expenditure on Beverages and Tobacco in the Domestic Market (Current Prices) (Straits $) |
|---|---|---|---|---|---|---|---|---|---|
| | Step 4 | Step 5 | Step 6 | Step 7 | | Step 8 | Step 9 | Step 10 | Step 11 |
| | [1] | [2] | [3] | [4] | [5] | [6] | [7] = [5] x [6] | [8] | [9] = [7] x [8] / 100 |
| 1947 | | 164.71 | | | 7.16 | 84,433 | 604,470 | 493.82 | 2,985,000 |
| 1948 | | 179.65 | 9.067% | 9.067% | 7.81 | 86,472 | 675,200 | 404.61 | 2,731,914 |
| 1949 | 9.56 | 220.02 | 22.473% | 22.473% | 9.56 | 88,083 | 842,345 | 417.66 | 3,518,157 |
| 1950 | | 203.15 | −7.666% | −7.666% | 8.83 | 91,989 | 812,264 | 444.64 | 3,611,639 |
| 1951 | | 181.26 | −10.776% | −10.776% | 7.88 | 96,129 | 757,354 | 506.62 | 3,836,933 |
| 1952 | | 176.19 | −2.797% | −2.797% | 7.66 | 101,430 | 776,764 | 514.31 | 3,994,994 |
| 1953 | | 206.53 | 17.217% | 17.217% | 8.98 | 107,262 | 962,855 | 521.93 | 5,025,422 |
| 1954 | | 208.97 | 1.183% | 1.183% | 9.08 | 112,338 | 1,020,348 | 542.23 | 5,532,675 |
| 1955 | | 204.74 | −2.023% | −2.023% | 8.90 | 117,495 | 1,045,601 | 540.39 | 5,650,294 |
| 1956 | | 230.57 | 12.617% | 12.617% | 10.02 | 123,444 | 1,237,146 | 542.24 | 6,708,259 |
| 1957 | | 215.81 | −6.401% | −6.401% | 9.38 | 144,593 | 1,356,338 | 549.94 | 7,459,072 |
| 1958 | | 215.37 | −0.205% | −0.205% | 9.36 | 151,400 | 1,417,274 | 550.13 | 7,796,871 |
| 1959 | | 194.19 | −9.837% | −9.837% | 8.44 | 157,960 | 1,333,227 | 547.50 | 7,299,441 |
| 1960 | | 230.48 | 18.691% | 18.691% | 10.02 | 163,410 | 1,637,015 | 547.21 | 8,957,982 |

*(Continued)*

**Appendix Table 6:** Singapore: Computation of PFCE in the Domestic Market, 1900–39 and 1948–60, Indian Labor Standard — Beverages and Tobacco in Current and 1914 Prices (Straits $)

| Year | Annual Per-Capita Private Final Consumption Expenditure in Real Terms (1914 Prices) (Straits $) | Weighted Real Wage Indices of Agriculture and Non-agriculture Sectors (1914 = 100) | Changes in Real Wages (%) | Changes in Real Consumption (%) | Real Per-Capita Private Final Consumption Expenditure Based on Real Wages and Income Elasticities of Demand (1914 Prices) (Straits $) | Indian Labor Population Standard (Numbers) | Total Real Private Final Consumption Expenditure on Beverage and Tobacco in the Domestic Market (1914 Prices) (Straits $) | Beverage and Tobacco Price Indices (1914 = 100) | Total Private Final Consumption Expenditure on Beverages and Tobacco in the Domestic Market (Current Prices) (Straits $) |
|---|---|---|---|---|---|---|---|---|---|
| | Step 4 | Step 5 | Step 6 | Step 7 | | Step 8 | Step 9 | Step 10 | Step 11 |
| | [1] | [2] | [3] | [4] | [5] | [6] | [7] = [5] x [6] | [8] | [9] = [7] x [8] / 100 |
| 1899 | | 116.03 | | | 8.94 | 15,945 | 142,574 | 81.32 | 115,943 |
| 1900 | | 113.92 | −1.814% | −1.814% | 8.78 | 15,827 | 138,949 | 83.55 | 116,087 |
| 1901 | | 112.77 | −1.008% | −1.008% | 8.69 | 16,229 | 141,044 | 81.61 | 115,107 |
| 1902 | | 108.67 | −3.637% | −3.637% | 8.37 | 16,696 | 139,820 | 86.19 | 120,516 |
| 1903 | | 107.35 | −1.214% | −1.214% | 8.27 | 17,173 | 142,072 | 91.42 | 129,879 |
| 1904 | | 107.24 | −0.106% | −0.106% | 8.26 | 17,664 | 145,981 | 86.94 | 126,910 |
| 1905 | | 105.29 | −1.816% | −1.816% | 8.11 | 18,171 | 147,446 | 89.41 | 131,830 |
| 1906 | | 106.94 | 1.562% | 1.562% | 8.24 | 18,693 | 154,048 | 86.21 | 132,805 |
| 1907 | | 107.05 | 0.102% | 0.102% | 8.25 | 19,230 | 158,636 | 89.90 | 142,614 |
| 1908 | | 107.87 | 0.772% | 0.772% | 8.31 | 19,784 | 164,464 | 90.40 | 148,668 |
| 1909 | | 110.50 | 2.437% | 2.437% | 8.52 | 20,353 | 173,318 | 87.90 | 152,352 |
| 1910 | | 108.44 | −1.861% | −1.861% | 8.36 | 20,937 | 174,972 | 90.09 | 157,633 |
| 1911 | | 98.90 | −8.802% | −8.802% | 7.62 | 21,586 | 164,522 | 88.10 | 144,939 |
| 1912 | | 97.22 | −1.696% | −1.696% | 7.49 | 22,304 | 167,109 | 88.64 | 148,125 |
| 1913 | | 95.24 | −2.036% | −2.036% | 7.34 | 23,042 | 169,122 | 99.12 | 167,628 |
| 1914 | | 100.00 | 4.995% | 4.995% | 7.71 | 23,800 | 183,415 | 100.00 | 183,415 |
| 1915 | | 93.86 | −6.142% | −6.142% | 7.23 | 24,580 | 177,790 | 91.83 | 163,256 |
| 1916 | | 88.38 | −5.833% | −5.833% | 6.81 | 25,382 | 172,883 | 135.91 | 234,973 |
| 1917 | | 100.72 | 13.954% | 13.954% | 7.76 | 26,208 | 203,414 | 127.84 | 260,045 |
| 1918 | | 104.36 | 3.614% | 3.614% | 8.04 | 27,057 | 217,597 | 174.54 | 379,801 |
| 1919 | | 92.87 | −11.007% | −11.007% | 7.16 | 27,931 | 199,900 | 201.99 | 403,783 |
| 1920 | | 89.13 | −4.028% | −4.028% | 6.87 | 28,829 | 198,021 | 236.50 | 468,319 |
| 1921 | | 112.82 | 26.583% | 26.583% | 8.69 | 34,162 | 297,027 | 237.22 | 704,595 |
| 1922 | | 123.66 | 9.603% | 9.603% | 9.53 | 35,714 | 340,340 | 233.57 | 794,938 |
| 1923 | | 126.94 | 2.658% | 2.658% | 9.78 | 37,023 | 362,196 | 201.55 | 730,023 |
| 1924 | | 127.47 | 0.412% | 0.412% | 9.82 | 38,357 | 376,788 | 188.81 | 711,412 |
| 1925 | | 124.53 | −2.308% | −2.308% | 9.60 | 40,018 | 384,037 | 186.19 | 715,022 |
| 1926 | | 120.44 | −3.285% | −3.285% | 9.28 | 41,613 | 386,223 | 187.93 | 725,839 |
| 1927 | | 127.57 | 5.925% | 5.925% | 9.83 | 43,253 | 425,230 | 180.99 | 769,611 |
| 1928 | | 131.90 | 3.394% | 3.394% | 10.16 | 44,915 | 456,557 | 181.13 | 826,975 |
| 1929 | | 131.51 | −0.296% | −0.296% | 10.13 | 46,602 | 472,298 | 176.61 | 834,148 |
| 1930 | | 129.23 | −1.734% | −1.734% | 9.96 | 46,035 | 458,465 | 170.09 | 779,795 |
| 1931 | | 115.38 | −10.717% | −10.717% | 8.89 | 50,658 | 450,439 | 174.80 | 787,372 |
| 1932 | | 122.09 | 5.817% | 5.817% | 9.41 | 49,139 | 462,349 | 168.76 | 780,264 |
| 1933 | 10.55 | 136.87 | 12.102% | 12.102% | 10.55 | 46,305 | 488,409 | 155.09 | 757,498 |
| 1934 | | 130.38 | −4.738% | −4.738% | 10.05 | 47,271 | 474,971 | 156.31 | 742,424 |
| 1935 | | 137.02 | 5.092% | 5.092% | 10.56 | 51,508 | 543,899 | 147.01 | 799,606 |
| 1936 | | 148.89 | 8.661% | 8.661% | 11.47 | 54,285 | 622,866 | 146.72 | 913,882 |
| 1937 | | 150.08 | 0.798% | 0.798% | 11.57 | 58,634 | 678,132 | 146.72 | 994,971 |
| 1938 | | 155.10 | 3.348% | 3.348% | 11.95 | 63,903 | 763,821 | 145.90 | 1,114,387 |
| 1939 | | 154.06 | −0.672% | −0.672% | 11.87 | 65,481 | 777,416 | 154.10 | 1,197,978 |

| Year | Annual Per-Capita Private Final Consumption Expenditure in Real Terms (1914 Prices) (Straits $) | Weighted Real Wage Indices of Agriculture and Non-agriculture Sectors (1914 = 100) | Changes in Real Wages (%) | Changes in Real Consumption (%) | Real Per-Capita Private Final Consumption Expenditure Based on Real Wages and Income Elasticities of Demand (1914 Prices) (Straits $) | Indian Labor Population Standard (Numbers) | Total Real Private Final Consumption Expenditure on Beverage and Tobacco in the Domestic Market (1914 Prices) (Straits $) | Beverage and Tobacco Price Indices (1914 = 100) | Total Private Final Consumption Expenditure on Beverages and Tobacco in the Domestic Market (Current Prices) (Straits $) |
|---|---|---|---|---|---|---|---|---|---|
| | Step 4 | Step 5 | Step 6 | Step 7 | | Step 8 | Step 9 | Step 10 | Step 11 |
| | [1] | [2] | [3] | [4] | [5] | [6] | [7] = [5] x [6] | [8] | [9] = [7] x [8] / 100 |
| 1947 | | 164.71 | | | 6.96 | 93,814 | 652,519 | 493.82 | 3,222,275 |
| 1948 | | 179.65 | 9.067% | 9.067% | 7.59 | 96,080 | 728,872 | 404.61 | 2,949,071 |
| 1949 | 9.29 | 220.02 | 22.473% | 22.473% | 9.29 | 97,870 | 909,302 | 417.66 | 3,797,812 |
| 1950 | | 203.15 | −7.666% | −7.666% | 8.58 | 102,210 | 876,830 | 444.64 | 3,898,726 |
| 1951 | | 181.26 | −10.776% | −10.776% | 7.65 | 106,810 | 817,555 | 506.62 | 4,141,928 |
| 1952 | | 176.19 | −2.797% | −2.797% | 7.44 | 112,700 | 838,509 | 514.31 | 4,312,553 |
| 1953 | | 206.53 | 17.217% | 17.217% | 8.72 | 119,180 | 1,039,392 | 521.93 | 5,424,888 |
| 1954 | | 208.97 | 1.183% | 1.183% | 8.82 | 124,820 | 1,101,455 | 542.23 | 5,972,463 |
| 1955 | | 204.74 | −2.023% | −2.023% | 8.65 | 130,550 | 1,128,715 | 540.39 | 6,099,432 |
| 1956 | | 230.57 | 12.617% | 12.617% | 9.74 | 137,160 | 1,335,486 | 542.24 | 7,241,494 |
| 1957 | | 215.81 | −6.401% | −6.401% | 9.11 | 144,593 | 1,317,737 | 549.94 | 7,246,790 |
| 1958 | | 215.37 | −0.205% | −0.205% | 9.09 | 151,400 | 1,376,939 | 550.13 | 7,574,974 |
| 1959 | | 194.19 | −9.837% | −9.837% | 8.20 | 157,960 | 1,295,284 | 547.50 | 7,091,701 |
| 1960 | | 230.48 | 18.691% | 18.691% | 9.73 | 163,410 | 1,590,426 | 547.21 | 8,703,041 |

*(Continued)*

## Appendix Table 6: Singapore: Computation of PFCE in the Domestic Market, 1900–39 and 1948–60, European Standard — Clothing in Current and 1914 Prices (Straits $)

| Year | Annual Per-Capita Private Final Consumption Expenditure in Real Terms (1914 Prices) (Straits $) | Weighted Real Wage Indices of Agriculture and Non-agriculture Sectors (1914 = 100) | Changes in Real Wages (%) | Changes in Real Consumption (%) | Real Per-Capita Private Final Consumption Expenditure Based on Real Wages and Income Elasticities of Demand (1914 Prices) (Straits $) | European Population Standard (Numbers) | Total Real Private Final Consumption Expenditure on Clothing in the Domestic Market (1914 Prices) (Straits $) | Clothing Price Indices (1914 = 100) | Total Private Final Consumption Expenditure on Clothing in the Domestic Market (Current Prices) (Straits $) |
|---|---|---|---|---|---|---|---|---|---|
| | Step 4 | Step 5 | STEP 6 | Step 7 | | Step 8 | Step 9 | Step 10 | Step 11 |
| | [1] | [2] | [3] | [4] | [5] | [6] | [7] = [5] x [6] | [8] | [9] = [7] x [8] / 100 |
| 1899 | | 116.03 | | | 184.96 | 13,667 | 2,527,895 | 76.31 | 1,928,921 |
| 1900 | | 113.92 | −1.814% | −1.814% | 181.60 | 13,566 | 2,463,621 | 78.94 | 1,944,855 |
| 1901 | | 112.77 | −1.008% | −1.008% | 179.77 | 13,911 | 2,500,760 | 84.45 | 2,111,789 |
| 1902 | | 108.67 | −3.637% | −3.637% | 173.23 | 14,310 | 2,479,068 | 86.79 | 2,151,594 |
| 1903 | | 107.35 | −1.214% | −1.214% | 171.13 | 14,720 | 2,518,992 | 92.79 | 2,337,290 |
| 1904 | | 107.24 | −0.106% | −0.106% | 170.95 | 15,141 | 2,588,296 | 90.19 | 2,334,473 |
| 1905 | | 105.29 | −1.816% | −1.816% | 167.85 | 15,575 | 2,614,278 | 87.98 | 2,300,023 |
| 1906 | | 106.94 | 1.562% | 1.562% | 170.47 | 16,023 | 2,731,334 | 84.42 | 2,305,847 |
| 1907 | | 107.05 | 0.102% | 0.102% | 170.64 | 16,483 | 2,812,687 | 82.99 | 2,334,320 |
| 1908 | | 107.87 | 0.772% | 0.772% | 171.96 | 16,958 | 2,916,007 | 86.31 | 2,516,708 |
| 1909 | | 110.50 | 2.437% | 2.437% | 176.15 | 17,445 | 3,072,991 | 76.42 | 2,348,477 |
| 1910 | | 108.44 | −1.861% | −1.861% | 172.87 | 17,946 | 3,102,323 | 84.38 | 2,617,633 |
| 1911 | | 98.90 | −8.802% | −8.802% | 157.66 | 18,503 | 2,917,040 | 84.03 | 2,451,054 |
| 1912 | | 97.22 | −1.696% | −1.696% | 154.98 | 19,118 | 2,962,911 | 83.07 | 2,461,380 |
| 1913 | | 95.24 | −2.036% | −2.036% | 151.83 | 19,750 | 2,998,597 | 99.53 | 2,984,482 |
| 1914 | | 100.00 | 4.995% | 4.995% | 159.41 | 20,400 | 3,252,027 | 100.00 | 3,252,027 |
| 1915 | | 93.86 | −6.142% | −6.142% | 149.62 | 21,069 | 3,152,293 | 138.32 | 4,360,216 |
| 1916 | | 88.38 | −5.833% | −5.833% | 140.89 | 21,756 | 3,065,285 | 161.28 | 4,943,690 |
| 1917 | | 100.72 | 13.954% | 13.954% | 160.55 | 22,464 | 3,606,604 | 144.02 | 5,194,086 |
| 1918 | | 104.36 | 3.614% | 3.614% | 166.36 | 23,192 | 3,858,088 | 189.80 | 7,322,652 |
| 1919 | | 92.87 | −11.007% | −11.007% | 148.05 | 23,941 | 3,544,313 | 229.60 | 8,137,742 |
| 1920 | | 89.13 | −4.028% | −4.028% | 142.08 | 24,711 | 3,510,990 | 291.60 | 10,238,046 |
| 1921 | | 112.82 | 26.583% | 26.583% | 179.85 | 27,757 | 4,992,118 | 237.20 | 11,841,303 |
| 1922 | | 123.66 | 9.603% | 9.603% | 197.12 | 29,018 | 5,720,077 | 182.80 | 10,456,300 |
| 1923 | | 126.94 | 2.658% | 2.658% | 202.36 | 30,082 | 6,087,408 | 163.60 | 9,958,999 |
| 1924 | | 127.47 | 0.412% | 0.412% | 203.20 | 31,165 | 6,332,657 | 157.10 | 9,948,604 |
| 1925 | | 124.53 | −2.308% | −2.308% | 198.51 | 32,515 | 6,454,486 | 158.10 | 10,204,542 |
| 1926 | | 120.44 | −3.285% | −3.285% | 191.99 | 33,811 | 6,491,229 | 157.50 | 10,223,685 |
| 1927 | | 127.57 | 5.925% | 5.925% | 203.36 | 35,143 | 7,146,810 | 155.40 | 11,106,142 |
| 1928 | | 131.90 | 3.394% | 3.394% | 210.27 | 36,493 | 7,673,324 | 151.90 | 11,655,779 |
| 1929 | | 131.51 | −0.296% | −0.296% | 209.64 | 37,864 | 7,937,891 | 141.00 | 11,192,426 |
| 1930 | 206.01 | 129.23 | −1.734% | −1.734% | 206.01 | 37,403 | 7,705,398 | 139.80 | 10,772,146 |
| 1931 | | 115.38 | −10.717% | −10.717% | 183.93 | 36,586 | 6,729,338 | 136.57 | 9,190,219 |
| 1932 | | 122.09 | 5.817% | 5.817% | 194.63 | 35,489 | 6,907,263 | 121.38 | 8,384,352 |
| 1933 | | 136.87 | 12.102% | 12.102% | 218.18 | 33,443 | 7,296,593 | 115.68 | 8,440,766 |
| 1934 | | 130.38 | −4.738% | −4.738% | 207.85 | 34,140 | 7,095,826 | 110.78 | 7,860,931 |
| 1935 | | 137.02 | 5.092% | 5.092% | 218.43 | 37,200 | 8,125,584 | 109.81 | 8,922,564 |
| 1936 | | 148.89 | 8.661% | 8.661% | 237.35 | 39,206 | 9,305,302 | 109.12 | 10,154,225 |
| 1937 | | 150.08 | 0.798% | 0.798% | 239.24 | 42,347 | 10,130,963 | 112.79 | 11,427,130 |
| 1938 | | 155.10 | 3.348% | 3.348% | 247.25 | 46,152 | 11,411,114 | 113.92 | 12,999,532 |
| 1939 | | 154.06 | −0.672% | −0.672% | 245.59 | 47,292 | 11,614,208 | 123.83 | 14,381,984 |

| Year | Annual Per-Capita Private Final Consumption Expenditure in Real Terms (1914 Prices) (Straits $) | Weighted Real Wage Indices of Agriculture and Non-agriculture Sectors (1914 = 100) | Changes in Real Wages (%) | Changes in Real Consumption (%) | Real Per-Capita Private Final Consumption Expenditure Based on Real Wages and Income Elasticities of Demand (1914 Prices) (Straits $) | European Population Standard (Numbers) | Total Real Private Final Consumption Expenditure on Clothing in the Domestic Market (1914 Prices) (Straits $) | Clothing Price Indices (1914 = 100) | Total Private Final Consumption Expenditure on Clothing in the Domestic Market (Current Prices) (Straits $) |
|---|---|---|---|---|---|---|---|---|---|
| | Step 4 | Step 5 | Step 6 | Step 7 | | Step 8 | Step 9 | Step 10 | Step 11 |
| | [1] | [2] | [3] | [4] | [5] | [6] | [7] = [5] x [6] | [8] | [9] = [7] x [8] / 100 |
| 1947 | | 164.71 | | | 226.14 | 56,289 | 12,729,149 | 628.50 | 80,002,359 |
| 1948 | 246.65 | 179.65 | 9.067% | 9.067% | 246.65 | 57,648 | 14,218,619 | 385.91 | 54,870,439 |
| 1949 | | 220.02 | 22.473% | 22.473% | 302.07 | 58,722 | 17,738,411 | 389.07 | 69,015,383 |
| 1950 | | 203.15 | −7.666% | −7.666% | 278.92 | 61,326 | 17,104,959 | 415.49 | 71,069,104 |
| 1951 | | 181.26 | −10.776% | −10.776% | 248.86 | 64,086 | 15,948,640 | 525.93 | 83,879,148 |
| 1952 | | 176.19 | −2.797% | −2.797% | 241.90 | 67,620 | 16,357,393 | 514.47 | 84,153,642 |
| 1953 | | 206.53 | 17.217% | 17.217% | 283.55 | 71,508 | 20,276,166 | 472.64 | 95,832,640 |
| 1954 | | 208.97 | 1.183% | 1.183% | 286.90 | 74,892 | 21,486,865 | 448.54 | 96,377,177 |
| 1955 | | 204.74 | −2.023% | −2.023% | 281.10 | 78,330 | 22,018,661 | 439.15 | 96,694,939 |
| 1956 | | 230.57 | 12.617% | 12.617% | 316.57 | 82,296 | 26,052,286 | 438.15 | 114,148,908 |
| 1957 | | 215.81 | −6.401% | −6.401% | 296.30 | 86,756 | 25,706,033 | 444.86 | 114,355,030 |
| 1958 | | 215.37 | −0.205% | −0.205% | 295.70 | 90,840 | 26,860,940 | 443.56 | 119,143,258 |
| 1959 | | 194.19 | −9.837% | −9.837% | 266.61 | 94,776 | 25,268,030 | 436.17 | 110,210,741 |
| 1960 | | 230.48 | 18.691% | 18.691% | 316.44 | 98,046 | 31,025,587 | 438.13 | 135,932,938 |

*(Continued)*

**Appendix Table 6:** Singapore: Computation of PFCE in the Domestic Market, 1900–39 and 1948–60, Eurasian Standard [1899–1939] Chinese, Indian and Eurasian Clerical Standard [1947–1960] — Clothing in Current and 1914 Prices (Straits $)

| Year | Annual Per-Capita Private Final Consumption Expenditure in Real Terms (1914 Prices) (Straits $) | Weighted Real Wage Indices of Agriculture and Non-agriculture Sectors (1914 = 100) | Changes in Real Wages (%) | Changes in Real Consumption (%) | Real Per-Capita Private Final Consumption Expenditure Based on Real Wages and Income Elasticities of Demand (1914 Prices) (Straits $) | Eurasian Population Standard (Numbers) | Total Real Private Final Consumption Expenditure on Clothing in the Domestic Market (1914 Prices) (Straits $) | Clothing Price Indices (1914 = 100) | Total Private Final Consumption Expenditure on Clothing in the Domestic Market (Current Prices) (Straits $) |
|---|---|---|---|---|---|---|---|---|---|
| | Step 4 | Step 5 | Step 6 | Step 7 | | Step 8 | Step 9 | Step 10 | Step 11 |
| | [1] | [2] | [3] | [4] | [5] | [6] | [7] = [5] x [6] | [8] | [9] = [7] x [8] / 100 |
| 1899 | | 116.03 | | | 20.04 | 2,278 | 45,643 | 76.31 | 34,828 |
| 1900 | | 113.92 | –1.814% | –1.814% | 19.67 | 2,261 | 44,482 | 78.94 | 35,115 |
| 1901 | | 112.77 | –1.008% | –1.008% | 19.48 | 2,318 | 45,153 | 84.45 | 38,130 |
| 1902 | | 108.67 | –3.637% | –3.637% | 18.77 | 2,385 | 44,761 | 86.79 | 38,848 |
| 1903 | | 107.35 | –1.214% | –1.214% | 18.54 | 2,453 | 45,482 | 92.79 | 42,201 |
| 1904 | | 107.24 | –0.106% | –0.106% | 18.52 | 2,523 | 46,733 | 90.19 | 42,150 |
| 1905 | | 105.29 | –1.816% | –1.816% | 18.18 | 2,596 | 47,202 | 87.98 | 41,528 |
| 1906 | | 106.94 | 1.562% | 1.562% | 18.47 | 2,670 | 49,316 | 84.42 | 41,633 |
| 1907 | | 107.05 | 0.102% | 0.102% | 18.49 | 2,747 | 50,785 | 82.99 | 42,147 |
| 1908 | | 107.87 | 0.772% | 0.772% | 18.63 | 2,826 | 52,650 | 86.31 | 45,441 |
| 1909 | | 110.50 | 2.437% | 2.437% | 19.08 | 2,908 | 55,485 | 76.42 | 42,403 |
| 1910 | | 108.44 | –1.861% | –1.861% | 18.73 | 2,991 | 56,014 | 84.38 | 47,263 |
| 1911 | | 98.90 | –8.802% | –8.802% | 17.08 | 3,084 | 52,669 | 84.03 | 44,255 |
| 1912 | | 97.22 | –1.696% | –1.696% | 16.79 | 3,186 | 53,497 | 83.07 | 44,442 |
| 1913 | | 95.24 | –2.036% | –2.036% | 16.45 | 3,292 | 54,141 | 99.53 | 53,886 |
| 1914 | | 100.00 | 4.995% | 4.995% | 17.27 | 3,400 | 58,717 | 100.00 | 58,717 |
| 1915 | | 93.86 | –6.142% | –6.142% | 16.21 | 3,511 | 56,916 | 138.32 | 78,726 |
| 1916 | | 88.38 | –5.833% | –5.833% | 15.26 | 3,626 | 55,345 | 161.28 | 89,261 |
| 1917 | | 100.72 | 13.954% | 13.954% | 17.39 | 3,744 | 65,119 | 144.02 | 93,782 |
| 1918 | | 104.36 | 3.614% | 3.614% | 18.02 | 3,865 | 69,660 | 189.80 | 132,215 |
| 1919 | | 92.87 | –11.007% | –11.007% | 16.04 | 3,990 | 63,995 | 229.60 | 146,931 |
| 1920 | | 89.13 | –4.028% | –4.028% | 15.39 | 4,118 | 63,393 | 291.60 | 184,854 |
| 1921 | | 112.82 | 26.583% | 26.583% | 19.48 | 4,270 | 83,202 | 237.20 | 197,355 |
| 1922 | | 123.66 | 9.603% | 9.603% | 21.36 | 4,464 | 95,335 | 182.80 | 174,272 |
| 1923 | | 126.94 | 2.658% | 2.658% | 21.92 | 4,628 | 101,457 | 163.60 | 165,983 |
| 1924 | | 127.47 | 0.412% | 0.412% | 22.01 | 4,795 | 105,544 | 157.10 | 165,810 |
| 1925 | | 124.53 | –2.308% | –2.308% | 21.51 | 5,002 | 107,575 | 158.10 | 170,076 |
| 1926 | | 120.44 | –3.285% | –3.285% | 20.80 | 5,202 | 108,187 | 157.50 | 170,395 |
| 1927 | | 127.57 | 5.925% | 5.925% | 22.03 | 5,407 | 119,113 | 155.40 | 185,102 |
| 1928 | | 131.90 | 3.394% | 3.394% | 22.78 | 5,614 | 127,889 | 151.90 | 194,263 |
| 1929 | | 131.51 | –0.296% | –0.296% | 22.71 | 5,825 | 132,298 | 141.00 | 186,540 |
| 1930 | 22.32 | 129.23 | –1.734% | –1.734% | 22.32 | 5,754 | 128,423 | 139.80 | 179,536 |
| 1931 | | 115.38 | –10.717% | –10.717% | 19.93 | 2,814 | 56,078 | 136.57 | 76,585 |
| 1932 | | 122.09 | 5.817% | 5.817% | 21.08 | 2,730 | 57,561 | 121.38 | 69,870 |
| 1933 | | 136.87 | 12.102% | 12.102% | 23.64 | 2,573 | 60,805 | 115.68 | 70,340 |
| 1934 | | 130.38 | –4.738% | –4.738% | 22.52 | 2,626 | 59,132 | 110.78 | 65,508 |
| 1935 | | 137.02 | 5.092% | 5.092% | 23.66 | 2,862 | 67,713 | 109.81 | 74,355 |
| 1936 | | 148.89 | 8.661% | 8.661% | 25.71 | 3,016 | 77,544 | 109.12 | 84,619 |
| 1937 | | 150.08 | 0.798% | 0.798% | 25.92 | 3,257 | 84,425 | 112.79 | 95,226 |
| 1938 | | 155.10 | 3.348% | 3.348% | 26.79 | 3,550 | 95,093 | 113.92 | 108,329 |
| 1939 | | 154.06 | –0.672% | –0.672% | 26.61 | 3,638 | 96,785 | 123.83 | 119,850 |

| Year | Annual Per-Capita Private Final Consumption Expenditure in Real Terms (1914 Prices) (Straits $) | Weighted Real Wage Indices of Agriculture and Non-agriculture Sectors (1914 = 100) | Changes in Real Wages (%) | Changes in Real Consumption (%) | Real Per-Capita Private Final Consumption Expenditure Based on Real Wages and Income Elasticities of Demand (1914 Prices) (Straits $) | Chinese, Indian, and Eurasian Clerical Population Standard (Numbers) | Total Real Private Final Consumption Expenditure on Clothing in the Domestic Market (1914 Prices) (Straits $) | Clothing Price Indices (1914 = 100) | Total Private Final Consumption Expenditure on Clothing in the Domestic Market (Current Prices) (Straits $) |
|---|---|---|---|---|---|---|---|---|---|
| | Step 4 | Step 5 | Step 6 | Step 7 | | Step 8 | Step 9 | Step 10 | Step 11 |
| | [1] | [2] | [3] | [4] | [5] | [6] | [7] = [5] x [6] | [8] | [9] = [7] x [8] / 100 |
| 1947 | | 164.71 | | | 13.39 | 14,072 | 188,357 | 628.50 | 1,183,817 |
| 1948 | 14.11 | 179.65 | 9.067% | 5.440% | 14.11 | 14,412 | 203,400 | 385.91 | 784,933 |
| 1949 | | 220.02 | 22.473% | 13.484% | 16.02 | 14,681 | 235,127 | 389.07 | 914,815 |
| 1950 | | 203.15 | –7.666% | –4.599% | 15.28 | 15,332 | 234,260 | 415.49 | 973,321 |
| 1951 | | 181.26 | –10.776% | –6.465% | 14.29 | 16,022 | 228,975 | 525.93 | 1,204,255 |
| 1952 | | 176.19 | –2.797% | –1.678% | 14.05 | 16,905 | 237,547 | 514.47 | 1,222,103 |
| 1953 | | 206.53 | 17.217% | 10.330% | 15.50 | 17,877 | 277,156 | 472.64 | 1,309,941 |
| 1954 | | 208.97 | 1.183% | 0.710% | 15.61 | 18,723 | 292,332 | 448.54 | 1,311,224 |
| 1955 | | 204.74 | –2.023% | –1.214% | 15.42 | 19,583 | 302,041 | 439.15 | 1,326,411 |
| 1956 | | 230.57 | 12.617% | 7.570% | 16.59 | 20,574 | 341,357 | 438.15 | 1,495,664 |
| 1957 | | 215.81 | –6.401% | –3.841% | 15.95 | 14,459 | 230,689 | 444.86 | 1,026,237 |
| 1958 | | 215.37 | –0.205% | –0.123% | 15.93 | 15,140 | 241,252 | 443.56 | 1,070,087 |
| 1959 | | 194.19 | –9.837% | –5.902% | 14.99 | 15,796 | 236,849 | 436.17 | 1,033,057 |
| 1960 | | 230.48 | 18.691% | 11.214% | 16.68 | 16,341 | 272,499 | 438.13 | 1,193,904 |

*(Continued)*

**Appendix Table 6:** Singapore: Computation of PFCE in the Domestic Market, 1900–39 and 1948–60, Asiatic Clerical Standard [1899–1939] Malay Clerical Standard [1947–1960] — Clothing in Current and 1914 Prices (Straits $)

| Year | Annual Per-Capita Private Final Consumption Expenditure in Real Terms (1914 Prices) (Straits $) | Weighted Real Wage Indices of Agriculture and Non-agriculture Sectors (1914 = 100) | Changes in Real Wages (%) | Changes in Real Consumption (%) | Real Per-Capita Private Final Consumption Expenditure Based on Real Wages and Income Elasticities of Demand (1914 Prices) (Straits $) | Asiatic Clerical Population Standard (Numbers) | Total Real Private Final Consumption Expenditure on Clothing in the Domestic Market (1914 Prices) (Straits $) | Clothing Price Indices (1914 = 100) | Total Private Final Consumption Expenditure on Clothing in the Domestic Market (Current Prices) (Straits $) |
|---|---|---|---|---|---|---|---|---|---|
| | Step 4 | Step 5 | Step 6 | Step 7 | | Step 8 | Step 9 | Step 10 | Step 11 |
| | [1] | [2] | [3] | [4] | [5] | [6] | [7]=[5]x[6] | [8] | [9]=[7]x[8]/100 |
| 1899 | | 116.03 | | | 20.04 | 19,362 | 387,962 | 76.31 | 296,036 |
| 1900 | | 113.92 | −1.814% | −1.814% | 19.67 | 19,219 | 378,097 | 78.94 | 298,481 |
| 1901 | | 112.77 | −1.008% | −1.008% | 19.48 | 19,707 | 383,797 | 84.45 | 324,101 |
| 1902 | | 108.67 | −3.637% | −3.637% | 18.77 | 20,273 | 380,468 | 86.79 | 330,210 |
| 1903 | | 107.35 | −1.214% | −1.214% | 18.54 | 20,853 | 386,595 | 92.79 | 358,709 |
| 1904 | | 107.24 | −0.106% | −0.106% | 18.52 | 21,449 | 397,232 | 90.19 | 358,277 |
| 1905 | | 105.29 | −1.816% | −1.816% | 18.18 | 22,065 | 401,219 | 87.98 | 352,990 |
| 1906 | | 106.94 | 1.562% | 1.562% | 18.47 | 22,699 | 419,184 | 84.42 | 353,883 |
| 1907 | | 107.05 | 0.102% | 0.102% | 18.49 | 23,351 | 431,669 | 82.99 | 358,253 |
| 1908 | | 107.87 | 0.772% | 0.772% | 18.63 | 24,023 | 447,526 | 86.31 | 386,245 |
| 1909 | | 110.50 | 2.437% | 2.437% | 19.08 | 24,714 | 471,619 | 76.42 | 360,426 |
| 1910 | | 108.44 | −1.861% | −1.861% | 18.73 | 25,423 | 476,120 | 84.38 | 401,734 |
| 1911 | | 98.90 | −8.802% | −8.802% | 17.08 | 27,137 | 463,485 | 84.03 | 389,445 |
| 1912 | | 97.22 | −1.696% | −1.696% | 16.79 | 28,039 | 470,774 | 83.07 | 391,086 |
| 1913 | | 95.24 | −2.036% | −2.036% | 16.45 | 28,967 | 476,444 | 99.53 | 474,201 |
| 1914 | | 100.00 | 4.995% | 4.995% | 17.27 | 29,920 | 516,711 | 100.00 | 516,711 |
| 1915 | | 93.86 | −6.142% | −6.142% | 16.21 | 30,901 | 500,864 | 138.32 | 692,790 |
| 1916 | | 88.38 | −5.833% | −5.833% | 15.26 | 31,909 | 487,040 | 161.28 | 785,497 |
| 1917 | | 100.72 | 13.954% | 13.954% | 17.39 | 32,947 | 573,049 | 144.02 | 825,283 |
| 1918 | | 104.36 | 3.614% | 3.614% | 18.02 | 34,015 | 613,007 | 189.80 | 1,163,488 |
| 1919 | | 92.87 | −11.007% | −11.007% | 16.04 | 35,113 | 563,152 | 229.60 | 1,292,997 |
| 1920 | | 89.13 | −4.028% | −4.028% | 15.39 | 36,243 | 557,857 | 291.60 | 1,626,712 |
| 1921 | | 112.82 | 26.583% | 26.583% | 19.48 | 46,973 | 915,222 | 237.20 | 2,170,906 |
| 1922 | | 123.66 | 9.603% | 9.603% | 21.36 | 49,107 | 1,048,681 | 182.80 | 1,916,988 |
| 1923 | | 126.94 | 2.658% | 2.658% | 21.92 | 50,907 | 1,116,025 | 163.60 | 1,825,816 |
| 1924 | | 127.47 | 0.412% | 0.412% | 22.01 | 52,741 | 1,160,987 | 157.10 | 1,823,911 |
| 1925 | | 124.53 | −2.308% | −2.308% | 21.51 | 55,025 | 1,183,322 | 158.10 | 1,870,833 |
| 1926 | | 120.44 | −3.285% | −3.285% | 20.80 | 57,218 | 1,190,059 | 157.50 | 1,874,342 |
| 1927 | | 127.57 | 5.925% | 5.925% | 22.03 | 59,473 | 1,310,248 | 155.40 | 2,036,126 |
| 1928 | | 131.90 | 3.394% | 3.394% | 22.78 | 61,758 | 1,406,776 | 151.90 | 2,136,893 |
| 1929 | | 131.51 | −0.296% | −0.296% | 22.71 | 64,077 | 1,455,280 | 141.00 | 2,051,945 |
| 1930 | 22.32 | 129.23 | −1.734% | −1.734% | 22.32 | 63,298 | 1,412,656 | 139.80 | 1,974,894 |
| 1931 | | 115.38 | −10.717% | −10.717% | 19.93 | 61,915 | 1,233,712 | 136.57 | 1,684,873 |
| 1932 | | 122.09 | 5.817% | 5.817% | 21.08 | 60,059 | 1,266,332 | 121.38 | 1,537,131 |
| 1933 | | 136.87 | 12.102% | 12.102% | 23.64 | 56,595 | 1,337,709 | 115.68 | 1,547,474 |
| 1934 | | 130.38 | −4.738% | −4.738% | 22.52 | 57,775 | 1,300,901 | 110.78 | 1,441,171 |
| 1935 | | 137.02 | 5.092% | 5.092% | 23.66 | 62,954 | 1,489,690 | 109.81 | 1,635,803 |
| 1936 | | 148.89 | 8.661% | 8.661% | 25.71 | 66,348 | 1,705,972 | 109.12 | 1,861,608 |
| 1937 | | 150.08 | 0.798% | 0.798% | 25.92 | 71,663 | 1,857,343 | 112.79 | 2,094,974 |
| 1938 | | 155.10 | 3.348% | 3.348% | 26.79 | 78,104 | 2,092,038 | 113.92 | 2,383,247 |
| 1939 | | 154.06 | −0.672% | −0.672% | 26.61 | 80,032 | 2,129,271 | 123.83 | 2,636,697 |

| Year | Annual Per-Capita Private Final Consumption Expenditure in Real Terms (1914 Prices) (Straits $) | Weighted Real Wage Indices of Agriculture and Non-agriculture Sectors (1914 = 100) | Changes in Real Wages (%) | Changes in Real Consumption (%) | Real Per-Capita Private Final Consumption Expenditure Based on Real Wages and Income Elasticities of Demand (1914 Prices) (Straits $) | Malay Clerical Population Standard (Numbers) | Total Real Private Final Consumption Expenditure on Clothing in the Domestic Market (1914 Prices) (Straits $) | Clothing Price Indices (1914 = 100) | Total Private Final Consumption Expenditure on Clothing in the Domestic Market (Current Prices) (Straits $) |
|---|---|---|---|---|---|---|---|---|---|
| | Step 4 | Step 5 | Step 6 | Step 7 | | Step 8 | Step 9 | Step 10 | Step 11 |
| | [1] | [2] | [3] | [4] | [5] | [6] | [7] = [5] x [6] | [8] | [9] = [7] x [8] / 100 |
| 1947 | | 164.71 | | | 13.72 | 126,649 | 1,737,312 | 628.50 | 10,918,961 |
| 1948 | 14.96 | 179.65 | 9.067% | 9.067% | 14.96 | 129,708 | 1,940,600 | 385.91 | 7,488,881 |
| 1949 | | 220.02 | 22.473% | 22.473% | 18.32 | 132,125 | 2,420,991 | 389.07 | 9,419,425 |
| 1950 | | 203.15 | −7.666% | −7.666% | 16.92 | 137,984 | 2,334,536 | 415.49 | 9,699,723 |
| 1951 | | 181.26 | −10.776% | −10.776% | 15.10 | 144,194 | 2,176,718 | 525.93 | 11,448,076 |
| 1952 | | 176.19 | −2.797% | −2.797% | 14.67 | 152,145 | 2,232,506 | 514.47 | 11,485,540 |
| 1953 | | 206.53 | 17.217% | 17.217% | 17.20 | 160,893 | 2,767,352 | 472.64 | 13,079,524 |
| 1954 | | 208.97 | 1.183% | 1.183% | 17.40 | 168,507 | 2,932,591 | 448.54 | 13,153,844 |
| 1955 | | 204.74 | −2.023% | −2.023% | 17.05 | 176,243 | 3,005,173 | 439.15 | 13,197,214 |
| 1956 | | 230.57 | 12.617% | 12.617% | 19.20 | 185,166 | 3,555,694 | 438.15 | 15,579,383 |
| 1957 | | 215.81 | −6.401% | −6.401% | 17.97 | 267,497 | 4,807,857 | 444.86 | 21,388,077 |
| 1958 | | 215.37 | −0.205% | −0.205% | 17.94 | 280,090 | 5,023,862 | 443.56 | 22,283,630 |
| 1959 | | 194.19 | −9.837% | −9.837% | 16.17 | 292,226 | 4,725,936 | 436.17 | 20,612,961 |
| 1960 | | 230.48 | 18.691% | 18.691% | 19.19 | 302,309 | 5,802,785 | 438.13 | 25,423,841 |

*(Continued)*

## Appendix Table 6: Singapore: Computation of PFCE in the Domestic Market, 1900–39 and 1948–60, Chinese Labor Standard — Clothing in Current and 1914 Prices (Straits $)

| Year | Annual Per-Capita Private Final Consumption Expenditure in Real Terms (1914 Prices) (Straits $) | Weighted Real Wage Indices of Agriculture and Non-agriculture Sectors (1914 = 100) | Changes in Real Wages (%) | Changes in Real Consumption (%) | Real Per-Capita Private Final Consumption Expenditure Based on Real Wages and Income Elasticities of Demand (1914 Prices) (Straits $) | Chinese Labor Population Standard (Numbers) | Total Real Private Final Consumption Expenditure on Clothing in the Domestic Market (1914 Prices) (Straits $) | Clothing Price Indices (1914 = 100) | Total Private Final Consumption Expenditure on Clothing in the Domestic Market (Current Prices) (Straits $) |
|---|---|---|---|---|---|---|---|---|---|
| | Step 4 | Step 5 | Step 6 | Step 7 | | Step 8 | Step 9 | Step 10 | Step 11 |
| | [1] | [2] | [3] | [4] | [5] | [6] | [7] = [5] x [6] | [8] | [9] = [7] x [8] / 100 |
| 1899 | | 116.03 | | | | 8.83 | 135,535 | 1,197,216 | 76.31 | 913,540 |
| 1900 | | 113.92 | −1.814% | −1.088% | | 8.74 | 134,530 | 1,175,398 | 78.94 | 927,894 |
| 1901 | | 112.77 | −1.008% | −0.605% | | 8.68 | 137,948 | 1,197,975 | 84.45 | 1,011,641 |
| 1902 | | 108.67 | −3.637% | −2.182% | | 8.49 | 141,912 | 1,205,513 | 86.79 | 1,046,270 |
| 1903 | | 107.35 | −1.214% | −0.728% | | 8.43 | 145,970 | 1,230,948 | 92.79 | 1,142,156 |
| 1904 | | 107.24 | −0.106% | −0.064% | | 8.43 | 150,145 | 1,265,352 | 90.19 | 1,141,265 |
| 1905 | | 105.29 | −1.816% | −1.089% | | 8.34 | 154,457 | 1,287,507 | 87.98 | 1,132,739 |
| 1906 | | 106.94 | 1.562% | 0.937% | | 8.41 | 158,890 | 1,336,879 | 84.42 | 1,128,620 |
| 1907 | | 107.05 | 0.102% | 0.061% | | 8.42 | 163,456 | 1,376,138 | 82.99 | 1,142,092 |
| 1908 | | 107.87 | 0.772% | 0.463% | | 8.46 | 168,162 | 1,422,316 | 86.31 | 1,227,553 |
| 1909 | | 110.50 | 2.437% | 1.462% | | 8.58 | 172,999 | 1,484,621 | 76.42 | 1,134,594 |
| 1910 | | 108.44 | −1.861% | −1.117% | | 8.49 | 177,962 | 1,510,162 | 84.38 | 1,274,222 |
| 1911 | | 98.90 | −8.802% | −5.281% | | 8.04 | 185,643 | 1,492,141 | 84.03 | 1,253,777 |
| 1912 | | 97.22 | −1.696% | −1.017% | | 7.96 | 191,815 | 1,526,064 | 83.07 | 1,267,747 |
| 1913 | | 95.24 | −2.036% | −1.221% | | 7.86 | 198,160 | 1,557,281 | 99.53 | 1,549,951 |
| 1914 | | 100.00 | 4.995% | 2.997% | | 8.09 | 204,683 | 1,656,756 | 100.00 | 1,656,756 |
| 1915 | | 93.86 | −6.142% | −3.685% | | 7.80 | 211,389 | 1,647,983 | 138.32 | 2,279,471 |
| 1916 | | 88.38 | −5.833% | −3.500% | | 7.52 | 218,286 | 1,642,200 | 161.28 | 2,648,538 |
| 1917 | | 100.72 | 13.954% | 8.372% | | 8.15 | 225,385 | 1,837,565 | 144.02 | 2,646,386 |
| 1918 | | 104.36 | 3.614% | 2.168% | | 8.33 | 232,691 | 1,938,270 | 189.80 | 3,678,837 |
| 1919 | | 92.87 | −11.007% | −6.604% | | 7.78 | 240,206 | 1,868,726 | 229.60 | 4,290,595 |
| 1920 | | 89.13 | −4.028% | −2.417% | | 7.59 | 247,933 | 1,882,231 | 291.60 | 5,488,584 |
| 1921 | | 112.82 | 26.583% | 15.950% | | 8.80 | 258,351 | 2,274,151 | 237.20 | 5,394,285 |
| 1922 | | 123.66 | 9.603% | 5.762% | | 9.31 | 270,088 | 2,514,449 | 182.80 | 4,596,412 |
| 1923 | | 126.94 | 2.658% | 1.595% | | 9.46 | 279,989 | 2,648,205 | 163.60 | 4,332,463 |
| 1924 | | 127.47 | 0.412% | 0.247% | | 9.48 | 290,074 | 2,750,374 | 157.10 | 4,320,837 |
| 1925 | | 124.53 | −2.308% | −1.385% | | 9.35 | 302,638 | 2,829,772 | 158.10 | 4,473,869 |
| 1926 | | 120.44 | −3.285% | −1.971% | | 9.17 | 314,698 | 2,884,543 | 157.50 | 4,543,156 |
| 1927 | | 127.57 | 5.925% | 3.555% | | 9.49 | 327,100 | 3,104,805 | 155.40 | 4,824,867 |
| 1928 | | 131.90 | 3.394% | 2.037% | | 9.69 | 339,668 | 3,289,765 | 151.90 | 4,997,153 |
| 1929 | | 131.51 | −0.296% | −0.178% | | 9.67 | 352,424 | 3,407,240 | 141.00 | 4,804,209 |
| 1930 | | 129.23 | −1.734% | −1.040% | | 9.57 | 348,138 | 3,330,790 | 139.80 | 4,656,444 |
| 1931 | | 115.38 | −10.717% | −6.430% | | 8.95 | 354,606 | 3,174,509 | 136.57 | 4,335,409 |
| 1932 | | 122.09 | 5.817% | 3.490% | | 9.26 | 343,972 | 3,186,794 | 121.38 | 3,868,276 |
| 1933 | | 136.87 | 12.102% | 7.261% | | 9.94 | 324,135 | 3,221,054 | 115.68 | 3,726,145 |
| 1934 | | 130.38 | −4.738% | −2.843% | | 9.65 | 330,894 | 3,194,742 | 110.78 | 3,539,215 |
| 1935 | | 137.02 | 5.092% | 3.055% | | 9.95 | 360,555 | 3,587,470 | 109.81 | 3,939,339 |
| 1936 | 10.47 | 148.89 | 8.661% | 5.196% | | 10.47 | 379,993 | 3,977,339 | 109.12 | 4,340,192 |
| 1937 | | 150.08 | 0.798% | 0.479% | | 10.52 | 410,436 | 4,316,545 | 112.79 | 4,868,808 |
| 1938 | | 155.10 | 3.348% | 2.009% | | 10.73 | 447,323 | 4,798,985 | 113.92 | 5,467,000 |
| 1939 | | 154.06 | −0.672% | −0.403% | | 10.68 | 458,365 | 4,897,616 | 123.83 | 6,064,765 |
| 1947 | | 164.71 | | | | 11.63 | 562,886 | 6,546,285 | 628.50 | 41,143,226 |
| 1948 | | 179.65 | 9.067% | 5.440% | | 12.26 | 576,480 | 7,069,120 | 385.91 | 27,280,126 |
| 1949 | 13.92 | 220.02 | 22.473% | 13.484% | | 13.92 | 587,220 | 8,171,768 | 389.07 | 31,794,152 |
| 1950 | | 203.15 | −7.666% | −4.599% | | 13.28 | 613,260 | 8,141,626 | 415.49 | 33,827,502 |
| 1951 | | 181.26 | −10.776% | −6.465% | | 12.42 | 640,860 | 7,957,961 | 525.93 | 41,853,538 |
| 1952 | | 176.19 | −2.797% | −1.678% | | 12.21 | 676,200 | 8,255,871 | 514.47 | 42,473,861 |
| 1953 | | 206.53 | 17.217% | 10.330% | | 13.47 | 715,080 | 9,632,474 | 472.64 | 45,526,626 |
| 1954 | | 208.97 | 1.183% | 0.710% | | 13.57 | 748,920 | 10,159,906 | 448.54 | 45,571,240 |
| 1955 | | 204.74 | −2.023% | −1.214% | | 13.40 | 783,300 | 10,497,341 | 439.15 | 46,099,065 |
| 1956 | | 230.57 | 12.617% | 7.570% | | 14.42 | 822,960 | 11,863,753 | 438.15 | 51,981,406 |
| 1957 | | 215.81 | −6.401% | −3.841% | | 13.86 | 788,031 | 10,923,900 | 444.86 | 48,595,710 |
| 1958 | | 215.37 | −0.205% | −0.123% | | 13.85 | 825,130 | 11,424,079 | 443.56 | 50,672,165 |
| 1959 | | 194.19 | −9.837% | −5.902% | | 13.03 | 860,882 | 11,215,593 | 436.17 | 48,918,686 |
| 1960 | | 230.48 | 18.691% | 11.214% | | 14.49 | 890,585 | 12,903,726 | 438.13 | 56,535,315 |

(*Continued*)

## Appendix Table 6: Singapore: Computation of PFCE in the Domestic Market, 1900–39 and 1948–60, Malay Labor Standard — Clothing in Current and 1914 Prices (Straits $)

| Year | Annual Per-Capita Private Final Consumption Expenditure in Real Terms (1914 Prices) (Straits $) | Weighted Real Wage Indices of Agriculture and Non-agriculture Sectors (1914 = 100) | Changes in Real Wages (%) | Changes in Real Consumption (%) | Real Per-Capita Private Final Consumption Expenditure Based on Real Wages and Income Elasticities of Demand (1914 Prices) (Straits $) | Malay Labor Population Standard (Numbers) | Total Real Private Final Consumption Expenditure on Clothing in the Domestic Market (1914 Prices) (Straits $) | Clothing Price Indices (1914 = 100) | Total Private Final Consumption Expenditure on Clothing in the Domestic Market (Current Prices) (Straits $) |
|---|---|---|---|---|---|---|---|---|---|
| | Step 4 | Step 5 | Step 6 | Step 7 | | Step 8 | Step 9 | Step 10 | Step 11 |
| | [1] | [2] | [3] | [4] | [5] | [6] | [7] = [5] x [6] | [8] | [9] = [7] x [8] / 100 |
| 1899 | | 116.03 | | | 8.96 | 41,002 | 367,190 | 76.31 | 280,186 |
| 1900 | | 113.92 | −1.814% | −1.088% | 8.86 | 40,698 | 360,499 | 78.94 | 284,588 |
| 1901 | | 112.77 | −1.008% | −0.605% | 8.80 | 41,732 | 367,423 | 84.45 | 310,274 |
| 1902 | | 108.67 | −3.637% | −2.182% | 8.61 | 42,931 | 369,735 | 86.79 | 320,894 |
| 1903 | | 107.35 | −1.214% | −0.728% | 8.55 | 44,159 | 377,536 | 92.79 | 350,303 |
| 1904 | | 107.24 | −0.106% | −0.064% | 8.54 | 45,422 | 388,088 | 90.19 | 350,030 |
| 1905 | | 105.29 | −1.816% | −1.089% | 8.45 | 46,726 | 394,883 | 87.98 | 347,415 |
| 1906 | | 106.94 | 1.562% | 0.937% | 8.53 | 48,068 | 410,025 | 84.42 | 346,152 |
| 1907 | | 107.05 | 0.102% | 0.061% | 8.54 | 49,449 | 422,066 | 82.99 | 350,283 |
| 1908 | | 107.87 | 0.772% | 0.463% | 8.57 | 50,873 | 436,229 | 86.31 | 376,495 |
| 1909 | | 110.50 | 2.437% | 1.462% | 8.70 | 52,336 | 455,338 | 76.42 | 347,984 |
| 1910 | | 108.44 | −1.861% | −1.117% | 8.60 | 53,837 | 463,172 | 84.38 | 390,808 |
| 1911 | | 98.90 | −8.802% | −5.281% | 8.15 | 52,424 | 427,194 | 84.03 | 358,952 |
| 1912 | | 97.22 | −1.696% | −1.017% | 8.07 | 54,167 | 436,906 | 83.07 | 362,951 |
| 1913 | | 95.24 | −2.036% | −1.221% | 7.97 | 55,959 | 445,844 | 99.53 | 443,745 |
| 1914 | | 100.00 | 4.995% | 2.997% | 8.21 | 57,801 | 474,323 | 100.00 | 474,323 |
| 1915 | | 93.86 | −6.142% | −3.685% | 7.90 | 59,695 | 471,811 | 138.32 | 652,604 |
| 1916 | | 88.38 | −5.833% | −3.500% | 7.63 | 61,642 | 470,155 | 161.28 | 758,266 |
| 1917 | | 100.72 | 13.954% | 8.372% | 8.27 | 63,647 | 526,088 | 144.02 | 757,650 |
| 1918 | | 104.36 | 3.614% | 2.168% | 8.44 | 65,710 | 554,919 | 189.80 | 1,053,237 |
| 1919 | | 92.87 | −11.007% | −6.604% | 7.89 | 67,832 | 535,009 | 229.60 | 1,228,381 |
| 1920 | | 89.13 | −4.028% | −2.417% | 7.70 | 70,014 | 538,875 | 291.60 | 1,571,360 |
| 1921 | | 112.82 | 26.583% | 15.950% | 8.92 | 55,513 | 495,416 | 237.20 | 1,175,127 |
| 1922 | | 123.66 | 9.603% | 5.762% | 9.44 | 58,035 | 547,764 | 182.80 | 1,001,313 |
| 1923 | | 126.94 | 2.658% | 1.595% | 9.59 | 60,163 | 576,903 | 163.60 | 943,813 |
| 1924 | | 127.47 | 0.412% | 0.247% | 9.61 | 62,330 | 599,160 | 157.10 | 941,280 |
| 1925 | | 124.53 | −2.308% | −1.385% | 9.48 | 65,030 | 616,456 | 158.10 | 974,618 |
| 1926 | | 120.44 | −3.285% | −1.971% | 9.29 | 67,621 | 628,388 | 157.50 | 989,711 |
| 1927 | | 127.57 | 5.925% | 3.555% | 9.62 | 70,286 | 676,372 | 155.40 | 1,051,081 |
| 1928 | | 131.90 | 3.394% | 2.037% | 9.82 | 72,986 | 716,664 | 151.90 | 1,088,613 |
| 1929 | | 131.51 | −0.296% | −0.178% | 9.80 | 75,727 | 742,256 | 141.00 | 1,046,581 |
| 1930 | | 129.23 | −1.734% | −1.040% | 9.70 | 74,807 | 725,601 | 139.80 | 1,014,391 |
| 1931 | | 115.38 | −10.717% | −6.430% | 9.08 | 56,287 | 510,857 | 136.57 | 697,674 |
| 1932 | | 122.09 | 5.817% | 3.490% | 9.39 | 54,599 | 512,834 | 121.38 | 622,501 |
| 1933 | | 136.87 | 12.102% | 7.261% | 10.07 | 51,450 | 518,347 | 115.68 | 599,628 |
| 1934 | | 130.38 | −4.738% | −2.843% | 9.79 | 52,523 | 514,113 | 110.78 | 569,547 |
| 1935 | | 137.02 | 5.092% | 3.055% | 10.09 | 57,231 | 577,312 | 109.81 | 633,937 |
| 1936 | 10.61 | 148.89 | 8.661% | 5.196% | 10.61 | 60,316 | 640,052 | 109.12 | 698,444 |
| 1937 | | 150.08 | 0.798% | 0.479% | 10.66 | 65,149 | 694,638 | 112.79 | 783,511 |
| 1938 | | 155.10 | 3.348% | 2.009% | 10.88 | 71,004 | 772,275 | 113.92 | 879,775 |
| 1939 | | 154.06 | −0.672% | −0.403% | 10.83 | 72,756 | 788,147 | 123.83 | 975,970 |

| Year | Annual Per-Capita Private Final Consumption Expenditure in Real Terms (1914 Prices) (Straits $) | Weighted Real Wage Indices of Agriculture and Non-agriculture Sectors (1914 = 100) | Changes in Real Wages (%) | Changes in Real Consumption (%) | Real Per-Capita Private Final Consumption Expenditure Based on Real Wages and Income Elasticities of Demand (1914 Prices) (Straits $) | Malay Labor Population Standard (Numbers) | Total Real Private Final Consumption Expenditure on Clothing in the Domestic Market (1914 Prices) (Straits $) | Clothing Price Indices (1914 = 100) | Total Private Final Consumption Expenditure on Clothing in the Domestic Market (Current Prices) (Straits $) |
|---|---|---|---|---|---|---|---|---|---|
| | Step 4 | Step 5 | Step 6 | Step 7 | | Step 8 | Step 9 | Step 10 | Step 11 |
| | [1] | [2] | [3] | [4] | [5] | [6] | [7] = [5] x [6] | [8] | [9] = [7] x [8] / 100 |
| 1947 | | 164.71 | | | 10.36 | 84,433 | 874,505 | 628.50 | 5,496,240 |
| 1948 | | 179.65 | 9.067% | 5.440% | 10.92 | 86,472 | 944,349 | 385.91 | 3,644,297 |
| 1949 | 12.39 | 220.02 | 22.473% | 13.484% | 12.39 | 88,083 | 1,091,650 | 389.07 | 4,247,316 |
| 1950 | | 203.15 | −7.666% | −4.599% | 11.82 | 91,989 | 1,087,623 | 415.49 | 4,518,948 |
| 1951 | | 181.26 | −10.776% | −6.465% | 11.06 | 96,129 | 1,063,088 | 525.93 | 5,591,129 |
| 1952 | | 176.19 | −2.797% | −1.678% | 10.87 | 101,430 | 1,102,885 | 514.47 | 5,673,997 |
| 1953 | | 206.53 | 17.217% | 10.330% | 12.00 | 107,262 | 1,286,783 | 472.64 | 6,081,810 |
| 1954 | | 208.97 | 1.183% | 0.710% | 12.08 | 112,338 | 1,357,241 | 448.54 | 6,087,770 |
| 1955 | | 204.74 | −2.023% | −1.214% | 11.94 | 117,495 | 1,402,318 | 439.15 | 6,158,281 |
| 1956 | | 230.57 | 12.617% | 7.570% | 12.84 | 123,444 | 1,584,855 | 438.15 | 6,944,091 |
| 1957 | | 215.81 | −6.401% | −3.841% | 12.35 | 144,593 | 1,785,079 | 444.86 | 7,941,043 |
| 1958 | | 215.37 | −0.205% | −0.123% | 12.33 | 151,400 | 1,866,813 | 443.56 | 8,280,357 |
| 1959 | | 194.19 | −9.837% | −5.902% | 11.60 | 157,960 | 1,832,744 | 436.17 | 7,993,820 |
| 1960 | | 230.48 | 18.691% | 11.214% | 12.90 | 163,410 | 2,108,603 | 438.13 | 9,238,457 |

(*Continued*)

**Appendix Table 6:** Singapore: Computation of PFCE in the Domestic Market, 1900–39 and 1948–60, Indian Labor Standard — Clothing in Current and 1914 Prices (Straits $)

| Year | Annual Per-Capita Private Final Consumption Expenditure in Real Terms (1914 Prices) (Straits $) | Weighted Real Wage Indices of Agriculture and Non-agriculture Sectors (1914 = 100) | Changes in Real Wages (%) | Changes in Real Consumption (%) | Real Per-Capita Private Final Consumption Expenditure Based on Real Wages and Income Elasticities of Demand (1914 Prices) (Straits $) | Indian Labor Population Standard (Numbers) | Total Real Private Final Consumption Expenditure on Clothing in the Domestic Market (1914 Prices) (Straits $) | Clothing Price Indices (1914 = 100) | Total Private Final Consumption Expenditure on Clothing in the Domestic Market (Current Prices) (Straits $) |
|---|---|---|---|---|---|---|---|---|---|
| | Step 4 | Step 5 | Step 6 | Step 7 | | Step 8 | Step 9 | Step 10 | Step 11 |
| | [1] | [2] | [3] | [4] | [5] | [6] | [7] = [5] x [6] | [8] | [9] = [7] x [8] / 100 |
| 1899 | | 116.03 | | | 7.46 | 15,945 | 118,954 | 76.31 | 90,768 |
| 1900 | | 113.92 | −1.814% | −1.814% | 7.32 | 15,827 | 115,929 | 78.94 | 91,518 |
| 1901 | | 112.77 | −1.008% | −1.008% | 7.25 | 16,229 | 117,677 | 84.45 | 99,373 |
| 1902 | | 108.67 | −3.637% | −3.637% | 6.99 | 16,696 | 116,656 | 86.79 | 101,247 |
| 1903 | | 107.35 | −1.214% | −1.214% | 6.90 | 17,173 | 118,535 | 92.79 | 109,985 |
| 1904 | | 107.24 | −0.106% | −0.106% | 6.90 | 17,664 | 121,796 | 90.19 | 109,852 |
| 1905 | | 105.29 | −1.816% | −1.816% | 6.77 | 18,171 | 123,019 | 87.98 | 108,231 |
| 1906 | | 106.94 | 1.562% | 1.562% | 6.88 | 18,693 | 128,527 | 84.42 | 108,505 |
| 1907 | | 107.05 | 0.102% | 0.102% | 6.88 | 19,230 | 132,355 | 82.99 | 109,845 |
| 1908 | | 107.87 | 0.772% | 0.772% | 6.94 | 19,784 | 137,217 | 86.31 | 118,428 |
| 1909 | | 110.50 | 2.437% | 2.437% | 7.10 | 20,353 | 144,604 | 76.42 | 110,511 |
| 1910 | | 108.44 | −1.861% | −1.861% | 6.97 | 20,937 | 145,984 | 84.38 | 123,177 |
| 1911 | | 98.90 | −8.802% | −8.802% | 6.36 | 21,586 | 137,266 | 84.03 | 115,338 |
| 1912 | | 97.22 | −1.696% | −1.696% | 6.25 | 22,304 | 139,424 | 83.07 | 115,824 |
| 1913 | | 95.24 | −2.036% | −2.036% | 6.12 | 23,042 | 141,103 | 99.53 | 140,439 |
| 1914 | | 100.00 | 4.995% | 4.995% | 6.43 | 23,800 | 153,029 | 100.00 | 153,029 |
| 1915 | | 93.86 | −6.142% | −6.142% | 6.03 | 24,580 | 148,336 | 138.32 | 205,177 |
| 1916 | | 88.38 | −5.833% | −5.833% | 5.68 | 25,382 | 144,242 | 161.28 | 232,633 |
| 1917 | | 100.72 | 13.954% | 13.954% | 6.48 | 26,208 | 169,714 | 144.02 | 244,416 |
| 1918 | | 104.36 | 3.614% | 3.614% | 6.71 | 27,057 | 181,548 | 189.80 | 344,578 |
| 1919 | | 92.87 | −11.007% | −11.007% | 5.97 | 27,931 | 166,783 | 229.60 | 382,934 |
| 1920 | | 89.13 | −4.028% | −4.028% | 5.73 | 28,829 | 165,215 | 291.60 | 481,767 |
| 1921 | | 112.82 | 26.583% | 26.583% | 7.25 | 34,162 | 247,819 | 237.20 | 587,826 |
| 1922 | | 123.66 | 9.603% | 9.603% | 7.95 | 35,714 | 283,956 | 182.80 | 519,072 |
| 1923 | | 126.94 | 2.658% | 2.658% | 8.16 | 37,023 | 302,191 | 163.60 | 494,385 |
| 1924 | | 127.47 | 0.412% | 0.412% | 8.20 | 38,357 | 314,366 | 157.10 | 493,869 |
| 1925 | | 124.53 | −2.308% | −2.308% | 8.01 | 40,018 | 320,414 | 158.10 | 506,574 |
| 1926 | | 120.44 | −3.285% | −3.285% | 7.74 | 41,613 | 322,238 | 157.50 | 507,524 |
| 1927 | | 127.57 | 5.925% | 5.925% | 8.20 | 43,253 | 354,782 | 155.40 | 551,331 |
| 1928 | | 131.90 | 3.394% | 3.394% | 8.48 | 44,915 | 380,919 | 151.90 | 578,617 |
| 1929 | | 131.51 | −0.296% | −0.296% | 8.46 | 46,602 | 394,053 | 141.00 | 555,615 |
| 1930 | | 129.23 | −1.734% | −1.734% | 8.31 | 46,035 | 382,512 | 139.80 | 534,751 |
| 1931 | | 115.38 | −10.717% | −10.717% | 7.42 | 50,658 | 375,815 | 136.57 | 513,249 |
| 1932 | | 122.09 | 5.817% | 5.817% | 7.85 | 49,139 | 385,752 | 121.38 | 468,243 |
| 1933 | 8.80 | 136.87 | 12.102% | 12.102% | 8.80 | 46,305 | 407,495 | 115.68 | 471,394 |
| 1934 | | 130.38 | −4.738% | −4.738% | 8.38 | 47,271 | 396,283 | 110.78 | 439,012 |
| 1935 | | 137.02 | 5.092% | 5.092% | 8.81 | 51,508 | 453,792 | 109.81 | 498,301 |
| 1936 | | 148.89 | 8.661% | 8.661% | 9.57 | 54,285 | 519,676 | 109.12 | 567,086 |
| 1937 | | 150.08 | 0.798% | 0.798% | 9.65 | 58,634 | 565,787 | 112.79 | 638,174 |
| 1938 | | 155.10 | 3.348% | 3.348% | 9.97 | 63,903 | 637,280 | 113.92 | 725,989 |
| 1939 | | 154.06 | −0.672% | −0.672% | 9.91 | 65,481 | 648,622 | 123.83 | 803,195 |

| Year | Annual Per-Capita Private Final Consumption Expenditure in Real Terms (1914 Prices) (Straits $) | Weighted Real Wage Indices of Agriculture and Non-agriculture Sectors (1914 = 100) | Changes in Real Wages (%) | Changes in Real Consumption (%) | Real Per-Capita Private Final Consumption Expenditure Based on Real Wages and Income Elasticities of Demand (1914 Prices) (Straits $) | Indian Labor Population Standard (Numbers) | Total Real Private Final Consumption Expenditure on Clothing in the Domestic Market (1914 Prices) (Straits $) | Clothing Price Indices (1914 = 100) | Total Private Final Consumption Expenditure on Clothing in the Domestic Market (Current Prices) (Straits $) |
|---|---|---|---|---|---|---|---|---|---|
| | Step 4 | Step 5 | Step 6 | Step 7 | | Step 8 | Step 9 | Step 10 | Step 11 |
| | [1] | [2] | [3] | [4] | [5] | [6] | [7] = [5] x [6] | [8] | [9] = [7] x [8] / 100 |
| 1947 | | 164.71 | | | 6.75 | 93,814 | 633,385 | 628.50 | 3,980,807 |
| 1948 | | 179.65 | 9.067% | 5.440% | 7.12 | 96,080 | 683,972 | 385.91 | 2,639,485 |
| 1949 | 8.08 | 220.02 | 22.473% | 13.484% | 8.08 | 97,870 | 790,658 | 389.07 | 3,076,239 |
| 1950 | | 203.15 | −7.666% | −4.599% | 7.71 | 102,210 | 787,742 | 415.49 | 3,272,975 |
| 1951 | | 181.26 | −10.776% | −6.465% | 7.21 | 106,810 | 769,971 | 525.93 | 4,049,534 |
| 1952 | | 176.19 | −2.797% | −1.678% | 7.09 | 112,700 | 798,796 | 514.47 | 4,109,553 |
| 1953 | | 206.53 | 17.217% | 10.330% | 7.82 | 119,180 | 931,989 | 472.64 | 4,404,923 |
| 1954 | | 208.97 | 1.183% | 0.710% | 7.88 | 124,820 | 983,020 | 448.54 | 4,409,239 |
| 1955 | | 204.74 | −2.023% | −1.214% | 7.78 | 130,550 | 1,015,669 | 439.15 | 4,460,309 |
| 1956 | | 230.57 | 12.617% | 7.570% | 8.37 | 137,160 | 1,147,876 | 438.15 | 5,029,454 |
| 1957 | | 215.81 | −6.401% | −3.841% | 8.05 | 144,593 | 1,163,604 | 444.86 | 5,176,372 |
| 1958 | | 215.37 | −0.205% | −0.123% | 8.04 | 151,400 | 1,216,883 | 443.56 | 5,397,554 |
| 1959 | | 194.19 | −9.837% | −5.902% | 7.56 | 157,960 | 1,194,675 | 436.17 | 5,210,775 |
| 1960 | | 230.48 | 18.691% | 11.214% | 8.41 | 163,410 | 1,374,494 | 438.13 | 6,022,092 |

*(Continued)*

**Appendix Table 6:** Singapore: Computation of PFCE in the Domestic Market, 1900–39 and 1948–60, European Standard — Rent in Current and 1914 Prices (Straits $)

| Year | Annual Per-Capita Private Final Consumption Expenditure in Real Terms (1914 Prices) (Straits $) | Weighted Real Wage Indices of Agriculture and Non-agriculture Sectors (1914 = 100) | Changes in Real Wages (%) | Changes in Real Consumption (%) | Real Per-Capita Private Final Consumption Expenditure Based on Real Wages and Income Elasticities of Demand (1914 Prices) (Straits $) | European Population Standard (Numbers) | Total Real Private Final Consumption Expenditure on Rent in the Domestic Market (1914 Prices) (Straits $) | Rent Price Indices (1914 = 100) | Total Private Final Consumption Expenditure on Rent in the Domestic Market (Current Prices) (Straits $) |
|---|---|---|---|---|---|---|---|---|---|
| | Step 4 | Step 5 | Step 6 | Step 7 | | Step 8 | Step 9 | Step 10 | Step 11 |
| | [1] | [2] | [3] | [4] | [5] | [6] | [7] = [5] x [6] | [8] | [9] = [7] x [8] / 100 |
| 1899 | | 116.03 | | | 102.34 | 13,667 | 1,398,722 | 75.02 | 1,049,375 |
| 1900 | | 113.92 | −1.814% | −1.451% | 100.85 | 13,566 | 1,368,195 | 76.46 | 1,046,185 |
| 1901 | | 112.77 | −1.008% | −0.806% | 100.04 | 13,911 | 1,391,648 | 77.93 | 1,084,573 |
| 1902 | | 108.67 | −3.637% | −2.910% | 97.13 | 14,310 | 1,389,990 | 79.43 | 1,104,127 |
| 1903 | | 107.35 | −1.214% | −0.971% | 96.19 | 14,720 | 1,415,847 | 80.96 | 1,146,330 |
| 1904 | | 107.24 | −0.106% | −0.085% | 96.11 | 15,141 | 1,455,109 | 82.53 | 1,200,835 |
| 1905 | | 105.29 | −1.816% | −1.452% | 94.71 | 15,575 | 1,475,151 | 84.12 | 1,240,873 |
| 1906 | | 106.94 | 1.562% | 1.250% | 95.89 | 16,023 | 1,536,461 | 85.74 | 1,317,418 |
| 1907 | | 107.05 | 0.102% | 0.081% | 95.97 | 16,483 | 1,581,902 | 87.40 | 1,382,617 |
| 1908 | | 107.87 | 0.772% | 0.618% | 96.56 | 16,958 | 1,637,498 | 89.09 | 1,458,920 |
| 1909 | | 110.50 | 2.437% | 1.950% | 98.45 | 17,445 | 1,717,441 | 86.37 | 1,483,334 |
| 1910 | | 108.44 | −1.861% | −1.489% | 96.98 | 17,946 | 1,740,410 | 86.05 | 1,497,671 |
| 1911 | | 98.90 | −8.802% | −7.042% | 90.15 | 18,503 | 1,668,057 | 84.75 | 1,413,662 |
| 1912 | | 97.22 | −1.696% | −1.357% | 88.93 | 19,118 | 1,700,133 | 85.45 | 1,452,722 |
| 1913 | | 95.24 | −2.036% | −1.629% | 87.48 | 19,750 | 1,727,760 | 90.86 | 1,569,881 |
| 1914 | | 100.00 | 4.995% | 3.996% | 90.98 | 20,400 | 1,855,955 | 100.00 | 1,855,955 |
| 1915 | | 93.86 | −6.142% | −4.914% | 86.51 | 21,069 | 1,822,581 | 100.28 | 1,827,636 |
| 1916 | | 88.38 | −5.833% | −4.666% | 82.47 | 21,756 | 1,794,230 | 102.44 | 1,838,075 |
| 1917 | | 100.72 | 13.954% | 11.163% | 91.68 | 22,464 | 2,059,383 | 102.29 | 2,106,508 |
| 1918 | | 104.36 | 3.614% | 2.891% | 94.33 | 23,192 | 2,187,614 | 114.34 | 2,501,224 |
| 1919 | | 92.87 | −11.007% | −8.806% | 86.02 | 23,941 | 2,059,410 | 124.90 | 2,572,247 |
| 1920 | | 89.13 | −4.028% | −3.222% | 83.25 | 24,711 | 2,057,170 | 160.76 | 3,307,149 |
| 1921 | | 112.82 | 26.583% | 21.267% | 100.95 | 27,757 | 2,802,144 | 168.16 | 4,712,102 |
| 1922 | | 123.66 | 9.603% | 7.682% | 108.71 | 29,018 | 3,154,495 | 186.66 | 5,888,314 |
| 1923 | | 126.94 | 2.658% | 2.127% | 111.02 | 30,082 | 3,339,684 | 209.64 | 7,001,195 |
| 1924 | | 127.47 | 0.412% | 0.330% | 111.39 | 31,165 | 3,471,381 | 217.54 | 7,551,596 |
| 1925 | | 124.53 | −2.308% | −1.846% | 109.33 | 32,515 | 3,554,879 | 225.57 | 8,018,871 |
| 1926 | | 120.44 | −3.285% | −2.628% | 106.46 | 33,811 | 3,599,400 | 236.04 | 8,496,106 |
| 1927 | | 127.57 | 5.925% | 4.740% | 111.50 | 35,143 | 3,918,585 | 253.41 | 9,930,205 |
| 1928 | | 131.90 | 3.394% | 2.715% | 114.53 | 36,493 | 4,179,648 | 275.75 | 11,525,328 |
| 1929 | | 131.51 | −0.296% | −0.237% | 114.26 | 37,864 | 4,326,329 | 277.40 | 12,001,198 |
| 1930 | 112.68 | 129.23 | −1.734% | −1.387% | 112.68 | 37,403 | 4,214,435 | 255.60 | 10,772,146 |
| 1931 | | 115.38 | −10.717% | −8.574% | 103.02 | 36,586 | 3,768,943 | 221.46 | 8,346,614 |
| 1932 | | 122.09 | 5.817% | 4.654% | 107.81 | 35,489 | 3,826,061 | 181.20 | 6,932,753 |
| 1933 | | 136.87 | 12.102% | 9.681% | 118.25 | 33,443 | 3,954,455 | 159.06 | 6,289,972 |
| 1934 | | 130.38 | −4.738% | −3.790% | 113.76 | 34,140 | 3,883,900 | 159.06 | 6,177,747 |
| 1935 | | 137.02 | 5.092% | 4.073% | 118.40 | 37,200 | 4,404,442 | 159.06 | 7,005,723 |
| 1936 | | 148.89 | 8.661% | 6.929% | 126.60 | 39,206 | 4,963,500 | 159.06 | 7,894,962 |
| 1937 | | 150.08 | 0.798% | 0.638% | 127.41 | 42,347 | 5,395,361 | 161.78 | 8,728,801 |
| 1938 | | 155.10 | 3.348% | 2.678% | 130.82 | 46,152 | 6,037,748 | 169.58 | 10,239,108 |
| 1939 | | 154.06 | −0.672% | −0.538% | 130.12 | 47,292 | 6,153,523 | 182.26 | 11,215,586 |

| Year | Annual Per-Capita Private Final Consumption Expenditure in Real Terms (1914 Prices) (Straits $) | Weighted Real Wage Indices of Agriculture and Non-agriculture Sectors (1914 = 100) | Changes in Real Wages (%) | Changes in Real Consumption (%) | Real Per-Capita Private Final Consumption Expenditure Based on Real Wages and Income Elasticities of Demand (1914 Prices) (Straits $) | European Population Standard (Numbers) | Total Real Private Final Consumption Expenditure on Rent in the Domestic Market (1914 Prices) (Straits $) | Rent Price Indices (1914 = 100) | Total Private Final Consumption Expenditure on Rent in the Domestic Market (Current Prices) (Straits $) |
|---|---|---|---|---|---|---|---|---|---|
| | Step 4 | Step 5 | Step 6 | Step 7 | | Step 8 | Step 9 | Step 10 | Step 11 |
| | [1] | [2] | [3] | [4] | [5] | [6] | [7] = [5] x [6] | [8] | [9] = [7] x [8] / 100 |
| 1947 | | 164.71 | | | 136.11 | 56,289 | 7,661,571 | 549.01 | 42,063,009 |
| 1948 | 145.99 | 179.65 | 9.067% | 7.254% | 145.99 | 57,648 | 8,415,776 | 460.76 | 38,776,736 |
| 1949 | | 220.02 | 22.473% | 17.978% | 172.23 | 58,722 | 10,113,781 | 510.58 | 51,639,140 |
| 1950 | | 203.15 | −7.666% | −6.132% | 161.67 | 61,326 | 9,914,543 | 527.05 | 52,254,829 |
| 1951 | | 181.26 | −10.776% | −8.621% | 147.73 | 64,086 | 9,467,595 | 642.35 | 60,814,625 |
| 1952 | | 176.19 | −2.797% | −2.238% | 144.43 | 67,620 | 9,766,131 | 680.78 | 66,485,468 |
| 1953 | | 206.53 | 17.217% | 13.774% | 164.32 | 71,508 | 11,750,190 | 719.21 | 84,508,170 |
| 1954 | | 208.97 | 1.183% | 0.946% | 165.87 | 74,892 | 12,422,689 | 735.68 | 91,390,893 |
| 1955 | | 204.74 | −2.023% | −1.618% | 163.19 | 78,330 | 12,782,712 | 724.70 | 92,635,925 |
| 1956 | | 230.57 | 12.617% | 10.094% | 179.66 | 82,296 | 14,785,499 | 768.62 | 113,644,003 |
| 1957 | | 215.81 | −6.401% | −5.121% | 170.46 | 86,756 | 14,788,541 | 790.58 | 116,915,026 |
| 1958 | | 215.37 | −0.205% | −0.164% | 170.18 | 90,840 | 15,459,313 | 807.05 | 124,764,207 |
| 1959 | | 194.19 | −9.837% | −7.870% | 156.79 | 94,776 | 14,859,864 | 818.03 | 121,558,016 |
| 1960 | | 230.48 | 18.691% | 14.953% | 180.23 | 98,046 | 17,671,171 | 818.03 | 144,555,328 |

*(Continued)*

**Appendix Table 6:** Singapore: Computation of PFCE in the Domestic Market, 1900–39 and 1948–60, Eurasian Standard [1899–1939] Chinese, Indian, and Eurasian Clerical Standard [1947–1960] — Rent in Current and 1914 Prices (Straits $)

| Year | Annual Per-Capita Private Final Consumption Expenditure in Real Terms (1914 Prices) (Straits $) | Weighted Real Wage Indices of Agriculture and Non-agriculture Sectors (1914 = 100) | Changes in Real Wages (%) | Changes in Real Consumption (%) | Real Per-Capita Private Final Consumption Expenditure Based on Real Wages and Income Elasticities of Demand (1914 Prices) (Straits $) | Eurasian Population Standard (Numbers) | Total Real Private Final Consumption Expenditure on Rent in the Domestic Market (1914 Prices) (Straits $) | Rent Price Indices (1914 = 100) | Total Private Final Consumption Expenditure on Rent in the Domestic Market (Current Prices) (Straits $) |
|---|---|---|---|---|---|---|---|---|---|
| | Step 4 | Step 5 | Step 6 | Step 7 | | Step 8 | Step 9 | Step 10 | Step 11 |
| | [1] | [2] | [3] | [4] | [5] | [6] | [7]=[5]x[6] | [8] | [9] = [7] x [8] / 100 |
| 1899 | | 116.03 | | | 25.58 | 2,278 | 58,280 | 75.02 | 43,724 |
| 1900 | | 113.92 | −1.814% | −1.451% | 25.21 | 2,261 | 57,008 | 76.46 | 43,591 |
| 1901 | | 112.77 | −1.008% | −0.806% | 25.01 | 2,318 | 57,985 | 77.93 | 45,191 |
| 1902 | | 108.67 | −3.637% | −2.910% | 24.28 | 2,385 | 57,916 | 79.43 | 46,005 |
| 1903 | | 107.35 | −1.214% | −0.971% | 24.05 | 2,453 | 58,994 | 80.96 | 47,764 |
| 1904 | | 107.24 | −0.106% | −0.085% | 24.03 | 2,523 | 60,630 | 82.53 | 50,035 |
| 1905 | | 105.29 | −1.816% | −1.452% | 23.68 | 2,596 | 61,465 | 84.12 | 51,703 |
| 1906 | | 106.94 | 1.562% | 1.250% | 23.97 | 2,670 | 64,019 | 85.74 | 54,892 |
| 1907 | | 107.05 | 0.102% | 0.081% | 23.99 | 2,747 | 65,913 | 87.40 | 57,609 |
| 1908 | | 107.87 | 0.772% | 0.618% | 24.14 | 2,826 | 68,229 | 89.09 | 60,788 |
| 1909 | | 110.50 | 2.437% | 1.950% | 24.61 | 2,908 | 71,560 | 86.37 | 61,806 |
| 1910 | | 108.44 | −1.861% | −1.489% | 24.25 | 2,991 | 72,517 | 86.05 | 62,403 |
| 1911 | | 98.90 | −8.802% | −7.042% | 22.54 | 3,084 | 69,502 | 84.75 | 58,903 |
| 1912 | | 97.22 | −1.696% | −1.357% | 22.23 | 3,186 | 70,839 | 85.45 | 60,530 |
| 1913 | | 95.24 | −2.036% | −1.629% | 21.87 | 3,292 | 71,990 | 90.86 | 65,412 |
| 1914 | | 100.00 | 4.995% | 3.996% | 22.74 | 3,400 | 77,331 | 100.00 | 77,331 |
| 1915 | | 93.86 | −6.142% | −4.914% | 21.63 | 3,511 | 75,941 | 100.28 | 76,151 |
| 1916 | | 88.38 | −5.833% | −4.666% | 20.62 | 3,626 | 74,760 | 102.44 | 76,586 |
| 1917 | | 100.72 | 13.954% | 11.163% | 22.92 | 3,744 | 85,808 | 102.29 | 87,771 |
| 1918 | | 104.36 | 3.614% | 2.891% | 23.58 | 3,865 | 91,151 | 114.34 | 104,218 |
| 1919 | | 92.87 | −11.007% | −8.806% | 21.51 | 3,990 | 85,809 | 124.90 | 107,177 |
| 1920 | | 89.13 | −4.028% | −3.222% | 20.81 | 4,118 | 85,715 | 160.76 | 137,798 |
| 1921 | | 112.82 | 26.583% | 21.267% | 25.24 | 4,270 | 107,775 | 168.16 | 181,235 |
| 1922 | | 123.66 | 9.603% | 7.682% | 27.18 | 4,464 | 121,327 | 186.66 | 226,474 |
| 1923 | | 126.94 | 2.658% | 2.127% | 27.76 | 4,628 | 128,449 | 209.64 | 269,277 |
| 1924 | | 127.47 | 0.412% | 0.330% | 27.85 | 4,795 | 133,515 | 217.54 | 290,446 |
| 1925 | | 124.53 | −2.308% | −1.846% | 27.33 | 5,002 | 136,726 | 225.57 | 308,418 |
| 1926 | | 120.44 | −3.285% | −2.628% | 26.61 | 5,202 | 138,438 | 236.04 | 326,773 |
| 1927 | | 127.57 | 5.925% | 4.740% | 27.88 | 5,407 | 150,715 | 253.41 | 381,931 |
| 1928 | | 131.90 | 3.394% | 2.715% | 28.63 | 5,614 | 160,756 | 275.75 | 443,282 |
| 1929 | | 131.51 | −0.296% | −0.237% | 28.57 | 5,825 | 166,397 | 277.40 | 461,585 |
| 1930 | 28.17 | 129.23 | −1.734% | −1.387% | 28.17 | 5,754 | 162,094 | 255.60 | 414,313 |
| 1931 | | 115.38 | −10.717% | −8.574% | 25.75 | 2,814 | 72,480 | 221.46 | 160,512 |
| 1932 | | 122.09 | 5.817% | 4.654% | 26.95 | 2,730 | 73,578 | 181.20 | 133,322 |
| 1933 | | 136.87 | 12.102% | 9.681% | 29.56 | 2,573 | 76,047 | 159.06 | 120,961 |
| 1934 | | 130.38 | −4.738% | −3.790% | 28.44 | 2,626 | 74,690 | 159.06 | 118,803 |
| 1935 | | 137.02 | 5.092% | 4.073% | 29.60 | 2,862 | 84,701 | 159.06 | 134,725 |
| 1936 | | 148.89 | 8.661% | 6.929% | 31.65 | 3,016 | 95,452 | 159.06 | 151,826 |
| 1937 | | 150.08 | 0.798% | 0.638% | 31.85 | 3,257 | 103,757 | 161.78 | 167,862 |
| 1938 | | 155.10 | 3.348% | 2.678% | 32.71 | 3,550 | 116,111 | 169.58 | 196,906 |
| 1939 | | 154.06 | −0.672% | −0.538% | 32.53 | 3,638 | 118,337 | 182.26 | 215,684 |

| Year | Annual Per-Capita Private Final Consumption Expenditure in Real Terms (1914 Prices) (Straits $) | Weighted Real Wage Indices of Agriculture and Non-agriculture Sectors (1914 = 100) | Changes in Real Wages (%) | Changes in Real Consumption (%) | Real Per-Capita Private Final Consumption Expenditure Based on Real Wages and Income Elasticities of Demand (1914 Prices) (Straits $) | Chinese, Indian, and Eurasian Clerical Population Standard (Numbers) | Total Real Private Final Consumption Expenditure on Rent in the Domestic Market (1914 Prices) (Straits $) | Rent Price Indices (1914 = 100) | Total Private Final Consumption Expenditure on Rent in the Domestic Market (Current Prices) (Straits $) |
|---|---|---|---|---|---|---|---|---|---|
| | Step 4 | Step 5 | Step 6 | Step 7 | | Step 8 | Step 9 | Step 10 | Step 11 |
| | [1] | [2] | [3] | [4] | [5] | [6] | [7]=[5]x[6] | [8] | [9]=[7]x[8]/100 |
| 1947 | | 164.71 | | | 12.24 | 14,072 | 172,288 | 549.01 | 945,883 |
| 1948 | 13.13 | 179.65 | 9.067% | 7.254% | 13.13 | 14,412 | 189,248 | 460.76 | 871,984 |
| 1949 | | 220.02 | 22.473% | 17.978% | 15.49 | 14,681 | 227,432 | 510.58 | 1,161,224 |
| 1950 | | 203.15 | −7.666% | −6.132% | 14.54 | 15,332 | 222,951 | 527.05 | 1,175,069 |
| 1951 | | 181.26 | −10.776% | −8.621% | 13.29 | 16,022 | 212,901 | 642.35 | 1,367,556 |
| 1952 | | 176.19 | −2.797% | −2.238% | 12.99 | 16,905 | 219,614 | 680.78 | 1,495,078 |
| 1953 | | 206.53 | 17.217% | 13.774% | 14.78 | 17,877 | 264,230 | 719.21 | 1,900,360 |
| 1954 | | 208.97 | 1.183% | 0.946% | 14.92 | 18,723 | 279,353 | 735.68 | 2,055,133 |
| 1955 | | 204.74 | −2.023% | −1.618% | 14.68 | 19,583 | 287,449 | 724.70 | 2,083,131 |
| 1956 | | 230.57 | 12.617% | 10.094% | 16.16 | 20,574 | 332,486 | 768.62 | 2,555,546 |
| 1957 | | 215.81 | −6.401% | −5.121% | 15.33 | 14,459 | 221,703 | 790.58 | 1,752,735 |
| 1958 | | 215.37 | −0.205% | −0.164% | 15.31 | 15,140 | 231,759 | 807.05 | 1,870,406 |
| 1959 | | 194.19 | −9.837% | −7.870% | 14.10 | 15,796 | 222,772 | 818.03 | 1,822,340 |
| 1960 | | 230.48 | 18.691% | 14.953% | 16.21 | 16,341 | 264,918 | 818.03 | 2,167,105 |

*(Continued)*

## Appendix Table 6: Singapore: Computation of PFCE in the Domestic Market, 1900–39 and 1948–60, Asiatic Clerical Standard [1899–1939] Malay Clerical Standard [1947–1960] — Rent in Current and 1914 Prices (Straits $)

| Year | Annual Per-Capita Private Final Consumption Expenditure in Real Terms (1914 Prices) (Straits $) | Weighted Real Wage Indices of Agriculture and Non-agriculture Sectors (1914 = 100) | Changes in Real Wages (%) | Changes in Real Consumption (%) | Real Per-Capita Private Final Consumption Expenditure Based on Real Wages and Income Elasticities of Demand (1914 Prices) (Straits $) | Asiatic Clerical Population Standard (Numbers) | Total Real Private Final Consumption Expenditure on Rent in the Domestic Market (1914 Prices) (Straits $) | Rent Price Indices (1914 = 100) | Total Private Final Consumption Expenditure on Rent in the Domestic Market (Current Prices) (Straits $) |
|---|---|---|---|---|---|---|---|---|---|
| | Step 4 | Step 5 | Step 6 | Step 7 | | Step 8 | Step 9 | Step 10 | Step 11 |
| | [1] | [2] | [3] | [4] | [5] | [6] | [7] = [5] x [6] | [8] | [9] = [7] x [8] / 100 |
| 1899 | | 116.03 | | | 25.58 | 19,362 | 495,381 | 75.02 | 371,654 |
| 1900 | | 113.92 | −1.814% | −1.451% | 25.21 | 19,219 | 484,569 | 76.46 | 370,524 |
| 1901 | | 112.77 | −1.008% | −0.806% | 25.01 | 19,707 | 492,875 | 77.93 | 384,120 |
| 1902 | | 108.67 | −3.637% | −2.910% | 24.28 | 20,273 | 492,288 | 79.43 | 391,045 |
| 1903 | | 107.35 | −1.214% | −0.971% | 24.05 | 20,853 | 501,446 | 80.96 | 405,992 |
| 1904 | | 107.24 | −0.106% | −0.085% | 24.03 | 21,449 | 515,351 | 82.53 | 425,296 |
| 1905 | | 105.29 | −1.816% | −1.452% | 23.68 | 22,065 | 522,449 | 84.12 | 439,476 |
| 1906 | | 106.94 | 1.562% | 1.250% | 23.97 | 22,699 | 544,163 | 85.74 | 466,586 |
| 1907 | | 107.05 | 0.102% | 0.081% | 23.99 | 23,351 | 560,257 | 87.40 | 489,677 |
| 1908 | | 107.87 | 0.772% | 0.618% | 24.14 | 24,023 | 579,947 | 89.09 | 516,701 |
| 1909 | | 110.50 | 2.437% | 1.950% | 24.61 | 24,714 | 608,260 | 86.37 | 525,347 |
| 1910 | | 108.44 | −1.861% | −1.489% | 24.25 | 25,423 | 616,395 | 86.05 | 530,425 |
| 1911 | | 98.90 | −8.802% | −7.042% | 22.54 | 27,137 | 611,621 | 84.75 | 518,343 |
| 1912 | | 97.22 | −1.696% | −1.357% | 22.23 | 28,039 | 623,382 | 85.45 | 532,665 |
| 1913 | | 95.24 | −2.036% | −1.629% | 21.87 | 28,967 | 633,512 | 90.86 | 575,623 |
| 1914 | | 100.00 | 4.995% | 3.996% | 22.74 | 29,920 | 680,517 | 100.00 | 680,517 |
| 1915 | | 93.86 | −6.142% | −4.914% | 21.63 | 30,901 | 668,280 | 100.28 | 670,133 |
| 1916 | | 88.38 | −5.833% | −4.666% | 20.62 | 31,909 | 657,884 | 102.44 | 673,961 |
| 1917 | | 100.72 | 13.954% | 11.163% | 22.92 | 32,947 | 755,107 | 102.29 | 772,386 |
| 1918 | | 104.36 | 3.614% | 2.891% | 23.58 | 34,015 | 802,125 | 114.34 | 917,116 |
| 1919 | | 92.87 | −11.007% | −8.806% | 21.51 | 35,113 | 755,117 | 124.90 | 943,157 |
| 1920 | | 89.13 | −4.028% | −3.222% | 20.81 | 36,243 | 754,296 | 160.76 | 1,212,621 |
| 1921 | | 112.82 | 26.583% | 21.267% | 25.24 | 46,973 | 1,185,522 | 168.16 | 1,993,582 |
| 1922 | | 123.66 | 9.603% | 7.682% | 27.18 | 49,107 | 1,334,594 | 186.66 | 2,491,210 |
| 1923 | | 126.94 | 2.658% | 2.127% | 27.76 | 50,907 | 1,412,943 | 209.64 | 2,962,044 |
| 1924 | | 127.47 | 0.412% | 0.330% | 27.85 | 52,741 | 1,468,661 | 217.54 | 3,194,906 |
| 1925 | | 124.53 | −2.308% | −1.846% | 27.33 | 55,025 | 1,503,987 | 225.57 | 3,392,599 |
| 1926 | | 120.44 | −3.285% | −2.628% | 26.61 | 57,218 | 1,522,823 | 236.04 | 3,594,507 |
| 1927 | | 127.57 | 5.925% | 4.740% | 27.88 | 59,473 | 1,657,863 | 253.41 | 4,201,241 |
| 1928 | | 131.90 | 3.394% | 2.715% | 28.63 | 61,758 | 1,768,312 | 275.75 | 4,876,100 |
| 1929 | | 131.51 | −0.296% | −0.237% | 28.57 | 64,077 | 1,830,370 | 277.40 | 5,077,430 |
| 1930 | 28.17 | 129.23 | −1.734% | −1.387% | 28.17 | 63,298 | 1,783,030 | 255.60 | 4,557,447 |
| 1931 | | 115.38 | −10.717% | −8.574% | 25.75 | 61,915 | 1,594,553 | 221.46 | 3,531,260 |
| 1932 | | 122.09 | 5.817% | 4.654% | 26.95 | 60,059 | 1,618,718 | 181.20 | 2,933,088 |
| 1933 | | 136.87 | 12.102% | 9.681% | 29.56 | 56,595 | 1,673,039 | 159.06 | 2,661,142 |
| 1934 | | 130.38 | −4.738% | −3.790% | 28.44 | 57,775 | 1,643,189 | 159.06 | 2,613,662 |
| 1935 | | 137.02 | 5.092% | 4.073% | 29.60 | 62,954 | 1,863,418 | 159.06 | 2,963,960 |
| 1936 | | 148.89 | 8.661% | 6.929% | 31.65 | 66,348 | 2,099,942 | 159.06 | 3,340,176 |
| 1937 | | 150.08 | 0.798% | 0.638% | 31.85 | 71,663 | 2,282,653 | 161.78 | 3,692,954 |
| 1938 | | 155.10 | 3.348% | 2.678% | 32.71 | 78,104 | 2,554,432 | 169.58 | 4,331,930 |
| 1939 | | 154.06 | −0.672% | −0.538% | 32.53 | 80,032 | 2,603,414 | 182.26 | 4,745,056 |

| Year | Annual Per-Capita Private Final Consumption Expenditure in Real Terms (1914 Prices) (Straits $) | Weighted Real Wage Indices of Agriculture and Non-agriculture Sectors (1914 = 100) | Changes in Real Wages (%) | Changes in Real Consumption (%) | Real Per-Capita Private Final Consumption Expenditure Based on Real Wages and Income Elasticities of Demand (1914 Prices) (Straits $) | Malay Clerical Population Standard (Numbers) | Total Real Private Final Consumption Expenditure on Rent in the Domestic Market (1914 Prices) (Straits $) | Rent Price Indices (1914 = 100) | Total Private Final Consumption Expenditure on Rent in the Domestic Market (Current Prices) (Straits $) |
|---|---|---|---|---|---|---|---|---|---|
| | Step 4 | Step 5 | Step 6 | Step 7 | | Step 8 | Step 9 | Step 10 | Step 11 |
| | [1] | [2] | [3] | [4] | [5] | [6] | [7] = [5] x [6] | [8] | [9] = [7] x [8] / 100 |
| 1947 | | 164.71 | | | 12.24 | 126,649 | 1,550,592 | 549.01 | 8,512,947 |
| 1948 | 13.13 | 179.65 | 9.067% | 7.254% | 13.13 | 129,708 | 1,703,232 | 460.76 | 7,847,853 |
| 1949 | | 220.02 | 22.473% | 17.978% | 15.49 | 132,125 | 2,046,884 | 510.58 | 10,451,018 |
| 1950 | | 203.15 | −7.666% | −6.132% | 14.54 | 137,984 | 2,006,561 | 527.05 | 10,575,625 |
| 1951 | | 181.26 | −10.776% | −8.621% | 13.29 | 144,194 | 1,916,105 | 642.35 | 12,308,004 |
| 1952 | | 176.19 | −2.797% | −2.238% | 12.99 | 152,145 | 1,976,524 | 680.78 | 13,455,701 |
| 1953 | | 206.53 | 17.217% | 13.774% | 14.78 | 160,893 | 2,378,069 | 719.21 | 17,103,236 |
| 1954 | | 208.97 | 1.183% | 0.946% | 14.92 | 168,507 | 2,514,173 | 735.68 | 18,496,200 |
| 1955 | | 204.74 | −2.023% | −1.618% | 14.68 | 176,243 | 2,587,037 | 724.70 | 18,748,177 |
| 1956 | | 230.57 | 12.617% | 10.094% | 16.16 | 185,166 | 2,992,372 | 768.62 | 22,999,910 |
| 1957 | | 215.81 | −6.401% | −5.121% | 15.33 | 267,497 | 4,101,502 | 790.58 | 32,425,590 |
| 1958 | | 215.37 | −0.205% | −0.164% | 15.31 | 280,090 | 4,287,536 | 807.05 | 34,602,508 |
| 1959 | | 194.19 | −9.837% | −7.870% | 14.10 | 292,226 | 4,121,283 | 818.03 | 33,713,292 |
| 1960 | | 230.48 | 18.691% | 14.953% | 16.21 | 302,309 | 4,900,980 | 818.03 | 40,091,441 |

*(Continued)*

## Appendix Table 6: Singapore: Computation of PFCE in the Domestic Market, 1900–39 and 1948–60, Chinese Labor Standard — Rent in Current and 1914 Prices (Straits $)

| Year | Annual Per-Capita Private Final Consumption Expenditure in Real Terms (1914 Prices) (Straits $) | Weighted Real Wage Indices of Agriculture and Non-agriculture Sectors (1914 = 100) | Changes in Real Wages (%) | Changes in Real Consumption (%) | Real Per-Capita Private Final Consumption Expenditure Based on Real Wages and Income Elasticities of Demand (1914 Prices) (Straits $) | Chinese Labor Population Standard (Numbers) | Total Real Private Final Consumption Expenditure on Rent in the Domestic Market (1914 Prices) (Straits $) | Rent Price Indices (1914 = 100) | Total Private Final Consumption Expenditure on Rent in the Domestic Market (Current Prices) (Straits $) |
|---|---|---|---|---|---|---|---|---|---|
| | Step 4 | Step 5 | Step 6 | Step 7 | | Step 8 | Step 9 | Step 10 | Step 11 |
| | [1] | [2] | [3] | [4] | [5] | [6] | [7] = [5] x [6] | [8] | [9] = [7] x [8] / 100 |
| 1899 | | 116.03 | | | 3.57 | 135,535 | 484,243 | 75.02 | 363,298 |
| 1900 | | 113.92 | -1.814% | -1.451% | 3.52 | 134,530 | 473,674 | 76.46 | 362,193 |
| 1901 | | 112.77 | -1.008% | -0.806% | 3.49 | 137,948 | 481,794 | 77.93 | 375,483 |
| 1902 | | 108.67 | -3.637% | -2.910% | 3.39 | 141,912 | 481,220 | 79.43 | 382,253 |
| 1903 | | 107.35 | -1.214% | -0.971% | 3.36 | 145,970 | 490,172 | 80.96 | 396,864 |
| 1904 | | 107.24 | -0.106% | -0.085% | 3.36 | 150,145 | 503,764 | 82.53 | 415,734 |
| 1905 | | 105.29 | -1.816% | -1.452% | 3.31 | 154,457 | 510,703 | 84.12 | 429,595 |
| 1906 | | 106.94 | 1.562% | 1.250% | 3.35 | 158,890 | 531,929 | 85.74 | 456,095 |
| 1907 | | 107.05 | 0.102% | 0.081% | 3.35 | 163,456 | 547,661 | 87.40 | 478,667 |
| 1908 | | 107.87 | 0.772% | 0.618% | 3.37 | 168,162 | 566,908 | 89.09 | 505,084 |
| 1909 | | 110.50 | 2.437% | 1.950% | 3.44 | 172,999 | 594,585 | 86.37 | 513,536 |
| 1910 | | 108.44 | -1.861% | -1.489% | 3.39 | 177,962 | 602,537 | 86.05 | 518,500 |
| 1911 | | 98.90 | -8.802% | -7.042% | 3.15 | 185,643 | 584,282 | 84.75 | 495,173 |
| 1912 | | 97.22 | -1.696% | -1.357% | 3.10 | 191,815 | 595,517 | 85.45 | 508,855 |
| 1913 | | 95.24 | -2.036% | -1.629% | 3.05 | 198,160 | 605,194 | 90.86 | 549,893 |
| 1914 | | 100.00 | 4.995% | 3.996% | 3.18 | 204,683 | 650,098 | 100.00 | 650,098 |
| 1915 | | 93.86 | -6.142% | -4.914% | 3.02 | 211,389 | 638,408 | 100.28 | 640,178 |
| 1916 | | 88.38 | -5.833% | -4.666% | 2.88 | 218,286 | 628,477 | 102.44 | 643,835 |
| 1917 | | 100.72 | 13.954% | 11.163% | 3.20 | 225,385 | 721,354 | 102.29 | 737,861 |
| 1918 | | 104.36 | 3.614% | 2.891% | 3.29 | 232,691 | 766,270 | 114.34 | 876,121 |
| 1919 | | 92.87 | -11.007% | -8.806% | 3.00 | 240,206 | 721,364 | 124.90 | 900,999 |
| 1920 | | 89.13 | -4.028% | -3.222% | 2.91 | 247,933 | 720,579 | 160.76 | 1,158,418 |
| 1921 | | 112.82 | 26.583% | 21.267% | 3.52 | 258,351 | 910,539 | 168.16 | 1,531,168 |
| 1922 | | 123.66 | 9.603% | 7.682% | 3.80 | 270,088 | 1,025,033 | 186.66 | 1,913,371 |
| 1923 | | 126.94 | 2.658% | 2.127% | 3.88 | 279,989 | 1,085,209 | 209.64 | 2,274,994 |
| 1924 | | 127.47 | 0.412% | 0.330% | 3.89 | 290,074 | 1,128,004 | 217.54 | 2,453,844 |
| 1925 | | 124.53 | -2.308% | -1.846% | 3.82 | 302,638 | 1,155,136 | 225.57 | 2,605,682 |
| 1926 | | 120.44 | -3.285% | -2.628% | 3.72 | 314,698 | 1,169,603 | 236.04 | 2,760,757 |
| 1927 | | 127.57 | 5.925% | 4.740% | 3.89 | 327,100 | 1,273,320 | 253.41 | 3,226,758 |
| 1928 | | 131.90 | 3.394% | 2.715% | 4.00 | 339,668 | 1,358,150 | 275.75 | 3,745,083 |
| 1929 | | 131.51 | -0.296% | -0.237% | 3.99 | 352,424 | 1,405,813 | 277.40 | 3,899,714 |
| 1930 | | 129.23 | -1.734% | -1.387% | 3.93 | 348,138 | 1,369,454 | 255.60 | 3,500,342 |
| 1931 | | 115.38 | -10.717% | -8.574% | 3.60 | 354,606 | 1,275,302 | 221.46 | 2,824,254 |
| 1932 | | 122.09 | 5.817% | 4.654% | 3.76 | 343,972 | 1,294,629 | 181.20 | 2,345,844 |
| 1933 | | 136.87 | 12.102% | 9.681% | 4.13 | 324,135 | 1,338,074 | 159.06 | 2,128,345 |
| 1934 | | 130.38 | -4.738% | -3.790% | 3.97 | 330,894 | 1,314,200 | 159.06 | 2,090,372 |
| 1935 | | 137.02 | 5.092% | 4.073% | 4.13 | 360,555 | 1,490,336 | 159.06 | 2,370,535 |
| 1936 | 4.42 | 148.89 | 8.661% | 6.929% | 4.42 | 379,993 | 1,679,505 | 159.06 | 2,671,428 |
| 1937 | | 150.08 | 0.798% | 0.638% | 4.45 | 410,436 | 1,825,635 | 161.78 | 2,953,575 |
| 1938 | | 155.10 | 3.348% | 2.678% | 4.57 | 447,323 | 2,043,000 | 169.58 | 3,464,619 |
| 1939 | | 154.06 | -0.672% | -0.538% | 4.54 | 458,365 | 2,082,175 | 182.26 | 3,795,031 |

| Year | Annual Per-Capita Private Final Consumption Expenditure in Real Terms (1914 Prices) (Straits $) | Weighted Real Wage ndices of Agriculture and Non-agriculture Sectors (1914 = 100) | Changes in Real Wages (%) | Changes in Real Consumption (%) | Real Per-Capita Private Final Consumption Expenditure Based on Real Wages and Income Elasticities of Demand (1914 Prices) (Straits $) | Chinese Labor Population Standard (Numbers) | Total Real Private Final Consumption Expenditure on Rent in the Domestic Market (1914 Prices) (Straits $) | Rent Price Indices (1914 = 100) | Total Private Final Consumption Expenditure on Rent in the Domestic Market (Current Prices) (Straits $) |
|---|---|---|---|---|---|---|---|---|---|
| | Step 4 | Step 5 | Step 6 | Step 7 | | Step 8 | Step 9 | Step 10 | Step 11 |
| | [1] | [2] | [3] | [4] | [5] | [6] | [7] = [5] x [6] | [8] | [9] = [7] x [8] / 100 |
| 1947 | | 164.71 | | | 5.10 | 562,886 | 2,872,240 | 549.01 | 15,768,966 |
| 1948 | | 179.65 | 9.067% | 7.254% | 5.47 | 576,480 | 3,154,983 | 460.76 | 14,536,978 |
| 1949 | 6.46 | 220.02 | 22.473% | 17.978% | 6.46 | 587,220 | 3,791,547 | 510.58 | 19,358,954 |
| 1950 | | 203.15 | -7.666% | -6.132% | 6.06 | 613,260 | 3,716,855 | 527.05 | 19,589,769 |
| 1951 | | 181.26 | -10.776% | -8.621% | 5.54 | 640,860 | 3,549,299 | 642.35 | 22,798,744 |
| 1952 | | 176.19 | -2.797% | -2.238% | 5.41 | 676,200 | 3,661,217 | 680.78 | 24,924,681 |
| 1953 | | 206.53 | 17.217% | 13.774% | 6.16 | 715,080 | 4,405,019 | 719.21 | 31,681,197 |
| 1954 | | 208.97 | 1.183% | 0.946% | 6.22 | 748,920 | 4,657,132 | 735.68 | 34,261,455 |
| 1955 | | 204.74 | -2.023% | -1.618% | 6.12 | 783,300 | 4,792,100 | 724.70 | 34,728,204 |
| 1956 | | 230.57 | 12.617% | 10.094% | 6.74 | 822,960 | 5,542,923 | 768.62 | 42,603,905 |
| 1957 | | 215.81 | -6.401% | -5.121% | 6.39 | 788,031 | 5,035,858 | 790.58 | 39,812,410 |
| 1958 | | 215.37 | -0.205% | -0.164% | 6.38 | 825,130 | 5,264,272 | 807.05 | 42,485,247 |
| 1959 | | 194.19 | -9.837% | -7.870% | 5.88 | 860,882 | 5,060,145 | 818.03 | 41,393,461 |
| 1960 | | 230.48 | 18.691% | 14.953% | 6.76 | 890,585 | 6,017,464 | 818.03 | 49,224,605 |

*(Continued)*

## Appendix Table 6: Singapore: Computation of PFCE in the Domestic Market, 1900–39 and 1948–60, Malay Labor Standard — Rent in Current and 1914 Prices (Straits $)

| Year | Annual Per-Capita Private Final Consumption Expenditure in Real Terms (1914 Prices) (Straits $) | Weighted Real Wage Indices of Agriculture and Non-agriculture Sectors (1914 = 100) | Changes in Real Wages (%) | Changes in Real Consumption (%) | Real Per-Capita Private Final Consumption Expenditure Based on Real Wages and Income Elasticities of Demand (1914 Prices) (Straits $) | Malay Labor Population Standard (Numbers) | Total Real Private Final Consumption Expenditure on Rent in the Domestic Market (1914 Prices) (Straits $) | Rent Price Indices (1914 = 100) | Total Private Final Consumption Expenditure on Rent in the Domestic Market (Current Prices) (Straits $) |
|---|---|---|---|---|---|---|---|---|---|
| | Step 4 | Step 5 | Step 6 | Step 7 | | Step 8 | Step 9 | Step 10 | Step 11 |
| | [1] | [2] | [3] | [4] | [5] | [6] | [7] = [5] x [6] | [8] | [9] = [7] x [8] / 100 |
| 1899 | | 116.03 | | | 2.83 | 41,002 | 116,071 | 75.02 | 87,081 |
| 1900 | | 113.92 | −1.814% | −1.451% | 2.79 | 40,698 | 113,538 | 76.46 | 86,817 |
| 1901 | | 112.77 | −1.008% | −0.806% | 2.77 | 41,732 | 115,484 | 77.93 | 90,002 |
| 1902 | | 108.67 | −3.637% | −2.910% | 2.69 | 42,931 | 115,347 | 79.43 | 91,625 |
| 1903 | | 107.35 | −1.214% | −0.971% | 2.66 | 44,159 | 117,493 | 80.96 | 95,127 |
| 1904 | | 107.24 | −0.106% | −0.085% | 2.66 | 45,422 | 120,751 | 82.53 | 99,650 |
| 1905 | | 105.29 | −1.816% | −1.452% | 2.62 | 46,726 | 122,414 | 84.12 | 102,973 |
| 1906 | | 106.94 | 1.562% | 1.250% | 2.65 | 48,068 | 127,502 | 85.74 | 109,325 |
| 1907 | | 107.05 | 0.102% | 0.081% | 2.65 | 49,449 | 131,273 | 87.40 | 114,735 |
| 1908 | | 107.87 | 0.772% | 0.618% | 2.67 | 50,873 | 135,886 | 89.09 | 121,067 |
| 1909 | | 110.50 | 2.437% | 1.950% | 2.72 | 52,336 | 142,520 | 86.37 | 123,093 |
| 1910 | | 108.44 | −1.861% | −1.489% | 2.68 | 53,837 | 144,426 | 86.05 | 124,283 |
| 1911 | | 98.90 | −8.802% | −7.042% | 2.49 | 52,424 | 130,732 | 84.75 | 110,794 |
| 1912 | | 97.22 | −1.696% | −1.357% | 2.46 | 54,167 | 133,246 | 85.45 | 113,855 |
| 1913 | | 95.24 | −2.036% | −1.629% | 2.42 | 55,959 | 135,411 | 90.86 | 123,037 |
| 1914 | | 100.00 | 4.995% | 3.996% | 2.52 | 57,801 | 145,458 | 100.00 | 145,458 |
| 1915 | | 93.86 | −6.142% | −4.914% | 2.39 | 59,695 | 142,842 | 100.28 | 143,239 |
| 1916 | | 88.38 | −5.833% | −4.666% | 2.28 | 61,642 | 140,620 | 102.44 | 144,057 |
| 1917 | | 100.72 | 13.954% | 11.163% | 2.54 | 63,647 | 161,402 | 102.29 | 165,095 |
| 1918 | | 104.36 | 3.614% | 2.891% | 2.61 | 65,710 | 171,451 | 114.34 | 196,030 |
| 1919 | | 92.87 | −11.007% | −8.806% | 2.38 | 67,832 | 161,404 | 124.90 | 201,597 |
| 1920 | | 89.13 | −4.028% | −3.222% | 2.30 | 70,014 | 161,228 | 160.76 | 259,194 |
| 1921 | | 112.82 | 26.583% | 21.267% | 2.79 | 55,513 | 155,022 | 168.16 | 260,686 |
| 1922 | | 123.66 | 9.603% | 7.682% | 3.01 | 58,035 | 174,515 | 186.66 | 325,757 |
| 1923 | | 126.94 | 2.658% | 2.127% | 3.07 | 60,163 | 184,760 | 209.64 | 387,324 |
| 1924 | | 127.47 | 0.412% | 0.330% | 3.08 | 62,330 | 192,046 | 217.54 | 417,774 |
| 1925 | | 124.53 | −2.308% | −1.846% | 3.02 | 65,030 | 196,665 | 225.57 | 443,625 |
| 1926 | | 120.44 | −3.285% | −2.628% | 2.94 | 67,621 | 199,128 | 236.04 | 470,027 |
| 1927 | | 127.57 | 5.925% | 4.740% | 3.08 | 70,286 | 216,786 | 253.41 | 549,365 |
| 1928 | | 131.90 | 3.394% | 2.715% | 3.17 | 72,986 | 231,229 | 275.75 | 637,611 |
| 1929 | | 131.51 | −0.296% | −0.237% | 3.16 | 75,727 | 239,344 | 277.40 | 663,938 |
| 1930 | | 129.23 | −1.734% | −1.387% | 3.12 | 74,807 | 233,154 | 255.60 | 595,943 |
| 1931 | | 115.38 | −10.717% | −8.574% | 2.85 | 56,287 | 160,391 | 221.46 | 355,197 |
| 1932 | | 122.09 | 5.817% | 4.654% | 2.98 | 54,599 | 162,821 | 181.20 | 295,029 |
| 1933 | | 136.87 | 12.102% | 9.681% | 3.27 | 51,450 | 168,285 | 159.06 | 267,675 |
| 1934 | | 130.38 | −4.738% | −3.790% | 3.15 | 52,523 | 165,283 | 159.06 | 262,899 |
| 1935 | | 137.02 | 5.092% | 4.073% | 3.28 | 57,231 | 187,435 | 159.06 | 298,135 |
| 1936 | 3.50 | 148.89 | 8.661% | 6.929% | 3.50 | 60,316 | 211,226 | 159.06 | 335,977 |
| 1937 | | 150.08 | 0.798% | 0.638% | 3.52 | 65,149 | 229,604 | 161.78 | 371,462 |
| 1938 | | 155.10 | 3.348% | 2.678% | 3.62 | 71,004 | 256,942 | 169.58 | 435,734 |
| 1939 | | 154.06 | −0.672% | −0.538% | 3.60 | 72,756 | 261,869 | 182.26 | 477,289 |

| Year | Annual Per-Capita Private Final Consumption Expenditure in Real Terms (1914 Prices) (Straits $) | Weighted Real Wage Indices of Agriculture and Non-agriculture Sectors (1914 = 100) | Changes in Real Wages (%) | Changes in Real Consumption (%) | Real Per-Capita Private Final Consumption Expenditure Based on Real Wages and Income Elasticities of Demand (1914 Prices) (Straits $) | Malay Labor Population Standard (Numbers) | Total Real Private Final Consumption Expenditure on Rent in the Domestic Market (1914 Prices) (Straits $) | Rent Price Indices (1914 = 100) | Total Private Final Consumption Expenditure on Rent in the Domestic Market (Current Prices) (Straits $) |
|---|---|---|---|---|---|---|---|---|---|
| | Step 4 | Step 5 | Step 6 | Step 7 | | Step 8 | Step 9 | Step 10 | Step 11 |
| | [1] | [2] | [3] | [4] | [5] | [6] | [7] = [5] x [6] | [8] | [9] = [7] x [8] / 100 |
| 1947 | | 164.71 | | | 3.55 | 84,433 | 299,869 | 549.01 | 1,646,320 |
| 1948 | | 179.65 | 9.067% | 7.254% | 3.81 | 86,472 | 329,388 | 460.76 | 1,517,697 |
| 1949 | 4.49 | 220.02 | 22.473% | 17.978% | 4.49 | 88,083 | 395,847 | 510.58 | 2,021,124 |
| 1950 | | 203.15 | −7.666% | −6.132% | 4.22 | 91,989 | 388,049 | 527.05 | 2,045,221 |
| 1951 | | 181.26 | −10.776% | −8.621% | 3.85 | 96,129 | 370,556 | 642.35 | 2,380,247 |
| 1952 | | 176.19 | −2.797% | −2.238% | 3.77 | 101,430 | 382,240 | 680.78 | 2,602,200 |
| 1953 | | 206.53 | 17.217% | 13.774% | 4.29 | 107,262 | 459,895 | 719.21 | 3,307,597 |
| 1954 | | 208.97 | 1.183% | 0.946% | 4.33 | 112,338 | 486,216 | 735.68 | 3,576,983 |
| 1955 | | 204.74 | −2.023% | −1.618% | 4.26 | 117,495 | 500,307 | 724.70 | 3,625,712 |
| 1956 | | 230.57 | 12.617% | 10.094% | 4.69 | 123,444 | 578,695 | 768.62 | 4,447,955 |
| 1957 | | 215.81 | −6.401% | −5.121% | 4.45 | 144,593 | 643,127 | 790.58 | 5,084,424 |
| 1958 | | 215.37 | −0.205% | −0.164% | 4.44 | 151,400 | 672,298 | 807.05 | 5,425,770 |
| 1959 | | 194.19 | −9.837% | −7.870% | 4.09 | 157,960 | 646,229 | 818.03 | 5,286,339 |
| 1960 | | 230.48 | 18.691% | 14.953% | 4.70 | 163,410 | 768,487 | 818.03 | 6,286,450 |

*(Continued)*

**Appendix Table 6:** Singapore: Computation of PFCE in the Domestic Market, 1900–39 and 1948–60, Indian Labor Standard — Rent in Current and 1914 Prices (Straits $)

| Year | Annual Per-Capita Private Final Consumption Expenditure in Real Terms (1914 Prices) (Straits $) | Weighted Real Wage Indices of Agriculture and Non-agriculture Sectors (1914 = 100) | Changes in Real Wages (%) | Changes in Real Consumption (%) | Real Per-Capita Private Final Consumption Expenditure Based on Real Wages and Income Elasticities of Demand (1914 Prices) (Straits $) | Indian Labor Population Standard (Numbers) | Total Real Private Final Consumption Expenditure on Rent in the Domestic Market (1914 Prices) (Straits $) | Rent Price Indices (1914 = 100) | Total Private Final Consumption Expenditure on Rent in the Domestic Market (Current Prices) (Straits $) |
|---|---|---|---|---|---|---|---|---|---|
| | Step 4 | Step 5 | Step 6 | Step 7 | | Step 8 | Step 9 | Step 10 | Step 11 |
| | [1] | [2] | [3] | [4] | [5] | [6] | [7] = [5] x [6] | [8] | [9] = [7] x [8] / 100 |
| 1899 | | 116.03 | | | 5.17 | 15,945 | 82,366 | 75.02 | 61,794 |
| 1900 | | 113.92 | −1.814% | −1.451% | 5.09 | 15,827 | 80,568 | 76.46 | 61,606 |
| 1901 | | 112.77 | −1.008% | −0.806% | 5.05 | 16,229 | 81,949 | 77.93 | 63,867 |
| 1902 | | 108.67 | −3.637% | −2.910% | 4.90 | 16,696 | 81,852 | 79.43 | 65,018 |
| 1903 | | 107.35 | −1.214% | −0.971% | 4.85 | 17,173 | 83,374 | 80.96 | 67,503 |
| 1904 | | 107.24 | −0.106% | −0.085% | 4.85 | 17,664 | 85,686 | 82.53 | 70,713 |
| 1905 | | 105.29 | −1.816% | −1.452% | 4.78 | 18,171 | 86,867 | 84.12 | 73,071 |
| 1906 | | 106.94 | 1.562% | 1.250% | 4.84 | 18,693 | 90,477 | 85.74 | 77,578 |
| 1907 | | 107.05 | 0.102% | 0.081% | 4.84 | 19,230 | 93,153 | 87.40 | 81,418 |
| 1908 | | 107.87 | 0.772% | 0.618% | 4.87 | 19,784 | 96,427 | 89.09 | 85,911 |
| 1909 | | 110.50 | 2.437% | 1.950% | 4.97 | 20,353 | 101,134 | 86.37 | 87,348 |
| 1910 | | 108.44 | −1.861% | −1.489% | 4.90 | 20,937 | 102,487 | 86.05 | 88,193 |
| 1911 | | 98.90 | −8.802% | −7.042% | 4.55 | 21,586 | 98,226 | 84.75 | 83,246 |
| 1912 | | 97.22 | −1.696% | −1.357% | 4.49 | 22,304 | 100,115 | 85.45 | 85,546 |
| 1913 | | 95.24 | −2.036% | −1.629% | 4.42 | 23,042 | 101,742 | 90.86 | 92,445 |
| 1914 | | 100.00 | 4.995% | 3.996% | 4.59 | 23,800 | 109,291 | 100.00 | 109,291 |
| 1915 | | 93.86 | −6.142% | −4.914% | 4.37 | 24,580 | 107,325 | 100.28 | 107,623 |
| 1916 | | 88.38 | −5.833% | −4.666% | 4.16 | 25,382 | 105,656 | 102.44 | 108,238 |
| 1917 | | 100.72 | 13.954% | 11.163% | 4.63 | 26,208 | 121,270 | 102.29 | 124,045 |
| 1918 | | 104.36 | 3.614% | 2.891% | 4.76 | 27,057 | 128,821 | 114.34 | 147,288 |
| 1919 | | 92.87 | −11.007% | −8.806% | 4.34 | 27,931 | 121,271 | 124.90 | 151,471 |
| 1920 | | 89.13 | −4.028% | −3.222% | 4.20 | 28,829 | 121,140 | 160.76 | 194,746 |
| 1921 | | 112.82 | 26.583% | 21.267% | 5.10 | 34,162 | 174,075 | 168.16 | 292,725 |
| 1922 | | 123.66 | 9.603% | 7.682% | 5.49 | 35,714 | 195,964 | 186.66 | 365,794 |
| 1923 | | 126.94 | 2.658% | 2.127% | 5.60 | 37,023 | 207,468 | 209.64 | 434,928 |
| 1924 | | 127.47 | 0.412% | 0.330% | 5.62 | 38,357 | 215,649 | 217.54 | 469,121 |
| 1925 | | 124.53 | −2.308% | −1.846% | 5.52 | 40,018 | 220,836 | 225.57 | 498,149 |
| 1926 | | 120.44 | −3.285% | −2.628% | 5.37 | 41,613 | 223,602 | 236.04 | 527,795 |
| 1927 | | 127.57 | 5.925% | 4.740% | 5.63 | 43,253 | 243,430 | 253.41 | 616,885 |
| 1928 | | 131.90 | 3.394% | 2.715% | 5.78 | 44,915 | 259,648 | 275.75 | 715,977 |
| 1929 | | 131.51 | −0.296% | −0.237% | 5.77 | 46,602 | 268,760 | 277.40 | 745,539 |
| 1930 | | 129.23 | −1.734% | −1.387% | 5.69 | 46,035 | 261,809 | 255.60 | 669,188 |
| 1931 | | 115.38 | −10.717% | −8.574% | 5.20 | 50,658 | 263,401 | 221.46 | 583,322 |
| 1932 | | 122.09 | 5.817% | 4.654% | 5.44 | 49,139 | 267,393 | 181.20 | 484,511 |
| 1933 | 5.97 | 136.87 | 12.102% | 9.681% | 5.97 | 46,305 | 276,366 | 159.06 | 439,589 |
| 1934 | | 130.38 | −4.738% | −3.790% | 5.74 | 47,271 | 271,435 | 159.06 | 431,746 |
| 1935 | | 137.02 | 5.092% | 4.073% | 5.98 | 51,508 | 307,815 | 159.06 | 489,611 |
| 1936 | | 148.89 | 8.661% | 6.929% | 6.39 | 54,285 | 346,886 | 159.06 | 551,758 |
| 1937 | | 150.08 | 0.798% | 0.638% | 6.43 | 58,634 | 377,067 | 161.78 | 610,032 |
| 1938 | | 155.10 | 3.348% | 2.678% | 6.60 | 63,903 | 421,962 | 169.58 | 715,584 |
| 1939 | | 154.06 | −0.672% | −0.538% | 6.57 | 65,481 | 430,053 | 182.26 | 783,827 |

| Year | Annual Per-Capita Private Final Consumption Expenditure in Real Terms (1914 Prices) (Straits $) | Weighted Real Wage Indices of Agriculture and Non-agriculture Sectors (1914 = 100) | Changes in Real Wages (%) | Changes in Real Consumption (%) | Real Per-Capita Private Final Consumption Expenditure Based on Real Wages and Income Elasticities of Demand (1914 Prices) (Straits $) | Indian Labor Population Standard (Numbers) | Total Real Private Final Consumption Expenditure on Rent in the Domestic Market (1914 Prices) (Straits $) | Rent Price Indices (1914 = 100) | Total Private Final Consumption Expenditure on Rent in the Domestic Market (Current Prices) (Straits $) |
|---|---|---|---|---|---|---|---|---|---|
| | Step 4 | Step 5 | Step 6 | Step 7 | | Step 8 | Step 9 | Step 10 | Step 11 |
| | [1] | [2] | [3] | [4] | [5] | [6] | [7] = [5] x [6] | [8] | [9] = [7] x [8] / 100 |
| 1947 | | 164.71 | | | 4.48 | 93,814 | 420,183 | 549.01 | 2,306,859 |
| 1948 | | 179.65 | 9.067% | 7.254% | 4.80 | 96,080 | 461,546 | 460.76 | 2,126,630 |
| 1949 | 5.67 | 220.02 | 22.473% | 17.978% | 5.67 | 97,870 | 554,669 | 510.58 | 2,832,042 |
| 1950 | | 203.15 | −7.666% | −6.132% | 5.32 | 102,210 | 543,743 | 527.05 | 2,865,808 |
| 1951 | | 181.26 | −10.776% | −8.621% | 4.86 | 106,810 | 519,231 | 642.35 | 3,335,252 |
| 1952 | | 176.19 | −2.797% | −2.238% | 4.75 | 112,700 | 535,603 | 680.78 | 3,646,258 |
| 1953 | | 206.53 | 17.217% | 13.774% | 5.41 | 119,180 | 644,415 | 719.21 | 4,634,676 |
| 1954 | | 208.97 | 1.183% | 0.946% | 5.46 | 124,820 | 681,297 | 735.68 | 5,012,145 |
| 1955 | | 204.74 | −2.023% | −1.618% | 5.37 | 130,550 | 701,041 | 724.70 | 5,080,426 |
| 1956 | | 230.57 | 12.617% | 10.094% | 5.91 | 137,160 | 810,880 | 768.62 | 6,232,571 |
| 1957 | | 215.81 | −6.401% | −5.121% | 5.61 | 144,593 | 811,047 | 790.58 | 6,411,963 |
| 1958 | | 215.37 | −0.205% | −0.164% | 5.60 | 151,400 | 847,834 | 807.05 | 6,842,435 |
| 1959 | | 194.19 | −9.837% | −7.870% | 5.16 | 157,960 | 814,959 | 818.03 | 6,666,598 |
| 1960 | | 230.48 | 18.691% | 14.953% | 5.93 | 163,410 | 969,139 | 818.03 | 7,927,838 |

*(Continued)*

## Appendix Table 6: Singapore: Computation of PFCE in the Domestic Market, 1900–39 and 1948–60, European Standard — Servant in Current and 1914 Prices (Straits $)

| Year | Annual Per-Capita Private Final Consumption Expenditure in Real Terms (1914 Prices) (Straits $) | Weighted Real Wage Indices of Agriculture and Non-agriculture Sectors (1914 = 100) | Changes in Real Wages (%) | Changes in Real Consumption (%) | Real Per-Capita Private Final Consumption Expenditure Based on Real Wages and Income Elasticities of Demand (1914 Prices) (Straits $) | European Population Standard (Numbers) | Total Real Private Final Consumption Expenditure on Servant in the Domestic Market (1914 Prices) (Straits $) | Servant Price Indices (1914 = 100) | Total Private Final Consumption Expenditure on Servant in the Domestic Market (Current Prices) (Straits $) |
|---|---|---|---|---|---|---|---|---|---|
|  | Step 4 | Step 5 | Step 6 | Step 7 |  | Step 8 | Step 9 | Step 10 | Step 11 |
|  | [1] | [2] | [3] | [4] | [5] | [6] | [7] = [5] x [6] | [8] | [9] = [7] x [8] / 100 |
| 1899 |  | 116.03 |  |  | 384.73 | 13,667 | 5,258,236 | 69.64 | 3,661,986 |
| 1900 |  | 113.92 | −1.814% | −1.814% | 377.75 | 13,566 | 5,124,542 | 75.00 | 3,843,406 |
| 1901 |  | 112.77 | −1.008% | −1.008% | 373.94 | 13,911 | 5,201,793 | 73.21 | 3,808,456 |
| 1902 |  | 108.67 | −3.637% | −3.637% | 360.34 | 14,310 | 5,156,672 | 82.14 | 4,235,837 |
| 1903 |  | 107.35 | −1.214% | −1.214% | 355.97 | 14,720 | 5,239,718 | 82.14 | 4,304,054 |
| 1904 |  | 107.24 | −0.106% | −0.106% | 355.59 | 15,141 | 5,383,876 | 78.57 | 4,230,188 |
| 1905 |  | 105.29 | −1.816% | −1.816% | 349.13 | 15,575 | 5,437,920 | 78.57 | 4,272,652 |
| 1906 |  | 106.94 | 1.562% | 1.562% | 354.59 | 16,023 | 5,681,407 | 82.14 | 4,666,870 |
| 1907 |  | 107.05 | 0.102% | 0.102% | 354.95 | 16,483 | 5,850,629 | 91.07 | 5,328,251 |
| 1908 |  | 107.87 | 0.772% | 0.772% | 357.69 | 16,958 | 6,065,542 | 91.07 | 5,523,976 |
| 1909 |  | 110.50 | 2.437% | 2.437% | 366.41 | 17,445 | 6,392,082 | 91.07 | 5,821,360 |
| 1910 |  | 108.44 | −1.861% | −1.861% | 359.59 | 17,946 | 6,453,095 | 91.07 | 5,876,926 |
| 1911 |  | 98.90 | −8.802% | −8.802% | 327.94 | 18,503 | 6,067,692 | 91.07 | 5,525,934 |
| 1912 |  | 97.22 | −1.696% | −1.696% | 322.38 | 19,118 | 6,163,108 | 91.07 | 5,612,830 |
| 1913 |  | 95.24 | −2.036% | −2.036% | 315.81 | 19,750 | 6,237,336 | 91.07 | 5,680,431 |
| 1914 |  | 100.00 | 4.995% | 4.995% | 331.59 | 20,400 | 6,764,493 | 100.00 | 6,764,493 |
| 1915 |  | 93.86 | −6.142% | −6.142% | 311.22 | 21,069 | 6,557,037 | 103.82 | 6,807,662 |
| 1916 |  | 88.38 | −5.833% | −5.833% | 293.07 | 21,756 | 6,376,054 | 103.82 | 6,619,761 |
| 1917 |  | 100.72 | 13.954% | 13.954% | 333.96 | 22,464 | 7,502,043 | 113.09 | 8,484,215 |
| 1918 |  | 104.36 | 3.614% | 3.614% | 346.03 | 23,192 | 8,025,152 | 116.80 | 9,373,377 |
| 1919 |  | 92.87 | −11.007% | −11.007% | 307.95 | 23,941 | 7,372,472 | 116.80 | 8,611,047 |
| 1920 |  | 89.13 | −4.028% | −4.028% | 295.54 | 24,711 | 7,303,157 | 155.50 | 11,356,409 |
| 1921 |  | 112.82 | 26.583% | 26.583% | 374.11 | 27,757 | 10,384,029 | 155.50 | 16,147,166 |
| 1922 |  | 123.66 | 9.603% | 9.603% | 410.03 | 29,018 | 11,898,246 | 155.50 | 18,501,772 |
| 1923 |  | 126.94 | 2.658% | 2.658% | 420.93 | 30,082 | 12,662,326 | 155.50 | 19,689,916 |
| 1924 |  | 127.47 | 0.412% | 0.412% | 422.67 | 31,165 | 13,172,465 | 155.50 | 20,483,183 |
| 1925 |  | 124.53 | −2.308% | −2.308% | 412.92 | 32,515 | 13,425,879 | 155.50 | 20,877,242 |
| 1926 |  | 120.44 | −3.285% | −3.285% | 399.35 | 33,811 | 13,502,307 | 155.50 | 20,996,088 |
| 1927 |  | 127.57 | 5.925% | 5.925% | 423.01 | 35,143 | 14,865,972 | 155.50 | 23,116,586 |
| 1928 |  | 131.90 | 3.394% | 3.394% | 437.37 | 36,493 | 15,961,166 | 155.50 | 24,819,613 |
| 1929 |  | 131.51 | −0.296% | −0.296% | 436.08 | 37,864 | 16,511,488 | 155.50 | 25,675,365 |
| 1930 | 428.52 | 129.23 | −1.734% | −1.734% | 428.52 | 37,403 | 16,027,883 | 152.90 | 24,506,633 |
| 1931 |  | 115.38 | −10.717% | −10.717% | 382.59 | 36,586 | 13,997,596 | 138.00 | 19,316,682 |
| 1932 |  | 122.09 | 5.817% | 5.817% | 404.85 | 35,489 | 14,367,695 | 124.70 | 17,916,516 |
| 1933 |  | 136.87 | 12.102% | 12.102% | 453.84 | 33,443 | 15,177,534 | 115.80 | 17,575,584 |
| 1934 |  | 130.38 | −4.738% | −4.738% | 432.34 | 34,140 | 14,759,922 | 123.70 | 18,258,023 |
| 1935 |  | 137.02 | 5.092% | 5.092% | 454.35 | 37,200 | 16,901,906 | 127.40 | 21,533,029 |
| 1936 |  | 148.89 | 8.661% | 8.661% | 493.70 | 39,206 | 19,355,820 | 125.70 | 24,330,265 |
| 1937 |  | 150.08 | 0.798% | 0.798% | 497.64 | 42,347 | 21,073,265 | 130.00 | 27,395,245 |
| 1938 |  | 155.10 | 3.348% | 3.348% | 514.30 | 46,152 | 23,736,088 | 128.20 | 30,429,665 |
| 1939 |  | 154.06 | −0.672% | −0.672% | 510.84 | 47,292 | 24,158,540 | 128.20 | 30,971,248 |

| Year | Annual Per-Capita Private Final Consumption Expenditure in Real Terms (1914 Prices) (Straits $) | Weighted Real Wage Indices of Agriculture and Non-agriculture Sectors (1914 = 100) | Changes in Real Wages (%) | Changes in Real Consumption (%) | Real Per-Capita Private Final Consumption Expenditure Based on Real Wages and Income Elasticities of Demand (1914 Prices) (Straits $) | European Population Standard (Numbers) | Total Real Private Final Consumption Expenditure on Servant in the Domestic Market (1914 Prices) (Straits $) | Servant Price Indices (1914 = 100) | Total Private Final Consumption Expenditure on Servant in the Domestic Market (Current Prices) (Straits $) |
|---|---|---|---|---|---|---|---|---|---|
|  | Step 4 | Step 5 | Step 6 | Step 7 |  | Step 8 | Step 9 | Step 10 | Step 11 |
|  | [1] | [2] | [3] | [4] | [5] | [6] | [7] = [5] x [6] | [8] | [9] = [7] x [8] / 100 |
| 1947 |  | 164.71 |  |  | 405.88 | 56,289 | 22,846,173 | 366.43 | 83,714,834 |
| 1948 | 442.68 | 179.65 | 9.067% | 9.067% | 442.68 | 57,648 | 25,519,462 | 306.70 | 78,268,306 |
| 1949 |  | 220.02 | 22.473% | 22.473% | 542.16 | 58,722 | 31,836,756 | 322.29 | 102,606,622 |
| 1950 |  | 203.15 | −7.666% | −7.666% | 500.60 | 61,326 | 30,699,842 | 334.74 | 102,765,611 |
| 1951 |  | 181.26 | −10.776% | −10.776% | 446.66 | 64,086 | 28,624,490 | 380.93 | 109,038,351 |
| 1952 |  | 176.19 | −2.797% | −2.797% | 434.16 | 67,620 | 29,358,116 | 423.69 | 124,388,376 |
| 1953 |  | 206.53 | 17.217% | 17.217% | 508.92 | 71,508 | 36,391,499 | 448.21 | 163,109,079 |
| 1954 |  | 208.97 | 1.183% | 1.183% | 514.93 | 74,892 | 38,564,451 | 454.64 | 175,329,712 |
| 1955 |  | 204.74 | −2.023% | −2.023% | 504.52 | 78,330 | 39,518,915 | 457.59 | 180,834,429 |
| 1956 |  | 230.57 | 12.617% | 12.617% | 568.17 | 82,296 | 46,758,431 | 459.05 | 214,645,047 |
| 1957 |  | 215.81 | −6.401% | −6.401% | 531.80 | 86,756 | 46,136,980 | 459.05 | 211,792,270 |
| 1958 |  | 215.37 | −0.205% | −0.205% | 530.71 | 90,840 | 48,209,797 | 459.05 | 221,307,556 |
| 1959 |  | 194.19 | −9.837% | −9.837% | 478.51 | 94,776 | 45,350,856 | 459.05 | 208,183,557 |
| 1960 |  | 230.48 | 18.691% | 18.691% | 567.94 | 98,046 | 55,684,472 | 459.05 | 255,620,125 |

*(Continued)*

**Appendix Table 6:** Singapore: Computation of PFCE in the Domestic Market, 1900–39 and 1948–60, Eurasian Standard [1899–1939] Chinese, Indian and Eurasian Clerical Standard [1947–1960] — Servant in Current and 1914 Prices (Straits $)

| Year | Annual Per-Capita Private Final Consumption Expenditure in Real Terms (1914 Prices) (Straits $) | Weighted Real Wage Indices of Agriculture and Non-agriculture Sectors (1914 = 100) | Changes in Real Wages (%) | Changes in Real Consumption (%) | Real Per-Capita Private Final Consumption Expenditure Based on Real Wages and Income Elasticities of Demand (1914 Prices) (Straits $) | Eurasian Population Standard (Numbers) | Total Real Private Final Consumption Expenditure on Servant in the Domestic Market (1914 Prices) (Straits $) | Servant Price Indices (1914 = 100) | Total Private Final Consumption Expenditure on Servant in the Domestic Market (Current Prices) (Straits $) |
|---|---|---|---|---|---|---|---|---|---|
| | Step 4 | Step 5 | Step 6 | | Step 7 | Step 8 | Step 9 | Step 10 | Step 11 |
| | [1] | [2] | [3] | [4] | [5] | [6] | [7] = [5] x [6] | [8] | [9] = [7] x [8] / 100 |
| 1899 | | 116.03 | | | 14.09 | 2,278 | 32,102 | 69.64 | 22,356 |
| 1900 | | 113.92 | −1.814% | −1.814% | 13.84 | 2,261 | 31,285 | 75.00 | 23,464 |
| 1901 | | 112.77 | −1.008% | −1.008% | 13.70 | 2,318 | 31,757 | 73.21 | 23,251 |
| 1902 | | 108.67 | −3.637% | −3.637% | 13.20 | 2,385 | 31,482 | 82.14 | 25,860 |
| 1903 | | 107.35 | −1.214% | −1.214% | 13.04 | 2,453 | 31,989 | 82.14 | 26,276 |
| 1904 | | 107.24 | −0.106% | −0.106% | 13.03 | 2,523 | 32,869 | 78.57 | 25,825 |
| 1905 | | 105.29 | −1.816% | −1.816% | 12.79 | 2,596 | 33,199 | 78.57 | 26,085 |
| 1906 | | 106.94 | 1.562% | 1.562% | 12.99 | 2,670 | 34,685 | 82.14 | 28,491 |
| 1907 | | 107.05 | 0.102% | 0.102% | 13.00 | 2,747 | 35,718 | 91.07 | 32,529 |
| 1908 | | 107.87 | 0.772% | 0.772% | 13.10 | 2,826 | 37,030 | 91.07 | 33,724 |
| 1909 | | 110.50 | 2.437% | 2.437% | 13.42 | 2,908 | 39,024 | 91.07 | 35,539 |
| 1910 | | 108.44 | −1.861% | −1.861% | 13.17 | 2,991 | 39,396 | 91.07 | 35,879 |
| 1911 | | 98.90 | −8.802% | −8.802% | 12.01 | 3,084 | 37,043 | 91.07 | 33,736 |
| 1912 | | 97.22 | −1.696% | −1.696% | 11.81 | 3,186 | 37,626 | 91.07 | 34,266 |
| 1913 | | 95.24 | −2.036% | −2.036% | 11.57 | 3,292 | 38,079 | 91.07 | 34,679 |
| 1914 | | 100.00 | 4.995% | 4.995% | 12.15 | 3,400 | 41,297 | 100.00 | 41,297 |
| 1915 | | 93.86 | −6.142% | −6.142% | 11.40 | 3,511 | 40,031 | 103.82 | 41,561 |
| 1916 | | 88.38 | −5.833% | −5.833% | 10.74 | 3,626 | 38,926 | 103.82 | 40,414 |
| 1917 | | 100.72 | 13.954% | 13.954% | 12.23 | 3,744 | 45,800 | 113.09 | 51,796 |
| 1918 | | 104.36 | 3.614% | 3.614% | 12.68 | 3,865 | 48,994 | 116.80 | 57,225 |
| 1919 | | 92.87 | −11.007% | −11.007% | 11.28 | 3,990 | 45,009 | 116.80 | 52,570 |
| 1920 | | 89.13 | −4.028% | −4.028% | 10.83 | 4,118 | 44,586 | 155.50 | 69,331 |
| 1921 | | 112.82 | 26.583% | 26.583% | 13.70 | 4,270 | 58,518 | 155.50 | 90,996 |
| 1922 | | 123.66 | 9.603% | 9.603% | 15.02 | 4,464 | 67,051 | 155.50 | 104,265 |
| 1923 | | 126.94 | 2.658% | 2.658% | 15.42 | 4,628 | 71,357 | 155.50 | 110,960 |
| 1924 | | 127.47 | 0.412% | 0.412% | 15.48 | 4,795 | 74,232 | 155.50 | 115,431 |
| 1925 | | 124.53 | −2.308% | −2.308% | 15.13 | 5,002 | 75,660 | 155.50 | 117,651 |
| 1926 | | 120.44 | −3.285% | −3.285% | 14.63 | 5,202 | 76,091 | 155.50 | 118,321 |
| 1927 | | 127.57 | 5.925% | 5.925% | 15.50 | 5,407 | 83,776 | 155.50 | 130,271 |
| 1928 | | 131.90 | 3.394% | 3.394% | 16.02 | 5,614 | 89,947 | 155.50 | 139,868 |
| 1929 | | 131.51 | −0.296% | −0.296% | 15.97 | 5,825 | 93,049 | 155.50 | 144,691 |
| 1930 | 15.70 | 129.23 | −1.734% | −1.734% | 15.70 | 5,754 | 90,323 | 152.90 | 138,104 |
| 1931 | | 115.38 | −10.717% | −10.717% | 14.01 | 2,814 | 39,441 | 138.00 | 54,429 |
| 1932 | | 122.09 | 5.817% | 5.817% | 14.83 | 2,730 | 40,484 | 124.70 | 50,483 |
| 1933 | | 136.87 | 12.102% | 12.102% | 16.62 | 2,573 | 42,766 | 115.80 | 49,523 |
| 1934 | | 130.38 | −4.738% | −4.738% | 15.84 | 2,626 | 41,589 | 123.70 | 51,446 |
| 1935 | | 137.02 | 5.092% | 5.092% | 16.64 | 2,862 | 47,624 | 127.40 | 60,674 |
| 1936 | | 148.89 | 8.661% | 8.661% | 18.08 | 3,016 | 54,539 | 125.70 | 68,555 |
| 1937 | | 150.08 | 0.798% | 0.798% | 18.23 | 3,257 | 59,378 | 130.00 | 77,191 |
| 1938 | | 155.10 | 3.348% | 3.348% | 18.84 | 3,550 | 66,881 | 128.20 | 85,742 |
| 1939 | | 154.06 | −0.672% | −0.672% | 18.71 | 3,638 | 68,071 | 128.20 | 87,268 |

| Year | Annual Per-Capita Private Final Consumption Expenditure in Real Terms (1914 Prices) (Straits $) | Weighted Real Wage Indices of Agriculture and Non-agriculture Sectors (1914 = 100) | Changes in Real Wages (%) | Changes in Real Consumption (%) | Real Per-Capita Private Final Consumption Expenditure Based on Real Wages and Income Elasticities of Demand (1914 Prices) (Straits $) | Chinese, Indian, and Eurasian Clerical Population Standard (Numbers) | Total Real Private Final Consumption Expenditure on Servant in the Domestic Market (1914 Prices) (Straits $) | Servant Price Indices (1914 = 100) | Total Private Final Consumption Expenditure on Servant in the Domestic Market (Current Prices) (Straits $) |
|---|---|---|---|---|---|---|---|---|---|
| | Step 4 | Step 5 | Step 6 | | Step 7 | Step 8 | Step 9 | Step 10 | Step 11 |
| | [1] | [2] | [3] | [4] | [5] | [6] | [7] = [5] x [6] | [8] | [9] = [7] x [8] / 100 |
| 1947 | | 164.71 | | | 32.31 | 14,072 | 454,667 | 366.43 | 1,666,027 |
| 1948 | 35.24 | 179.65 | 9.067% | 9.067% | 35.24 | 14,412 | 507,868 | 306.70 | 1,557,634 |
| 1949 | | 220.02 | 22.473% | 22.473% | 43.16 | 14,681 | 633,590 | 322.29 | 2,041,996 |
| 1950 | | 203.15 | −7.666% | −7.666% | 39.85 | 15,332 | 610,964 | 334.74 | 2,045,160 |
| 1951 | | 181.26 | −10.776% | −10.776% | 35.56 | 16,022 | 569,662 | 380.93 | 2,169,995 |
| 1952 | | 176.19 | −2.797% | −2.797% | 34.56 | 16,905 | 584,262 | 423.69 | 2,475,479 |
| 1953 | | 206.53 | 17.217% | 17.217% | 40.51 | 17,877 | 724,235 | 448.21 | 3,246,068 |
| 1954 | | 208.97 | 1.183% | 1.183% | 40.99 | 18,723 | 767,479 | 454.64 | 3,489,274 |
| 1955 | | 204.74 | −2.023% | −2.023% | 40.16 | 19,583 | 786,474 | 457.59 | 3,598,824 |
| 1956 | | 230.57 | 12.617% | 12.617% | 45.23 | 20,574 | 930,549 | 459.05 | 4,271,696 |
| 1957 | | 215.81 | −6.401% | −6.401% | 42.33 | 14,459 | 612,121 | 459.05 | 2,809,948 |
| 1958 | | 215.37 | −0.205% | −0.205% | 42.25 | 15,140 | 639,622 | 459.05 | 2,936,192 |
| 1959 | | 194.19 | −9.837% | −9.837% | 38.09 | 15,796 | 601,691 | 459.05 | 2,762,070 |
| 1960 | | 230.48 | 18.691% | 18.691% | 45.21 | 16,341 | 738,792 | 459.05 | 3,391,433 |

*(Continued)*

**Appendix Table 6:** Singapore: Computation of PFCE in the Domestic Market, 1900–39 and 1948–60, Asiatic Clerical Standard [1899–1939] Malay Clerical Standard [1947–1960] — Servant in Current and 1914 Prices (Straits $)

| Year | Annual Per-Capita Private Final Consumption Expenditure in Real Terms (1914 Prices) (Straits $) | Weighted Real Wage Indices of Agriculture and Non-agriculture Sectors (1914 = 100) | Changes in Real Wages (%) | Changes in Real Consumption (%) | Real Per-Capita Private Final Consumption Expenditure Based on Real Wages and Income Elasticities of Demand (1914 Prices) (Straits $) | Asiatic Clerical Population Standard (Numbers) | Total Real Private Final Consumption Expenditure on Servant in the Domestic Market (1914 Prices) (Straits $) | Servant Price Indices (1914 = 100) | Total Private Final Consumption Expenditure on Servant in the Domestic Market (Current Prices) (Straits $) |
|---|---|---|---|---|---|---|---|---|---|
| | Step 4 | Step 5 | Step 6 | Step 7 | | Step 8 | Step 9 | Step 10 | Step 11 |
| | [1] | [2] | [3] | [4] | [5] | [6] | [7] = [5] x [6] | [8] | [9] = [7] x [8] / 100 |
| 1899 | | 116.03 | | | 14.09 | 19,362 | 272,863 | 69.64 | 190,030 |
| 1900 | | 113.92 | −1.814% | −1.814% | 13.84 | 19,219 | 265,926 | 75.00 | 199,444 |
| 1901 | | 112.77 | −1.008% | −1.008% | 13.70 | 19,707 | 269,934 | 73.21 | 197,630 |
| 1902 | | 108.67 | −3.637% | −3.637% | 13.20 | 20,273 | 267,593 | 82.14 | 219,808 |
| 1903 | | 107.35 | −1.214% | −1.214% | 13.04 | 20,853 | 271,902 | 82.14 | 223,348 |
| 1904 | | 107.24 | −0.106% | −0.106% | 13.03 | 21,449 | 279,383 | 78.57 | 219,515 |
| 1905 | | 105.29 | −1.816% | −1.816% | 12.79 | 22,065 | 282,188 | 78.57 | 221,719 |
| 1906 | | 106.94 | 1.562% | 1.562% | 12.99 | 22,699 | 294,823 | 82.14 | 242,176 |
| 1907 | | 107.05 | 0.102% | 0.102% | 13.00 | 23,351 | 303,604 | 91.07 | 276,497 |
| 1908 | | 107.87 | 0.772% | 0.772% | 13.10 | 24,023 | 314,756 | 91.07 | 286,653 |
| 1909 | | 110.50 | 2.437% | 2.437% | 13.42 | 24,714 | 331,701 | 91.07 | 302,085 |
| 1910 | | 108.44 | −1.861% | −1.861% | 13.17 | 25,423 | 334,868 | 91.07 | 304,969 |
| 1911 | | 98.90 | −8.802% | −8.802% | 12.01 | 27,137 | 325,981 | 91.07 | 296,876 |
| 1912 | | 97.22 | −1.696% | −1.696% | 11.81 | 28,039 | 331,107 | 91.07 | 301,544 |
| 1913 | | 95.24 | −2.036% | −2.036% | 11.57 | 28,967 | 335,095 | 91.07 | 305,176 |
| 1914 | | 100.00 | 4.995% | 4.995% | 12.15 | 29,920 | 363,416 | 100.00 | 363,416 |
| 1915 | | 93.86 | −6.142% | −6.142% | 11.40 | 30,901 | 352,271 | 103.82 | 365,735 |
| 1916 | | 88.38 | −5.833% | −5.833% | 10.74 | 31,909 | 342,547 | 103.82 | 355,640 |
| 1917 | | 100.72 | 13.954% | 13.954% | 12.23 | 32,947 | 403,040 | 113.09 | 455,806 |
| 1918 | | 104.36 | 3.614% | 3.614% | 12.68 | 34,015 | 431,144 | 116.80 | 503,576 |
| 1919 | | 92.87 | −11.007% | −11.007% | 11.28 | 35,113 | 396,079 | 116.80 | 462,620 |
| 1920 | | 89.13 | −4.028% | −4.028% | 10.83 | 36,243 | 392,355 | 155.50 | 610,112 |
| 1921 | | 112.82 | 26.583% | 26.583% | 13.70 | 46,973 | 643,699 | 155.50 | 1,000,951 |
| 1922 | | 123.66 | 9.603% | 9.603% | 15.02 | 49,107 | 737,564 | 155.50 | 1,146,912 |
| 1923 | | 126.94 | 2.658% | 2.658% | 15.42 | 50,907 | 784,929 | 155.50 | 1,220,564 |
| 1924 | | 127.47 | 0.412% | 0.412% | 15.48 | 52,741 | 816,552 | 155.50 | 1,269,738 |
| 1925 | | 124.53 | −2.308% | −2.308% | 15.13 | 55,025 | 832,261 | 155.50 | 1,294,165 |
| 1926 | | 120.44 | −3.285% | −3.285% | 14.63 | 57,218 | 836,998 | 155.50 | 1,301,533 |
| 1927 | | 127.57 | 5.925% | 5.925% | 15.50 | 59,473 | 921,531 | 155.50 | 1,432,981 |
| 1928 | | 131.90 | 3.394% | 3.394% | 16.02 | 61,758 | 989,421 | 155.50 | 1,538,550 |
| 1929 | | 131.51 | −0.296% | −0.296% | 15.97 | 64,077 | 1,023,535 | 155.50 | 1,591,598 |
| 1930 | 15.70 | 129.23 | −1.734% | −1.734% | 15.70 | 63,298 | 993,557 | 152.90 | 1,519,149 |
| 1931 | | 115.38 | −10.717% | −10.717% | 14.01 | 61,915 | 867,701 | 138.00 | 1,197,427 |
| 1932 | | 122.09 | 5.817% | 5.817% | 14.83 | 60,059 | 890,643 | 124.70 | 1,110,632 |
| 1933 | | 136.87 | 12.102% | 12.102% | 16.62 | 56,595 | 940,845 | 115.80 | 1,089,498 |
| 1934 | | 130.38 | −4.738% | −4.738% | 15.84 | 57,775 | 914,957 | 123.70 | 1,131,802 |
| 1935 | | 137.02 | 5.092% | 5.092% | 16.64 | 62,954 | 1,047,737 | 127.40 | 1,334,817 |
| 1936 | | 148.89 | 8.661% | 8.661% | 18.08 | 66,348 | 1,199,854 | 125.70 | 1,508,216 |
| 1937 | | 150.08 | 0.798% | 0.798% | 18.23 | 71,663 | 1,306,317 | 130.00 | 1,698,212 |
| 1938 | | 155.10 | 3.348% | 3.348% | 18.84 | 78,104 | 1,471,383 | 128.20 | 1,886,313 |
| 1939 | | 154.06 | −0.672% | −0.672% | 18.71 | 80,032 | 1,497,571 | 128.20 | 1,919,886 |

| Year | Annual Per-Capita Private Final Consumption Expenditure in Real Terms (1914 Prices) (Straits $) | Weighted Real Wage Indices of Agriculture and Non-agriculture Sectors (1914 = 100) | Changes in Real Wages (%) | Changes in Real Consumption (%) | Real Per-Capita Private Final Consumption Expenditure Based on Real Wages and Income Elasticities of Demand (1914 Prices) (Straits $) | Malay Clerical Population Standard (Numbers) | Total Real Private Final Consumption Expenditure on Servant in the Domestic Market (1914 Prices) (Straits $) | Servant Price Indices (1914 = 100) | Total Private Final Consumption Expenditure on Servant in the Domestic Market (Current Prices) (Straits $) |
|---|---|---|---|---|---|---|---|---|---|
| | Step 4 | Step 5 | Step 6 | Step 7 | | Step 8 | Step 9 | Step 10 | Step 11 |
| | [1] | [2] | [3] | [4] | [5] | [6] | [7] = [5] x [6] | [8] | [9] = [7] x [8] / 100 |
| 1947 | | 164.71 | | | 32.31 | 126,649 | 4,091,999 | 366.43 | 14,994,239 |
| 1948 | 35.24 | 179.65 | 9.067% | 9.067% | 35.24 | 129,708 | 4,570,814 | 306.70 | 14,018,707 |
| 1949 | | 220.02 | 22.473% | 22.473% | 43.16 | 132,125 | 5,702,310 | 322.29 | 18,377,964 |
| 1950 | | 203.15 | −7.666% | −7.666% | 39.85 | 137,984 | 5,498,676 | 334.74 | 18,406,441 |
| 1951 | | 181.26 | −10.776% | −10.776% | 35.56 | 144,194 | 5,126,958 | 380.93 | 19,529,957 |
| 1952 | | 176.19 | −2.797% | −2.797% | 34.56 | 152,145 | 5,258,359 | 423.69 | 22,279,314 |
| 1953 | | 206.53 | 17.217% | 17.217% | 40.51 | 160,893 | 6,518,114 | 448.21 | 29,214,614 |
| 1954 | | 208.97 | 1.183% | 1.183% | 40.99 | 168,507 | 6,907,313 | 454.64 | 31,403,462 |
| 1955 | | 204.74 | −2.023% | −2.023% | 40.16 | 176,243 | 7,078,268 | 457.59 | 32,389,417 |
| 1956 | | 230.57 | 12.617% | 12.617% | 45.23 | 185,166 | 8,374,945 | 459.05 | 38,445,267 |
| 1957 | | 215.81 | −6.401% | −6.401% | 42.33 | 267,497 | 11,324,242 | 459.05 | 51,984,046 |
| 1958 | | 215.37 | −0.205% | −0.205% | 42.25 | 280,090 | 11,833,011 | 459.05 | 54,319,556 |
| 1959 | | 194.19 | −9.837% | −9.837% | 38.09 | 292,226 | 11,131,289 | 459.05 | 51,098,293 |
| 1960 | | 230.48 | 18.691% | 18.691% | 45.21 | 302,309 | 13,667,657 | 459.05 | 62,741,517 |

*(Continued)*

**Appendix Table 6:** Singapore: Computation of PFCE in the Domestic Market, 1900–39 and 1948–60, European Standard — Transport in Current and 1914 Prices (Straits $)

| Year | Annual Per-Capita Private Final Consumption Expenditure in Real Terms (1914 Prices) (Straits $) | Weighted Real Wage Indices of Agriculture and Non-agriculture Sectors (1914=100) | Changes in Real Wages (%) | Changes in Real Consumption (%) | Real Per-Capita Private Final Consumption Expenditure Based on Real Wages and Income Elasticities of Demand (1914 Prices) (Straits $) | European Population Standard (Numbers) | Total Real Private Final Consumption Expenditure on Transport in the Domestic Market (1914 Prices) (Straits $) | Transport Price Indices (1914 = 100) | Total Private Final Consumption Expenditure on Transport in the Domestic Market (Current Prices) (Straits $) |
|---|---|---|---|---|---|---|---|---|---|
| | Step 4 | Step 5 | Step 6 | Step 7 | | Step 8 | Step 9 | Step 10 | Step 11 |
| | [1] | [2] | [3] | [4] | [5] | [6] | [7] = [5] x [6] | [8] | [9] = [7] x [8] / 100 |
| 1899 | | 116.03 | | | 202.12 | 13,667 | 2,762,442 | 109.66 | 3,029,367 |
| 1900 | | 113.92 | −1.814% | −1.814% | 198.45 | 13,566 | 2,692,205 | 107.87 | 2,904,213 |
| 1901 | | 112.77 | −1.008% | −1.008% | 196.45 | 13,911 | 2,732,789 | 107.44 | 2,936,201 |
| 1902 | | 108.67 | −3.637% | −3.637% | 189.31 | 14,310 | 2,709,085 | 107.23 | 2,904,887 |
| 1903 | | 107.35 | −1.214% | −1.214% | 187.01 | 14,720 | 2,752,714 | 107.34 | 2,954,639 |
| 1904 | | 107.24 | −0.106% | −0.106% | 186.81 | 15,141 | 2,828,448 | 107.23 | 3,032,877 |
| 1905 | | 105.29 | −1.816% | −1.816% | 183.42 | 15,575 | 2,856,840 | 107.12 | 3,060,240 |
| 1906 | | 106.94 | 1.562% | 1.562% | 186.28 | 16,023 | 2,984,757 | 107.23 | 3,200,484 |
| 1907 | | 107.05 | 0.102% | 0.102% | 186.47 | 16,483 | 3,073,659 | 105.07 | 3,229,497 |
| 1908 | | 107.87 | 0.772% | 0.772% | 187.91 | 16,958 | 3,186,564 | 104.64 | 3,334,377 |
| 1909 | | 110.50 | 2.437% | 2.437% | 192.49 | 17,445 | 3,358,114 | 103.67 | 3,481,281 |
| 1910 | | 108.44 | −1.861% | −1.861% | 188.91 | 17,946 | 3,390,168 | 103.24 | 3,499,882 |
| 1911 | | 98.90 | −8.802% | −8.802% | 172.28 | 18,503 | 3,187,694 | 102.91 | 3,280,539 |
| 1912 | | 97.22 | −1.696% | −1.696% | 169.36 | 19,118 | 3,237,821 | 103.02 | 3,335,619 |
| 1913 | | 95.24 | −2.036% | −2.036% | 165.91 | 19,750 | 3,276,817 | 99.46 | 3,259,143 |
| 1914 | | 100.00 | 4.995% | 4.995% | 174.20 | 20,400 | 3,553,762 | 100.00 | 3,553,762 |
| 1915 | | 93.86 | −6.142% | −6.142% | 163.50 | 21,069 | 3,444,774 | 101.83 | 3,507,813 |
| 1916 | | 88.38 | −5.833% | −5.833% | 153.97 | 21,756 | 3,349,694 | 103.13 | 3,454,539 |
| 1917 | | 100.72 | 13.954% | 13.954% | 175.45 | 22,464 | 3,941,238 | 108.64 | 4,281,761 |
| 1918 | | 104.36 | 3.614% | 3.614% | 181.79 | 23,192 | 4,216,056 | 112.50 | 4,743,063 |
| 1919 | | 92.87 | −11.007% | −11.007% | 161.78 | 23,941 | 3,873,167 | 122.90 | 4,760,122 |
| 1920 | | 89.13 | −4.028% | −4.028% | 155.27 | 24,711 | 3,836,752 | 126.80 | 4,865,002 |
| 1921 | | 112.82 | 26.583% | 26.583% | 196.54 | 27,757 | 5,455,304 | 122.80 | 6,699,114 |
| 1922 | | 123.66 | 9.603% | 9.603% | 215.41 | 29,018 | 6,250,806 | 112.00 | 7,000,903 |
| 1923 | | 126.94 | 2.658% | 2.658% | 221.14 | 30,082 | 6,652,219 | 94.80 | 6,306,304 |
| 1924 | | 127.47 | 0.412% | 0.412% | 222.05 | 31,165 | 6,920,224 | 99.40 | 6,878,702 |
| 1925 | | 124.53 | −2.308% | −2.308% | 216.93 | 32,515 | 7,053,356 | 105.30 | 7,427,184 |
| 1926 | | 120.44 | −3.285% | −3.285% | 209.80 | 33,811 | 7,093,508 | 103.50 | 7,341,781 |
| 1927 | | 127.57 | 5.925% | 5.925% | 222.23 | 35,143 | 7,809,917 | 94.20 | 7,356,941 |
| 1928 | | 131.90 | 3.394% | 3.394% | 229.78 | 36,493 | 8,385,282 | 93.10 | 7,806,698 |
| 1929 | | 131.51 | −0.296% | −0.296% | 229.10 | 37,864 | 8,674,397 | 89.70 | 7,780,935 |
| 1930 | 225.12 | 129.23 | −1.734% | −1.734% | 225.12 | 37,403 | 8,420,333 | 85.50 | 7,199,385 |
| 1931 | | 115.38 | −10.717% | −10.717% | 201.00 | 36,586 | 7,353,711 | 96.20 | 7,074,270 |
| 1932 | | 122.09 | 5.817% | 5.817% | 212.69 | 35,489 | 7,548,144 | 89.00 | 6,717,849 |
| 1933 | | 136.87 | 12.102% | 12.102% | 238.43 | 33,443 | 7,973,597 | 85.40 | 6,809,452 |
| 1934 | | 130.38 | −4.738% | −4.738% | 227.13 | 34,140 | 7,754,203 | 84.50 | 6,552,301 |
| 1935 | | 137.02 | 5.092% | 5.092% | 238.70 | 37,200 | 8,879,506 | 82.40 | 7,316,713 |
| 1936 | | 148.89 | 8.661% | 8.661% | 259.37 | 39,206 | 10,168,682 | 80.00 | 8,134,945 |
| 1937 | | 150.08 | 0.798% | 0.798% | 261.44 | 42,347 | 11,070,951 | 81.40 | 9,011,754 |
| 1938 | | 155.10 | 3.348% | 3.348% | 270.19 | 46,152 | 12,469,879 | 81.50 | 10,162,951 |
| 1939 | | 154.06 | −0.672% | −0.672% | 268.37 | 47,292 | 12,691,816 | 82.18 | 10,429,918 |

| Year | Annual Per-Capita Private Final Consumption Expenditure in Real Terms (1914 Prices) (Straits $) | Weighted Real Wage Indices of Agriculture and Non-agriculture Sectors (1914 = 100) | Changes in Real Wages (%) | Changes in Real Consumption (%) | Real Per-Capita Private Final Consumption Expenditure Based on Real Wages and Income Elasticities of Demand (1914 Prices) (Straits $) | European Population Standard (Numbers) | Total Real Private Final Consumption Expenditure on Transport in the Domestic Market (1914 Prices) (Straits $) | Transport Price Indices (1914 = 100) | Total Private Final Consumption Expenditure on Transport in the Domestic Market (Current Prices) (Straits $) |
|---|---|---|---|---|---|---|---|---|---|
| | Step 4 | Step 5 | Step 6 | Step 7 | | Step 8 | Step 9 | Step 10 | Step 11 |
| | [1] | [2] | [3] | [4] | [5] | [6] | [7] = [5] x [6] | [8] | [9] = [7] x [8] / 100 |
| 1947 | | 164.71 | | | 283.86 | 56,289 | 15,978,038 | 181.50 | 28,999,745 |
| 1948 | 309.60 | 179.65 | 9.067% | 9.067% | 309.60 | 57,648 | 17,847,669 | 151.91 | 27,113,007 |
| 1949 | | 220.02 | 22.473% | 22.473% | 379.17 | 58,722 | 22,265,825 | 150.46 | 33,502,172 |
| 1950 | | 203.15 | −7.666% | −7.666% | 350.11 | 61,326 | 21,470,696 | 155.63 | 33,413,802 |
| 1951 | | 181.26 | −10.776% | −10.776% | 312.38 | 64,086 | 20,019,247 | 173.46 | 34,725,344 |
| 1952 | | 176.19 | −2.797% | −2.797% | 303.64 | 67,620 | 20,532,327 | 171.95 | 35,304,987 |
| 1953 | | 206.53 | 17.217% | 17.217% | 355.92 | 71,508 | 25,451,297 | 166.69 | 42,424,734 |
| 1954 | | 208.97 | 1.183% | 1.183% | 360.13 | 74,892 | 26,971,005 | 164.20 | 44,287,727 |
| 1955 | | 204.74 | −2.023% | −2.023% | 352.85 | 78,330 | 27,638,533 | 165.87 | 45,843,506 |
| 1956 | | 230.57 | 12.617% | 12.617% | 397.37 | 82,296 | 32,701,669 | 168.29 | 55,035,046 |
| 1957 | | 215.81 | −6.401% | −6.401% | 371.93 | 86,756 | 32,267,041 | 174.01 | 56,147,121 |
| 1958 | | 215.37 | −0.205% | −0.205% | 371.17 | 90,840 | 33,716,717 | 174.83 | 58,946,746 |
| 1959 | | 194.19 | −9.837% | −9.837% | 334.65 | 94,776 | 31,717,246 | 177.47 | 56,287,324 |
| 1960 | | 230.48 | 18.691% | 18.691% | 397.20 | 98,046 | 38,944,316 | 179.24 | 69,804,046 |

*(Continued)*

## Appendix Table 6: Singapore: Computation of PFCE in the Domestic Market, 1900–39 and 1948–60, Eurasian Standard [1899–1939] Chinese, Indian and Eurasian Clerical Standard [1947–1960] — Transport in Current and 1914 Prices (Straits $)

| Year | Annual Per-Capita Private Final Consumption Expenditure in Real Terms (1914 Prices) (Straits $) | Weighted Real Wage Indices of Agriculture and Non-agriculture Sectors (1914 = 100) | Changes in Real Wages (%) | Changes in Real Consumption (%) | Real Per-Capita Private Final Consumption Expenditure Based on Real Wages and Income Elasticities of Demand (1914 Prices) (Straits $) | Eurasian Population Standard (Numbers) | Total Real Private Final Consumption Expenditure on Transport in the Domestic Market (1914 Prices) (Straits $) | Transport Price Indices (1914 = 100) | Total Private Final Consumption Expenditure on Transport in the Domestic Market (Current Prices) (Straits $) |
|---|---|---|---|---|---|---|---|---|---|
| | Step 4 | Step 5 | Step 6 | Step 7 | | Step 8 | Step 9 | Step 10 | Step 11 |
| | [1] | [2] | [3] | [4] | [5] | [6] | [7] = [5] x [6] | [8] | [9] = [7] x [8] / 100 |
| 1899 | | 116.03 | | | 27.82 | 2,278 | 63,378 | 109.66 | 69,502 |
| 1900 | | 113.92 | −1.814% | −1.814% | 27.32 | 2,261 | 61,766 | 107.87 | 66,630 |
| 1901 | | 112.77 | −1.008% | −1.008% | 27.04 | 2,318 | 62,697 | 107.44 | 67,364 |
| 1902 | | 108.67 | −3.637% | −3.637% | 26.06 | 2,385 | 62,154 | 107.23 | 66,646 |
| 1903 | | 107.35 | −1.214% | −1.214% | 25.74 | 2,453 | 63,155 | 107.34 | 67,787 |
| 1904 | | 107.24 | −0.106% | −0.106% | 25.72 | 2,523 | 64,892 | 107.23 | 69,582 |
| 1905 | | 105.29 | −1.816% | −1.816% | 25.25 | 2,596 | 65,543 | 107.12 | 70,210 |
| 1906 | | 106.94 | 1.562% | 1.562% | 25.64 | 2,670 | 68,478 | 107.23 | 73,428 |
| 1907 | | 107.05 | 0.102% | 0.102% | 25.67 | 2,747 | 70,518 | 105.07 | 74,093 |
| 1908 | | 107.87 | 0.772% | 0.772% | 25.87 | 2,826 | 73,108 | 104.64 | 76,499 |
| 1909 | | 110.50 | 2.437% | 2.437% | 26.50 | 2,908 | 77,044 | 103.67 | 79,870 |
| 1910 | | 108.44 | −1.861% | −1.861% | 26.00 | 2,991 | 77,779 | 103.24 | 80,297 |
| 1911 | | 98.90 | −8.802% | −8.802% | 23.72 | 3,084 | 73,134 | 102.91 | 75,264 |
| 1912 | | 97.22 | −1.696% | −1.696% | 23.31 | 3,186 | 74,284 | 103.02 | 76,528 |
| 1913 | | 95.24 | −2.036% | −2.036% | 22.84 | 3,292 | 75,179 | 99.46 | 74,773 |
| 1914 | | 100.00 | 4.995% | 4.995% | 23.98 | 3,400 | 81,533 | 100.00 | 81,533 |
| 1915 | | 93.86 | −6.142% | −6.142% | 22.51 | 3,511 | 79,032 | 101.83 | 80,479 |
| 1916 | | 88.38 | −5.833% | −5.833% | 21.19 | 3,626 | 76,851 | 103.13 | 79,256 |
| 1917 | | 100.72 | 13.954% | 13.954% | 24.15 | 3,744 | 90,422 | 108.64 | 98,235 |
| 1918 | | 104.36 | 3.614% | 3.614% | 25.02 | 3,865 | 96,727 | 112.50 | 108,818 |
| 1919 | | 92.87 | −11.007% | −11.007% | 22.27 | 3,990 | 88,861 | 122.90 | 109,210 |
| 1920 | | 89.13 | −4.028% | −4.028% | 21.37 | 4,118 | 88,025 | 126.80 | 111,616 |
| 1921 | | 112.82 | 26.583% | 26.583% | 27.05 | 4,270 | 115,531 | 122.80 | 141,873 |
| 1922 | | 123.66 | 9.603% | 9.603% | 29.65 | 4,464 | 132,378 | 112.00 | 148,264 |
| 1923 | | 126.94 | 2.658% | 2.658% | 30.44 | 4,628 | 140,880 | 94.80 | 133,554 |
| 1924 | | 127.47 | 0.412% | 0.412% | 30.57 | 4,795 | 146,555 | 99.40 | 145,676 |
| 1925 | | 124.53 | −2.308% | −2.308% | 29.86 | 5,002 | 149,375 | 105.30 | 157,292 |
| 1926 | | 120.44 | −3.285% | −3.285% | 28.88 | 5,202 | 150,225 | 103.50 | 155,483 |
| 1927 | | 127.57 | 5.925% | 5.925% | 30.59 | 5,407 | 165,397 | 94.20 | 155,804 |
| 1928 | | 131.90 | 3.394% | 3.394% | 31.63 | 5,614 | 177,582 | 93.10 | 165,329 |
| 1929 | | 131.51 | −0.296% | −0.296% | 31.54 | 5,825 | 183,705 | 89.70 | 164,783 |
| 1930 | 30.99 | 129.23 | −1.734% | −1.734% | 30.99 | 5,754 | 178,324 | 85.50 | 152,467 |
| 1931 | | 115.38 | −10.717% | −10.717% | 27.67 | 2,814 | 77,868 | 96.20 | 74,909 |
| 1932 | | 122.09 | 5.817% | 5.817% | 29.28 | 2,730 | 79,927 | 89.00 | 71,135 |
| 1933 | | 136.87 | 12.102% | 12.102% | 32.82 | 2,573 | 84,432 | 85.40 | 72,105 |
| 1934 | | 130.38 | −4.738% | −4.738% | 31.27 | 2,626 | 82,109 | 84.50 | 69,382 |
| 1935 | | 137.02 | 5.092% | 5.092% | 32.86 | 2,862 | 94,024 | 82.40 | 77,476 |
| 1936 | | 148.89 | 8.661% | 8.661% | 35.70 | 3,016 | 107,675 | 80.00 | 86,140 |
| 1937 | | 150.08 | 0.798% | 0.798% | 35.99 | 3,257 | 117,229 | 81.40 | 95,425 |
| 1938 | | 155.10 | 3.348% | 3.348% | 37.19 | 3,550 | 132,042 | 81.50 | 107,615 |
| 1939 | | 154.06 | −0.672% | −0.672% | 36.94 | 3,638 | 134,393 | 82.18 | 110,441 |

| Year | Annual Per-Capita Private Final Consumption Expenditure in Real Terms (1914 Prices) (Straits $) | Weighted Real Wage Indices of Agriculture and Non-agriculture Sectors (1914 = 100) | Changes in Real Wages (%) | Changes in Real Consumption (%) | Real Per-Capita Private Final Consumption Expenditure Based on Real Wages and Income Elasticities of Demand (1914 Prices) (Straits $) | Chinese, Indian, and Eurasian Clerical Population Standard (Numbers) | Total Real Private Final Consumption Expenditure on Transport in the Domestic Market (1914 Prices) (Straits $) | Transport Price Indices (1914 = 100) | Total Private Final Consumption Expenditure on Transport in the Domestic Market (Current Prices) (Straits $) |
|---|---|---|---|---|---|---|---|---|---|
| | Step 4 | Step 5 | Step 6 | Step 7 | | Step 8 | Step 9 | Step 10 | Step 11 |
| | [1] | [2] | [3] | [4] | [5] | [6] | [7] = [5] x [6] | [8] | [9] = [7] x [8] / 100 |
| 1947 | | 164.71 | | | 43.51 | 14,072 | 612,284 | 181.50 | 1,111,280 |
| 1948 | 47.46 | 179.65 | 9.067% | 9.067% | 47.46 | 14,412 | 683,928 | 151.91 | 1,038,979 |
| 1949 | | 220.02 | 22.473% | 22.473% | 58.12 | 14,681 | 853,234 | 150.46 | 1,283,814 |
| 1950 | | 203.15 | −7.666% | −7.666% | 53.66 | 15,332 | 822,764 | 155.63 | 1,280,428 |
| 1951 | | 181.26 | −10.776% | −10.776% | 47.88 | 16,022 | 767,144 | 173.46 | 1,330,686 |
| 1952 | | 176.19 | −2.797% | −2.797% | 46.54 | 16,905 | 786,805 | 171.95 | 1,352,898 |
| 1953 | | 206.53 | 17.217% | 17.217% | 54.56 | 17,877 | 975,302 | 166.69 | 1,625,729 |
| 1954 | | 208.97 | 1.183% | 1.183% | 55.20 | 18,723 | 1,033,538 | 164.20 | 1,697,120 |
| 1955 | | 204.74 | −2.023% | −2.023% | 54.08 | 19,583 | 1,059,117 | 165.87 | 1,756,738 |
| 1956 | | 230.57 | 12.617% | 12.617% | 60.91 | 20,574 | 1,253,138 | 168.29 | 2,108,961 |
| 1957 | | 215.81 | −6.401% | −6.401% | 57.01 | 14,459 | 824,322 | 174.01 | 1,434,384 |
| 1958 | | 215.37 | −0.205% | −0.205% | 56.89 | 15,140 | 861,357 | 174.83 | 1,505,906 |
| 1959 | | 194.19 | −9.837% | −9.837% | 51.30 | 15,796 | 810,277 | 177.47 | 1,437,966 |
| 1960 | | 230.48 | 18.691% | 18.691% | 60.88 | 16,341 | 994,906 | 179.24 | 1,783,276 |

*(Continued)*

**Appendix Table 6:** Singapore: Computation of PFCE in the Domestic Market, 1900–39 and 1948–60, Asiatic Clerical Standard [1899–1939] Malay Clerical Standard [1947–1960] — Transport in Current and 1914 Prices (Straits $)

| Year | Annual Per-Capita Private Final Consumption Expenditure in Real Terms (1914 Prices) (Straits $) | Weighted Real Wage Indices of Agriculture and Non-agriculture Sectors (1914 = 100) | Changes in Real Wages (%) | Changes in Real Consumption (%) | Real Per-Capita Private Final Consumption Expenditure Based on Real Wages and Income Elasticities of Demand (1914 Prices) (Straits $) | Asiatic Clerical Population Standard (Numbers) | Total Real Private Final Consumption Expenditure on Transport in the Domestic Market (1914 Prices) (Straits $) | Transport Price Indices (1914 = 100) | Total Private Final Consumption Expenditure on Transport in the Domestic Market (Current Prices) (Straits $) |
|---|---|---|---|---|---|---|---|---|---|
| | Step 4 | Step 5 | Step 6 | Step 7 | | Step 8 | Step 9 | Step 10 | Step 11 |
| | [1] | [2] | [3] | [4] | [5] | [6] | [7]=[5]x[6] | [8] | [9]=[7]x[8]/100 |
| 1899 | | 116.03 | | | 27.82 | 19,362 | 538,711 | 109.66 | 590,764 |
| 1900 | | 113.92 | −1.814% | −1.814% | 27.32 | 19,219 | 525,014 | 107.87 | 566,358 |
| 1901 | | 112.77 | −1.008% | −1.008% | 27.04 | 19,707 | 532,928 | 107.44 | 572,596 |
| 1902 | | 108.67 | −3.637% | −3.637% | 26.06 | 20,273 | 528,305 | 107.23 | 566,489 |
| 1903 | | 107.35 | −1.214% | −1.214% | 25.74 | 20,853 | 536,813 | 107.34 | 576,191 |
| 1904 | | 107.24 | −0.106% | −0.106% | 25.72 | 21,449 | 551,583 | 107.23 | 591,449 |
| 1905 | | 105.29 | −1.816% | −1.816% | 25.25 | 22,065 | 557,119 | 107.12 | 596,785 |
| 1906 | | 106.94 | 1.562% | 1.562% | 25.64 | 22,699 | 582,065 | 107.23 | 624,134 |
| 1907 | | 107.05 | 0.102% | 0.102% | 25.67 | 23,351 | 599,402 | 105.07 | 629,792 |
| 1908 | | 107.87 | 0.772% | 0.772% | 25.87 | 24,023 | 621,420 | 104.64 | 650,245 |
| 1909 | | 110.50 | 2.437% | 2.437% | 26.50 | 24,714 | 654,874 | 103.67 | 678,893 |
| 1910 | | 108.44 | −1.861% | −1.861% | 26.00 | 25,423 | 661,125 | 103.24 | 682,521 |
| 1911 | | 98.90 | −8.802% | −8.802% | 23.72 | 27,137 | 643,580 | 102.91 | 662,325 |
| 1912 | | 97.22 | −1.696% | −1.696% | 23.31 | 28,039 | 653,701 | 103.02 | 673,446 |
| 1913 | | 95.24 | −2.036% | −2.036% | 22.84 | 28,967 | 661,574 | 99.46 | 658,006 |
| 1914 | | 100.00 | 4.995% | 4.995% | 23.98 | 29,920 | 717,488 | 100.00 | 717,488 |
| 1915 | | 93.86 | −6.142% | −6.142% | 22.51 | 30,901 | 695,484 | 101.83 | 708,211 |
| 1916 | | 88.38 | −5.833% | −5.833% | 21.19 | 31,909 | 676,287 | 103.13 | 697,455 |
| 1917 | | 100.72 | 13.954% | 13.954% | 24.15 | 32,947 | 795,717 | 108.64 | 864,467 |
| 1918 | | 104.36 | 3.614% | 3.614% | 25.02 | 34,015 | 851,202 | 112.50 | 957,602 |
| 1919 | | 92.87 | −11.007% | −11.007% | 22.27 | 35,113 | 781,974 | 122.90 | 961,046 |
| 1920 | | 89.13 | −4.028% | −4.028% | 21.37 | 36,243 | 774,622 | 126.80 | 982,221 |
| 1921 | | 112.82 | 26.583% | 26.583% | 27.05 | 46,973 | 1,270,846 | 122.80 | 1,560,599 |
| 1922 | | 123.66 | 9.603% | 9.603% | 29.65 | 49,107 | 1,456,163 | 112.00 | 1,630,903 |
| 1923 | | 126.94 | 2.658% | 2.658% | 30.44 | 50,907 | 1,549,675 | 94.80 | 1,469,092 |
| 1924 | | 127.47 | 0.412% | 0.412% | 30.57 | 52,741 | 1,612,108 | 99.40 | 1,602,435 |
| 1925 | | 124.53 | −2.308% | −2.308% | 29.86 | 55,025 | 1,643,122 | 105.30 | 1,730,208 |
| 1926 | | 120.44 | −3.285% | −3.285% | 28.88 | 57,218 | 1,652,476 | 103.50 | 1,710,312 |
| 1927 | | 127.57 | 5.925% | 5.925% | 30.59 | 59,473 | 1,819,367 | 94.20 | 1,713,844 |
| 1928 | | 131.90 | 3.394% | 3.394% | 31.63 | 61,758 | 1,953,402 | 93.10 | 1,818,618 |
| 1929 | | 131.51 | −0.296% | −0.296% | 31.54 | 64,077 | 2,020,754 | 89.70 | 1,812,616 |
| 1930 | 30.99 | 129.23 | −1.734% | −1.734% | 30.99 | 63,298 | 1,961,568 | 85.50 | 1,677,140 |
| 1931 | | 115.38 | −10.717% | −10.717% | 27.67 | 61,915 | 1,713,092 | 96.20 | 1,647,994 |
| 1932 | | 122.09 | 5.817% | 5.817% | 29.28 | 60,059 | 1,758,386 | 89.00 | 1,564,964 |
| 1933 | | 136.87 | 12.102% | 12.102% | 32.82 | 56,595 | 1,857,498 | 85.40 | 1,586,303 |
| 1934 | | 130.38 | −4.738% | −4.738% | 31.27 | 57,775 | 1,806,389 | 84.50 | 1,526,398 |
| 1935 | | 137.02 | 5.092% | 5.092% | 32.86 | 62,954 | 2,068,535 | 82.40 | 1,704,473 |
| 1936 | | 148.89 | 8.661% | 8.661% | 35.70 | 66,348 | 2,368,856 | 80.00 | 1,895,085 |
| 1937 | | 150.08 | 0.798% | 0.798% | 35.99 | 71,663 | 2,579,045 | 81.40 | 2,099,343 |
| 1938 | | 155.10 | 3.348% | 3.348% | 37.19 | 78,104 | 2,904,934 | 81.50 | 2,367,521 |
| 1939 | | 154.06 | −0.672% | −0.672% | 36.94 | 80,032 | 2,956,636 | 82.18 | 2,429,713 |

| Year | Annual Per-Capita Private Final Consumption Expenditure in Real Terms (1914 Prices) (Straits $) | Weighted Real Wage Indices of Agriculture and Non-agriculture Sectors (1914 = 100) | Changes in Real Wages (%) | Changes in Real Consumption (%) | Real Per-Capita Private Final Consumption Expenditure Based on Real Wages and Income Elasticities of Demand (1914 Prices) (Straits $) | Malay Clerical Population Standard (Numbers) | Total Real Private Final Consumption Expenditure on Transport in the Domestic Market (1914 Prices) (Straits $) | Transport Price Indices (1914 = 100) | Total Private Final Consumption Expenditure on Transport in the Domestic Market (Current Prices) (Straits $) |
|---|---|---|---|---|---|---|---|---|---|
| | Step 4 | Step 5 | Step 6 | Step 7 | | Step 8 | Step 9 | Step 10 | Step 11 |
| | [1] | [2] | [3] | [4] | [5] | [6] | [7] = [5] x [6] | [8] | [9] = [7] x [8] / 100 |
| 1947 | | 164.71 | | | 48.94 | 126,649 | 6,198,403 | 181.50 | 11,249,949 |
| 1948 | 53.38 | 179.65 | 9.067% | 9.067% | 53.38 | 129,708 | 6,923,694 | 151.91 | 10,518,022 |
| 1949 | | 220.02 | 22.473% | 22.473% | 65.38 | 132,125 | 8,637,641 | 150.46 | 12,996,588 |
| 1950 | | 203.15 | −7.666% | −7.666% | 60.36 | 137,984 | 8,329,185 | 155.63 | 12,962,306 |
| 1951 | | 181.26 | −10.776% | −10.776% | 53.86 | 144,194 | 7,766,120 | 173.46 | 13,471,096 |
| 1952 | | 176.19 | −2.797% | −2.797% | 52.35 | 152,145 | 7,965,161 | 171.95 | 13,695,958 |
| 1953 | | 206.53 | 17.217% | 17.217% | 61.37 | 160,893 | 9,873,390 | 166.69 | 16,457,941 |
| 1954 | | 208.97 | 1.183% | 1.183% | 62.09 | 168,507 | 10,462,934 | 164.20 | 17,180,657 |
| 1955 | | 204.74 | −2.023% | −2.023% | 60.84 | 176,243 | 10,721,890 | 165.87 | 17,784,194 |
| 1956 | | 230.57 | 12.617% | 12.617% | 68.51 | 185,166 | 12,686,046 | 168.29 | 21,349,893 |
| 1957 | | 215.81 | −6.401% | −6.401% | 64.13 | 267,497 | 17,153,529 | 174.01 | 29,848,453 |
| 1958 | | 215.37 | −0.205% | −0.205% | 63.99 | 280,090 | 17,924,193 | 174.83 | 31,336,766 |
| 1959 | | 194.19 | −9.837% | −9.837% | 57.70 | 292,226 | 16,861,251 | 177.47 | 29,922,986 |
| 1960 | | 230.48 | 18.691% | 18.691% | 68.48 | 302,309 | 20,703,245 | 179.24 | 37,108,630 |

*(Continued)*

## Appendix Table 6: Singapore: Computation of PFCE in the Domestic Market, 1900–39 and 1948–60, European Standard — Club in Current and 1914 Prices (Straits $)

| Year | Annual Per-Capita Private Final Consumption Expenditure in Real Terms (1914 Prices) (Straits $) | Weighted Real Wage Indices of Agriculture and Non-agriculture Sectors (1914 = 100) | Changes in Real Wages (%) | Changes in Real Consumption (%) | Real Per-Capita Private Final Consumption Expenditure Based on Real Wages and Income Elasticities of Demand (1914 Prices) (Straits $) | European Population Standard (Numbers) | Total Real Private Final Consumption Expenditure on Club in the Domestic Market (1914 Prices) (Straits $) | Club Price Indices (1914 = 100) | Total Private Final Consumption Expenditure on Club in the Domestic Market (Current Prices) (Straits $) |
|---|---|---|---|---|---|---|---|---|---|
| | Step 4 | Step 5 | Step 6 | Step 7 | | Step 8 | Step 9 | Step 10 | Step 11 |
| | [1] | [2] | [3] | [4] | [5] | [6] | [7] = [5] x [6] | [8] | [9] = [7] x [8] / 100 |
| 1899 | | 116.03 | | | 126.30 | 13,667 | 1,726,248 | 88.18 | 1,522,127 |
| 1900 | | 113.92 | −1.814% | −1.814% | 124.01 | 13,566 | 1,682,357 | 88.88 | 1,495,309 |
| 1901 | | 112.77 | −1.008% | −1.008% | 122.76 | 13,911 | 1,707,718 | 89.10 | 1,521,632 |
| 1902 | | 108.67 | −3.637% | −3.637% | 118.30 | 14,310 | 1,692,905 | 90.99 | 1,540,360 |
| 1903 | | 107.35 | −1.214% | −1.214% | 116.86 | 14,720 | 1,720,168 | 91.66 | 1,576,648 |
| 1904 | | 107.24 | −0.106% | −0.106% | 116.74 | 15,141 | 1,767,494 | 91.97 | 1,625,589 |
| 1905 | | 105.29 | −1.816% | −1.816% | 114.62 | 15,575 | 1,785,237 | 93.74 | 1,673,405 |
| 1906 | | 106.94 | 1.562% | 1.562% | 116.41 | 16,023 | 1,865,172 | 92.14 | 1,718,521 |
| 1907 | | 107.05 | 0.102% | 0.102% | 116.53 | 16,483 | 1,920,727 | 91.55 | 1,758,489 |
| 1908 | | 107.87 | 0.772% | 0.772% | 117.43 | 16,958 | 1,991,281 | 92.28 | 1,837,625 |
| 1909 | | 110.50 | 2.437% | 2.437% | 120.29 | 17,445 | 2,098,482 | 91.37 | 1,917,380 |
| 1910 | | 108.44 | −1.861% | −1.861% | 118.05 | 17,946 | 2,118,513 | 92.28 | 1,954,977 |
| 1911 | | 98.90 | −8.802% | −8.802% | 107.66 | 18,503 | 1,991,987 | 99.88 | 1,989,693 |
| 1912 | | 97.22 | −1.696% | −1.696% | 105.83 | 19,118 | 2,023,312 | 101.47 | 2,052,994 |
| 1913 | | 95.24 | −2.036% | −2.036% | 103.68 | 19,750 | 2,047,680 | 102.43 | 2,097,491 |
| 1914 | | 100.00 | 4.995% | 4.995% | 108.86 | 20,400 | 2,220,743 | 100.00 | 2,220,743 |
| 1915 | | 93.86 | −6.142% | −6.142% | 102.17 | 21,069 | 2,152,636 | 91.31 | 1,965,530 |
| 1916 | | 88.38 | −5.833% | −5.833% | 96.21 | 21,756 | 2,093,221 | 103.77 | 2,172,126 |
| 1917 | | 100.72 | 13.954% | 13.954% | 109.64 | 22,464 | 2,462,876 | 113.88 | 2,804,673 |
| 1918 | | 104.36 | 3.614% | 3.614% | 113.60 | 23,192 | 2,634,610 | 134.00 | 3,530,377 |
| 1919 | | 92.87 | −11.007% | −11.007% | 101.10 | 23,941 | 2,420,339 | 147.40 | 3,567,579 |
| 1920 | | 89.13 | −4.028% | −4.028% | 97.03 | 24,711 | 2,397,583 | 163.50 | 3,920,048 |
| 1921 | | 112.82 | 26.583% | 26.583% | 122.82 | 27,757 | 3,409,015 | 176.70 | 6,023,730 |
| 1922 | | 123.66 | 9.603% | 9.603% | 134.61 | 29,018 | 3,906,123 | 177.40 | 6,929,463 |
| 1923 | | 126.94 | 2.658% | 2.658% | 138.19 | 30,082 | 4,156,966 | 169.20 | 7,033,587 |
| 1924 | | 127.47 | 0.412% | 0.412% | 138.76 | 31,165 | 4,324,442 | 164.10 | 7,096,409 |
| 1925 | | 124.53 | −2.308% | −2.308% | 135.56 | 32,515 | 4,407,636 | 164.20 | 7,237,339 |
| 1926 | | 120.44 | −3.285% | −3.285% | 131.10 | 33,811 | 4,432,727 | 161.70 | 7,167,720 |
| 1927 | | 127.57 | 5.925% | 5.925% | 138.87 | 35,143 | 4,880,410 | 159.50 | 7,784,254 |
| 1928 | | 131.90 | 3.394% | 3.394% | 143.59 | 36,493 | 5,239,956 | 159.50 | 8,357,730 |
| 1929 | | 131.51 | −0.296% | −0.296% | 143.16 | 37,864 | 5,420,624 | 155.30 | 8,418,228 |
| 1930 | 140.68 | 129.23 | −1.734% | −1.734% | 140.68 | 37,403 | 5,261,859 | 156.10 | 8,213,762 |
| 1931 | | 115.38 | −10.717% | −10.717% | 125.60 | 36,586 | 4,595,328 | 160.50 | 7,375,501 |
| 1932 | | 122.09 | 5.817% | 5.817% | 132.91 | 35,489 | 4,716,829 | 160.10 | 7,551,643 |
| 1933 | | 136.87 | 12.102% | 12.102% | 148.99 | 33,443 | 4,982,694 | 158.40 | 7,892,588 |
| 1934 | | 130.38 | −4.738% | −4.738% | 141.93 | 34,140 | 4,845,595 | 159.50 | 7,728,723 |
| 1935 | | 137.02 | 5.092% | 5.092% | 149.16 | 37,200 | 5,548,796 | 157.70 | 8,750,451 |
| 1936 | | 148.89 | 8.661% | 8.661% | 162.08 | 39,206 | 6,354,401 | 157.40 | 10,001,827 |
| 1937 | | 150.08 | 0.798% | 0.798% | 163.37 | 42,347 | 6,918,228 | 157.70 | 10,910,045 |
| 1938 | | 155.10 | 3.348% | 3.348% | 168.84 | 46,152 | 7,792,417 | 159.40 | 12,421,112 |
| 1939 | | 154.06 | −0.672% | −0.672% | 167.71 | 47,292 | 7,931,105 | 152.87 | 12,124,274 |

| Year | Annual Per-Capita Private Final Consumption Expenditure in Real Terms (1914 Prices) (Straits $) | Weighted Real Wage Indices of Agriculture and Non-agriculture Sectors (1914 = 100) | Changes in Real Wages (%) | Changes in Real Consumption (%) | Real Per-Capita Private Final Consumption Expenditure Based on Real Wages and Income Elasticities of Demand (1914 Prices) (Straits $) | European Population Standard (Numbers) | Total Real Private Final Consumption Expenditure on Club in the Domestic Market (1914 Prices) (Straits $) | Club Price Indices (1914 = 100) | Total Private Final Consumption Expenditure on Club in the Domestic Market (Current Prices) (Straits $) |
|---|---|---|---|---|---|---|---|---|---|
| | Step 4 | Step 5 | Step 6 | Step 7 | | Step 8 | Step 9 | Step 10 | Step 11 |
| | [1] | [2] | [3] | [4] | [5] | [6] | [7] = [5] x [6] | [8] | [9] = [7] x [8] / 100 |
| 1947 | | 164.71 | | | 94.15 | 56,289 | 5,299,353 | 423.73 | 22,454,709 |
| 1948 | 102.68 | 179.65 | 9.067% | 9.067% | 102.68 | 57,648 | 5,919,444 | 444.09 | 26,287,488 |
| 1949 | | 220.02 | 22.473% | 22.473% | 125.76 | 58,722 | 7,384,791 | 437.21 | 32,286,894 |
| 1950 | | 203.15 | −7.666% | −7.666% | 116.12 | 61,326 | 7,121,074 | 469.31 | 33,419,962 |
| 1951 | | 181.26 | −10.776% | −10.776% | 103.61 | 64,086 | 6,639,680 | 546.51 | 36,286,513 |
| 1952 | | 176.19 | −2.797% | −2.797% | 100.71 | 67,620 | 6,809,850 | 564.09 | 38,413,686 |
| 1953 | | 206.53 | 17.217% | 17.217% | 118.05 | 71,508 | 8,441,300 | 556.45 | 46,971,319 |
| 1954 | | 208.97 | 1.183% | 1.183% | 119.44 | 74,892 | 8,945,334 | 546.51 | 48,887,140 |
| 1955 | | 204.74 | −2.023% | −2.023% | 117.03 | 78,330 | 9,166,729 | 544.22 | 49,886,891 |
| 1956 | | 230.57 | 12.617% | 12.617% | 131.79 | 82,296 | 10,845,993 | 549.57 | 59,606,038 |
| 1957 | | 215.81 | −6.401% | −6.401% | 123.36 | 86,756 | 10,701,842 | 558.74 | 59,795,428 |
| 1958 | | 215.37 | −0.205% | −0.205% | 123.10 | 90,840 | 11,182,649 | 561.80 | 62,823,782 |
| 1959 | | 194.19 | −9.837% | −9.837% | 110.99 | 94,776 | 10,519,494 | 567.15 | 59,661,041 |
| 1960 | | 230.48 | 18.691% | 18.691% | 131.74 | 98,046 | 12,916,459 | 572.82 | 73,987,920 |

**Appendix Table 7:** Total Private Final Consumption Expenditure by Major Object of Consumption and Standard in Constant Prices, Singapore, 1900–39 and 1947–1960

(Straits $)

| Year | Food Total | | | | | | | Beverages and Tobacco | | | | | | |
|---|---|---|---|---|---|---|---|---|---|---|---|---|---|---|
| | European Standard | Eurasian Standard | Asiatic Clerical Standard | Chinese Labor Standard | Malay Labor Standard | Indian Labour Standard | Total | European Standard | Eurasian Standard | Asiatic Clerical Standard | Chinese Labor Standard | Malay Labor Standard | Indian Labor Standard | Total |
| 1899 | 5,439,107 | 294,754 | 2,365,451 | 10,676,299 | 3,102,431 | 1,353,955 | 23,231,996 | 1,237,123 | 10,389 | 88,304 | 634,748 | 240,359 | 142,574 | 2,353,498 |
| 1900 | 5,330,194 | 288,852 | 2,318,085 | 10,462,517 | 3,040,308 | 1,326,844 | 22,766,800 | 1,205,668 | 10,125 | 86,059 | 623,181 | 235,979 | 138,949 | 2,299,961 |
| 1901 | 5,427,068 | 294,102 | 2,360,215 | 10,652,668 | 3,095,564 | 1,350,958 | 23,180,574 | 1,223,844 | 10,277 | 87,356 | 635,151 | 240,512 | 141,044 | 2,338,184 |
| 1902 | 5,440,909 | 294,852 | 2,366,234 | 10,679,836 | 3,103,458 | 1,354,404 | 23,239,693 | 1,213,228 | 10,188 | 86,598 | 639,147 | 242,025 | 139,820 | 2,331,007 |
| 1903 | 5,548,916 | 300,705 | 2,413,206 | 10,891,840 | 3,165,065 | 1,381,290 | 23,701,021 | 1,232,766 | 10,352 | 87,993 | 652,633 | 247,132 | 142,072 | 2,372,949 |
| 1904 | 5,703,397 | 309,076 | 2,480,389 | 11,195,067 | 3,253,180 | 1,419,745 | 24,360,854 | 1,266,683 | 10,637 | 90,414 | 670,873 | 254,039 | 145,981 | 2,438,627 |
| 1905 | 5,792,605 | 313,911 | 2,519,186 | 11,370,172 | 3,304,063 | 1,441,951 | 24,741,887 | 1,279,398 | 10,744 | 91,322 | 682,620 | 258,487 | 147,446 | 2,470,016 |
| 1906 | 6,024,044 | 326,453 | 2,619,838 | 11,824,459 | 3,436,075 | 1,499,563 | 25,730,431 | 1,336,684 | 11,225 | 95,411 | 708,796 | 268,399 | 154,048 | 2,574,563 |
| 1907 | 6,201,579 | 336,074 | 2,697,047 | 12,172,938 | 3,537,340 | 1,543,757 | 26,488,733 | 1,376,497 | 11,559 | 98,252 | 729,611 | 276,281 | 158,636 | 2,650,837 |
| 1908 | 6,414,603 | 347,618 | 2,789,691 | 12,591,079 | 3,658,847 | 1,596,785 | 27,398,623 | 1,427,061 | 11,984 | 101,862 | 754,094 | 285,552 | 164,464 | 2,745,015 |
| 1909 | 6,711,682 | 363,717 | 2,918,889 | 13,174,207 | 3,828,299 | 1,670,737 | 28,667,532 | 1,503,887 | 12,629 | 107,345 | 787,127 | 298,060 | 173,318 | 2,882,366 |
| 1910 | 6,814,297 | 369,278 | 2,963,516 | 13,375,628 | 3,886,830 | 1,696,281 | 29,105,829 | 1,518,242 | 12,749 | 108,370 | 800,668 | 303,188 | 174,972 | 2,918,190 |
| 1911 | 6,592,851 | 357,277 | 2,968,406 | 13,093,203 | 3,551,601 | 1,641,156 | 28,204,494 | 1,427,567 | 11,988 | 105,494 | 791,114 | 279,638 | 164,522 | 2,780,323 |
| 1912 | 6,731,180 | 364,774 | 3,030,688 | 13,367,921 | 3,626,119 | 1,675,590 | 28,796,272 | 1,450,015 | 12,176 | 107,153 | 809,099 | 285,995 | 167,109 | 2,831,548 |
| 1913 | 6,854,720 | 371,468 | 3,086,311 | 13,613,267 | 3,692,671 | 1,706,343 | 29,324,781 | 1,467,479 | 12,323 | 108,444 | 825,651 | 291,845 | 169,122 | 2,874,864 |
| 1914 | 7,327,950 | 397,113 | 3,299,381 | 14,553,088 | 3,947,602 | 1,824,144 | 31,349,279 | 1,591,505 | 13,365 | 117,609 | 878,391 | 310,488 | 183,415 | 3,094,773 |
| 1915 | 7,242,660 | 392,491 | 3,260,980 | 14,383,705 | 3,901,656 | 1,802,913 | 30,984,406 | 1,542,697 | 12,955 | 114,002 | 873,739 | 308,843 | 177,790 | 3,030,026 |
| 1916 | 7,173,622 | 388,750 | 3,229,896 | 14,246,597 | 3,864,465 | 1,785,727 | 30,689,057 | 1,500,116 | 12,597 | 110,855 | 870,673 | 307,760 | 172,883 | 2,974,884 |
| 1917 | 8,130,391 | 440,599 | 3,660,677 | 16,146,711 | 4,379,881 | 2,023,895 | 34,782,154 | 1,765,031 | 14,822 | 130,432 | 974,253 | 344,372 | 203,414 | 3,432,324 |
| 1918 | 8,606,305 | 466,390 | 3,874,956 | 17,091,862 | 4,636,258 | 2,142,365 | 36,818,134 | 1,888,105 | 15,855 | 139,527 | 1,027,646 | 363,245 | 217,597 | 3,651,976 |
| 1919 | 8,199,725 | 444,356 | 3,691,895 | 16,284,408 | 4,417,232 | 2,041,155 | 35,078,771 | 1,734,547 | 14,566 | 128,179 | 990,775 | 350,212 | 199,900 | 3,418,179 |
| 1920 | 8,224,894 | 445,720 | 3,703,227 | 16,334,393 | 4,430,791 | 2,047,420 | 35,186,445 | 1,718,239 | 14,429 | 126,974 | 997,935 | 352,743 | 198,021 | 3,408,340 |
| 1921 | 10,957,825 | 548,144 | 5,692,752 | 20,188,023 | 4,166,847 | 2,877,603 | 44,431,195 | 2,443,086 | 18,938 | 208,314 | 1,205,725 | 324,295 | 297,027 | 4,497,385 |
| 1922 | 12,225,691 | 611,566 | 6,351,428 | 22,523,862 | 4,648,969 | 3,210,554 | 49,572,071 | 2,799,341 | 21,699 | 238,691 | 1,333,129 | 358,562 | 340,340 | 5,091,761 |
| 1923 | 12,909,727 | 645,784 | 6,706,794 | 23,784,087 | 4,909,082 | 3,390,186 | 52,345,661 | 2,979,109 | 23,093 | 254,019 | 1,404,044 | 377,635 | 362,196 | 5,400,096 |
| 1924 | 13,413,301 | 670,974 | 6,968,408 | 24,711,841 | 5,100,572 | 3,522,428 | 54,387,524 | 3,099,131 | 24,023 | 264,253 | 1,458,213 | 392,205 | 376,788 | 5,614,612 |
| 1925 | 13,768,225 | 688,728 | 7,152,797 | 25,365,732 | 5,235,537 | 3,615,634 | 55,826,654 | 3,158,753 | 24,485 | 269,336 | 1,500,309 | 403,527 | 384,037 | 5,740,447 |
| 1926 | 13,987,688 | 699,707 | 7,266,811 | 25,770,056 | 5,318,990 | 3,673,266 | 56,716,518 | 3,176,734 | 24,625 | 270,870 | 1,529,348 | 411,338 | 386,223 | 5,799,137 |
| 1927 | 15,141,927 | 757,445 | 7,866,456 | 27,896,556 | 5,757,904 | 3,976,378 | 61,396,665 | 3,497,568 | 27,111 | 298,226 | 1,646,128 | 442,747 | 425,230 | 6,337,010 |
| 1928 | 16,097,336 | 805,238 | 8,362,805 | 29,656,743 | 6,121,210 | 4,227,275 | 65,270,606 | 3,755,238 | 29,109 | 320,197 | 1,744,191 | 469,122 | 456,557 | 6,774,414 |
| 1929 | 16,667,209 | 833,744 | 8,658,862 | 30,706,641 | 6,337,911 | 4,376,928 | 67,581,294 | 3,884,714 | 30,112 | 331,237 | 1,806,475 | 485,874 | 472,298 | 7,010,712 |
| 1930 | 16,264,686 | 813,609 | 8,449,746 | 29,965,058 | 6,184,846 | 4,271,222 | 65,949,168 | 3,770,935 | 29,230 | 321,535 | 1,765,942 | 474,972 | 458,465 | 6,821,080 |
| 1931 | 14,715,907 | 368,067 | 7,645,132 | 28,232,001 | 4,304,542 | 4,347,565 | 59,613,214 | 3,293,262 | 12,764 | 280,806 | 1,683,084 | 334,402 | 450,439 | 6,054,758 |
| 1932 | 14,855,891 | 371,568 | 7,717,856 | 28,500,555 | 4,345,488 | 4,388,921 | 60,180,279 | 3,380,337 | 13,101 | 288,230 | 1,689,597 | 335,696 | 462,349 | 6,169,311 |
| 1933 | 15,185,011 | 379,800 | 7,888,838 | 29,131,961 | 4,441,759 | 4,486,154 | 61,513,524 | 3,570,870 | 13,840 | 304,476 | 1,707,761 | 339,305 | 488,409 | 6,424,663 |
| 1934 | 14,987,527 | 374,861 | 7,786,242 | 28,753,094 | 4,383,993 | 4,427,810 | 60,713,527 | 3,472,617 | 13,459 | 296,099 | 1,693,811 | 336,534 | 474,971 | 6,287,491 |
| 1935 | 16,913,087 | 423,022 | 8,786,599 | 32,447,220 | 4,947,238 | 4,996,684 | 68,513,850 | 3,976,569 | 15,412 | 339,069 | 1,902,031 | 377,904 | 543,899 | 7,154,884 |
| 1936 | 18,905,496 | 472,855 | 9,821,685 | 36,269,593 | 5,530,036 | 5,585,307 | 76,584,972 | 4,553,910 | 17,650 | 388,297 | 2,108,734 | 418,972 | 622,866 | 8,110,429 |
| 1937 | 20,534,128 | 513,590 | 10,667,783 | 39,394,071 | 6,006,426 | 6,066,459 | 83,182,457 | 4,957,979 | 19,216 | 422,751 | 2,288,577 | 454,704 | 678,132 | 8,821,359 |
| 1938 | 22,904,054 | 572,865 | 11,898,996 | 43,940,700 | 6,699,652 | 6,766,614 | 92,782,881 | 5,584,471 | 21,644 | 476,170 | 2,544,360 | 505,524 | 763,821 | 9,895,990 |
| 1939 | 23,359,018 | 584,244 | 12,135,356 | 44,813,534 | 6,832,733 | 6,901,025 | 94,625,911 | 5,683,862 | 22,029 | 484,644 | 2,596,653 | 515,914 | 777,416 | 10,080,519 |

| Year | Food Total | | | | | | | Beverages and Tobacco | | | | | | |
|---|---|---|---|---|---|---|---|---|---|---|---|---|---|---|
| | European Standard | Malay Clerical Standard | Chinese. Indian. Eurasian Clerical Grades Standard | Chinese Labor Standard | Malay Labor Standard | Indian Labor Standard | Total | European Standard | Malay Clerical Standard | Chinese. Indian. Eurasian Clerical Grades Standard | Chinese Labor Standard | Malay Labor Standard | Indian Labor Standard | Total |
| 1947 | 18,255,364 | 1,536,486 | 14,880,415 | 48,347,790 | 6,119,372 | 9,228,276 | 98,367,703 | 9,042,300 | 66,009 | 594,080 | 3,664,934 | 604,470 | 652,519 | 14,624,311 |
| 1948 | 19,882,898 | 1,673,470 | 16,207,060 | 52,658,176 | 6,664,937 | 10,051,011 | 107,137,551 | 10,100,362 | 73,733 | 663,595 | 4,093,777 | 675,200 | 728,872 | 16,335,539 |
| 1949 | 23,439,406 | 1,972,808 | 19,106,061 | 62,077,288 | 7,857,112 | 11,848,863 | 126,301,538 | 12,600,687 | 91,985 | 827,866 | 5,107,184 | 842,345 | 909,302 | 20,379,370 |
| 1950 | 23,165,302 | 1,949,738 | 18,882,632 | 61,351,347 | 7,765,230 | 11,710,300 | 124,824,549 | 12,150,708 | 88,700 | 798,302 | 4,924,803 | 812,264 | 876,830 | 19,651,608 |
| 1951 | 22,381,866 | 1,883,799 | 18,244,033 | 59,276,484 | 7,502,615 | 11,314,265 | 120,603,062 | 11,329,303 | 82,704 | 744,336 | 4,591,879 | 757,354 | 817,555 | 18,323,131 |
| 1952 | 23,153,681 | 1,948,759 | 18,873,159 | 61,320,570 | 7,761,334 | 11,704,426 | 124,761,929 | 11,619,665 | 84,824 | 763,413 | 4,709,566 | 776,764 | 838,509 | 18,792,741 |
| 1953 | 27,435,948 | 2,309,182 | 22,363,745 | 72,661,792 | 9,196,791 | 13,869,156 | 147,836,614 | 14,403,412 | 105,145 | 946,305 | 5,837,846 | 962,855 | 1,039,392 | 23,294,955 |
| 1954 | 28,972,205 | 2,438,483 | 23,615,987 | 76,730,440 | 9,711,759 | 14,645,750 | 156,114,625 | 15,263,446 | 111,423 | 1,002,810 | 6,186,426 | 1,020,348 | 1,101,455 | 24,685,908 |
| 1955 | 29,873,146 | 2,514,312 | 24,350,367 | 79,116,505 | 10,013,763 | 15,101,185 | 160,969,277 | 15,641,213 | 114,181 | 1,027,629 | 6,339,539 | 1,045,601 | 1,128,715 | 25,296,880 |
| 1956 | 34,157,654 | 2,874,923 | 27,842,779 | 90,463,664 | 11,449,971 | 17,267,048 | 184,056,039 | 18,506,546 | 135,098 | 1,215,881 | 7,500,887 | 1,237,146 | 1,335,486 | 29,931,045 |
| 1957 | 34,395,185 | 1,929,943 | 38,420,248 | 82,742,576 | 12,810,660 | 17,387,123 | 187,685,735 | 18,260,581 | 88,868 | 1,644,063 | 6,722,752 | 1,356,338 | 1,317,737 | 29,390,339 |
| 1958 | 35,962,661 | 2,017,896 | 40,171,155 | 86,513,364 | 13,394,474 | 18,179,498 | 196,239,048 | 19,080,983 | 92,861 | 1,717,926 | 7,024,789 | 1,417,274 | 1,376,939 | 30,710,772 |
| 1959 | 34,937,265 | 1,960,360 | 39,025,764 | 84,046,628 | 13,012,560 | 17,661,150 | 190,643,727 | 17,949,441 | 87,354 | 1,616,050 | 6,608,204 | 1,333,227 | 1,295,284 | 28,889,559 |
| 1960 | 40,871,439 | 2,293,332 | 45,654,378 | 98,322,138 | 15,222,773 | 20,660,936 | 223,024,995 | 22,039,388 | 107,258 | 1,984,282 | 8,113,945 | 1,637,015 | 1,590,426 | 35,472,315 |

*(Continued)*

**Appendix Table 7:** Total Private Final Consumption Expenditure by Major Object of Consumption and Standard in Current Prices, Singapore, 1900–39 and 1947–1960

(Straits $)

### Food Total

| Year | European Standard | Eurasian Standard | Asiatic Clerical Standard | Chinese Labor Standard | Malay Labor Standard | Indian Labor Standard | Total |
|---|---|---|---|---|---|---|---|
| 1899 | 4,412,406 | 239,115 | 1,918,941 | 8,661,010 | 2,516,807 | 1,098,379 | 18,846,658 |
| 1900 | 4,369,042 | 236,765 | 1,900,083 | 8,575,892 | 2,492,072 | 1,087,584 | 18,661,438 |
| 1901 | 4,499,325 | 243,826 | 1,956,742 | 8,831,623 | 2,566,385 | 1,120,016 | 19,217,917 |
| 1902 | 4,652,316 | 252,117 | 2,023,278 | 9,131,925 | 2,653,650 | 1,158,099 | 19,871,385 |
| 1903 | 4,744,669 | 257,121 | 2,063,442 | 9,313,202 | 2,706,328 | 1,181,089 | 20,265,850 |
| 1904 | 4,977,968 | 269,764 | 2,164,903 | 9,771,141 | 2,839,400 | 1,239,164 | 21,262,341 |
| 1905 | 5,223,634 | 283,077 | 2,271,742 | 10,253,353 | 2,979,527 | 1,300,318 | 22,311,651 |
| 1906 | 5,289,017 | 286,620 | 2,300,177 | 10,381,691 | 3,016,820 | 1,316,593 | 22,590,920 |
| 1907 | 5,313,974 | 287,973 | 2,311,031 | 10,430,678 | 3,031,056 | 1,322,806 | 22,697,516 |
| 1908 | 5,582,067 | 302,501 | 2,427,624 | 10,956,913 | 3,183,974 | 1,389,542 | 23,842,622 |
| 1909 | 5,760,682 | 312,181 | 2,505,303 | 11,307,512 | 3,285,855 | 1,434,005 | 24,605,538 |
| 1910 | 5,934,800 | 321,616 | 2,581,026 | 11,649,283 | 3,385,171 | 1,477,348 | 25,349,243 |
| 1911 | 6,778,183 | 367,321 | 3,051,851 | 13,461,266 | 3,651,440 | 1,687,291 | 28,997,351 |
| 1912 | 7,124,071 | 386,065 | 3,207,586 | 14,148,191 | 3,837,772 | 1,773,393 | 30,477,078 |
| 1913 | 7,203,681 | 390,379 | 3,243,430 | 14,306,294 | 3,880,658 | 1,793,210 | 30,817,653 |
| 1914 | 7,327,950 | 397,113 | 3,299,381 | 14,553,088 | 3,947,602 | 1,824,144 | 31,349,279 |
| 1915 | 7,585,155 | 411,052 | 3,415,187 | 15,063,889 | 4,086,160 | 1,888,170 | 32,449,613 |
| 1916 | 7,638,020 | 413,917 | 3,438,989 | 15,168,877 | 4,114,638 | 1,901,330 | 32,675,770 |
| 1917 | 9,412,300 | 510,068 | 4,237,852 | 18,692,545 | 5,070,452 | 2,343,001 | 40,266,218 |
| 1918 | 12,003,667 | 650,498 | 5,404,605 | 23,838,921 | 6,466,434 | 2,988,069 | 51,352,193 |
| 1919 | 15,077,106 | 817,053 | 6,788,409 | 29,942,678 | 8,122,110 | 3,753,139 | 64,500,495 |
| 1920 | 20,066,803 | 1,087,453 | 9,035,001 | 39,852,067 | 10,810,085 | 4,995,223 | 85,846,631 |
| 1921 | 18,404,853 | 920,667 | 9,561,594 | 33,907,970 | 6,998,671 | 4,833,245 | 74,627,000 |
| 1922 | 17,628,945 | 881,853 | 9,158,498 | 32,478,485 | 6,703,623 | 4,629,487 | 71,480,891 |
| 1923 | 18,626,209 | 931,739 | 9,676,592 | 34,315,783 | 7,082,845 | 4,891,375 | 75,524,543 |
| 1924 | 19,396,465 | 970,270 | 10,076,751 | 35,734,856 | 7,375,744 | 5,093,650 | 78,647,736 |
| 1925 | 20,594,430 | 1,030,196 | 10,699,112 | 37,941,912 | 7,831,285 | 5,408,244 | 83,505,179 |
| 1926 | 22,169,479 | 1,108,985 | 11,517,373 | 40,843,686 | 8,430,216 | 5,821,863 | 89,891,602 |
| 1927 | 23,446,884 | 1,172,884 | 12,181,004 | 43,197,098 | 8,915,965 | 6,157,319 | 95,071,153 |
| 1928 | 24,270,469 | 1,214,082 | 12,608,868 | 44,714,421 | 9,229,144 | 6,373,598 | 98,410,583 |
| 1929 | 24,622,799 | 1,231,707 | 12,791,909 | 45,363,531 | 9,363,121 | 6,466,122 | 99,839,190 |
| 1930 | 22,486,856 | 1,124,861 | 11,682,255 | 41,428,401 | 8,550,903 | 5,905,208 | 91,178,483 |
| 1931 | 15,391,167 | 384,956 | 7,995,939 | 29,527,465 | 4,502,062 | 4,547,059 | 62,348,648 |
| 1932 | 13,248,386 | 331,362 | 6,882,733 | 25,416,607 | 3,875,278 | 3,914,011 | 53,668,377 |
| 1933 | 12,505,866 | 312,791 | 6,496,983 | 23,992,107 | 3,658,084 | 3,694,646 | 50,660,477 |
| 1934 | 12,950,916 | 323,922 | 6,728,193 | 24,845,921 | 3,788,265 | 3,826,128 | 52,463,346 |
| 1935 | 16,013,727 | 400,528 | 8,319,369 | 30,721,827 | 4,684,166 | 4,730,984 | 64,870,600 |
| 1936 | 17,432,618 | 436,016 | 9,056,503 | 33,443,923 | 5,099,205 | 5,150,171 | 70,618,437 |
| 1937 | 20,895,697 | 522,633 | 10,855,624 | 40,087,730 | 6,112,188 | 6,173,279 | 84,647,151 |
| 1938 | 21,596,868 | 540,170 | 11,219,893 | 41,432,906 | 6,317,288 | 6,380,428 | 87,487,553 |
| 1939 | 21,445,527 | 536,385 | 11,141,269 | 41,142,562 | 6,273,019 | 6,335,717 | 86,874,479 |

| Year | European Standard | Malay Clerical Standard | Chinese, Indian, Eurasian Clerical Grades Standard | Chinese Labor Standard | Malay Labor Standard | Indian Labor Standard | Total |
|---|---|---|---|---|---|---|---|
| 1947 | 71,954,987 | 6,056,184 | 58,652,354 | 190,566,709 | 24,119,997 | 36,373,992 | 387,724,223 |
| 1948 | 71,818,963 | 6,044,736 | 58,541,478 | 190,206,461 | 24,074,400 | 36,305,230 | 386,991,268 |
| 1949 | 78,941,707 | 6,644,231 | 64,347,408 | 209,070,446 | 26,462,012 | 39,905,851 | 425,371,655 |
| 1950 | 83,489,050 | 7,026,964 | 68,054,065 | 221,113,702 | 27,986,325 | 42,204,580 | 449,874,685 |
| 1951 | 107,486,516 | 9,046,742 | 87,615,014 | 284,668,964 | 36,030,503 | 54,335,548 | 579,183,286 |
| 1952 | 116,261,314 | 9,785,284 | 94,767,577 | 307,908,275 | 38,971,899 | 58,771,299 | 626,465,648 |
| 1953 | 130,950,539 | 11,021,621 | 106,741,141 | 346,811,448 | 43,895,867 | 66,196,855 | 705,617,470 |
| 1954 | 125,527,001 | 10,565,142 | 102,320,276 | 332,447,666 | 42,077,846 | 63,455,200 | 676,393,132 |
| 1955 | 124,269,457 | 10,459,300 | 101,295,220 | 329,117,168 | 41,656,305 | 62,819,499 | 669,616,949 |
| 1956 | 142,939,681 | 12,030,703 | 116,513,798 | 378,563,678 | 47,914,742 | 72,257,490 | 770,220,091 |
| 1957 | 150,249,636 | 8,430,637 | 167,832,451 | 361,447,159 | 55,961,232 | 75,952,748 | 819,873,862 |
| 1958 | 154,652,705 | 8,677,697 | 172,750,785 | 372,039,375 | 57,601,177 | 78,178,545 | 843,900,284 |
| 1959 | 146,586,615 | 8,225,101 | 163,740,769 | 352,635,234 | 54,596,921 | 74,101,053 | 799,885,694 |
| 1960 | 171,204,779 | 9,606,448 | 191,239,850 | 411,857,778 | 63,766,080 | 86,545,791 | 934,220,726 |

### Beverages and Tobacco

| Year | European Standard | Eurasian Standard | Asiatic Clerical Standard | Chinese Labor Standard | Malay Labor Standard | Indian Labor Standard | Total |
|---|---|---|---|---|---|---|---|
| 1899 | 1,006,048 | 8,448 | 71,810 | 516,187 | 195,464 | 115,943 | 1,913,901 |
| 1900 | 1,007,297 | 8,459 | 71,899 | 520,648 | 197,153 | 116,087 | 1,921,544 |
| 1901 | 998,791 | 8,387 | 71,292 | 518,353 | 196,284 | 115,107 | 1,908,216 |
| 1902 | 1,045,724 | 8,781 | 74,642 | 550,904 | 208,610 | 120,516 | 2,009,177 |
| 1903 | 1,126,968 | 9,464 | 80,441 | 596,623 | 225,922 | 129,879 | 2,169,297 |
| 1904 | 1,101,209 | 9,247 | 78,603 | 583,233 | 220,852 | 126,910 | 2,120,055 |
| 1905 | 1,143,900 | 9,606 | 81,650 | 610,325 | 231,111 | 131,830 | 2,208,422 |
| 1906 | 1,152,353 | 9,677 | 82,253 | 611,052 | 231,386 | 132,805 | 2,219,527 |
| 1907 | 1,237,471 | 10,392 | 88,329 | 655,920 | 248,376 | 142,614 | 2,383,102 |
| 1908 | 1,289,998 | 10,833 | 92,078 | 681,666 | 258,126 | 148,668 | 2,481,368 |
| 1909 | 1,321,965 | 11,101 | 94,360 | 691,910 | 262,005 | 152,352 | 2,533,693 |
| 1910 | 1,367,792 | 11,486 | 97,631 | 721,326 | 273,144 | 157,633 | 2,629,012 |
| 1911 | 1,257,645 | 10,561 | 92,937 | 696,949 | 246,353 | 144,939 | 2,449,384 |
| 1912 | 1,285,291 | 10,793 | 94,980 | 717,184 | 253,505 | 148,125 | 2,509,879 |
| 1913 | 1,454,517 | 12,214 | 107,486 | 818,358 | 289,267 | 167,628 | 2,849,470 |
| 1914 | 1,591,505 | 13,365 | 117,609 | 878,391 | 310,488 | 183,415 | 3,094,773 |
| 1915 | 1,416,584 | 11,896 | 104,682 | 802,313 | 283,596 | 163,256 | 2,782,327 |
| 1916 | 2,038,877 | 17,121 | 150,669 | 1,183,372 | 418,290 | 234,973 | 4,043,304 |
| 1917 | 2,256,424 | 18,948 | 166,745 | 1,245,490 | 440,247 | 260,045 | 4,387,899 |
| 1918 | 3,295,554 | 27,674 | 243,534 | 1,793,684 | 634,019 | 379,801 | 6,374,266 |
| 1919 | 3,503,645 | 29,422 | 258,912 | 2,001,285 | 707,401 | 403,783 | 6,904,447 |
| 1920 | 4,063,634 | 34,124 | 300,294 | 2,360,115 | 834,237 | 468,319 | 8,060,724 |
| 1921 | 5,795,380 | 44,923 | 494,153 | 2,860,168 | 769,279 | 704,595 | 10,668,498 |
| 1922 | 6,538,468 | 50,683 | 557,514 | 3,113,811 | 837,499 | 794,938 | 11,892,913 |
| 1923 | 6,004,534 | 46,544 | 511,987 | 2,829,917 | 761,142 | 730,023 | 10,884,148 |
| 1924 | 5,851,452 | 45,358 | 498,934 | 2,753,243 | 740,520 | 711,412 | 10,600,918 |
| 1925 | 5,881,150 | 45,588 | 501,466 | 2,793,363 | 751,310 | 715,022 | 10,687,900 |
| 1926 | 5,970,117 | 46,277 | 509,052 | 2,874,142 | 773,037 | 725,839 | 10,898,465 |
| 1927 | 6,330,153 | 49,068 | 539,751 | 2,979,282 | 801,316 | 769,611 | 11,469,181 |
| 1928 | 6,801,976 | 52,726 | 579,982 | 3,159,306 | 849,736 | 826,975 | 12,270,701 |
| 1929 | 6,860,973 | 53,183 | 585,013 | 3,190,499 | 858,125 | 834,148 | 12,381,941 |
| 1930 | 6,413,916 | 49,718 | 546,894 | 3,003,659 | 807,872 | 779,795 | 11,601,853 |
| 1931 | 5,756,654 | 22,311 | 490,851 | 2,942,047 | 584,539 | 787,372 | 10,583,774 |
| 1932 | 5,704,685 | 22,110 | 486,420 | 2,851,379 | 566,524 | 780,264 | 10,411,382 |
| 1933 | 5,538,235 | 21,465 | 472,227 | 2,648,650 | 526,245 | 757,498 | 9,964,319 |
| 1934 | 5,428,029 | 21,038 | 462,830 | 2,647,587 | 526,034 | 742,424 | 9,827,942 |
| 1935 | 5,846,102 | 22,658 | 498,478 | 2,796,246 | 555,570 | 799,606 | 10,518,660 |
| 1936 | 6,681,596 | 25,896 | 569,718 | 3,093,981 | 614,725 | 913,882 | 11,899,799 |
| 1937 | 7,274,456 | 28,194 | 620,269 | 3,357,850 | 667,152 | 994,971 | 12,942,892 |
| 1938 | 8,147,533 | 31,578 | 694,713 | 3,712,126 | 737,541 | 1,114,387 | 14,437,878 |
| 1939 | 8,758,684 | 33,947 | 746,824 | 4,001,375 | 795,010 | 1,197,978 | 15,533,818 |

| Year | European Standard | Malay Clerical Standard | Chinese, Indian, Eurasian Clerical Grades Standard | Chinese Labor Standard | Malay Labor Standard | Indian Labor Standard | Total |
|---|---|---|---|---|---|---|---|
| 1947 | 44,652,793 | 325,966 | 2,933,692 | 18,098,222 | 2,985,000 | 3,222,275 | 72,217,948 |
| 1948 | 40,866,858 | 298,328 | 2,684,956 | 16,563,744 | 2,731,914 | 2,949,071 | 66,094,871 |
| 1949 | 52,628,319 | 384,187 | 3,457,684 | 21,330,782 | 3,518,157 | 3,797,812 | 85,116,942 |
| 1950 | 54,026,729 | 394,396 | 3,549,560 | 21,897,571 | 3,611,639 | 3,898,726 | 87,378,621 |
| 1951 | 57,396,914 | 418,998 | 3,770,982 | 23,263,541 | 3,836,933 | 4,141,928 | 92,829,296 |
| 1952 | 59,761,353 | 436,258 | 3,926,325 | 24,221,871 | 3,994,994 | 4,312,553 | 96,653,355 |
| 1953 | 75,175,582 | 548,782 | 4,939,041 | 30,469,411 | 5,025,422 | 5,424,888 | 121,583,127 |
| 1954 | 82,763,618 | 604,175 | 5,437,576 | 33,544,918 | 5,532,675 | 5,972,463 | 133,855,426 |
| 1955 | 84,523,091 | 617,019 | 5,553,173 | 34,258,050 | 5,650,294 | 6,099,432 | 136,701,060 |
| 1956 | 100,349,254 | 732,550 | 6,592,953 | 40,672,552 | 6,708,259 | 7,241,494 | 162,297,063 |
| 1957 | 100,422,640 | 488,724 | 9,041,395 | 36,971,252 | 7,459,072 | 7,246,790 | 161,629,873 |
| 1958 | 104,970,472 | 510,857 | 9,450,852 | 38,645,566 | 7,796,871 | 7,574,974 | 168,949,592 |
| 1959 | 98,273,495 | 478,265 | 8,847,900 | 36,180,030 | 7,299,441 | 7,091,701 | 158,170,832 |
| 1960 | 120,602,695 | 586,934 | 10,858,275 | 44,400,671 | 8,957,982 | 8,703,041 | 194,109,598 |

(Continued)

**Appendix Table 7:** Total Private Final Consumption Expenditure by Major Object of Consumption and Standard in Constant Prices, Singapore, 1900–39 and 1947–1960

(Straits $)

| Year | Clothing | | | | | | | Rent | | | | | | |
|---|---|---|---|---|---|---|---|---|---|---|---|---|---|---|
| | European Standard | Eurasian Standard | Asiatic Clerical Standard | Chinese Labor Standard | Malay Labor Standard | Indian Labor Standard | Total | European Standard | Eurasian Standard | Asiatic Clerical Standard | Chinese Labor Standard | Malay Labor Standard | Indian Labor Standard | Total |
| 1899 | 2.527.895 | 45.643 | 387.962 | 1.197.216 | 367.190 | 118.954 | 4,644,859 | 1.398.722 | 58.280 | 495.381 | 484.243 | 116.071 | 82.366 | 2,635,062 |
| 1900 | 2.463.621 | 44.482 | 378.097 | 1.175.398 | 360.499 | 115.929 | 4,538,027 | 1.368.195 | 57.008 | 484.569 | 473.674 | 113.538 | 80.568 | 2,577,553 |
| 1901 | 2.500.760 | 45.153 | 383.797 | 1.197.975 | 367.423 | 117.677 | 4,612,785 | 1.391.648 | 57.985 | 492.875 | 481.794 | 115.484 | 81.949 | 2,621,735 |
| 1902 | 2.479.068 | 44.761 | 380.468 | 1.205.513 | 369.735 | 116.656 | 4,596,200 | 1.389.990 | 57.916 | 492.288 | 481.220 | 115.347 | 81.852 | 2,618,613 |
| 1903 | 2.518.992 | 45.482 | 386.595 | 1.230.948 | 377.536 | 118.535 | 4,678,089 | 1.415.847 | 58.994 | 501.446 | 490.172 | 117.493 | 83.374 | 2,667,324 |
| 1904 | 2.588.296 | 46.733 | 397.232 | 1.265.352 | 388.088 | 121.796 | 4,807,497 | 1.455.109 | 60.630 | 515.351 | 503.764 | 120.751 | 85.686 | 2,741,291 |
| 1905 | 2.614.278 | 47.202 | 401.219 | 1.287.507 | 394.883 | 123.019 | 4,868,108 | 1.475.151 | 61.465 | 522.449 | 510.703 | 122.414 | 86.867 | 2,779,049 |
| 1906 | 2.731.334 | 49.316 | 419.184 | 1.336.879 | 410.025 | 128.527 | 5,075,265 | 1.536.461 | 64.019 | 544.163 | 531.929 | 127.502 | 90.477 | 2,894,550 |
| 1907 | 2.812.687 | 50.785 | 431.669 | 1.376.138 | 422.066 | 132.355 | 5,225,701 | 1.581.902 | 65.913 | 560.257 | 547.661 | 131.273 | 93.153 | 2,980,158 |
| 1908 | 2.916.007 | 52.650 | 447.526 | 1.422.316 | 436.229 | 137.217 | 5,411,945 | 1.637.498 | 68.229 | 579.947 | 566.908 | 135.886 | 96.427 | 3,084,894 |
| 1909 | 3.072.991 | 55.485 | 471.619 | 1.484.621 | 455.338 | 144.604 | 5,684,657 | 1.717.441 | 71.560 | 608.260 | 594.585 | 142.520 | 101.134 | 3,235,500 |
| 1910 | 3.102.323 | 56.014 | 476.120 | 1.510.162 | 463.172 | 145.984 | 5,753,775 | 1.740.410 | 72.517 | 616.395 | 602.537 | 144.426 | 102.487 | 3,278,773 |
| 1911 | 2.917.040 | 52.669 | 463.485 | 1.492.141 | 427.194 | 137.266 | 5,489,796 | 1.668.057 | 69.502 | 611.621 | 584.282 | 130.732 | 98.226 | 3,162,420 |
| 1912 | 2.962.911 | 53.497 | 470.774 | 1.526.064 | 436.906 | 139.424 | 5,589,576 | 1.700.133 | 70.839 | 623.382 | 595.517 | 133.246 | 100.115 | 3,223,231 |
| 1913 | 2.998.597 | 54.141 | 476.444 | 1.557.281 | 445.844 | 141.103 | 5,673,410 | 1.727.760 | 71.990 | 633.512 | 605.194 | 135.411 | 101.742 | 3,275,610 |
| 1914 | 3.252.027 | 58.717 | 516.711 | 1.656.756 | 474.323 | 153.029 | 6,111,564 | 1.855.955 | 77.331 | 680.517 | 650.098 | 145.458 | 109.291 | 3,518,650 |
| 1915 | 3.152.293 | 56.916 | 500.864 | 1.647.983 | 471.811 | 148.336 | 5,978,203 | 1.822.581 | 75.941 | 668.280 | 638.408 | 142.842 | 107.325 | 3,455,377 |
| 1916 | 3.065.285 | 55.345 | 487.040 | 1.642.200 | 470.155 | 144.242 | 5,864,267 | 1.794.230 | 74.760 | 657.884 | 628.477 | 140.620 | 105.656 | 3,401,628 |
| 1917 | 3.606.604 | 65.119 | 573.049 | 1.837.565 | 526.088 | 169.714 | 6,778,139 | 2.059.383 | 85.808 | 755.107 | 721.354 | 161.402 | 121.270 | 3,904,324 |
| 1918 | 3.858.088 | 69.660 | 613.007 | 1.938.270 | 554.919 | 181.548 | 7,215,494 | 2.187.614 | 91.151 | 802.125 | 766.270 | 171.451 | 128.821 | 4,147,432 |
| 1919 | 3.544.313 | 63.995 | 563.152 | 1.868.726 | 535.009 | 166.783 | 6,741,977 | 2.059.410 | 85.809 | 755.117 | 721.364 | 161.404 | 121.271 | 3,904,374 |
| 1920 | 3.510.990 | 63.393 | 557.857 | 1.882.231 | 538.875 | 165.215 | 6,718,560 | 2.057.170 | 85.715 | 754.296 | 720.579 | 161.228 | 121.140 | 3,900,127 |
| 1921 | 4.992.118 | 83.202 | 915.222 | 2.274.151 | 495.416 | 247.819 | 9,007,927 | 2.802.144 | 107.775 | 1.185.522 | 910.539 | 155.022 | 174.075 | 5,335,077 |
| 1922 | 5.720.077 | 95.335 | 1.048.681 | 2.514.449 | 547.764 | 283.956 | 10,210,261 | 3.154.495 | 121.327 | 1.334.594 | 1.025.033 | 174.515 | 195.964 | 6,005,927 |
| 1923 | 6.087.408 | 101.457 | 1.116.025 | 2.648.205 | 576.903 | 302.191 | 10,832,188 | 3.339.684 | 128.449 | 1.412.943 | 1.085.209 | 184.760 | 207.468 | 6,358,513 |
| 1924 | 6.332.657 | 105.544 | 1.160.987 | 2.750.374 | 599.160 | 314.366 | 11,263,088 | 3.471.381 | 133.515 | 1.468.661 | 1.128.004 | 192.046 | 215.649 | 6,609,256 |
| 1925 | 6.454.486 | 107.575 | 1.183.322 | 2.829.772 | 616.456 | 320.414 | 11,512,025 | 3.554.879 | 136.726 | 1.503.987 | 1.155.136 | 196.665 | 220.836 | 6,768,230 |
| 1926 | 6.491.229 | 108.187 | 1.190.059 | 2.884.543 | 628.388 | 322.238 | 11,624,644 | 3.599.400 | 138.438 | 1.522.823 | 1.169.603 | 199.128 | 223.602 | 6,852,995 |
| 1927 | 7.146.810 | 119.113 | 1.310.248 | 3.104.805 | 676.372 | 354.782 | 12,712,131 | 3.918.585 | 150.715 | 1.657.863 | 1.273.320 | 216.786 | 243.430 | 7,460,699 |
| 1928 | 7.673.324 | 127.889 | 1.406.776 | 3.289.765 | 716.664 | 380.919 | 13,595,337 | 4.179.648 | 160.756 | 1.768.312 | 1.358.150 | 231.229 | 259.648 | 7,957,744 |
| 1929 | 7.937.891 | 132.298 | 1.455.280 | 3.407.240 | 742.256 | 394.053 | 14,069,019 | 4.326.329 | 166.397 | 1.830.370 | 1.405.813 | 239.344 | 268.760 | 8,237,013 |
| 1930 | 7.705.398 | 128.423 | 1.412.656 | 3.330.790 | 725.601 | 382.512 | 13,685,380 | 4.214.435 | 162.094 | 1.783.030 | 1.369.454 | 233.154 | 261.809 | 8,023,976 |
| 1931 | 6.729.338 | 56.078 | 1.233.712 | 3.174.509 | 510.857 | 375.815 | 12,080,310 | 3.768.943 | 72.480 | 1.594.553 | 1.275.302 | 160.391 | 263.401 | 7,135,068 |
| 1932 | 6.907.263 | 57.561 | 1.266.332 | 3.186.794 | 512.834 | 385.752 | 12,316,535 | 3.826.061 | 73.578 | 1.618.718 | 1.294.629 | 162.821 | 267.393 | 7,243,200 |
| 1933 | 7.296.593 | 60.805 | 1.337.709 | 3.221.054 | 518.347 | 407.495 | 12,842,002 | 3.954.455 | 76.047 | 1.673.039 | 1.338.074 | 168.285 | 276.366 | 7,486,266 |
| 1934 | 7.095.826 | 59.132 | 1.300.901 | 3.194.742 | 514.113 | 396.283 | 12,560,997 | 3.883.900 | 74.690 | 1.643.189 | 1.314.200 | 165.283 | 271.435 | 7,352,698 |
| 1935 | 8.125.584 | 67.713 | 1.489.690 | 3.587.470 | 577.312 | 453.792 | 14,301,562 | 4.404.442 | 84.701 | 1.863.418 | 1.490.336 | 187.435 | 307.815 | 8,338,147 |
| 1936 | 9.305.302 | 77.544 | 1.705.972 | 3.977.339 | 640.052 | 519.676 | 16,225,885 | 4.963.500 | 95.452 | 2.099.942 | 1.679.505 | 211.226 | 346.886 | 9,396,511 |
| 1937 | 10.130.963 | 84.425 | 1.857.343 | 4.316.545 | 694.638 | 565.787 | 17,649,701 | 5.395.361 | 103.757 | 2.282.653 | 1.825.635 | 229.604 | 377.067 | 10,214,077 |
| 1938 | 11.411.114 | 95.093 | 2.092.038 | 4.798.985 | 772.275 | 637.280 | 19,806,784 | 6.037.748 | 116.111 | 2.554.432 | 2.043.000 | 256.942 | 421.962 | 11,430,193 |
| 1939 | 11.614.208 | 96.785 | 2.129.271 | 4.897.616 | 788.147 | 648.622 | 20,174,650 | 6.153.523 | 118.337 | 2.603.414 | 2.082.175 | 261.869 | 430.053 | 11,649,370 |

| Year | Clothing | | | | | | | Rent | | | | | | |
|---|---|---|---|---|---|---|---|---|---|---|---|---|---|---|
| | European Standard | Malay Clerical Standard | Chinese, Indian, Eurasian Clerical Grades Standard | Chinese Labor Standard | Malay Labor Standard | Indian Labor Standard | Total | European Standard | Malay Clerical Standard | Chinese, Indian, Eurasian Clerical Grades Standard | Chinese Labor Standard | Malay Labor Standard | Indian Labor Standard | Total |
| 1947 | 12.729.149 | 188.357 | 1.737.312 | 6.546.285 | 874.505 | 633.385 | 22,708,993 | 7.661.571 | 172.288 | 1.550.592 | 2.872.240 | 299.869 | 420.183 | 12,976,743 |
| 1948 | 14.218.619 | 203.400 | 1.940.600 | 7.069.120 | 944.349 | 683.972 | 25,060,060 | 8.415.776 | 189.248 | 1.703.232 | 3.154.983 | 329.388 | 461.546 | 14,254,174 |
| 1949 | 17.738.411 | 235.127 | 2.420.991 | 8.171.768 | 1.091.650 | 790.658 | 30,448,605 | 10.113.781 | 227.432 | 2.046.884 | 3.791.547 | 395.847 | 554.669 | 17,130,160 |
| 1950 | 17.104.959 | 234.260 | 2.334.536 | 8.141.626 | 1.087.623 | 787.742 | 29,690,745 | 9.914.543 | 222.951 | 2.006.561 | 3.716.855 | 388.049 | 543.743 | 16,792,701 |
| 1951 | 15.948.640 | 228.975 | 2.176.718 | 7.957.961 | 1.063.088 | 769.971 | 28,145,354 | 9.467.595 | 212.901 | 1.916.105 | 3.549.299 | 370.556 | 519.231 | 16,035,686 |
| 1952 | 16.357.393 | 237.547 | 2.232.506 | 8.255.871 | 1.102.885 | 798.796 | 28,984,997 | 9.766.131 | 219.614 | 1.976.524 | 3.661.217 | 382.240 | 535.603 | 16,541,329 |
| 1953 | 20.276.166 | 277.156 | 2.767.352 | 9.632.474 | 1.286.783 | 931.989 | 35,171,919 | 11.750.190 | 264.230 | 2.378.069 | 4.405.019 | 459.895 | 644.415 | 19,901,819 |
| 1954 | 21.486.865 | 292.332 | 2.932.591 | 10.159.906 | 1.357.241 | 983.020 | 37,211,956 | 12.422.689 | 279.353 | 2.514.173 | 4.657.132 | 486.216 | 681.297 | 21,040,860 |
| 1955 | 22.018.661 | 302.041 | 3.005.173 | 10.497.341 | 1.402.318 | 1.015.669 | 38,241,202 | 12.782.712 | 287.449 | 2.587.037 | 4.792.100 | 500.307 | 701.041 | 21,650,647 |
| 1956 | 26.052.286 | 341.357 | 3.555.694 | 11.863.753 | 1.584.855 | 1.147.876 | 44,545,819 | 14.785.499 | 332.486 | 2.992.372 | 5.542.923 | 578.695 | 810.880 | 25,042,856 |
| 1957 | 25.706.033 | 230.689 | 4.807.857 | 10.923.900 | 1.785.079 | 1.163.604 | 44,617,162 | 14.788.541 | 221.703 | 4.101.502 | 5.035.858 | 643.127 | 811.047 | 25,601,778 |
| 1958 | 26.860.940 | 241.252 | 5.023.862 | 11.424.079 | 1.866.813 | 1.216.883 | 46,633,828 | 15.459.313 | 231.759 | 4.287.536 | 5.264.272 | 672.298 | 847.834 | 26,763,010 |
| 1959 | 25.268.030 | 236.849 | 4.725.936 | 11.215.593 | 1.832.744 | 1.194.675 | 44,473,828 | 14.859.864 | 222.772 | 4.121.283 | 5.060.145 | 646.229 | 814.959 | 25,725,251 |
| 1960 | 31.025.587 | 272.499 | 5.802.785 | 12.903.726 | 2.108.603 | 1.374.494 | 53,487,692 | 17.671.171 | 264.918 | 4.900.980 | 6.017.464 | 768.487 | 969.139 | 30,592,159 |

*(Continued)*

**Appendix Table 7:** Total Private Final Consumption Expenditure by Major Object of Consumption and Standard in Current Prices, Singapore, 1900–39 and 1947–1960

(Straits $)

| | Clothing | | | | | | | Rent | | | | | | |
|---|---|---|---|---|---|---|---|---|---|---|---|---|---|---|
| Year | European Standard | Eurasian Standard | Asiatic Clerical Standard | Chinese Labor Standard | Malay Labor Standard | Indian Labor Standard | Total | European Standard | Eurasian Standard | Asiatic Clerical Standard | Chinese Labor Standard | Malay Labor Standard | Indian Labor Standard | Total |
| 1899 | 1,928.921 | 34.828 | 296.036 | 913.540 | 280.186 | 90.768 | 3,544.279 | 1,049.375 | 43.724 | 371.654 | 363.298 | 87.081 | 61.794 | 1,976.925 |
| 1900 | 1,944.855 | 35.115 | 298.481 | 927.894 | 284.588 | 91.518 | 3,582.451 | 1,046.185 | 43.591 | 370.524 | 362.193 | 86.817 | 61.606 | 1,970.915 |
| 1901 | 2,111.789 | 38.130 | 324.101 | 1,011.641 | 310.274 | 99.373 | 3,895.308 | 1,084.573 | 45.191 | 384.120 | 375.483 | 90.002 | 63.867 | 2,043.236 |
| 1902 | 2,151.594 | 38.848 | 330.210 | 1,046.270 | 320.894 | 101.247 | 3,989.063 | 1,104.127 | 46.005 | 391.045 | 382.253 | 91.625 | 65.018 | 2,080.073 |
| 1903 | 2,337.290 | 42.201 | 358.709 | 1,142.156 | 350.303 | 109.985 | 4,340.644 | 1,146.330 | 47.764 | 405.992 | 396.864 | 95.127 | 67.503 | 2,159.579 |
| 1904 | 2,334.473 | 42.150 | 358.277 | 1,141.265 | 350.030 | 109.852 | 4,336.047 | 1,200.835 | 50.035 | 425.296 | 415.734 | 99.650 | 70.713 | 2,262.263 |
| 1905 | 2,300.023 | 41.528 | 352.990 | 1,132.739 | 347.415 | 108.231 | 4,282.927 | 1,240.873 | 51.703 | 439.476 | 429.595 | 102.973 | 73.071 | 2,337.691 |
| 1906 | 2,305.847 | 41.633 | 353.883 | 1,128.620 | 346.152 | 108.505 | 4,284.640 | 1,317.418 | 54.892 | 466.586 | 456.095 | 109.325 | 77.578 | 2,481.895 |
| 1907 | 2,334.320 | 42.147 | 358.253 | 1,142.092 | 350.283 | 109.845 | 4,336.941 | 1,382.617 | 57.609 | 489.677 | 478.667 | 114.735 | 81.418 | 2,604.723 |
| 1908 | 2,516.708 | 45.441 | 386.245 | 1,227.553 | 376.495 | 118.428 | 4,670.869 | 1,458.920 | 60.788 | 516.701 | 505.084 | 121.067 | 85.911 | 2,748.470 |
| 1909 | 2,348.477 | 42.403 | 360.426 | 1,134.594 | 347.984 | 110.511 | 4,344.395 | 1,483.334 | 61.806 | 525.347 | 513.536 | 123.093 | 87.348 | 2,794.464 |
| 1910 | 2,617.633 | 47.263 | 401.734 | 1,274.222 | 390.808 | 123.177 | 4,854.838 | 1,497.671 | 62.403 | 530.425 | 518.500 | 124.283 | 88.193 | 2,821.474 |
| 1911 | 2,451.054 | 44.255 | 389.445 | 1,253.777 | 358.952 | 115.338 | 4,612.821 | 1,413.662 | 58.903 | 518.343 | 495.173 | 110.794 | 83.246 | 2,680.120 |
| 1912 | 2,461.380 | 44.442 | 391.086 | 1,267.747 | 362.951 | 115.824 | 4,643.429 | 1,452.722 | 60.530 | 532.665 | 508.855 | 113.855 | 85.546 | 2,754.173 |
| 1913 | 2,984.482 | 53.886 | 474.201 | 1,549.951 | 443.745 | 140.439 | 5,646.705 | 1,569.881 | 65.412 | 575.623 | 549.893 | 123.037 | 92.445 | 2,976.292 |
| 1914 | 3,252.027 | 58.717 | 516.711 | 1,656.756 | 474.323 | 153.029 | 6,111.564 | 1,855.955 | 77.331 | 680.517 | 650.098 | 145.458 | 109.291 | 3,518.650 |
| 1915 | 4,360.216 | 78.726 | 692.790 | 2,279.471 | 652.604 | 205.177 | 8,268.983 | 1,827.636 | 76.151 | 670.133 | 640.178 | 143.239 | 107.623 | 3,464.960 |
| 1916 | 4,943.690 | 89.261 | 785.497 | 2,648.538 | 758.266 | 232.633 | 9,457.886 | 1,838.075 | 76.586 | 673.961 | 643.835 | 144.057 | 108.238 | 3,484.752 |
| 1917 | 5,194.086 | 93.782 | 825.283 | 2,646.386 | 757.650 | 244.416 | 9,761.603 | 2,106.508 | 87.771 | 772.386 | 737.861 | 165.095 | 124.045 | 3,993.667 |
| 1918 | 7,322.652 | 132.215 | 1,163.488 | 3,678.837 | 1,053.237 | 344.578 | 13,695.007 | 2,501.224 | 104.218 | 917.116 | 876.121 | 196.030 | 147.288 | 4,741.997 |
| 1919 | 8,137.742 | 146.931 | 1,292.997 | 4,290.595 | 1,228.381 | 382.934 | 15,479.580 | 2,572.247 | 107.177 | 943.157 | 900.999 | 201.597 | 151.471 | 4,876.648 |
| 1920 | 10,238.046 | 184.854 | 1,626.712 | 5,488.584 | 1,571.360 | 481.767 | 19,591.322 | 3,307.149 | 137.798 | 1,212.621 | 1,158.418 | 259.194 | 194.746 | 6,269.926 |
| 1921 | 11,841.303 | 197.355 | 2,170.906 | 5,394.285 | 1,175.127 | 587.826 | 21,366.802 | 4,712.102 | 181.235 | 1,993.582 | 1,531.168 | 260.686 | 292.725 | 8,971.498 |
| 1922 | 10,456.300 | 174.272 | 1,916.988 | 4,596.412 | 1,001.313 | 519.072 | 18,664.358 | 5,888.314 | 226.474 | 2,491.210 | 1,913.371 | 325.757 | 365.794 | 11,210.919 |
| 1923 | 9,958.999 | 165.983 | 1,825.816 | 4,332.463 | 943.813 | 494.385 | 17,721.459 | 7,001.195 | 269.277 | 2,962.044 | 2,274.994 | 387.324 | 434.928 | 13,329.763 |
| 1924 | 9,948.604 | 165.810 | 1,823.911 | 4,320.837 | 941.280 | 493.869 | 17,694.311 | 7,551.596 | 290.446 | 3,194.906 | 2,453.844 | 417.774 | 469.121 | 14,377.686 |
| 1925 | 10,204.542 | 170.076 | 1,870.833 | 4,473.869 | 974.618 | 506.574 | 18,200.511 | 8,018.871 | 308.418 | 3,392.599 | 2,605.682 | 443.625 | 498.149 | 15,267.344 |
| 1926 | 10,223.685 | 170.395 | 1,874.342 | 4,543.156 | 989.711 | 507.524 | 18,308.814 | 8,496.106 | 326.773 | 3,594.507 | 2,760.757 | 470.027 | 527.795 | 16,175.965 |
| 1927 | 11,106.142 | 185.102 | 2,036.126 | 4,824.867 | 1,051.081 | 551.331 | 19,754.651 | 9,930.205 | 381.931 | 4,201.241 | 3,226.758 | 549.365 | 616.885 | 18,906.384 |
| 1928 | 11,655.779 | 194.263 | 2,136.893 | 4,997.153 | 1,088.613 | 578.617 | 20,651.318 | 11,525.328 | 443.282 | 4,876.100 | 3,745.083 | 637.611 | 715.977 | 21,943.381 |
| 1929 | 11,192.426 | 186.540 | 2,051.945 | 4,804.209 | 1,046.581 | 555.615 | 19,837.316 | 12,001.198 | 461.585 | 5,077.430 | 3,899.714 | 663.938 | 745.539 | 22,849.404 |
| 1930 | 10,772.146 | 179.536 | 1,974.894 | 4,656.444 | 1,014.391 | 534.751 | 19,132.162 | 10,772.146 | 414.313 | 4,557.447 | 3,500.342 | 595.943 | 669.188 | 20,509.379 |
| 1931 | 9,190.219 | 76.585 | 1,684.873 | 4,335.409 | 697.674 | 513.249 | 16,498.009 | 8,346.614 | 160.512 | 3,531.260 | 2,824.254 | 355.197 | 583.322 | 15,801.159 |
| 1932 | 8,384.352 | 69.870 | 1,537.131 | 3,868.276 | 622.501 | 468.243 | 14,950.374 | 6,932.753 | 133.322 | 2,933.088 | 2,345.844 | 295.029 | 484.511 | 13,124.547 |
| 1933 | 8,440.766 | 70.340 | 1,547.474 | 3,726.145 | 599.628 | 471.394 | 14,855.747 | 6,289.972 | 120.961 | 2,661.142 | 2,128.345 | 267.675 | 439.589 | 11,907.684 |
| 1934 | 7,860.931 | 65.508 | 1,441.171 | 3,539.215 | 569.547 | 439.012 | 13,915.383 | 6,177.747 | 118.803 | 2,613.662 | 2,090.372 | 262.899 | 431.746 | 11,695.229 |
| 1935 | 8,922.564 | 74.355 | 1,635.803 | 3,939.339 | 633.937 | 498.301 | 15,704.299 | 7,005.723 | 134.725 | 2,963.960 | 2,370.535 | 298.135 | 489.611 | 13,262.689 |
| 1936 | 10,154.225 | 84.619 | 1,861.608 | 4,340.192 | 698.444 | 567.086 | 17,706.173 | 7,894.962 | 151.826 | 3,340.176 | 2,671.428 | 335.977 | 551.758 | 14,946.127 |
| 1937 | 11,427.130 | 95.226 | 2,094.974 | 4,868.808 | 783.511 | 638.174 | 19,907.823 | 8,728.801 | 167.862 | 3,692.954 | 2,953.575 | 371.462 | 610.032 | 16,524.686 |
| 1938 | 12,999.532 | 108.329 | 2,383.247 | 5,467.000 | 879.775 | 725.989 | 22,563.871 | 10,239.108 | 196.906 | 4,331.930 | 3,464.619 | 435.734 | 715.584 | 19,383.882 |
| 1939 | 14,381.984 | 119.850 | 2,636.697 | 6,064.765 | 975.970 | 803.195 | 24,982.460 | 11,215.586 | 215.684 | 4,745.056 | 3,795.031 | 477.289 | 783.827 | 21,232.473 |

| | Clothing | | | | | | | Rent | | | | | | |
|---|---|---|---|---|---|---|---|---|---|---|---|---|---|---|
| Year | European Standard | Malay Clerical Standard | Chinese, Indian, Eurasian Clerical Grades Standard | Chinese Labor Standard | Malay Labor Standard | Indian Labor Standard | Total | European Standard | Malay Clerical Standard | Chinese, Indian, Eurasian Clerical Grades Standard | Chinese Labor Standard | Malay Labor Standard | Indian Labor Standard | Total |
| 1947 | 80,002.359 | 1,183.817 | 10,918.961 | 41,143.226 | 5,496.240 | 3,980.807 | 142,725.410 | 42,063.009 | 945.883 | 8,512.947 | 15,768.966 | 1,646.320 | 2,306.859 | 71,243.984 |
| 1948 | 54,870.439 | 784.933 | 7,488.881 | 27,280.126 | 3,644.297 | 2,639.485 | 96,708.161 | 38,776.736 | 871.984 | 7,847.853 | 14,536.978 | 1,517.697 | 2,126.630 | 65,677.877 |
| 1949 | 69,015.383 | 914.815 | 9,419.425 | 31,794.152 | 4,247.316 | 3,076.239 | 118,467.331 | 51,639.140 | 1,161.224 | 10,451.018 | 19,358.954 | 2,021.124 | 2,832.042 | 87,463.502 |
| 1950 | 71,069.104 | 973.321 | 9,699.723 | 33,827.502 | 4,518.948 | 3,272.975 | 123,361.573 | 52,254.829 | 1,175.069 | 10,575.625 | 19,589.769 | 2,045.221 | 2,865.808 | 88,506.322 |
| 1951 | 83,879.148 | 1,204.255 | 11,448.076 | 41,853.538 | 5,591.129 | 4,049.534 | 148,025.680 | 60,814.625 | 1,367.556 | 12,308.004 | 22,798.744 | 2,380.247 | 3,335.252 | 103,004.428 |
| 1952 | 84,153.642 | 1,222.103 | 11,485.540 | 42,473.861 | 5,673.997 | 4,109.553 | 149,118.696 | 66,485.468 | 1,495.078 | 13,455.701 | 24,924.681 | 2,602.200 | 3,646.258 | 112,609.386 |
| 1953 | 95,832.640 | 1,309.941 | 13,079.524 | 45,526.626 | 6,081.810 | 4,404.923 | 166,235.464 | 84,508.170 | 1,900.360 | 17,103.236 | 31,681.197 | 3,307.597 | 4,634.676 | 143,135.235 |
| 1954 | 96,377.177 | 1,311.224 | 13,153.844 | 45,571.240 | 6,087.770 | 4,409.239 | 166,910.495 | 91,390.893 | 2,055.133 | 18,496.200 | 34,261.455 | 3,576.983 | 5,012.145 | 154,792.809 |
| 1955 | 96,694.939 | 1,326.411 | 13,197.214 | 46,099.065 | 6,158.281 | 4,460.309 | 167,936.219 | 92,635.925 | 2,083.131 | 18,748.177 | 34,728.204 | 3,625.712 | 5,080.426 | 156,901.576 |
| 1956 | 114,148.908 | 1,495.664 | 15,579.383 | 51,981.406 | 6,944.091 | 5,029.454 | 195,178.906 | 113,644.003 | 2,555.546 | 22,999.910 | 42,603.905 | 4,447.955 | 6,232.571 | 192,483.889 |
| 1957 | 114,355.030 | 1,026.237 | 21,388.077 | 48,595.710 | 7,941.043 | 5,176.372 | 198,482.469 | 116,915.026 | 1,752.735 | 32,425.590 | 39,812.410 | 5,084.424 | 6,411.963 | 202,402.147 |
| 1958 | 119,143.258 | 1,070.087 | 22,283.630 | 50,672.165 | 8,280.357 | 5,397.554 | 206,847.051 | 124,764.207 | 1,870.406 | 34,602.508 | 42,485.247 | 5,425.770 | 6,842.435 | 215,990.572 |
| 1959 | 110,210.741 | 1,033.057 | 20,612.961 | 48,918.686 | 7,993.820 | 5,210.775 | 193,980.042 | 121,558.016 | 1,822.340 | 33,713.292 | 41,393.461 | 5,286.339 | 6,666.598 | 210,440.046 |
| 1960 | 135,932.938 | 1,193.904 | 25,423.841 | 56,535.315 | 9,238.457 | 6,022.092 | 234,346.547 | 144,555.328 | 2,167.105 | 40,091.441 | 49,224.605 | 6,286.450 | 7,927.838 | 250,252.768 |

*(Continued)*

**Appendix Table 7:** Total Private Final Consumption Expenditure by Major Object of Consumption and Standard in Constant Prices, Singapore, 1900–39 and 1947–1960

(Straits $)

| Year | Servant European Standard | Servant Eurasian Standard | Servant Asiatic Clerical Standard | Servant Total | Transport European Standard | Transport Eurasian Standard | Transport Asiatic Clerical Standard | Transport Total | Clubbing European Standard | Clubbing Total | Total from Indirect Approach |
|---|---|---|---|---|---|---|---|---|---|---|---|
| 1899 | 5,258,236 | 32,102 | 272,863 | 5,563,201 | 2,762,442 | 63,378 | 538,711 | 3,364,531 | 1,726,248 | 1,726,248 | 43,519,395 |
| 1900 | 5,124,542 | 31,285 | 265,926 | 5,421,753 | 2,692,205 | 61,766 | 525,014 | 3,278,985 | 1,682,357 | 1,682,357 | 42,565,436 |
| 1901 | 5,201,793 | 31,757 | 269,934 | 5,503,484 | 2,732,789 | 62,697 | 532,928 | 3,328,415 | 1,707,718 | 1,707,718 | 43,292,894 |
| 1902 | 5,156,672 | 31,482 | 267,593 | 5,455,746 | 2,709,085 | 62,154 | 528,305 | 3,299,543 | 1,692,905 | 1,692,905 | 43,233,707 |
| 1903 | 5,239,718 | 31,989 | 271,902 | 5,543,609 | 2,752,714 | 63,155 | 536,813 | 3,352,682 | 1,720,168 | 1,720,168 | 44,035,842 |
| 1904 | 5,383,876 | 32,869 | 279,383 | 5,696,128 | 2,828,448 | 64,892 | 551,583 | 3,444,922 | 1,767,494 | 1,767,494 | 45,256,813 |
| 1905 | 5,437,920 | 33,199 | 282,188 | 5,753,306 | 2,856,840 | 65,543 | 557,119 | 3,479,503 | 1,785,237 | 1,785,237 | 45,877,106 |
| 1906 | 5,681,407 | 34,685 | 294,823 | 6,010,915 | 2,984,757 | 68,478 | 582,065 | 3,635,300 | 1,865,172 | 1,865,172 | 47,786,197 |
| 1907 | 5,850,629 | 35,718 | 303,604 | 6,189,951 | 3,073,659 | 70,518 | 599,402 | 3,743,578 | 1,920,727 | 1,920,727 | 49,199,686 |
| 1908 | 6,065,542 | 37,030 | 314,756 | 6,417,329 | 3,186,564 | 73,108 | 621,420 | 3,881,092 | 1,991,281 | 1,991,281 | 50,930,179 |
| 1909 | 6,392,082 | 39,024 | 331,701 | 6,762,807 | 3,358,114 | 77,044 | 654,874 | 4,090,032 | 2,098,482 | 2,098,482 | 53,421,376 |
| 1910 | 6,453,095 | 39,396 | 334,868 | 6,827,359 | 3,390,168 | 77,779 | 661,125 | 4,129,072 | 2,118,513 | 2,118,513 | 54,131,509 |
| 1911 | 6,067,692 | 37,043 | 325,981 | 6,430,716 | 3,187,694 | 73,134 | 643,580 | 3,904,408 | 1,991,987 | 1,991,987 | 51,964,143 |
| 1912 | 6,163,108 | 37,626 | 331,107 | 6,531,840 | 3,237,821 | 74,284 | 653,701 | 3,965,806 | 2,023,312 | 2,023,312 | 52,961,585 |
| 1913 | 6,237,336 | 38,079 | 335,095 | 6,610,510 | 3,276,817 | 75,179 | 661,574 | 4,013,570 | 2,047,680 | 2,047,680 | 53,820,424 |
| 1914 | 6,764,493 | 41,297 | 363,416 | 7,169,206 | 3,553,762 | 81,533 | 717,488 | 4,352,783 | 2,220,743 | 2,220,743 | 57,816,998 |
| 1915 | 6,557,037 | 40,031 | 352,271 | 6,949,339 | 3,444,774 | 79,032 | 695,484 | 4,219,290 | 2,152,636 | 2,152,636 | 56,769,278 |
| 1916 | 6,376,054 | 38,926 | 342,547 | 6,757,527 | 3,349,694 | 76,851 | 676,287 | 4,102,832 | 2,093,221 | 2,093,221 | 55,883,416 |
| 1917 | 7,502,043 | 45,800 | 403,040 | 7,950,883 | 3,941,238 | 90,422 | 795,717 | 4,827,377 | 2,462,876 | 2,462,876 | 64,138,077 |
| 1918 | 8,025,152 | 48,994 | 431,144 | 8,505,289 | 4,216,056 | 96,727 | 851,202 | 5,163,985 | 2,634,610 | 2,634,610 | 68,136,920 |
| 1919 | 7,372,472 | 45,009 | 396,079 | 7,813,560 | 3,873,167 | 88,861 | 781,974 | 4,744,002 | 2,420,339 | 2,420,339 | 64,121,202 |
| 1920 | 7,303,157 | 44,586 | 392,355 | 7,740,098 | 3,836,752 | 88,025 | 774,622 | 4,699,399 | 2,397,583 | 2,397,583 | 64,050,554 |
| 1921 | 10,384,029 | 58,518 | 643,699 | 11,086,246 | 5,455,304 | 115,531 | 1,270,846 | 6,841,682 | 3,409,015 | 3,409,015 | 84,608,527 |
| 1922 | 11,898,246 | 67,051 | 737,564 | 12,702,861 | 6,250,806 | 132,378 | 1,456,163 | 7,839,348 | 3,906,123 | 3,906,123 | 95,328,352 |
| 1923 | 12,662,326 | 71,357 | 784,929 | 13,518,611 | 6,652,219 | 140,880 | 1,549,675 | 8,342,774 | 4,156,966 | 4,156,966 | 100,954,809 |
| 1924 | 13,172,465 | 74,232 | 816,552 | 14,063,248 | 6,920,224 | 146,555 | 1,612,108 | 8,678,887 | 4,324,442 | 4,324,442 | 104,941,058 |
| 1925 | 13,425,879 | 75,660 | 832,261 | 14,333,800 | 7,053,356 | 149,375 | 1,643,122 | 8,845,853 | 4,407,636 | 4,407,636 | 107,434,644 |
| 1926 | 13,502,307 | 76,091 | 836,998 | 14,415,397 | 7,093,508 | 150,225 | 1,652,476 | 8,896,209 | 4,432,727 | 4,432,727 | 108,737,627 |
| 1927 | 14,865,972 | 83,776 | 921,531 | 15,871,278 | 7,809,917 | 165,397 | 1,819,367 | 9,794,681 | 4,880,410 | 4,880,410 | 118,452,875 |
| 1928 | 15,961,166 | 89,947 | 989,421 | 17,040,534 | 8,385,282 | 177,582 | 1,953,402 | 10,516,267 | 5,239,956 | 5,239,956 | 126,394,859 |
| 1929 | 16,511,488 | 93,049 | 1,023,535 | 17,628,073 | 8,674,397 | 183,705 | 2,020,754 | 10,878,856 | 5,420,624 | 5,420,624 | 130,825,590 |
| 1930 | 16,027,883 | 90,323 | 993,557 | 17,111,764 | 8,420,333 | 178,324 | 1,961,568 | 10,560,225 | 5,261,859 | 5,261,859 | 127,413,452 |
| 1931 | 13,997,596 | 39,441 | 867,701 | 14,904,738 | 7,353,711 | 77,868 | 1,713,092 | 9,144,670 | 4,595,328 | 4,595,328 | 113,528,085 |
| 1932 | 14,367,695 | 40,484 | 890,643 | 15,298,822 | 7,548,144 | 79,927 | 1,758,386 | 9,386,457 | 4,716,829 | 4,716,829 | 115,311,434 |
| 1933 | 15,177,534 | 42,766 | 940,845 | 16,161,144 | 7,973,597 | 84,432 | 1,857,498 | 9,915,527 | 4,982,694 | 4,982,694 | 119,325,820 |
| 1934 | 14,759,922 | 41,589 | 914,957 | 15,716,468 | 7,754,203 | 82,109 | 1,806,389 | 9,642,700 | 4,845,595 | 4,845,595 | 117,119,474 |
| 1935 | 16,901,906 | 47,624 | 1,047,737 | 17,997,268 | 8,879,506 | 94,024 | 2,068,535 | 11,042,065 | 5,548,796 | 5,548,796 | 132,896,572 |
| 1936 | 19,355,820 | 54,539 | 1,199,854 | 20,610,212 | 10,168,682 | 107,675 | 2,368,856 | 12,645,213 | 6,354,401 | 6,354,401 | 149,927,623 |
| 1937 | 21,073,265 | 59,378 | 1,306,317 | 22,438,960 | 11,070,951 | 117,229 | 2,579,045 | 13,767,226 | 6,918,228 | 6,918,228 | 162,992,008 |
| 1938 | 23,736,088 | 66,881 | 1,471,383 | 25,274,352 | 12,469,879 | 132,042 | 2,904,934 | 15,506,855 | 7,792,417 | 7,792,417 | 182,489,473 |
| 1939 | 24,158,540 | 68,071 | 1,497,571 | 25,724,182 | 12,691,816 | 134,393 | 2,956,636 | 15,782,844 | 7,931,105 | 7,931,105 | 185,968,581 |

| Year | Servant European Standard | Servant Malay Clerical Standard | Servant Chinese, Indian, Eurasian Clerical Grades Standard | Servant Total | Transport European Standard | Transport Malay Clerical Standard | Transport Chinese, Indian, Eurasian Clerical Grades Standard | Transport Total | Clubbing European Standard | Clubbing Total | Total from Indirect Approach |
|---|---|---|---|---|---|---|---|---|---|---|---|
| 1947 | 22,846,173 | 454,667 | 4,091,999 | 27,392,838 | 15,978,038 | 612,284 | 6,198,403 | 22,788,724 | 5,299,353 | 5,299,353 | 204,158,665 |
| 1948 | 25,519,462 | 507,868 | 4,570,814 | 30,598,144 | 17,847,669 | 683,928 | 6,923,694 | 25,455,291 | 5,919,444 | 5,919,444 | 224,760,204 |
| 1949 | 31,836,756 | 633,590 | 5,702,310 | 38,172,656 | 22,265,825 | 853,234 | 8,637,641 | 31,756,699 | 7,384,791 | 7,384,791 | 271,573,818 |
| 1950 | 30,699,842 | 610,964 | 5,498,676 | 36,809,482 | 21,470,696 | 822,764 | 8,329,185 | 30,622,644 | 7,121,074 | 7,121,074 | 265,512,804 |
| 1951 | 28,624,490 | 569,662 | 5,126,958 | 34,321,110 | 20,019,247 | 767,144 | 7,766,120 | 28,552,511 | 6,639,680 | 6,639,680 | 252,620,534 |
| 1952 | 29,358,116 | 584,262 | 5,258,359 | 35,200,737 | 20,532,327 | 786,805 | 7,965,161 | 29,284,293 | 6,809,850 | 6,809,850 | 260,375,877 |
| 1953 | 36,391,499 | 724,235 | 6,518,114 | 43,633,848 | 25,451,297 | 975,302 | 9,873,390 | 36,299,989 | 8,441,300 | 8,441,300 | 314,580,444 |
| 1954 | 38,564,451 | 767,479 | 6,907,313 | 46,239,244 | 26,971,005 | 1,033,538 | 10,462,934 | 38,467,477 | 8,945,334 | 8,945,334 | 332,705,404 |
| 1955 | 39,518,915 | 786,474 | 7,078,268 | 47,383,657 | 27,638,533 | 1,059,117 | 10,721,890 | 39,419,541 | 9,166,729 | 9,166,729 | 342,127,933 |
| 1956 | 46,758,431 | 930,549 | 8,374,945 | 56,063,925 | 32,701,669 | 1,253,138 | 12,686,046 | 46,640,853 | 10,845,993 | 10,845,993 | 397,126,531 |
| 1957 | 46,136,980 | 612,121 | 11,324,242 | 58,073,343 | 32,267,041 | 824,322 | 17,153,529 | 50,244,893 | 10,701,842 | 10,701,842 | 406,315,093 |
| 1958 | 48,209,797 | 639,622 | 11,833,011 | 60,682,431 | 33,716,717 | 861,357 | 17,924,193 | 52,502,267 | 11,182,649 | 11,182,649 | 424,714,005 |
| 1959 | 45,350,856 | 601,691 | 11,131,289 | 57,083,836 | 31,717,246 | 810,277 | 16,861,251 | 49,388,773 | 10,519,494 | 10,519,494 | 406,724,469 |
| 1960 | 55,684,472 | 738,792 | 13,667,657 | 70,090,921 | 38,944,316 | 994,906 | 20,703,245 | 60,642,467 | 12,916,459 | 12,916,459 | 486,227,008 |

(*Continued*)

**Appendix Table 7:** Total Private Final Consumption Expenditure by Major Object of Consumption and Standard in Current Prices, Singapore, 1900–39 and 1947–1960

(Straits $)

| Year | Servant | | | | Transport | | | | Clubbing | | Total from Indirect Approach |
|---|---|---|---|---|---|---|---|---|---|---|---|
| | European Standard | Eurasian Standard | Asiatic Clerical Standard | Total | European Standard | Eurasian Standard | Asiatic Clerical Standard | Total | European Standard | Total | |
| 1899 | 3,661,986 | 22,356 | 190,030 | 3,874,372 | 3,029,367 | 69,502 | 590,764 | 3,689,633 | 1,522,127 | 1,522,127 | 35,367,896 |
| 1900 | 3,843,406 | 23,464 | 199,444 | 4,066,315 | 2,904,213 | 66,630 | 566,358 | 3,537,200 | 1,495,309 | 1,495,309 | 35,235,172 |
| 1901 | 3,808,456 | 23,251 | 197,630 | 4,029,337 | 2,936,201 | 67,364 | 572,596 | 3,576,161 | 1,521,632 | 1,521,632 | 36,191,806 |
| 1902 | 4,235,837 | 25,860 | 219,808 | 4,481,506 | 2,904,887 | 66,646 | 566,489 | 3,538,022 | 1,540,360 | 1,540,360 | 37,509,586 |
| 1903 | 4,304,054 | 26,276 | 223,348 | 4,553,679 | 2,954,639 | 67,787 | 576,191 | 3,598,617 | 1,576,648 | 1,576,648 | 38,664,316 |
| 1904 | 4,230,188 | 25,825 | 219,515 | 4,475,529 | 3,032,877 | 69,582 | 591,449 | 3,693,908 | 1,625,589 | 1,625,589 | 39,775,731 |
| 1905 | 4,272,652 | 26,085 | 221,719 | 4,520,455 | 3,060,240 | 70,210 | 596,785 | 3,727,235 | 1,673,405 | 1,673,405 | 41,061,784 |
| 1906 | 4,666,870 | 28,491 | 242,176 | 4,937,537 | 3,200,484 | 73,428 | 624,134 | 3,898,046 | 1,718,521 | 1,718,521 | 42,131,085 |
| 1907 | 5,328,251 | 32,529 | 276,497 | 5,637,277 | 3,229,497 | 74,093 | 629,792 | 3,933,382 | 1,758,489 | 1,758,489 | 43,351,429 |
| 1908 | 5,523,976 | 33,724 | 286,653 | 5,844,353 | 3,334,377 | 76,499 | 650,245 | 4,061,122 | 1,837,625 | 1,837,625 | 45,486,428 |
| 1909 | 5,821,360 | 35,539 | 302,085 | 6,158,985 | 3,481,281 | 79,870 | 678,893 | 4,240,044 | 1,917,380 | 1,917,380 | 46,594,498 |
| 1910 | 5,876,926 | 35,879 | 304,969 | 6,217,773 | 3,499,882 | 80,297 | 682,521 | 4,262,699 | 1,954,977 | 1,954,977 | 48,090,016 |
| 1911 | 5,525,934 | 33,736 | 296,876 | 5,856,545 | 3,280,539 | 75,264 | 662,325 | 4,018,129 | 1,989,693 | 1,989,693 | 50,604,042 |
| 1912 | 5,612,830 | 34,266 | 301,544 | 5,948,640 | 3,335,619 | 76,528 | 673,446 | 4,085,593 | 2,052,994 | 2,052,994 | 52,471,788 |
| 1913 | 5,680,431 | 34,679 | 305,176 | 6,020,286 | 3,259,143 | 74,773 | 658,006 | 3,991,922 | 2,097,491 | 2,097,491 | 54,399,818 |
| 1914 | 6,764,493 | 41,297 | 363,416 | 7,169,206 | 3,553,762 | 81,533 | 717,488 | 4,352,783 | 2,220,743 | 2,220,743 | 57,816,998 |
| 1915 | 6,807,662 | 41,561 | 365,735 | 7,214,958 | 3,507,813 | 80,479 | 708,211 | 4,296,503 | 1,965,530 | 1,965,530 | 60,442,874 |
| 1916 | 6,619,761 | 40,414 | 355,640 | 7,015,815 | 3,454,539 | 79,256 | 697,455 | 4,231,250 | 2,172,126 | 2,172,126 | 63,080,903 |
| 1917 | 8,484,215 | 51,796 | 455,806 | 8,991,818 | 4,281,761 | 98,235 | 864,467 | 5,244,463 | 2,804,673 | 2,804,673 | 75,450,340 |
| 1918 | 9,373,377 | 57,225 | 503,576 | 9,934,178 | 4,743,063 | 108,818 | 957,602 | 5,809,483 | 3,530,377 | 3,530,377 | 95,437,500 |
| 1919 | 8,611,047 | 52,570 | 462,620 | 9,126,238 | 4,760,122 | 109,210 | 961,046 | 5,830,378 | 3,567,579 | 3,567,579 | 110,285,366 |
| 1920 | 11,356,409 | 69,331 | 610,112 | 12,035,852 | 4,865,002 | 111,616 | 982,221 | 5,958,838 | 3,920,048 | 3,920,048 | 141,683,342 |
| 1921 | 16,147,166 | 90,996 | 1,000,951 | 17,239,112 | 6,699,114 | 141,873 | 1,560,599 | 8,401,586 | 6,023,730 | 6,023,730 | 147,298,227 |
| 1922 | 18,501,772 | 104,265 | 1,146,912 | 19,752,948 | 7,000,903 | 148,264 | 1,630,903 | 8,780,069 | 6,929,463 | 6,929,463 | 148,711,561 |
| 1923 | 19,689,916 | 110,960 | 1,220,564 | 21,021,441 | 6,306,304 | 133,554 | 1,469,092 | 7,908,950 | 7,033,587 | 7,033,587 | 153,423,890 |
| 1924 | 20,483,183 | 115,431 | 1,269,738 | 21,868,351 | 6,878,702 | 145,676 | 1,602,435 | 8,626,814 | 7,096,409 | 7,096,409 | 158,912,225 |
| 1925 | 20,877,242 | 117,651 | 1,294,165 | 22,289,059 | 7,427,184 | 157,292 | 1,730,208 | 9,314,683 | 7,237,339 | 7,237,339 | 166,502,015 |
| 1926 | 20,996,088 | 118,321 | 1,301,533 | 22,415,942 | 7,341,781 | 155,483 | 1,710,312 | 9,207,576 | 7,167,720 | 7,167,720 | 174,066,084 |
| 1927 | 23,116,586 | 130,271 | 1,432,981 | 24,679,838 | 7,356,941 | 155,804 | 1,713,844 | 9,226,590 | 7,784,254 | 7,784,254 | 186,892,052 |
| 1928 | 24,819,613 | 139,868 | 1,538,550 | 26,498,031 | 7,806,698 | 165,329 | 1,818,618 | 9,790,645 | 8,357,730 | 8,357,730 | 197,922,388 |
| 1929 | 25,675,365 | 144,691 | 1,591,598 | 27,411,653 | 7,780,935 | 164,783 | 1,812,616 | 9,758,334 | 8,418,228 | 8,418,228 | 200,496,066 |
| 1930 | 24,506,633 | 138,104 | 1,519,149 | 26,163,886 | 7,199,385 | 152,467 | 1,677,140 | 9,028,992 | 8,213,762 | 8,213,762 | 185,828,517 |
| 1931 | 19,316,682 | 54,429 | 1,197,427 | 20,568,538 | 7,074,270 | 74,909 | 1,647,994 | 8,797,173 | 7,375,501 | 7,375,501 | 141,972,802 |
| 1932 | 17,916,516 | 50,483 | 1,110,632 | 19,077,631 | 6,717,849 | 71,135 | 1,564,964 | 8,353,947 | 7,551,643 | 7,551,643 | 127,137,902 |
| 1933 | 17,575,584 | 49,523 | 1,089,498 | 18,714,605 | 6,809,452 | 72,105 | 1,586,303 | 8,467,860 | 7,892,588 | 7,892,588 | 122,463,280 |
| 1934 | 18,258,023 | 51,446 | 1,131,802 | 19,441,270 | 6,552,301 | 69,382 | 1,526,398 | 8,148,081 | 7,728,723 | 7,728,723 | 123,219,974 |
| 1935 | 21,533,029 | 60,674 | 1,334,817 | 22,928,520 | 7,316,713 | 77,476 | 1,704,473 | 9,098,661 | 8,750,451 | 8,750,451 | 145,133,879 |
| 1936 | 24,330,265 | 68,555 | 1,508,216 | 25,907,036 | 8,134,945 | 86,140 | 1,895,085 | 10,116,171 | 10,001,827 | 10,001,827 | 161,195,569 |
| 1937 | 27,395,245 | 77,191 | 1,698,212 | 29,170,648 | 9,011,754 | 95,425 | 2,099,343 | 11,206,522 | 10,910,045 | 10,910,045 | 185,309,768 |
| 1938 | 30,429,665 | 85,742 | 1,886,313 | 32,401,719 | 10,162,951 | 107,615 | 2,367,521 | 12,638,087 | 12,421,112 | 12,421,112 | 201,334,103 |
| 1939 | 30,971,248 | 87,268 | 1,919,886 | 32,978,401 | 10,429,918 | 110,441 | 2,429,713 | 12,970,073 | 12,124,274 | 12,124,274 | 206,695,978 |

| Year | Servant | | | | Transport | | | | Clubbing | | Total from Indirect Approach |
|---|---|---|---|---|---|---|---|---|---|---|---|
| | European Standard | Malay Clerical Standard | Chinese, Indian, Eurasian Clerical Grades Standard | Total | European Standard | Malay Clerical Standard | Chinese, Indian, Eurasian Clerical Grades Standard | Total | European Standard | Total | |
| 1947 | 83,714,834 | 1,666,027 | 14,994,239 | 100,375,099 | 28,999,745 | 1,111,280 | 11,249,949 | 41,360,973 | 22,454,709 | 22,454,709 | 838,102,346 |
| 1948 | 78,268,306 | 1,557,634 | 14,018,707 | 93,844,646 | 27,113,007 | 1,038,979 | 10,518,022 | 38,670,008 | 26,287,488 | 26,287,488 | 774,274,320 |
| 1949 | 102,606,622 | 2,041,996 | 18,377,964 | 123,026,582 | 33,502,172 | 1,283,814 | 12,996,588 | 47,782,574 | 32,286,894 | 32,286,894 | 919,515,480 |
| 1950 | 102,765,611 | 2,045,160 | 18,406,441 | 123,217,212 | 33,413,802 | 1,280,428 | 12,962,306 | 47,656,536 | 33,419,962 | 33,419,962 | 953,414,910 |
| 1951 | 109,038,351 | 2,169,995 | 19,529,957 | 130,738,304 | 34,725,344 | 1,330,686 | 13,471,096 | 49,527,127 | 36,286,513 | 36,286,513 | 1,139,594,633 |
| 1952 | 124,388,376 | 2,475,479 | 22,279,314 | 149,143,169 | 35,304,987 | 1,352,898 | 13,695,958 | 50,353,844 | 38,413,686 | 38,413,686 | 1,222,757,783 |
| 1953 | 163,109,079 | 3,246,068 | 29,214,614 | 195,569,761 | 42,424,734 | 1,625,729 | 16,457,941 | 60,508,404 | 46,971,319 | 46,971,319 | 1,439,620,781 |
| 1954 | 175,329,712 | 3,489,274 | 31,403,462 | 210,222,447 | 44,287,727 | 1,697,120 | 17,180,657 | 63,165,504 | 48,887,140 | 48,887,140 | 1,454,226,953 |
| 1955 | 180,834,429 | 3,598,824 | 32,389,417 | 216,822,670 | 45,843,506 | 1,756,738 | 17,784,194 | 65,384,438 | 49,886,891 | 49,886,891 | 1,463,249,803 |
| 1956 | 214,645,047 | 4,271,696 | 38,445,267 | 257,362,011 | 55,035,046 | 2,108,961 | 21,349,893 | 78,493,899 | 59,606,038 | 59,606,038 | 1,715,641,898 |
| 1957 | 211,792,270 | 2,809,948 | 51,984,046 | 266,586,264 | 56,147,121 | 1,434,384 | 29,848,453 | 87,429,958 | 59,795,428 | 59,795,428 | 1,796,200,000 |
| 1958 | 221,307,556 | 2,936,192 | 54,319,556 | 278,563,305 | 58,946,746 | 1,505,906 | 31,336,766 | 91,789,418 | 62,823,782 | 62,823,782 | 1,868,864,003 |
| 1959 | 208,183,557 | 2,762,070 | 51,098,293 | 262,043,920 | 56,287,324 | 1,437,966 | 29,922,986 | 87,648,276 | 59,661,041 | 59,661,041 | 1,771,829,851 |
| 1960 | 255,620,125 | 3,391,433 | 62,741,517 | 321,753,075 | 69,804,046 | 1,783,276 | 37,108,630 | 108,695,952 | 73,987,920 | 73,987,920 | 2,117,366,586 |

**Appendix Table 8:** Singapore: Percentage Share of Expenditure Incurred in Relation to Straits Settlements by Class of Account and Department for the Period 1900–09

| Department | Year | Personal Emoluments | | | | | | | Intermediate Consumption | Construction | Machinery and Equipment | Transfers |
|---|---|---|---|---|---|---|---|---|---|---|---|---|
| | | 1.1 | 1.2 | 1.3 | 1.4 | 1.5 | 1.6 | 1.9 | 2 | 3 | 4 | 9 |
| Analyst | 1900 | 100% | 100% | | | | | | 100% | | | |
| | 1901 | 100% | | | | | 100% | | 100% | | | |
| | 1902 | 100% | | | | | 100% | | 100% | | | |
| | 1903 | 100% | 100% | | | | | | 100% | | | |
| | 1904 | 100% | 100% | | | | | | 100% | | | |
| | 1905 | 100% | 100% | | | | | | 100% | | | |
| | 1906 | 100% | 100% | | | | | | 100% | | | |
| | 1907 | 100% | 100% | | | | | | 100% | | | |
| | 1908 | 100% | 100% | | | | | | 100% | | | |
| | 1909 | 78% | 85% | | | | | | 74% | | 100% | |
| | | 78% | 85% | | | | 0% | | 74% | | 100% | |
| Audit Department | 1900 | 72% | 92% | | | | | | 71% | | | |
| | 1901 | 57% | | | | | 91% | | 81% | | | |
| | 1902 | 70% | | | | | 93% | | 76% | | | |
| | 1903 | 71% | 94% | | | | | | 73% | | | |
| | 1904 | 69% | 92% | | | | | | 80% | | 100% | |
| | 1905 | 59% | 95% | | | | | | 82% | | 0% | |
| | 1906 | 68% | 96% | | | | | | 91% | | | |
| | 1907 | 69% | 96% | | | | | | 82% | | | |
| | 1908 | 65% | 95% | | | | | | 83% | | 0% | |
| | 1909 | 66% | 87% | | | | | | 85% | | | |
| | | 67% | 94% | | | | 92% | | 80% | | 80% | |
| Bankruptcy | 1900 | 87% | 63% | | | | | | 89% | | | |
| | 1901 | 84% | | | | | 67% | | 81% | | | |
| | 1902 | 89% | | | | | 65% | | 85% | | | |
| | 1903 | 91% | 78% | | | | | | 78% | | | |
| | 1904 | 90% | 75% | | | | | | 96% | | | |
| | 1905 | 80% | | | | | | | 18% | | | |
| | 1906 | 87% | | | | | | | 30% | | | |
| | 1907 | 82% | | | | | | | 50% | | | |
| | 1908 | 83% | | | | | | | 79% | | 0% | 100% |
| | 1909 | 76% | | | | | | | 70% | | | 100% |
| | | 85% | 72% | | | | 66% | | 68% | | 68% | 100% |
| Botanical Gardens | 1900 | 71% | 87% | | | | | | 32% | | | 100% |
| | 1901 | 67% | 62% | | | | | | 46% | | | 100% |
| | 1902 | 66% | 59% | | | | | | 32% | | | 100% |
| | 1903 | 77% | 45% | | | | | | 69% | 0% | | 0% |
| | 1904 | 69% | 60% | | | | | | 39% | | 100% | 100% |
| | 1905 | 66% | 48% | | | | | | 39% | | | 100% |
| | 1906 | 71% | 42% | | | | | | 20% | | 100% | 100% |
| | 1907 | 70% | 34% | | | | | | 7% | 100% | | 100% |
| | 1908 | 72% | 61% | | | | | | 7% | | | 100% |
| | 1909 | 73% | 82% | | | | | | 7% | | | 100% |
| | | 70% | 58% | | | | | | 30% | 30% | 30% | 100% |
| Colonial Secretary | 1909 | 100% | 13% | | | | | | 77% | | 61% | |
| | | 100% | 13% | 0% | | | 0% | | 77% | 0% | 61% | 0% |
| Ecclesiastical | 1900 | 40% | 46% | | | | | | 31% | | | 0% |
| | 1901 | 45% | 45% | | | | | | 32% | | | 0% |
| | 1902 | 40% | 45% | | | | | | 31% | | | 0% |
| | 1903 | 36% | 46% | | | | | | 11% | | 0% | 0% |
| | 1904 | 43% | 46% | | | | | | 42% | | | 0% |
| | 1905 | 55% | 60% | | | | | | 36% | | | 0% |
| | 1906 | 51% | 49% | | | | | | 31% | | | 0% |
| | 1907 | 47% | 44% | | | | | | 31% | | | 0% |
| | 1908 | 48% | 44% | | | | | | 31% | | | 75% |
| | 1909 | 47% | 44% | | | | | | 31% | | | 57% |
| | | 45% | 47% | | | | | | 31% | | 31% | 31% |
| Education | 1900 | 35% | 18% | | | | | | 47% | | | 60% |
| | 1901 | 36% | | | | | 11% | | 56% | | | 67% |
| | 1902 | 0% | | | | | 16% | | 47% | | | 69% |
| | 1903 | 49% | 19% | | | | | | 28% | | | 66% |
| | 1904 | 49% | 21% | | | | | | 39% | | | 62% |
| | 1905 | 0% | 20% | | | | | | 38% | | 100% | 49% |
| | 1906 | 48% | 26% | 100% | | | | | 39% | 15% | 100% | 58% |
| | 1907 | 78% | 85% | | | | | | 74% | | 100% | |
| | 1908 | 50% | 34% | | | | | | 48% | 100% | 7% | 41% |
| | 1909 | 51% | 37% | | | | | | 41% | | 61% | 53% |
| | | 49% | 33% | 100% | | | 14% | | 46% | 46% | 74% | 58% |
| Forest | 1903 | 44% | 24% | | | | | | 2% | 0% | 0% | |
| | 1904 | 33% | 27% | | | | | | 12% | | | |
| | 1905 | 0% | 26% | | | | | | 8% | 0% | | |
| | 1906 | 32% | 18% | | | | | | 14% | | | |
| | 1907 | 32% | 30% | | | | | | 33% | | | |
| | 1908 | 31% | 38% | | | | | | 18% | | 100% | |
| | 1909 | 32% | 44% | | | | | | 33% | | 38% | |
| | | 34% | 30% | | | | | | 17% | 17% | 46% | 17% |

The percentage data were not taken into account for the computation of the expenditure incurred by class of account.

(*Continued*)

## Appendix Table 8:  *(Continued)*

| | | Personal Emoluments | | | | | | | Intermediate Consumption | Construction | Machinery and Equipment | Transfers |
|---|---|---|---|---|---|---|---|---|---|---|---|---|
| | | 1.1 | 1.2 | 1.3 | 1.4 | 1.5 | 1.6 | 1.9 | 2 | 3 | 4 | 9 |
| Indian Immigration Department | 1900 | 4% | 0% | | | | | | 1% | | | |
| | 1901 | 45% | | | | | 0% | | 76% | | | |
| | 1902 | 4% | | | | | 0% | | 6% | | | |
| | 1903 | 3% | 0% | | | | | | 8% | | 0% | |
| | 1904 | 3% | 0% | | | | | | 7% | | | |
| | 1905 | 4% | 0% | | | | | | 1% | | 0% | |
| | 1906 | 3% | 0% | | | | | | 1% | | | |
| | 1907 | 4% | 0% | | | | | | 1% | | | |
| | 1908 | 7% | | | | | | | 1% | | | |
| | | 4% | 0% | | | | 0% | | 3% | | 3% | |
| Marine | 1900 | 70% | 59% | | | | | | 70% | | 63% | |
| | 1901 | 70% | | | | | 60% | | 74% | | 87% | |
| | 1902 | 69% | | | | | 60% | | 74% | | 100% | |
| | 1903 | 72% | 58% | | | | | | 87% | 86% | 49% | |
| | 1904 | 74% | 58% | | | | | | 73% | 75% | 55% | |
| | 1905 | 73% | 68% | | | | | | 72% | 68% | 25% | 9% |
| | 1906 | 70% | 70% | | | | | | 72% | | 33% | |
| | 1907 | 68% | 71% | | | | | | 75% | 100% | 91% | |
| | 1908 | 69% | 66% | 100% | | | | | 67% | 22% | 63% | |
| | 1909 | 67% | 59% | | | | | | 71% | | 43% | |
| | | 70% | 64% | 100% | | | 60% | | 73% | 70% | 61% | 9% |
| Medical | 1900 | 52% | 41% | | | | | | 53% | | 90% | 100% |
| | 1901 | 54% | | | | | 36% | | 54% | | 89% | 100% |
| | 1902 | 0% | 0% | 0% | | | 0% | | 0% | 0% | 0% | 0% |
| | 1903 | 55% | 43% | | | | | | 60% | | 47% | 0% |
| | 1904 | 55% | 48% | | | | | | 59% | | 85% | 84% |
| | 1905 | 56% | 43% | | | | | | 58% | | 68% | 83% |
| | 1906 | 56% | 48% | | | | | | 59% | | 78% | 98% |
| | 1907 | 57% | 36% | 100% | | | | | 58% | | 70% | 99% |
| | 1908 | 56% | 30% | | | | | | 58% | | 87% | 99% |
| | 1909 | 58% | 35% | | | | | | 60% | 100% | 40% | 99% |
| | | 55% | 36% | 55% | | | 36% | | 58% | 58% | 73% | 85% |
| Miscellaneous | 1900 | | 68.4% | | | | | | 70.3% | | | 49.4% |
| | 1901 | | | | | | 60.2% | | 50.4% | | 100.0% | 61.6% |
| | 1902 | | | | | | 52.4% | | 65.6% | | 100.0% | 39.3% |
| | 1903 | | 52.3% | | | | | | 67.6% | | | 93.6% |
| | 1904 | | 48.9% | | | | | | 67.8% | 79.6% | | 93.8% |
| | 1905 | | 52.1% | 45.0% | | | | | 81.8% | 100.0% | | 70.7% |
| | 1906 | | 58.1% | 100.0% | | | | | 76.7% | 13.4% | | 78.1% |
| | 1907 | | 49.4% | 100.0% | | | | | 72.8% | 100.0% | | 76.7% |
| | 1908 | 63.7% | 100.0% | 100.0% | | | | | 82.7% | | 0.9% | 72.9% |
| | | 63.7% | 61.3% | 86.2% | | | 56.3% | 0.0% | 70.6% | 73.3% | 67.0% | 70.7% |
| Police | 1900 | 47% | 48% | | | | | | 56% | | 59% | |
| | 1901 | 46% | | | | | 54% | | 57% | | 66% | |
| | 1902 | 49% | | | | | 53% | | 66% | | 77% | |
| | 1903 | 50% | 54% | | | | | | 62% | | 62% | |
| | 1904 | 50% | 53% | | | | | | 64% | | 96% | |
| | 1905 | 50% | 58% | | | | | | 60% | | 58% | |
| | 1906 | 49% | 56% | | | | | | 62% | | 46% | |
| | 1907 | 48% | 54% | | | | | | 61% | | 72% | |
| | 1908 | 48% | 55% | 0% | | | | | 59% | | 52% | |
| | 1909 | 49% | 52% | 0% | | | | | 49% | | 51% | |
| | | 49% | 54% | 0% | | | 53% | | 60% | | 64% | |
| Post Office | 1900 | 68% | | 0% | | 60% | | | 89% | | 100% | 61% |
| | 1901 | 69% | | 0% | | 62% | | | 87% | | | 58% |
| | 1902 | 62% | | 0% | | | 42% | | 81% | | | 64% |
| | 1903 | 62% | 55% | 0% | | | | | 80% | 78% | 100% | 65% |
| | 1904 | 62% | 45% | 0% | | | | | 81% | 76% | 100% | 64% |
| | 1905 | 59% | 39% | 0% | | | | | 79% | 62% | 99% | 98% |
| | 1906 | 61% | 46% | 0% | | | | | 87% | | 79% | 87% |
| | 1907 | 61% | 42% | 0% | | | | | 85% | 100% | 86% | 88% |
| | 1908 | 60% | 41% | 0% | | | | | 77% | | 30% | 97% |
| | 1909 | 60% | 27% | 0% | | | | | 41% | 56% | 26% | 98% |
| | | 62% | 42% | 0% | | 61% | 42% | | 79% | 75% | 77% | 78% |
| Prisons | 1900 | 70% | 69% | | | | | | 76% | | 0% | 87% |
| | 1901 | 71% | | | | | 65% | | 75% | | | 85% |
| | 1902 | 73% | | | | | 65% | | 78% | | | 90% |
| | 1903 | 74% | 67% | | | | | | 80% | | | 92% |
| | 1904 | 74% | 79% | | | | | | 76% | | 85% | 87% |
| | 1905 | 72% | 81% | | | | | | 76% | 100% | 100% | 91% |
| | 1906 | 74% | 81% | | | | | | 78% | | | 93% |
| | 1907 | 0% | 0% | 0% | | | 0% | | 0% | 0% | 0% | 0% |
| | 1908 | 73% | 79% | 0% | | | | | 78% | | | 94% |
| | 1909 | 74% | 100% | | | | | | 79% | | | 79% |
| | | 73% | 62% | 0% | | | 14% | | 77% | 77% | 77% | 89% |
| Treasury | 1900 | 68% | 47% | | | | | | 99% | | | |
| | 1901 | 71% | | | | | 41% | | 99% | | 100% | |
| | 1902 | 68% | | | | | 53% | | 99% | | | |
| | 1903 | 71% | 69% | | | | | | 100% | | 100% | |
| | 1904 | 71% | 72% | | | | | | 100% | | 99% | |
| | 1905 | 64% | 100% | | | | | | 97% | | 34% | |
| | 1906 | 69% | 100% | | | | | | 53% | | 100% | |
| | 1907 | 67% | 100% | | | | | | 96% | | | |
| | 1908 | 67% | 100% | | | | | | 94% | | 0% | |
| | 1909 | 70% | 100% | | | | | | 10% | | | |
| | | 69% | 86% | | | | 47% | | 85% | | 72% | |

**Appendix Table 9:** Methodology Adopted to Identify the Share of Expenditure Assigned to Singapore in Relation to Straits Settlements by Departments for the Period 1910–39

**Step 1**

| | Major Code | Sub Code | Actual SS | Malacca | Penang | Singapore | Singapore (Proper) | Penang + Malacca | Sum Average %applied to S'pore | Major Code | Sub Code |
|---|---|---|---|---|---|---|---|---|---|---|---|
| Item A | 1 | 1 | 1,000.00 | | | | 500.00 | 500.00 | 50.00% | 1 | 1 |
| Item B | 2 | | 100.00 | 20.00 | 30.00 | 50.00 | 50.00 | 13,796.14 | | 2 | |
| Item C | 4 | 1 | 2,000.00 | | | | | | | 4 | 1 |
| Item D | 3 | 1 | 300.00 | | | 300.00 | 300.00 | - | | 3 | 1 |
| Item E | 2 | | 1,000.00 | | | | | | | 2 | |
| Item F | 2 | | 100.00 | 20.00 | 30.00 | 50.00 | 50.00 | 17,165.04 | | 2 | |
| Item G | 2 | | 100.00 | 20.00 | 30.00 | 50.00 | 50.00 | 9,616.47 | | 2 | |
| Item H | 2 | | 100.00 | 20.00 | 30.00 | 50.00 | 50.00 | 7,187.00 | | 2 | |
| Item I | 9 | | 150.00 | | | | | | | 9 | |
| Item J | 2 | | 2,000.00 | | | | | | | 2 | |
| Item K | 1 | 2 | 400.00 | | | | 200.00 | 200.00 | 50.00% | 1 | 2 |
| Item L | 4 | 1 | 50.00 | 20.00 | 10.00 | 20.00 | 20.00 | 30.00 | | 4 | 1 |

**Step 1** Distribution of compensation of employees (Major Code 1) was based on the known distribution of intermediate consumption (Major Code 2) for the respective Settlements

**Step 2**

| | Major Code | Sub Code | Actual SS | Malacca | Penang | Singapore | Singapore (Proper) | Penang + Malacca | Sum Average %applied to S'pore | Major Code | Sub Code |
|---|---|---|---|---|---|---|---|---|---|---|---|
| Item A | 1 | 1 | 1,000.00 | | | | 500.00 | 500.00 | 50.00% | 1 | 1 |
| Item B | 2 | | 100.00 | 20.00 | 30.00 | 50.00 | 50.00 | 13,796.14 | | 2 | |
| Item C | 4 | 1 | 2,000.00 | | | | | | | 4 | 1 |
| Item D | 3 | 1 | 300.00 | | | 300.00 | 300.00 | - | | 3 | 1 |
| Item E | 2 | | 1,000.00 | | | | 500.00 | 500.00 | 50.00% | 2 | |
| Item F | 2 | | 100.00 | 20.00 | 30.00 | 50.00 | 50.00 | 17,165.04 | | 2 | |
| Item G | 2 | | 100.00 | 20.00 | 30.00 | 50.00 | 50.00 | 9,616.47 | | 2 | |
| Item H | 2 | | 100.00 | 20.00 | 30.00 | 50.00 | 50.00 | 7,187.00 | | 2 | |
| Item I | 9 | | 150.00 | | | | | | | 9 | |
| Item J | 2 | | 2,000.00 | | | | 1,000.00 | 1,000.00 | 50.00% | 2 | |
| Item K | 1 | 2 | 400.00 | | | | 200.00 | 200.00 | 50.00% | 1 | 2 |
| Item L | 4 | 1 | 50.00 | 20.00 | 10.00 | 20.00 | 20.00 | 30.00 | | 4 | 1 |

**Step 2** Distribution of intermediate consumption (Major Code 2) was based on the known distribution of intermediate consumption (Major Code 2) for the respective Settlements

**Step 3**

| | Major Code | Sub Code | Actual SS | Malacca | Penang | Singapore | Singapore (Proper) | Penang + Malacca | Sum Average %applied to S'pore | Major Code | Sub Code |
|---|---|---|---|---|---|---|---|---|---|---|---|
| Item A | 1 | 1 | 1,000.00 | | | | 500.00 | 500.00 | 50.00% | 1 | 1 |
| Item B | 2 | | 100.00 | 20.00 | 30.00 | 50.00 | 50.00 | 13,796.14 | | 2 | |
| Item C | 4 | 1 | 2,000.00 | | | | 800.00 | 1,200.00 | 40.00% | 4 | 1 |
| Item D | 3 | 1 | 300.00 | | | 300.00 | 300.00 | - | | 3 | 1 |
| Item E | 2 | | 1,000.00 | | | | 500.00 | 500.00 | 50.00% | 2 | |
| Item F | 2 | | 100.00 | 20.00 | 30.00 | 50.00 | 50.00 | 50.00 | | 2 | |
| Item G | 2 | | 100.00 | 20.00 | 30.00 | 50.00 | 50.00 | 50.00 | | 2 | |
| Item H | 2 | | 100.00 | 20.00 | 30.00 | 50.00 | 50.00 | 50.00 | | 2 | |
| Item I | 9 | | 150.00 | | | | | | | 9 | |
| Item J | 2 | | 2,000.00 | | | | 1,000.00 | 1,000.00 | 50.00% | 2 | |
| Item K | 1 | 2 | 400.00 | | | | 200.00 | 200.00 | 50.00% | 1 | 2 |
| Item L | 4 | 1 | 50.00 | 20.00 | 10.00 | 20.00 | 20.00 | 30.00 | | 4 | 1 |

**Step 3** Distribution of Transport Equipment (Code 4.1) was based on the known distribution of Transport Equipment (Code 4.1). The same methodology was applied for Major Codes 3, 4, and 9

**Step 4**

| | Major Code | Sub Code | Actual SS | Malacca | Penang | Singapore | Singapore (Proper) | Penang + Malacca | Sum Average %applied to S'pore | Major Code | Sub Code |
|---|---|---|---|---|---|---|---|---|---|---|---|
| Item A | 1 | 1 | 1,000.00 | | | | 500.00 | 500.00 | 50.00% | 1 | 1 |
| Item B | 2 | | 100.00 | 20.00 | 30.00 | 50.00 | 50.00 | 13,796.14 | | 2 | |
| Item C | 4 | 1 | 2,000.00 | | | | 800.00 | 1,200.00 | 40.00% | 4 | 1 |
| Item D | 3 | 1 | 300.00 | | | 300.00 | 300.00 | - | | 3 | 1 |
| Item E | 2 | | 1,000.00 | | | | 500.00 | 500.00 | 50.00% | 2 | |
| Item F | 2 | | 100.00 | 20.00 | 30.00 | 50.00 | 50.00 | 50.00 | | 2 | |
| Item G | 2 | | 100.00 | 20.00 | 30.00 | 50.00 | 50.00 | 50.00 | | 2 | |
| Item H | 2 | | 100.00 | 20.00 | 30.00 | 50.00 | 50.00 | 50.00 | | 2 | |
| Item I | 9 | | 150.00 | | | | 75.00 | 75.00 | 50.00% | 9 | |
| Item J | 2 | | 2,000.00 | | | | 1,000.00 | 1,000.00 | 50.00% | 2 | |
| Item K | 1 | 2 | 400.00 | | | | 200.00 | 200.00 | 50.00% | 1 | 2 |
| Item L | 4 | 1 | 50.00 | 20.00 | 10.00 | 20.00 | 20.00 | 30.00 | | 4 | 1 |

**Step 4** In cases where the distribution of a particular code (other than Major Code 2) was not known entirely for a particular year by Department, the distribution of Code 2 was utilized for the distribution of share of expenditure for all other codes

**Appendix Table 10:** Percentage Share of Expenditure Incurred in Singapore in Relation to Straits Settlements by Class of Account and Department

| | | Share of Singapore (%) |
|---|---|---|
| Agricultural Department | 1919–1939 | 25 |
| Civil Services | 1905, 1921–1934 | 75 |
| Colonial Development Fund, Grants-in-aid | 1931–1939 | 75 |
| Cooperative Societies | 1927–1939 | 25 |
| Director of supplies, SS and FMS | 1921 | 75 |
| Fisheries | 1923–1939 | 25 |
| General Clerical Service | 1927–1939 | 25 |
| Immigration | 1934–1939 | 50 |
| Imports, Exports, and Statistics | 1922–1923 | 75 |
| Malayan Civil Service | 1934–1935 | 25 |
| Malayan Establishments | 1934–1937 | 25 |
| Museum and Library | 1900–1939 | 100 |
| Pensions and Allowances | 1910–1939 | 50 |
| Political Intelligence | 1926–1929 | 25 |
| Printing | 1910–1939 | 100 |
| Public Trustee | 1939 | 50 |
| Straits Settlements Civil Services | 1935–1939 | 75 |
| Subventions | 1939 | 75 |
| Survey Department | 1920–1939 | 50 |
| Survey Department: Meteorological Branch | 1937–1938 | 50 |
| Veterinary (Principal Veterinary Officer SS and FMS) | 1933 | 25 |
| War Expenditure | 1914–1920 | 75 |

Case 1: All Capitalized construction work and machinery and equipment (M&E) was purchased from private contractors

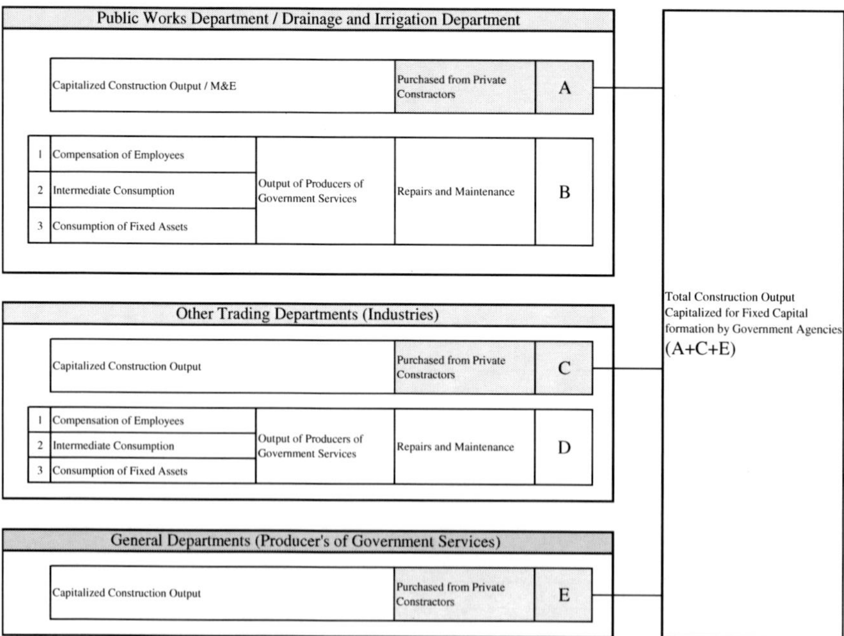

Case 2: Construction work and capital formation in machinery and equipment (M&E) was partially done by PWD and the rest was purchased from private contractors

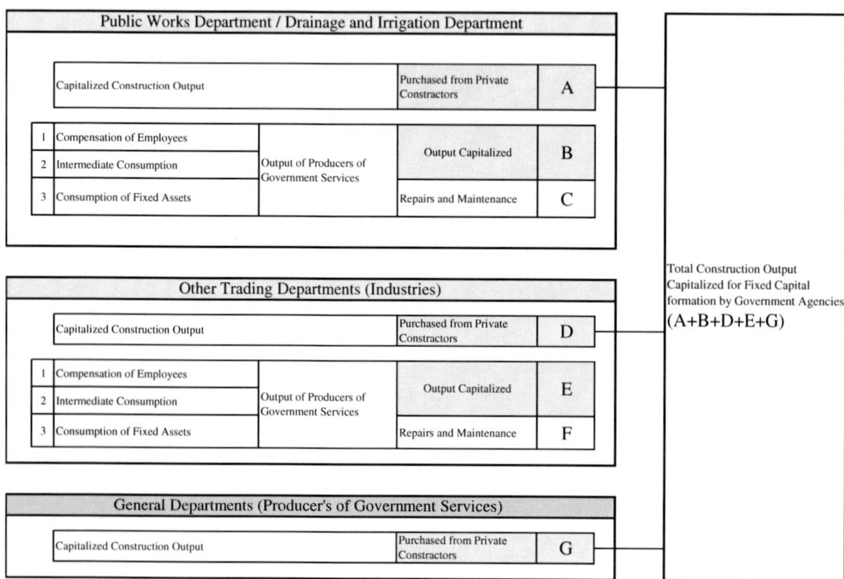

**Appendix Figure 1:**

# Bibliography

## Published Official Records

### *Annual Reports*

*Annual Administration Report, City Council of Singapore*, 1947–59.

———. *Singapore Municipality*, 1899–1902, 1904–09, 1911–39.

———. *Malacca*, 1918, 1920, 1922.

———. *Penang*, 1918–22.

*Annual Report, Chinese Protectorates Department, Straits Settlements*, 1901, 1903–08, 1910–11, 1913, 1915, 1919–30, 1933.

———. *Colony of Singapore*, 1948–56.

———. *Education Department, Colony of Singapore*, 1948–56.

———. *Education Department, State of Singapore*, 1957–60.

———. *Education Department, Straits Settlements*, 1899–1905, 1907–13, 1915–16, 1918–24, 1926–27, 1929–38.

———. *Electrical Department, Federation of Malaya*, 1948.

———. *Electrical Department, Malayan Union*, 1946–47.

———. *Financial Statements, Colony of Singapore*, 1948–56.

———. *Financial Statements, State of Singapore*, 1957–60.

———. *Financial Statements, Straits Settlements*, 1939.

———. *Foreign Trade of Malaya*, 1929–30, 1932, 1934, 1936–39.

———. *Forest Department, Straits Settlements*, 1899, 1905–06, 1910, 1914, 1918, 1920–24, 1926, 1932–38.

———. *Government Monopoly Department, Straits Settlements*, 1910–15, 1918–27, 1932–34.

———. *Indian Immigration Department, Straits Settlements*, 1901–02, 1905–07, 1909–11.

———. *Johore*, 1933.

———. *Labour Department, Colony of Singapore*, 1949.

———. *Land Office, Straits Settlements*, 1899, 1901–07, 1909–27, 1933–36.

———. *Malayan Agricultural Statistics*, 1931–39, 1947–49.

———. *Medical Department, Straits Settlements*, 1911, 1913–15, 1923–38.

———. *Medical Department, Colony of Singapore*, 1948–56.

———. *Medical Department, State of Singapore*, 1957–60.

———. *Post and Telegraphs Department, Straits Settlements*, 1899, 1902, 1905–07, 1910–16, 1918–27, 1933–38.

———. *Public Work, Straits Settlements*, 1899, 1901–15, 1918–38.

———. *Registration of Births and Deaths Department, Straits Settlements*, 1902–03, 1905–07, 1910–35, 1938.

———. *Registration of Births and Deaths, Malayan Union*, 1940–46.

———. *Returns of Imports and Exports, British Malaya*, 1921–37.

———. *Singapore's External Trade*, 1956–60.

———. *Singapore Harbour Board*, 1929, 1936, 1940, 1963.

———. *State of Singapore*, 1957–60.

———. *Straits Settlements*, 1899–1938.

———. *Trade and Custom, Federated Malay States*, 1903–32.

*Appendices to the Report on the Trade, Straits Settlements*, 1899–1906, 1908–17, 1921–27.

*Blue Book, Straits Settlements*, annual series, 1900–38.

*Malayan Year Book*, 1939.

*Statistical Tables Relating to British Self-Governing Dominions, Crown Colonies, Possessions and Protectorates*, 1908–12.

*Statistical Tables Relating to the Colonial and Other Possessions and Protectorates*, 1902–07.

*Statistical Tables Relating to the Colonial and Other Possessions of the United Kingdom*, 1899–1901.

*Yearbook of Statistics, Singapore*, 1998, 2002.

## Monthly Bulletins

*Monthly Statistical Bulletin, Federation of Malaya*, 1948–53.

*Malayan Statistics Monthly Digest of Economic and Social Statistics Relating to the Colony of Singapore and the Federation of Malaya,* 1958–60.

## Population Census Reports

Cavendish A (1911). *Report on the Census of Kedah and Perlis, 1911,* Penang: The Criterion Press Ltd.

Chua, SC (1957). *Report on the Census of Population, 1957,* Singapore: State of Singapore.

Del Tufo, MV (1949). *A Report on the 1947 Census of Population, Malaya (Comprising Federation of Malaya and the Colony of Singapore),* London: The Crown Agents for the Colonies.

Innes, JR (1901). *Report on the Census of the Straits Settlements, 1901,* Singapore: Government Printing Office.

Marriot, H (1912). *Census Report of the Straits Settlements, 1911,* Singapore: Government Printing Office.

Nathan, JE (1922). *The Census of British Malaya (the Straits Settlements, Federated Malay States and Protected States of Johore, Kedah, Perlis, Kelantan, Trengganu and Brunei), 1921,* London: Waterloo & Sons Limited.

Vlieland, CA (1932). *A Report on the 1931 Census and on Certain Problems of Vital Statistics, British Malaya (the Colony of the Straits Settlements and the Malay States under British Protection, namely the Federated Malay States of Perak, Selangor, Negeri Sembilan and Pahang and the States of Johore, Kedah, Kelantan, Trengganu, Perlis and Brunei),* London: The Crown Agents for the Colonies.

## Special Reports

Allen, LA (1938). *Proclamations, Order, Notices, Rules, Regulations, Declarations, Appointments, Forms and By-Laws in Force on 31st day of December 1935 Made under the Laws of the Federated Malay States and of Each of Them Prepared under the Authority of the Revised Edition of the Laws Enactment, 1932, Vol. V Containing the Subsidiary Legislation Made under Enactments, Chapters 138–161 (Diet Scales of Government Hospitals 1936- Chapter 154.)*, Kuala Lumpur: Government Printer.

Commission Appointed to Inquire into Matters Relating to the Use of Opium in the Straits Settlements and the Federated Malay States and British Malaya Opium Committee (1924). *Proceedings of the British Malaya Opium Committee*, Singapore: Government Printing Office.

Department for Economic and Social Affairs, Statistics Division, United Nations (1999). *Studies in Methods, Handbook of National Accounting, Series F, No. 77, A Systems Approach to National Accounts Compilation, A Technical Report*, New York: United Nations.

Department of Economic and Social Affairs, Statistical Office of the United Nations (1968). *A System of National Accounts, (SNA68), Studies in Methods, Series F, No. 2, Rev. 3*, New York: United Nations.

Department of International Economic and Social Affairs, United Nations (1986). *Studies in Methods, Series F, No. 39, Handbook of National Accounting, Accounting for Production: Sources and Methods*, New York: United Nations.

Department of Economic and Social Affairs, Statistics Division, United Nations (1997). *Principles and Recommendations for Population and Housing Censuses, Revision 1, Statistical Papers, Series M, No. 67, Rev. 1*, New York: United Nations.

Department of Statistics, Federation of Malaya (1949). *Average Prices, Declared Trade Values, Exchange, Currency and Cost of Living, 1948, Malaya*, Singapore: Government Printing Office.

————. Federation of Malaya (1952). *Average Prices, Declared Trade Values, Exchange and Currency, Volume and Average Values of Imports and Exports, Market Prices, and Cost of Living for the year 1951, Malaya*, Singapore: Government Printing Office.

————. International Monetary Fund (2001). Government Finance Statistics Manual 2001 (GFSM 2001), Washington, DC: IMF.

————. Malaysia (1999). *Malaysia Economic Statistics Time Series, 1999*, Kuala Lumpur: Government Printing Office.

————. Singapore (1952). *Average Prices, Declared Trade Values, Exchange and Currency, Volume and Average Values of Imports and Exports, Market Prices, and Cost of Living for the year 1951, Malaya*, Singapore: Government Printing Office.

————. Singapore (1975). S*ingapore National Accounts, 1960–1973*, Singapore: Government Printing Office.

————. Singapore (1983). *Economic & Social Statistics Singapore 1960–1982*, Singapore: Government Printer.

————. Singapore (1996). *Singapore System of National Accounts 1995*, Singapore: Government Printer.

————. Singapore (2008). *Import and Export Price Indices, January 2008*, Singapore: Government Printing Office.

————. Straits Settlements and Federated Malay States (1940). *Average Prices, Declared Trade Values, Exchange and Currency for the year 1939, Malaya*, Singapore: Government Printing Office.

————. Malayan Union (1947). *Report on the Registration of Births and Deaths, Malayan Union, 1940–1946*, Kuala Lumpur: Government Press.

Federated Malay States (1932). *Third Inter-Departmental Agricultural Conference*, Kuala Lumpur: Government Printing Office.

International Monetary Fund (2001). The Government Finance Statistics Manual, New York: IMF.

Milles, JI (1931). *Report of the Commission on the Temporary Allowances, Family Budget 1930*, Singapore: Government Printing Office.

OECD (2007). *OECD Fact Book 2007: Economic, Environmental and Social Statistics*, Paris: OECD.

Straits Settlements (1909). *Proceeding's of the Legislative Council of the Straits Settlements for the year 1908*, Singapore: Government Printing Office.

———— (1910). *Proceeding's of the Legislative Council of the Straits Settlements for the year 1909*, Singapore: Government Printing Office.

Straits Settlements and Federated Malay States Opium Commission (1908). *Proceedings of the Commission Appointed to Inquire into Matters Relating to the Use of Opium in the Straits Settlements and the Federated Malay States*, Singapore: Government Printing Office.

The Commissions Appointed by the Excellency the Governor of the Straits Settlements and the High Commissioner of the Federated Malay States (1919). *To enquire into Certain Matters Relating to the Public Service, to Wit, the Salaries, and the Conditions of Service as Affecting Such Salaries of Certain Officers in the Public Service of the Straits Settlements and the Federated Malay States, and the Provision of Free Passages to Such Officers and to Their Wives and Children When Proceeding from and Returning to the Straits Settlements and Federated Malay States on Leave of Absence*, Singapore: Government Printing Office.

## Books and Articles

Abeysinghe, T and KM Choy (2007). *The Singapore Economy: An Econometric Perspective (Routledge Studies in the Growth Economies of Asia)*, London: Routledge.

Abizadeh, S and J Gray (1985). Wagner's Law: A Pooled Time-Series, Cross-section Comparison, *National Tax Journal,* (38), 209–218.

Abraha, GG (2004). *Export Instability and Economic Growth in Ethiopia*, Dakar: African Institute for Economic Development and Planning.

Afxentiou, PC and A Serletis (1996). Government Expenditures In The European Union: Do They Converge Or Follow Wagner's Law?. *International Economic Journal, Korean International Economic Association*, 10(3), 33–47.

Agénor, P-R, CJ McDermott and ES Prasad (2000). Macroeconomic Fluctuations in Developing Countries: Some Stylized Facts, *The World Bank Economic Review*, 14(2), 251–285.

Ahmed, S, AT Levin and BA Wilson (2004). Recent US Macroeconomic Stability: Good Policies, Good Practices, or Good Luck? *Review of Economics and Statistics*, 86(3), 824–832.

Ahsan, SM, ACC Kwan and BS Sahni (1989). Causality between Government Consumption Expenditure and National Income: OECD Countries, *Public Finance*, 2, 204–224.

——— (1996). Cointegration and Wagner's Hypothesis: Time Series Evidence for Canada, *Applied Economics*, 28, 1055–1058.

Heston, A, R Summers and B Aten (2002). *Penn World Table Version 6.1*, Center for International Comparisons at the University of Pennsylvania (CICUP).

Alexander, WR (1990). Growth: Some Combined Cross-Sectional and Time Series Evidence from OECD Countries, *Applied Economics*, 22(9), 1197–1204.

Ansari, MI, DV Gordon and C Akuamoah (1997). Keynes versus Wagner: Public Expenditure and National Income for Three African Countries. *Applied Economics*, 29(4) 543–550.

Ashworth, J (1994). Spurious in Mexico: A Comment on Wagner's Law, *Public Finance*, 49,(2)282–286.

Backus, DK and PJ Kehoe (1992). International Evidence on the Historical Properties of Business Cycles, *The American Economic Review*, 82(4), 864–888.

Barrell, R and S Gottschalk (2004). The Volatility of the Output Gap in the G7, *National Institute of Economic and Social Research Discussion Paper* No. 230.

Barro, R (1991). Economic Growth in a Cross-Section of Countries, *Quarterly Journal of Economics*, 106(2), 407–443.

Basu, S and A Taylor (1999). Business Cycles in International Historical Perspective, *The Journal of Economic Perspectives*, 13(2), 45–68.

Bauer, PT (1948). *The Rubber Industry: A Study in Competition and Monopoly*, Cambridge: Harvard University Press.

Baxter, M and RG King (1995). Measuring Business-cycles: Approximate Band-Pass Filters for Economic Time Series, *NBER Working Paper* No. 5022.

Benham, F (1951). *The National Income of Malaya, 1947–1949*, Singapore: Government Printer.

——— (1959). *The National Income of Singapore 1956*, London: Oxford University Press.

Bergman, UM, MD Bordo and L Jonung (1998). Historical Evidence on Business Cycles: The International Experience, *Working Paper Series in Economics and Finance, No. 255, Stockholm School of Economics*.

Bird, RM (1971). Wagner's Law of Expanding State Activity, *Public Finance*, 26, 1–26.

Biswal, B, U Dhawan and H-Y Lee (1999). Testing Wagner versus Keynes Using Disaggregated Public Expenditure Data for Canada, *Applied Economics*, 31, 1283–1291.

Blake, DJ (1968). Patterns of Singapore's Trade, 1961–66. *Malayan Economic Review*, 13(1), 39–69.

Blanchard, O and J Simon (2001). The Long and Large Decline in U.S. Output volatility, *Brookings Papers on Economic Activity*, 1, 135–164.

Blattman, C, J Hwang and JG Williamson (2004). The Impact of the Terms of Trade on Economic Development in the Periphery, 1870–1939: Volatility and Secular Change, *NBER Working Paper No. 10600*.

Bleaney, M and D Greenaway (2001). The Impact of Terms of Trade and Real Exchange Rate Volatility on Investment and Growth in Sub-Saharan Africa, *Journal of Development Economics*, 65, 491–500.

Booth, A (1990). The Evolution of Fiscal Policy and the Role of Government in the Colonial Economy, in Booth A, WJO' Malley and A Weidemann (eds.), *Indonesian Economic History in the Dutch Colonial Era*, Monograph Series 35, New Haven: Yale University, Southeast Asian Studies.

———— (2002). Growth Collapses in Indonesia: A Comparison of the 1930s and the 1990s, *Itinerario (European Journal of Overseas History)*, 3(4), 73–99.

Broadberry, SN (1986). *The British Economy Between the Wars: A Macroeconomic Survey*, Oxford: Blackwell.

Broadberry, SN (1988). The Impact of the World Wars on the Long Run Performance of the British Economy, *Oxford Review of Economic Policy*, 4(1), 25–37.

Broadberry, SN (1997a). Anglo-German Productivity Differences, 1870–1990: A Sectoral Analysis, *European Review of Economic History*, 1(2), 247–267.

Broadberry, SN (1997b). The Long-Run Growth and Productivity Performance of the United Kingdom, *Scottish Journal of Political Economy*, 44(4), 403–424.

Brown, I (1994). The British Merchant Community in Singapore and Japanese Commercial Expansion in the 1930s, in Sugiyama, S and MC Guerrero (eds.), *International Commercial Rivalry in*

*Southeast Asia in the Interwar Period*, New Haven: Yale Centre for International and Area Studies, 111–132.

Buchanan, JM (1975). *The Limits of Liberty, Between Anarchy and Leviathan*, Chicago: University of Chicago Press.

Carrera, J, M Feliz and D Panigo (1999). Unit Roots and Cycles in the Main Macroeconomic Variables for Argentina, *XXXIV Reunión Annual de la Asociación Argentina de Economía Política*.

Carter, SB, *et al.* (2006). *Historical Statistics of the United States, Earliest Times to the Present, Millennial Edition, Volume Three, Part C Economic Structure and Performance*, New York: Cambridge University Press.

Cecchetti, SG, A Flores-Lagunes and S Krause (2006). Assessing the Sources of Changes in the Volatility of Real Growth, *NBER Working Paper* No. 11946, National Bureau of Economic Research, Inc.

Cheng, UW (1961). Opium in the Straits Settlements, 1867–1910, *Journal of Southeast Asian History*, 2(1), 57–75.

Chiang, HD (1963). *A History of Straits Settlements Foreign Trade, 1870–1915*, Singapore: National Museum, Singapore.

Chin, YF (1965). The statistics of the Straits Settlements Foreign Trade, 1870–1915, *Malayan Economic Review*, 10(1), 73–83.

Chletsos, M and C Kollias (1997). Testing Wagner's Law Using Disaggregated Public Expenditure Data in the Case of Greece: 1958–93, *Applied Economics*, 29(3), 371–377.

Romer, CD (1986). Spurious Volatility in Historical Unemployment Data. *Journal of Political Economy*, 94(1), 1–37.

——— (1989). The Prewar Business Cycle Reconsidered: New Estimates of Gross National Product, 1869–1908, *Journal of Political Economy*, 97(1), 1–37.

Clarida, R, J Gali and M Gertler (2000). Monetary Policy Rules and Macroeconomic Stability: Evidence and Some Theory, *Quarterly Journal of Economics*, 115(1), 147–180.

Clark, C (1937). *National Income and Outlay*, London: Macmillan Press Ltd.

Courakis, AS, F Moura-Roque and G Tridimas (1993). Public Expenditure Growth in Greece and Portugal: Wagner's Law and Beyond, *Applied Economics*, 25, 125–134.

Crafts, NFR (1984). Economic Growth in France and Britain, 1830–1910: A Review of the Evidence, *Journal of Economic History*, 44, 49–67.

——— (1987). British Economic Growth, 1700–1850: Some Difficulties of Interpretation, *Explorations in Economic History*, 24, 245–68.

——— (1988). The Assessment: British Economic Growth over the Long Run, *Oxford Review of Economic Policy*, 4(1), i–xxi.

——— (1995). Recent Research on the National Accounts of the UK, 1700–1939, *Scandinavian Economic History Review*, 43, 17–29.

——— (1997). Economic Growth in East Asia and Western Europe Since 1950: Implications for Living Standards, *National Institute Economic Review*, 162, 75–84.

——— (1999). Economic Growth in the Twentieth Century, *Oxford Review of Economic Policy*, 15(4), 18–34.

Craft, NFR and SN Broadberry (1990a). European Productivity in the Twentieth Century: Introduction, *Oxford Bulletin of Economic and Statistics*, 52(4), 331–41.

Craft, NFR (2002). *Britain's Relative Economic Performance, 1870–1999*, London: IEA.

——— (1990b). Explaining Anglo-American Productivity Differences in the Mid-Twentieth Century, *Oxford Bulletin of Economics and Statistics*, 52, 375–402.

Creutzberg, P and P Boomgaard (eds.) (1975–96). *Changing Economy in Indonesia: A Selection of Statistical Resource Material from the Early 19th century up to 1940*, 16 volumes, Amsterdam: Royal Tropical Institute.

Da Costa, M (2007). Colonial Origins, Institutions and Economic Performance in the Caribbean: Guyana and Barbados, *IMF Working Paper* No. 07/43.

Dawe, DC (1996). A New Look at the Effect of Export Instability on Investment and Growth, *World Development*, 24(12), 1905–1914.

De Ferranti D, G Perry, I Gill and L Serven (2000). Securing our future in a global economy, *World Bank Latin America and Caribbean Studies*.

De Long, JB and L Summers (1991). Equipment Investment and Economic Growth, *Quarterly Journal of Economics*, 106, 445–502.

De Long, JB, L Summers and AB Abel (1992). Equipment Investment and Economic Growth: How Robust Is the Nexus? *Brookings Papers on Economic Activity*, 157–211.

Demirbas, S (1999). Cointegration Analysis-Causality Testing and Wagner's Law: The Case of Turkey, 1950–1990, *Annual Meeting of the European Public Choice Society*, Lisbon.

Derksen, JBD and J Tinbergen (1945). *Berekeningen over de economische betekenis van Nederlandsch–Indi·voor Nederland* (Calculations of the Economic Significance of the Netherlands Indies to the Netherlands) Maandschrift van het Centraal Bureau voor de Statistiek [Monthly bulletin of the Central Bureau of Statistics] 40.

Devarajan, S and S Vinaya (1993). What do Governments Buy? The composition of Public Spending and Economic Performance, Policy Research Working Paper, *The World Bank, Working Paper* No. 1082.

Dickey, DA and WA Fuller (1979). Distributions of the Estimators for Autoregressive Time Series with a Unit Root, *Journal of the American Statistical Association*, 74, 427–31.

——— (1981). The Likelihood Ratio Statistics for Autoregressive Time Series with a Unit Root, *Econometrica*, 49(4), 1057–72.

Dickey, DA, DW Jansen and DC Thornton (1991). A Primer on Cointegration with an Application to Money and Income, *Review Federal Reserve Bank of St. Louis*, 73(2), 58–78.

Drabble, JH (2000). *An Economic History of Malaysia, c.1800–1990*, London: Macmillan Press Ltd.

Dupasquier, C and PN Osakwe (2006). Trade Regimes, Liberalization and Macroeconomic Instability in Africa, Department of Economics, *Singapore Centre for Applied and Policy Economics Working Paper Series*, No. 2006/04, National University of Singapore.

Dynan, KE, Elmendorf and DE Sichel (2006). Can Financial Innovation Explain the Reduced Volatility of Economic Activity?, *Journal of Monetary Economics*, 53(1), 123–150.

Edward, CT (1970). *Public Finance in Malaya and Singapore*, Canberra: ANU Press.

Emerson, R (1969). *Malaysia: Study in Direct and Indirect Rule,* 3rd ed., Kuala Lumpur: University of Malaya Press.

Eng, P Van Der (2002). Halting Progress: Indonesia's Development Experience Since 1880, *Itinerario, European Journal of Overseas History*, 26(3), 15–34.

Engle, RF and CWJ Granger (1987). Cointegration and Error Correction: Representation, Estimation and Testing, *Econometrica*, 55, 251–276.

Feder, G (1984). On Exports and Economic Growth, *Journal of Development Economics*, 12, 59–73.

Feinstein, CH (1972). *National Income, Expenditure and Output of the United Kingdom, 1855–1965*, Cambridge: Cambridge University Press.

Figart, DM (1925). *The Plantation Rubber Industry in the Middle East*, Washington: Government Printing Office, Department of Commerce, Bureau of Foreign and Domestic Commerce.

Fukao, K and D Ma (2006). Real GDP in Pre-War East Asia: A 1934–36 Benchmark Purchasing Power Parity Comparison with the U.S. *Discussion Paper Series No. 132, Hitotsubashi University Research Unit for Statistical Analysis in Social Sciences (A COE Program)*, Tokyo: Hitotsubashi University, The Institute of Economic Research.

Fukao, K, D Ma and T Yuan (2006). International Comparison in Historical Perspective: Reconstructing the 1934–36 Benchmark Purchasing Power Parity for Japan, Korea and Taiwan, *Discussion Paper Series A*, No. 442, Tokyo: Hitotsubashi University, The Institute of Economic Research.

Ganti, S and BR Kalluri (1978). Wagner's Law of Public Expenditures: Some Efficient Results for the United States, *Public Finance*, 34, 225–33.

Ghali, KH (1999). Government Size and Economic Growth: Evidence from a Multivariate Cointegration Analysis, *Applied Economics*, 31, 975–987.

Ghesquiere, H (2007). *Singapore's Success, Engineering Economic Growth*, Singapore: Thomson.

Glezakos, C (1973). Export Instability and Economic Growth: A Statistical Verification, *Economic Development and Cultural Change*, 21(4), 670–678.

Goffiman, IJ and DJ Mahar (1971). The Growth of Public Expenditures in Selected Developing Nations: Six Caribbean Countries 1940–65, *Public Finance*, 26, 57–74.

Goh, KS (1995). *The Practice of Economic Growth,* Singapore: Marshall Cavendish.

Gonzalo, J (1994). Five Alternative Methods of Estimating Long-Run Equilibrium Relationships, *Journal of Econometrics*, 60, 203–233.

Goode, R (1984). *Government Finance in Developing Countries,* Washington DC: The Brookings Institution.

Granger, CW (1981). Some Properties of Time Series Data and Their Use in Econometric Model Specification, *Journal of Econometrics*, 16, 121–130.

Grist, DH (1950). *An Outline of Malayan Agriculture, Malayan Planting Manual, No. 2,* London: Grand City Press Limited.

Gupta, SP (1967). Public Expenditure and Economic Growth: A Time-Series Analysis, *Public Finance*, 22(4), 423–466.

Gyles, AF (1991). A Time-domain Transfer Function Model of Wagner's Law: The Case of the United Kingdom Economy, *Applied Economics*, 23, 327–330.

Halicioğlu, F (2003). Testing Wagner's Law for Turkey, 1960–2000, *Review of Middle East Economics and Finance*, 1(2), 129–140.

Haque, ME and DR Osborn (2007). Public Expenditure and Economic Growth: A Disaggregated Analysis for Developing Countries, *Manchester School*, 75(5), 533–556.

Havinden, M and D Meredith (eds.) (1996). *Colonialism and Development: Britain and Its Tropical Colonies, 1850–1960,* London: Routledge.

Hayo, B (1994). No Further Evidence of Wagner's Law for Mexico, *Public Finance*, 49, 287–294.

Heikkinen, S and JL van Zanden (eds.) (2004). *Explorations in Economic Growth, Essays in Measurement and Analysis,* Amsterdam: Aksant Academic Publishers.

Helms, LJ (1985). The Effect of State and Local Taxes on Economic Growth: A Time Series-Cross Section Approach, *Review of Economics and Statistics*, 67 (3), 574–582.

Henrekson, M (1993). Wagner's Law — A Spurious Relationship, *Public Finance*, 48(3), 406–415.

Hicks, GL (eds.) (1993). *Overseas Chinese Remittances from Southeast Asia, 1910–1940*, Singapore: Select Books.

Hjerppe, R (1996). *Finland's Historical National Accounts 1860–1994: Calculation Methods and Statistical Tables*, Jyväskylä: Jyväskylä University, Department of History, Publications of the Finnish History 24.

Hodrick, R and EC Prescott (1980). Post-War U.S. Business Cycles: An Empirical Investigation, *Journal of Money, Credit & Banking*, 24(1), 1–17.

Hondroyiannis, G and E Papapetrou (1995). An Examination of Wagner's Law for Greece: A Cointegration Analysis, *Public Finance*, 48(2), 406–415.

Hooley, R (2005). American economic policy in the Philippines, 1902–1940: Exploring a Dark Age in Colonial Statistics, *Journal of Asian Economics*, 16, 464–488.

Hsieh, E and Kon S Lai (1994). Government Spending and Economic Growth: The G-7 Experience, *Applied Economics*, 26(5), 535–542.

Huang, C-J (2006). Testing Wagner's Law Using Bounds Test and a New Granger Non-Causality Test: Evidence for Taiwan, *The Journal of American Academy of Business*, 8(2), 86–90.

Huff, WG (1993). The Development of the Rubber Market in Pre-World War II Singapore, *Journal of Southeast Asian Studies*, 24(2), 285–306.

——— (1997). *The Economic growth of Singapore, Trade and development in the Twentieth Century*, Cambridge: Cambridge University Press.

——— (2001). Entitlements, Destitution, and Emigration in the 1930s Singapore Great Depression, *Economic History Review*, 54(2), 290–323.

———— (2003a). Currency Boards and Chinese Banks in Malaya and the Philippines before World War II, *Australian Economic History Review*, 43(2), 125–139.

———— (2003b). Monetization and Financial Development in Southeast Asia before the Second World War, *Economic History Review*, 56(2), 300–345.

Huff, WG and G Caggiano (2007). Globalization, Immigration, and Lewisian Elastic Labor in Pre–World War II Southeast Asia, *The Journal of Economic History*, 67(1), 33–68.

International Bank for Reconstruction and Development (IBRD) (1955). *The Economic Development of Malaya, Report of a Mission organized by the International Bank for Reconstruction and Development (IBRD) at the request of the Government of the Federation of Malaya, the Crown Colony of Singapore and the United Kingdom*, Baltimore: The Johns Hopkins Press.

Islam, AM (2001). Wagner's Law Revisited: Cointegration and Exogeneity Test for the USA, *Applied Economics Letter*, 8(8), 509–515.

Smits, J-P, E Horlings and JL van Zanden (2000). *Dutch GNP and Its Components, 1800–1913*, Groningen: Groningen Growth and Development Centre, Monograph Series No. 5.

Jang, BK and S Nakabayashi (2005). Some Issues in Medium-Term Fiscal Policy, *Singapore: Selected Issues, IMF Country Report 05/140*, Washington DC: International Monetary Fund.

Johansen, S (1988). Statistical Analysis of Cointegration Vectors, *Journal of Economic Dynamics and Control*, 12, 231–54.

Johansen, S and K Juselius (1990). Maximum Likelihood Estimation and Inference on Cointegration — With Applications to the Demand for Money, *Oxford Bulletin of Economics and Statistics*, 52, 169–210.

Kahn, JA, MM McConnell and GP Quiros (2002). On the Causes of the Increased Stability of the U.S. Economy, *Economic Policy Review of the Federal Reserve Bank of New York*, 8(1), 183–206.

Karavitis, N (1987). The Causal Factors of Government Expenditure Growth in Greece, 1950–80, *Applied Economics*, 19(6), 789–807.

Kent, C, K Smith and J Holloway (2005). Declining Output Volatility, What Role for Structural Change?, *Research Discussion Paper, 2005–08, Economic Group, Reserve Bank of Australia.*

Khan, AH (1990). Wagner's Law and the Developing Economy: A Time-Series Evidence from Pakistan, *The Indian Journal of Economics,* 38, 115–123.

Kneller, R, MF Bleany and N Germell (1999a). Growth, Public Policy and the Government Budget Constraint: Evidence from OECD Countries, *Discussion Papers in Economics,* DP 98/14, University of Nottingham.

——— (1999b). Fiscal Policy and Growth: Evidence from OECD Countries, *Journal of Public Economics,* 74, 171–190.

Knudsen, O and A Parnes (1975). *Trade Instability and Economic Development, Lexington,* Massachusetts: Heath-Lexington Press.

Kolluri, BR, MJ Panik and MS Wahab (2000). Government Expenditure and Economic Growth: Evidence from G7 Countries, *Applied Economics,* 32, 1059–1068.

Kormendi, RC and PG Meguire (1985). Macroeconomic Determinants of Growth: Cross-Country Evidence, *Journal of Monetary Economics,* 16, 141–163.

Kratoska, PH (1990). The British Empire and the Southeast Asian Rice Crisis of 1919–1921, *Modern Asian Studies,* 24(1), 115–146.

——— (2000). Imperial Unity Versus Local Autonomy, British Malaya and the Depression of the 1930s, Boomgaard, and Brown (eds.), In *Weathering the Storm: The Economies of Southeast Asia in the 1930s Depression,* Singapore: Institute of Southeast Asian Studies, 229–298.

Krause, LB, AT Koh and Y Lee (Tsao) (1987). *The Singapore Economy Reconsidered,* Singapore: Institute of Southeast Asian Studies.

Kravis, IB, Z Kenessey, A Heston and R Summers (1975). *A System of International Comparisons of Gross Product and Purchasing Power,* Baltimore: Johns Hopkins University Press.

Kremers, JM, NR Erisccos and JJ Dolado (1992). The Power of Cointegration Test, *Oxford Bulletin of Economics and Statistics,* 54, 325–348.

Kuznets, S (1934). National Income, 1929–1932, *NBER Bulletin*, No. 49, 1–12.

Kydland, FE and EC Prescott (1982). Time to Build and Aggregate Fluctuations, *Econometrica*, 50(6), 1345–1370.

Landau, D (1983). Government Expenditure and Economic Growth: A Cross — Country Study, *Southern Economic Journal*, 49(3), 783–792.

———— (1986). Government and Economic Growth in the Less Developed Countries: An Empirical Study for 1960–1980, *Economic Development and Cultural Change*, 35, 35–75.

Lee, KY (2000). *From Third World to First, the Singapore Story: 1965–2000*, Singapore: Harper Collins.

Lee, SY (1990). *The Monetary and Banking Development of Singapore and Malaysia*, 3rd ed., Singapore: Singapore University Press.

Lee, SA (1974). *Economic Growth and the Public Sector in Malaya and Singapore, 1948–1960*, Singapore: Oxford University Press.

Levine, R and D Renelt (1992). A Sensitivity Analysis of Cross-Country Growth Regressions, *American Economic Review*, 82(4), 942–963.

Lim CY (1967). *Economic Development of Modern Malaya*, Kuala Lumpur: Oxford University Press.

———— (2004). *Southeast Asia the Long Road Ahead*, 2nd ed., Singapore: World Scientific.

Lim, D (1974). Export Instability and Economic Development: The Example of West Malaysia, *Oxford Economic Papers*, 54(2), (March), 78–92.

———— (1976). Export Instability and Economic Growth: A Return to Fundamentals, *Oxford Bulletin of Economics and Statistics*, 38(4), 311–322.

Lin, SAY (1994). Government Spending and Economic Growth, *Applied Economics*, 26, 83–94.

Lindblad, JT (1997). Foreign Investment in Southeast Asia in Historical Perspective, *Asian Economic Journal*, 11(1), 61–80.

———— (1998). *Foreign Investment in Southeast Asia in the Twentieth Century*, London: Macmillan.

Lloyd, PJ and RJ Sandilands (1986). The Trade Sector in a Very Open Re-Export Economy, in Lim C-Y and P Lloyd (eds.), *Resources and Growth in Singapore*, Singapore: Oxford University Press.

Loh, WL (2005). *Centering the Periphery: New Forays in Malaysian Economic History*, Kuala Lumpur: Inaugural Lecture, Faculty of Arts and Social Sciences, University of Malaya.

Love, J (1977). The Decline in Export Instability?, *Oxford Bulletin of Economics and Statistics*, 39(4), 355–359.

——— (1987). Export Instability in Less Developed Countries: Consequences and Causes, *Journal of Economic Studies*, 14(2), 73–80.

——— (1992). Export Instability and the Domestic Economy: Questions of Causality, *Journal of Development Studies* 28(4), 735–742.

Low, L (1998). *The Political Economy of a City-State, Government-Made Singapore*, Singapore: Oxford University Press.

Maddison, A (1998). *Chinese Economic Performance in the Long-Run*, Paris: OECD.

——— (2001). *The World Economy, A Millennial Perspective*, Development Centre Seminars, Paris: OECD.

——— (2003). *The World Economy, Historical Statistics*, Paris: OECD.

Maede, J and R Stone (1941). The Construction of Tables on National Income, Expenditure, Savings and Investment, *Economic Journal*, 51, 216–233.

Mann, AJ (1980). Wagner's Law: An Econometric Test for Mexico, 1925–1976, *National Tax Journal*, 33, 189–201.

Manning, LM and D Adriacanos (1993). Dollar Movements and Inflation: A Cointegration Analysis, *Applied Economics*, 25, 1483–1488.

Martin, B and R Rowthorn (2004). Will Stability Last?, *UBS Global Asset Management Research*.

MacBean, AI (1966). *Export Instability and Economic Development*, Cambridge: Harvard University Press.

McConnell, MM, P Mosser and G Perez-Quiros (1999). A Decomposition of the Increased Stability of GDP Growth, *Current Issues in Economics and Finance, Federal Reserve Bank of New York*, 5(13),

McConnell, MM and G Perez-Quiros (2000). Output Fluctuations in the United States: What Has Changed Since the Early 1980s?, *American Economic Review*, 90(5), 1464–1476.

Mendoza, E (1994). Terms-of-Trade Uncertainty and Economic Growth: are Risk Indicators Significant in Growth Regressions?, *International Finance Discussion Papers*, No. 491.

—— (1995). The Terms of Trade, the Real Exchange Rate, and Economic Fluctuations, *International Economic Review*, 36, 101–137.

Mills, LA (1942). *British Rule in Eastern Asia: A Study of Contemporary Government and Economic Development in British Malaya and Hong Kong*, London: Oxford University Press.

Mizoguchi, T and M Umemura (eds.) (1988). *Basic Economic Statistics of Former Japanese Colonies 1895–1938: Estimates and Findings*, Tokyo: Toyo Keizai Shinposha.

Mofidi, A and J Stone (1990). Do State and Local Taxes affect Economic Growth?, *Review of Economics and Statistics*, 72(4), 686–691.

Moran, C (1983). Export Fluctuations and Economic Growth: An Empirical Analysis, *Journal of Development Economics*, 12, 195–218.

Muhsam, HV (1960). Population Estimates Based on Census Enumeration and Coverage Check, *Population Studies*, 13(3), 278–281.

Mullor-Sebastian, A (January 1988). A New Approach to the Relationship between Export Instability and Economic Development, *Economic Development and Cultural Change*, 36, 217–236.

Murthy, NRV (1993). Further Evidence of Wagner's Law for Mexico: An Application of Cointegration Analysis, *Public Finance*, 48, 92–96.

Musgrave, RA (1969). *Fiscal System*, New Haven: Yale University Press.

Nagarajan, P and A Spears (1990). An Econometric Test of Wagner's Law for Mexico: A Re-Examination, *Public Finance*, 45, 165–168.

Balke NS and RJ Gordon (1989). The Estimation of Prewar Gross National Product: Methodology and New Evidence, *Journal of Political Economy*, 97(1), 38–92.

Nelson, C and C Plosser (1982). Trends and Random Walks in Macroeconomic Time Series: Some Evidence and Implications, *Journal of Monetary Economics*, 10, 139–162.

Nomura, M (1995). Wagner's Hypothesis and Displacement Effect in Japan, 1960–1991, *Public Finance*, 50(1), 121–135.

Noriega, A and A Ramirez-Zamora (1999). Unit Roots and Multiple Structural Breaks in Real Output: How Long Does An Economy Remain Stationary?, *Estudios Económicos*, 14(2), 163–188.

Odaka, K (2007). Exploring and Sharing Asian Economic History: An Interim Report on the Asian Historical Statistics Database Project, *Discussion Paper Series, No. 227, Hitotsubashi University Research Unit for Statistical Analysis in Social Sciences (A 21st-Century COE Program)*, Hitotsubashi University, Institute of Economic Research.

Ohkawa, K, M Shinohara and M Umemura (eds.) (1966). *Estimates of Long-Term Economic Statistics of Japan since 1868, Vol. 1, National Income*, Tokyo: Toyo Keizai Shinposha.

Oshima, HT (1997). Fulfilling Kuznets Dream: Comments on the Asian Historical Statistics Project, *Asian Historical Statistics Project, Project Newsletter*, No. 7, Hitotsubashi University, Institute of Economic Research.

Oxley, L (1994). Cointegration, Causality and Wagner's Law: A Test for Britain 1870–1913, *Scottish Journal of Political Economy*, 41(3), 286–298.

Ozler, S and J Harrigan (1988). Export Instability and Growth, *Department of Economics Working Paper,* No. 486, Los Angeles: University of California.

Pack, H and LE Westphal (1986). Industrial Strategy and Technological Change: Theory versus Reality, *Journal of Development Economics*, 22(1), 87–128.

Peacock, AT and J Wiseman (1961). *The Growth of Public Expenditure in the United Kingdom*. London: National Bureau of Economic Research.

———— (1968). Economic Growth and the Principles of Educational Finance in Developed Countries, in *Financing of Education for Economic Growth*, Paris: OECD, 89–101.

Peebles, G and P Wilson (1996). *The Singapore Economy*, Cheltenham: Edward Elgar.

——— (2002). *Economic Growth and Development in Singapore: Past and Future*, Cheltenham: Edward Elgar.

Philips, PCB and P Perron (1988). Testing for a Unit Root in Time Series Regression, *Biometrica*, 75, 335–346.

Pluta, JE (1979). Wagner's Law, Public Sector Patterns, and Growth of Public Enterprises in Taiwan, *Public Finance Quarterly*, 7(1), 25–46.

Premchand, A (1983). *Government Budgeting and Expenditure Controls: Theory and Practice*, Washington, DC: International Monetary Fund.

Prest, AR and AA Adams (1954). *Consumers' Expenditure in the United Kingdom, 1900–1919*, Cambridge: Cambridge University Press.

Pryor, FL (1968). *Public Expenditures in Communist and Capitalist Nations*, London: Allen & Unwin.

Ram, R (1986). Government Size and Economic Growth: A New Framework and Some Evidence from Cross-Section and Time-Series Data, *American Economic Review*, 76(1), 191–203.

——— (1987). Wagner's Hypothesis in Time Series and Cross-Section Perspectives: Evidence from Real Data for 115 Countries, *The Review of Economics and Statistics*, 69(2), 194–204.

Ramey, G and VA Ramey, (1994). Cross-Country Evidence on the Link between Volatility and Growth, *American Economic Review*, 85(5), 1138–1151.

Rangarajan, C and V Sundararajan, (1976). Impact of Export Fluctuations on Income: A Cross Country Analysis, *The Review of Economics and Statistics*, 58(3), 368–372.

Rao, VVB (1976). *National Accounts of West Malaysia, 1947–1971*, Singapore: Heinemann Educational Books (Asia) Ltd.

Rapach, D (2002). Are Real GDP Levels Nonstationary? Evidence from Panel Data Tests, *Southern Economic Journal*, 68(3), 473–495.

de Rouvray, C (2004). Seeing the World through a National Accounting Framework: Economic History Becomes Quantitative, in *Programme Including New Researchers Paper & Abstracts of the Other Academic Papers, the Economic History Society Annual Conference 2004*, London: The Economic History Society, 157–164.

Sachs, JD and A Warner (1995). Economic Reform and the Process of Global Integration, *Brookings Papers on Economic Activity*, 1.

Saw, SH (1999). *The Population of Singapore*, Singapore: Institute of Southeast Asian Studies.

Sharom A (1965). American Trade with Singapore, 1819–1865, *Journal of the Malaysian Branch of the Royal Asiatic Society*, 38(2), 241–257.

Sheffrin, SM (1988). Have Economic Fluctuations Been Dampened? A Look at Evidence Outside the United States, *Journal of Monetary Economics*, 21(1), 73–83.

Hiroshi, S and H Hitoshi (1999). *Japan and Singapore in the World Economy: Japan's Economic Advance into Singapore, 1870–1965*, London: Routledge.

Simon, JL (1986). *Theory of Population and Economic Growth*, New York: Blackwell.

Singh, A and S Fagernäs (2006). Globalisation, Instability and Economic Insecurity, *Centre for Business Research, Working Paper*, No. 328, University of Cambridge.

Singh, B and SS Balbir (1984). Causality between Public Expenditure and National Income, *The Review of Economics and Statistics*, 66(4), 630–644.

Singh, G (1996). Wagner's Law: A Time Series Evidence from the Indian Economy, *The Indian Journal of Economics*, 38, 115–125.

Sinha, D (1999). Export Instability, Investment and Economic Growth in Asian Countries: A Time Series Analysis, *Center Discussion Paper* No. 799, Economic Growth Center, Yale University.

Sivasubramonian, S (2000). *The National Income of India in the Twentieth Century*, New Delhi: Oxford University Press.

Snodgrass, DR (1966). *Ceylon: An Export Economy in Transition*, Illinois: Irwin.

Sosa-Escudero, W (1997). Testing for Unit Roots and Trend-Breaks in Argentine Real GDP, *Económica*, 43, 123–142.

Stock, JH and MW Watson (1988). Variable Trends in Economic Time Series, *Journal of Economic Perspectives*, 2(3), 147–174.

———— (1999). Business Cycle Fluctuations in US Macroeconomic Time Series, in JB Taylor and M Woodford (eds.), *Handbook of Macroeconomics*, Vol. 1A, Amsterdam: Elsevier BV.

Straits Settlements and Federated Malay States (1909). *Agricultural Bulletin*, 8(5), Appendix B, 237–238.

Sugihara, K (1980). Patterns of Intra-Asian Trade, 1898–1913, *Osaka City University Economic Review*, 55–76.

———— (1996). *Ajiakan Boeki no Keisei to Kozo* (Formation and Structure of Intra-Asian Trade), Kyoto: Mineruva Shobo.

———— (1998). Intra-Asian Trade and East Asia's Industrialisation, 1919–1939, in G Austin (ed.), *Industrial Growth in the Third World, c.1870–c.1990: Depressions, Intra-regional Trade, and Ethnic Networks*, LSE Working Papers in Economic History, 44/98, London School of Economics and Political Science, London, 25–57.

Sugimoto I (2005). The Construction of GDP Estimates of Singapore, 1900–1939 and 1950–1960, Progress and Prospects, in *Programme including New Researchers Paper & Abstracts of the other Academic Papers, the Economic History Society Annual Conference 2005*, Leicester: The Economic History Society, 103–111.

———— (2007a). An Analysis of the State of Johore Government Finance, 1910–1939, *Journal of Malayan Branch of the Royal Asiatic Society*, 80, Part 2, 67–87.

Sun, KN (1997). A Political/Economic Analysis of Taiwan Government Spending Growth, *Public Finance Review*, 29, 1–20.

Tan, EC (2003). Does Wagner's Law or the Keynesian Paradigm Hold in the Case of Malaysia?, *Thammasat Review*, 8(1), 62–75.

Tan, S-h (1997). Budgetary Guidelines and Fiscal Performance in Hong Kong, *International Journal of Public Sector Management*, 10(7), 547–571.

Tanzi, V and L Schuknecht (2000). *Public Spending in the 20th Century, A Global Perspective*, Cambridge: Cambridge University Press.

Taylor, WC (1949). *Local Government in Malaya*, Alor Star: Kedah Government Press.

Thornton, J (1999). Cointegration, Causality and Wagner's Law in 19th Century Europe, *Applied Economics Letters*, 6(7), 413–416.

——— (2001). Population growth and economic growth: long-run evidence from Latin America, *Southern Economic Journal*, 68(2), 464–468.

Tirthankar, R (2000), *The Economic History of India, 1857–1947*, New Delhi: Oxford University Press.

Trocki, CA (1990). *Opium and Empire: Chinese Society in Colonial Singapore, 1800–1910*, Ithaca, NY: Cornell University Press.

Chang, T (2002). An Economic Test of Wagner's Law for Six Countries Based on Cointegration and Error-Correction Modeling Techniques, *Applied Economics*, 34, 1157–1169.

Turnovsky, SJ and P Chattopadhyay (2003). Volatility and Growth in Developing Economies: Some Numerical Results and Empirical Evidence, *Journal of International Economics*, 59, 267–295.

Vatter, HG and JF Walker (1986). Real Public Sector Employment Growth, Wagner's Law, and Economic Growth in the United States, *Public Finance*, 41, 117–137.

Voivodas, CS (1974). The Effect of Foreign Exchange Instability on Growth, *The Review of Economic and Statistics*, 51(3), 410–412.

Wagner, RE and WE Weber (1977). Wagner's Law, Fiscal Institutions and the Growth of Government, *National Tax Journal*, 30, 59–68.

Wahab, M (2004). Economic Growth and Government Expenditure: Evidence from a New Test Specification, *Applied Economics*, 36, 2125–2135.

Warren, JF (1986). *Rickshaw Coolie: a People's History of Singapore 1900–1940*, Singapore: Oxford University Press.

Westphal, L, L Kim and C Dahlman (1985). Reflections on the Republic of Korea's Acquisition of Technological Capability, in N Rosenberg and C Frischtak (eds.), *International Technology Transfer: Concepts, Measures and Comparisons*, New York: Praeger, 167–221.

Wilson, P (1994). Export Earnings Instability of Singapore, 1957–1988: Time Series Analysis, *Journal of Asian Economics*, 5, 399–412.

Wilson, P and G Peebles (2005). Don't Frighten the Horses — The Political Economy of Singapore's Foreign Exchange Rate Regime since 1981, *Singapore Centre for Applied and Policy Economics (SCAPE) Working Paper No. 2005/06*.

Yuk, W (2005). Government Size and Economic Growth: Time-Series Evidence for the United Kingdom, 1830–1993, *Econometric Working Paper EWP0501*, Department of Economics, University of Victoria.

Wong LK (1978). Singapore's Growth as an Entrepot Port 1819–1941, *Journal of Southeast Asian Studies*, 9(1), 50–85.

―――― (1979). Twentieth Century Malayan Economic History: A Select Bibliographic Survey, *The Journal of Southeast Asian Studies*, 10(1), 1–24.

―――― (1991). Commercial Growth Before the Second World War, in Chew, ECT and E Lee (eds.), *A History of Singapore, Singapore*: Oxford University Press, 41–65.

Yeoh, BSA (1993). Urban Sanitation, Health and Water Supply in Later Nineteenth and Early Twentiedh Century Colonial Singapore, *South East Asia Research*, 1(2), 143–172.

―――― (1996). *Contesting Space: Power Relations and the Urban Built Environment in Colonial Singapore*, Kuala Lumpur: Oxford University Press.

Yousefi, M and S Abizadeh (1992). Growth of State Government Expenditures Empirical Evidence from the United States, *Public Finance Review*, 47, 322–339.

## Unpublished Sources

Choo, EK (1976). *The Singapore Trade Depression, 1920–22*, Academic Exercise, Department of History, National University of Singapore.

Dawe, DC (1993). *Essays on Price Stabilization and Macroeconomy in Low Income Countries*, PhD Thesis, Department of Economics, Harvard University.

Goh, KS (1956). *Techniques of National Income Estimation in Under-Developed Territories, with Special Reference to Asia and Africa*, PhD Thesis, University of London, London School of Economics.

Hanizah, I (1995). *Pembangunan dan Perkembangan Infrastruktur Pelabohan Singapore, 1819–1941 (Construction and Development of*

*Singapore Port Infrastructure, Singapore, 1819–1941*), MA Thesis, Department of Southeast Asian Studies, University of Malaya.

Hernaikh, SD (1989). *Poverty in Singapore in the 1920s and 1930s*, Academic exercise, Department of History, National University of Singapore.

Khoo, KK (1960). *The Municipal Government of Singapore, 1887–1940*, Academic Exercise, Department of History, University of Malaya.

Nazrin, R (2000). *Essays of Economic Growth of Malaysia in the Twentieth Century*, PhD Thesis, Harvard University.

——— (2002). Historical GDP Statistics of Malaya, 1900–1939: Progress and Perspectives, paper presented at *XIII International Economic History Congress*, Session 30, Modern Economic Growth and Distribution in Asia, Latin America and the European Periphery: A Historical National Accounts Approach, July 22–26, 2002, Buenos Aires: International Economic History Association.

——— (2006). Methodology for Deriving the Domestic Private Final Consumption Expenditure Series of Malaya, 1900–1939, paper presented at *XIV International Economic History Congress*, Session 103, New Experiences with Historical National Accounts: Methodologies and Analysis, August 21–25, 2006, Helsinki: International Economic History Association.

Oshima, HT (1956). *A Critique of the National Income Statistics of Selected Asian Countries*, PhD Thesis, Columbia University.

Ruhana P (1999). *Perbekalan Air Johor-Singapura* (*Water Supply from State of Johore to Singapore*), MA Thesis, Department of Southeast Asian Studies, Faculty of Arts and Social Sciences, Kuala Lumpur: University of Malaya.

Sugimoto, I (1997). *Analysis Struktur Pentadbiran Kewangan British di Negeri Johor, 1896–1957* (*Analysis of British Colonial Government Finance Structure in the State of Johore, 1896–1957*), MA Thesis, Department of Southeast Asian Studies, Faculty of Arts and Social Sciences, Kuala Lumpur: University of Malaya.

——— (2007b). Historical GDP in the Colony of Singapore: Methodologies of Construction and Overall Patterns of Growth, 1900–1939 and 1950–1960, paper presented at *Singapore Economic Review Conference 2007*, Session 9: Empirical Macroeconomics,

August 2–4, 2007, Singapore: Singapore Economic Review and Brooks World Poverty Institute.

——— (2007c). *Eiryo shokuminchi Singapore niokeru Minkan Saishu Shishutu Suikei, 1900–39, 1948–60 (Methodology Employed for the Estimation of Private Final Consumption Expenditure by Resident Household, 1900–39, 1948–60)*, paper presented at 76th The Socio-Economic History Society, Annual Conference, May 26–27, 2007, Tokyo: Nihon-Keizaishi Gakkai (The Socio-Economic History Society).

Teo, M, KT Cel (1962). *The Development of the Port of Singapore, 1819–1959*, Academic Exercise, Department of Geography, University of Malaya.

## Online Sources

National Institute of Health and Nutrition (NIHN), Japan (1995). *Health and Nutrition Information Infrastructure Database System.* Available at: http://health02.nutritio.net:8888/nns/owa/nns_index_e.nk1100 (accessed January 6, 2008).

Asian Development Bank (2001). Key Indicators of Developing Asian and Pacific Countries. Available at: http://www.adb.org/Documents/Books/Key_Indicators/2001/sin_ki2001.xls (accessed January 6, 2008).

Asian Development Bank (2005). Key Indicators of Developing Asian and Pacific Countries. Available at: http://www.adb.org/Documents/Books/Key_Indicators/2005/xls/SIN.xls (accessed January 6, 2008).

## CD-ROM

International Monetary Fund, Department of Statistics (2006). *International Financial Statistics CD-ROM Subscription*, New York: IMF.